Healthy People 2010

Conference Edition-Volume I

Includes

◆ **Understanding and Improving Health**

◆ **Objectives for Improving Health (Part A)**

U. S. Department of Health and Human Services
January 2000

Message from the Secretary

Healthy People 2010 provides our Nation with the wide range of public health opportunities that exist in the first decade of the 21st century. With 467 objectives in 28 focus areas, Healthy People 2010 will be a tremendously valuable asset to health planners, medical practitioners, educators, elected officials, and all of us who work to improve health. Healthy People 2010 reflects the very best in public health planning—it is comprehensive, it was created by a broad coalition of experts from many sectors, it has been designed to measure progress over time, and, most important, it clearly lays out a series of objectives to bring better health to all people in this country.

Achieving the vision of "Healthy People in Healthy Communities" represents an opportunity for individuals to make healthy lifestyle choices for themselves and their families. It challenges clinicians to put prevention into their practices. It requires communities and businesses to support health-promoting policies in schools, worksites, and other settings. It calls for scientists to pursue new research. Above all, it demands that all of us work together, using both traditional and innovative approaches, to help the American public achieve the 10-year targets defined by Healthy People 2010.

The 20th century brought remarkable and unprecedented improvements in the lives of the people of the United States. We saw the infant mortality rate plummet and life expectancy increase by 30 years. While we recognize that most of the advances came from prevention efforts, we also saw almost unimaginable improvements in medical technologies and health care. The challenge for the 21st century is twofold. First, we must ensure that this rate of advancement continues unabated. Second, we must make certain that all Americans benefit from advancements in quality of life, regardless of their race, ethnicity, gender, disability status, income, or educational level. These challenges are substantial, but with the objectives defined by Healthy People 2010, they are achievable.

I wholeheartedly commend Healthy People 2010, and I challenge all of us to work together to achieve its ambitious and important vision.

Donna E. Shalala
Secretary of Health and Human Services

Foreword

We have witnessed a great deal of progress in public health and medicine since our Nation first embarked on the national planning process for the Healthy People initiative. The process began in 1979 with *Healthy People: The Surgeon General's Report on Health Promotion and Disease Prevention*, which was followed in 1990 by *Healthy People 2000*. Healthy People 2010 represents the third time that the U.S. Department of Health and Human Services (HHS) has developed 10-year health objectives for the Nation.

Healthy People 2010 reflects the scientific advances that have taken place over the past 20 years in preventive medicine, disease surveillance, vaccine and therapeutic development, and information technology. It also mirrors the changing demographics of our country, the changes that have taken place in health care, and the growing impact of global forces on our national health status.

Healthy People 2010 incorporates input from a broad cross-section of people. Scientific experts from many Federal agencies took the lead in developing the focus areas and objectives. The Secretary's Council on National Health Promotion and Disease Prevention Objectives for 2010 and the Healthy People Steering Committee provided guidance to steer the process. The HHS Office of Public Health and Science, particularly the Office of Disease Prevention and Health Promotion, expertly managed the process. But perhaps most important to the success of this effort was the overwhelming and enthusiastic contribution made by the Healthy People Consortium and the public. We received more than 11,000 comments from people in every State by fax, Internet, letter, and in person through several public meetings.

The knowledge, commitment, and collaboration of these groups have combined to produce national health objectives that are even more comprehensive than their predecessors. There are 467 objectives in 28 focus areas, making Healthy People 2010 an encyclopedic compilation of health improvement opportunities for the next decade. Building on two decades of success in Healthy People initiatives, Healthy People 2010 is poised to address the concerns of the 21st century. Two major goals reflect the Nation's changing demographics. The first goal, which addresses the fact that we are growing older as a Nation, is to increase the quality and years of healthy life. The second goal, which addresses the diversity of our population, is to eliminate health disparities.

And, for the first time, a set of Leading Health Indicators will help individuals and communities target the actions to improve health. The Leading Health Indicators also will help communities track the success of these actions.

I sincerely appreciate the number of people, institutions, and organizations that have worked together to create this important document. But our journey has just begun. I encourage you to stay the course as we pursue the vision of Healthy People 2010 to create tomorrow's healthier people today.

David Satcher, M.D., Ph.D.
Assistant Secretary for Health and
Surgeon General

Contents

Healthy People 2010, Volume II

Healthy People 2010: Objectives for Improving Health (Part B)

Healthy People 2010

Understanding
and Improving Health

Introduction

Healthy People 2010 outlines a comprehensive, nationwide health promotion and disease prevention agenda. It is designed to serve as a roadmap for improving the health of all people in the United States during the first decade of the 21st century.

Like the preceding Healthy People 2000 initiative—which was driven by an ambitious, yet achievable, 10-year strategy for improving the Nation's health by the end of the 20th century—Healthy People 2010 is committed to a single, overarching purpose: promoting health and preventing illness, disability, and premature death.

The History Behind the Healthy People 2010 Initiative

Healthy People 2010 builds on initiatives pursued over the past two decades. In 1979, *Healthy People: The Surgeon General's Report on Health Promotion and Disease Prevention* provided national goals for reducing premature deaths and preserving independence for older adults. In 1980, another report, *Promoting Health/Preventing Disease: Objectives for the Nation*, outlined 226 targeted health objectives for the Nation to achieve over the next 10 years.

Healthy People 2000: National Health Promotion and Disease Prevention Objectives, released in 1990, identified health improvement goals and objectives to be reached by the year 2000. The Healthy People 2010 initiative continues in this tradition as an instrument to improve health for the first decade of the 21st century.

Healthy People 2010 is grounded in science, built through public consensus, and designed to measure progress.

The Way Healthy People 2010 Goals and Objectives Were Developed

Healthy People 2010 represents the ideas and expertise of a diverse range of individuals and organizations concerned about the Nation's health. The Healthy People Consortium—an alliance of more than 350 national organizations and 250 State public health, mental health, substance abuse, and environmental agencies—conducted 3 national meetings on the development of Healthy People 2010. In addition, many individuals and organizations gave testimony about health priorities at five Healthy People 2010 regional meetings held in late 1998.

On two occasions—in 1997 and in 1998—the American public was given the opportunity to share its thoughts and ideas. More than 11,000 comments on draft materials were received by mail or via the Internet from individuals in every State, the District of Columbia, and Puerto Rico. All the comments received during the development of Healthy People 2010 can be viewed on the Healthy People Website: http://www.health.gov/healthypeople.

The final Healthy People 2010 objectives were developed by teams of experts from a variety of Federal agencies under the direction of Health and Human Services Secretary Donna Shalala, Assistant Secretary for Health and Surgeon General David Satcher, and former Assistant Secretaries for Health. The process was coordinated by the Office of Disease Prevention and Health Promotion, U.S. Department of Health and Human Services.

The Central Goals of Healthy People 2010

Healthy People 2010 is designed to achieve two overarching goals:

- Increase quality and years of healthy life

- Eliminate health disparities

These two goals are supported by specific objectives in 28 focus areas (see page 17). Each objective was developed with a target to be achieved by the year 2010. A full explanation of the two goals can be found in the next section of this document: "A Systematic Approach to Health Improvement."

The Relationship Between Individual and Community Health

Over the years, it has become clear that individual health is closely linked to community health—the health of the community and environment in which individuals live, work, and play. Likewise, community health is profoundly affected by the collective behaviors, attitudes, and beliefs of everyone who lives in the community.

Community health is profoundly affected by the collective behaviors, attitudes, and beliefs of everyone who lives in the community.

Indeed, the underlying premise of Healthy People 2010 is that the health of the individual is almost inseparable from the health of the larger community and that the health of every community in every State and territory determines the overall health status of the Nation. That is why the vision for Healthy People 2010 is "Healthy People in Healthy Communities."

How Healthy People 2010 Will Improve the Nation's Health

One of the most compelling and encouraging lessons learned from the Healthy People 2000 initiative is that we, as a Nation, can make dramatic progress in improving the Nation's health in a relatively short period of time. For example, during the last decade, we achieved significant reductions in infant mortality. Childhood vaccinations are at the highest levels ever recorded in the United States. Fewer teenagers are becoming parents. Overall, alcohol, tobacco, and illicit drug use is leveling off. Death rates for coronary heart disease and stroke have declined. Significant advances have been made in the diagnosis and treatment of cancer and in reducing unintentional injuries.

But we still have a long way to go. Diabetes and other chronic conditions continue to present a serious obstacle to public health. Violence and abusive behavior continue to ravage homes and communities across the country. Mental disorders continue to go undiagnosed and untreated. Obesity in adults has increased 50 percent over the past two decades. Nearly 40 percent of adults engage in no leisure time physical activity. Smoking among adolescents has increased in the past decade. And HIV/AIDS remains a serious health problem, now disproportionately affecting women and communities of color.

Healthy People 2010 will be the guiding instrument for addressing these and other new health issues, reversing unfavorable trends, and expanding past achievements in health.

The Key Role of Community Partnerships

Community partnerships, particularly when they reach out to nontraditional partners, can be among the most effective tools for improving health in communities.

For the past two decades, Healthy People has been used as a strategic management tool for the Federal Government, States, communities, and many other public- and private-sector partners. Virtually all States, the District of Columbia, and Guam have developed their own Healthy People plans modeled after the national plan. Most States have tailored the national objectives to their specific needs.

Partnerships are effective tools for improving health in communities.

Businesses; local governments; and civic, professional, and religious organizations have also been inspired by Healthy People to print immunization reminders, set up hotlines, change cafeteria menus, begin community recycling, establish worksite fitness programs, assess school health education curriculums, sponsor health fairs, and engage in myriad other activities.

Everyone Can Help Achieve the Healthy People 2010 Objectives

Addressing the challenge of health improvement is a shared responsibility that requires the active participation and leadership of the Federal Government, States, local governments, policymakers, health care providers, professionals, business executives, educators, community leaders, and the American public itself. Although administrative responsibility for the Healthy People 2010 initiative rests in the U.S. Department of Health and Human Services, representatives of all these diverse groups shared their experience, expertise, and ideas in developing the Healthy People 2010 goals and objectives.

Healthy People 2010, however, is just the beginning. The biggest challenges still stand before us, and we all share a role in building a healthier Nation.

Regardless of your age, gender, education level, income, race, ethnicity, cultural customs, language, religious beliefs, disability, sexual orientation, geographic location, or occupation, Healthy People 2010 is designed to be a valuable resource in determining how you can participate most effectively in improving the Nation's health. Perhaps you will recognize the need to be a more active participant in decisions affecting your own health or the health of your children or loved ones. Perhaps you will assume a leadership role in promoting healthier behaviors in your neighborhood or community. Or perhaps you will use your influence and social stature to advocate for and implement policies and programs that can dramatically improve the health of dozens, hundreds, thousands, or even millions of people.

Whatever your role, this document is designed to help you determine what *you* can do—in your home, community, business, or State—to help improve the Nation's health.

Other Information Is Available About Healthy People 2010

Healthy People 2010: Understanding and Improving Health is the first of three parts in the Healthy People 2010 series. The second part, *Healthy People 2010: Objectives for Improving Health*, contains detailed descriptions of 467 objectives to improve health. These objectives are organized into 28 specific focus areas. The third part, *Tracking Healthy People 2010*, provides a comprehensive review of the statistical measures that will be used to evaluate progress.

To receive more information about the Healthy People 2010 initiative, visit the Website at http://www.health.gov/healthypeople, or call 1-800-367-4725.

Healthy People 2010: Objectives for Improving Health **contains 467 objectives to improve health, organized into 28 focus areas.**

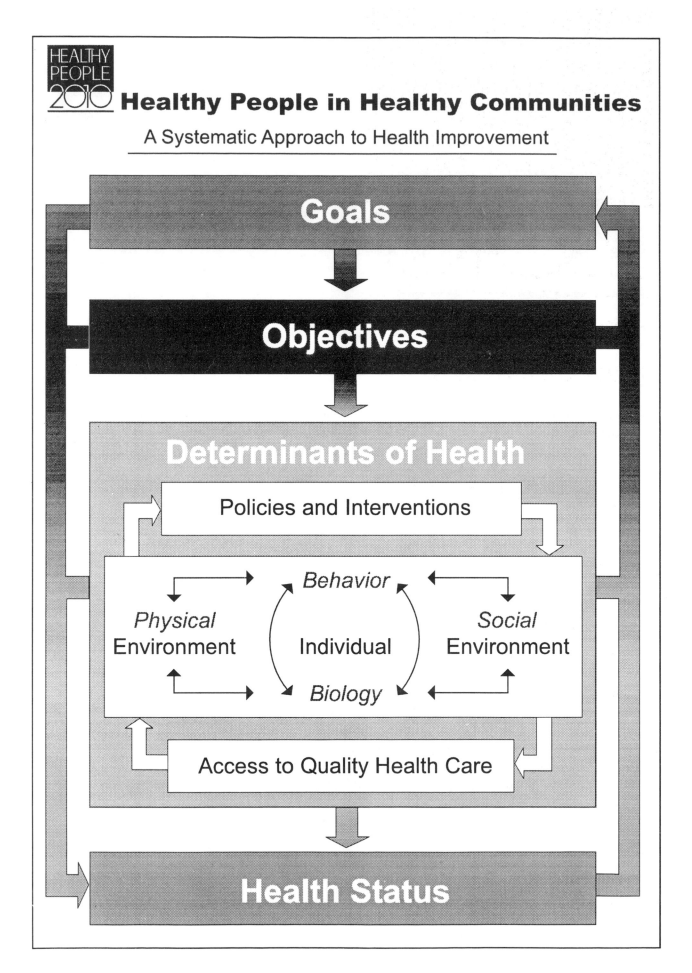

HEALTHY PEOPLE 2010

Healthy People in Healthy Communities

A Systematic Approach to Health Improvement

Goals

Objectives

Determinants of Health

Policies and Interventions

Behavior

Physical Environment

Individual

Social Environment

Biology

Access to Quality Health Care

Health Status

A Systematic Approach to Health Improvement

Healthy People 2010 is about improving health—the health of each individual, the health of communities, and the health of the Nation. However, the Healthy People 2010 goals and objectives cannot by themselves improve the health status of the Nation. Instead, they should be recognized as part of a larger, systematic approach to health improvement.

This systematic approach to health improvement is composed of four key elements:

- Goals
- Objectives
- Determinants of health
- Health status

Whether this systematic approach is used to improve health on a national level, as in Healthy People 2010, or to organize community action on a particular health issue, such as promoting smoking cessation, the components remain the same. The goals provide a general focus and direction. The goals, in turn, serve as a guide for developing a set of objectives that will actually measure progress within a specified amount of time. The objectives focus on the determinants of health, which encompass the combined effects of individual and community physical and social environments and the policies and interventions used to promote health, prevent disease, and ensure access to quality health care. The ultimate measure of success in any health improvement effort is the health status of the target population.

> Successful community partnerships use a systematic approach to health improvement.

Healthy People 2010 is built on this systematic approach to health improvement.

Goal 1: Increase Quality and Years of Healthy Life

The first goal of Healthy People 2010 is to help individuals of all ages increase life expectancy *and* improve their quality of life.

Life Expectancy

Life expectancy is the average number of years people born in a given year are expected to live based on a set of age-specific death rates. At the beginning of the 20th century, life expectancy at birth was 47.3 years. Fortunately, life expectancy has dramatically increased over the past 100 years (see figure 1). Today, the average life expectancy at birth is nearly 77 years.

Figure 1. Past and projected female and male life expectancy at birth, United States, 1900-2050

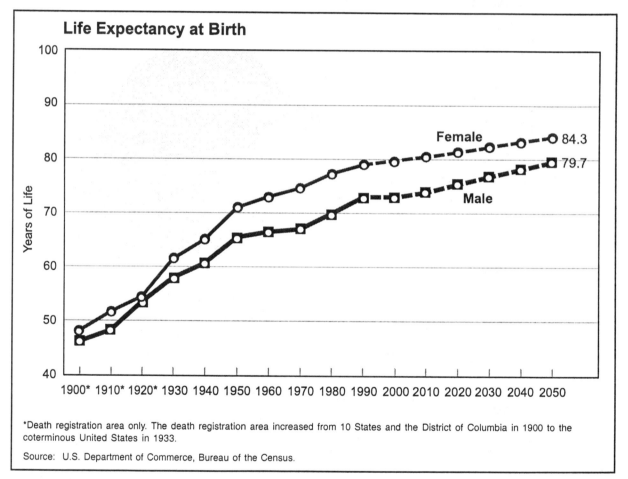

*Death registration area only. The death registration area increased from 10 States and the District of Columbia in 1900 to the coterminous United States in 1933.

Source: U.S. Department of Commerce, Bureau of the Census.

Life expectancy for persons at every age group has also increased during the past century. Based on today's age-specific death rates, individuals aged 65 years can be expected to live an average of 18 more years, for a total of 83 years. Those aged 75 years can be expected to live an average of 11 more years, for a total of 86 years.

Differences in life expectancy between populations, however, suggest a substantial need and opportunity for improvement. At least 18 countries with populations of 1 million or more have life expectancies greater than the United States for both men and women (see figure 2).

Life Expectancy by Country

FEMALE		MALE	
Country	**Years of Life Expectancy**	**Country**	**Years of Life Expectancy**
Japan	82.9	Japan	76.4
France	82.6	Sweden	76.2
Switzerland	81.9	Israel	75.3
Sweden	81.6	Canada	75.2
Spain	81.5	Switzerland	75.1
Canada	81.2	Greece	75.1
Australia	80.9	Australia	75.0
Italy	80.8	Norway	74.9
Norway	80.7	Netherlands	74.6
Netherlands	80.4	Italy	74.4
Greece	80.3	England and Wales	74.3
Finland	80.3	France	74.2
Austria	80.1	Spain	74.2
Germany	79.8	Austria	73.5
Belgium	79.8	Singapore	73.4
England and Wales	79.6	Germany	73.3
Israel	79.3	New Zealand	73.3
Singapore	79.0	Northern Ireland	73.1
United States	**78.9**	Belgium	73.0
		Cuba	73.0
		Costa Rica	73.0
		Finland	72.8
		Denmark	72.8
		Ireland	72.5
		United States	**72.5**

Source: World Health Organization. United Nations. Centers for Disease Control and Prevention. National Center for Health Statistics. National Vital Statistics System. 1990-1995 and unpublished data.

There are substantial differences in life expectancy among different population groups within the United States. For example, women outlive men by an average of 6 years. White women currently have the greatest life expectancy in the United States. The life expectancy for African American women has risen to be higher today than that for white men. People from households with an annual income of at least $25,000 live an average of 3 to 7 years longer, depending on gender and race, than people from households with annual incomes of less than $10,000.

Quality of Life

Quality of life reflects a general sense of happiness and satisfaction with our lives and environment. General quality of life encompasses all aspects of life, including health, recreation, culture, rights, values, beliefs, aspirations, and the conditions that support a life containing these elements. *Health-related quality of life* reflects a personal sense of physical and mental health and the ability to react to factors in the physical and social environments. Health-related quality of life is inherently more subjective than life expectancy and therefore can be more difficult to measure. Some tools, however, have been developed to measure health-related quality of life.

Global assessments, in which a person rates his or her health as "poor," "fair," "good," "very good," or "excellent," can be reliable indicators of a person's perceived health. In 1996, 90 percent of people in the United States reported their health as good, very good, or excellent.

Healthy days is another measure of health-related quality of life that estimates the number of days of poor physical and mental health in the past 30 days. In 1998, 82 percent of adults reported having no days in the past month where poor physical or mental health impaired their usual activities. The proportions of days that are reported "unhealthy" are the result more often of mentally unhealthy days for younger adults and physically unhealthy days for older adults.

Years of healthy life is a combined measure developed for the Healthy People initiative. The difference between life expectancy and years of healthy life reflects the average amount of time spent in less than optimal health because of chronic or acute limitations. After decreasing in the early 1990s, years of healthy life increased to a level in 1996 that was only slightly above that at the beginning of the decade (64.0 years in 1990 to 64.2 years in 1996). During the same period, life expectancy increased a full year.

As with life expectancy, various population groups can show dramatic differences in quality of life. For example, people in the lowest income households are five times more likely to report their health as fair or poor than people in the highest income households (see figure 3). A higher percentage of women report their health as fair or poor compared to men. Adults in rural areas are 36 percent more likely to report their health status as fair or poor than are adults in urban areas.

Achieving a Longer and Healthier Life—the Healthy People Perspective

Healthy People 2010 seeks to increase life expectancy and quality of life over the next 10 years by helping individuals gain the knowledge, motivation, and opportunities they need to make informed decisions about their health. At the same time, Healthy People 2010 encourages local and State leaders to develop communitywide and statewide efforts that promote healthy behaviors, create healthy environments, and increase access to high-quality health care. Given the fact that individual and community health are virtually inseparable, it is critical that both the individual and the community do their parts to increase life expectancy and improve quality of life.

Figure 3. Percentage of persons with fair or poor perceived health status by household income, United States, 1995.

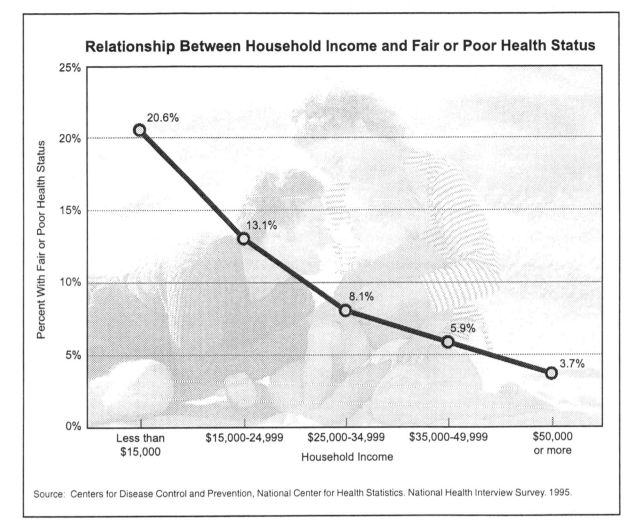

Relationship Between Household Income and Fair or Poor Health Status

Percent With Fair or Poor Health Status

- 20.6%
- 13.1%
- 8.1%
- 5.9%
- 3.7%

Less than $15,000 | $15,000-24,999 | $25,000-34,999 | $35,000-49,999 | $50,000 or more

Household Income

Source: Centers for Disease Control and Prevention, National Center for Health Statistics. National Health Interview Survey. 1995.

Goal 2: Eliminate Health Disparities

The second goal of Healthy People 2010 is to eliminate health disparities among different segments of the population. These include differences that occur by gender, race or ethnicity, education or income, disability, living in rural localities, or sexual orientation. This section highlights ways in which health disparities can occur among various demographic groups in the United States.

Gender

Whereas some differences in health between men and women are the result of biological differences, others are more complicated and require greater attention and scientific exploration. Some health differences are obviously gender specific, such as cervical and prostate cancers.

Overall, men have a life expectancy that is 6 years less than women and have higher death rates for each of the 10 leading causes of death. For example, men are two times more likely than women to die from unintentional injuries and four times more likely than women to die from firearm-related injuries. Although overall death rates for women may currently be lower than for men, women have shown increased death rates over the past decade in areas where men have experienced improvements, such as lung cancer. Women are also at greater risk for Alzheimer's disease than men and twice as likely as men to be affected by major depression.

Race and Ethnicity

Current information about the biologic and genetic characteristics of African Americans, Hispanics, American Indians, Alaska Natives, Asians, Native Hawaiians, and Pacific Islanders does not explain the health disparities experienced by these groups compared with the white, non-Hispanic population in the United States. These disparities are believed to be the result of the complex interaction among genetic variations, environmental factors, and specific health behaviors.

Even though the Nation's infant mortality rate is down, the infant death rate among African Americans is still more than double that of whites. Heart disease death rates are more than 40 percent higher for African Americans than for whites. The death rate for all cancers is 30 percent higher for African Americans than for whites; for prostate cancer, it is more than double that for whites. African American women have a higher death rate from breast cancer despite having a mammography screening rate that is higher than that for white women. The death rate from HIV/AIDS for African Americans is more than seven times that for whites; the rate of homicide is six times that for whites.

Hispanics living in the United States are almost twice as likely to die from diabetes than are non-Hispanic whites. Although constituting only 11 percent of the total population in 1996, Hispanics accounted for 20 percent of the new cases of tuberculosis. Hispanics also have higher rates of high blood pressure and obesity than non-Hispanic whites. There are differences among Hispanic populations as well. For example, whereas the rate of low-birth-weight infants is lower for the total Hispanic population compared with whites, Puerto Ricans have a low-birth-weight rate that is 50 percent higher than that for whites.

American Indians and Alaska Natives have an infant death rate almost double that for whites. The rate of diabetes for this population group is more than twice that for whites. The Pima of Arizona have one of the highest rates of diabetes in the world. American Indians and Alaska Natives also have disproportionately high death rates from unintentional injuries and suicide.

Asians and Pacific Islanders, on average, have indicators of being one of the healthiest population groups in the United States. However, there is great diversity within this population group, and health disparities for some specific groups are quite marked. Women of Vietnamese origin, for example, suffer from cervical cancer at nearly five times the rate for white women. New cases of hepatitis and tuberculosis are also higher in Asians and Pacific Islanders living in the United States than in whites.

Income and Education

Inequalities in income and education underlie many health disparities in the United States. Income and education are intrinsically related and often serve as proxy measures for each other (see figure 4). In general, population groups that suffer the worst health status are also those that have the highest poverty rates and least education. Disparities in income and education levels are associated with differences in the occurrence of illness and death, including heart disease, diabetes, obesity, elevated blood lead level, and low birth weight. Higher incomes permit increased access to medical care, enable one to afford better housing and live in safer neighborhoods, and increase the opportunity to engage in health-promoting behaviors.

Figure 4. Relationship between education and median household income among adults 25 years and older, by gender, United States, 1996

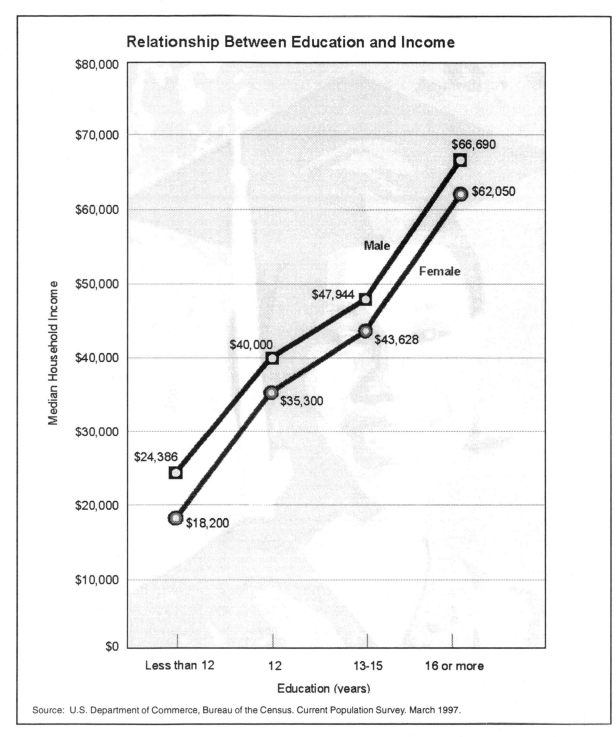

Relationship Between Education and Income

Source: U.S. Department of Commerce, Bureau of the Census. Current Population Survey. March 1997.

Income inequality in the United States has increased over the past three decades. There are distinct demographic differences in poverty by race, ethnicity, and household composition (see figure 5) as well as geographical variations in poverty across the United States. Recent health gains for the U.S. population as a whole appear to reflect achievements among the higher socioeconomic groups; lower socioeconomic groups continue to lag behind.

Figure 5. Percentage of persons below the poverty level by race/ethnic group and type of household, United States, 1996

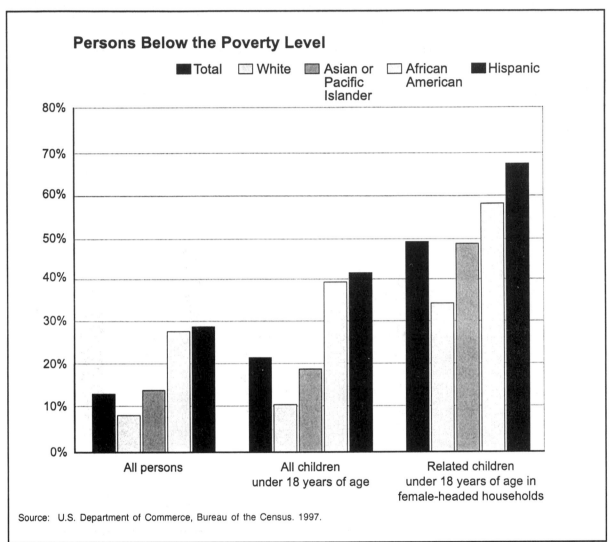

Persons Below the Poverty Level

■ Total ▨ White ▨ Asian or Pacific Islander □ African American ■ Hispanic

Source: U.S. Department of Commerce, Bureau of the Census. 1997.

Overall, those with higher incomes tend to fare better than those with lower incomes. For example, among white men aged 65 years, those in the highest income families could expect to live more than 3 years longer than those in the lowest income families. The percentage of people in the lowest income families reporting limitation in activity caused by chronic disease is three times that of people in the highest income families.

The average level of education in the U.S. population has steadily increased over the past several decades—an important achievement given that more years of education usually translate into more years of life. For women, the amount of education achieved is a key determinant of the welfare and survival of their children. Higher levels of education may also increase the likelihood of obtaining or understanding health-related information needed to develop health-promoting behaviors and beliefs in prevention.

Figure 6. Percentage of adults aged 25 to 64 years by educational level, race and ethnicity, United States, 1996

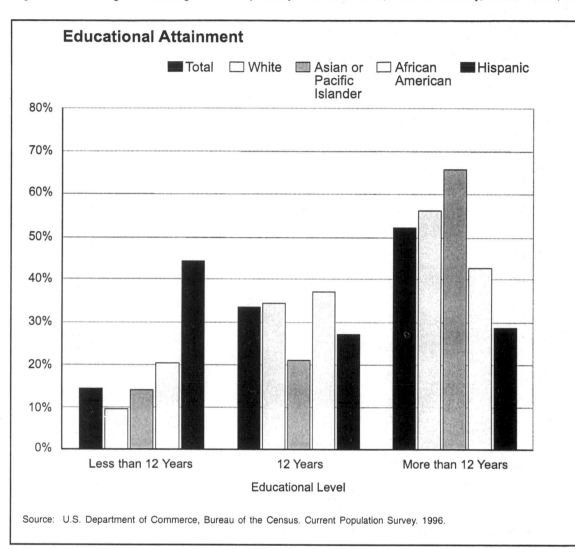

Educational Attainment

Legend: ■ Total □ White ▨ Asian or Pacific Islander □ African American ■ Hispanic

Source: U.S. Department of Commerce, Bureau of the Census. Current Population Survey. 1996.

But again, educational attainment differs by race and ethnicity (figure 6). Among people aged 25 to 64 years in the United States, the overall death rate for those with less than 12 years of education is more than twice that for people with 13 or more years of education. The infant mortality rate is almost double for infants of mothers with less than 12 years of education when compared with those with an education of 13 or more years.

Disability

People with disabilities are identified as persons having an activity limitation, who use assistance, or who perceive themselves as having a disability. In 1994, 54 million people in the United States, or roughly 21 percent of the population, had some level of disability. Although rates of disability are relatively stable or falling slightly for people aged 45 years and older, rates are on the rise among the younger population. People with disabilities tend to report more anxiety, pain, sleeplessness, and days of depression and fewer days of vitality than do people without activity limitations. People with disabilities also have other disparities, including lower rates of physical activity and higher rates of obesity. Many people with disabilities lack access to health services and medical care.

Rural Localities

Twenty-five percent of Americans live in rural areas, that is, places with fewer that 2,500 residents. Injury-related death rates are 40 percent higher in rural populations than in urban populations. Heart disease, cancer, and diabetes rates exceed those for urban areas. People living in rural areas are less likely to use preventive screening services, exercise regularly, or wear seat belts. In 1996, 20 percent of the rural population was uninsured compared with 16 percent of the urban population. Timely access to emergency services and the availability of specialty care are other issues for this population group.

Sexual Orientation

America's gay and lesbian population comprises a diverse community with disparate health concerns. Major health issues for gay men are HIV/AIDS and other sexually transmitted diseases, substance abuse, depression, and suicide. Gay male adolescents are two to three times more likely than their peers to attempt suicide. Some evidence suggests lesbians have higher rates of smoking, obesity, alcohol abuse, and stress than heterosexual women. The issues surrounding personal, family, and social acceptance of sexual orientation can place a significant burden on mental health and personal safety.

Achieving Equity—The Healthy People Perspective

Although the diversity of the American population may be one of our Nation's greatest assets, diversity also presents a range of health improvement challenges—challenges that must be addressed by individuals, the community and State in which they live, and the Nation as a whole.

Healthy People 2010 recognizes that communities, States, and national organizations will need to take a multidisciplinary approach to achieving health equity that involves improving health, education, housing, labor, justice, transportation, agriculture, and the environment. However, our greatest opportunities for reducing health disparities are in empowering individuals to make informed health care decisions and in promoting communitywide safety, education, and access to health care.

Healthy People 2010 is firmly dedicated to the principle that—regardless of age, gender, race, ethnicity, income, education, geographic location, disability, and sexual orientation—every person in every community across the Nation deserves equal access to comprehensive, culturally competent, community-based health care systems that are committed to serving the needs of the individual and promoting community health.

Objectives

The Nation's progress in achieving the two goals of Healthy People 2010 will be monitored through 467 objectives in 28 focus areas. Many objectives focus on interventions designed to reduce or eliminate illness, disability, and premature death among individuals and communities. Others focus on broader issues, such as improving access to quality health care, strengthening public health services, and improving the availability and dissemination of health-related information. Each objective has a target for specific improvements to be achieved by the year 2010.

Together, these objectives reflect the depth of scientific knowledge as well as the breadth of diversity in the Nation's communities. More importantly, they are designed to help the Nation achieve its two overarching goals and realize the vision of healthy people living in healthy communities.

A list of the short titles of all Healthy People 2010 objectives by focus area can be found in the Appendix. In addition, *Healthy People 2010: Objectives for Improving Health* provides an overview of the issues, trends, and opportunities for action in each of the 28 focus areas. It also contains detailed language of each objective, the rationale behind its focus, the target for the year 2010, and national data tables of its measures.

Healthy People 2010 Focus Areas

1. Access to Quality Health Services
2. Arthritis, Osteoporosis, and Chronic Back Conditions
3. Cancer
4. Chronic Kidney Disease
5. Diabetes
6. Disability and Secondary Conditions
7. Educational and Community-Based Programs
8. Environmental Health
9. Family Planning
10. Food Safety
11. Health Communication
12. Heart Disease and Stroke
13. HIV
14. Immunization and Infectious Diseases
15. Injury and Violence Prevention
16. Maternal, Infant, and Child Health
17. Medical Product Safety
18. Mental Health and Mental Disorders
19. Nutrition and Overweight
20. Occupational Safety and Health
21. Oral Health
22. Physical Activity and Fitness
23. Public Health Infrastructure
24. Respiratory Diseases
25. Sexually Transmitted Diseases
26. Substance Abuse
27. Tobacco Use
28. Vision and Hearing

Objectives

The depth of topics covered by the objectives in Healthy People 2010 reflect the array of critical influences that determine the health of individuals and communities.

For example, individual behaviors and environmental factors are responsible for about 70 percent of all premature deaths in the United States. Developing and implementing policies and preventive interventions that effectively address these determinants of health can reduce the burden of illness, enhance quality of life, and increase longevity.

Individual *biology* and *behaviors* influence health through their interaction with each other and with the individual's *social* and *physical environments*. In addition, *policies and interventions* can improve health by targeting factors related to individuals and their environments, including *access to quality health care* (see figure 7).

Figure 7. Determinants of Health

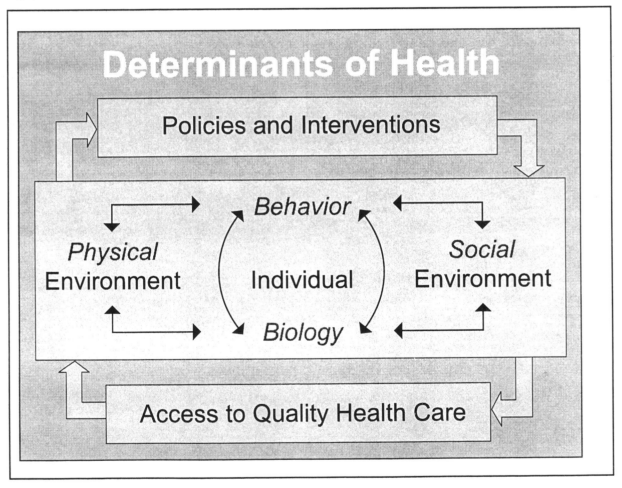

Biology refers to the individual's genetic makeup (those factors with which he or she is born), family history (which may suggest risk for disease), and the physical and mental health problems acquired during life. Aging, diet, physical activity, smoking, stress, alcohol or illicit drug abuse, injury or violence, or an infectious or toxic agent may result in illness or disability and can produce a "new" biology for the individual.

Behaviors are individual responses or reactions to internal stimuli and external conditions. Behaviors can have a reciprocal relationship to biology; in other words, each can react to the other. For example, smoking (behavior) can alter the cells in the lung and result in shortness of breath, emphysema, or cancer (biology) that may then lead an individual to stop smoking (behavior). Similarly, a family history that includes heart disease (biology) may motivate an individual to develop good eating habits, avoid tobacco, and maintain an active lifestyle (behaviors), which may prevent his or her own development of heart disease (biology).

Personal choices and the social and physical environments surrounding individuals can shape behaviors. The social and physical environments include all factors that affect the life of individuals, positively or negatively, many of which may not be under their immediate or direct control.

The **social environment** includes interactions with family, friends, coworkers, and others in the community. It also encompasses social institutions, such as law enforcement, the workplace, places of worship, and schools. Housing, public transportation, and the presence or absence of violence in the community are among other components of the social environment. The social environment has a profound effect on individual health, as well as on the health of the larger community, and is unique because of cultural customs; language; and personal, religious, or spiritual beliefs. At the same time, individuals and their behaviors contribute to the quality of the social environment.

The **physical environment** can be thought of as that which can be seen, touched, heard, smelled, and tasted. However, the physical environment also contains less tangible elements, such as radiation and ozone. The physical environment can harm individual and community health, especially when individuals and communities are exposed to toxic substances; irritants; infectious agents; and physical hazards in homes, schools, and worksites. The physical environment can also promote good health, for example, by providing clean and safe places for people to work, exercise, and play.

Policies and interventions can have a powerful and positive effect on the health of individuals and the community. Examples include health promotion campaigns to prevent smoking; policies mandating child restraints and seat belt use in automobiles; disease prevention services, such as immunization of children, adolescents, and adults; and clinical services, such as enhancing mental health care. Policies and interventions that promote individual and community health may be implemented by a variety of agencies, such as transportation, education, energy, housing, labor, justice, and other venues, or through places of worship, community-based organizations, civic groups, and businesses.

The health of individuals and communities also depends greatly on **access to quality health care**. Expanding access to quality health care is important to eliminate health disparities and to increase the quality and years of healthy life for all people living in the United States. Health care in the broadest sense not only includes services received through health care providers but also health information and services received through other venues in the community.

The determinants of health—individual biology and behavior, the physical and social environments, policies and interventions, and access to quality health care—have a profound effect on the health of individuals, communities, and the Nation. An evaluation of these determinants is an important part of developing any strategy to improve health.

Our understanding of these determinants and how they relate to one another, coupled with our understanding of how individual and community health determines the health of the Nation, is perhaps the most important key to achieving our Healthy People 2010 goals of increasing the quality and years of life and of eliminating the Nation's health disparities.

To completely understand the health status of a population, it is essential to monitor and evaluate the consequences of the determinants of health.

The health status of the United States is a description of the health of the total population using information that is representative of most people living in this country. For relatively small population groups, however, it may not be possible to draw accurate conclusions about their health using current data collection methods. The goal of eliminating health disparities will necessitate improved collection and use of standardized data to correctly identify disparities among select population groups.

Health status can be measured by birth and death rates, life expectancy, quality of life, morbidity from specific diseases, risk factors, use of ambulatory care and inpatient care, accessibility of health personnel and facilities, financing of health care, health insurance coverage, and many other factors. The information used to report health status comes from a variety of sources, including birth and death records; hospital discharge data; and health information collected from health care records, personal interviews, physical examinations, and telephone surveys. These measures are monitored on an annual basis in the United States and are reported in a variety of publications, including *Health, United States* and *Healthy People Reviews*.

The leading causes of death are frequently used to describe the health status of the Nation. The Nation has seen a great deal of change over the past 100 years in the leading causes of death (see figure 8). At the beginning of the 1900s, infectious diseases ran rampant in the United States and worldwide and topped the leading causes of death. A century later, with the control of many infectious agents and the increasing age of the population, chronic diseases top the list.

A very different picture emerges when the leading causes of death are viewed for various subgroups. Unintentional injuries, mainly motor vehicle crashes, are the fifth leading cause of death for the total population, but they are the leading cause of death for people aged 1 to 44 years. Similarly, HIV/AIDS is the 14th leading cause of death for the total population but the leading cause of death for African American men aged 25 to 44 years (figure 9).

The leading causes of death in the United States generally result from a mix of behaviors; injury, violence, and other factors in the environment; and the unavailability or inaccessibility of quality health services. Understanding and monitoring behaviors, environmental factors, and community health systems may prove more useful to monitoring the Nation's *true* health, and in driving health improvement activities, than the death rates that reflect the cumulative impact of these factors. This approach has served as the basis for developing the Leading Health Indicators.

Figure 8. The 10 leading causes of death as a percentage of all deaths in the United States, 1900 and 1997

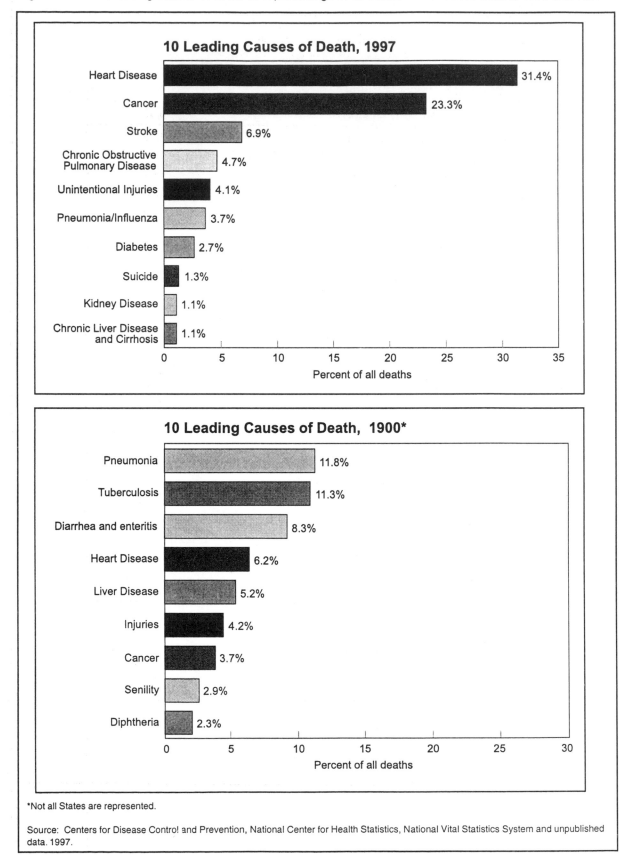

10 Leading Causes of Death, 1997

Cause	Percent
Heart Disease	31.4%
Cancer	23.3%
Stroke	6.9%
Chronic Obstructive Pulmonary Disease	4.7%
Unintentional Injuries	4.1%
Pneumonia/Influenza	3.7%
Diabetes	2.7%
Suicide	1.3%
Kidney Disease	1.1%
Chronic Liver Disease and Cirrhosis	1.1%

Percent of all deaths

10 Leading Causes of Death, 1900*

Cause	Percent
Pneumonia	11.8%
Tuberculosis	11.3%
Diarrhea and enteritis	8.3%
Heart Disease	6.2%
Liver Disease	5.2%
Injuries	4.2%
Cancer	3.7%
Senility	2.9%
Diphtheria	2.3%

Percent of all deaths

*Not all States are represented.

Source: Centers for Disease Control and Prevention, National Center for Health Statistics, National Vital Statistics System and unpublished data. 1997.

Figure 9. The 3 leading causes of death by age group, United States, 1997

Leading Causes of Death by Age Group

Younger Than 1 Year	Number of Deaths
Birth defects	6,178
Disorders related to premature birth	3,925
Sudden infant death syndrome	2,991
1-4 Years	
Unintentional Injuries	2,005
Birth defects	589
Cancer	438
5-14 Years	
Unintentional Injuries	3,371
Cancer	1,030
Homicide	457
15-24 Years	
Unintentional Injuries	13,367
Homicide	6,146
Suicide	4,186
25-44 Years	
Unintentional Injuries	27,129
Cancer	21,706
Heart disease	16,513
45-64 Years	
Cancer	131,743
Heart disease	101,235
Unintentional Injuries	17,521
65 Years and Older	
Heart disease	606,913
Cancer	382,913
Stroke	140,366

Source: Centers for Disease Control and Prevention, National Center for Health Statistics. National Vital Statistics Systems. 1999.

Health Status

Leading Health Indicators

The Leading Health Indicators reflect the major public health concerns in the United States and were chosen based on their ability to motivate action, the availability of data to measure their progress, and their relevance as broad public health issues.

The Leading Health Indicators illuminate individual behaviors, physical and social environmental factors, and important health system issues that greatly affect the health of individuals and communities. Underlying each of these indicators is the significant influence of income and education (see Income and Education, page 12).

The process of selecting the Leading Health Indicators mirrored the collaborative and extensive efforts undertaken to develop Healthy People 2010. The process was led by an interagency work group within the U.S. Department of Health and Human Services. Individuals and organizations provided comments at national and regional meetings or via mail and the Internet. A report by the Institute of Medicine, National Academy of Sciences, provided several scientific models on which to support a set of indicators. Focus groups were used to ensure that the indicators are meaningful and motivating to the public.

Leading Health Indicators

- **Physical activity**
- **Overweight and obesity**
- **Tobacco use**
- **Substance abuse**
- **Responsible sexual behavior**
- **Mental health**
- **Injury and violence**
- **Environmental quality**
- **Immunization**
- **Access to health care**

For each of the Leading Health Indicators, specific objectives derived from Healthy People 2010 will be used to track progress. This small set of measures will provide a snapshot of the health of the Nation. Tracking and communicating progress on the Leading Health Indicators through national- and State-level report cards will spotlight achievements and challenges in the next decade. The Leading Health Indicators serve as a link to the 467 objectives in *Healthy People 2010: Objectives for Improving Health* and can become the basic building blocks for community health initiatives.

A major challenge throughout the history of Healthy People has been to balance a comprehensive set of health objectives with a smaller set of health priorities.

The Leading Health Indicators are intended to help everyone more easily understand the importance of health promotion and disease prevention and to encourage wide participation in improving health in the next decade. Developing strategies and action plans to address one or more of these indicators can have a profound effect on increasing the quality of life and the years of healthy life and on eliminating health disparities—creating *healthy people in healthy communities*.

Physical Activity

Regular physical activity throughout life is important for maintaining a healthy body, enhancing psychological well-being, and preventing premature death.

In 1997, 64 percent of adolescents engaged in the recommended amount of physical activity. In the same year, only 15 percent of adults performed the recommended amount of physical activity and 40 percent of adults engaged in no leisure-time physical activity.

Participation in regular physical activity, United States, 1990-1997

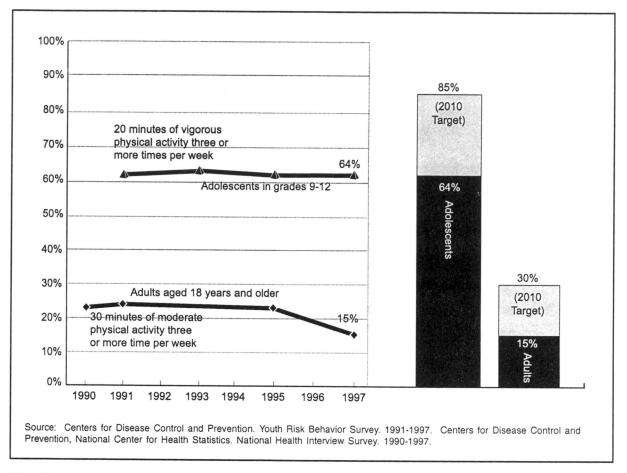

Source: Centers for Disease Control and Prevention. Youth Risk Behavior Survey. 1991-1997. Centers for Disease Control and Prevention, National Center for Health Statistics. National Health Interview Survey. 1990-1997.

The objectives selected to measure progress among adolescents and adults for this Leading Health Indicator are presented below. These are only indicators and do not represent all the physical activity and fitness objectives included in Healthy People 2010.

22-7. Increase the proportion of adolescents who engage in vigorous physical activity that promotes cardiorespiratory fitness 3 or more days per week for 20 or more minutes per occasion.

22-2. Increase the proportion of adults who engage regularly, preferably daily, in moderate physical activity for at least 30 minutes per day.

Health Impact of Physical Activity

Regular physical activity is associated with lower death rates for adults of any age, even when only moderate levels of physical activity are performed. Regular physical activity decreases the risk of death from heart disease, lowers the risk of developing diabetes, and is associated with a decreased risk of colon cancer. Regular physical activity helps prevent high blood pressure and helps reduce blood pressure in persons with elevated levels.

Regular physical activity also:

■ Increases muscle and bone strength

■ Increases lean muscle and helps decrease body fat

■ Aids in weight control and is a key part of any weight loss effort

■ Enhances psychological well-being and may even reduce the risk of developing depression

■ Appears to reduce symptoms of depression and anxiety and to improve mood

In addition, children and adolescents need weight-bearing exercise for normal skeletal development, and young adults need such exercise to achieve and maintain peak bone mass. Older adults can improve and maintain strength and agility with regular physical activity. This can reduce the risk of falling, helping older adults maintain an independent living status. Regular physical activity also increases the ability of people with certain chronic, disabling conditions to perform activities of daily living.

Populations With Low Rates of Physical Activity

■ Women are less active than men at all ages.

■ People with lower incomes and less education are typically not as physically active as those with higher incomes and education.

■ African Americans and Hispanics are generally less physically active than whites.

■ Adults in northeastern and southern States tend to be less active than adults in north-central and western States.

■ People with disabilities are less physically active than people without disabilities.

■ By age 75, one in three men and one in two women engage in *no* regular physical activity.

Other Issues

The major barriers most people face when trying to increase physical activity are lack of time, access to convenient facilities, and safe environments in which to be active.

For more information on Healthy People 2010 objectives or on physical activity and fitness, visit www.health.gov/healthypeople/ or call 1-800-336-4797.

Overweight and Obesity

Overweight and obesity are major contributors to many preventable causes of death. On average, higher body weights are associated with higher death rates. The number of overweight children, adolescents, and adults has risen over the past four decades. Total costs (medical cost and lost productivity) attributable to obesity alone amounted to an estimated $99 billion in 1995.

During 1988-1994, 11 percent of children and adolescents aged 6 to 19 years were overweight or obese. During the same years, 23 percent of adults aged 20 and older were considered obese.

Overweight and obesity, United States, 1988-1994

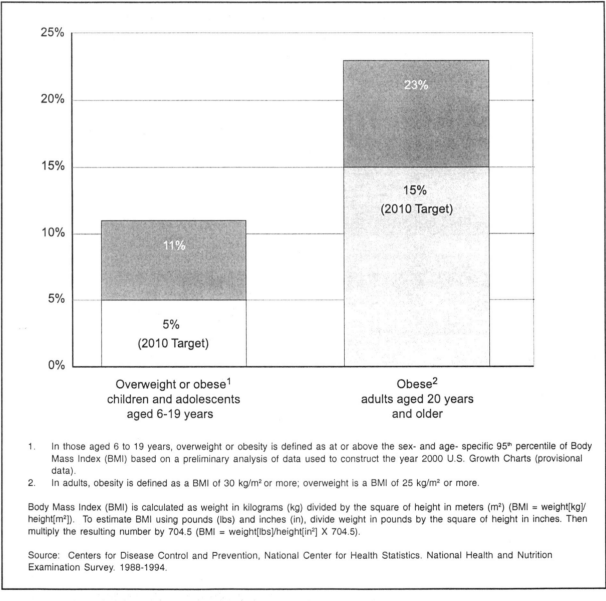

1. In those aged 6 to 19 years, overweight or obesity is defined as at or above the sex- and age- specific 95th percentile of Body Mass Index (BMI) based on a preliminary analysis of data used to construct the year 2000 U.S. Growth Charts (provisional data).
2. In adults, obesity is defined as a BMI of 30 kg/m² or more; overweight is a BMI of 25 kg/m² or more.

Body Mass Index (BMI) is calculated as weight in kilograms (kg) divided by the square of height in meters (m²) (BMI = weight[kg]/height[m²]). To estimate BMI using pounds (lbs) and inches (in), divide weight in pounds by the square of height in inches. Then multiply the resulting number by 704.5 (BMI = weight[lbs]/height[in²] X 704.5).

Source: Centers for Disease Control and Prevention, National Center for Health Statistics. National Health and Nutrition Examination Survey. 1988-1994.

The objectives selected to measure progress among children, adolescents, and adults for this Leading Health Indicator are presented below. These are only indicators and do not represent all the nutrition and overweight objectives included in Healthy People 2010.

19-3c. Reduce the proportion of children and adolescents who are overweight or obese.

19-2. Reduce the proportion of adults who are obese.

Health Impact of Overweight and Obesity

Overweight and obesity substantially raise the risk of illness from high blood pressure; high cholesterol; Type 2 diabetes; heart disease and stroke; gallbladder disease; arthritis; sleep disturbances and problems breathing; and endometrial, breast, prostate, and colon cancers.

Obese individuals may also suffer from social stigmatization, discrimination, and lowered self-esteem.

Populations With High Rates of Overweight and Obesity

An estimated 107 million adults in the United States are overweight or obese. The proportion of adolescents from poor households who are overweight is almost twice that of adolescents from middle- and high-income households. Overweight is especially prevalent among women with lower incomes and less education. Obesity is more common among African American and Hispanic women than among white women. Among African Americans, the proportion of women who are obese is 80 percent higher than the proportion of men who are obese. This gender difference is also seen among Hispanic women and men, but the percentage of white, non-Hispanic women and men who are obese is about the same.

Reducing Overweight and Obesity

The development of obesity is a complex result of a variety of social, behavioral, cultural, environmental, physiological, and genetic factors. For example, a healthy diet and regular physical activity are both important for maintaining a healthy weight. Once overweight is established during adolescence, it is likely to remain in adulthood. For many overweight and obese individuals, substantial change in eating, shopping, exercising, and even social behaviors may be necessary to develop a healthier lifestyle.

Other Important Nutrition Issues

The quality of food consumed in terms of the proportion of calories from fat, protein, and carbohydrate sources; salt, mineral, and vitamin content; and amount of dietary fiber plays a critical role in disease prevention. The *Dietary Guidelines for Americans* recommend that, to stay healthy, one should eat a variety of foods and choose a diet that is plentiful in grain products, vegetables, and fruits; moderate in salt, sodium, and sugars; and low in fat, saturated fat, and cholesterol.

Nutritional Challenges

Although much progress has been made in making nutrition information available and in providing reduced-fat foods and other healthful food choices in supermarkets, challenges remain. One challenge is the composition of foods eaten away from home. As much as 40 percent of a family's food budget is spent in restaurants and on carry-out meals. Foods eaten away from home are generally higher in fat, saturated fat, cholesterol, and sodium and are lower in fiber and calcium than foods prepared and eaten at home.

For more information on Healthy People 2010 objectives or on nutrition and overweight, visit www.health.gov/healthypeople/ or call 1-800-336-4797.

Tobacco Use

Leading Health Indicator

Cigarette smoking is the single most preventable cause of disease and death in the United States. Smoking results in more deaths each year in the United States than AIDS, alcohol, cocaine, heroin, homicide, suicide, motor vehicle crashes, and fires—combined.

Tobacco-related deaths number more than 430,000 per year among U.S. adults, representing more than 5 million years of potential life lost. Direct medical costs attributable to smoking total at least $50 billion per year.

In 1997, 36 percent of adolescents were current smokers. In the same year, 24 percent of adults were current smokers.

Cigarette smoking, United States, 1990-1997

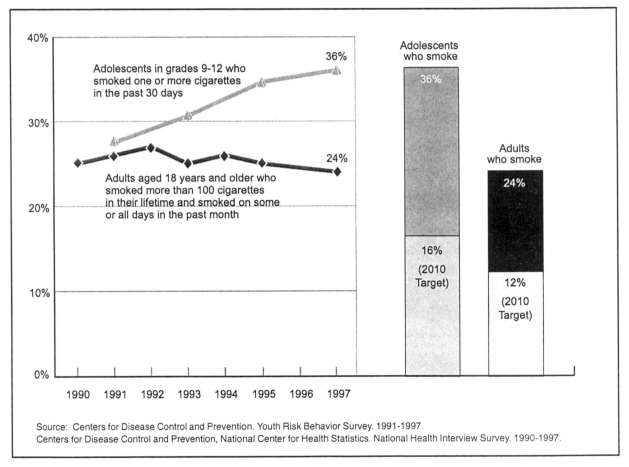

Source: Centers for Disease Control and Prevention. Youth Risk Behavior Survey. 1991-1997.
Centers for Disease Control and Prevention, National Center for Health Statistics. National Health Interview Survey. 1990-1997.

The objectives selected to measure progress among adolescents and adults for this Leading Health Indicator are presented below. These are only indicators and do not represent all the tobacco use objectives included in Healthy People 2010.

27-3b. Reduce cigarette smoking by adolescents.
27-1a. Reduce cigarette smoking by adults.

Health Impact of Cigarette Smoking

Smoking is a major risk factor for heart disease, stroke, lung cancer, and chronic lung diseases—all leading causes of death. Smoking during pregnancy can result in miscarriages, premature delivery, and sudden infant death syndrome. Other health effects of smoking result from injuries and environmental damage caused by fires.

Environmental tobacco smoke (ETS) increases the risk of heart disease and significant lung conditions, especially asthma and bronchitis in children. ETS is responsible for an estimated 3,000 lung cancer deaths each year among adult nonsmokers.

Trends in Cigarette Smoking

Adolescents. Overall, the percentage of adolescents in grades 9 through 12 who smoked in the past month increased in the 1990s. Every day, an estimated 3,000 young persons start smoking. These trends are disturbing because the vast majority of adult smokers tried their first cigarette before age 18 years; more than half of adult smokers became daily smokers before this same age. Almost half of adolescents who continue smoking regularly will eventually die from a smoking-related illness.

Adults. Following years of steady decline, rates of smoking among adults appear to have leveled off in the 1990s.

Populations With High Rates of Smoking

Adolescents. Adolescent rates of cigarette smoking have increased in the 1990s among white, African American, and Hispanic high school students after years of declining rates during the 1970s and 1980s. In 1997, 40 percent of white high school students currently smoked cigarettes compared with 34 percent for Hispanics and 23 percent for African Americans. Among African Americans in 1997 only 17 percent of high school girls, compared with 28 percent of boys, currently smoked cigarettes. Rates of smoking cigarettes in white and Hispanic high school girls and boys are not substantially different.

Adults. Overall, American Indians and Alaska Natives, blue-collar workers, and military personnel have the highest rates of smoking in adults. Rates of smoking in Asian and Pacific Islander men are more than four times higher than for women of the same race. Men have only somewhat higher rates of smoking than women within the total U.S. population. Low-income adults are about twice as likely to smoke as are high-income adults. The percentage of people aged 25 years and older with less than 12 years of education who are current smokers is nearly three times that for persons with 16 or more years of education.

Other Important Tobacco Issues

There is no safe tobacco alternative to cigarettes. Spit tobacco (chew) causes cancer of the mouth, inflammation of the gums, and tooth loss. Cigar smoking causes cancer of the mouth, throat, and lungs and can increase the risk of heart disease and chronic lung problems.

For more information on Healthy People 2010 objectives or on tobacco use, visit www.health.gov/healthypeople/ or call 1-800-336-4797.

Substance Abuse

Alcohol and illicit drug use are associated with many of this country's most serious problems, including violence, injury, and HIV infection. The annual economic costs to the United States from alcohol abuse were estimated to be $167 billion in 1995, and the costs from drug abuse were estimated to be $110 billion.

In 1997, 77 percent of adolescents aged 12 to 17 years reported that they did *not* use alcohol or illicit drugs in the past month. In the same year, 6 percent of adults aged 18 years and older reported using illicit drugs in the past month; 16 percent reported binge drinking in the past month, which is defined as consuming five or more drinks on one occasion.

Use of alcohol and/or illicit drugs, United States, 1994-1997

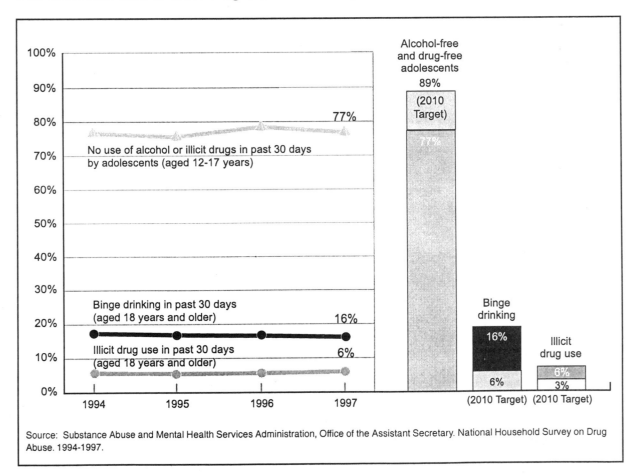

Source: Substance Abuse and Mental Health Services Administration, Office of the Assistant Secretary. National Household Survey on Drug Abuse. 1994-1997.

The objectives selected to measure progress among adolescents and adults for this Leading Health Indicator are presented below. These are only indicators and do not represent all the substance abuse objectives in Healthy People 2010.

26-10a. Increase the proportion of adolescents not using alcohol or any illicit drugs during the past 30 days.

26-10c. Reduce the proportion of adults using any illicit drug during the past 30 days.

26-11c. Reduce the proportion of adults engaging in binge drinking of alcoholic beverages during the past month.

Health Impact of Substance Abuse

Alcohol and illicit drug use are associated with child and spousal abuse; sexually transmitted diseases, including HIV infection; teen pregnancy; school failure; motor vehicle crashes; escalation of health care costs; low worker productivity; and homelessness. Alcohol and illicit drug use also can result in substantial disruptions in family, work, and personal life.

Alcohol abuse alone is associated with motor vehicle crashes, homicides, suicides, and drowning—leading causes of death among youth. Long-term heavy drinking can lead to heart disease, cancer, alcohol-related liver disease, and pancreatitis. Alcohol use during pregnancy is known to cause fetal alcohol syndrome, a leading cause of preventable mental retardation.

Trends of Substance Abuse

Adolescents. Although the trend from 1994 to 1997 has shown some fluctuations, about 77 percent of adolescents aged 12 to 17 years report being both alcohol-free and drug-free in the past month.

Alcohol is the drug most frequently used by adolescents aged 12 to 17 years. In 1997, 21 percent of adolescents aged 12 to 17 years reported drinking alcohol in the past month. Alcohol use in the past month for this age group has remained at about 20 percent since 1992. Eight percent of this age group reported binge drinking, and 3 percent were heavy drinkers (five or more drinks on the same occasion on each of five or more days in the past 30 days).

Data from 1998 show that 10 percent of adolescents aged 12 to 17 reported using illicit drugs in the past 30 days. This rate is significantly lower than in the previous year and remains well below the all-time high of 16 percent in 1979. Current illicit drug use had nearly doubled for those aged 12 to 13 years between 1996 and 1997 but then decreased between 1997 and 1998. Youth are experimenting with a variety of illicit drugs, including marijuana, cocaine, crack, heroin, acid, inhalants, and methamphetamines, as well as misuse of prescription drugs and other "street" drugs. The younger a person becomes a habitual user of illicit drugs, the stronger the addiction becomes and the more difficult it is to stop use.

Adults. Binge drinking has remained at the same approximate level of 16 percent for all adults since 1988, with the highest current rate of 32 percent among adults aged 18 to 25 years. Illicit drug use has been near the present rate of 6 percent since 1980. Men continue to have higher rates of illicit drug use than women, and rates of illicit drug use in urban areas are higher than in rural areas.

For more information on Healthy People 2010 objectives or on substance abuse, visit www.health.gov/healthypeople/ or call 1-800-336-4797.

Leading Health Indicator

Responsible
Sexual Behavior

Unintended pregnancies and sexually transmitted diseases (STDs), including infection with the human immunodeficiency virus that causes AIDS, can result from unprotected sexual behaviors. Abstinence is the only method of complete protection. Condoms, if used correctly and consistently, can help prevent both unintended pregnancy and STDs.

In 1997, 85 percent of adolescents abstained from sexual intercourse or used condoms if they were sexually active. In the same year, 23 percent of sexually active adults used condoms.

Responsible sexual behavior, United States, 1995 and 1997

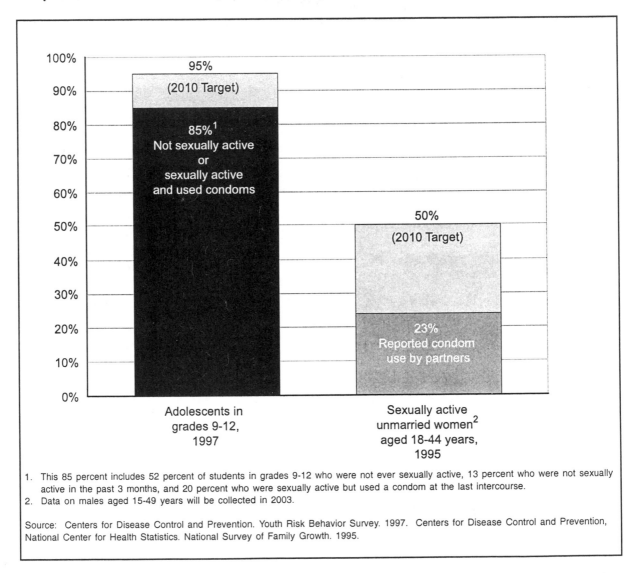

1. This 85 percent includes 52 percent of students in grades 9-12 who were not ever sexually active, 13 percent who were not sexually active in the past 3 months, and 20 percent who were sexually active but used a condom at the last intercourse.
2. Data on males aged 15-49 years will be collected in 2003.

Source: Centers for Disease Control and Prevention. Youth Risk Behavior Survey. 1997. Centers for Disease Control and Prevention, National Center for Health Statistics. National Survey of Family Growth. 1995.

The objectives selected to measure progress among adolescents and adults for this Leading Health Indicator are presented below. These are only indicators and do not represent all the responsible sexual behavior objectives in Healthy People 2010.

25-11.   **Increase the proportion of adolescents who abstain from sexual intercourse or use condoms if currently sexually active.**

13-6.   **Increase the proportion of sexually active persons who use condoms.**

Trends in Sexual Behavior

In the past 6 years there has been both an increase in abstinence among all youth and an increase in condom use among those young people who are sexually active. Research has clearly shown that the most effective school-based programs are comprehensive ones that include a focus on abstinence *and* condom use. Condom use in sexually active adults has remained steady at about 25 percent.

Unintended Pregnancies

Half of all pregnancies in the United States are unintended, that is, at the time of conception the pregnancy was not planned or not wanted. Unintended pregnancy rates in the United States have been declining. The rates remain highest among women aged 20 years or younger, women aged 40 years or older, and low income African American women. Approximately 1 million teenage girls each year in the United States have unintended pregnancies. Nearly half of all unintended pregnancies end in abortion.

The cost to U.S. taxpayers for adolescent pregnancy is estimated at between $7 billion and $15 billion a year.

Sexually Transmitted Diseases

Sexually transmitted diseases are common in the United States, with an estimated 15 million new cases of STDs reported each year. Almost 4 million of the new cases of STDs each year occur in adolescents. Women generally suffer more serious STD complications than men, including pelvic inflammatory disease, ectopic pregnancy, infertility, chronic pelvic pain, and cervical cancer from the human papilloma virus. African Americans and Hispanics have higher rates of STDs than whites.

The total cost of the most common STDs and their complications is conservatively estimated at $17 billion annually.

HIV/AIDS

Nearly 700,000 cases of AIDS have been reported in the United States since the HIV/AIDS epidemic began in the 1980s. The latest estimates indicate that 650,000 to 900,000 people in the United States are currently infected with HIV. The lifetime cost of health care associated with HIV infection, in light of recent advances in HIV diagnostics and therapies, is $155,000 or more per person.

About one-half of all new HIV infections in the United States are among people aged 25 years and under, and the majority are infected through sexual behavior. HIV infection is the leading cause of death for African American men aged 25 to 44 years. Compelling worldwide evidence indicates that the presence of other STDs increases the likelihood of both transmitting and acquiring HIV infection.

For more information on Healthy People 2010 objectives or on responsible sexual behavior, visit www.health.gov/healthypeople/ or call 1-800-336-4797.

Approximately 20 percent of the U.S. population are affected by mental illness during a given year; no one is immune. Of all mental illnesses, depression is the most common disorder. More than 19 million adults in the United States suffer from depression. Major depression is the leading cause of disability and is the cause of more that two-thirds of suicides each year.

In 1997, only 23 percent of adults diagnosed with depression received treatment.

Adults with depression[1] who received treatment,[2] United States, 1994-1997

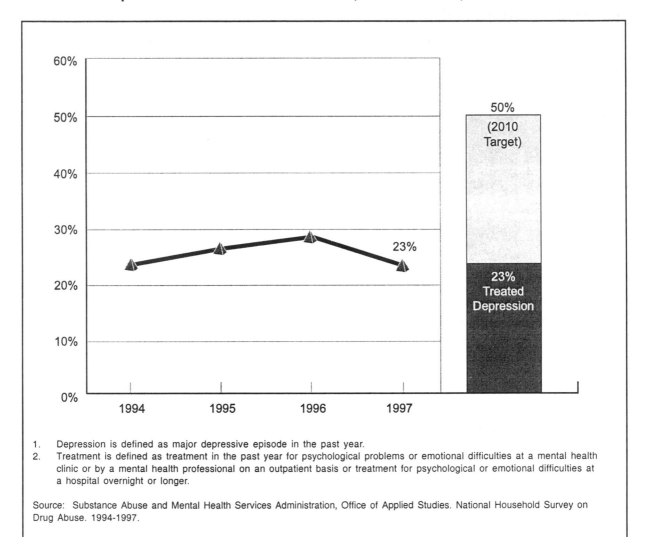

1. Depression is defined as major depressive episode in the past year.
2. Treatment is defined as treatment in the past year for psychological problems or emotional difficulties at a mental health clinic or by a mental health professional on an outpatient basis or treatment for psychological or emotional difficulties at a hospital overnight or longer.

Source: Substance Abuse and Mental Health Services Administration, Office of Applied Studies. National Household Survey on Drug Abuse. 1994-1997.

The objective selected to measure progress among adults for this Leading Health Indicator is presented below. This is only an indicator and does not represent all the mental health objectives in Healthy People 2010.

18-9b. Increase the proportion of adults with recognized depression who receive treatment.

Definition of Mental Health

Mental health is sometimes thought of as simply the absence of a mental illness but is actually much broader. Mental health is a state of successful mental functioning, resulting in productive activities, fulfilling relationships, and the ability to adapt to change and cope with adversity. Mental health is indispensable to personal well-being, family and interpersonal relationships, and one's contribution to society.

Impact of Depression

A person with a depressive disorder is often unable to fulfill the daily responsibilities of being a spouse, partner, or parent. The misunderstanding of mental illness and the associated stigmatization prevent many persons with depression from seeking professional help. Many people will be incapacitated for weeks or months because their depression goes untreated.

Depression is also associated with other medical conditions, such as heart disease, cancer, and diabetes as well as anxiety and eating disorders. Depression has also been associated with alcohol and illicit drug abuse. An estimated 8 million persons aged 15 to 54 years had coexisting mental and substance abuse disorders within the past year.

The total estimated direct and indirect cost of mental illness in the United States in 1996 was $150 billion.

Treatment of Depression

Depression is treatable. Available medications and psychological treatments, alone or in combination, can help 80 percent of those with depression. With adequate treatment, future episodes of depression can be prevented or reduced in severity. Treatment for depression can enable people to return to satisfactory, functioning lives.

Populations With High Rates of Depression

Serious mental illness clearly affects mental health and can affect children, adolescents, adults, and older adults of all ethnic and racial groups, both genders, and people at all educational and income levels.

Adults and older adults have the highest rates of depression. Major depression affects approximately twice as many women as men. Women who are poor, on welfare, less educated, unemployed, and from minority populations are more likely to experience depression. In addition, depression rates are higher among older adults with coexisting medical conditions. For example, 12 percent of older persons hospitalized for problems such as hip fracture or heart disease are diagnosed with depression. Rates of depression for older persons in nursing homes range from 15 to 25 percent.

For more information on Healthy People 2010 objectives or on mental health, visit www.health.gov/healthypeople/ or call 1-800-336-4797.

Injury and Violence

Leading Health Indicator

More than 400 Americans die each day from injuries due primarily to motor vehicle crashes, firearms, poisonings, suffocation, falls, fires, and drowning. The risk of injury is so great that most persons sustain a significant injury at some time during their lives.

Motor vehicle crashes are the most common cause of serious injury. In 1997 there were 15.8 deaths from motor vehicle crashes per 100,000 persons.

Because no other crime is measured as accurately and precisely, homicide is a reliable indicator of all violent crime. In 1997, the murder rate in the United States fell to its lowest level in 3 decades, 7.2 homicides per 100,000 persons.

Motor vehicle deaths and homicides, United States, 1997

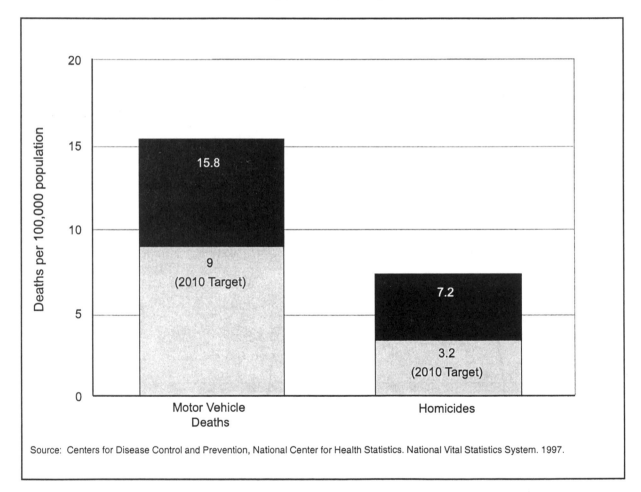

Source: Centers for Disease Control and Prevention, National Center for Health Statistics. National Vital Statistics System. 1997.

The objectives selected to measure progress for this Leading Health Indicator are presented below. These are only indicators and do not represent all the injury and violence prevention objectives in Healthy People 2010.

15-15. Reduce deaths caused by motor vehicle crashes.
15-32. Reduce homicides.

Impact of Injury and Violence

The cost of injury and violence in the United States is estimated at more than $224 billion per year, an increase of 42 percent over the last decade. These costs include direct medical care and rehabilitation as well as productivity losses to the Nation's workforce. The total societal cost of motor vehicle crashes alone exceeds $150 billion annually.

Motor Vehicle Crashes

Motor vehicle crashes are often predictable and preventable. Increased use of seat belts and reductions in driving while impaired are two of the most effective means to reduce the risk of death and serious injury of occupants in motor vehicle crashes.

Death rates associated with motor vehicle-traffic injuries are highest in the age group 15 to 24 years. In 1996, teenagers accounted for only 10 percent of the U.S. population but 15 percent of the deaths from motor vehicle crashes. Those aged 75 years and older had the second highest rate of motor vehicle-related deaths.

Nearly 40 percent of traffic fatalities in 1997 were alcohol-related. Each year in the United States it is estimated that more than 120 million episodes of impaired driving occur among adults. In 1996, 21 percent of traffic fatalities of children under age 14 years involved alcohol; 60 percent of the time it was the driver of the child's car who was impaired.

The highest intoxication rates in fatal crashes in 1995 were recorded for drivers aged 21 to 24 years. Young drivers who have been arrested for driving while impaired are more than four times as likely to die in future alcohol-related crashes.

Homicides

In 1997, 32,436 individuals died from firearm injuries; of this number, 42 percent were victims of homicide. In 1997, homicide was the third leading cause of death for children aged 5 to 14 years, an increasing trend in childhood violent deaths. In 1996, more than 80 percent of infant homicides were considered to be fatal child abuse.

Many factors that contribute to injuries are also closely associated with violent and abusive behavior, such as low income, discrimination, lack of education, and lack of employment opportunities.

Males are most often the victims and the perpetrators of homicides. African Americans are seven times more likely than whites to be murdered. There has been a decline in the homicide of intimates, including spouses, partners, boyfriends, and girlfriends, over the past decade, but this problem remains significant.

For more information on Healthy People 2010 objectives or on injury and violence, visit www.health.gov/healthypeople/ or call 1-800-336-4797.

Environmental Quality

An estimated 25 percent of preventable illnesses worldwide can be attributed to poor environmental quality. In the United States, air pollution alone is estimated to be associated with 50,000 premature deaths and an estimated $40 billion to $50 billion in health-related costs annually. Two indicators of air quality are ozone (outdoor) and environmental tobacco smoke (indoor).

In 1997, approximately 43 percent of the U.S. population lived in areas designated as nonattainment areas for established health-based standards for ozone. During the years 1988 to 1994, 65 percent of nonsmokers were exposed to environmental tobacco smoke (ETS).

Ozone and environmental tobacco smoke exposure, United States, 1988-1994, 1997

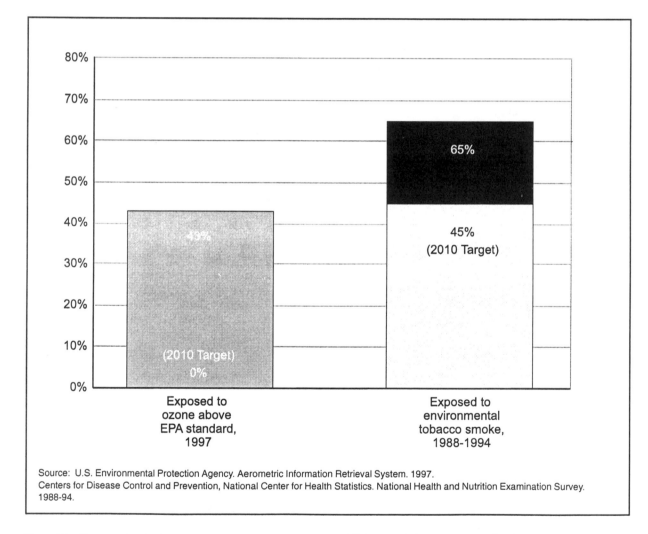

Source: U.S. Environmental Protection Agency. Aerometric Information Retrieval System. 1997.
Centers for Disease Control and Prevention, National Center for Health Statistics. National Health and Nutrition Examination Survey. 1988-94.

The objectives selected to measure progress among children, adolescents, and adults for this Leading Health Indicator are presented below. These are only indicators and do not represent all the environmental quality objectives in Healthy People 2010.

8-1a.   **Reduce the proportion of persons exposed to air that does not meet the U.S. Environmental Protection Agency's health-based standards for ozone.**

27-10. **Reduce the proportion of nonsmokers exposed to environmental tobacco smoke.**

Defining the Environment

Physical and social environments play major roles in the health of individuals and communities. The physical environment includes the air, water, and soil, through which exposure to chemical, biological, and physical agents may occur. The social environment includes housing, transportation, urban development, land-use, industry, and agriculture and results in exposures such as work-related stress, injury, and violence.

Global Concern

Environmental quality is a global concern. Ever-increasing numbers of people and products cross national borders and may transfer health risks such as infectious diseases and chemical hazards. For example, pesticides that are not registered or are restricted for use in the United States potentially could be imported in the fruits, vegetables, and seafood produced abroad.

Health Impact of Poor Air Quality

Poor air quality contributes to respiratory illness, cardiovascular disease, and cancer. For example, asthma can be triggered or worsened by exposure to ozone and ETS. The overall death rate from asthma increased 52 percent between 1980 and 1993, and for children it increased 67 percent.

Air Pollution. Dramatic improvements in air quality in the United States have occurred over the past three decades. Between 1970 and 1997, total emissions of the six principal air pollutants decreased 31 percent. Still, million of tons of toxic pollutants are released into the air each year from automobiles, industry, and other sources. In 1997, despite continued improvements in air quality, approximately 120 million people lived in areas with unhealthy air based on established standards for one or more commonly found air pollutants, including ozone. In 1996, a disproportionate number of Hispanics and Asian and Pacific Islanders lived in areas that failed to meet these standards compared with whites, African Americans, and American Indians or Alaska Natives.

Tobacco Smoke. Exposure to ETS, or secondhand smoke, among nonsmokers is widespread. Home and workplace environments are major sources of exposure. A total of 15 million children are estimated to have been exposed to secondhand smoke in their homes in 1996. ETS increases the risk of heart disease and respiratory infections in children and is responsible for an estimated 3,000 cancer deaths of adult nonsmokers.

Improvement in Environmental Quality

In the United States, ensuring clean water, safe food, and effective waste management has contributed greatly to a declining threat from many infectious diseases; however, there is still more that can be done. Work to improve the air quality and to better understand threats such as chronic, low-level exposures to hazardous substances must also continue.

For more information on Healthy People 2010 objectives or on environmental quality, visit www.health.gov/healthypeople/ or call 1-800-336-4797.

Immunization

Vaccines are among the greatest public health achievements of the 20th century. Immunizations can prevent disability and death from infectious diseases for individuals and can help control the spread of infections within communities.

In 1998, 73 percent of children received all vaccines recommended for universal administration for at least 5 years.

In 1997, influenza immunization rates were 63 percent in adults aged 65 and older, almost double the 1989 immunization rate of 33 percent. In 1997, only 43 percent of persons aged 65 and older had ever received a pneumococcal vaccine.

Immunization coverage, United States, 1991-1998

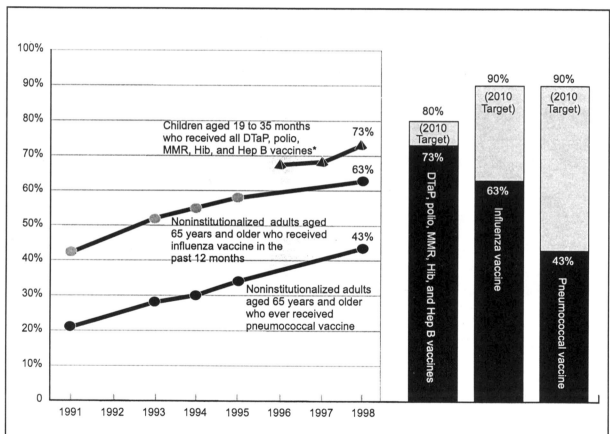

*Four or more doses of diphtheria/tetanus/acellular pertussis (DTaP) vaccine, three or more doses of polio vaccine, one or more dose measles/mumps/rubella (MMR) vaccine, three or more doses of *Haemophilus influenzae* type b (Hib) vacccine, and three or more doses or hepatitis B (Hep B) vaccine

Source: Centers for Disease Control and Prevention, National Center for Health Statistics and National Immunization Program. National Immunization Survey. 1996-1998. Centers for Disease Control and Prevention, National Center for Health Statistics. National Health Interview Survey. 1991-1997.

The objectives selected to measure progress among children and adults for this Leading Health Indicator are presented below. These are only indicators and do not represent all the immunization and infectious diseases objectives in Healthy People 2010.

14-24.   **Increase the proportion of young children who receive all vaccines that have been recommended for universal administration for at least 5 years.**

14-29a,b.   **Increase the proportion of noninstitutionalized adults who are vaccinated annually against influenza and ever vaccinated against pneumococcal disease.**

_____Leading Health Indicator

Impact of Immunization

Many once-common vaccine-preventable diseases are now controlled. Smallpox has been eradicated, poliomyelitis has been eliminated from the Western Hemisphere, and measles cases in the United States are at a record low.

Immunizations against influenza and pneumococcal disease can prevent serious illness and death. Pneumonia and influenza deaths together constitute the sixth leading cause of death in the United States. Influenza causes an average of 110,000 hospitalizations and 20,000 deaths annually; pneumococcal disease causes 10,000 to 14,000 deaths annually.

Recommended Immunizations

As of November 1, 1999, all children born in the United States (11,000 per day) should be receiving 12 to 16 doses of vaccine by age 2 years to be protected against 10 vaccine-preventable childhood diseases. This recommendation will change in the years ahead as new vaccines are developed, including combinations of current vaccines that may even reduce the number of necessary shots.

Recommended immunizations for adults aged 65 years and older include a yearly immunization against influenza (the "flu-shot") and a one-time immunization against pneumococcal disease. Most of the deaths and serious illnesses caused by influenza and pneumococcal disease occur in older adults and others at increased risk for complications of these diseases due to other risk factors or medical conditions.

Trends in Immunization

National coverage levels in children are now greater than 90 percent for each immunization recommended during the first 2 years of life, except for hepatitis B and varicella vaccines. The hepatitis B immunization rate in children was 87 percent in 1998, the highest level ever reported. In 1996, 69 percent of children aged 19 to 35 months from the lowest income households received the combined series of recommended immunizations compared with 80 percent of children from higher income households.

Both influenza and pneumococcal immunization rates are signigicatly lower for African American and Hispanic adults than for white adults.

Other Immunization Issues

Coverage levels for immunizations in adults are not as high as those achieved in children, yet the health effects may be just as great. Barriers to adult immunization include not knowing immunizations are needed, misconceptions about vaccines, and lack of recommendations from health care providers.

For more information on Healthy People 2010 objectives or on immunization and infectious diseases, visit www.health.gov/healthypeople/ or call 1-800-336-4797.

Access to Health Care

Leading Health Indicator

Strong predictors of access to quality health care include having health insurance, a higher income level, and a regular primary care provider or other source of ongoing health care. Use of clinical preventive services, such as early prenatal care, can serve as indicators of access to quality health care services.

In 1997, 86 percent of all individuals had health insurance, and 86 percent had a usual source of health care. Also in that year, 83 percent of pregnant women received prenatal care in the first trimester of pregnancy.

Access to health care, United States, 1997

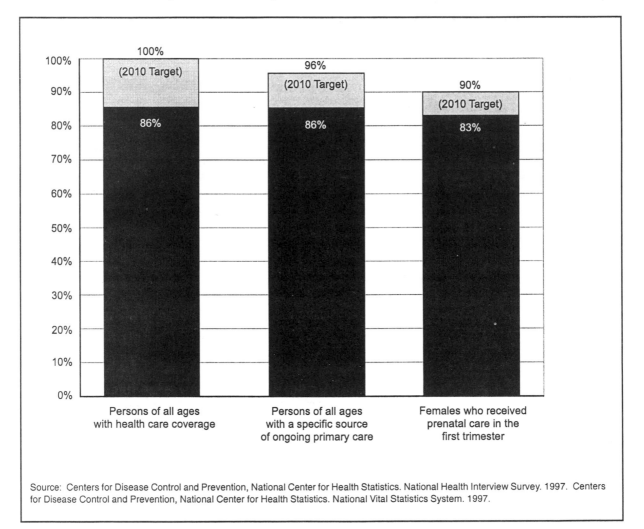

Source: Centers for Disease Control and Prevention, National Center for Health Statistics. National Health Interview Survey. 1997. Centers for Disease Control and Prevention, National Center for Health Statistics. National Vital Statistics System. 1997.

The objectives selected to measure progress for this Leading Health Indicator are presented below. These are only indicators and do not represent all the access to quality health care objectives in Healthy People 2010.

1-1.   Increase the proportion of persons with health insurance.
1-4a.   Increase the proportion of persons who have a specific source of ongoing care.
16-6a.   Increase the proportion of pregnant women who begin prenatal care in the first trimester of pregnancy.

Health Insurance

Health insurance provides access to health care. Persons with health insurance are more likely to have a primary care provider and to have received appropriate preventive care such as a recent Pap test, immunization, or early prenatal care. Adults with health insurance are twice as likely to receive a routine checkup as are adults without health insurance.

More than 44 million persons in the United States do not have health insurance, including 11 million uninsured children. Over the past decade, the proportion of persons aged 65 years and under with health insurance remained steady at about 85 percent. About one-third of adults 65 years and under below the poverty level were uninsured. For persons of Hispanic origin, approximately one in three was without health insurance coverage in 1997. Mexican Americans had one of the highest uninsured rates at 38 percent.

Ongoing Sources of Primary Care

More than 40 million Americans do not have a particular doctor's office, clinic, health center, or other place where they usually go to seek health care or health-related advice. Even among privately insured persons, a significant number lacked a usual source of care or reported difficulty in accessing needed care due to financial constraints or insurance problems.

People aged 18 to 24 years were the most likely to lack a usual source of ongoing primary care. Only 76 percent of individuals below the poverty level and 74 percent of Hispanics had a usual source of ongoing primary care.

Barriers to Access

Financial, structural, and personal barriers can limit access to health care. Financial barriers include not having health insurance, not having enough health insurance to cover needed services, or not having the financial capacity to cover services outside a health plan or insurance program. Structural barriers include the lack of primary care providers, medical specialists, or other health care professionals to meet special needs or the lack of health care facilities. Personal barriers include cultural or spiritual differences, language barriers, not knowing what to do or when to seek care, or concerns about confidentiality or discrimination.

For more information on Healthy People 2010 objectives or on access to health care, visit www.health.gov/healthypeople/ or call 1-800-336-4797.

Bibliography

Introduction

McGinnis JM and Maiese DR. Defining mission, goals, and objectives. In: *Principles of Public Health Practice.* Scutchfield FD and Keck CW (eds.). Albany, NY: Delmar Publishers, 1997, pp. 140-141.

A Systematic Approach to Health Improvement

Goals

American College of Physicians. Rural primary care. *Ann Inter Med* 122(5):380-390, 1995.

American Medical Association Council Report. Health care needs of gay men and lesbians in the United States. *JAMA* 247:1354-1359, 1996.

Centers for Disease Control and Prevention. BRFSS Prevalence Data, 1998. <http://ww2.cdc.gov/ nccdphp/brfss/ index.asp>.

Centers for Disease Control and Prevention. Health-related quality of life and activity limitation—eight states, 1995. *MMWR* 47(7):134-140, 1998.

Centers for Disease Control and Prevention. Health-related quality-of-life measures—United States, 1993. *MMWR* 44:195-200, 1995.

Definitions: Healthy People 2010, Disability and Secondary Conditions Focus Area.

Institute of Medicine. *Improving Health in the Community.* Washington, DC: National Academy Press, 1997, pp. 48-56.

National Center for Health Statistics. *Health, United States, 1999, With Health and Aging Chartbook.* Hyattsville, MD: U.S. Department of Health and Human Services, 1999.

National Center for Health Statistics. *Healthy People 2000 Review, 1998-99.* Hyattsville, MD: Public Health Service, 1999.

Tissue T. Another look at self-rated health among the elderly. *J Gerontol* (27):91-94, 1972.

Barker WH. Prevention of disability in older persons. In: *Public Health and Preventive Medicine, Fourteenth Edition,* Wallace RB (ed.). Stamford, CT: Appleton & Lange, 1998, p. 1063.

Braden J, Beauregard K. *Health Status and Access to Care of Rural and Urban Populations.* AHCPR Pub. no. 94-0031. National Medical Expenditure Survey Research Findings 18. Rockville, MD: Public Health Service, Agency for Health Care Policy and Research, 1994.

Catalan J, Pugh K. Suicidal behaviour and HIV infection—is there a link? *AIDS Care* 7(Suppl 2):S117-S121, 1995.

Cochran SD, Mays VM. Depressive distress among homosexually active African American men and women. *Am J Psychiatry* 151:524-529, 1994.

Davidson L, Linnoila M (eds.). *Report of the Secretary's Task Force on Youth Suicide, 2: Risk Factors for Youth Suicide.* Washington, DC: U.S. Department of Health and Human Services, Public Health Service, 1989.

Frumkin H and Walker ED. Minority workers and communities. In: *Public Health and Preventive Medicine, Fourteenth Edition,* Wallace RB (ed.). Stamford, CT: Appleton & Lange, 1998, p. 685.

Hoyert DL, Kochanek KD, Murphy SL. Deaths: final data for 1997. *National Vital Statistics Reports.* Vol. 47, no. 19. Hyattsville, MD: National Center for Health Statistics, 1999.

Idler EL and Benyamini Y. Self-rated health and mortality: a review of twenty-seven community studies. *J Health Soc Behav* 38:21-37, 1997.

LaPlante MP, Rice DP, Cyril J. Health insurance coverage of people with disabilities in the U.S. *Disability Statistics Abstract.* Disability Statistics Rehabilitation. San Francisco, CA: Research and Training Center, September 1994.

Last JM. The determinants of health. In: *Principles of Public Health Practice,* Scutchfield FD and Keck CW (eds.). Albany, NY: Delmar Publishers, 1997, pp. 33-34.

Luepker RV. Heart disease. In: *Public Health and Preventive Medicine. Fourteenth Edition,* Wallace RB (ed.). Stamford, CT: Appleton & Lange, 1998, pp. 939-940.

McNeil JM. Americans with disabilities: 1994-95. *Current Population Reports.* Bureau of the Census (P70-61). Washington, DC: U.S. Department of Commerce, August 1997.

Pamuk E, Makuc D, Heck K, Reuben C, Lochner K. *Socioeconomic Status and Health Chartbook. Health, United States, 1998.* Hyattsville, MD: National Center for Health Statistics, 1998.

Pearson TA, Lewis C. Rural epidemiology: insights from a rural population laboratory. *Am J Epidemiol* 148(10):949-957, 1998.

Solarz, A (ed.). *Lesbian Health: current Assessment and Directions for the Future.* Washington, DC: Institute of Medicine, 1997.

Syme SL and Balfour JL. Social determinants of disease. In: *Public Health and Preventive Medicine, Fourteenth Edition,* Wallace RB (ed.). Stamford, CT: Appleton & Lange, 1998, pp. 800-801.

Vistnes JP and Monheit AC. *Health Insurance Status of the Civilian Noninstitutionalized Population.* Medical Expenditure Panel Survey Research Findings 1. AHCPR Pub. no. 97-0030. Rockville, MD: Agency for Health Care Policy and Research, August 1997.

Determinants of Health

Institute of Medicine. *Improving Health in the Community.* Washington, DC: National Academy Press, 1997, pp. 48-56.

McGinnis JM, Maiese DR. Defining mission, goals, and objectives. In: *Principles of Public Health Practice,* Scutchfield FD and Keck CW (eds.). Albany, NY: Delmar Publishers, 1997, pp. 136-145.

Syme SL and Balfour JL. Social determinants of disease. In: *Public Health and Preventive Medicine, Fourteenth Edition,* Wallace RB (ed.). Stamford, CT: Appleton & Lange, 1998, p. 795.

Health Status

National Center for Health Statistics. *Health, United States, 1999, With Health and Aging Chartbook.* Hyattsville, MD: U.S. Department of Health and Human Services, 1999.

Leading Health Indicators

Physical Activity

Centers for Disease Control and Prevention. Physical activity and the prevention of coronary heart disease. *MMWR* 42:669-672, 1993.

Centers for Disease Control and Prevention. Prevalence of sedentary leisure-time behavior among adults in the United States. *Health E-Stats.* Atlanta, GA: Centers for Disease Control and Prevention, National Center for Health Statistics, 1999.

National Center for Health Statistics. *Health, United States, 1999, With Health and Aging Chartbook.* Hyattsville, MD: U.S. Department of Health and Human Services, 1999.

National Center for Health Statistics. *Healthy People 2000 Review, 1998-99.* Hyattsville, MD: U.S. Department of Health and Human Services, 1999.

U.S. Department of Health and Human Services. *Physical Activity and Health: A Report of the Surgeon General.* Atlanta, GA: Centers for Disease Control and Prevention, National Center for Chronic Disease Prevention and Health Promotion, 1996.

Pamuk E, Makuc D, Heck K, Reuben C, Lochner K. *Socioeconomic Status and Health Chartbook. Health, United States, 1998.* Hyattsville, MD: National Center for Health Statistics, 1998.

Overweight and Obesity

Agricultural Research Service. Research News. Press Release. U.S. Department of Agriculture, Washington, DC, November 20, 1996.

National Center for Health Statistics. *Health, United States, 1999, With Health and Aging Chartbook.* Hyattsville, MD: U.S. Department of Health and Human Services, 1999.

National Center for Health Statistics. *Healthy People 2000 Review, 1998-99.* Hyattsville, MD: U.S. Department of Health and Human Services, 1999.

National Institutes of Health. *Statistics Related to Overweight and Obesity.* NIH Publication No. 96-4158. National Institute of Diabetes and Digestive and Kidney Diseases. Bethesda, MD: U.S. Department of Health and Human Services, July 1996.

U.S. Department of Agriculture/U.S. Department of Health and Human Services. *Dietary Guidelines for Americans. Fourth Edition.* USDA Home and Garden Bulletin No. 232. December 1995.

Pamuk E, Makuc D, Heck K, Reuben C, Lochner K. *Socioeconomic Status and Health Chartbook. Health, United States, 1998.* Hyattsville, MD: National Center for Health Statistics, 1998.

Lin BH and Frazao E. Nutritional quality of foods at and away from home. *FoodReview* 20(2):33-40, 1997.

Wolf AM, Colditz GA. Current estimates of the economic cost of obesity in the United States. *Obesity Research* 6(2):97-106, 1998.

Tobacco Use

Centers for Disease Control and Prevention. Guidelines for school health programs to prevent tobacco use and addiction. *MMWR* 43(no. RR-2):1994.

Centers for Disease Control and Prevention. Smoking-attributable mortality and years of potential life lost—United States, 1984. *MMWR* 46(20):441-451, 1997.

Centers for Disease Control and Prevention. *Targeting Tobacco Use: The Nation's Leading Cause of Death.* Atlanta, GA: U.S. Department of Health and Human Services, CDC, 1999.

Centers for Disease Control and Prevention. Youth Risk Behavior Surveillance—United States, 1997. *MMWR* 47(SS-3):1998.

National Center for Health Statistics. *Health, United States, 1999, With Health and Aging Chartbook.* Hyattsville, MD: U.S. Department of Health and Human Services, 1999.

National Cancer Institute. *Cigars: Health Effects and Trends.* Bethesda, MD: U.S. Department of Health and Human Services, National Institutes of Health, 1998.

U.S. Environmental Protection Agency. *Respiratory Health Effects of Passive Smoking: Fact Sheet.* EPA Pub. No. EPA-43-F-93-003. Washington, DC: EPA, 1993.

U.S. Department of Health and Human Services. *Tobacco Use Among U.S. Racial/Ethnic Minority Groups—African Americans, American Indians and Alaska Natives, Asian Americans and Pacific Islanders, and Hispanics: A Report of the Surgeon General.* Atlanta, Georgia: U.S. Department of Health and Human Services, Centers for Disease Control and Prevention, National Center for Chronic Disease Prevention and Health Promotion, Office on Smoking and Health, 1998.

Substance Abuse

National Clearinghouse for Alcohol and Drug Information. *Health Care Costs, the Deficit, & Alcohol, Tobacco, and Other Drugs.* Rockville, MD: NCADI Inventory Number ML007, 1995.

Substance Abuse and Mental Health Services Administration. *Summary of Findings From the 1998 National Household Survey on Drug Abuse.* Rockville, MD: U.S. Department of Health and Human Services, SAMHSA, Office of Applied Studies, 1999.

Harwood H, Fountain D, Livermore G. *The Economic Costs of Alcohol and Drug Abuse in the United States, 1992*. NIH Publication Number 98-4327. Rockville, MD: U.S. Department of Health and Human Services, National Institutes of Health, 1998.

Responsible Sexual Behavior

American Social Health Association. *Sexually Transmitted Diseases in America: How Many Cases and at What Cost?* Menlo Park, CA: Kaiser Family Foundation, 1998.

Centers for Disease Control and Prevention. *Fact sheet: Youth Risk Behavior Trends*. Atlanta, GA: U.S. Department of Health and Human Services, Centers for Disease Control and Prevention. National Center for Chronic Disease Prevention and Health Promotion, 1999.

Centers for Disease Control and Prevention. *From Data to Action: CDC's Public Health Surveillance for Women, Infants, and Children*. Atlanta, GA: U.S. Department of Health and Human Services, Centers for Disease Control and Prevention, National Center for Chronic Disease Prevention and Health Promotion, 1994.

Centers for Disease Control and Prevention. *HIV/AIDS Surveillance Report, Midyear edition*. Atlanta, GA: U.S. Department of Health and Human Services, Centers for Disease Control and Prevention, 1999.

Centers for Disease Control and Prevention. *PRAMS 1996 Surveillance Report*. Atlanta, GA: Centers for Disease Control and Prevention, National Center for Chronic Disease Prevention and Health Promotion, Division of Reproductive Health, 1999.

Centers for Disease Control and Prevention. Trends in sexual risk behaviors among high school students—United States, 1991-1997. *MMWR* 47(36):749-752, 1998.

Centers for Disease Control and Prevention. Young people at risk—epidemic shifts further toward young women and minorities. In: *CDC Update*. Atlanta, GA: U.S. Department of Health and Human Services, Centers for Disease Control and Prevention, National Center for HIV, TB & STD Prevention, 1999.

Division of STD Prevention. *Sexually Transmitted Disease Surveillance, 1998*. Atlanta, GA: U.S. Department of Health and Human Services, Centers for Disease Control and Prevention, September 1999.

National Center for Health Statistics. *Healthy People 2000 Review, 1998-99*. Hyattsville, MD: U.S. Department of Health and Human Services, 1999.

Holtgrave DR, Pinkerton SD. Updates of cost of illness and quality of life estimates for use in economic evaluations of HIV prevention programs. *J Acquir Immune Defic Syndr Hum Retrovirol* 16(1):54-62, 1997.

Hoyert DL, Kochanek KD, Murphy SL. Deaths: final data for 1997. *National Vital Statistics Reports*. Vol. 47, no. 19. Hyattsville, MD: National Center for Health Statistics, 1999.

Maynard RA (ed.). *Kids Having Kids; Economic Costs and Cocial Consequences of Teen Pregnancy*. Washington, DC: Urban Institute Press, 1997.

St. Louis ME, Wasserheit JN, Gayle HD. Janus considers the HIV pandemic-harnessing recent advances to enhance AIDS prevention. *Am J Public Health* 87(1):10-12, 1997.

Mental Health

National Center for Health Statistics. *Healthy People 2000 Review, 1998-99.* Hyattsville, MD: U.S. Department of Health and Human Services, 1999.

National Institutes of Health, Consensus Development Panel on Depression in Late Life, Diagnosis and treatment of depression in late life. *JAMA* 268:1018-1024, 1992.

National Institute of Mental Health. *Depression.* Fact sheet. http://www.nimh.nih.gov/depression/index.htm. Bethesda, MD: U.S. Department of Health and Human Services, National Institutes of Health, 1999.

National Institute of Mental Health. *The Invisible Disease—Depression.* Fact sheet. <http://www.nimh.nih.gov/publicat/invisible.cfm>. Bethesda, MD: U.S. Department of Health and Human Services, National Institutes of Health, 1999.

Office of Applied Statistics. *Statistics Source Book, 1998,* Rouse BA (ed.). Substance Abuse and Mental Health Services Administration. Rockville, MD: U.S. Department of Health and Human Services, 1998.

Substance Abuse and Mental Health Services Administration. *Mental Health: A Report of the Surgeon General.* Rockville, MD: U.S. Department of Health and Human Services, National Institutes of Health, 1999.

Bromet EJ. Psychiatric disorders. In: *Public Health and Preventive Medicine, Fourteenth Edition,* Wallace RB (ed.). Stamford, CT: Appleton & Lange, 1998, p. 1037.

Greenberg PE, Stiglin LE, Finkelstein SN, Berndt ER. The economic burden of depression in 1990. *J Clin Psychiatry* 54:405-418, 1993.

Koenig HG and Blazer DG. Mood disorders and suicide. In: *Handbook of Mental Health and Aging, Second Edition,* Birren JE, Sloane RB, Cohen GD (eds.). San Diego, CA: Academic Press, 1992, 379-407.

Weissman MM and Klerman JK. Depression: current understanding and changing trends. *Ann Rev Public Health* 13:319-339, 1992.

Injury and Violence

National Center for Health Statistics. *Healthy People 2000 Review, 1998-99.* Hyattsville, MD: U.S. Department of Health and Human Services, 1999.

National Center for Injury Prevention and Control. *Impaired Driving Fact Sheet.* Atlanta, GA: U.S. Department of Health and Human Services, Centers for Disease Control and Prevention, 1999.

National Highway Traffic Safety Administration. *Traffic Safety Facts, 1998.* Washington, DC: U.S. Department of Transportation, 1998.

National Safety Council, *Accident Facts.* Washington, DC: National Safety Council, 1995.

Baker SP, O'Neill B, Ginsburg MJ, Li G. *The Injury Fact Book, 2nd Edition,* New York, NY: Oxford University Press, 1992.

Fox JA and Zawitz MW. *Homicide Trends in the United States.* U.S. Department of Justice, Bureau of Justice Statistics, 1999.

Hoyert DL, Kochanek KD, Murphy SL. Deaths: final data for 1997. *National Vital Statistics Reports.* Vol. 47, no. 19. Hyattsville, MD: National Center for Health Statistics, 1999.

Environmental Quality

American Lung Association. *Health Costs of Air Pollution.* Washington, DC: American Lung Association, 1990.

California Environmental Protection Agency, *Health Effects of Exposure to Environmental Tobacco Smoke.* Final Report. Sacramento, CA: California Environmental Protection Agency, Office of Environmental Health Hazard Assessment, 1997.

Centers for Disease Control and Prevention. Progress toward the elimination of tuberculosis—United States, 1998. *MMWR* 48:732-736, 1999.

Centers for Disease Control and Prevention. State-specific prevalence of cigarette smoking among adults, and children's and adolescent's exposure to environmental tobacco smoke—United States. *MMWR* 46:1038-1043, 1997.

National Center for Health Statistics. *Health, United States, 1999, With Health and Aging Chartbook.* Hyattsville, MD: U.S. Department of Health and Human Services, 1999.

U.S. Environmental Protection Agency. *National Air Quality and Trends Report.* Office of Air and Radiation. Washington, DC: EPA, 1997.

U.S. Environmental Protection Agency. *Respiratory Health Effects of Passive Smoking: Lung Cancer and Other Disorders.* EPA Pub. No. EPA/600/6-90/006F. Washington, DC: EPA, 1992.

World Health Organization. Fact Sheet 170, June 1997.

Weiss KB, Gergen PJ, Hodgson TA. An economic evaluation of asthma in the United States. *N Engl J Med* 326:862-866, 1992.

Immunization

Centers for Disease Control and Prevention. National Immunization Program, Immunization Services Division, Health Services Research and Evaluation Branch. Unpublished data. Atlanta, GA, 1999.

Centers for Disease Control and Prevention. National vaccination coverage levels among children aged 19-35 months—United States, 1998. *MMWR* 48:829-830, 1999.

Centers for Disease Control and Prevention. Prevention and control of influenza: recommendations of the Advisory Committee on Immunization Practices (ACIP). *MMWR* 48(no. RR-4), 1999.

Centers for Disease Control and Prevention. Prevention of pneumococcal disease: recommendations of the Advisory Committee on Immunization Practices (ACIP). *MMWR* 46(no. RR-8), 1997.

Centers for Disease Control and Prevention. Reasons reported by Medicare beneficiaries for not receiving influenza and pneumococcal vaccinations—United States, 1996. *MMWR* 48:886-890, 1999.

Centers for Disease Control and Prevention. Recommended childhood immunization schedule—United States, 1999. *MMWR* 48:12-16, 1999.

Centers for Disease Control and Prevention. Ten great public health achievements—United States, 1900-1999. *MMWR* 48:241-248, 1999.

National Center for Health Statistics. *Health, United States, 1999, With Health and Aging Chartbook.* Hyattsville, MD: U.S. Department of Health and Human Services, 1999.

Feiken DR, Schuchat A, Kolczak M, et al. Mortality from invasive pneumococcal pneumonia in the era of antibiotic resistance, 1995-1997. *Am J Public Health,* in press.

Pamuk E, Makuc D, Heck K, Reuben C, Lochner K. *Socioeconomic Status and Health Chartbook. Health, United States, 1998.* Hyattsville, MD: National Center for Health Statistics, 1998.

Access to Health Care

Centers for Disease Control and Prevention. Health insurance coverage and receipt of preventive health services—United States, 1993. *MMWR* 44(11):219-225, 1995.

National Center for Health Statistics. *Health, United States, 1999, With Health and Aging Chartbook.* Hyattsville, MD: U.S. Department of Health and Human Services, 1999.

U.S. General Accounting Office. *Health Insurance: Coverage Leads to Increased Health Care Access for Children.* GAO/HEHS-98-14. Washington, DC: GAO, 1998, pp. 4-20.

Healthy People 2010

Objectives for
Improving Health (Part A)

Reader's Guide

Each focus area chapter contains the following sections:

Lead Agency Designation

Each focus area is managed by a designated lead agency or co-lead agencies of the U.S. Department of Health and Human Services (HHS). For certain focus areas, the lead agency responsibilities are shared by other Federal Departments. In particular, the Disability and Secondary Conditions focus area is co-led by the Centers for Disease Control and Prevention and the U.S. Department of Education. The Food Safety focus area is co-led by the Food and Drug Administration and the Food Safety and Inspection Service of the U.S. Department of Agriculture. Lead agencies are responsible for undertaking activities to move the Nation toward achieving the year 2010 goals and for reporting progress on the focus area objectives over the course of the decade.

Contents

This brief list details the specific organization of each chapter, including the descriptive headings for the types of objectives that are contained in this focus area.

Goal Statement

Each chapter contains a concise goal statement. This statement frames the overall purpose of the focus area.

Overview

The Overview provides the context and background for the objectives and identifies opportunities for prevention or interventions. The Overview addresses the following topics: nature of the issues; key trends or developments in the focus area; costs and other pertinent information; relevant disparities among population groups (including race and ethnicity, gender, age, disability status, and socioeconomic status) or between geographic areas; and implications of such factors for prevention or other improvements, with explicit reference to the objectives and promising research.

Interim Progress Toward Year 2000 Objectives

Because Healthy People 2010 builds on the experience of the preceding decade, this section provides a brief description of progress to date on year 2000 objectives pertaining to the focus area. A final report on the year 2000 objectives, *Healthy People 2000 Review,* will be published by the National Center for Health Statistics of the Centers for Disease Control and Prevention.

Healthy People 2010 Objectives

This section begins with a restatement of the focus area goal and a list of short titles for all objectives in the focus area. Where appropriate, objectives are organized into sections with headings. These headings provide structure and appear in the list of short titles.

Objectives were developed by work groups (see Appendix E and Appendix F) for each focus area, with broad public input. Each objective is designed to drive action. Therefore, objectives begin with a verb, followed by the subject.

Each objective is numbered for reference purposes. Numbering does not imply priority or importance. Explanatory text follows objectives as needed.

Criteria for Developing Objectives

Criteria first published in *Developing Objectives for Healthy People 2010* in September 1997 call for objectives to be useful to national, State, and local agencies as well as to the private sector and the public. The objectives must have certain attributes, including the following:

- The result to be achieved should be **important and understandable** to a broad audience and relate to the two overarching Healthy People 2010 goals.

- Objectives should be **prevention oriented** and should address health improvements that can be achieved through population-based and health-service interventions.

- Objectives should **drive action** and suggest a set of interim steps that will achieve the proposed targets within the specified timeframe.

- Objectives should be **useful and relevant**. States, localities, and the private sector should be able to use the objectives to target efforts in schools, communities, worksites, health practices, and other settings.

- Objectives should be **measurable** and include a range of measures—health outcomes, behavioral and health-service interventions, and community capacity—directed toward improving health outcomes and quality of life. They should count assets and achievements and look to the positive.

- **Continuity** and **comparability** are important. Whenever possible, objectives should build upon Healthy People 2000 and those goals and performance measures already established.

- Objectives must be supported by sound **scientific evidence.**

Types of Objectives

There are two types of objectives—measurable and developmental.

Measurable objectives. Measurable objectives provide direction for action. For measurable objectives, the current status is expressed with a national baseline. The baseline represents the starting point for action to move the Nation toward the desired end. The baselines use valid and reliable data derived from currently established, nationally representative data systems. These baseline data provide the point from which a 2010 target is set. Where possible, objectives are measured with nationally representative data systems. Some of these systems build on, or are comparable with, State and local data systems. However, State data are not a prerequisite to developing an objective. Non-national data may be used where national data are not available. These situations are noted in the baseline data for the objective. The data source for each measurable objective is identified.

Developmental objectives. Developmental objectives provide a vision for a desired outcome or health status. Current national surveillance systems do not provide data on these subjects. The purpose of developmental objectives is to identify areas of emerging importance and to drive the development of data systems to measure them. Most developmental objectives have a potential data source with reasonable expectation of data points by the year 2004 to facilitate setting year 2010 targets in the mid-decade review. Developmental objectives that do not have a baseline at the midcourse will be dropped.

Population Group Data Table

Because eliminating health disparities is a goal of Healthy People 2010, a standard data table is used to display the current status of population groups for population-based objectives. This standard table consists of a set of population variables that are to be considered a minimum breakout set for data collection. Within each category in the table, groups are alphabetized. Some objectives show more detailed or additional breakouts of population groups.

Sample Population-Based Table

	Percent of Persons With Health Insurance
TOTAL	
Race and ethnicity	
American Indian or Alaska Native	
Asian or Pacific Islander	
Asian	
Native Hawaiian and other Pacific Islander	

Black or African American	
White	
Hispanic or Latino	
Not Hispanic or Latino	
Black or African American	
White	
Gender	
Female	
Male	
Family income level	
Poor	
Near poor	
Middle/high income	
Education level	
Less than high school	
High school graduate	
At least some college	
The following are additional categories included where appropriate.	
Geographic location	
Urban	
Rural	
Health insurance status	
Private health insurance	
Public health insurance	
Medicare	
Medicaid	
No health insurance	
Disability status	
Persons with disabilities or activity limitations	
Persons without disabilities or activity limitations	
Select populations	
Age groups	
School grade levels	
Persons with select medical conditions	

DNA = Data have not been analyzed. DNC = Data are not collected. DSU = Data are statistically unreliable.
Note: Age adjusted to the year 2000 standard population.

Race and ethnicity. Following guidance issued by the Office of Management and Budget (OMB), Healthy People 2010 sets forth the new categories for reporting race and ethnicity. Federal data systems have until January 2003 to comply with these standards. "More than one race" will be displayed in this category when data are available at the midcourse review.

Gender. Gender follows race and ethnicity in the template. In many instances, where the unique problem for each gender needs to be highlighted, data for all population groups in the template are presented for both genders.

Socioeconomic status (SES). SES is shown as income level or education breakouts or both. If education was selected, data are presented in three groups: less than high school, high school graduate, and at least some college. If income was selected, the three groups are poor, near poor, and middle/high income. In some objectives, programmatic data considerations may result in different income categories being displayed.

Age. Age is not included in the minimum template for the table, because to show inclusive age categories would add considerable complexity to the minimum set. Furthermore, age often is in the objective (for example, mammograms for women aged 40 years and over), and many objectives are relevant only for a subset of age groups. Age breakouts have been added to objectives where relevant and may not be inclusive of the total population. For example, data lines for elderly persons or children could be added to selected objectives without adding other groups. Age adjustment here is indicated for those objectives. The statistical compendium, Tracking Healthy People 2010, covers this subject in greater detail.

Several other population groups are shown in various objectives. These include the following: urban/rural populations, health insurance status, and persons with disabilities or activity limitations.

The following abbreviations in the data tables indicate where data are not available:

DNA = Data have not been analyzed.

DNC = Data are not collected.

DSU = Data are statistically unreliable. The data set produces the figure, but the number of respondents is too small to be valid, the proportion of respondents with missing information is too large, or the survey does not have representative data for certain population groups.

NA = Not applicable.

Targets for Measurable Objectives

As a general rule, one target is set for all population groups to reach by the year 2010. This supports the overarching goal of eliminating health disparities. The guidelines used to develop targets are as follows:

- One national target for the year 2010 is set for all measurable objectives and is applicable to all population groups. This target setting method supports the goal of eliminating health disparities and improving health for all segments of the total population.

- For those measures contained in the HHS Initiative to Eliminate Racial and Ethnic Disparities in Health, the targets are set at "better than the best."

- For those objectives that in the short term can be influenced by lifestyle choices, behaviors, and health services (in other words, using existing and known interventions), the target also is set at "better than the best" currently achieved by any population group.

- For objectives for which it is unlikely to achieve an equal health outcome within 10 years by applying known health interventions, the target is set at levels that represent improvements for a substantial proportion of the population. These targets are regarded as minimally acceptable improvements. Explicit recognition is made that population groups already better than the identified target should continue to improve.

The following target setting methods have been used:

(1) Better than the best group.

(2) __ percent improvement.

(3) "Total coverage" or "Complete elimination" (for targets like 0 percent, 100 percent, all States, etc.).

(4) Consistent with _____ (another national program, for example, national education goals).

(5) Retain year 2000 target (the Healthy People 2000 target has been retained).

Data Source/Potential Data Source

Data source is defined as the instrument that reports the measure indicated. Measurable objectives cite the data source for the baseline.

(1) For HHS data sets, surveys, and reports, the citation includes the name of the data set, the HHS agency, and institute or center that serves as the source—for example, National Health Interview Survey, CDC, NCHS.

(2) For non-HHS or non-Federal data sets, surveys, and reports, the citation includes the name of the data set, cabinet-level agency, and bureau/agency/organization—for example, Fatality Analysis Reporting System, DOT, NHTSA.

Related Objectives

Each objective is placed in only one focus area, meaning there are no duplicate objectives in Healthy People 2010. There are, however, numerous linkages among focus areas, and these are represented in the list of related objectives from other focus areas.

Terminology

Terms are set up as dictionary definitions in alphabetical order. These definitions enable the reader to understand the concepts used in the chapter. A master list of abbreviations and acronyms used throughout the book appears in Appendix K. For more information on measuring the objectives, technical notes, or operational definitions, refer to the statistical compendium, Tracking Healthy People 2010.

References

The references cited throughout both the text and the objectives are listed at the end of each chapter.

1

Access to Quality Health Services

Co-Lead Agencies: Agency for Healthcare Research and Quality;
Health Resources and Services Administration

Contents

Goal

Improve access to comprehensive, high-quality health care services.

Overview

Access to quality care is important to eliminate health disparities and increase the quality and years of healthy life for all Americans. This chapter focuses on four components of the health care system: clinical preventive care, primary care, emergency services, and long-term and rehabilitative care. Together with health care delivered by specialists and care received in hospital settings, these elements represent major components of the continuum of care. The public health system is important in each of these areas because it educates people about prevention and addresses the need to eliminate disparities by easing access to preventive services for people less able to use existing health services. It ensures the availability of primary care through direct funding of clinics and providers or by providing public insurance. It coordinates emergency services systems and oversees long-term and rehabilitative care. Tertiary services (for example, hospital and specialty care) currently are not included among the Healthy People 2010 objectives. The Agency for Healthcare Research and Quality (AHRQ), formerly the Agency for Health Care Policy and Research, is working in conjunction with the Centers for Disease Control and Prevention and other agencies of the U.S. Department of Health and Human Services to develop a *National Report on Healthcare Quality*, which will report annually on a broader array of quality measures that will complement Healthy People 2010.

Issues

Access to quality care across each of the components in the continuum of care must be improved to realize the full potential of prevention. For example, success in reducing the burden of heart disease and narrowing the gap in heart disease outcomes between different racial groups will depend on several factors. These factors include ensuring access to clinical preventive services, such as blood pressure and cholesterol screening; effective primary care to educate people about modifiable risk factors, such as smoking, and to manage effectively chronic conditions like hypertension; high-quality emergency services to improve outcomes of acute cardiac events; and access to rehabilitative and long-term care for heart disease patients.

Major changes in the structure of the U.S. health care system, including the increasing influence of market forces, changes in payment and delivery systems, and welfare reform, have significant implication for vulnerable and at-risk populations. In light of these systems changes, Federal, State, and local public health agencies must redouble their efforts to address access barriers and reduce disparities for these populations. It is increasingly important that health care communication and services be provided in a culturally and linguistically sensitive manner. Adequate access to health care and related services can increase appropriate patient use of the health care system and, ultimately, improve health outcomes. Consequently, measures of access across a continuum of care are an important way to evaluate the quality of the Nation's health care system.

Clinical preventive care. Clinical preventive services have a substantial impact on many of the leading causes of disease and death. People must have access to clinical preventive services that are effective in preventing disease (primary prevention) or in detecting asymptomatic disease or risk factors at early, treatable stages (secondary prevention). As in Healthy People 2000, the recommendations of the U.S. Preventive Services Task Force[1] serve as a guide to quality preventive health care. The task force was reconvened in 1998 and, in conjunction with the Evidence-Based Practice Centers (EPCs) of the Agency for Healthcare Research and Quality, will provide additional information regarding the effectiveness and cost-effectiveness of individual clinical preventive services.

Improving access to appropriate preventive care requires addressing many barriers, including those that involve the patient, provider, and system of care.[2, 3] Patient barriers include lack of knowledge, skepticism about the effectiveness of prevention, lack of a usual source of primary care, and lack of money to pay for preventive care. Although patient awareness and acceptance of some interventions are high, such as screening for breast cancer, other interventions (for example, colorectal cancer screening and sexually transmitted disease [STD] screening) are less uniformly accepted. A small but significant number of patients remain skeptical of even widely accepted preventive measures, such as immunizations. Having health insurance, a high income, and a primary care provider are strong predictors that a person will receive appropriate preventive care. Although reimbursement for common screening tests, such as mammograms and Pap smears, is provided by most health insurance plans (and is required by law in some States), reimbursement for effective counseling interventions, such as smoking cessation, is less common.[4]

Health provider barriers include limited time, lack of training in prevention, lack of perceived effectiveness of selected preventive services, and practice environments that fail to facilitate prevention. Although consensus is growing regarding the value of a range of preventive services, providers identify lack of time and reimbursement as specific barriers to more consistent delivery of counseling about behavioral risk factors such as diet and exercise.[5] Computerized or manual tracking systems, patient and clinician reminders, guidelines, and patient information materials can help providers improve delivery of necessary preventive care.[6]

System barriers can include lack of resources or attention devoted to prevention, lack of coverage or inadequate reimbursement for services, and lack of systems to track the quality of care.[3] Systems interventions that can increase delivery of health care include offering clinical preventive services among standard covered benefits, providing feedback on performance to providers and practices, offering incentives for improved performance, and developing and implementing systems to identify and provide outreach to patients in need of services.[2]

Measuring and reporting how well preventive care is provided under different systems are essential first steps in motivating those systems that are not performing well to develop the information, tools, and incentives to improve care.[7] Significant progress in the delivery of clinical preventive services (CPS) is unlikely without appropriate data systems to allow providers and administrators to identify those services and populations most in need of better delivery. To be effective, preventive care also must be linked to systems to ensure appropriate followup services or counseling for patients identified by risk assessment or screening. Comprehensive national data to track what systems of care are doing to monitor and improve the delivery of CPS will not be available in the first half of the decade. Thus, this issue is not addressed in this focus area's objectives but represents an important research and data collection agenda for the coming decade.

Primary care. Improving primary care across the Nation depends in part on ensuring that people have a usual source of care. Having a primary care provider as the usual source of care is especially important because of the beneficial attributes of primary care. These benefits include the provision of integrated, accessible health care services by clinicians who are accountable for addressing a large majority of personal health care needs, developing a sustained partnership with patients, and practicing in the context of family and community.[8] Increasing the number and proportion of members of underrepresented racial and ethnic groups who are primary care providers also is important because they are more likely to practice in areas where health services are in short supply and are more likely to practice in areas with high percentages of underrepresented racial and ethnic populations.

Emergency services. Prehospital emergency medical services (EMS), poison control centers (PCCs), and hospital-based emergency departments (EDs) are the most commonly sought sources of emergency care. Each year, they provide prompt first-contact care for millions of Americans regardless of their socioeconomic status, age, or special need. For many severely ill and injured persons, they are a crucial link in the chain of survival between the onset of symptoms and treatment in a hospital. For persons whose health problems are less pressing but who believe they need urgent medical attention, emergency services are a gateway to additional health care.

In addition to their central role in secondary and tertiary prevention, emergency services are increasingly contributing to primary prevention by providing immunizations and other preventive care in association with treatment for acute health problems.

Within the current health care delivery system, EDs are the only institutional providers required by Federal law to evaluate anyone seeking care.[9] They are expected at least to stabilize the most severely ill and injured patients, and they provide walk-in care for vast numbers of persons who face financial or other barriers to receiving care elsewhere.

Long-term care and rehabilitative services. People with physical or mental conditions that limit their capacity for self-care need long-term care and rehabilitative services. This population covers persons of all ages, from those who were born with physical or mental limitations or who developed such limitations later on in life, including those injured at any age, to those with diminishing functioning at older ages.[10] About 40 percent of the people in this population are under age 65 years.[11] The long-term care population includes individuals who need help or supervision to perform activities of daily living or instrumental activities of daily living.

The goals of long-term care services are to improve functioning, maintain existing functioning, or slow deterioration in functioning while delivering care in the least restrictive environment. Rehabilitative services, a critical component of long-term care, strive to return individuals to their optimal level of functioning. People in the long-term care population need access to a range of services, including nursing home care, home health care, adult day care, assisted living, and hospice care.

Trends

A significant measure of the access problem is the proportion of people who have health insurance. Following declines in the proportion of people with health insurance during the 1980s, the proportion has remained essentially level, at 85 percent in 1997 for persons under age 65 years.[12] Approximately 44.3 million persons lacked health insurance in 1998, continuing an increase in the number of uninsured. At the same time, the proportion with a usual source of care—an important predictor of access to needed services—fell from 83 percent to 78 percent between 1987 and 1992 before rising to 84 percent in 1997.[13] Although the lack of health insurance is clearly a major factor impeding access to care, having health insurance does not guarantee that health care will be accessible or affordable. Significant numbers of privately insured persons lack a usual source of care or report delays or difficulties in accessing needed care due to affordability or insurance problems.[14]

As a result of growing scientific evidence on the effectiveness of certain preventive services, 82 percent of employer-sponsored insurance plans include childhood immunizations, and 90 percent include Pap tests and mammograms. Nonetheless, gaps persist in coverage for effective preventive services, especially counseling.[4]

Concerns increasingly are focused on access to quality emergency services, long-term care, and rehabilitative services. Although emergency services are widely available in the United States, the range of services varies in accessibility and quality from region to region and, often, from neighborhood to neighborhood, raising additional concerns about care for vulnerable underserved populations. As the proportion of older Americans in the total population increases, the demand for quality long-term care services and facilities also will increase. Quality rehabilitative care needs are evident across all populations, and access to rehabilitative care is a significant problem for people who lack health insurance or who are underinsured and are unable to pay for the type and quality of health care they need.

During the 1990s, increased attention has been paid at all levels of government as well as by the private sector to health care quality improvement. The National Committee for Quality Assurance (NCQA), a managed care accreditation group, has led a collaborative effort to develop the Health Plan Employer Data and Information Set (HEDIS), a widely used tool for evaluating health plan performance.[15] The Joint Commission for the Accreditation of Healthcare Organizations (JCAHO) also has developed performance measures. The Agency for Healthcare Research and Quality has developed the Consumer Assessment of Health Plans Survey (CAHPS), an instrument to assess consumer experiences with health plans, and the Healthcare Cost and Utilization Project (HCUP), which makes available State and nationwide estimates of hospital use. These data can be used with the HCUP Quality Indicators, providing measures of ambulatory-care sensitive conditions, which can uncover potential problems in access to primary care services. Quality monitoring systems tend to emphasize measures that focus on delivery rates for clinical preventive services because access to and use of these services are an important indicator of the quality of health care providers and of delivery systems. The complementary *National Report on Healthcare Quality* will explore methods for integrating the data from these quality monitoring systems with population-based data collected by the public sector.

The Federal Advisory Commission on Consumer Protection and Quality in the Health Care Industry was established in 1997 to study changes occurring in the health care system and recommend ways to ensure consumer protection and quality health care. The Commission's report provides a foundation for the emerging issues of the next decade in monitoring and reporting on quality of health care. It also includes a "Consumer Bill of Rights and Responsibilities,"[16] which is designed to strengthen consumer confidence in the health care system while holding participants in the system accountable for improving quality.[17]

The Institute of Medicine issued a report in December 1999 documenting the magnitude of medical errors in U.S. hospitals. The report recommended strategies to reduce such errors.[18]

Disparities

Limitations in access to care extend beyond basic causes, such as a shortage of health care providers or a lack of facilities. Individuals also may lack a usual source of care or may face other barriers to receiving services, such as financial barriers (having no health insurance or being underinsured), structural barriers (no facilities or health care professionals nearby), and personal barriers (cultural differences, language differences, not knowing what to do, or environmental challenges for people with disabilities). Patients with disabilities may face additional barriers arising from facilities that are not physically accessible or attitudes of clinicians. Hispanics, young adults, and uninsured persons are least likely to have a usual source of care.[12] Hispanic persons and those with less than 12 years of education are least likely to have a usual primary care provider.[19] Certain people, such as those who are disabled, elderly, chronically ill, or HIV-infected, require access to health care providers who have the knowledge and skills to address their special needs.[20]

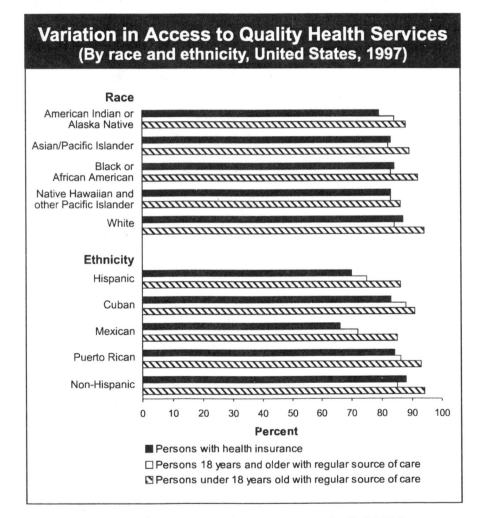

Variation in Access to Quality Health Services
(By race and ethnicity, United States, 1997)

■ Persons with health insurance
□ Persons 18 years and older with regular source of care
▨ Persons under 18 years old with regular source of care

Source: National Health Interview Survey, CDC, NCHS, 1997 (age adjusted to the year 2000 population).

Data as of November 30, 1999

Substantial disparities remain in health insurance coverage for certain populations. Among the nonelderly population, approximately 31 percent of Hispanic persons lacked coverage in 1997, a rate that is double the national average. Mexican Americans had one of the highest uninsured rates at 35 percent. For adults under age 65 years, 33 percent of those below the poverty level were uninsured. Similar disparities exist in access to a specific source of ongoing care. An average of 84 percent of adults identified a specific source of ongoing care in 1997, but the proportions dropped to 75 percent for Hispanics and 75 percent for those below the poverty level.[12]

Opportunities

Increasing recognition of the critical role of preventive services across the continuum of care and the need for providers to incorporate preventive services into patient visits has led to the development of tools and projects designed to help providers and patients shift to a prevention-oriented health care system. HEDIS reports on the delivery of many clinical preventive services provided by health maintenance organizations (HMOs). The 1999 reporting set for HEDIS contained several measures of clinical preventive services, including childhood immunizations, adolescent immunizations, smoking cessation advice, influenza vaccinations for older adults, breast cancer screening, cervical cancer screening, and prenatal care in the first trimester. A CDC grant to the State of Massachusetts for a health assessment partnership has resulted in a collaborative effort in New England to increase HMO participation in HEDIS. The specific tools developed include the increased use of electronic birth certificates, which have assisted outreach programs to teach new mothers the value of periodic checkups for their infants.

One of the earliest and most recognized tool kits is the *Clinician's Handbook of Preventive Services,*[6] developed by the Office of Disease Prevention and Health Promotion and now the responsibility of AHRQ. It was produced as a companion to *Healthy People 2000* and the U.S. Preventive Services Task Force *Guide to Clinical Preventive Services.*[1] Under development is the CDC *Guide to Community Preventive Services,* due to be released in 2001.[21] The *Guide* will assess the effectiveness of preventive services and interventions in community settings and at the clinical systems level. It will cover 15 topics in three areas: changing risk behaviors, such as eliminating tobacco use and increasing physical activity; reducing specific diseases and injuries, such as cancer and injuries from motor vehicle crashes; and addressing environmental challenges, such as changing the sociocultural environment.

Continued progress in the delivery of clinical preventive services will require better collection and reporting of data on the delivery of recommended services by providers and health plans. This information will allow providers and administrators to identify the services and groups of people where the biggest gaps exist in receiving needed health care services. The best information systems allow both cross-sectional comparisons of performance by providers, plans, systems, and localities as well as long-term analyses of the health and health care of individuals. These systems can facilitate interventions such as reminders, audit, and feedback, which have been shown to improve rates of immunization and screening.[22, 23]

In centralized health systems with stable populations (people who stay with one provider or health plan, for example), tracking of individuals has been used effectively for a limited number of services, primarily immunizations and cancer screenings. Expanding effective data collection efforts to cover additional services and to include more providers and health care systems is the current challenge. Measuring how well preventive care is provided under different systems is an essential first step in motivating those systems that are not performing well to develop the information, tools, and incentives to improve care.

Into the next decade, Healthy People and its partners will continue to promote communitywide efforts to provide clinical preventive services, using local leadership and insights to tailor and increase the accessibility of these services. Efforts will continue to promote the development of local prevention coalitions that include health departments, businesses, community institutions, and individuals from each community. Healthy People also will work to strengthen the capacity or ability of States and localities to collect health data and conduct community health assessments for small geographic areas.

Advances in the use of genetic information may improve both clinical and preventive care by helping to identify high-risk individuals and populations who will benefit most from preventive services and other clinical interventions. It will be essential to develop policies that will ensure appropriate evaluation of new genetic services, quality assurance of available genetic technology, and access to genetic services of proven benefit.

Overcoming technological, financial, or organizational barriers that can slow or block access to emergency services and improving emergency care accessibility and quality will require the combined effort of health care providers, health plans, and health care consumers as well as government agencies at the Federal, Tribal, State, and local levels.

Data as of November 30, 1999

The proportion of adults under age 65 years without health care coverage has remained essentially the same, while the total number of uninsured persons has continued to increase. The proportion of the adult population with a specific source of primary care has increased, although Hispanic and African American adults and other subgroups continue to be less likely to have a specific source of primary care. Compared to 1991 and 1992 baseline data, the proportion of adults in 1995 who received selected recommended clinical preventive services (including tetanus boosters and routine mammograms) has increased. Progress also has been made in improving racial and ethnic representation in the health professions.

Note: Unless otherwise noted, data are from Centers for Disease Control and Prevention, National Center for Health Statistics, *Healthy People 2000 Review, 1998-99.*

Access to Quality Health Services

Goal: Improve access to comprehensive, high-quality health care services.

Number   Objective

Clinical Preventive Care

1-1   Persons with health insurance

1-2   Health insurance coverage for clinical preventive services

1-3   Counseling about health behaviors

Primary Care

1-4   Source of ongoing care

1-5   Usual primary care provider

1-6   Difficulties or delays in obtaining needed health care

1-7   Core competencies in health provider training

1-8   Racial and ethnic representation in health professions

1-9   Hospitalization for ambulatory-care-sensitive conditions

Emergency Services

1-10   Delay or difficulty in getting emergency care

1-11   Rapid prehospital emergency care

1-12   Single toll-free number for poison control centers

1-13   Trauma care systems

1-14   Special needs of children

Long-Term Care and Rehabilitative Services

1-15   Long-term care services

1-16   Pressure ulcers among nursing home residents

Clinical Preventive Care

1-1. Increase the proportion of persons with health insurance.

Target: 100 percent.

Baseline: 86 percent of the population was covered by health insurance in 1997 (age adjusted to the year 2000 standard population).

Target setting method: Total coverage.

Data source: National Health Interview Survey (NHIS), CDC, NCHS.

Total Population, 1997	Health Insurance Percent
TOTAL	86
Race and ethnicity	
American Indian or Alaska Native	79
Asian or Pacific Islander	83
Asian	83
Native Hawaiian and other Pacific Islander	83
Black or African American	84
White	87
Hispanic or Latino	70
Cuban	83
Mexican American	66
Puerto Rican	84
Not Hispanic or Latino	88
Black or African American	84
White	89
Gender	
Female	87
Male	85

Total Population, 1997	Health Insurance Percent
Family income level	
Poor	70
Near poor	74
Middle/high income	93
Location of residence	
Within metropolitan statistical area	86
Outside metropolitan statistical area	84
Disability status	
Persons with disabilities	85
Persons without disabilities	86

DNA = Data have not been analyzed. DNC = Data are not collected. DSU = Data are statistically unreliable.
Note: Age adjusted to the year 2000 standard population.

Access to health services—including preventive care, primary care, and tertiary care—often depends on whether a person has health insurance.[24, 25, 26] Uninsured people are less than half as likely as people with health insurance to have a primary care provider; to have received appropriate preventive care, such as recent mammograms or Pap tests; or to have had any recent medical visits.[24] Lack of insurance also affects access to care for relatively serious medical conditions. Evidence suggests that lack of insurance over an extended period significantly increases the risk of premature death and that death rates among hospitalized patients without health insurance are significantly higher than among patients with insurance.[27] As demonstrated by a study of data from the National Health Interview Survey, Medicaid expansions that increase the proportion of a State's population eligible for Medicaid lead to increases in enrollment, enhanced utilization of medical services, and lower child death rates.[28] Another study showed that the chronically ill are even less likely than those with acute conditions to get health care services they need.[29]

1-2.   (Developmental) Increase the proportion of insured persons with coverage for clinical preventive services.

Potential data source: Medical Expenditure Panel Survey (MEPS), AHRQ.

Insurance coverage for clinical preventive services improved substantially during the 1990s, but significant variations remain in the services covered, depending on the plan and type of insurance. In 1988, among employers who offer health insurance, only 26 percent of their employees were covered for adult physical examinations, 35 percent for well-child care (including immunizations), and 43 percent for preventive screening tests.[30] In contrast, a 1997 national survey of over 3,000 employers found that 88 percent of employer-sponsored plans covered well-baby care, 89 percent covered adult physical examinations, 92 percent covered gynecologic examinations, and 89 and 91 percent covered Pap tests and mammograms, respectively. Coverage was highest in HMO plans and lowest in indemnity insurance plans.[4]

Including effective clinical preventive services among the services routinely covered by insurance is an effective way to emphasize the importance of clinical preventive services as an integral part of health care.[31] The Balanced Budget Act of 1997 (Public Law 105-33) added colorectal cancer screening among other new preventive benefits under the Medicare program and expanded Medicare coverage of mammography and cervical cancer screening. Although health insurance by itself is not sufficient to eliminate existing gaps in the delivery of preventive services, it is an important factor in influencing who gets recommended services.[32, 33]

Selected clinical preventive services have a positive influence on personal health, and many are cost-effective in comparison with the treatment of disease.[1, 34] Insurance coverage is especially problematic for counseling services, in part because of the difficulty in proving the benefits of some counseling interventions. For example, only 22 percent of employer-sponsored plans cover medications or counseling for smoking cessation.[4] The effectiveness of smoking cessation counseling, however, is supported by strong evidence, with more intensive interventions having the greatest impact and most favorable cost-effectiveness ratio.[35]

1-3. (Developmental) Increase the proportion of persons appropriately counseled about health behaviors.

Potential data source: National Health Interview Survey (NHIS), CDC, NCHS.

Substantial gaps remain in the delivery of appropriate screening and counseling services related to health behaviors. Unhealthy diets, smoking, physical inactivity, and alcohol use account for a majority of preventable deaths in the United States.[36] Data indicate that risk assessment and counseling interventions are delivered less frequently than other preventive interventions (for example, cancer screenings).[12] In addition, the attention physicians give to specific health-risk behaviors appears to be influenced by the socioeconomic status of their patients.[37] Although time is an important constraint in the primary care setting, evidence demonstrates that brief clinician counseling is effective in getting patients to stop smoking and reduce problem drinking.[1, 38] In addition, more intensive dietary counseling can lead to reduced dietary fat and cholesterol intake and increased fruit and vegetable consumption.[1] Effective primary care-based interventions to increase physical activity have been more difficult to identify.[1, 39]

Some evidence shows that provider counseling can increase the use of seat belts, child safety seats, and bicycle helmets, especially when directed to parents of infants and young children.[1] Brief counseling interventions aimed at high-risk individuals can increase condom use and prevent new sexually transmitted diseases.[40]

Clinician counseling should be tailored to the individual risk factors, needs, preferences, and abilities of each patient.[1] For some preventive interventions, such as hormone therapy in post-menopausal women, the optimal strategy depends on how individual patients value potential benefits and risks. Counseling of peri-menopausal and postmenopausal women should encourage shared decisionmaking based on individual risk factors and patient preferences.[1]

Primary Care

1-4. Increase the proportion of persons who have a specific source of ongoing care.

Target and baseline:

Objective	Increase in Persons With Specific Source of Ongoing Care	1997 Baseline*	2010 Target
		Percent	
1-4a.	All ages	86	96
1-4b.	Children and youth aged 17 years and under	93	96
1-4c.	Adults aged 18 years and older	84	96

*Age adjusted to the year 2000 standard population.

Target setting method: Better than the best.

Data source: National Health Interview Survey (NHIS), CDC, NCHS.

Population by Age Group, 1997	Specific Source of Ongoing Care		
	1-4a. All Ages	1-4b. Aged 17 Years and Under	1-4c. Aged 18 Years and Older
	Percent		
TOTAL	86	93	84
Race and ethnicity			
American Indian or Alaska Native	86	88	84
Asian or Pacific Islander	84	89	82
Asian	84	90	82

Population by Age Group, 1997	Specific Source of Ongoing Care		
	1-4a. All Ages	1-4b. Aged 17 Years and Under	1-4c. Aged 18 Years and Older
	Percent		
Native Hawaiian and other Pacific Islander	84	86	83
Black or African American	85	92	83
White	87	94	84
Hispanic or Latino	78	86	75
Cuban	89	91	88
Mexican American	75	85	72
Puerto Rican	88	93	86
Not Hispanic or Latino	87	94	85
Black or African American	85	92	83
White	88	95	86
Gender			
Female	90	93	89
Male	82	93	79
Family income level			
Poor	78	86	75
Near poor	81	90	78
Middle/high income	90	96	87
Geographic location			
Urban	86	93	83
Rural	88	94	86
Disability status			
Persons with disabilities	89	95	86
Persons without disabilities	86	93	84

DNA = Data have not been analyzed. DNC = Data are not collected. DSU = Data are statistically unreliable.

Note: Age adjusted to the year 2000 standard population.

Access to care depends in part on access to an ongoing source of care. People with a usual source of health care are more likely than those without a usual source of care to receive a variety of preventive health care services.[41, 42] An estimated 16 percent of adults in the Unites States lack a usual source of care. Thus, more than 40 million Americans have no particular doctor's office, clinic, health center, or other place where they go for health care advice. The National Health Interview Survey (NHIS) does not count emergency departments as a usual source of care.[12]

An estimated 93 percent of children aged 17 years and under have a specific source of ongoing care. The implementation of the Children's Health Insurance Program in 1999 provides a mechanism for increasing the proportion of children with an ongoing source of care.

The usual source of care can vary among groups according to their age, race and ethnicity, and health insurance coverage. Young children and elderly adults aged 65 years and older are most likely to have a usual source of care, and adults aged 18 to 64 years are least likely. Young adults aged 18 to 24 years are the least likely of any age group to have a usual source of care. Among racial and ethnic groups, Hispanic persons are the least likely to have a usual source of care. Some 25 percent of the adult Hispanic population (and 28 percent of the Mexican American population) lack a usual source of care, compared to 17 percent of African Americans and 16 percent of the total adult population.

Some 88 percent of persons with a usual source use an office-based provider, and 11 percent use a hospital outpatient department or clinic. African Americans and Hispanics are more likely to use hospital-based providers (including hospital clinics and outpatient departments) as their usual source of care.[14]

Uninsured persons under age 65 years are more likely to lack a usual source of care (38 percent) than those who have either public or private insurance. When compared with their counterparts who have private health insurance, uninsured people under age 65 years are 2.6 times more likely to lack a usual source of care.

1-5. Increase the proportion of persons with a usual primary care provider.

Target: 85 percent.

Baseline: 77 percent of the population had a usual primary care provider in 1996.

Target setting method: Better than the best.

Data source: Medical Expenditure Panel Survey (MEPS), AHRQ.

Total Population, 1996	1-5. Have a Usual Primary Care Provider	Provider Has Office Hours at Night or on Weekends*	Provider Usually Asks About Prescription Medications and Treatments by Other Doctors*
		Percent	
TOTAL	77	37	59
Race and ethnicity			
American Indian or Alaska Native	79	37	64
Asian or Pacific Islander	72	36	57
Asian	DNC	DNC	DNC
Native Hawaiian and other Pacific Islander	DNC	DNC	DNC
Black or African American	74	34	60
White	77	37	59
Hispanic or Latino	64	32	52
Not Hispanic or Latino	78	37	60
Black or African American	74	34	60
White	79	38	60
Gender			
Female	80	37	61
Male	73	36	57
Education level (aged 18 years and older)			
Less than high school	69	24	53
High school graduate	74	32	58
At least some college	74	34	59
Geographic location			
Urban (MSA)	76	39	59
Rural (non-MSA)	78	29	60
Disability status			
Persons with activity limitations	DNA	DNA	DNA
Persons without activity limitations	DNA	DNA	DNA

DNA = Data have not been analyzed. DNC = Data are not collected. DSU = Data are statistically unreliable.

*Data for office hours, prescription medications, and treatments are displayed to further characterize the practices of primary care providers.

A usual source of primary care helps people clarify the nature of their health problems and can direct them to appropriate health services, including specialty care.[43]

Primary care also emphasizes continuity, which implies that individuals use their primary source of care over time for most of their health care needs. More after-hours care, shorter travel time to a practice site, and shorter office waits have been associated with patients' beginning an acute episode of care with primary care physicians. Greater continuity has been observed for individuals with shorter appointment waits, insurance, and access to more after-hours care.[44] Other advantages of primary care are that a primary care provider deals with all common health needs (comprehensiveness) and coordinates health care services, such as referrals to specialists. Evidence suggests that first contact care provided by an individual's primary care provider leads to less costly medical care.[45]

1-6. Reduce the proportion of families that experience difficulties or delays in obtaining health care or do not receive needed care for one or more family members.

Target: 7 percent.

Baseline: 12 percent of families experienced difficulties or delays in obtaining health care or did not receive needed care in 1996.

Target setting method: Better than the best.

Data source: Medical Expenditure Panel Survey (MEPS), AHRQ.

Families, 1996	Experienced Difficulty or Delay in Receiving Health Care or Received No Health Care
	Percent
TOTAL	12
Race and ethnicity (head of household)	
American Indian or Alaska Native	15
Asian or Pacific Islander	14
Asian	DNC
Native Hawaiian and other Pacific Islander	DNC
Black or African American	10
White	12
Hispanic or Latino	15
Not Hispanic or Latino	11
Black or African American	10
White	11

Data as of November 30, 1999

Families, 1996	Experienced Difficulty or Delay in Receiving Health Care or Received No Health Care
	Percent
Gender (head of household)	
Female	DNA
Male	DNA
Family income level	
Below poverty	17
Near poverty	17
Middle/high income	9
Geographic location	
Urban (in MSA)	12
Rural (non-MSA)	12
Disability status	
Persons with activity limitations	DNA
Persons without activity limitations	DNA
Health insurance status of family	
All members private insurance	7
All members public insurance	12
All members uninsured	27

DNA = Data have not been analyzed. DNC = Data are not collected. DSU = Data are statistically unreliable.

In 1996, according to the Medical Expenditure Panel Survey, 12.8 million families (11.6 percent) for a variety of reasons experienced difficulty or delay in obtaining care or did not receive needed health care services they thought they needed. In addition to a lack of insurance or underinsurance, barriers include a lack of appropriate referrals, travel distance to the provider, lack of transportation, and unavailability of specialists. Families experience barriers to care for a variety of reasons: inability to afford health care (60 percent); insurance-related causes (20 percent), including (1) the insurance company not approving, covering, or paying for care, (2) preexisting conditions for which insurance coverage often is restricted, (3) lack of access to required referrals, and (4) clinicians refusing to accept the family's insurance plan; and other problems (21 percent), such as transportation, physical barriers, communication problems, child care limitations, lack of time or information, or refusal of services.[14]

An additional source of information is the Robert Wood Johnson National Access to Care Survey. Results of the 1994 National Access to Care Survey suggest that some studies have missed substantial components of unmet needs by failing to include specific questions about supplementary health care services, such as prescription drugs, eyeglasses, dental care, and mental health care or counseling.[46] When specific questions were added about these services, the findings showed that 16.1 percent of respondents (approximately 41 million Americans) were unable to obtain at least one service they believed they needed. The highest reported unmet need was for dental care. This problem can be attributed partly to insufficient provider reimbursement, which discourages participation in plans even when the service is covered.

1-7. (Developmental) Increase the proportion of schools of medicine, schools of nursing, and other health professional training schools whose basic curriculum for health care providers includes the core competencies in health promotion and disease prevention.

Potential data source: Adaptation of the Prevention Self-Assessment Analysis, Association of Teachers of Preventive Medicine (ATPM).

Significant changes in the health care system and in the expectations of consumers are influencing the education of health care providers in the United States. For example, many medical schools are assessing the content of their predoctoral and postgraduate curricula.[47] Medical educators and medical schools are recognizing that physicians will need to be prepared to provide population-based preventive health care as well as high quality medical care to their patients.[48] This challenge exists for other health professionals, including nurses, nurse practitioners, physician assistants, and allied health personnel. This link between medicine and public health is essential to provide the highest quality health care possible to the U.S. population.

A core set of competencies for medical students in health promotion and disease prevention was developed by a task force established by the Association of Teachers of Preventive Medicine (ATPM) and the U.S. Department of Health and Human Services' Health Resources and Services Administration. The competencies, derived from the ATPM *Inventory of Knowledge and Skills Relating to Health Promotion and Disease Prevention,*[49] cover four categories: clinical prevention, quantitative skills, health services organization and delivery, and community dimensions of medical practice. Together, they address a wide spectrum of topics, including environmental health hazards and asthma management. This set of competencies will provide medical educators with measurable education outcomes in prevention education. The core competencies will be evaluated for potential adaptability to health provider education curricula in schools of nursing and health professional schools. The core competencies also will be reviewed for potential expansion to cover emerging issues and competencies in evaluating and responding to environmental health concerns and natural and man-made disasters. Because health care providers will have to address new health issues, policies, technologies, and practice guidelines over their careers, continuing education programs also need to be updated periodically.

1-8. In the health professions, allied and associated health profession fields, and the nursing field, increase the proportion of all degrees awarded to members of under-represented racial and ethnic groups.

Target and baseline:

Objective	Increase in Degrees Awarded to Under-represented Populations	1995–96 Baseline	2010 Target
		Percent	
	Health professions, allied and associated health fields*		
1-8a.	American Indian or Alaska Native	0.5	1.0
1-8b.	Asian or Pacific Islander	4.0	4.0
1-8c.	Black or African American	6.6	13.0
1-8d.	Hispanic or Latino	3.8	12.0
	Nursing		
1-8e.	American Indian or Alaska Native	0.7	1.0
1-8f.	Asian or Pacific Islander	3.2	4.0
1-8g.	Black or African American	6.9	13.0
1-8h.	Hispanic or Latino	3.4	12.0
1-8i.	**Medicine**	Developmental	
1-8j.	**Dentistry**	Developmental	
1-8k.	**Pharmacy**	Developmental	

*For the baselines, health professions includes dentistry.

Target setting method: Targets based on U.S. Bureau of the Census projections of the proportions of racial and ethnic groups in the population for the year 2000.

Data source: Data Systems of HRSA, Bureau of Health Professions.

Certain racial and ethnic groups and low-income communities lag behind the overall U.S. population on virtually all health status indicators, including life expectancy and infant death. Furthermore, access to health care is a problem, and these groups often lack a specific source of care. Increasing the number of health professionals from certain racial and ethnic groups is viewed as an integral part of the solution to improving access to care.

Members of underrepresented racial or ethnic groups make up about 25 percent of the U.S. population. Their representation among health professionals, however, is in the range of 10 percent. Several studies have shown that minority health professionals are more likely to serve areas with high proportions of underrepresented racial and ethnic groups and to practice in or near designated health care shortage areas.[50, 51]

Despite considerable efforts to increase the number of representatives of racial or ethnic groups in health profession schools (medicine, dentistry, nursing, pharmacy, and allied and associated health professions), the percentage of such entrants, enrollees, and graduates has not advanced significantly and in some cases has not advanced at all since 1990. The targets set for Healthy People 2000 for such enrollment and graduation were not achieved, and achieving the revised targets by 2010 presents a significant challenge. Additional attention will need to be given to such efforts as providing financial assistance for underrepresented racial and ethnic group students to pursue health care degrees, encouraging mentor relationships, promoting the early recruiting of students from racial and ethnic groups before they graduate, and increasing the number of racial and ethnic group faculty and administrative staff members in schools that train health care professionals. Other suggested approaches to improving culturally appropriate care for ethnic and minority populations include increasing cultural competency among all health workers and increasing the number of lay health workers from underrepresented racial and ethnic groups.

1-9. Reduce hospitalization rates for three ambulatory-care-sensitive conditions—pediatric asthma, uncontrolled diabetes, and immunization-preventable pneumonia and influenza in older adults.

Target and baseline:

Objective	Reduction in Hospitalizations for Ambulatory-Care-Sensitive Conditions	1996 Baseline	2010 Target
		Admissions per 10,000 Population	
1-9a.	Pediatric asthma—persons under age 18 years	23.0	17.3
1-9b.	Uncontrolled diabetes—persons aged 18 to 64 years	7.2	5.4
1-9c.	Immunization-preventable pneumonia or influenza—persons aged 65 years and older	10.6	8.0

Target setting method: 25 percent improvement.

Data source: Healthcare Cost and Utilization Project (HCUP), AHRQ.

Persons With Ambulatory-Care-Sensitive Conditions by Age Group, 1996	Hospitalizations		
	1-9a. Persons Under Age 18 Years With Asthma	1-9b. Persons Aged 18 to 64 Years With Diabetes	1-9c.Persons Aged 65 Years and Older With Preventable Pneumonia or Influenza
	Admissions per 10,000		
TOTAL	23.0	7.2	10.6
Race and ethnicity			
American Indian or Alaska Native	DNC	DNC	DNC
Asian or Pacific Islander	DNC	DNC	DNC
Asian	DNC	DNC	DNC
Native Hawaiian and other Pacific Islander	DNC	DNC	DNC
Black or African American	DNC	DNC	DNC
White	DNC	DNC	DNC
Hispanic or Latino	DNC	DNC	DNC
Not Hispanic or Latino	DNC	DNC	DNC
Black or African American	DNC	DNC	DNC
White	DNC	DNC	DNC
Gender			
Female	18.2	7.0	9.1
Male	27.6	7.4	12.6
ZIP code income level *			
$25,000 or less	52.0	18.8	21.1
$25,001 to $35,000	22.3	6.7	9.2
More than $35,000	10.6	2.9	6.0
Insurance status			
Private	15.7	3.7	DNA
Medicaid	45.9	23.5	DNA
Uninsured	8.3	6.3	NA

*Income of patient is the median income for the postal ZIP Code of residence.

DNA = Data have not been analyzed. DNC = Data are not collected. DSU = Data are statistically unreliable. NA = Not applicable.

Comprehensive primary care services can reduce the severity of certain illnesses. Hospital admission rates for "ambulatory-care-sensitive conditions" serve as an indicator for both limited access to primary care and evidence of low-quality primary care. Disparities in hospital admission rates for racial and ethnic groups and low-income populations have been well documented.[52, 53]

The three indicators selected here represent common problems encountered in primary care and allow monitoring of hospitalization rates for children (asthma), working-age adults (diabetes), and elderly persons (pneumonia and influenza). For each of these conditions, interventions can reduce hospitalization rates. Advances in the management of asthma have reduced its adverse health effects. Primary care can prevent both acute problems and long-term consequences of diabetes. Illness and death from preventable pneumonia and influenza among elderly persons can be avoided through the use of pneumococcal and influenza vaccines. These three conditions have been chosen because coordination of community preventive services, public health interventions, clinical preventive services, and primary care can reduce levels of these illnesses. To be effective, these services must be culturally competent and linguistically appropriate.[54]

This objective can be achieved by targeting high-risk populations. Because multiple factors besides access and quality contribute to the admission rates for ambulatory-care-sensitive conditions, each State will need to examine its rates and interpret them in the context of its population, health system, and community characteristics, and need to implement corresponding strategies. The objective is to improve primary care and preventive services and thereby reduce the need for hospital admission and the extended illness and costs associated with hospitalization.[55, 56, 57, 58]

It should be noted that the privately insured have admission rates that are half those of the national average, indicating what is potentially achievable. Because of data limitations and potential access barriers to hospital admission among the uninsured, the Medicaid rate is artificially high and the uninsured rate is artificially low. (See Volume III for more information.) Data by race are not included because these data are reported at the State level. State-level hospital discharge databases can provide accurate estimates of racial and ethnic disparities in hospital admission rates at the State level. There are substantial disparities in hospital admission rates for pediatric asthma and uncontrolled diabetes by race and ethnicity. The magnitude of this disparity also fluctuates by State, suggesting that access to care and quality may play a role. Specifically, among seven States for which rates were determined, the age- and gender-adjusted relative risk of hospitalization for pediatric asthma ranged from 2.3 to 5.8 for African Americans and 1.3 to 2.6 for Hispanics compared to non-Hispanic whites. For uncontrolled diabetes, the relative risk of hospitalization ranged from 3.0 to 4.4 for African Americans and 1.2 to 2.0 for Latinos compared to non-Hispanic whites. AHRQ is developing a Minority National Inpatient Sample as part of HCUP that will provide national estimates of disparities in avoidable hospitalization rates by race and ethnicity.

Data as of November 30, 1999

Emergency Services

1-10. (Developmental) Reduce the proportion of persons who delay or have difficulty in getting emergency medical care.

Potential data source: National Health Interview Survey (NHIS), CDC, NCHS.

Emergency services are a vital part of access to health care in the United States. All population groups, regardless of their socioeconomic, health, or insurance status, want to know that emergency services will be available and will function quickly and effectively when needed.[59] This broadly shared social expectation was reinforced by landmark Federal legislation, the Emergency Medical Treatment and Active Labor Act (EMTALA) of 1986. EMTALA stipulates that anyone seeking care at a hospital emergency department (ED) must receive a medical screening examination for an emergency medical condition and appropriate stabilizing measures.[60]

For many people, however, a variety of barriers continue to block access to emergency departments when the need for emergency medical care arises.[9] Among these barriers are psychological and cultural factors that may keep some people, even if insured, from seeking care promptly; financial constraints that may inhibit some people, even if insured, from seeking care promptly; and shortcomings in the number, location, or capability of EDs in a specified geographic area.

A significant component of this objective is to reduce the proportion of people whose access to emergency services is blocked by their health insurance coverage or payment policies. These policies affect access to hospital emergency departments and, in some instances, use of prehospital emergency services.[61] Typically, these policies stipulate that unless an enrollee's condition is life threatening, the enrollee or the ED must obtain authorization before an ED visit or risk that a claim for services will be denied. In some cases, claims for ED visits can be denied retroactively if they are deemed medically unnecessary. The rationale for these coverage and payment policies is clear: to manage care and contain costs. These policies, however, discourage some enrollees from receiving emergency treatment when and where it is warranted.[62]

Concerns about access barriers have prompted Federal, State, and organizational groups to seek assurances that health coverage or payment policies will provide payment when people go to an ED with acute symptoms of sufficient severity—including severe pain—such that a prudent layperson could reasonably expect that the lack of medical attention could result in serious jeopardy, serious impairment to bodily functions, or serious dysfunction of any bodily organ or part.

1-11. (Developmental) Increase the proportion of persons who have access to rapidly responding prehospital emergency medical services.

Potential data source: Annual Survey of EMS Operations, International Association of Fire Fighters.

The outcome of many medical emergencies depends on the prompt availability of appropriately trained and properly equipped prehospital emergency medical care providers. In urban areas, this capability is defined by an interval of less than 5 minutes from the time an emergency call is placed to arrival on the scene for at least 90 percent of first-responder emergency medical services and less than 8 minutes for at least 90 percent of transporting EMS. In rural areas, this capability is defined as an interval of less than 10 minutes from the time an emergency call is placed to arrival on the scene for at least 80 percent of EMS responses.

Assuring a prompt response requires a well-coordinated system of care involving a variety of organizations and agencies, some of which are outside the traditional health care arena. The components include public awareness of how and whom to call for emergency assistance and public education concerning initial lifesaving emergency care procedures to be followed until the arrival of EMS providers. They also include access via a 911 or enhanced 911 system or, in rural areas, a uniform addressing system that allows emergency responders to locate quickly the person requesting emergency assistance; the availability of well-trained and appropriately certified response personnel, who are frequently from law enforcement or fire services; transportation (ground, air, or water ambulance); medical direction and oversight; and destination hospitals that are well-equipped and appropriately staffed.

1-12. Establish a single toll-free telephone number for access to poison control centers on a 24-hour basis throughout the United States.

Target: 100 percent.

Baseline: 15 percent of poison control centers shared a single toll-free number in 1999.

Target setting method: Total coverage.

Data source: Annual Survey of U.S. Poison Control Centers, American Association of Poison Control Centers.

Poison control centers (PCCs) are staffed on a 24-hour basis by toxicologists and specialists in poison information who respond to requests from the general public and health care professionals for immediate information and treatment advice about poisonings and toxic exposures. Local or toll-free telephone calls to PCC hotline numbers provide primary access to these services. Each year more than 2 million callers seek telephone assistance from PCCs throughout the United

States.[63] When a caller reports a poisoning or toxic exposure, a PCC toxicologist or specialist in poison information assesses the severity of the incident, advises the caller about treatment, and makes referrals for further medical attention when necessary. PCCs respond to inquiries in languages other than English by using language-translation services, interpreters, or bilingual staff members. PCCs manage most incidents by providing telephone advice to a caregiver at home, avoiding the need for more costly care at a hospital emergency department or another health care facility.

Linking all PCCs in the United States through a single toll-free telephone number and consolidating several key PCC functions can make contacting PCCs easier and more cost-effective.[64, 65] When PCCs are linked through a common telephone number, callers can be routed automatically to the nearest PCC based on their area code, telephone exchange number, and ZIP Code. Educational efforts could focus on a single easy-to-remember emergency number that permits callers to access PCCs quickly. Incorporating all PCCs under the umbrella of a toll-free nationwide telephone number will help ensure access to poison control services when and where they are needed.

1-13. Increase the number of Tribes, States, and the District of Columbia with trauma care systems that maximize survival and functional outcomes of trauma patients and help prevent injuries from occurring.

Target: All Tribes, States, and the District of Columbia.

Baseline: 5 States had trauma care systems in 1998.

Target setting method: Total coverage.

Data sources: State EMS Directors Survey, National Association of State EMS Directors; IHS (Tribal data are developmental).

A trauma care system is an organized and coordinated effort in a defined geographic area to deliver the full spectrum of care to injured patients. The main goals of the system are to match the available trauma care resources in a community, region, or State with the needs of individual patients and to ensure that patients have rapid access to the acute care facility and rehabilitation services they need. In a trauma care system, prehospital, acute care, and rehabilitation services are integrated and administered by a public agency that provides leadership, coordinates service delivery, establishes minimum standards of care, designates trauma centers (which offer 24-hour specialized treatment for the most severely injured patients), and fosters ongoing system evaluation and quality improvement.

Trauma care systems traditionally have focused on preventing adverse outcomes in the event of injury. Many trauma care professionals and people in the public health field believe that trauma care systems also should contribute to the prevention of injuries.[66] Trauma care professionals are in a good position to provide leadership in injury surveillance, clinical preventive services, and communitywide injury prevention programs. Recent Federal initiatives in trauma care have resulted in the design of a model system that incorporates public information, education, and prevention of injuries as key features.[67]

Results of a national survey conducted in 1993 indicated that only 5 States had complete trauma systems, but 19 other States and the District of Columbia had at least some trauma system components in place.[68] A survey of all 50 States and the District of Columbia in 1998 again indicated that only 5 States satisfied all trauma care system criteria.[69] However, results from this survey also showed that 37 other States and the District of Columbia had at least some trauma system components in place.

1-14. Increase the number of States and the District of Columbia that have implemented guidelines for prehospital and hospital pediatric care.

1-14a. Increase the number of States and the District of Columbia that have implemented statewide pediatric protocols for online medical direction.

Target: All States and the District of Columbia.

Baseline: 18 States had implemented statewide pediatric protocols for online medical direction in 1997.

Target setting method: Total coverage.

Data source: Emergency Medical Services for Children Annual Grantees Survey, HRSA.

Emergency medical service systems try to bring essential prehospital medical treatment to patients as quickly as possible. Emergency care of children present a particular challenge since prehospital providers often treat fewer children and have limited pediatric experience and assessment skills. It can be more difficult to assess the severity of illness or injury since characteristic changes in vital signs that signal deterioration in adults may not occur in children. Important anatomic, physiologic, and developmental differences exist between children and adults that affect their responses to medical care and their risk of injury and illness.[70] Most EMS systems operate independently of hospitals or other facilities and typically have few physicians to ensure appropriateness of care.

Experienced providers can offer medical direction in two ways, either online or offline. Online direction involves direct communication (for example, voice) between EMS medical directors (for example, at hospitals) and emergency medical technicians (EMTs) and paramedics to authorize and guide the care of patients at the scene and during transport. Offline medical direction includes the development of guidelines, protocols, procedures, and policies, as well as planning for, training in, and evaluation of their use.

1-14b. Increase the number of States and the District of Columbia that have adopted and disseminated pediatric guidelines that categorize acute care facilities with the equipment, drugs, trained personnel, and other resources necessary to provide varying levels of pediatric emergency and critical care.

Target: All States and the District of Columbia.

Baseline: 11 States had adopted and disseminated pediatric guidelines that categorize acute care facilities with the equipment, drugs, trained personnel, and other resources necessary to provide varying levels of pediatric emergency and critical care in 1997.

Target setting method: Total coverage.

Data source: Emergency Medical Services for Children Annual Grantees Survey, HRSA.

Emergency care for life-threatening pediatric illness and injury requires specialized resources, medical direction, equipment, drugs, trained personnel, and properly staffed and equipped hospitals.[70] Children, however, receive emergency care in a variety of settings—from rural community hospitals to large urban medical centers. Hospitals vary in terms of their readiness to treat children's emergencies. If the hospitals are properly equipped and staffed, children frequently can receive the care that they need at local hospitals, but some children require the advanced care available only at regional specialty centers. Categorization is essentially an effort to identify the readiness and capability of a hospital and its staff to provide optimal emergency care.[71] Compliance can be voluntary or assigned by official agencies.

Long-Term Care and Rehabilitative Services

1-15. **(Developmental) Increase the proportion of persons with long-term care needs who have access to the continuum of long-term care services.**

Potential data source: National Health Interview Survey (NHIS), CDC, NCHS.

The long-term care population needs access to a range of services, including nursing home care, home health care, adult day care, assisted living, and hospice care.[72] Persons with long-term care needs require the help of other persons to perform activities of daily living (personal care activities) and instrumental activities of daily living (routine needs). Access problems are viewed as a need for specified long-term care services that were not received in the past 12 months.

Long-term care crosses the boundaries of different types of care—from health to social—and intensity of services—from periodic home health and homemaker visits to round-the-clock subacute care. Access to the full range of long-term care services continues to be a problem because of financial barriers and the limited availability of specific services.[11, 73] Although people in the long-term care population and their caregivers prefer long-term care to be delivered in the least restrictive environment, limited access and limited knowledge about care options can result in a long-term care population that is more dependent than necessary. The long-term care services selected cover key services in institutions, in the home, and in the community. Access to this range of services in rural areas is often difficult.

1-16. Reduce the proportion of nursing home residents with a current diagnosis of pressure ulcers.

Target: 8 diagnoses per 1,000 residents.

Baseline: 16 diagnoses of pressure ulcer per 1,000 nursing home residents in 1997.

Target setting method: Better than the best.

Data source: National Nursing Home Survey (NNHS), CDC, NCHS.

Nursing Home Residents, 1997	Pressure Ulcers Diagnoses per 1,000
TOTAL	16
Race and ethnicity	
American Indian or Alaska Native	DSU
Asian or Pacific Islander	DSU
Asian	DSU
Native Hawaiian and other Pacific Islander	DSU
Black or African American	DSU
White	14
Hispanic or Latino	DSU
Not Hispanic or Latino	15
Black or African American	DSU
White	13
Gender	
Female	14
Male	20

Nursing Home Residents, 1997	Pressure Ulcers Diagnoses per 1,000
Education level	
Less than high school	DNA
High school graduate	DNA
At least some college	DNA
Geographic location	
Urban	17
Rural	12
Disability status	
Persons with disabilities	16
Persons without disabilities	DSU

DNA = Data have not been analyzed. DNC = Data are not collected. DSU = Data are statistically unreliable.

Pressure ulcers in all settings are sufficiently common to warrant concern, particularly as a quality-of-care issue. A significant number of people are at risk for pressure ulcers in nursing homes. Older adults are particularly prone to pressure ulcers as a result of decreased mobility, multiple contributing diagnoses, loss of muscle mass, and poor nutrition. About 24 percent of the Nation's 1.4 million nursing home residents require the assistance of another person to transfer from bed to chair.

According to studies of the treatment of pressure ulcers, it is difficult to determine the exact extent of the problem, including the number of new cases and the number of people who have pressure ulcers. Pressure ulcers have long been recognized as a serious quality-of-care problem in both acute care facilities and nursing homes.[74, 75] The prevention of pressure ulcers depends on close observation, appropriate nutrition, and effective nursing care. The number of new cases of pressure ulcers could indicate the overall quality of care provided to nursing home residents. Evidence-based guidelines have been issued on the prevention and treatment of pressure ulcers.[76]

Related Objectives From Other Focus Areas

2. Arthritis, Osteopororis, and Chronic Back Conditions

2-2.	Activity limitations due to arthritis
2-3.	Personal care limitations
2-6.	Racial differences in total knee replacement
2-7.	Seeing a health care provider
2-11.	Activity limitations due to chronic back conditions

3. Cancer

3-10. Provider counseling about preventive measures
3-11. Pap tests
3-12. Colorectal cancer screening
3-13. Mammogram

5. Diabetes

5-1. Diabetes education
5-4. Diagnosis of diabetes
5-11. Annual urinary microalbumin measurement
5-12. Annual glycosylated hemoglobin measurement
5-13. Annual dilated eye examination
5-14. Annual foot examinations
5-15. Aspirin therapy

6. Disability and Secondary Conditions

6-7. Congregate care of children and adults with disabilities
6-10. Accessibility of health and wellness programs

7. Educational and Community-Based Programs

7-2. School health education
7-3. Health-risk behavior information for college and university students
7-5. Worksite health promotion programs
7-7. Patient and family education
7-8. Satisfaction with patient education
7-12. Older adult participation in community health promotion activities

9. Family Planning

9-1. Intended pregnancy
9-2. Birth spacing
9-3. Contraceptive use
9-5. Emergency contraception
9-6. Male involvement
9-10. Pregnancy prevention and sexually transmitted disease protection
9-11. Pregnancy prevention education
9-13. Insurance coverage for contraceptive supplies and services

11. Health Communication

11-2 Health literacy
11-6 Satisfaction with providers' communication skills

12. Heart Disease and Stroke

12-1. Coronary hearth disease (CHD) deaths
12-15. Blood cholesterol screening

13. HIV

13-6. Condom use
13-8. HIV counseling and education for persons in substance abuse treatment
13-9. HIV/AIDS, STD, and TB education in State prisons
13-10. HIV counseling and testing in State prisons

14. Immunization and Infectious Diseases

14-5. Invasive pneumococcal infections
14-22. Universally recommended vaccination of children aged 19 to 35 months
14-23. Vaccination coverage for children in day care, kindergarten, and first grade
14-24. Fully immunized children aged 19 to 35 months
14-25. Providers who measure childhood vaccination coverage levels
14-26. State/community population-based immunization registries for children
14-27. Vaccination coverage among adolescents
14-28. Hepatitis B vaccination among high-risk groups
14-29. Flu and pneumococcal vaccination of high-risk adults

15. Injury and Violence Prevention

15-7.   Nonfatal poisoning

15-8.   Deaths from poisoning

15-10. Emergency department surveillance systems

15-12. Emergency department visits

15-19. Safety belts

15-20. Child restraints

15-21. Motorcycle helmet use

15-23. Bicycle helmet use

15-24. Bicycle helmet laws

16. Maternal, Infant, and Child Health

16-1.   Fetal and infant deaths

16-2.   Child deaths

16-3.   Adolescent and young adult deaths

16-17. Prenatal substance exposure

16-18. Fetal alcohol syndrome

16-20. Newborn bloodspot screening

16-22. Medical home for children with special health care needs

16-23. Service systems for children with special health care needs

17. Medical Product Safety

17-3.   Provider review of medications taken by patients

17-5.   Receipt of oral counseling from prescribers and dispensers

18. Mental Health and Mental Disorders

18-6.   Primary care screening and assessment

18-7.   Treatment for children with mental health needs

18-8.   Juvenile justice facility screening

18-9.   Treatment for adults with mental disorders

18-10. Treatment for both co-occurring disorders

18-11. Adult jail diversion

18-12. State tracking of consumer satisfaction

18-13. State plans addressing cultural competence

18-14. State plans addressing elderly persons

19. Nutrition and Overweight

19-1.   Healthy weight in adults

19-2.   Obesity in adults

19-3.   Overweight or obesity in children and adolescents

19-4.   Growth retardation in children

19-17. Nutrition counseling for medical conditions

19-18. Food security

21. Oral Health

21-7.   Annual examinations for oral and pharyngeal cancer

21-10. Use of oral health care system

21-11. Use of oral health care system by residents in long-term care facilities

21-13. School-based health centers with oral health component

21-14. Health centers with oral health service components

21-15. Referral for cleft lip or palate

21-16. State-based surveillance system

21-17. Tribal, State, and local dental programs

22. Physical Activity and Fitness

22-12. School physical activity facilities

22-13.	Worksite physical activity and fitness
22-14.	Community walking
22-15.	Community bicycling

23. Public Health Infrastructure

23-1.	Public health employee access to Internet
23-2.	Public access to information and surveillance data
23-3.	Use of geocoding in health data systems
23-8.	Competencies for public health workers
23-9.	Training in essential public health services
23-10.	Continuing education and training by public health agencies
23-12.	Health improvement plans
23-13.	Access to public health laboratory services
23-14.	Access to epidemiology services

24. Respiratory Diseases

24-6.	Patient education
24-7.	Appropriate asthma care
24-11.	Medical evaluation and followup

25. Sexually Transmitted Diseases

25-11.	Responsible adolescent sexual behavior
25-13.	Hepatitis B vaccine services in STD clinics
25-14.	Screening in youth detention facilities and jails
25-15.	Contracts to treat nonplan partners of STD patients
25-16.	Annual screening for genital chlamydia
25-17.	Screening of pregnant women
25-18.	Compliance with recognized STD treatment standards
25-19.	Provider referral services for sex partners

26. Substance Abuse

26-18.	Treatment gap for illicit drugs
26-20.	Treatment of injection drug users
26-21.	Treatment gap for problem alcohol use
26-22.	Hospital emergency department referrals

27. Tobacco Use

27-6.	Smoking cessation by adults
27-7.	Smoking cessation by adolescents
27-8.	Insurance coverage of cessation treatment

28. Vision and Hearing

28-1.	Dilated eye examination
28-2.	Vision screening for children
28-10.	Vision rehabilitation services and devices
28-11.	Newborn hearing screening
28-13.	Rehabilitation for hearing impairment
28-14.	Hearing examination
28-15.	Evaluation and treatment referrals

Terminology

(A listing of all abbreviations and acronyms used in this publication appears in Appendix K.)

Access: According to the Institute of Medicine, "The timely use of personal health services to achieve the best possible health outcomes."[59] This definition includes both the use and effectiveness of health services. The concept of access also encompasses physical accessibility of facilities.

Activities of daily living (ADL): Personal care activities, such as bathing, dressing, eating, and getting around (with special equipment, if needed) inside the home

Acute care facility: A health facility that provides care on a short-term basis. Included are community hospitals with an average length of stay of less than 30 days for all patients.

Ambulatory care: Health care that does not require the patient to stay in a hospital or other facility, such as care provided on an outpatient basis.

Ambulatory-care-sensitive conditions: Conditions resulting in hospitalization that could potentially have been prevented if the person had improved access to high-quality primary care services outside the hospital setting.

Asymptomatic: Without symptoms. This term may apply either to healthy persons or to persons with preclinical (prior to clinical diagnosis) disease in whom symptoms are not yet apparent.

Clinical care: The provision of health care services to individual patients by trained health care professionals.

Clinical preventive services (CPS): Common screening tests, immunizations, risk assessment, counseling about health risk behaviors, and other preventive services routinely delivered in the clinical setting for the primary prevention of disease or for the early detection of disease in persons with no symptoms of illness.

Continuum of care: The array of health services and care settings that address health promotion, disease prevention, and the diagnosis, treatment, management, and rehabilitation of disease, injury, and disability. In-

cluded are primary care and specialized clinical services provided in community and primary care settings, hospitals, trauma centers, and rehabilitation and long-term care facilities.

Core competencies: A defined set of skills and knowledge considered necessary in the educational curricula for training health care providers. Examples of core competencies include skills in prevention education; skills in using sources of health data to identify what clinical preventive services should be delivered to the individual patient based on that person's age, gender, and risk factor status; an understanding of the U.S. public health system (local and State health departments) and its role in monitoring and maintaining the health of the community; and skills to evaluate and translate medical and scientific research reports into clinical practice.

Emergency services: Health care services that are needed or appear to be needed immediately because of injury or sudden illness that threatens serious impairment of any bodily function or serious dysfunction of any bodily part or organ.[17]

Functional assessment: A health care provider's review of a patient for the ability to perform activities of daily living (personal care activities) and instrumental activities (routine needs) of daily living. (See also *Persons with long-term care needs*.)

Health intervention: Any measure taken to improve or promote health or to prevent, diagnose, treat, or manage disease, injury, or disability.

Health outcomes: The results or consequences of a process of care. Health outcomes may include satisfaction with care as well as the use of health care resources. Included are clinical outcomes, such as changes in health status and changes in the length and quality of life as a result of detecting or treating disease.

Instrumental activities for daily living: Routine activities, such as everyday household chores, shopping, or getting around for other purposes, that enable a person to live independently in the community.

Long-term care (LTC): A broad range of health and social services delivered in institutions, in the community, and at home. Long-term care services include institutional services, such as those delivered in nursing homes, rehabilitation hospitals, subacute care facilities, hospice facilities, and assisted living facilities; services delivered in the home, such as home health and personal care, hospice, homemaker, and meals; and community-based services, such as adult day care, social services, congregate meals, transportation and escort services, legal protective services, and counseling for clients as well as their caregivers.[10]

Managed care: According to the Institute of Medicine, "a set of techniques used by or on behalf of purchasers of health care benefits to manage health care costs by influencing patient care decisionmaking through case-by-case assessments of the appropriateness of care prior to its provision."[77]

Patient barriers: Any mental, physical, or psychosocial condition that prevents an individual from accessing needed health care. Examples include attitudes or biases, mental disorders or illnesses, behavioral disorders, physical limitations, cultural or linguistic factors, sexual orientation, and financial constraints.

Persons with long-term care needs: Persons who need the help of other persons to perform activities of daily living (personal care activities) and instrumental activities of daily living (routine needs).

Primary care: According to the Institute of Medicine, "The provision of integrated, accessible health care services by clinicians who are accountable for addressing a large majority of personal health care needs, developing a sustained partnership with patients, and practicing in the context of family and community."[8]

Primary care provider: A physician who specializes in general and family practice, general internal medicine, or general pediatrics; a nonphysician health care provider, such as a nurse practitioner, physician assistant, or certified nurse midwife.

Primary prevention: Measures such as health care services, medical tests, counseling, and health education designed to prevent the onset of a targeted condition. Routine immunization of healthy individuals is an example of primary prevention.[1]

Provider barriers: Any mental, physical, psychosocial, or environmental condition that prevents or discourages health care providers from offering preventive services. Examples of provider barriers include a poor practice environment, lack of knowledge, and lack of efficacy studies.

Quality: According to the Institute of Medicine, "The degree to which health services for individuals and populations increase the likelihood of desired health outcomes and are consistent with current professional knowledge."[78] Simply stated, it is doing the right thing, for the right patient, at the right time, with the right outcome.

Rehabilitative services: Services to restore specific skills, including overall physical mobility and functional abilities.

Secondary prevention: Measures such as health care services designed to identify or treat individuals who have a disease or risk factors for a disease but who are not yet experiencing symptoms of the disease. Pap tests and high blood pressure screening are examples of secondary prevention.[1]

System barriers: Conditions within a health care system that prevent people from accessing needed services or prevent health care providers from delivering those services. System barriers include physical, cultural, linguistic, and financial barri-

ers as well as the availability of health care facilities or providers with special skills, such as eye, ear, nose, and throat specialists.

Tertiary prevention: Preventive health care measures or services that are part of the treatment and management of persons with clinical illnesses. Examples of tertiary prevention include cholesterol reduction in patients with coronary heart disease and insulin therapy to prevent complications of diabetes.[1]

Usual source of care: A particular doctor's office, clinic, health center, or other health care facility to which an individual usually would go to obtain health care services. Having a usual source of care is associated with improved access to preventive services and followup care.

Vulnerable and at-risk populations: High-risk groups of people who have multiple health and social needs. Examples include pregnant women, people with human immunodeficiency virus infection, substance abusers, migrant farm workers, homeless people, poor people, infants and children, elderly people, people with disabilities, people with mental illness or mental health problems or disorders, and people from certain ethnic or racial groups who do not have the same access to quality health care services as other populations.

References

1. U.S. Preventive Services Task Force. *Guide to Clinical Preventive Services,* 2nd ed. Washington, DC: U.S. Department of Health and Human Services, 1995.

2. Thompson, R.S.; Taplin, S.H.; McAfee, T.A.; et al. Primary and secondary prevention services in clinical practice. Twenty years' experience in development, implementation, and evalua-

tion. *Journal of the American Medical Association* 273:1130-1135, 1995.

3. Solberg, L.I.; Kottke, T.E.; Brake, M.L.; et al. The case of the missing clinical preventive services systems.

Effective Clinical Practice 1(1):33-38, August/ September 1998.

4. Partnership for Prevention. Results from the William M. Mercer Survey of Employer Sponsored Health Plans. Washington, DC: the Partnership, 1999.

5. American College of Preventive Medicine. *1998 National Prevention in Primary Care Study.* Washington, DC: the College, November 1998.

6. U.S. Department of Health and Human Services. *Clinician's Handbook of Preventive Services,* 2nd Ed. Washington, DC: U.S. Department of Health and Human Services, 1998.

7. National Committee for Quality Assurance. The State of Managed Care Quality. 1999.

8. Donaldson, M.S.; Yordy, K.D.; Lohr, K.N. (eds.). Institute of Medicine. *Primary Care: America's Health in a New Era.* Washington, DC: National Academy Press, 1996.

9. Josiah Macy, Jr. Foundation. The role of emergency medicine in the future of American medical care: Summary of the conference. *Annals of Emergency Medicine* 25:230-233, 1995.

10. Krane, R.A., and Kane, R.L. Long Term Care: Principles, Programs, and Policies. New York: Springer, 1987.

11. Wiener, J.M.; Illston, L.H.; and Hanley, R.J. Sharing the Burden: Strategies for Public and Private Long Term Care Insurance. Washington, DC: The Brookings Institution, 1994.

12. CDC, National Center for Health Statistics. *National Health Interview Survey.* Hyattsville, MD: National Center for Health Statistics, unpublished.

13. Benson, V., and Marano, M.A. Current estimates from the National Health Interview Survey, 1995. *Vital Health Statistics* 10(199), 1998.

14. Weinick, R.M.; Zuvekas, S.H.; and Drilea, S.K. *Access to Health Care—Sources and Barriers, 1996.* MEPS Research Findings No. 3. AHCPR Pub. No. 98-0001. Rockville, MD: The Agency for Health Care Policy and Research, 1997.

15. National Committee on Quality Assurance. *Health Plan Employer Data and Information Set (HEDIS 3.0).* Washington, DC: National Committee on Quality Assurance, 1997.

16. Advisory Commission on Consumer Protection and Quality in the Health Care Industry. *Consumer Bill of Rights and Responsibilities—Report to the President.* Washington, DC: Advisory Commission, November 1997.

17. President's Advisory Commission on Consumer Protection and Quality in the Health Care Industry. *Quality First: Better Health Care for All Americans: Final Report to the President of the United States.* Washington, DC: United States Government Printing Office, 1998.

18. Kohn, L.; Corrigan, J.; and Donaldson, M. (eds.). Committee on Quality of Health Care in America. *To Err Is Human: Building a Safer Health System.* Washington, DC: Institute of Medicine, 1999.

19. Agency for Healthcare Research and Quality. Unpublished tabulations of *Medical Expenditure Panel Survey* (MEDS) data, 1996.

20. Bierman, A.S. *Journal of Ambulatory Care Management* 21(3):17-26, 1998.

21. Truman, B.I.; Smith-Akin, C.K.; Hinman, A.R.; et al. Developing the *Guide to Community Preventive Services*—Overview and Rationale. *American Journal of Preventive Medicine.* January 2000 (In press).

22. Centers for Disease Control and Prevention. Vaccine-Preventable Diseases: Improving Vaccination Coverage in Children, Adolescents, and Adults. A Report on Recommendations of the Task Force on Community Preventive Services. *Morbidity and Mortality Weekly Report* 48(No. RR-8):1-16, 1999.

23. National Health Service, Center for Reviews and Dissemination. Getting Evidence Into Practice. *Effective Health Care.* 5(1), February, 1999.

24. Centers for Disease Control and Prevention. Health insurance coverage and receipt of preventive health services—United States, 1993. *Morbidity and Mortality Weekly Report* 44:219-225, 1995.

25. Weissman, J.S., and Epstein, A.M. The insurance gap: Does it make a difference? *Annual Review of Public Health* 14:243-270, 1993.

26. U.S. General Accounting Office. *Health Insurance: Coverage Leads to Increased Health Care Access for Children.* GAO/HEHS-98-14. Washington, DC: General Accounting Office, 1998.

27. Reinhardt, U.E. Coverage and access in health care reform. *New England Journal of Medicine* 330:1452-1453, 1994.

28. Currie, J., and Gruber, J. Health insurance eligibility, utilization of medical care, and child health. *Quarterly Journal of Economics* 111(2):431-466, May 1996.

29. Hafner-Eaton, C. Physician utilization disparities between the uninsured and insured: comparisons of the chronically ill, acutely ill, and well nonelderly populations. *Journal of the American Medical Association* 269:787-792, 1993.

30. Health Insurance Association of America. Research Bulletin: A Profile of Employer-Sponsored Group Health Insurance. Washington, DC: The Association, 1989.

31. Davis, K.; Bialek, R.; Parkinson, M.; Smith, and J.; Vellozzi, C. Paying for preventive care: moving the debate forward. *American Journal of Preventive Medicine* 64(suppl.):7-30, 1990.

32. Faust, H.S. Strategies for obtaining preventive services reimbursement. *American Journal of Preventive Medicine* 64(suppl.):1-5, 1990.

33. Faulkner, L.A., and Schauffler, H.H. The effect of health insurance coverage on the appropriate use of recommended clinical preventive services. *American Journal of Preventive Medicine* 13(6):453-458, November/December 1997.

34. Tengs, T.O.; Adams, M.E.; Pliskin, J.S.; et al. Five-hundred life-saving interventions and their cost-effectiveness. *Risk Analysis* 15:369-390, 1995.

35. Cromwell, J.; Bartosch, W.J.; Fiore, M.C.; Hasselblad, V.; and Baker, T. Cost-effectiveness of the clinical practice recommendations in the AHCPR guideline for smoking cessation. *Journal of the American Medical Association* 278:1759-1766, 1997.

36. McGinnis, J.M., and Foege, W.H. Actual causes of death in the United States. *Journal of the American Medical Association* 270:2207-2212, 1993.

37. Taira, D.A.; Safran, D.G.; Seto, T.B.; Rogers, W.H.; and Tarlov, A.R. The relationship between patient income and physician discussion of health risk behaviors. *Journal of the American Medical Association* 278:1412-1417, 1997.

38. Fiore, M.C.; Bailey, W.C.; Cohen, S.J.; et al. *Smoking Cessation. Clinical Practice Guideline No. 18.* AHCPR Pub. No. 96-0692. Rockville, MD: U.S. Department of Health and Human Services, Agency for Health Care Policy and Research, 1996.

39. U.S. Department of Health and Human Services. *Physical Activity and Health: A Report of the Surgeon General.* Atlanta, GA: U.S. Department of Health and Human Services, Centers for Disease Control and Prevention, National Center for Chronic Disease Prevention and Health Promotion, 1996.

40. Kamb, M.L.; Fishbein, M.; Douglas, J.M.; Rhodes, F.; et al. Efficiency of risk reduction counseling to prevent human immunodeficiency virus and sexually transmitted diseases. *JAMA* 280:1161-1167, 1998.

41. Moy, E.; Bartman, B.A.; and Weir, M.R. Access to hypertensive care: effects of income, insurance, and source of care. *Archives of Internal Medicine* 155(14):1497-1502, 1995.

42. Ettner, S.L. The timing of preventive services for women and children: the effect of having a usual source of care. *American Journal of Public Health* 86:1748-1754, 1996.

43. Starfield, B. *Primary Care: Balancing Health Needs, Services and Technology.* New York: Oxford University Press; 1998.

44. Forrest, C.B., and Starfield, B. Entry into primary care and continuity: the affects of access. *American Journal of Public Health* 88:1334, 1998.

45. Forrest, C.B., and Starfield, B. The effect of first-contact care with primary care clinicians on ambulatory health care expenditures. *Journal of Family Practice* 43:40-48, 1996.

46. Berk, M.L.; Schur, C.L.; and Cantor, J.C. Ability to obtain health care: Recent estimates from the RWJF National Access to Care Survey. *Health Affairs* 14(3):139-146, 1995.

47. Wallace, R.B.; Wiese, W.H.; Lawrence, R.S.; Runyan, J.W.; and Tilson, H.H. Inventory of knowledge and skills relating to disease prevention and health promotion. *American Journal of Preventive Medicine* 6:51-56, 1990.

48. Report on the population health perspective panel. *Academic Medicine* 74:138-141, 1999.

49. Wallace, R.B.; Wiese, W.H.; Lawrence, R.S.; et al. Inventory of knowledge and skills relating to disease prevention and health promotion. *American Journal of Preventive Medicine* 6:51-56, 1990.

50. Komaromy, M.; Grumbach, K.; Drake, M.; et al. The role of Black and Hispanic physicians in providing health care for under served populations. *New England Journal of Medicine* 334:1305-1310, 1996.

51. Cooper-Patrick, L.; Gallo, J.; Gonzales, J.; et al. Race, gender, and partnership in the patient-physician relationship. *Journal of the American Medical Association* 282:583-589, 1999.

52. Goodman, D.C.; Stukel, T.A.; and Chang, C.H. Trends in pediatric asthma hospitalization rates: regional and socioeconomic differences. *Pediatrics* 101:208-213, 1998.

53. Pappas, G.; Hadden, W.C.; Kozak, L.J.; and Fisher, G.F. Potentially avoidable hospitalizations: inequalities in rates between U.S. socioeconomic groups. *American Journal of Public Health* 87:811-816, 1997.

54. Carillo, J.E.; Green, A.R.; and Betancourt, J.R. Cross-cultural primary care: a patient-based approach. *Annals of Internal Medicine* 130(1):829-834, 1999.

55. Billings, J.; Anderson, G.M.; and Newman, L.S. Recent findings on preventable hospitalizations. *Health Affairs* 15(3):239-249, 1996.

56. Billings, J.; Zeitel, L.; Lukomnik, J.; Carey, T.S.; Blank, A.E.; and Newman, L. Impact of socioeconomic status on hospital use in New York City. *Health Affairs* 12(1):162-173, 1993.

57. Bindman, A.B.; Grumbach, K.; Osmond, D.; Komaromy, M.; Vranizan, K.; Lurie, N.; Billings, J.; and Stewart, A. Preventable hospitalizations and access to health care. *Journal of the American Medical Association* 274(4):305-311, 1995.

58. Weissman, J.S.; Gatsonis, C.; and Epstein, A.M. Rates of avoidable hospitalization by insurance status in Massachusetts and Maryland. *Journal of the American Medical Association* 268(17):2388-2394, 1992.

59. Millman, M., ed. Institute of Medicine. *Access to Health Care in America*. Washington, DC: National Academy Press, 1993.

60. Dane, L.A. The Emergency Medical Treatment and Active Labor Act: The anomalous right to health care. *Health Matrix* 8:3-28, 1998.

61. Young, C.J. Emergency! Says who?: Analysis of the legal issues concerning managed care and emergency medical services. *Journal of Contemporary Health Law and Policy* 13:553-579, 1997.

62. Young G.P., and Lowe R.A. Adverse outcomes of managed care gatekeeping. *Academic Emergency Medicine* 4:1129-1136, 1997.

63. Litovitz, T.L.; Klein-Schwartz, W.; Caravati, E.M.; et al. Annual Report of the American Association of Poison Control Centers: Toxic Exposure Surveillance System. *American Journal of Emergency Medicine* 17:435-487, 1999.

64. Zuvekas, A.; Nolan, L.S.; Azzouzi, A.; Tumaylle, C.; and Ellis, J. *An Analysis of Potential Economies of Scale in Poison Control Centers: Final Report.* Washington, DC: Center for Health Policy Research, Georgetown University Medical Center, 1997.

65. Poison Control Center Advisory Work Group. *Final Report*. Atlanta, GA, and Rockville, MD: National Center for Injury Prevention and Control, Centers for Disease Control and Prevention, and Maternal and Child Health Bureau, Health Resources and Services Administration, 1997.

66. Institute of Medicine, Committee on Injury Prevention and Control. In: Bonnie, R.J.; Fulco, C.E.; Liverman, C.T., eds. *Reducing the Burden of Injury: Advancing Treatment and Prevention.*

Washington, DC: National Academy Press, 1999.

67. Health Resources and Services Administration. *Model Trauma Care System Plan*. Rockville, MD: Health Resources and Services Administration, Division of Trauma and Emergency Medical Systems, 1992.

68. Bazzoli, G.J.; Madura, K.J.; Cooper, G.F.; MacKenzie, E.J.; and Maier, R.V. Progress in the development of trauma systems in the United States: Results of a national survey. *Journal of the American Medical Association* 273:395-401, 1995.

69. Bass, R.R.; Gainer, P.S.; and Carlini, A.R. Update on trauma system development in the United States. *Journal of Trauma* 47(3 Suppl):515-521, 1999.

70. Institute of Medicine, Committee on Pediatric Emergency Medical Services. In: Durch, J.S., and Lohr, K.N., eds. *Emergency Medical Services for Children*. Washington, DC: National Academy Press, 1993.

71. American Academy of Pediatrics. Guidelines for pediatric emergency care facilities. *Pediatrics* 96:526-537, 1995.

72. Havens, B., and Beland, F., eds. Long-term care in five countries. *Canadian Journal on Aging* 15(suppl. 1):1-102, 1996.

73. Estes, C.L., and Swann, J.H. The Long Term Care Crisis. Newbury Park, CA: Sage Publications, 1993.

74. Spector, W., and Fortinsky, W. Pressure ulcer prevalence in Ohio nursing homes. *Journal of Aging and Health* 10(1):62-80, 1998.

75. Spector, W. Correlates of pressure sores in nursing homes: Evidence from the

National Medical Expenditure Survey. *Journal of Investigative Dermatology* 102(6):425-455, 1994.

76. The Pressure Ulcer Guideline Panel. *Treating Pressure Ulcers: Guideline Technical Report, No. 15, Volumes 1 and 2.* AHCPR Pub. No. 96-N014. Rockville, MD: Agency for Health Care Policy and Research, 1996.

77. Halverson, P.K.; Kaluzny, A.D.; and McLaughln, C.P.; Gaithersburg, MD: with Mays, G.P.; eds. *Managed Care and Public Health.* Aspen Publishers, Inc., 1998.

78. Institute of Medicine. *Medicare: A Strategy for Quality Assurance,* Vol. I. Lohr, K.N., ed. Washington, DC: National Academy Press, 1990.

2
Arthritis, Osteoporosis, and Chronic Back Conditions

Co-Lead Agencies: Centers for Disease Control and Prevention;
National Institutes of Health

Contents

Goal

Prevent illness and disability related to arthritis and other rheumatic conditions, osteoporosis, and chronic back conditions.

Overview

The current and projected growth in the number of people aged 65 years and older in the United States has focused attention on preserving quality of life as well as length of life. Chief among the factors involving preserving quality of life are the prevention and treatment of musculoskeletal conditions—the major causes of disability in the United States. Among musculoskeletal conditions, arthritis and other rheumatic conditions, osteoporosis, and chronic back conditions have the greatest impact on public health and quality of life.

Demographic trends suggest that people will need to continue working at older ages (for example, beyond age 65 years), increasing the adverse social and economic consequences of the high rates of activity limitation and disability of older persons with these conditions. At the same time, effective public health interventions exist to reduce the burden of all three conditions. (See Focus Area 6: Disability and Secondary Conditions.)

Issues and Trends

Arthritis

The various forms of arthritis affect more than 15 percent of the U.S. population—over 43 million persons—and more than 20 percent of the adult population, making arthritis one of the most common conditions in the United States.[1, 2, 3, 4]

The significant public health impact of arthritis is reflected in a variety of measures. First, arthritis is the leading cause of disability.[5] Arthritis limits the major activities (for example, working, housekeeping, school) of nearly 3 percent of the entire U.S. population (7 million persons), including nearly 1 out of every 5 persons with arthritis.[1, 2, 3] Arthritis trails only heart disease as a cause of work disability.[6] As a consequence, arthritis limits the independence of affected persons and disrupts the lives of family members and other care givers.

Second, health-related quality-of-life measures are consistently worse for persons with arthritis, whether the measure is healthy days in the past 30 days, days without severe pain, "ability days" (that is, days without activity limitations), or difficulty in performing personal care activities.[7, 8]

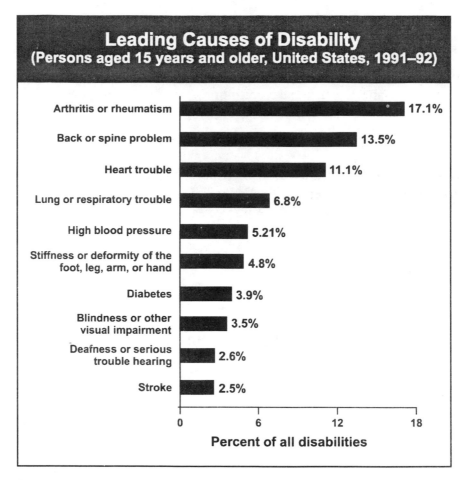

Leading Causes of Disability
(Persons aged 15 years and older, United States, 1991–92)

Cause	Percent
Arthritis or rheumatism	17.1%
Back or spine problem	13.5%
Heart trouble	11.1%
Lung or respiratory trouble	6.8%
High blood pressure	5.21%
Stiffness or deformity of the foot, leg, arm, or hand	4.8%
Diabetes	3.9%
Blindness or other visual impairment	3.5%
Deafness or serious trouble hearing	2.6%
Stroke	2.5%

Percent of all disabilities

Source: CDC. Prevalence of disabilities and associated health conditions—United States, 1991–92. *Morbidity and Mortality Weekly Report* 43(40):730-731, 737-739, 1994.

Third, arthritis has a sizable economic impact. Arthritis is the source of at least 44 million visits to a health care provider, 744,000 hospitalizations, and 4 million days of hospital care per year.[4, 9] Estimated medical care costs for persons with arthritis were $15 billion, and total costs (medical care plus lost productivity) were $65 billion in 1992.[10] This latter amount is equal to 1.1 percent of the gross domestic product. Nearly 60 percent of persons with arthritis are in the working-aged population[1, 2, 3] and they have a low rate of labor force participation.[11]

Fourth, arthritis, like other chronic pain conditions, has an important negative effect on a person's mental health.[12, 13]

Fifth, although death is not a frequent outcome of arthritis, persons with certain forms of arthritis do have higher death rates than the general population. For example, the 2 million persons in the United States with rheumatoid arthritis are at greater risk of premature death from respiratory and infectious diseases than the overall U.S. population.[14]

A variety of demographic trends indicate that the impact of arthritis will only increase.[15] Given current population projections, arthritis will affect over 18 percent of all persons in the United States (nearly 60 million persons) in the year 2020 and will limit the major activities of nearly 4 percent (11.6 million).[1, 2, 3] Direct and indirect costs are expected to rise proportionately.

Osteoporosis

About 13 to 18 percent of women aged 50 years and older and 3 to 6 percent of men aged 50 years and older have osteoporosis, a reduction in bone mass or density that leads to deteriorated and fragile bones. These rates correspond to 4 million to 6 million women and 1 million to 2 million men in the United States who have osteoporosis.[16] Another 37 to 50 percent of women aged 50 years and older and 28 to 47 percent of men of the same age group have some degree of osteopenia, reduction in bone mass that is not as severe as osteoporosis.

The major health consequence of osteoporosis is an increased risk of fractures. Approximately 1.5 million fractures per year are attributed to osteoporosis.[17] One in three women and one in eight men aged 50 years and older will experience an osteoporotic-related fracture in their lifetime.[17] Health care costs for these fractures are estimated at $13.8 billion per year in 1996 dollars.[18]

The risk of any fracture increases with the presence of osteoporosis, but hip fractures represent the most serious impact in terms of health care costs and consequences for the individual. In 1994, there were 281,000 hospital discharges for hip fracture among people aged 45 years and older. Of these, 74,000, or 26 percent, were men.[16] In all, 1 out of 6 white women and 1 out of 17 white men will experience a hip fracture by the time they reach age 90 years.[19] Although the hip fracture rate among women seems relatively constant, the rate among men seems to be increasing over time.[20]

An average of 24 percent of hip fracture patients aged 50 years and older die in the year following fracture, with higher death rates among men than among women.[21] Also, hip fracture was more likely to lead to functional impairment than were other serious medical conditions, including heart attack, stroke, and cancer.[21] For example, half of all hip fracture patients will be unable to walk without assistance.[17]

Chronic Back Conditions

Chronic low back pain is described in different ways, such as the occurrence of back pain lasting for more than 7 to 12 weeks, back pain lasting beyond the expected period of healing, or frequently recurring back pain. Moreover, a wide range of outcome measures are used to describe chronic back problems, such as low back pain (LBP), activity limitation, impairment and disability. Compounding the problem is the lack of a single data source to track chronic back problems. Sources that have been used include workers compensation data, Occupational

Safety and Health Administration (OSHA) and Bureau of Labor Statistics records, and data from national health surveys.

Chronic back conditions are both common and debilitating. Back pain occurs in 15 to 45 percent of people each year,[22, 23, 24, 25, 26] and 70 to 85 percent of people have back pain some time in their life. In the United States, back pain is the most frequent cause of activity limitation in people under age 45 years, [27, 28] the second most frequent reason for physician visits, the fifth-ranking reason for hospitalization and the third most common reason for surgical procedures.[29]

Work-related risk factors, such as heavy physical work, lifting and forceful movements, awkward postures, and whole body vibration, are associated with low back disorders. Work-related risk factors account for 28 percent to 50 percent of the low back problem in an adult population.[30] A number of personal factors may be risk factors for low back pain. These include nonmodifiable factors, such as age and gender, some anthropometric characteristics (for example, height and body build), previous history of low back problems, and spinal abnormalities as well as modifiable factors, such as weight, physical fitness, smoking, some aspects of lumbar flexibility, trunk muscle strength, and hamstring elasticity. A history of previous low back problems is one of the most reliable predictors of subsequent back problems.[31]

Disparities

Arthritis is a leading health problem among all demographic groups, although significant and sometimes surprising disparities exist. Arthritis affects 50 percent of people aged 65 years and older. However, most people with arthritis are younger than age 65 years and of working age.[1, 2, 3] Arthritis also affects 285,000 children,[32] making it one of the more common chronic conditions of childhood. Arthritis is more common in women aged 18 years and older than in men and is the leading chronic condition and cause of activity limitation among women.[33, 34]

Whites and African Americans have similar rates of disease, but African Americans have greater rates of activity limitation.[1, 2, 3] For African Americans, arthritis is the third most common chronic condition and the leading cause of activity limitation.[35] For Hispanics and American Indians or Alaska Natives, arthritis is the second most common chronic condition and the second leading cause of activity limitation.[35] For Asians or Pacific Islanders, arthritis is the fourth most common chronic condition and the second leading cause of activity limitation.[35] For whites, arthritis is the most common chronic condition and the second leading cause of activity limitation.[35]

The rate of arthritis and its associated disabilities is higher among persons with low education and low income.[1, 2, 3] African Americans have lower rates of total joint replacement, a surgical procedure that is highly successful in reducing the impact of arthritis in persons with severe pain or disability, than do whites.[36]

Certain types of jobs, such as shipyard work, farm work, and occupations that place high knee-bending demands on the workers, increase the risks for osteoarthritis.[37, 38]

Osteoporosis is more common among women than men. The rates of disease increase markedly with increasing age. Rates are higher among non-Hispanic white Americans than among non-Hispanic African Americans or Mexican Americans.[16] White postmenopausal women are at highest risk of the disease.

The risk for chronic back pain increases with age. Although back pain appears to be equally common in men and women, impairment from back and spine conditions is more common in women.

Opportunities

The importance of physical activity for bone and joint health was highlighted in a 1996 report *Physical Activity and Health: A Report of the Surgeon General.*[39] Although behavioral interventions seem to have potential benefits, risk factors for the various types of arthritis need to be identified. Recreational or occupational joint injury has been identified as a risk factor for later osteoarthritis, and overweight is a risk factor for osteoarthritis of the knee and possibly the hip and hand.[40] Overweight appears to be a risk factor associated with the progression and severity of osteoarthritis.[40, 41]

Genetic research may soon identify persons at high risk for certain types of arthritis and thereby offer a better target for interventions. Current medical care offers considerable relief from pain and other symptoms for all types of arthritis. Available interventions often are not used, however, because of the popular belief that arthritis is part of normal aging, that a person can do nothing about it, and that it affects only old persons. But early diagnosis and aggressive treatment of rheumatoid arthritis with disease-modifying drugs, for example, appear to reduce its symptoms and related disability.[42, 43, 44, 45, 46, 47]

Educational and behavioral interventions also can relieve symptoms and reduce disability. Telephone contacts with clinicians and several land-based and water exercise programs have had beneficial outcomes.[48, 49, 50, 51] The Arthritis Self-Help Course, a 6-week, 2-hour per week educational intervention, has been shown to reduce pain up to 20 percent beyond what was achieved through conventional medical care.[52] The course has the additional benefit of reducing medical care costs by reducing the number of physician visits for arthritis.[52, 53] These and other effective interventions are currently underused, with some reaching less than 1 percent of target populations.[54] Countering myths about arthritis and applying available interventions can help reduce the impact of this health problem. (See Focus Area 6. Disability and Secondary Conditions.)

Interventions for osteoporosis and fractures can be designed to prevent the development of the disease, reduce further bone loss after the occurrence of the disease, and lessen the risk of fractures. Opportunities for primary prevention occur throughout the lifespan and include programs to promote exercise, avoid smoking, reduce excessive alcohol consumption, and improve nutrition, particularly the amount of calcium and vitamin D in the diet. (See Focus Area 19. Nutrition and Overweight.) These approaches can be important in achieving a high peak bone mass during adolescence to delay the onset of osteoporosis as bone mass declines with age. The approaches also can reduce the rate of bone loss later in life.

Women need to be particularly concerned about bone loss occurring at the time of menopause, when bone can be lost at the rate of 2 to 4 percent per year. Women should be counseled on methods to minimize their bone loss. Evidence indicates that older persons, even those who have had a fracture, can benefit from treatment to prevent further bone loss or restore some lost bone to decrease the risk of subsequent fractures.[55]

A wide range of interventions prevent or reduce low back problems. These interventions may include activities designed to reduce the physical demands of work activities by redesigning the task or to address the individual's specific needs, such as strength or endurance training or counseling for nutrition and lifestyle changes. Ergonomic interventions that are directed at changing the job or work environment have proven effective in reducing risk of occupational low back pain. (See Focus Area 20. Occupational Safety and Health.) Thus, it is reasonable to assume that ergonomic approaches would be effective in preventing chronic LBP as well. Even in a nonwork environment, the physical demands of the activity can be reduced by using ergonomic principles. Interventions involving training in proper lifting techniques, physical conditioning, and weight loss have been investigated in programmatically oriented studies. These have shown that workplace interventions may have an effect on low back disorders.[56] The overall benefits of exercise, nutrition and lifestyle changes on an individual's health and well-being would certainly justify efforts in this area. Also, interventions directed at improving strength and endurance may have an important impact on reducing activity limitations due to chronic low back pain.

Because national data systems will not be available in the first half of the decade for tracking progress, four subjects of interest concerning arthritis and osteoporosis are not covered in this focus area's objectives. Representing a research and data collection agenda for the coming decade, the topics involve appropriate management, patient education, provider counseling, and bone fracture prevention. The first addresses persons with systemic rheumatic disease who receive an early specific diagnosis and appropriate management plan. The second topic concerns hospitals, managed care organizations, and large group practices that provide effective, evidence-based arthritis education (including information about community and self-help resources) for patients to use as an integral part of the management of their condition. The third topic concerns health care provider counseling for persons at risk for or who have arthritis. Women

Data as of November 30, 1999

aged 65 years and older, eligible under Medicare criteria, who have an initial bone density measurement are the focus of the fourth topic about bone fracture prevention.

Interim Progress Toward Year 2000 Objectives

The national health objectives for the year 2000 included two objectives for osteoporosis, one objective for chronic back conditions, and no objectives for arthritis. The objective of increasing the proportion of women of menopausal age who have been counseled about estrogen replacement therapy for the prevention of osteoporosis had no data subsequent to the 1994 baseline to chart progress. Annual hip fracture rates increased among people aged 65 years and older and rates of activity limitation due to chronic back conditions increased from the 1986-88 baseline.

Note: Unless otherwise noted, data are from Centers for Disease Control and Prevention, National Center for Health Statistics, *Healthy People 2000 Review, 1998-99.*

Arthritis, Osteoporosis, and Chronic Back Conditions

Goal: Prevent illness and disability related to arthritis and other rheumatic conditions, osteoporosis, and chronic back conditions.

Number	Objective
Arthritis and Other Rheumatic Conditions	
2-1	Mean days without severe pain
2-2	Activity limitations due to arthritis
2-3	Personal care limitations
2-4	Help in coping
2-5	Employment rates
2-6	Racial differences in total knee replacement
2-7	Seeing a health care provider
2-8	Arthritis education
Osteoporosis	
2-9	Cases of osteoporosis
2-10	Hospitalization for vertebral fracture
Chronic Back Conditions	
2-11	Activity limitations due to chronic back conditions

Arthritis and Other Rheumatic Conditions

2-1. **(Developmental) Increase the mean number of days without severe pain among adults who have chronic joint symptoms.**

Potential data sources: Behavioral Risk Factor Surveillance System (BRFSS), CDC, NCCDPHP; National Health Interview Survey (NHIS), CDC, NCHS.

Public health researchers measure days without severe pain by asking "During the past 30 days, for about how many days did pain make it hard for you to do your usual activities, such as self-care, work, or recreation?" Pain is the most important symptom among persons with arthritis, resulting in the widespread use of conventional prescription and nonprescription medications, surgical interventions, and alternative medical treatments. A measure of pain-free days provides a pertinent and understandable performance-based approach for tracking this key health-related quality of life (HRQOL) determinant for persons with arthritis. Increasing days without severe pain is a feasible target, given more widespread use of available interventions (medical, educational, exercise, nutritional) that are likely to affect this measure. Health surveys variously ask about chronic joint symptoms or arthritis in addressing arthritis and other rheumatic conditions, which is why both terms are used for these objectives.

2-2. **Reduce the proportion of adults with chronic joint symptoms who experience a limitation in activity due to arthritis.**

Target: 21 percent.

Baseline: 27 percent of adults aged 18 years and older with chronic joint symptoms experienced a limitation in activity due to arthritis in 1997. (Age adjusted to the year 2000 standard population.)

Target setting method: Better than the best.

Data sources: National Health Interview Survey (NHIS), CDC, NCHS; National Health and Nutrition Examination Survey (NHANES), CDC, NCHS.

Adults Aged 18 Years and Older With Chronic Joint Symptoms, 1997	Experienced Limitation in Activity Due to Arthritis
	Percent
TOTAL	27
Race and ethnicity	
American Indian or Alaska Native	27
Asian or Pacific Islander	18
Asian	16
Native Hawaiian and other Pacific Islander	DSU
Black or African American	32
White	27
Hispanic or Latino	28
Not Hispanic or Latino	27
Black or African American	32
White	27
Gender	
Female	31
Male	22
Family income level	
Poor	36
Near poor	30
Middle/high income	24
Education level (aged 25 years and older)	
Less than high school	34
High school graduate	32
At least some college	26

DNA = Data have not been analyzed. DNC = Data are not collected. DSU = Data are statistically unreliable.
Note: Age adjusted to the year 2000 standard population.

2-3. **Reduce the proportion of all adults with chronic joint symptoms who have difficulty in performing two or more personal care activities, thereby preserving independence.**

Target: 1.4 percent.

Baseline: 2.0 percent of adults aged 18 years and older with chronic joint symptoms experienced difficulty performing two or more personal care activities in 1997. (Age adjusted to the year 2000 standard population.)

Target setting method: Better than the best.

Data source: National Health Interview Survey (NHIS), CDC, NCHS.

Adults Aged 18 Years and Older With Chronic Joint Symptoms, 1997	Personal Care Limitations Percent
TOTAL	2.0
Race and ethnicity	
American Indian or Alaska Native	DSU
Asian or Pacific Islander	DSU
Asian	DSU
Native Hawaiian and other Pacific Islander	DSU
Black or African American	3.6
White	1.8
Hispanic or Latino	3.5
Not Hispanic or Latino	1.9
Black or African American	3.4
White	1.7
Gender	
Female	2.2
Male	1.6
Family income level	
Poor	5.4
Near poor	2.4
Middle/high income	0.9

Adults Aged 18 Years and Older With Chronic Joint Symptoms, 1997	Personal Care Limitations Percent
Education level (aged 25 years and older)	
Less than high school	3.4
High school graduate	2.2
At least some college	1.4

DNA = Data have not been analyzed. DNC = Data are not collected. DSU = Data are statistically unreliable.
Note: Age adjusted to the year 2000 standard population.

Arthritis and other rheumatic conditions affect quality of life in many ways and are key items of personal interest to individuals with these conditions.[7, 8, 57, 58, 59, 60, 61] From a public health perspective, validated measures of HRQOL are essential for monitoring the impact of clinical and public health interventions.

Activity limitation occurs frequently among persons with arthritis and is an important functional element that can compromise independence. Activity limitation affects 27 percent of all persons who have arthritis,[1] making it the number one cause of activity limitations in the United States.[5] The activity limitations of arthritis also indirectly affect health and independence by decreasing physical activity, increasing weight, and placing persons at higher risk for all the adverse outcomes of those risk factors.

As the leading cause of disability, arthritis is a leading cause of difficulty in performing personal care activities and thereby a leading cause of loss of independence. Therefore, maintaining independence, especially in personal care, is important for persons with arthritis.

2-4. (Developmental) Increase the proportion of adults aged 18 years and older with arthritis who seek help in coping if they experience personal and emotional problems.

Potential data sources: National Health Interview Survey (NHIS), CDC, NCHS; Behavioral Risk Factor Surveillance System (BRFSS), CDC, NCCDPHP.

Coping difficulties, depression, anxiety, and low self-efficacy are recognized as major personal and emotional problems among persons with arthritis.[12] These problems are especially frequent among persons who experience physical pain. Because arthritis is a leading cause of chronic pain, monitoring these mental health outcomes can help assess the success of applied interventions.[13]

2-5. Increase the employment rate among adults with arthritis in the working-age population.

Target: 78 percent.

Baseline: 67 percent of adults aged 18 to 64 years with arthritis were employed in the past week in 1997. (Age adjusted to the year 2000 standard population.)

Target setting method: Better than the best.

Data source: National Health Interview Survey (NHIS), CDC, NCHS.

Adults Aged 18 to 64 Years With Arthritis, 1997	Employed in Past Week Percent
TOTAL	67
Race and ethnicity	
American Indian or Alaska Native	46
Asian or Pacific Islander	56
Asian	54
Native Hawaiian and other Pacific Islander	DSU
Black or African American	52
White	69
Hispanic or Latino	60
Not Hispanic or Latino	67
Black or African American	53
White	70
Gender	
Female	60
Male	74
Family income level	
Poor	39
Near poor	54
Middle/high income	77
Education level (aged 25 to 64 years)	
Less than high school	47
High school graduate	65
At least some college	78

DNA = Data have not been analyzed. DNC = Data are not collected. DSU = Data are statistically unreliable.
Note: Age adjusted to the year 2000 standard population.

Labor force participation rates (which parallel employment rates) for all persons of work age (18 to 64 years) in 1994 were 70.6 percent for females and 86.9 percent for males.[11] Rates for persons with arthritis, however, are far below these numbers.[11] A part of this low rate may be increased through early diagnosis and appropriate management, improved self-management, and improved job retention efforts. Raising this low rate will help foster independence for affected persons and reduce the demands on families and society. Reducing demands on families and society is particularly important as demographic changes lead to fewer workers for each nonworker.

2-6. (Developmental) Eliminate racial disparities in the rate of total knee replacements.

Potential data sources: Medicare data, HCFA; National Hospital Discharge Survey (NHDS), CDC, NCHS; Hospital Cost and Utilization Project (HCUP), AHRQ.

Studies have shown that African Americans have much lower rates of total knee replacement than whites, even when adjusted for age, gender, and insurance coverage.[36] The reasons for this difference are unclear, but the effect is that many persons are not getting needed interventions to reduce pain and disability. This is one component of a more widespread problem of racial differences in medical care that is difficult to explain by financial or access-to-care issues.

2-7. (Developmental) Increase the proportion of adults who have seen a health care provider for their chronic joint symptoms.

Potential data source: National Health Interview Survey (NHIS) CDC, NCHS.

Studies using the 1989 National Health Interview Survey have shown that 16 percent of adults aged 18 years and older have not seen a doctor for their arthritis.[62] Appropriate medical management, patient and provider education, improved self-management, and physical activity—all encouraged by providers—can reduce arthritis pain and disability. Increasing the percentage of persons who seek a diagnosis and treatment from a health care provider for their chronic joint symptoms is an objective amenable to public awareness campaigns to counter the myths that arthritis is part of normal aging and nothing can be done for it. This objective is especially important for the working-aged population, the upper age limit of which is likely to rise as the overall population ages through the 2030s.

2-8. **(Developmental) Increase the proportion of persons with arthritis who have had effective, evidence-based arthritis education as an integral part of the management of their condition.**

Potential data sources: National Health Interview Survey (NHIS), CDC, NCHS; Behavioral Risk Factor Surveillance System (BRFSS), CDC, NCCDPHP.

Existing evidence-based education interventions, such as the Arthritis Self-Help Course, are effective in reducing arthritis pain and reducing physician visits for arthritis.[52] These beneficial interventions, which include information about community and self-help resources, are estimated to reach less than 1 percent of the population with arthritis.[54] Expanding the dissemination of the benefits of interventions currently available offers the opportunity of quickly improving the health of all persons with arthritis and reducing the impact of arthritis nationally. Education efforts should be provided in a culturally and linguistically competent manner.

Osteoporosis

2-9. Reduce the overall number of cases of osteoporosis.

Target: 8 percent of adults.

Baseline: 10 percent of adults aged 50 years and older had osteoporosis as measured by low total femur bone mineral density (BMD) in 1988-94. (Age adjusted to the year 2000 standard population.)

Target setting method: 20 percent improvement.

Data sources: National Health and Nutrition Examination Survey (NHANES), CDC, NCHS.

Adults Aged 50 Years and Older, 1988–94	Osteoporosis as Measured by Low Bone Mineral Density Percent
TOTAL	10
Race and ethnicity	
American Indian or Alaska Native	DSU
Asian or Pacific Islander	DSU
Asian	DNC
Native Hawaiian and other Pacific Islander	DNC

Adults Aged 50 Years and Older, 1988–94	Osteoporosis as Measured by Low Bone Mineral Density
	Percent
Black or African American	7
White	10
Hispanic or Latino	DSU
Mexican American	10
Not Hispanic or Latino	DNA
Black or African American	7
White	10
Gender	
Female	16
Male	3
Education level	
Less than high school	11
High school graduate	11
At least some college	9

DNA = Data have not been analyzed. DNC = Data are not collected. DSU = Data are statistically unreliable.

Note: Age adjusted to the year 2000 standard population.

BMD has been identified as one of the primary predictive factors for osteoporosis-related fractures.[63, 64, 65] Osteoporosis is defined as a BMD value that is more than 2.5 standard deviations below that of an average young adult.[66]

The proportion of adults 50 years and older with osteoporosis in the total femur region is 10 percent (16 percent in women and 3 percent in men). Osteoporosis occurs in nonwhite women and in men, although the rates of disease are not as high as the rates found among white women. These estimates are based on the total femur; estimates based on a different skeletal site (or combination of sites) may differ. For example, the proportion of white women with osteoporosis in Olmsted County, Minnesota, was established to be approximately 16 to 17 percent at the femur, lumbar spine, or wrist when each site was considered separately. However, 30 percent of women had osteoporosis in at least one of the three sites.[67]

Osteoporosis is a major risk factor for hip fracture. Virtually all persons with a hip fracture are hospitalized for treatment.[21] Two-thirds of persons who fracture a hip do not return to their prefracture level of functioning. Health care expenditures for hip fractures in 1995 have been estimated at $8.7 billion.[18] Interventions that reduce the rate of osteoporosis should have a marked impact on the rate of hip

Data as of November 30, 1999

fractures. Estimates indicate that osteoporosis contributes to 90 percent of hip fractures in women and 80 percent of hip fractures in men.[65] Increasing BMD by 5 percent may decrease the risk of fractures by 25 percent.[68]

Although osteoporosis increases the risk of fractures, most hip fractures result from falls.[66] Some risk factors associated with falls may be amenable to interventions. These risk factors include impaired vision, use of long-acting psychotropic drugs, physical inactivity, muscle weakness, and poor health.[69] (See Focus Area 15. Injury and Violence Prevention.)

2-10. Reduce the proportion of adults who are hospitalized for vertebral fractures associated with osteoporosis.

Target: 11.6 hospitalization per 10,000 population aged 65 years and older.

Baseline: 14.5 per 10,000 adults aged 65 years and older were hospitalized for vertebral fractures associated with osteoporosis in 1997. (Age adjusted to the year 2000 standard population.)

Target setting method: 20 percent improvement.

Data source: National Hospital Discharge Survey (NHDS), CDC, NCHS.

Adults Aged 65 Years and Older, 1997	Hospitalizations for Vertebral Fractures Associated With Osteoporosis Rate per 10,000
TOTAL	14.5
Race and ethnicity	
American Indian or Alaska Native	DSU
Asian or Pacific Islander	DSU
Asian	DNC
Native Hawaiian and other Pacific Islander	DNC
Black or African American	6.5
White	11.1
Hispanic or Latino	DSU
Not Hispanic or Latino	DSU
Black or African American	DSU
White	DSU

Adults Aged 65 Years and Older, 1997	Hospitalizations for Vertebral Fractures Associated With Osteoporosis Rate per 10,000
Gender	
Female	15.2
Male	13.0
Age	
65 to 74 years	5.5
75 to 84 years	16.5
85 years and older	47.6

DNA = Data have not been analyzed. DNC = Data are not collected. DSU = Data are statistically unreliable.

Note: Age adjusted to the year 2000 standard population.

Vertebral fractures are the most common fracture due to osteoporosis.[70] About 30 to 50 percent of women and 20 to 30 percent of men will experience vertebral fractures in their lifetime.[70] The overall number of cases of these fractures rises rapidly with increasing age. Among white women, the rate rises from 6 percent among those aged 50 to 59 years to about 75 percent among those aged 90 years and older.[71] Most of these fractures cause little difficulty and go unrecognized. However, 33 percent of the fractures will be diagnosed clinically, 8 percent will require hospitalization,[72] and about 2 percent will require long-term nursing care.[73]

The most common symptom of vertebral fractures is back pain, which is reported in about half of the cases. People with these fractures are more likely to have difficulty performing activities of daily living, such as bending, reaching above the head, and walking. Changes in the outward appearance of people experiencing these fractures is a loss of height and the development of a humped back.[70]

Interventions that reduce the number of persons with osteoporosis should reduce the rates of vertebral fractures. Falls associated with fractures at other sites do not play a prominent role in these fractures. Normal daily activities can place sufficient stress on the vertebra to cause fractures.[71]

For discussion of calcium and vitamin D, see Focus Area 19. Nutrition and Overweight.

Chronic Back Conditions

2-11. Reduce activity limitation due to chronic back conditions.

Target: 25 adults per 1,000 population aged 18 years and older.

Baseline: 32 adults per 1,000 population aged 18 years and older experienced activity limitations due to chronic back conditions in 1997 (age adjusted to the year 2000 standard population).

Target setting method: Better than the best.

Data source: National Health Interview Survey (NHIS), CDC, NCHS.

Adults Aged 18 Years and Older, 1997	Experienced Limitation of Activity Due to Chronic Back Conditions Rate per 1,000
TOTAL	32
Race and ethnicity	
American Indian or Alaska Native	68
Asian or Pacific Islander	18
Asian	15
Native Hawaiian and other Pacific Islander	DSU
Black or African American	36
White	31
Hispanic or Latino	28
Not Hispanic or Latino	32
Black or African American	36
White	32
Gender	
Female	32
Male	31
Family income level	
Poor	77
Near poor	53
Middle/high income	24

Adults Aged 18 Years and Older, 1997	Experienced Limitation of Activity Due to Chronic Back Conditions Rate per 1,000
Education level (aged 25 years and older)	
Less than high school	54
High school graduate	35
At least some college	28

DNA = Data have not been analyzed. DNC = Data are not collected. DSU = Data are statistically unreliable.
Note: Age adjusted to the year 2000 standard population.

Persons who are overweight and persons who frequently bend over or lift heavy objects are at risk for low back injuries.[74] Occupations that require repetitive lifting, particularly in a forward bent and twisted position, place employees at especially high risk. Other risk factors for low back injury include exposure to vibration produced by vehicles or industrial machinery, prolonged vehicle driving, and certain sports activities.[24, 25, 26, 75, 76] Predictors of back problems may include diminished lumbar flexibility, trunk muscle strength, and hamstring elasticity.[77] Osteoporosis increases the risk of vertebral compression, which may account for the increase in reported low back pain in older females.[78, 79] Increased age also is associated with back pain.[80] In addition, persons who have experienced back problems in the past are at increased risk for future injury.[80, 81]

Related Objectives From Other Focus Areas

1. Access to Quality Health Services

1-3.   Counseling about health behaviors

3. Cancer

3-10.   Provider counseling about preventive measures

6. Disability and Secondary Conditions

6-4.   Social participation among adults with disabilities

6-5.   Sufficient emotional support among adults with disabilities

6-8.   Employment parity

7. Education and Community-Based Programs

7-5.   Worksite health promotion programs

7-6.   Participation in employer-sponsored health promotion activities

7-10.   Community health promotion programs

7-12.   Older adult participation in community health promotion activities

15. Injury and Violence Prevention

15-28.   Hip fractures

19. Nutrition and Overweight

19-1.   Healthy weight in adults

19-2.   Obesity in adults

19-11.   Calcium intake

19-16.   Worksite promotion of nutrition education and weight management

19-17.   Nutrition counseling for medical conditions

20. Occupational Safety and Health

20-2.   Work-related injuries

20-3.   Overexertion or repetitive motion

22. Physical Activity and Fitness

22-1.   No leisure-time physical extivity

22-2.   Moderate physical activity

22-3.   Vigorous physical activity

22-4.   Muscular strength and endurance

22-5.   Flexibility

22-8.   Physical education requirements in schools

22-10.   Physical activity in physical education class

27. Tobacco Use

27-1.   Adult tobacco use

27-5.   Smoking cessation by adults

27-7.   Smoking cessation by adolescents

27-17.   Adolescent disapproval of smoking

Terminology

(A listing of all abbreviations and acronyms used in this publication appears in Appendix K.)

Activity limitations: Problems in a person's performance of everyday functions such as communication, self-care, mobility, learning, and behavior.

Arthritis: Shorthand for arthritis and other rheumatic conditions.

Arthritis and other rheumatic conditions: More than 100 conditions (or diseases or problems) that primarily affect the joints, muscles, fascia, tendons, bursa, ligaments, and other connective tissues of the body.

Bone mineral density (BMD): Measurement used to determine the presence of osteoporosis.

Chronic back conditions: Low back pain and other conditions affecting only the back.

Chronic joint symptoms: Pain, aching, stiffness, or swelling in or around a joint that was present on most days for at least 1 month in the past 12 months.

Disability: The general term used to represent the interactions between individuals with a health condition and barriers in their environment. The term disability is operationalized as self-reported activity limitations or use of assistive devices or equipment related to an activity limitation.

Musculoskeletal conditions: Problems that affect the skeleton, joints, muscles, and connective tissues of the body.

Osteoarthritis: A slowly progressive, degenerative joint disease that results from the breakdown of cartilage and leads to pain and stiffness; usually affects the knees, hips, and hands; the most common form of arthritis.

Osteoporosis: Bone disease characterized by a reduction of bone mass and a deterioration of the microarchitecture of the bone leading to bone fragility.

Osteopenia: A condition similar to osteoporosis except the reduction in bone mass is not as severe.

Personal care activities: Eating, bathing, dressing, or getting around inside the home, including getting in or out of bed or chairs and using the toilet (including getting to the toilet).

Rheumatoid arthritis: A chronic, inflammatory disease of the body that produces its most prominent manifestations in joints, often leading to joint pain, stiffness, and deformity.

Work disability: Limited in the amount or kind of work; unable to work.

References

1.   Centers for Disease Control and Prevention (CDC). Arthritis prevalence and activity limitations— United States, 1990. *Morbidity and Mortality Weekly Report* 43(24):433-438, 1994.

2.   Lawrence, R.C.; Helmick, C.G.; Arnett, F.C.; et al. Estimates of the prevalence of arthritis and selected musculoskeletal disorders in the United States. *Arthritis & Rheumatism* 41(5):778-799, 1998.

3.   Helmick, C.G.; Lawrence, R.C.; Pollard, R.A., et al. Arthritis and other rheumatic conditions: Who is affected now, who will be affected later? *National Arthritis Data Workgroup Arthritis Care and Research* 8:203-211, 1995.

4.   CDC. Impact of arthritis and other rheumatic conditions on the health-care system. *Morbidity and Mortality Weekly Report* 48(17):349-353, 1999.

5.   CDC. Current Trends: Prevalence of disabilities and associated health conditions—United States, 1991-1992. *Morbidity and Mortality Weekly Report* 43(40):730-731, 737-739, 1994.

6.   LaPlante, M.P. Data on Disability from the National Health Interview Survey, 1983-1985. Washington, DC:

U.S. National Institute on Disability and Rehabilitation Research, U.S. Department of Education, 1988.

7.   CDC. Health-related quality of life and activity limitation—8 states, 1995. *Morbidity and Mortality Weekly Report* 47(67):134-140, 1998.

8.   CDC. State differences in reported healthy days among adults—United States, 1993-1996. *Morbidity and Mortality Weekly Report* 47(12):239-243, 1998.

9.   CDC. *Targeting Arthritis: The Nation's Leading Cause of Disability. At-a-Glance, 1998.* Atlanta, GA: Technical Information and Editorial Services Branch, National Center for Chronic Disease Prevention and Health Promotion, Centers for Disease Control and Prevention, 1998.

10.   Yelin, E., and Callahan, L.F. for the National Arthritis Data Workgroup. The economic cost and social and psychological impact of musculoskeletal conditions. *Arthritis & Rheumatism* 38(10):1351-1362, 1995.

11.   Trupin, L.; Sebesta, D.S.; Yelin, E.; and LaPlante, M.P. Trends in Laborforce Participation Among Persons With Disability, 1983-1994. Disability Statistics Report 10. Washington, DC: U.S. Department of Education, National Institute on

Disability and Rehabilitation Research, 1997.

12.   Frank, R.G., and Hagglund, K.J. Mood disorders. In: Wegener, S.T. (ed.). *Clinical Care in the Rheumatic Diseases.* Atlanta, GA: American College of Rheumatology, 1996, 125-130.

13.   Bradley, L.A. Wegener. S.T.; Belza, B.L.; and Gall, E.P. Pain management interventions for patients with rheumatic diseases. In: Melvin, J., and Jensen, G. (eds.). *Rheumatologic Rehabilitation Series Volume I: Assessment and Management.* Rockville, MD: American Occupational Therapy Association, 1998, 259-278.

14.   Wolf, F. The natural history of rheumatoid arthritis. *Journal of Rheumathology,* 23(suppl. 44):13-22, 1996

15.   Boult, C.; Altmann, M.; Gilbertson, D.; Yu, C.; and Kane, R.L. Decreasing disability in the 21st century: The future effects of controlling six fatal and non-fatal conditions. *American Journal of Public Health* 86:1388-1393, 1996.

16.   Looker, A.C.; Orwoll, E.S.; Johnston, C.C.; et al. Prevalence of low femoral bone density in older U.S. adults from NHANES III. *Journal of Bone and Mineral*

Research 12(11):1761-1768, 1997.

17. Riggs, B.L., and Melton, III, L.J. The worldwide problem of osteoporosis: Insights afforded by epidemiology. *Bone* 17(5 suppl):505S-511S, 1995.

18. Ray, N.F.; Chan, J.K.; Thamer, M.; and Melton, III, L.J. Medical expenditures for the treatment of osteoporotic fractures in the United States in 1995: Report from the National Osteoporosis Foundation. *Journal of Bone and Mineral Research* 12(1):24-35, 1997.

19. Melton, III, L.J; Chrischilles, E.A.; Cooper, C.; et al. How many women have osteoporosis? *Journal of Bone and Mineral Research* 7:1005-1010, 1992.

20. Bacon, W.E. Secular trends in hip fracture occurrence and survival: Age and sex differences. *Journal of Aging Health* 8(4):538-553, 1996.

21. U.S. Congress, Office of Technology Assessment. *Hip Fracture Outcomes in People Age 50 and Over—Background Paper*. OTA-BP-H-120. Washington, DC: U.S. Government Printing Office, July 1994.

22. Anderson, G.B.J. The epidemology of spinal disorders. In: Frymoyer, J.W., (ed). *The Adult Spine: Principles and Practice, 2nd ed.* Raven, Philadelphia, PA: LIPPENCOTT-Raven, 1997.

23. Biering-Sorensen, F. Physical measurements as risk indicators for low-back trouble over a one year period. *Spine* 9:106-119, 1984.

24. Frymoyer, J.W.; Pope, M.H.; Clements, J.H.; et al. Risk factors in low-back pain: An epidemiological survey. *Journal of Bone and Joint*

Surgery 65(2):213-218, 1983.

25. Frymoyer, J.W. Back pain and sciatica. *New England Journal of Medicine* 318(5):291-300, 1988.

26. Svensson, H.O., and Anderson, G.B.J. Low-back pain in 40- to 47-year old men: Work history and work environment factors. *Spine* 8(3):272-276, 1983.

27. Anderson, G.B. Epidemiological aspects on low back pain in industry. *Spine* 6(1):53-60, 1981.

28. Kelsey, J.L.; White, A.A.; Pastides, H.; et al. The impact of musculoskeletal disorders on the population of the United States. *Journal of Bone and Joint Surgery* 61(7):959-964, 1979.

29. Praemer, A.; Furner, S.; and Rice, D.P. Musculoskeletal conditions in the United States. Park Ridge, IL: American Academy of Orthoscopic Surgery, 1992.

30. Wegman, D.H., and Fine, L.J. Occupational and Environmental Medicine. *Journal of the American Medical Association* 275(23):1831-1832, 1996.

31. Shelerud, R. Epidemiology of Occupational Low Back Pain. In: *Occupational Medicine: State of the Art Reviews*. Philadelphia, PA: Hanley and Belfus 1998, 1-22.

32. CDC. NCCDPHP, DACH, HCASB, Atlanta, GA, unpublished data.

33. CDC. Prevalence and impact of arthritis among women. United States, 1989-1991. *Morbidity and Mortality Weekly Report* 44(17):329-334, 517-518, 1995.

34. Callahan, L.F.; Rao, J.; and Boutaugh, M. Arthritis and women's health: Prevalence, impact, and prevention. *American*

Journal of Preventive Medicine 12(5):401-409, 1996.

35. CDC. Prevalence and impact of arthritis by race and ethnicity—United States, 1989-1991. *Morbidity and Mortality Weekly Report* 45(18):373-378, 1996.

36. Wilson, M.G.; May, D.S.; and Kelly, J.J. Racial differences in the use of total knee arthroplasty for osteoarthritis among older Americans. *Ethnicity & Disease* 4(1):57-67, 1994.

37. Hochberg, J.C. Osteoarthritis. In: Silman, A.J., and Hochberg, J.C. (eds.). *Epidemiology of the Rheumatic Diseases*. Oxford: Oxford University Press, 1993, 257-288.

38. Felson, D.T. Epidemiology of hip and knee osteoarthritis. *Epidemiologic Reviews* 10:1-28, 1988.

39. U.S. Department of Health and Human Services (HHS). *Physical Activity and Health: A Report of the Surgeon General*. Atlanta, GA: HHS, CDC, 1996.

40. Felson, D.T., and Zhang, Y. Personal Communication. An update on the epidemiology of knee and hip osteoarthritis with a view to prevention. August 1998.

41. Felson, D.T.; Zhang, Y.; Anthony, J.M.; et al. Weight loss reduces the risk for symptomatic knee osteoarthritis in women. The Framingham Study. *Annals of Internal Medicine* 116(7):535-539, 1992.

42. Weinblatt, M.E. Rheumatoid arthritis: Treat now, not later! (Editorial). *Annals of Internal Medicine* 124:773-774, 1996.

43. Van der Heide, A.; Jacobs, J.W.; Bijlsma, J.W.; et al. The effectiveness of early treatment with "second-

line" antirheumatic drugs. A randomized, controlled trial. *Annals of Internal Medicine* 124(8):699-707, 1996.

44. Fries, J.F.; Williams, C.A.; Morrfeld, D.; Singh, G.; and Sibley, J. Reduction in long-term disability in patients with rheumatoid arthritis by disease-modifying antirheumatic drug-based treatment strategies. *Arthritis & Rheumatism* 39:616-622, 1996.

45. Egsmose, C.; Lund, B.; Borg, G.; et al. Patients with rheumatoid arthritis benefit from early 2nd line therapy: 5-year follow up of a prospective double blind placebo controlled study. *Journal of Rheumatology* 22:2208-2213, 1995.

46. Kirwan, J.R. The Arthritis and Rheumatism Council, Low-Dose Glucocorticoid Study Group. The effect of glucocorticoids on joint destruction in rheumatoid arthritis. *New England Journal of Medicine* 333(3):142-146, 1995.

47. Emery, P., and Salmon, M. Early rheumatoid arthritis: Time to aim for remission? *Annals of Rheumatic Diseases* 54:944-947, 1995.

48. Maisiak, R.; Austin, J.; and Heck, L. Health outcomes of two telephone interventions for patients with rheumatoid arthritis or osteoarthritis. *Arthritis & Rheumatism* 39:1391-1399, 1996.

49. Minor, M.A. Arthritis and exercise: The times they are a-changin' (Editorial). *Arthritis Care and Research* 9:9-81, 1996.

50. Minor, M.A., and Kay, D.R. Arthritis. In: *Exercise Management for Persons With Chronic Diseases and Disabilities*. Champaign, IL: Human Kinetics, 1997.

51. Puett, D.W., and Griffin, M.R. Published trials of nonmedicinal and noninvasive therapies for hip and knee osteoarthritis. *Annals of Internal Medicine* 121(2):133-140, 1994.

52. Lorig, K.R.; Mazonson, P.D.; and Holman, H.R. Evidence suggesting that health education for self-management in patients with chronic arthritis has sustained health benefits while reducing health care costs. *Arthritis & Rheumatism* 36(4):439-446, 1993.

53. Kruger, J.M.S.; Helmick, C.G.; Callahan, L.F.; and Haddix, A.C. Cost-effectiveness of the Arthritis Self-Help Course. *Archives of Internal Medicine,* 1998.

54. Boutaugh, M. Personal communication. Arthritis Foundation. August 1999.

55. Seeman, E. Introduction. *American Journal of Medicine* 103(Suppl 2a):1s-2s, 1997.

56. Violinn, E. Do workplace interventions prevent low-back disorders? If so: Why?: a methodological commentary. *Erognomics* 42(1):258-272, 1999.

57. Hennessy, C.H.; Moriarty, D.G.; Zack, M.M.; Scherr, P.A.; and Brackbill, R. Measuring health-related quality of life for public health surveillance. *Public Health Reports* 109(5):665-672, 1994.

58. CDC. Quality of life as a new public health measure—Behavioral Risk Factor Surveillance System, 1993. *Morbidity and Mortality Weekly Report* 43(20):375-380, 1994.

59. CDC. Health-related quality-of-life measures—United States, 1993. *Morbidity and Mortality Weekly Report* 44(11):195-200, 1995.

60. Newschaffer, C.J. *Validation of BRFSS HRQOL Measures in a Statewide Sample*. Atlanta, GA: HHS, Public Health Service, CDC, National Center for Chronic Disease Prevention and Health Promotion, 1998.

61. Verbrugge, L.M.; Merrill, S.S.; and Liu, X. Measuring Disability With Parsimony. *Disability Rehabilitation* 21(5-6):295-306, 1999.

62. Rao, J.K.; Callahan, L.F.; and Helmick, C.G. Characteristics of persons with self-reported arthritis and other rheumatic conditions who do not see a doctor. *Journal of Rheumatology* 24:169-173, 1997.

63. Cummings, S.R.; Black, D.M.; Nevitt, M.C.; et al., for the Study of Osteoporotic Fracture Group. Bone density at various sites for prediction of hip fractures. *Lancet* 341(8837):72-75, 1993.,

64. Melton, III, L.J.; Atkinson, E.J.; O'Fallon, W.M.; Wahner, H.W.; and Riggs, B.L. Long-term fracture prediction by bone mineral assessed at different skeletal sites. *Journal of Bone and Mineral Research* 8(10):1227-1233, 1993.

65. Melton, III, L.J.; Thamer, M.; Ray, N.F.; et al. Fractures attributable to osteoporosis: Report from the National Osteoporosis Foundation. *Journal of Bone and Mineral Research* 12(1):16-23, 1997.

66. World Health Organization (WHO). *Assessment of Fracture Risk and Its Application to Screening for Postmenopausal Osteoporosis*. Technical Report Series No. 843. Geneva, Switzerland: the Organization, 1994.

67. Melton, III, L.J. How many women have osteoporosis now? *Journal*

of *Bone and Mineral Research* 10(2):175-177, 1995.

68. Lips, P. Prevention of hip fractures: Drug therapy. *Bone* 18(3 suppl.):159S-163S, 1996.

69. Cummings, S.R. Treatable and untreatable risk factors for hip fracture. *Bone* 18:165s-176s, 1996.

70. Ross P.D. Clinical consequences of vertebral fractures. *American Journal of Medicine* 103:30S-43S, 1997.

71. Melton, III, L.J.; Kan, S.H.; Frye, M.A.; Wahner, H.W.; O'Fallon, W.M.; and Riggs, B.L. Epidemiology of vertebral fractures in women. *American Journal of Epidemiology* 129:1000-1011, 1989.

72. Jacobsen, S.J.; Cooper, C.; Gottlieb, M.S.; Goldberg, J.; Yahnke, D.P.; and Melton III, L.J. Hospitalization with vertebral fracture among the aged: a national population-based study 1986-1989. *Epidemiology* 3(6):515-518, 1992.

73. Chrischilles, E.A.; Butler, C.D.; Davis, S.C.; and Wallace, R.B. A model of lifetime osteoporosis impact. *Archives of Internal Medicine* 151(10):2026-2032, 1991.

74. Schuchmann, J.A. Low back pain: A comprehensive approach. *Comprehensive Therapy* 14(1):14-18, 1988.

75. Kelsey, J.L.; Githens, P.B.; White, III, A.A.; et al. An epidemiologic study of lifting and twisting on the job and risk for acute, prolapsed lumbar vertebral disc. *Journal of Orthopaedic Research* 2(1):61-66, 1984.

76. Kelsey, J.L.; Githens, P.B.; O'Conner, T.; et al. Acute prolapsed lumbar intervertebral disc. An epidemiologic study with special reference to driving automobiles and cigarette smoking. *Spine* 9(6):608-613, 1984.

77. Parnianpour, M.; Bejjani, F.J.; Pavlidis, L. Worker training: The fallacy of single, correct lifting technique. *Ergonomics* 30(2):331-334, 1987.

78. Porter, R.W.; Hibbert, C.; Wellman, P. Backache and the lumbar spinal canal. *Spine* 5(2):99-105, 1980.

79. Buchanan, J.R.; Myers, C.; Greer, III, R.B.; et al. Assessment of the risk of vertebral fracture in menopausal women. *Journal of Bone and Joint Surgery* 69(2):212-218, 1987.

80. Chaffin, D.B., and Park, K.S. A longitudinal study of low back pain as associated with occupational weight lifting factors. *American Industrial Hygiene Association Journal* 34(12):513-525, 1973.

81. Venning, P.J.; Walter, S.D.; and Stitt, L.W. Personal and job-related factors as determinants of incidence of back injuries among nursing personnel. *Journal of Occupational Medicine* 29(10).820-825, 1987.

3
Cancer

Co-Lead Agencies: Centers for Disease Control and Prevention;
National Institutes of Health

Contents

Goal

Reduce the number of new cancer cases as well as the illness, disability, and death caused by cancer.

Overview

Cancer is the second leading cause of death in the United States. During 1999, an estimated 1,221,800 persons in the United States were diagnosed with cancer; 563,100 persons were expected to die from cancer.[1] These estimates did not include most skin cancers, and new cases of skin cancer are estimated to exceed 1 million per year. One-half of new cases of cancer occur in people aged 65 years and over.[2]

About 491,400 Americans who get cancer in a given year, or 4 in 10 patients, are expected to be alive 5 years after diagnosis. When adjusted for normal life expectancy (accounting for factors such as dying of heart disease, injuries, and diseases of old age), a "relative" 5-year survival rate of 60 percent is seen for all cancers.[1] This rate means that the chance of a person recently diagnosed with cancer being alive in 5 years is 60 percent of the chance of someone not diagnosed with cancer. Five-year relative survival rates commonly are used to monitor progress in the early detection and treatment of cancer and include persons who are living 5 years after diagnosis, whether in remission, disease free, or under treatment.

Issues and Trends

Cancer death rates for all sites combined decreased an average of 0.6 percent per year from 1990 to 1996.[3] This decrease occurred after rates had increased by 0.4 percent per year from 1973 to 1990.[4] Death rates for male lung, female breast, prostate, and colorectal cancers decreased significantly during the 1990-96 period.[3] The lung and bronchus, prostate, female breast, and colon and rectum were the most common cancer sites for all racial and ethnic populations in the United States and together accounted for approximately 54 percent of all newly diagnosed cancers.[1]

In addition to the human toll of cancer, the financial costs of cancer are substantial.[5] The overall annual costs for cancer are estimated at $107 billion, with $37 billion for direct medical costs (the total of all health expenditures), $11 billion for costs of illness (the cost of low productivity due to illness), and $59 billion for costs of death (the cost of lost productivity due to death). Treatment for lung, breast, and prostate cancers alone accounts for more than half of the direct medical costs.

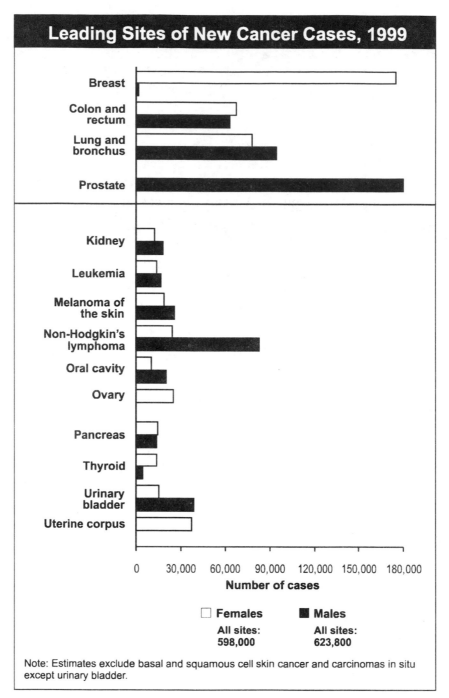

Leading Sites of New Cancer Cases, 1999

Breast
Colon and rectum
Lung and bronchus
Prostate

Kidney
Leukemia
Melanoma of the skin
Non-Hodgkin's lymphoma
Oral cavity
Ovary
Pancreas
Thyroid
Urinary bladder
Uterine corpus

0   30,000   60,000   90,000   120,000   150,000   180,000

Number of cases

☐ Females   ■ Males

All sites: 598,000   All sites: 623,800

Note: Estimates exclude basal and squamous cell skin cancer and carcinomas in situ except urinary bladder.

Source: American Cancer Society, *Surveillance Research,* 1999.

Disparities

Cancer death rates vary by gender, race, and ethnicity.[3] Male cancer death rates peaked in 1990 at 220.8 per 100,000, and female death rates peaked a year later at 142.2 per 100,000. After the peak year, through 1996, male cancer deaths for all sites decreased on average by 1 percent per year, and female deaths decreased on average by 0.4 percent per year. There were significant decreases in mortality for lung, prostate, brain, and other nervous system cancers in males and a significant decrease in breast cancer mortality for females.[3] Among males, lung cancer death rates have declined since 1990. In contrast, lung cancer death rates have continued to increase among females. Since 1987, more females have died from lung cancer than breast cancer.

African Americans are about 34 percent more likely to die of cancer than are whites and more than two times more likely to die of cancer than are Asian/Pacific Islanders, American Indians, and Hispanics.[1] African American women are more likely to die of breast and colon cancers than are women of any other racial and ethnic group, and they have approximately the same lung cancer mortality rates as white women. African American men have the highest mortality rates of colon and rectum, lung, and prostate cancers. Age-adjusted lung cancer death rates are approximately 40 percent higher among African American males than white males. Little difference in age-adjusted lung cancer death rates has been observed between African American females and white females. Hispanics have higher rates of cervical, esophageal, gallbladder, and stomach cancers. Similarly, some specific forms of cancer affect other ethnic groups at rates higher than the national average (for example, stomach and liver cancers among Asian American populations and colon and rectum cancer among Alaska Natives). Racial and ethnic groups have lower survival rates than whites for most cancers.[1]

Differences between the races represent both a challenge to understand the reasons and an opportunity to reduce illness and death and to improve survival rates.

The Hispanic cancer experience also differs from that of the non-Hispanic white population, with Hispanics having higher rates of cervical, esophageal, gallbladder, and stomach cancers. New cases of female breast and lung cancers are increasing among Hispanics, who are diagnosed at later stages and have lower survival rates than whites.

The recent decrease in deaths from breast cancer in white females is attributed to greater use of breast cancer screening in regular medical care. However, new cases of breast cancer in African American females continue to increase, and deaths continue to increase as well, in part, because breast cancer is diagnosed at later stages in African American females.[1]

Data on colorectal cancer (CRC) show a decline in new cases and death rates in white males and females, stable new case rates in African Americans, and a continued rise in death rates in African American males. Five-year survival rates are 64 percent in whites and 52 percent in African Americans (1989-94). Early detection and treatment play a key role in these survival rates.

New cases of prostate cancer peaked in 1992 at 190.8 per 100,000 people and declined on average by 8.5 percent each year from 1992 to 1996. Prostate cancer death rates peaked in 1991 at 26.7 per 100,000 people; rates decreased on average by 2.1 percent each year from 1991 to 1995. Causes of the trends are unclear but may be attributed to a number of factors that are under investigation.

Data as of November 30, 1999

Possible disparities regarding the health status of lesbian women and possible barriers to access to health services by lesbians have been identified by the Institute of Medicine as a research priority.[6]

Opportunities

Evidence suggests that several types of cancer can be prevented and that the prospects for surviving cancer continue to improve. The ability to reduce cancer death rates depends, in part, on the existence and application of various types of resources. First, the means to provide culturally and linguistically appropriate information on prevention, early detection, and treatment to the public and to health care professionals are essential. Second, mechanisms or systems must exist for providing people with access to state-of-the-art preventive services and treatment. Where suitable, participation in clinical trials also should be encouraged. Third, a mechanism for maintaining continued research progress and for fostering new research is essential. Genetic information that can be used to improve disease prevention strategies is emerging for many cancers and may provide the foundation for improved effectiveness in clinical and preventive medicine services.

To provide new opportunities for cancer prevention and control in the future, there is a continuing and vital need to foster new, innovative research on both the causes of cancer (including genetic and environmental causes) and on methods to translate biologic and epidemiologic findings into effective prevention and control programs for use by government and community organization to further reduce the Nation's cancer burden.

These needs can be met, in part, with the network of cancer control resources now in place. This network has the organizational and personnel capabilities for various cancer interventions. Despite the extent of these resources, they alone are insufficient to reduce deaths from cancer. Gaps exist in information transfer, optimal practice patterns, research capabilities, and other areas. These must be recognized and filled to meet cancer prevention and control needs.

It is estimated that as much as 50 percent or more of cancer can be prevented through smoking cessation and improved dietary habits, such as reducing fat consumption and increasing fruit and vegetable consumption.[7, 8] Physical activity and weight control also can contribute to cancer prevention.[9, 10]

Scientific data from randomized trials of cancer prevention together with expert opinions suggest that compliance with screening recommendations for cancer of the breast, cervix, and colon/rectum could reduce deaths from these cancers.

To reduce breast cancer deaths, a high percentage of females in the United States aged 40 years and older need to comply with screening recommendations. A reduction in breast cancer deaths could be expected to occur after a delay of roughly 7 years.[11] To reduce cervical cancer deaths, a high percentage of females in the United States who are aged 18 years and older need to comply with screening recommendations. Evidence from randomized preventive trials is unavailable, but expert opinion suggests that a beneficial impact on cervical cancer death rates would be expected to occur after a delay of a few years.

Evidence shows that a reduction in CRC deaths can be achieved through detection and removal of precancerous polyps and treatment of CRC in its earliest stages. The findings from three randomized controlled trials indicate that biennial screening with fecal occult blood tests (FOBT) can reduce deaths from CRC by 15 to 21 percent in people aged 45 to 80 years.[12, 13, 14] One trial[15] reported a 33 percent reduction in deaths with annual screening in the same age groups, and a simulation model showed a 56 percent reduction.[16] The efficacy of sigmoidoscopy has been supported by three case-control studies[17, 18, 19] that showed 59 to 79 percent reductions in CRC deaths from cancers within reach of the sigmoidoscope in age groups 45 years and older.

Prostate cancer interventions that include preventive strategies are not available at this time because it is unclear whether any of the factors that increase the risk of prostate cancer can be changed. Race and age are risk factors: African Americans and older men are at higher risk. Widespread prostate cancer screening should be approached with caution until the results of clinical trials provide evidence that screening does more good than harm.[20] Some advocates favor screening programs targeting high-risk groups, including African Americans and males with a positive family history of prostate cancer. However, there is no clinical evidence that screening tests should be performed with these high-risk groups.

Melanoma and other skin cancers were expected to claim the lives of almost 9,200 persons in 1999.[1] Insufficient evidence exists to determine whether routine skin examinations (self or physician) decrease deaths from melanoma or other skin cancers. However, many of the skin cancers diagnosed each year could be prevented by limiting exposure to the sun, by wearing protective clothing, and by using sunscreen. Research into the genetic risk of disease may provide the basis for identifying the individuals most at risk and the preventive methods best tailored for reducing those risks.

For all cancers, treatments designed to increase survival are needed along with improved access to state-of-the-art care. In addition to measurements of survival, indices of quality of life for both the short term and long term are regarded as important considerations.

Interim Progress Toward Year 2000 Objectives

The Healthy People 2000 objective for total cancer deaths was achieved for the total population by 1995. Lung cancer deaths declined for the first time in 50 years in 1991, declined again in 1992, remained level in 1993, and then dropped again in 1994, 1995, and 1996. The decline in the age-adjusted death rate for CRC for

Data as of November 30, 1999

the total population has gone beyond the year 2000 target, but declines in death rates have not been as substantial for the black population. Improvements were observed in cancer risk factors, such as tobacco use and dietary fat intake. Data also showed some improvement in the proportion of women receiving mammograms and Pap tests. In addition, for both mammograms and Pap tests, the disparity in use rates for most of the population subgroups and those for all women either has been reduced or eliminated.

Note: Unless otherwise noted, data are from Centers for Disease Control and Prevention, National Center for Health Statistics, *Healthy People 2000 Review, 1998-99.*

Cancer

Goal: Reduce the number of new cancer cases as well as the illness, disability, and death caused by cancer.

Number	Objective
3-1	Cancer deaths
3-2	Lung cancer deaths
3-3	Breast cancer deaths
3-4	Cervical cancer deaths
3-5	Colorectal cancer deaths
3-6	Oropharyngeal cancer deaths
3-7	Prostate cancer deaths
3-8	Melanoma cancer deaths
3-9	Sun exposure
3-10	Provider counseling about preventive measures
3-11	Pap tests
3-12	Colorectal cancer screening
3-13	Mammograms
3-14	Statewide cancer registries
3-15	Cancer survival

3-1. Reduce the overall cancer death rate.

Target: 158.7 cancer deaths per 100,000 population.

Baseline: 201.4 cancer deaths per 100,000 population in 1998 (preliminary data; age adjusted to the year 2000 standard population).

Target setting method: 21 percent improvement.

Data source: National Vital Statistics System (NVSS), CDC, NCHS.

Total Population, 1997*	Cancer Deaths Rate per 100,000
TOTAL	205.7
Race and ethnicity	
American Indian or Alaska Native	131.8
Asian or Pacific Islander	127.2
Asian	DNC
Native Hawaiian and other Pacific Islander	DNC
Black or African American	262.1
White	202.2
Hispanic or Latino	125.5
Not Hispanic or Latino	210.4
Black or African American	268.5
White	205.7
Gender	
Female	171.6
Male	258.0
Education level (aged 25 to 64 years)	
Less than high school	137.1
High school graduate	141.6
At least some college	82.3

DNA = Data have not been analyzed. DNC = Data are not collected. DSU = Data are statistically unreliable.
Note: Age adjusted to the year 2000 standard population.
*New data for population groups will be added when available.

3-2. Reduce the lung cancer death rate.

Target: 44.8 deaths per 100,000 population.

Baseline: 57.4 lung cancer deaths per 100,000 population in 1998 (preliminary data; age adjusted to the year 2000 standard population).

Target setting method: 22 percent improvement.

Data source: National Vital Statistics System (NVSS), CDC, NCHS.

Total Population, 1997*	Lung Cancer Deaths Rate per 100,000
TOTAL	58.1
Race and ethnicity	
American Indian or Alaska Native	36.3
Asian or Pacific Islander	28.9
Asian	DNC
Native Hawaiian and other Pacific Islander	DNC
Black or African American	67.9
White	58.0
Hispanic or Latino	23.9
Not Hispanic or Latino	60.2
Black or African American	69.6
White	59.9
Gender	
Female	41.4
Male	81.6
Education level (aged 25 to 64 years)	
Less than high school	48.3
High school graduate	42.0
At least some college	18.4

DNA = Data have not been analyzed. DNC = Data are not collected. DSU = Data are statistically unreliable.
Note: Age adjusted to the year 2000 standard population.
*New data for population groups will be added when available.

Lung cancer is the most common cause of cancer death among both females and males in the United States. Estimates indicated that 171,600 (77,600 females and 94,000 males) new cases of lung cancer would be diagnosed in 1999; 158,900

Data as of November 30, 1999

persons (68,000 females and 90,900 males) would die from lung cancer in 1999, accounting for 28 percent of all cancer deaths.[1]

Cigarette smoking is the most important risk factor for lung cancer, accounting for 68 to 78 percent of lung cancer deaths among females and 88 to 91 percent of lung cancer deaths among males.[21] Other risk factors include occupational exposures (radon, asbestos) and indoor and outdoor air pollution (radon, environmental tobacco smoke).[22] One to two percent of lung cancer deaths are attributable to air pollution.[23] Smoking cessation decreases the risk of lung cancer to 30-50 percent of that of continuing smokers after 10 years of abstinence.[7]

3-3.   Reduce the breast cancer death rate.

Target: 22.2 deaths per 100,000 females.

Baseline: 27.7 breast cancer deaths per 100,000 females in 1998 (preliminary data; age adjusted to the year 2000 standard population).

Target setting method: 20 percent improvement.

Data source: National Vital Statistics System (NVSS), CDC, NCHS.

Females, 1997*	Breast Cancer Deaths Rate per 100,000
TOTAL	28.6
Race and ethnicity	
American Indian or Alaska Native	13.1
Asian or Pacific Islander	12.6
Asian	DNC
Native Hawaiian and other Pacific Islander	DNC
Black or African American	37.7
White	28.0
Hispanic or Latino	17.8
Not Hispanic or Latino	29.2
Black or African American	38.7
White	28.4

Females, 1997*	Breast Cancer Deaths Rate per 100,000
Education level (aged 25 to 64 years)	
Less than high school	21.2
High school graduate	29.6
At least some college	22.9

DNA = Data have not been analyzed. DNC = Data are not collected. DSU = Data are statistically unreliable.

Note: Age adjusted to the year 2000 standard population.

*New data for population groups will be added when available.

Breast cancer is the most common cancer among women in the United States. An estimated 175,000 new cases were expected to be diagnosed in 1999. About 43,700 U.S. women were expected to die from breast cancer in 1999, accounting for about 16.5 percent of cancer deaths among women.[1] Death from breast cancer can be reduced substantially if the tumor is discovered at an early stage. Mammography is the most effective method for detecting these early malignancies. Clinical trials have demonstrated that mammography screening can reduce breast cancer deaths by 20 to 39 percent in women aged 50 to 74 years and about 17 percent in women aged 40 to 49 years.[24] Breast cancer deaths can be reduced through increased adherence with recommendations for regular mammography screening.

Many breast cancer risk factors, such as age, family history of breast cancer, reproductive history, mammographic densities, previous breast disease, and race and ethnicity, are not subject to intervention.[25, 26] However, being overweight is a well-established breast cancer risk for post-menopausal women that can be addressed.[25] Avoiding weight gain is one method by which older women may reduce their risk of developing breast cancer.

3-4. Reduce the death rate from cancer of the uterine cervix.

Target: 2.0 deaths per 100,000 females.

Baseline: 3.0 cervical cancer deaths per 100,000 females in 1998 (preliminary data; age adjusted to the year 2000 standard population).

Target setting method: Better than the best.

Data source: National Vital Statistics System (NVSS), CDC, NCHS.

Females, 1997*	Cervical Cancer Deaths Rate per 100,000
TOTAL	3.2
Race and ethnicity	
American Indian or Alaska Native	4.0
Asian or Pacific Islander	3.0
Asian	DNC
Native Hawaiian and other Pacific Islander	DNC
Black or African American	6.5
White	2.8
Hispanic or Latino	3.8
Not Hispanic or Latino	3.1
Black or African American	6.7
White	2.7
Education level (aged 25 to 64 years)	
Less than high school	7.7
High school graduate	5.1
At least some college	2.1

DNA = Data have not been analyzed. DNC = Data are not collected. DSU = Data are statistically unreliable.
Note: Age adjusted to the year 2000 standard population.
*New data for population groups will be added when available.

Cervical cancer is the 10th most common cancer among females in the United States, with an estimated 12,800 new cases in 1999. The number of new cases of cervical cancer is higher among racial and ethnic minority females than among white females. An estimated 4,800 U.S. females were expected to die from cervical cancer in 1999.[1] Cervical cancer accounts for about 1.8 percent of cancer deaths among females. Infections of the cervix with certain types of sexually transmitted human papilloma virus increases risk of cervical cancer and may be responsible for most cervical cancer in the United States.[27]

Considerable evidence suggests that screening can reduce the number of deaths from cervical cancer. Invasive cervical cancer is preceded in a large proportion of cases by precancerous changes in cervical tissue that can be identified with a Pap test. If cervical cancer is detected early, the likelihood of survival is almost 100 percent with appropriate treatment and followup; that is, almost all cervical cancer deaths could be avoided if all females complied with screening and followup recommendations.[28] Risk is substantially decreased among former smokers in comparison to continuing smokers.[7]

3-5. Reduce the colorectal cancer death rate.

Target: 13.9 deaths per 100,000 population.

Baseline: 21.1 colorectal cancer deaths per 100,000 population in 1998 (preliminary data; age adjusted to the year 2000 standard population).

Target setting method: 34 percent improvement.

Data source: National Vital Statistics System (NVSS), CDC, NCHS.

Total Population, 1997*	Colorectal Cancer Deaths Rate per 100,000
TOTAL	21.6
Race and ethnicity	
American Indian or Alaska Native	14.5
Asian or Pacific Islander	13.5
Asian	DNC
Native Hawaiian and other Pacific Islander	DNC
Black or African American	28.8
White	21.1
Hispanic or Latino	12.8
Not Hispanic or Latino	22.1
Black or African American	29.5
White	21.4
Gender	
Female	18.4
Male	26.0
Education level (aged 25 to 64 years)	
Less than high school	10.4
High school graduate	12.0
At least some college	7.7

DNA = Data have not been analyzed. DNC = Data are not collected. DSU = Data are statistically unreliable.
Note: Age adjusted to the year 2000 standard population.
*New data for population groups will be added when available.

Colorectal cancer is the second leading cause of cancer-related deaths in the United States. An estimated 129,400 cases (67,000 females, 62,400 males) of CRC and 56,600 deaths (28,800 females, 27,800 males) from CRC were expected to occur in 1999. When cancer-related deaths are estimated separately for males and females, however, CRC becomes the third leading cause of cancer death behind lung and breast cancer for females and behind lung and prostate cancer for males.[1]

Risk factors for CRC may include age, personal and family history of polyps or colorectal cancer, inflammatory bowel disease, inherited syndromes, physical inactivity (colon only), obesity, alcohol use, and a diet high in fat and low in fruits and vegetables.[29] Detecting and removing precancerous colorectal polyps and detecting and treating the disease in its earliest stages will reduce deaths from CRC. FOBT and sigmoidoscopy are widely used to screen for CRC, and barium enema and colonoscopy are used as diagnostic tests.

3-6. Reduce the oropharyngeal cancer death rate.

Target: 2.6 deaths per 100,000 population.

Baseline: 2.9 oropharyngeal deaths per 100,000 population in 1998 (preliminary data; age adjusted to the year 2000 standard population).

Target setting method: 10 percent improvement.

Data source: National Vital Statistics System (NVSS), CDC, NCHS.

Total Population, 1997*	Oropharyngeal Cancer Deaths
	Rate per 100,000
TOTAL	3.0
Race and ethnicity	
American Indian or Alaska Native	2.6
Asian or Pacific Islander	2.5
Asian	DNC
Native Hawaiian and other Pacific Islander	DNC
Black or African American	4.7
White	2.8
Hispanic or Latino	1.8
Not Hispanic or Latino	3.1
Black or African American	4.8
White	2.9
Gender	
Female	1.8
Male	4.6

Total Population, 1997*	Oropharyngeal Cancer Deaths Rate per 100,000
Education level (aged 25 to 64 years)	
Less than high school	3.5
High school graduate	3.0
At least some college	1.3

DNA = Data have not been analyzed. DNC = Data are not collected. DSU = Data are statistically unreliable.

Note: Age adjusted to the year 2000 standard population.

*New data for population groups will be added when available.

Oral and pharyngeal cancers comprise a diversity of malignant tumors that affect the oral cavity and pharynx; the overwhelming majority of these tumors are squamous cell carcinomas. In 1999, 29,000 new cases of oropharyngeal cancer were expected to be diagnosed, and approximately 8,100 deaths were expected to occur from the disease. Oropharyngeal cancer is the 10th most common cancer among U.S. men and the 14th most common among U.S. women.[1] Its 5-year survival rate is only 53 percent. The risk of oral cancer is increased in current smokers. Alcohol consumption is an independent risk factor, and when alcohol is combined with use of tobacco products, 90 percent of all oral cancers are explained.[30]

3-7.   Reduce the prostate cancer death rate.

Target: 28.7 deaths per 100,000 males.

Baseline: 31.9 prostate cancer deaths per 100,000 males in 1998 (preliminary data; age adjusted to the year 2000 standard population).

Target setting method: 10 percent improvement.

Data source: National Vital Statistics System (NVSS), CDC, NCHS.

Males, 1997*	Prostate Cancer Deaths Rate per 100,000
TOTAL	33.8
Race and ethnicity	
American Indian or Alaska Native	19.3
Asian or Pacific Islander	14.5
Asian	DNC
Native Hawaiian and other Pacific Islander	DNC

Males, 1997*	Prostate Cancer Deaths Rate per 100,000
Black or African American	71.1
White	31.1
Hispanic or Latino	20.8
Not Hispanic or Latino	34.4
Black or African American	72.5
White	31.5
Education level (aged 25 to 64 years)	
Less than high school	4.2
High school graduate	4.6
At least some college	3.1

DNA = Data have not been analyzed. DNC = Data are not collected. DSU = Data are statistically unreliable.

Note: Age adjusted to the year 2000 standard population.

*New data for population groups will be added when available.

Prostate cancer is the most commonly diagnosed form of cancer (other than skin cancer) in males and the second leading cause of cancer death among males in the United States. Prostate cancer was expected to account for an estimated 179,300 cases and 37,000 deaths in 1999, or about 27 percent and 14 percent of the cases and deaths due to all cancers, respectively.[1] Prostate cancer is most common in men aged 65 years and older, who account for approximately 80 percent of all cases of prostate cancer.

Digital rectal examination (DRE) and the prostate-specific antigen (PSA) test are two commonly used methods for detecting prostate cancer. Clinical trials of the benefits of DRE and PSA screening are under way, with results expected in the early 21st century.

Although several treatment alternatives are available for prostate cancer, their impact on reducing death from prostate cancer when compared with no treatment in patients with operable cancer is uncertain.[31, 32, 33] Efforts aimed at reducing deaths through screening and early detection remain controversial because of the uncertain benefits and potential risks of screening, diagnosis, and treatment.

3-8.   Reduce the rate of melanoma cancer deaths.

Target: 2.5 deaths per 100,000 population.

Baseline: 2.8 melanoma cancer deaths per 100,000 population in 1998 (preliminary data; age adjusted to the year 2000 standard population).

Data as of November 30, 1999

Target setting method: 11 percent improvement.

Data source: National Vital Statistics System (NVSS), CDC, NCHS.

Total Population, 1997*	Melanoma Cancer Deaths Rate per 100,000
TOTAL	2.8
Race and ethnicity	
American Indian or Alaska Native	DSU
Asian or Pacific Islander	0.6
Asian	DNC
Native Hawaiian and other Pacific Islander	DNC
Black or African American	0.6
White	3.1
Hispanic or Latino	0.8
Not Hispanic or Latino	2.8
Black or African American	0.6
White	3.3
Gender	
Female	1.9
Male	4.0
Education level (aged 25 to 64 years)	
Less than high school	1.8
High school graduate	2.8
At least some college	2.3

DNA = Data have not been analyzed. DNC = Data are not collected. DSU = Data are statistically unreliable.
Note: Age adjusted to the year 2000 standard population.
*New data for population groups will be added when available.

Melanoma, the deadliest of all skin cancers, accounted for an estimated 44,200 new cancer cases and 7,300 deaths in 1999.[1] Trends show annual rises in the number of new cases of 4.3 percent (1973-90) and 2.5 percent (1990-95) and an annual rise in deaths of 1.7 percent (1973-90) followed by a decline of 0.4 percent in 1990-95. In whites, the population at highest risk, death rates are twice as high in males as in females.[3]

Although the cause of melanoma is unknown, risk factors include a personal or family history of melanoma, the presence of atypical moles, a large number of moles, intermittent sun exposure, a history of sunburns early in life, freckles, and sun-sensitive skin (as measured by poor tanning ability and light skin, eye, or hair color).[34] Evidence is insufficient to determine whether early detection through routine skin examination (self or physician) decreases the number of deaths from melanoma, but reduced ultraviolet exposure is likely to have a beneficial impact on the risk of melanoma and other skin cancers (basal and squamous cell skin cancers).[33]

3-9. **Increase the proportion of persons who use at least one of the following protective measures that may reduce the risk of skin cancer: avoid the sun between 10 a.m. and 4 p.m., wear sun-protective clothing when exposed to sunlight, use sunscreen with a sun protective factor (SPF) of 15 or higher, and avoid artificial sources of ultraviolet light.**

3-9a. (Developmental) Increase the proportion of adolescents in grades 9 through 12 who follow protective measures that may reduce the risk of skin cancer.

Potential data source: Youth Risk Behavioral Surveillance System (YRBSS), CDC, NCCDPHP.

3-9b. Increase the proportion of adults aged 18 years and older who follow protective measures that may reduce the risk of skin cancer.

Target: 75 percent of adults aged 18 years and older use at least one of the identified protective measures.

Baseline: 49 percent of adults aged 18 years and older regularly used at least one protective measure in 1998 (preliminary data; age adjusted to the year 2000 standard population).

Target setting method: Better than the best.

Data source: National Health Interview Survey (NHIS), CDC, NCHS. Data on artificial ultraviolet light source are developmental.

Persons Aged 18 Years and Older, 1992*	Type of Protective Measure			
	3-9b. Regularly Used At Least One Protective Measure	Limited Sun Exposure†	Wore Protective Clothing†	Used Sun-screen†
	Percent			
TOTAL	54	32	29	29
Race and ethnicity				
American Indian or Alaska Native	42	DSU	DSU	DSU
Asian or Pacific Islander	52	38	35	16
Asian	DNA	DNA	DNA	DNA
Native Hawaiian and other Pacific Islander	DNA	DNA	DNA	DNA
Black or African American	54	45	30	9
White	54	30	29	32
Hispanic or Latino	47	35	26	20
Not Hispanic or Latino	54	32	29	29
Black or African American	54	46	31	9
White	54	30	29	33
Gender				
Female	61	39	29	37
Male	46	24	28	20
Education level (aged 25 years and older)				
Less than high school	52	38	30	17
High school graduate	54	34	30	29
Some college	60	32	35	37
Family income level				
Poor	52	39	27	17
Near poor	54	36	30	22
Middle/high income	56	30	29	34
Geographic location				
Urban	54	33	28	30
Rural	52	29	31	26

Data as of November 30, 1999

Persons Aged 18 Years and Older, 1992*	Type of Protective Measure			
	3-9b. Regularly Used At Least One Protective Measure	Limited Sun Exposure†	Wore Protective Clothing†	Used Sun-screen†
	Percent			
Disability status				
With activity limitations	57	38	33	27
Without activity limitations	53	31	28	29

DNA = Data have not been analyzed. DNC = Data are not collected. DSU = Data are statistically unreliable.

Note: Age adjusted to the year 2000 standard population.

*New data for population groups will be added when available.

†Data for limit sun exposure, use sunscreen, and wear protective clothing are displayed to further characterize the issue.

3-10. Increase the proportion of physicians and dentists who counsel their at-risk patients about tobacco use cessation, physical activity, and cancer screening.

Target and baseline:

Objective	Increase Counseling About Tobacco Use Cessation, Physical Activity, and Cancer Screening	1988 Baseline (unless noted)	2010 Target
		Percent	
3-10a.	Internists who counsel about smoking cessation	50	85
3-10b.	Family physicians who counsel about smoking cessation	43	85
3-10c.	Dentists who counsel about smoking cessation	59 (1997)	85
3-10d.	Primary care providers who counsel about blood stool tests	56	85
3-10e.	Primary care providers who counsel about protoscopic examinations	23	85
3-10f.	Primary care providers who counsel about mammograms	37	85
3-10g.	Primary care providers who counsel about Pap tests	55	85
3-10h.	Primary care providers who counsel about physical activity	22 (1995)	85

Data as of November 30, 1999

Target setting method: Better than the best.

Data sources: Survey of Physicians' Attitudes and Practices in Early Cancer Detection, NIH, NCI; National Ambulatory Medical Care Survey (NAMCS), CDC, NCHS; Survey of Current Issues in Dentistry, American Dental Association.

Smoking cessation,[7, 21] adoption of healthy diets,[8] increased physical activity,[9, 10] and increased cancer screening[11, 12, 13, 14, 15, 16, 17, 18, 19] can all contribute to reduced numbers of cancer deaths. Experts recommend that providers screen patients for breast, cervical, and colorectal cancers and counsel patients to prevent or reduce tobacco use, promote physical activity, and promote a healthy diet.[33] Provider counseling should be conducted in a linguistically and culturally appropriate manner.

3-11. Increase the proportion of women who receive a Pap test.

Target and baseline:

Objective	Pap Test	1998 Baseline*	2010 Target
		Percent	
3-11a.	Women aged 18 years and older who have ever received a Pap test.	92	97
3-11b.	Women aged 18 years and older who received a Pap test within the preceding 3 years.	79	90

*Preliminary data; age adjusted to the year 2000 standard population. Includes women without a uterine cervix.

Target setting method: Better than the best.

Data source: National Health Interview Survey (NHIS), CDC, NCHS.

Women Aged 18 Years and Older, 1994*	3-11a. Pap Test Ever	3-11b. Pap Test in Past 3 Years
	Percent	
TOTAL	94	77
Race and ethnicity		
American Indian or Alaska Native	93	68
Asian or Pacific Islander	82	63
Asian	DNA	DNA
Native Hawaiian and other Pacific Islander	DNA	DNA
Black or African American	96	81
White	95	77

Women Aged 18 Years and Older, 1994*	3-11a. Pap Test Ever	3-11b. Pap Test in Past 3 Years
	Percent	
Hispanic or Latino	91	71
Not Hispanic or Latino	95	77
Black or African American	96	82
White	95	77
Education level (aged 25 years and older)		
Less than high school	94	66
High school graduate	97	76
At least some college	97	83
Disability status		
With activity limitations	95	74
Without activity limitations	94	78
Family income level		
Poor	91	69
Near poor	94	72
Middle/high income	96	82
Geographic location		
Urban	94	77
Rural	95	76

DNA = Data have not been analyzed. DNC = Data are not collected. DSU = Data are statistically unreliable.

Note: Age adjusted to the year 2000 standard population. Includes women without a uterine cervix.

*New data for population groups will be added when available.

3-12. Increase the proportion of adults who receive a colorectal cancer screening examination.

Target and baseline:

Objective	Colorectal Cancer Screening	1998 Baseline*	2010 Target
		Percent	
3-12a.	Adults aged 50 years and older who have received a fecal occult blood test (FOBT) within the preceding 2 years.	34	50
3-12b.	Adults aged 50 years and older who have ever received a sigmoidoscopy	38	50

*Preliminary data; age adjusted to the year 2000 standard population.

Target setting method: Better than the best.

Data source: National Health Interview Survey (NHIS), CDC, NCHS.

Adults Aged 50 Years and Older, 1992*	3-12a. Fecal Occult Blood Test	3-12b. Sigmoidoscopy
	Percent	
TOTAL	30	33
Race and ethnicity		
American Indian or Alaska Native	DSU	DSU
Asian or Pacific Islander	DSU	DSU
Asian	DSU	DSU
Native Hawaiian and other Pacific Islander	DSU	DSU
Black or African American	25	27
White	30	34
Hispanic or Latino	22	28
Not Hispanic or Latino	30	33
Black or African American	25	27
White	31	34
Gender		
Female	30	31
Male	30	36

Adults Aged 50 Years and Older, 1992*	3-12a. Fecal Occult Blood Test	3-12b. Sigmoidoscopy
	Percent	
Education level		
Less than high school	23	28
High school graduate	29	30
At least some college	38	43
Disability status		
Persons with activity limitations	32	37
Persons without activity limitations	28	31
Family income level		
Poor	22	28
Near poor	28	33
Middle/high income	34	36
Geographic location		
Urban	31	34
Rural	25	31

DNA = Data have not been analyzed. DNC = Data are not collected. DSU = Data are statistically unreliable.

Note: crude rates; data are not age adjusted.

*New data for population groups will be added when available.

3-13. Increase the proportion of women aged 40 years and older who have received a mammogram within the preceding 2 years.

Target: 70 percent.

Baseline: 68 percent of women aged 40 years and older received a mammogram within the preceding 2 years in 1998 (preliminary data, age adjusted to the year 2000 standard population).

Target setting method: Better than the best.

Data source: National Health Interview Survey (NHIS), CDC, NCHS.

Women Aged 40 Years and Older, 1994*	Mammogram
	Percent
TOTAL	59
Race and ethnicity	
American Indian or Alaska Native	DSU
Asian or Pacific Islander	49
Asian	DSU
Native Hawaiian and other Pacific Islander	DSU
Black or African American	61
White	59
Hispanic or Latino	51
Not Hispanic or Latino	60
Black or African American	60
White	61
Education level	
Less than high school	47
High school graduate	59
At least some college	67
Family income level	
Poor	43
Near poor	48
Middle/high income	67
Geographic location	
Urban	60
Rural	57
Disability status	
With activity limitations	55
Without activity limitations	61

DNA = Data have not been analyzed. DNC = Data are not collected. DSU = Data are statistically unreliable.

Note: Age adjusted to the year 2000 standard population.

*New data for population groups will be added when available.

3-14. **Increase the number of States that have a statewide population-based cancer registry that captures case information on at least 95 percent of the expected number of reportable cancers.**

Target: 45 States.

Baseline: 21 States in 1999.

Target setting method: 114 percent improvement.

Data sources: National Program of Cancer Registries, CDC; SEER Program, NIH, NCI.

Cancer surveillance serves as the foundation for a national comprehensive strategy to reduce illness and death from cancer. Such surveillance is the indispensable tool that enables public health professionals at the national, State, and community levels to better understand and tackle the cancer burden while advancing clinical, epidemiological, and health services research. In addition, surveillance data from cancer registries, such as cancer incidence and deaths, stage at diagnosis, treatment, and demographics of cancer patients, are essential for planning and evaluating cancer control programs, allocating preventive and treatment resources, targeting and conducting research, and responding to concerns from citizens about the occurrence of cancer in their communities.

Population-based State cancer registries that provide accurate, complete, and timely data are a critical component of the public health infrastructure in the United States. The National Program of Cancer Registries (NPCR) provides funds to 45 States to assist in planning or enhancing cancer registries; develop model legislation and regulations for programs to increase the viability of registry operations; set standards for data quality, completeness, and timeliness; provide training for registry personnel; and help establish computerized reporting and data processing systems. The National Cancer Institute's SEER Program covers the remaining 5 States.

3-15. **Increase the proportion of cancer survivors who are living 5 years or longer after diagnosis.**

Target: 70 percent.

Baseline: 59 percent of persons with invasive cancer of any type were living 5 years or longer after diagnosis in 1989–95.

Target setting method: 19 percent improvement.

Data source: Surveillance, Epidemiology, and End Results (SEER), NIH, NCI.

Persons With Invasive Cancer of Any Type, 1989-95	5 Years or Longer Survival Percent
TOTAL	59
Race and ethnicity	
American Indian or Alaska Native	DNA
Asian or Pacific Islander	DNA
Asian	DNA
Native Hawaiian and other Pacific Islander	DNA
Black or African American	48
White	61
Hispanic or Latino	DNA
Not Hispanic or Latino	DNA
Black or African American	DNA
White	DNA
Gender	
Female	61
Male	58
Education level (aged 25 to 64 years)	
Less than high school	DNA
High school graduate	DNA
At least some college	DNA

DNA = Data have not been analyzed. DNC = Data are not collected. DSU = Data are statistically unreliable.

Related Objectives From Other Focus Areas

19. Nutrition and Overweight

19-5.   Fruit intake

19-6.   Vegetable intake

19-8.   Saturated fat intake

19-9.   Total fat intake

21. Oral Health

21-6.   Early detection of oral and pharyngeal cancer

21-17.   Annual examinations for oral and pharyngeal cancer

27. Tobacco Use

27-1.   Adult tobacco use

27-2.   Youth tobacco use

27-5.   Smoking cessation by adults

Data as of November 30, 1999

Terminology

(A listing of all abbreviations and acronyms used in this publication appears in Appendix K.)

Cancer: A term for diseases in which abnormal cells divide without control. Cancer cells can invade nearby tissue and can spread through the bloodstream and lymphatic system to other parts of the body.

Cancer screening: Checking for changes in tissue, cells, or fluids that may indicate the possibility of cancer when there are no symptoms.

Carcinoma: Cancer that begins in the epithelial tissue that lines or covers an organ.

Clinical trials: Research studies that evaluate the effectiveness of new treatment or disease prevention methods on patients.

Digital rectal exam (DRE): A test in which the health care provider inserts a lubricated, gloved finger into the rectum to feel for abnormal areas.

Fecal occult blood test (FOBT): A test to check for small amounts of hidden blood in stool.

Grade: A system for classifying cancer cells in terms of how abnormal they appear under a microscope. The grading system provides information about the probable growth rate of the tumor and its tendency to spread. The systems used to grade tumors vary with each type of cancer. Grading plays a role in treatment decisions.

Malignant: Cancerous.

Mammogram: An x-ray of the breast.

Melanoma: Cancer of the cells that produce pigment in the skin.

Pap (Papanicolaou) test: Microscopic examination of cells collected from the cervix. The Pap test is used to detect cancer, changes in the cervix that may lead to cancer, and noncancerous conditions, such as infection or inflammation.

PSA (prostate-specific antigen) test: A test that measures the level of an enzyme (PSA) in the blood that increases due to diseases of the prostate gland, including prostate cancer.

Risk factor: Something that increases a person's chance of developing a disease.

Sigmoidoscopy: A procedure in which the physician or health care provider looks inside the rectum and the lower part of the colon (sigmoid colon) through a flexible lighted tube. During the procedure, the physician or health care provider may collect samples of tissues or cells for closer examination.

Squamous cells: Flat cells that look like fish scales. These cells are found in the tissue that forms the surface of the skin, the lining of the hollow organs of the body, and the passages of the respiratory and digestive tracts.

Stage: The size and extent of a cancer, including whether the disease has spread from the original site into surrounding tissue and other parts of the body.

References

1.   Landis, S.H.; Murray, T.; Bolden, S.; and Wingo, P.A. Cancer statistics, 1999. *CA: A Cancer Journal for Clinicians* 49(1):8-31, 1999.

2.   Ries, L.A.G.; Kosary, C.L.; Hankey, B.F. et al. SEER Cancer Statistics Review, 1973-1996, Bethesda, MD: National Cancer Institute, 1999.

3.   Wingo, P.A.; Ries, L.A.G.; Giovino, G.A. et al. Annual report to the nation on the status of cancer, 1973-1996, with a special section on lung cancer and tobacco smoking. *Journal of the National Cancer Institute,* 91(8):675-690, 1999.

4.   Wingo, P.A.; Ries, L.A.; Rosenberg, H.M.; Miller, D.S.; and Edwards, B.K. Cancer incidence and mortality 1973-1995: A report card for the U.S. *Cancer* 82(6):1197-1207, 1998.

5. Brown, M.L.; Hodgson, T.A.; and Rice, D.P. Economic impact of cancer in the United States. In: Schottenfeld, D.. and Fraumen, Jr., J.F., eds. *Cancer Epidemiology and Prevention*, 2nd ed. New York, NY: Oxford University Press, 1996.

6. Solarz, A., ed. *Lesbian Health: Current Assessment and Directions for the Future 1999.* Washington, DC. National Academy Press, 1999.

7. U.S. Department of Health and Human Services (HHS). *The Health Benefits of Smoking Cessation.* Public Health Service, Centers for Disease Control, Center for Chronic Disease Prevention and Health Promotion, Office on Smoking and Health. DHHS Publication No. CDC 90-8416, 1990.

8. Willet. W. Diet and Nutrition. In: Schottenfield, D., and Fraumeni, J.F., eds. Cancer *Epidemiology and Prevention*, 2nd ed. New York: Oxford University Press, 1996, 438-461.

9. Greenwald, P.; Kramer, B.; and Weed, D.L., eds. *Cancer Prevention and Control.* New York: Marcel Dekker, 1995, 303-327.

10. HHS. *Physical Activity and Health: A Report of the Surgeon General.* Atlanta, GA: Centers for Disease Control and Prevention, 1996.

11. Fletcher, S.W.; Black, W.; Harris, R.; et al. Report of the International Workshop on Screening for Breast Cancer. *Journal of the National Cancer Institute* 85(20):1644-1656, 1993.

12. Kronborg, O.; Fenger, C.; Olsen, J.; Jorgensen O.D.; and Sondergaard. Randomized study of screening for colorectal cancer with faecal-occult-blood test. *Lancet* 348(9640):1467-1471, 1996.

13. Hardcastle, J.D.; Chamberlain, J.O.; Robinson, M.H.E.; et al. Randomized controlled trial of faecal-occult-blood screening for colorectal cancer. *Lancet* 348(9040):1472-1477, 1996.

14. Mandel, J.S. Reducing mortality from colorectal cancer by screening for fecal occult blood: Update, personal communication, 1997.

15. Mandel, J.S.; Bond, J.H.; Church T.R.; et al. Reducing mortality from colorectal cancer by screening for fecal occult blood. *New England Journal of Medicine* 328(19):1365-1371, 1993.

16. Winawer, S.; Fletcher, R.; Miller, L. et al. Colorectal cancer screening: clinical guidelines and rationale. *Gerontology* 112:594-642, 1997.

17. Selby, J.V.; Freidman, G.D.; Quesenberry, C.P., Jr.; and Weiss, N.S. A case-control study of screening sigmoidoscopy and mortality from colorectal cancer. *New England Journal of Medicine* 326(10):653-657, 1992.

18. Muller, A.D., and Sonnenberg, A. Protection by endoscopy against death from colorectal cancer—A case-control study among veterans. *Archives of Internal Medicine* 155:1741-1748, 1995.

19. Newcomb, P.A.; Norfleet, R.G.; Storer, B.E.; Surawicz, T.S.; and Marcus, P.M. Screening sigmoidoscopy and colorectal cancer mortality. *Journal of the National Cancer Institute* 84(20):1572-1575, 1992.

20. Alexander, F.E.; Edinburgh, G.L.; Andriole, G.L. et al. Rationale for randomized trials of prostate cancer screening. *European Journal of Cancer* 35(2):262-271, 1999.

21. Centers for Disease Control and Prevention.

Cigarette smoking-attributable mortality and years of potential life lost—United States, 1990. *Morbidity and Mortality Weekly Report* 42(33):645-649, 1993.

22. Greenwald, P.; Kramer, B.S.; and Weed, D.L., eds. *Cancer Prevention and Control.* New York: Marcel Dekker, 1995, 568-569.

23. Doll, R., and Peto, R. The Causes of Cancer. Quantitative Estimates of Avoidable Risks of Cancer in the United States Today. New York: Oxford University Press, 1981.

24. Kerlikowske, K.; Grady, D.; Rubin, S.M.; et al. Efficacy of screening mammography. A meta-analysis. *Journal of the American Medical Association* 273:149-154, 1995.

25. Henderson, B.E.; Pike, M.C.; Bernstein, L.; and Ross, R.K. Breast cancer. In: Schottenfeld, D., and Fraumeni, J.F., Jr., eds. *Cancer Epidemiology and Prevention*, 2nd ed. New York: Oxford University Press, 1996, 1022-1039.

26. Harvard report on cancer prevention, Vol. 1. Causes of human cancer. *Cancer Causes & Control* 7(1 suppl.):1-59, 1996.

27. National Institutes of Health. *Cervical Cancer. NIH Consensus Statement* 14(1):1-38, 1996.

28. Schiffman, M.H.; Brinton, L.A.; Devesa, S.S.; and Fraumeni, J.F., Jr. Cervical cancer. In: Schottenfeld, D., and Fraumeni, J.F., Jr. (eds.). *Cancer Epidemiology and Prevention*, 2nd ed. New York: Oxford University Press, 1996, 1090-1116.

29. Schottenfeld, D., and Winawer, S.J. Cancers of the large intestine. In: Schottenfeld, D., and Fraumeri, J.F. Jr. (eds.). *Cancer Epidemiology and Prevention,*

2nd ed. New York: Oxford University Press, 1996, 813-840.

30. Silverman, S. Oral Cancer, 4th ed. Hamilton, Ontario, Canada: American Cancer Society, B.C. Decker, Inc., 1998.

31. Chodak, G.W.; Thisted, R.A.; Gerber, G.S.; Johansson, J.E.; Adolfsson J.; Jones, G.W.; et al. Results of conservative management of clinically localized prostate cancer. *New England Journal of Medicine* 330(4):242-248, 1994.

32. Gerber, G.S.; Thisted, R.A.; Scardino, P.T.; et al. Results of radical prostatectomy in men with clinically localized prostate cancer: Multi-institutional pooled analysis. *Journal of the American Medical Association* 276(8):615-619, 1996.

33. HHS. *Report of the U.S. Preventive Services Task Force: Guide to Clinical Preventive Services*, 2nd ed. Washington, DC: Government Printing Office, 1996.

34. Armstrong, B.K., and English, D.R. Cutaneous malignant melanoma. In: Schottenfeld, D., and Fraumeni, J.F. (eds.). *Cancer Epidemiology and Prevention*, 2nd ed. New York: Oxford University Press, 1996, 1282-1312.

4

Chronic Kidney Disease

Lead Agency: National Institutes of Health

Contents

Goal

Reduce new cases of chronic kidney disease and its complications, disability, death, and economic costs.

Overview

Issues and Trends

Chronic kidney failure is the most significant result of chronic kidney disease. When kidney function has deteriorated and is no longer adequate to sustain life and the process is considered irreversible, renal replacement therapy (RRT)—dialysis or transplantation—becomes necessary to maintain life. Treated chronic kidney failure, also called end-stage renal disease, is the most feared consequence of kidney disease. Chronic renal insufficiency, however, is more common than treated chronic kidney failure and can also severely affect health and well-being. Therefore, ideally, programs should be directed at preventing the development of chronic renal insufficiency and its subsequent progression to end-stage renal disease.

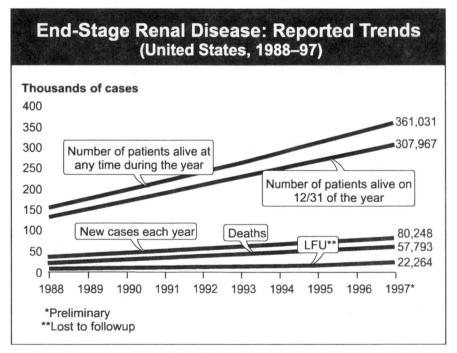

Source: NIH. U.S. Renal Data System, *1999 Annual Data Report*.

Unfortunately, chronic renal insufficiency is usually asymptomatic, and the exact number of people affected is unknown. The best available estimates are based on national surveys. Current estimates indicate approximately 10 million persons aged 12 years and older have some form of chronic kidney disease.[1] People with end-stage kidney failure represent a small fraction of all individuals with chronic kidney disease. A significant proportion of people with chronic kidney failure progress to end stage. The challenge is to initiate effective programs to prevent progression of established kidney disease and to institute methods to assess the progress of such initiatives.

In 1997, 80,248 new cases of end-stage kidney failure were reported.[2] Virtually all of these patients became permanently dependent on renal replacement therapy to stay alive.

Dialysis and kidney transplantation are the two methods of treatment available to people with kidney disease when they reach end stage. In 1997, 361,031 people in the United States depended on either dialysis or transplants to replace the function of their own failed kidneys.[3] Although these treatments are life-saving, dialysis and transplants have substantial limitations. Neither treatment restores normal health, and both are expensive.[4] The rates of illness, disability, and death experienced by individuals with treated chronic kidney failure are substantially higher than those of the general population.[5]

In most instances, terminal kidney failure develops as the result of progressive damage to the kidneys over a decade or more. A number of underlying diseases can cause progressive kidney failure. The two most important of these are diabetes, which in 1997 accounted for 42 percent of the new cases of chronic kidney failure, and high blood pressure, which was responsible for 26 percent of the new cases.[6] Other conditions that contribute significantly include glomerulonephritis, vasculitis, interstitial nephritis, and genetic and congenital disorders, particularly polycystic kidney disease.[7]

Chronic kidney failure affects people of all ages. The number of new cases peaks in the sixth decade of life, but 25 percent of persons arriving at end-stage in 1997 were under age 45 years, and 1.5 percent—nearly 1,100—were under age 20 years.[6] Kidney failure is particularly devastating in childhood, often resulting in impaired growth and development.

A worrisome increase in the number of new cases of kidney failure occurred between 1987 and 1997. The rate increased from 142 per million population in 1987 to 296 per million population in 1997,[8] representing an increase in the annual number of new cases from 34,797 to 80,248,[9] respectively.

This relentless growth in new cases of kidney failure has occurred in spite of the fact that death rates from other diseases, especially cardiovascular diseases, have declined.[10] The increase has not been confined to a single age group. Although the rates of new cases have grown slightly more rapidly for individuals aged 75 years and older, sizable increases have been noted in every age group.[11]

The causes of these increases are not completely understood, but one major factor appears to be an increase in the number of new cases of diabetes, particularly type

Data as of November 30, 1999

2 diabetes.[12, 13] In 1987, the rate of new cases of treated chronic kidney failure due to diabetes was 45 per million population. By 1997, the rate had increased to 124 per million population.[14]

Treatment for end-stage kidney failure has a substantial impact on Federal resources for health care. The 1972 Social Security Amendment (Public Law 92-603) instituted federally financed health care coverage for dialysis and renal transplantation, effective July 1, 1973. The cost of this program has far exceeded original expectations. Medicare spending in 1996 was estimated to be $10.96 billion, a 12.5 percent increase from the $9.74 billion spent in 1995. The total expenditure by all payers for treating these patients in 1996 was estimated at $14.55 billion, up from $13.05 billion in 1995.[15] Although this patient population made up only 0.6 percent of the total Medicare population in 1994, it consumed 5.1 percent of Medicare expenditures.[16] The increases in the cost per patient have been modest, but the driving force behind the growth in these expenditures has been the growing number of patients.

Kidney disease develops and progresses more rapidly to end stage in people with a variety of chronic health problems, such as type 1 or type 2 diabetes and high blood pressure, and family history of genetic kidney diseases. Therefore, people with these chronic health problems require counseling about the possibility of kidney disease and the steps they must take to avoid serious kidney complications. Also, people who have proteinuria and/or elevated serum creatinine have a greater likelihood of developing serious cardiovascular disease complications. Therefore, cardiovascular risk assessment and management should include kidney function to prevent the consequences of kidney failure. Because national data systems will not be available in the fist half of the decade to track progress, these issues are not addressed in the chapter.

Disparities

Kidney disease has a disproportionate impact on certain racial and ethnic groups, especially African Americans and American Indians or Alaska Natives. African Americans have the highest overall risk of chronic kidney disease. The reasons are not entirely explained by the higher number of persons in this population who have diabetes and high blood pressure.[17, 18] On average, African Americans develop end-stage kidney failure at an earlier age than whites (55.8 years compared to 62.2 years).[19] American Indians or Alaska Natives have a much higher risk of chronic kidney disease due to diabetes than whites. Overall, the rates of new cases are 4 times higher in African Americans and American Indians or Alaska Natives and 1.5 times higher in Asians or Pacific Islanders than in whites.

Annual increases in end-stage renal disease (ESRD) rates are greater in certain racial and ethnic populations than in white populations. Rates of new cases are increasing by 7 percent per year for African Americans, 10 percent per year for American Indians or Alaska Natives, and 11 percent for Asians or Pacific Islanders, compared to 6 percent per year for whites. Two communities of an American Indian Tribe, the Zuni Pueblo in New Mexico and in Sacaton, Arizona, may have the highest rates of chronic kidney failure in the world, at 12.6 and 14.0 times the overall average U.S. rate, respectively. Projections indicate that increases in the rates of new cases will continue in American Indians or Alaska Natives.

Although complete data are not yet available, some evidence indicates that persons of Mexican ancestry also may have a high risk of developing chronic kidney failure, particularly due to diabetes.[20, 21] In 1995, the Health Care Financing Administration changed the way in which data on race and ethnicity are collected on the Medical Evidence Form used to enroll patients into the Medicare End-Stage Renal Disease Program. Data from 1997 suggest that 7 percent of the ESRD patients are of Mexican ancestry and another 4 percent are of Hispanic ancestry from areas other than Mexico.[22]

The disproportionately high rates of chronic kidney failure among racial and ethnic minority groups have resulted in a greater burden of disease in these communities. In 1996, African Americans constituted 12.6 percent of the U.S. population but 29.8 percent of ESRD patients; American Indians or Alaska Natives constituted 0.9 percent of the U.S. population but 1.7 percent of those receiving renal replacement therapy.[23] On December 31, 1996, the point-prevalent rate per million population (adjusted for age and gender) was 3,404 in African Americans and 2,761 in American Indians or Alaska Natives, compared to 754 in whites, differences of 4.5- and 3.7-fold, respectively.[24] Data on persons of Asian or Pacific Islander ancestry indicate slightly higher incidence and prevalence rates than those for whites.[25]

There is a slight preponderance of kidney failure in men. In 1997, the incidence of treated chronic kidney failure was 322 per million population in men, compared with 271 per million in women.[8]

Renal transplantation is an important life-saving renal replacement therapy and has been shown to offer many advantages when compared with dialysis.[26, 27] In 1997, 12,445 transplants were performed in the United States. There was significant gender discrepancy, with 7,352 transplants for men, compared with 4,948 for women.[28] Racial and ethnic disparities also exist. Between 1994 and 1997, the first cadaveric transplantation rates (per 100 patient years) in the pediatric age group were 31 for black males, 28 for white males, 19 for black females, and 26 for white females. For recipients between the ages of 20 and 44 years, the rates were 7 for black males, 17 for white males, 7 for black females, and 15 for white females. In the 45- to 65-year age group, the rates were 4 for black males, 8 for white males, 2 for black females, and 6 for white females.[29] The data from the USRDS database also confirms that the transplantation rate is lower for Native Americans. The transplantation rate in Asians is equivalent to the rate in whites.[30] Reasons for the racial and ethnic disparities in the rate of transplantation are varied and include differences in finding HLA matches, cultural attitudes and beliefs on the

Data as of November 30, 1999

part of both patients and health care providers, socioeconomic status, rates of organ donation, and geographic location.

Opportunities

Major risk factors for the development and progression of chronic kidney disease include diabetes, high blood pressure, environmental exposures, proteinuria, family history of kidney disease, and increasing age. African Americans and American Indians or Alaska Natives who have these risk factors are especially susceptible to the development of chronic and progressive kidney disease.[31, 32] Strategies for preventing the development of chronic kidney disease, therefore, should use appropriate methods to target these populations.

Under certain circumstances, the progression of kidney disease to end stage can be slowed or halted. Three interventions are effective in certain defined populations: glycemic control (for patients with diabetes), blood pressure control (for patients with high blood pressure), and use of angiotensin-converting enzyme (ACE) inhibitors. Interventions to slow the progression of kidney disease and prevent chronic kidney failure are likely to have the greatest impact if applied early in the course of the disease. Unfortunately, because kidney disease in its early stages is generally asymptomatic, many people who would benefit from these interventions are not identified. Early identification of patients at risk for chronic kidney disease is essential in reducing the growth in the number of new cases of treated chronic kidney failure. For example, microalbuminuria screening and more intensive treatment of patients with microalbuminuria are an important part of a strategy to reduce nephropathy in persons with type 1 diabetes, both in terms of economic indices and clinical outcomes.[33, 34, 35] This strategy also may be useful in type 2 diabetes.

Patient care must continue to emphasize interventions to conserve residual renal function. At a certain stage, however, providing appropriate preparation for renal replacement therapy becomes advisable. Several studies show that many patients with chronic kidney failure do not receive optimum preparation for treated chronic kidney failure in the year prior to the commencement of renal replacement therapy. This lack of optimal preparation has a substantial effect on the cost of care and on illness and disability at the time of renal replacement therapy.[36]

Kidney transplantation has emerged as the preferred therapy for many patients with treated chronic kidney failure, particularly children. Kidney transplantation confers a survival advantage over dialysis.[37] Over the past decade, transplantation success rates, especially 1-year patient and graft survival, have improved steadily. This improvement has been observed in both cadaveric and living-related transplants.[38, 39] For young children, kidney transplantation results in improved rates of growth.[40] Because of accumulating evidence on the advantages of transplantation, equal access of all population groups to transplantation is a substantial concern.

Certain racial and ethnic groups and women consistently have longer waiting times and lower rates of kidney transplantation than white males.[41, 42, 43, 44, 45, 46]

Attention to risk factors for kidney disease and interventions to slow its progression are urgently needed. This need is driven by the increasing number of cases of treated chronic kidney failure, its disproportionate effect on certain racial and ethnic groups, the high societal cost of the disease, and the impact on Federal health care resources.

Interim Progress Toward Year 2000 Objectives

Healthy People 2000 did not include a chapter on chronic kidney disease. However, objectives relating to chronic kidney disease were included in several chapters. Since the mid-1980s, the number of new cases of ESRD has grown steadily. One objective concerning diabetes addressed ESRD. Results show that ESRD among people with diabetes has more than doubled since its baseline and is moving away from the target. Subobjectives tracking ESRD due to diabetes among African Americans and American Indians or Alaska Natives also are moving away from their targets.

Note: Unless otherwise noted, data are from Centers for Disease Control and Prevention, National Center for Health Statistics, *Healthy People 2000 Review, 1998-99*.

Chronic Kidney Disease

Goal: Reduce new cases of chronic kidney disease and its complications, disability, death, and economic costs.

Number	Objective
4-1	End-stage renal disease
4-2	Cardiovascular disease deaths in persons with chronic kidney failure
4-3	Counseling for chronic kidney failure care
4-4	Use of arteriovenous fistulas
4-5	Registration for kidney transplantation
4-6	Waiting time for transplantation
4-7	Kidney failure due to diabetes
4-8	Medical therapy for persons with diabetes and proteinuria

4-1.   **Reduce the rate of new cases of end-stage renal disease (ESRD).**

Target: 217 new cases per million population.

Baseline: 289 new cases of end-stage renal disease per million population in 1997.

Target setting method: Better than the best.

Data source: U.S. Renal Data System (USRDS), NIH, NIDDK.

Total Population, 1997	New Cases of End-Stage Renal Disease Rate per Million
TOTAL	289
Race and ethnicity	
American Indian or Alaska Native	586
Asian or Pacific Islander	344
Asian	DNC
Native Hawaiian and other Pacific Islander	DNC
Black or African American	873
White	218
Hispanic or Latino	DNA
Not Hispanic or Latino	DNA
Black or African American	DNA
White	DNA
Gender	
Female	242
Male	348
Age	
Under 20 years	13
20 to 44 years	109
45 to 64 years	545
65 to 74 years	1,296
75 years and older	1,292

Total Population, 1997	New Cases of End-Stage Renal Disease Rate per Million
Family income level	
Poor	DNC
Near poor	DNC
Middle/high income	DNC

DNA = Data have not been analyzed. DNC = Data are not collected. DSU = Data are statistically unreliable.

The current average annual increase in new cases of treated chronic kidney failure rates is 6 percent. Therefore, the expected rate in 2010 would be 612 new cases per million population. Without improvements in prevention and because of changes in demographics and increases in the number of cases of diabetes, rates of new cases of treated chronic kidney failure are expected to continue to rise 5 to 8 percent per year.

4-2. Reduce deaths from cardiovascular disease in persons with chronic kidney failure.

Target: 52 deaths per 1,000 patient years at risk.

Baseline: 70 deaths from cardiovascular disease per 1,000 patient years at risk (in persons with ESRD) in 1997.

Target setting method: Better than the best.

Data source: U.S. Renal Data System (USRDS), NIH, NIDDK.

Persons With Treated Chronic Kidney Failure, 1997	Deaths From Cardiovascular Disease Per 1,000 Patient Years at Risk
TOTAL	70
Race and ethnicity	
American Indian or Alaska Native	63
Asian or Pacific Islander	60
Asian	DNC
Native Hawaiian and other Pacific Islander	DNC
Black or African American	62
White	75

Persons With Treated Chronic Kidney Failure, 1997	Deaths From Cardiovascular Disease Per 1,000 Patient Years at Risk
Hispanic or Latino	DNA
Not Hispanic or Latino	DNA
Black or African American	DNA
White	DNA
Gender	
Female	73
Male	67
Family income level	
Poor	DNC
Near poor	DNC
Middle/high income	DNC

DNA = Data have not been analyzed. DNC = Data are not collected. DSU = Data are statistically unreliable.

Cardiovascular disease (CVD) is the major cause of death among patients with chronic renal failure and ESRD. Therefore, targeting reduction in CVD deaths will lead to a significant decrease in deaths for this population. The increased risk of CVD in kidney disease patients is evident before the onset of terminal kidney failure. Increases in the number of CVD deaths also are seen in individuals with proteinuria or elevated creatinine (both are markers of declining kidney function). CVD death rates in the treated chronic kidney failure population are estimated to be 30-fold higher than in the general population.[47] The known risk factors for cardiovascular disease in the general population include age, male gender, diabetes, elevated cholesterol, high blood pressure, smoking, and family history. Elevated homocysteine levels in the blood also may be an important risk factor in treated chronic kidney failure patients and at earlier stages in the progression of kidney disease.[48, 49, 50] Strategies to reduce CVD deaths should target risk reduction before terminal kidney failure.[51] All responsible health care providers can initiate the strategies to reduce CVD deaths as suggested in published guidelines.[51]

Data as of November 30, 1999

4-3. **Increase the proportion of treated chronic kidney failure patients who have received counseling on nutrition, treatment choices, and cardiovascular care 12 months before the start of renal replacement therapy.**

Target: 60 percent.

Baseline: 45 percent of newly diagnosed patients with treated chronic kidney failure received counseling on nutrition, treatment choices, and cardiovascular care in 1996.

Target setting method: 33 percent improvement (Better than the best will be used when data are available).

Data source: U.S. Renal Data System, (USRDS), NIH, NIDDK.

Patients Newly Diagnosed With Treated Chronic Kidney Failure, 1996	Received Counseling Prior to Renal Replacement Therapy Percent
TOTAL	45
Race and ethnicity	
American Indian or Alaska Native	DNA
Asian or Pacific Islander	DNA
Asian	DNC
Native Hawaiian and other Pacific Islander	DNC
Black or African American	DNA
White	DNA
Hispanic or Latino	DNA
Not Hispanic or Latino	DNA
Black or African American	DNA
White	DNA
Gender	
Female	DNA
Male	DNA
Family income level	
Poor	DNC
Near poor	DNC
Middle/high income	DNC

DNA = Data have not been analyzed. DNC = Data are not collected. DSU = Data are statistically unreliable.

Medically appropriate care of kidney disease patients within 12 months before the start of renal replacement therapy reduces the substantial illness, disability, and death associated with treated chronic kidney failure.[52] Appropriate preparation for RRT includes reduction in cardiovascular disease risk factors, treatment of anemia, optimum therapy to preserve residual renal function, consultation about nutrition, and patient education about RRT methods. Patients should be seen by a specialist in RRT at least 12 months prior to initiation of RRT for general counseling. However, specific issues—such as vascular access and estimation of residual renal function—need to be addressed at least 6 months prior to RRT. Many patients with chronic renal failure are not seen by health care professionals who have RRT expertise until very near the time that RRT will be required. In a USRDS survey of 3,468 new dialysis patients, 55 percent had not been seen by a nephrologist 1 year prior to the start of RRT, and 33 percent had not been seen even 3 months before RRT.[53] Although control of diet is a major aspect of care for patients with chronic kidney failure and terminal kidney failure, by the start of RRT, 46 percent of the patients had not seen a dietitian.

4-4. Increase the proportion of new hemodialysis patients who use arteriovenous fistulas as the primary mode of vascular access.

Target: 50 percent.

Baseline: 29 percent of newly diagnosed patients with treated chronic kidney failure on hemodialysis used arteriovenous fistulas as the primary mode of vascular access in 1997.

Target setting method: 72 percent improvement (consistent with Dialysis Outcomes Quality Initiative (DOQI) guidelines). (Better than the best will be used when data are available).

Data source: U.S. Renal Data System, (USRDS), NIH, NIDDK.

Newly Diagnosed Chronic Kidney Failure Patients on Hemodialysis, 1997	Arteriovenous Fistula Use Percent
TOTAL	29
Race and ethnicity	
American Indian or Alaska Native	DNA
Asian or Pacific Islander	DNA
Asian	DNC
Native Hawaiian and other Pacific Islander	DNC
Black or African American	DNA

Data as of November 30, 1999

Newly Diagnosed Chronic Kidney Failure Patients on Hemodialysis, 1997	Arteriovenous Fistula Use Percent
White	DNA
Hispanic or Latino	DNA
Not Hispanic or Latino	DNA
Black or African American	DNA
White	DNA
Gender	
Female	DNA
Male	DNA
Family income level	
Poor	DNC
Near poor	DNC
Middle/high income	DNC

DNA = Data have not been analyzed. DNC = Data are not collected. DSU = Data are statistically unreliable.

Patients receiving renal replacement therapy as of December 31, 1997, were treated predominantly (72 percent) with dialysis. Of these, 88 percent were on hemodialysis. Vascular access is the major lifeline for hemodialysis patients. The presence of a functioning vascular access site represents a critical factor in the well-being of these patients. Unfortunately, however, it also is the largest single cause of illness and disability in patients receiving hemodialysis for renal replacement therapy, accounting for nearly 25 percent of all hospitalizations. Complications and problems related to vascular access have been estimated to account for as much as 17 percent of the health care costs associated with treated chronic kidney failure.[55]

Monitoring the type of vascular access for dialysis in new patients is an important method to assess the adequacy of preparation for renal replacement therapy. Clinical evidence shows that patients with endogenous arteriovenous fistulas experience lower complication rates than patients with synthetic grafts. In the United States, the use rate for arteriovenous fistulas is under 30 percent.[54] Arteriovenous fistulas, ideally, should be placed at least 6 months before the start of dialysis. Early placement of arteriovenous fistulas is particularly important for elderly persons, because atherosclerotic vessels may take a much longer time to dilate to a usable diameter.

4-5. Increase the proportion of dialysis patients registered on the waiting list for transplantation.

Target: 66 percent of dialysis patients.

Baseline: 20 percent of newly diagnosed treated chronic kidney failure patients under age 70 years were registered on the waiting list in 1994-96.

Target setting method: Better than the best.

Data source: U.S. Renal Data System (USRDS), NIH, NIDDK.

Dialysis Patients Under Age 70 Years, 1994–96	Transplant Waiting List Percent
TOTAL	20
Race and ethnicity	
American Indian or Alaska Native	2
Asian or Pacific Islander	4
Asian	DNC
Native Hawaiian and other Pacific Islander	DNC
Black or African American	29
White	65
Hispanic or Latino	12
Not Hispanic or Latino	DNA
Black or African American	DNA
White	DNA
Gender	
Female	40
Male	60
Family income level	
Poor	DNC
Near poor	DNC
Middle/high income	DNC
Age groups	
Under 20 years	3
20 to 39 years	31
40 to 59 years	51
60 to 69 years	15

DNA = Data have not been analyzed. DNC = Data are not collected. DSU = Data are statistically unreliable.

Successful renal transplantation confers many advantages, including improvements in physical and psychological growth in children and improved survival and quality of life for recipients in general. The prospects of receiving a kidney transplant, however, are determined by a number of factors. These factors include age, primary cause of kidney failure, race and ethnic origin, gender, geographic location, and availability of suitable donors. Any combination of these factors may directly influence the first important step in the process of receiving a kidney transplant—namely, being registered on the waiting list. Significant disparities exist in the people who are registered on the waiting list. Women and people from select racial and ethnic groups—particularly, African Americans—are less likely than other kidney transplant candidates to be registered on the waiting list.[55, 56, 57]

4-6. Increase the proportion of patients with treated chronic kidney failure who receive a transplant within 3 years of registration on the waiting list.

Target: 51 registrants per 1,000 patient years at risk.

Baseline: 41 registrants per 1,000 patient years at risk (since placed on dialysis) received a transplant within 3 years in 1995-97.

Target setting method: Better than the best.

Data source: U.S. Renal Data System (USRDS), NIH, NIDDK.

Renal Transplant Waiting List Registrants, 1995–97	Transplant Within 3 Years Rate per 1,000 Patient Years
TOTAL	41
Race and ethnicity	
American Indian or Alaska Native	30
Asian or Pacific Islander	DNA
Asian	50
Native Hawaiian and other Pacific Islander	DNA
Black or African American	30
White	49
Hispanic or Latino	DNA

Data as of November 30, 1999

Renal Transplant Waiting List Registrants, 1995–97	Transplant Within 3 Years Rate per 1,000 Patient Years
Not Hispanic or Latino	DNA
Black or African American	DNA
White	DNA
Gender	
Female	33
Male	49
Age	
Under 20 years	282
20 to 44 years	110
45 to 64 years	52
65 years and older	6
Family income level	
Poor	DNC
Near poor	DNC
Middle/high income	DNC

DNA = Data have not been analyzed. DNC = Data are not collected. DSU = Data are statistically unreliable.

Individuals from certain racial and ethnic populations (specifically, African Americans) move up the waiting list to receive kidney transplants at a slower rate than whites.[58, 59] The exact causes are unclear. Racial and ethnic disparities in waiting times may be influenced by genetic and biological factors (such as HLA types),[60] the request and consent procedures of organ procurement organizations, patient registration practices for a center or region, organ acceptance practices at each transplant center, geographic location, socioeconomic status, cultural attitudes and beliefs about organ donation, rates of organ donation within each local area, and the donor pool.[42, 61]

Reports also have documented a lower rate of transplantation in women.[55] The U.S. Department of Health and Human Services (HHS) is working toward the goal of making sure that all persons in the United States have an equal opportunity to receive a transplant, regardless of who they are or where they live. To increase access to transplantation, HHS launched the National Organ and Tissue Donation Initiative to increase overall organ and tissue donation. One aspect of the initiative is to learn more about the factors that influence organ and tissue donation, with a special emphasis on certain racial and ethnic minority communities. Health care workers, particularly in the area of transplantation, need to understand the various obstacles to organ donation and transplantation, especially in the groups with

Data as of November 30, 1999

which they work, and to initiate programs and policies that are culturally sensitive and meaningful.

4-7. Reduce kidney failure due to diabetes.

Target: 78 diabetic persons with ESRD per million population.

Baseline: 113 diabetic persons with ESRD per million population in 1996.

Target setting method: Better than the best.

Data source: U.S. Renal Data System (USRDS), NIH, NIDDK.

Persons With Diabetes, 1996	New Cases of ESRD Rate per Million
TOTAL	113
Race and ethnicity	
American Indian or Alaska Native	482
Asian or Pacific Islander	156
Asian	DNC
Native Hawaiian and other Pacific Islander	DNC
Black or African American	329
White	79
Hispanic or Latino	DNA
Not Hispanic or Latino	DNA
Black or African American	DNA
White	DNA
Gender	
Female	103
Male	112
Age	
Under 20 years	0
20 to 44 years	35
45 to 64 years	276
65 to 74 years	514
75 years and older	263

Persons With Diabetes, 1996	New Cases of ESRD
	Rate per Million
Family income level	
Poor	DNC
Near poor	DNC
Middle/high income	DNC

DNA = Data have not been analyzed. DNC = Data are not collected. DSU = Data are statistically unreliable.

Convincing, consistent, and continuing scientific evidence shows that with secondary and tertiary prevention, microvascular complications of diabetes, especially diabetic kidney disease, can be reduced substantially. Enhanced quality of life, reductions in death rates, and reduced costs can result from improved clinical and public health diabetes prevention strategies directed at kidney disease and other microvascular and metabolic complications of diabetes. Monitoring the consequences of these strategies, including reductions in the magnitude of chronic renal insufficiency, terminal kidney failure, and other microvascular complications, should be an important component of an effective national public health program.

4-8. **(Developmental) Increase the proportion of persons with type 1 or type 2 diabetes and proteinuria who receive recommended medical therapy to reduce progression to chronic renal insufficiency.**

Potential data sources: National Ambulatory Medical Care Survey (NAMCS), CDC, NCHS; National Hospital Ambulatory Care Survey (NHAMCS), CDC, NCHS.

Related Objectives From Other Focus Areas

1. Access to Quality Health Services

1-2.   Health insurance coverage for clinical preventive services

1-3.   Counseling about health behaviors

1-7.   Core competencies in health provider training

5. Diabetes

5-2.   Prevent diabetes

5-3.   Reduce diabetes

5-4.   Diagnosis of diabetes

5-7.   Cardiovascular deaths in persons with diabetes

5-11.   Annual urinary microalbumin measurement

5-12.   Annual glycosylated hemoglobin measurement

6. Disability and Secondary Conditions

6-1.   Standard definition of people with disabilities in data sets

6-2.   Feelings and depression among children with disabilities

6-3.   Feelings and depression interfering with activities among adults with disabilities

6-5.   Sufficient emotional support among adults with disabilities

6-6.   Satisfaction with life among adults with disabilities

6-8.   Employment parity

7. Educational and Community-Based Programs

7-7.   Patient and family education

7-8.   Satisfaction with patient education

7-9.   Health care organization sponsorship of community health promotion activities

7-10.   Community health promotion programs

7-11.   Culturally appropriate community health promotion programs

8. Environmental Health

8-11.   Elevated blood lead levels in children

8-14.   Toxic pollutants

8-20.   School policies to protect against environmental hazards

8-22.   Lead-based paint testing

8-25.   Exposure to heavy metals and other toxic chemicals

8-26.   Information systems used for environmental health

8-27.   Monitoring environmentally related diseases

8-29.   Global burden of disease

10. Food Safety

10-1.   Foodborne infections

10-2.   Outbreaks of foodborne infections

10-5.   Consumer food safety practices

10-6   Safe food preparation practices in retail establishments

11. Health Communication

11-2.   Health literacy

11-4.   Quality of Internet health information sources

11-6.   Satisfaction with providers' communication skills

12. Heart Disease and Stroke

12-1.   Coronary heart disease (CHD) deaths

12-2.   Knowledge of symptoms of heart attack and importance of dialing 911

12-6.   Heart failure hospitalizations

12-8.   Knowledge of early warning symptoms of stroke

12-9.   High blood pressure

12-10.   High blood pressure control

12-11.   Action to help control blood pressure

12-12.   Blood pressure monitoring

12-16.   LDL-cholesterol level in CHD patients

13. HIV

13-1.   New AIDS cases

13-3.   AIDS cases among persons who inject drugs

13-5.   New HIV cases

13-8.   HIV counseling and education for persons in substance abuse treatment

13-12.   Screening for STDs and immunization for hepatitis B

13-17.   Perinatally acquired HIV infection

14. Immunization and Infectious Diseases

14-1.   Vaccine-preventable diseases

14-2.   Hepatitis B in infants and young children

14-3.   Hepatitis B in adults and high-risk groups

14-9.   Hepatitis C

14-10.   Identification of persons with chronic hepatitis C

14-16.   Invasive early-onset group B streptococcal disease

14-28.   Hepatitis B vaccination among high-risk groups

16. Maternal, Infant, and Child Health

16-10.   Low birth weight and very low birth weight

17. Medical Product Safety

17-1.   Monitoring of adverse medical events

17-2.   Linked, automated information systems

17-3.   Provider review of medications taken by patients

17-6.   Blood donations

19. Nutrition and Overweight

19-1.   Healthy weight in adults

19-2.   Obesity in adults

19-8.   Saturated fat intake

19-17.   Nutrition counseling for medical conditions

20. Occupational Safety and Health

20-7.   Elevated blood lead levels from work exposure

22. Physical Activity and Fitness

22-2.   Moderate physical activity

22-3.   Vigorous physical activity

22-13.   Worksite physical activity and fitness

23. Public Health Infrastructure

23-2.   Public access to information and surveillance data

23-3.   Use of geocoding in health data systems

23-4.   Data for all population groups

23-5.   Data for Leading Health Indicators, Health Status Indicators, and Priority Data Needs at State, Tribal, and local levels

Terminology

(A listing of all abbreviations and acronyms used in this publication appears in Appendix K.)

Arteriovenous fistulas: The type of vascular access created by joining a person's own (endogenous) artery to the nearby vein. The increase in blood flow in the vein leads to marked dilation of the vein and permits an easier insertion of needles for dialysis.

Chronic renal insufficiency, chronic renal failure, and end-stage renal disease (ESRD) (defined in this chapter as treated chronic renal failure): Terms describing the continuum of increasing renal dysfunction and decreasing glomerular filtration rate (GFR). Because of the progressive nature of kidney disease, these terms represent successive stages of disease in most patients.

Chronic renal insufficiency: The stage in chronic renal disease in which damage to the kidney already has resulted in significant impairment of renal function, but systemic manifestations are minimal. Most patients who have chronic renal insufficiency are asymptomatic. Chronic renal insufficiency usually is identified because the serum creatinine is slightly elevated (greater than 1.5 mg/dL in males or 1.2 mg/dL in females and greater than age-specific normative values in children). The serum creatinine test is insensitive and does not identify all persons who have chronic renal insufficiency. Although precise GFR limits cannot be assigned to this stage of disease, typically patients with chronic renal insufficiency have a GFR between 30 ml/min and 75 ml/min.

Chronic renal failure: The stage in chronic renal disease in which renal dysfunction has progressed to a level resulting in systemic manifestations. These manifestations include a rise in the blood concentration of urea, creatinine, and phosphate, which are removed by the kidneys, and other problems, such as anemia, bone disease, acidosis, and salt and fluid retention. Growth failure may be seen in children. Most patients with chronic renal failure progress to treated chronic renal failure (end-stage renal disease).

Diabetes (diabetes mellitus): A chronic disease due to insulin deficiency or resistance to insulin action and associated with hyperglycemia (elevated blood glucose levels). Over time, without proper preventive treatment, organ complications related to diabetes develop, including heart, nerve, foot, eye, and kidney damage as well as problems with pregnancy. Diabetes is classified into two major categories.

Type 1 diabetes (previously called insulin-dependent diabetes mellitus [IDDM] or juvenile-onset diabetes [JODM]): Represents clinically about 5 percent of all persons with diagnosed diabetes. Its clinical onset typically occurs at ages under 30 years, with more gradual development after age 30. Most often type 1 diabetes represents an autoimmune destructive disease in the beta (insulin-producing) cells of the pancreas in genetically susceptible individuals. Insulin therapy always is required to sustain life and maintain diabetes control.

Type 2 diabetes (previously called noninsulin-dependent diabetes mellitus [NIDDM] or adult-onset diabetes [AODM]): Refers to the most common form of diabetes in the United States and the world, especially in certain racial and ethnic groups and in elderly persons. Women who develop diabetes during pregnancy also are at increased risk of developing this type of diabetes later in life. In the United States, approximately 95 percent of all persons with diagnosed diabetes (10. 5 million) and 100 percent of all persons with undiagnosed (5.5 million) diabetes probably have type 2 diabetes.

Diabetic kidney disease: Kidney disease and resultant kidney functional impairment due to the longstanding effects of diabetes on the microvasculature of the kidney. Features include increased urine protein and decreased kidney function.

Dialysis: The process by which metabolic waste products are removed by cleansing of the blood directly through extracorporeal filtration membranes (hemodialysis) or indirectly by diffusion of waste products through the peritoneal membranes into instilled fluids (peritoneal dialysis).

End-stage renal disease (referred to in this focus area as treated chronic kidney failure):

The stage in chronic renal disease in which renal replacement therapy, dialysis, or kidney transplantation is needed to sustain life. Treated chronic kidney failure is generally an irreversible state. The glomerular filtration rate is usually less than 10 ml/min.

Glomerular filtration: The process by which the kidneys filter the blood, clearing it of toxins.

Glomerular filtration rate (GFR): The rate at which the blood is cleared by glomerular filtration and an important measure of kidney function. Normal GFR values in adults are between 100 and 150 ml/min. One of the most important hallmarks of chronic renal disease is a progressive decline in the rate of glomerular filtration. Generally, a GFR below 75 ml/min represents clinically significant renal insufficiency. A GFR of less than 10 ml/min represents kidney failure severe enough to require renal replacement therapy to maintain life.

Hemodialysis: The process by which biologic waste products are removed from the body through external blood circuit and external (artificial) membranes.

Glomerulonephritis: Inflammation in the primary filtration units (glomeruli) of the kidneys. Typically, this process leads to loss of blood, blood products, and protein into the urine. Unchecked or without effective treatment, this process could lead ultimately to permanent kidney damage and loss of kidney function and chronic kidney failure.

Incidence rate: A measure of the number of new cases of disease occurring in a specific population over a specific period of time, usually 1 year. For end-stage renal disease, the best information is based on the incidence of treated end-stage renal disease

reported through Medicare to the U.S. Renal Data System. Available data exclude those patients who die without receiving treatment.

Interstitial nephritis: Inflammation in the supporting matrix of the kidneys. This process could result from damage caused by microorganisms (such as bacteria and viruses) or from toxic reaction to drugs or other substances such as lead and mercury.

Microalbuminuria: Abnormally elevated levels of albumin in the urine—but at levels too low to be detectable by the dipstick method used to test for protein in the urine. Increased urinary excretion of albumin, even if the concentration is too low to be detectable as dipstick proteinuria, has been associated with increased risk of progressive kidney disease in people with diabetes[6,7] and increased risk of subsequent death in persons with[8] and without diabetes[9,10] and in elderly individuals.[11] Microalbuminuria can be measured in several ways. If a random urine sample is used, the albumin concentration in the first-voided morning urine or the ratio of urine albumin to urine creatinine can be used. If a timed urine collection is available, an albumin excretion rate can be determined. Urine albumin concentrations of 30-300 μg/ml, urinary albumin to creatinine ratios of less than 3.5 mg/mmol, and urine albumin excretion rates of less than 15 μg/min all have been used as cutoff values for detection of microalbuminuria.

Patient year (at risk): A measure of the duration (in years) a patient has been exposed to the effects of a particular biologic or physiologic condition, such as chronic renal insufficiency or the effects of dialysis.

Polycystic kidney disease: A disorder (usually inherited) of the kidneys in which the normal kidney structures (particularly, the tubules) are replaced by sacs (or cysts) that ultimately increase in size and lead to further destruction of the supporting matrix of the kidneys. The most common variety is the adult polycystic kidney disease (ADPKD), which is inherited as an autosomal dominant genetic disease. ADPKD is usually characterized by elevated blood pressure, pain from enlarged cysts, blood in the urine, and a relentless progression to terminal kidney failure.

Prevalence rate: A measure of the total number of cases of disease existing in a specific population at a certain point in time (point prevalence) or over a certain period of time (period prevalence). Point prevalence rates reflect the number of individuals at the stated date.

Proteinuria: Abnormal levels of protein in the urine. Proteinuria is a marker for structural kidney damage or inflammation and also may be involved in the pathogenesis of progressive renal injury. Increased risks of developing progressive renal disease,[1, 2] of death,[3, 4] and of death due to cardiovascu-

lar disease[5] have been documented in persons with persistent proteinuria. Urine protein can be estimated by a dipstick method, which provides a semiquantitative estimate of concentration. More accurate measures include determining the ratio of urine protein to urine creatinine or the amount of protein excreted by a person in a 24-hour period.

Renal disease: A synonym for kidney disease.

Serum creatinine: A blood chemistry measurement used to estimate the level of kidney function. Serum creatinine is an important index for monitoring progression of disease in persons with chronic renal disease. Elevations in serum creatinine are an insensitive marker of early chronic renal insufficiency. In advanced renal failure, however, a change in serum creatinine is a more reliable indicator. This test remains the most widely available method used to estimate the glomerular filtration rate or to monitor changes in level of renal function.[12]

U.S. Renal Data System (USRDS): A national database of information on treated chronic kidney failure patients—new cases, illness, disability, and death out-

comes. USRDS is based predominantly on data collected by the Health Care Financing Administration's Medicare treated chronic kidney failure program and is funded by a contract from the National Institutes of Health.[13] This database contains information on approximately 93 percent of all patients treated for treated chronic kidney failure in the United States. Most of the data cited in this focus area derive from USRDS reports. As noted, these numbers reflect reported cases of treated end-stage renal disease and, therefore, do not include patients who die without treatment or patients whose care is not reported to USRDS.

Vascular access: The means by which blood is removed from a person for cleansing during dialysis and safely and easily returned, when cleaned, into the body.

Vasculitis: Inflammation of the blood vessels. Typically, the cause of this process is unknown. Untreated, it leads to progression to relentless and specific organ failures, including chronic kidney failure, or death.

References

1. Jones, C.A.; McQuillan, G.M.; Kusek, J.W.; et al. Serum Creatinine Levels in the U.S. Population: Third National Health and Nutrition Examination Survey, *American Journal of Kidney Disease* 32:992-999, 1998.

2. U.S. Renal Data System (USRDS). 1999 *Annual Data Report.* Bethesda, MD: National Institutes of Health, National Institute of Diabetes and Digestive and Kidney

Diseases, April 1999, Appendix, Table A-1.

3. USRDS. *1999 ADR,* Bethesda, MD: National Institutes of Health, National Institute of Diabetes and Digestive and Kidney Diseases, April 1999, Appendix, Table A- 1. Appendix, Table B-3.

4. USRDS. *1999 ADR,* Bethesda, MD: National Institutes of Health, National Institute of Diabetes and

Digestive and Kidney Diseases, April 1999, Chapter X. 133-148.

5. USRDS. *1999 ADR,* Bethesda, MD: National Institutes of Health, National Institute of Diabetes and Digestive and Kidney Diseases, April 1999, Chapter V. 63-78.

6. USRDS. *1999 ADR,* Bethesda, MD: National Institutes of Health, National Institute of Diabetes and

Digestive and Kidney Diseases, April 1999, Appendix, Table A-1.

7. USRDS. *1999 ADR,* Bethesda, MD: National Institutes of Health, National Institute of Diabetes and Digestive and Kidney Diseases, April 1999, Appendix, Table A- 15.

8. USRDS. *1999 ADR,* Bethesda, MD: National Institutes of Health, National Institute of Diabetes and Digestive and Kidney Diseases, April 1999, Appendix, Table A-3.

9. USRDS. *1999 ADR,* Bethesda, MD: National Institutes of Health, National Institute of Diabetes and Digestive and Kidney Diseases, April 1999, Appendix, Table A- 1.

10. National Heart, Lung, and Blood Institute. *Morbidity and Mortality Chartbook on Cardiovascular Disease, Lung and Blood Diseases.* Bethesda, MD: Public Health Service, 1998.

11. USRDS. *1999 ADR,* Bethesda, MD: National Institutes of Health, National Institute of Diabetes and Digestive and Kidney Diseases, April 1999, Appendix, Tables A-1, A-2, and A-3.

12. Clark, C. How should we respond to the worldwide diabetes epidemic? *Diabetes Care* 21:475-476, 1998.

13. Centers for Disease Control and Prevention (CDC). *National Diabetes Fact Sheet: National Estimates and General Information on Diabetes in the United States.* Atlanta, GA: U.S. Department of Health and Human Services, 1997.

14. USRDS. *1999 ADR,* Bethesda, MD: National Institutes of Health, National Institute of Diabetes and Digestive and Kidney Diseases, April 1999, Appendix, Table A-6.

15. Eggers, P.W. Personal Communication. Health Care Financing Administration. 1999.

16. Perneger, T.V.; Klag, M.J.; Feldman, H.I.; and Whelton, P.K. Projection of hypertension related renal disease in middle-aged residents of the United States. *Journal of the American Medical Association* 269(10):1272-1277, 1993.

17. Whittle, J.C.; Whelton, P.K.; Seidler, AJ.; and Klag, M.J. Does racial variation in risk factors explain black-white differences in the incidence of hypertensive end-stage renal disease? *Archives of Internal Medicine* 151:1359-1364, 1991.

18. Brancati, F.L.; Whittle, J.C.; Whelton, P.K.; Seidler, A.J.; and Klag, M.J. The excess incidence of diabetic end-stage renal disease among blacks. A population based study of potential explanatory factors. *Journal of the American Medical Association* 268:3079-3084, 1992.

19. USRDS. *1999 ADR,* Bethesda, MD: National Institutes of Health, National Institute of Diabetes and Digestive and Kidney Diseases, April 1999, Appendix, Table A- 1. Appendix, Table A-14.

20. Gonzales Villalpano, C.G.; Stern, M.P.; Arrendondo Perez, B.; Martinez Diaz, S.; et al. Nephropathy in low income diabetics: the Mexico City Diabetes Study. *Archives of Medical Research* 27:367-372, 1996.

21. Pugh, J.A.; Stern, M.P.; Haffner, S.M.; Eifler, C.W.; and Zapata, M. Excess incidence of treatment of end-stage renal disease in Mexican Americans. *American Journal of Epidemiology* 127:135-144, 1998.

22. Agodoa, L.Y.C.; Roys, E.C.; Wolfe, R.A.; et al. ESRD among Hispanics in the U.S. *Journal of the American Society of Nephrology* 10:232A, 1999.

23. USRDS. *1999 ADR,* Bethesda, MD: National Institutes of Health, National Institute of Diabetes and Digestive and Kidney Diseases, April 1999, Appendix, Table B-3.

24. USRDS. *1999 ADR,* Bethesda, MD: National Institutes of Health, National Institute of Diabetes and Digestive and Kidney Diseases, April 1999, Appendix, Table ES-1.

25. USRDS. *1999 ADR,* Bethesda, MD: National Institutes of Health, National Institute of Diabetes and Digestive and Kidney Diseases, April 199, Appendix, Table A.6.

26. Rettig, R., and Levinsky, N.G. Kidney failure and the Federal Government. Washington, DC: National Academy Press, 1991.

27. Port, F.K.; Wolfe, B.A.; Mauger, E.A.; et al. Comparison of survival probabilities for dialysis patients vs. cadaveric renal transplant recipients. *Journal of the American Medical Association* 270(11):1339-1343, 1993.

28. USRDS, *1999 ADR,* Appendix, Table F-1.

29. USRDS, *1999 ADR,* Chapter VII, 104-106.

30. USRDS, *1999 ADR,* Appendix, Table F-2.

31. Freedman, B.I.; Tuttle, A.B.; and Spray, B.J. Familial predisposition to nephropathy in African Americans with non-insulin-dependent diabetes mellitus. *Kidney Diseases* 25(5):710-713, 1995.

32. Siegel, J.; Krolewski, A.; Warran, J.; and Weinstein, M. Cost-effectiveness of screening and early treatment of nephropathy in pa-

tients with insulin-dependent diabetes mellitus. *Journal of the American Society of Nephrology* 3:S111 -S119, 1992.

33. Kiberd, B., and Jindal, K. Screening to prevent renal failure in insulin dependent diabetic patients: An economic evaluation. *British Medical Journal* 311:1595-1599, 1995.

34. Borch-Johnsen, K.; Wenzel, H.; Viberti, G.; and Mogensen, C. Is screening and intervention for microalbuminuria worthwhile in patients with insulin dependent diabetes? *British Medical Journal* 306:1722-1725, 1993.

35. Ifudu, O.; Dawood, M.; Homel, P.; and Friedman, E.A. Excess morbidity in patients starting uremia therapy without prior care by a nephrologist. *American Journal of Kidney Diseases* 28:841-845, 1996.

36. USRDS. *1997 Annual Data Report.* Bethesda, MD: National Institutes of Health, National Institute of Diabetes and Digestive and Kidney Diseases, April 1997, 49-60.

37. USRDS. *1998 Annual Data Report.* Table G.19.

38. USRDS. *1998 ADR,* Bethesda, MD: National Institutes of Health, National Institute of Diabetes and Digestive and Kidney Diseases, April 1998, Appendix, Table G.43.

39. Turenne, M.N.; Port, F.K.; Strawderman, R.L.; Ettenger, R.B.; Alexander, S.R.; Lewy, J.E.; Jones, C.A; Agodoa, L.Y.; and Held, P.J. Growth rates in pediatric dialysis patients and renal transplant recipients. *American Journal of Kidney Diseases* 30(2):193-203, 1997.

40. United Network for Organ Sharing (UNOS). *1997 Report of the Organ Procurement and Transplantation Network: Waiting List Activity and Donor Procurement,* Richmond, VA: United Network for Organ Sharing, 1997. Executive Summary, Kidney Volume. Rockville, MD: Health Resources and Services Administration, 1997.

41. Alexander, G.C., and Sehgal, A.R. Barriers to cadaveric renal transplantation among blacks, women, and the poor. *Journal of the American Medical Association* 280(13):1148-1152, 1998.

42. Bloembergen, W.E.; Mauger, E.A.; and Wolfe, R.A. Association of gender and access to cadaveric renal transplantation. *American Journal of Kidney Diseases* 30(6):733-738, 1997.

43. Narva, A.; Stiles, S.; Karp, S.; and Turak, A. Access of Native Americans to renal transplantation in Arizona and New Mexico. *Blood Purification* 14:293-304, 1996.

44. Ozminkowski, R.J.; White, A.J.; Hassol, M.S.P.H; and Murphy, M. Minimizing racial disparity regarding receipt of a cadaver kidney transplant. *American Journal of Kidney Disease* 30:749-759, 1997.

45. USRDS. *1997 ADR,* Bethesda, MD: National Institutes of Health, National Institute of Diabetes and Digestive and Kidney Diseases, April 1997, 107-112.

46. Levey, A.S.; Beto, J.A.; Coronado, B.E.; et al. Controlling the epidemic of cardiovascular disease in chronic renal disease. What do we know? What do we need to learn? Where do we go from here? *Report of the National Kidney Foundation Task Force on Cardiovascular Disease.* New York: National Kidney Foundation, July 1998.

47. Bostom, A.G.; Shemin, D.; Verhoef, P.; Nadeau, M.R.; Jacques, P.F; Selhub, J.; Dworkin, L.; and Rosenberg, I.H. Elevated fasting total plasma homocysteine levels and cardiovascular disease outcomes in maintenance dialysis patients: A prospective study. *Arteriosclerosis, Thrombosis, and Vascular Biology* 17(11):2554-2558, 1997.

48. Bostom, A.G., and Lathrop, L. Hyperhomocysteinemia in end-stage renal disease: Prevalence, etiology, and potential relationship to arteriosclerotic outcomes. *Kidney International* 52(I):10-20, 1997.

49. Bostom, A.G.; Shemin, D.; Lapane, K.L.; Sutherland, P.; Nadeau, M.R.; Wilson, P.W.; Yoburn, D.; Bausserman, L.; Tofler, G.; Jacques, P.F.; Selhub, J.; and Rosenberg, I.H. Hyperhomocysteinemia, hyperfibrinogenemia, and lipoprotein (a) excess in maintenance dialysis patients: A matched case-control study. *Arteriosclerosis* 125(I):91-101, 1996.

50. Perneger, T.V.; Klag, M.J.; and Whelton, P.K. Cause of death in patients with end-stage renal disease: Death certificates vs. registry reports. *American Journal of Public Health* 83(12):1735-1738, 1993.

51. USRDS. *1997 ADR,* Bethesda, MD: National Institutes of Health, National Institute of Diabetes and Digestive and Kidney Diseases, April 1997, April, 1997, Figure IV-3, 52.

52. National Kidney Foundation. Dialysis Outcomes, Quality Initiatives, Clinical Practice Guidelines, Executive Summaries. National Kidney Foundation, 1997.

53. USRDS, *1999 ADR,* Bethesda, MD: National Institutes of Health, National Institute of Diabetes and

Digestive and Kidney Diseases, April 1999, 159.

54. Hirth, R.A.; Turenne, M.N.; Woods, J.D.; Young, E.W.; Port, F.K.; Pauly, F.K.; and Held, P.J. Vascular access in newly treated U.S. hemodialysis patients: Predictors and trends. *Journal of the American Medical Association* 276:1303-1308, 1996.

55. Soucie, M.J.; Neylan, J.F.; and McClellan, W. Race and sex differences in the identification of candidates for renal transplantation. *American Journal of Kidney Diseases* 19:414-419, 1992.

56. Kasiske, B.L.; London, W.; and Ellison, M.D. Race and socioeconomic factors influencing early placement on the kidney transplant waiting list. *Journal of the American Society of Nephrology* 9:2142-2147, 1998.

57. United Network for Organ Sharing (UNOS). 1997 Report of the Organ Procurement and Transplantation Network: Waiting List Activity and Donor Procurement, Executive Summary, Kidney Volume. Rockville, MD: Health Resources and Services Administration, 1997.

58. Ellison, M.D.; Breen, T.J.; Guo, T.G.; Cunningham, P.R.G.; and Daily, O.P. Blacks and whites on the UNOS renal waiting list: Waiting times and patient demographics compared. *Transplantation Proceedings* 25(4):2462-2466, 1993.

59. Thompson, J.S. American society of histocompatibility and immunogenetics crossmatch study. *Transplantation* 59(11):1636-1638, 1995.

60. Sanfilippo, F.P.; Vaughn, W.K.; Peters, T.G.; Shield C.F.; Adams, P.L.; Lorber, M.I.; and Williams, M. Factors affecting the waiting time of cadaveric kidney transplant candidates in the United States. *Journal of the American Medical Association* 267:247-252, 1992.

61. McCauley, J.; Irish, W.; Thompson, L.; Stevenson, J.; Lockett, R.; Bussard, R.; and Washington, M. Factors determining the rate of referral, transplantation, and survival on dialysis in women with ESRD. *American Journal of Kidney Diseases* 30:739-748, 1997.

5

Diabetes

Co-Lead Agencies: Centers for Disease Control and Prevention;
National Institutes of Health

Contents

Goal

Through prevention programs, reduce the disease and economic burden of diabetes, and improve the quality of life for all persons who have or are at risk for diabetes.

Overview

Diabetes poses a significant public health challenge for the United States. Some 800,000 new cases are diagnosed each year, or 2,200 per day.[1, 2] The changing demographic patterns in the United States are expected to increase the number of people who are at risk for diabetes and who eventually develop the disease. Diabetes is a chronic disease that usually manifests itself as one of two major types: type 1, mainly occurring in children and adolescents 18 years and younger, in which the body does not produce insulin and thus insulin administration is required to sustain life; or type 2 occurring usually in adults over 30 years of age in which the body's tissues become unable to use its own limited amount of insulin effectively. While all persons with diabetes require self-management training, treatment for type 2 diabetes usually consists of a combination of physical activity, proper nutrition, oral tablets and insulin. Type 1 diabetes has been sometimes referred to as juvenile or insulin-dependent diabetes; and type 2 diabetes has been referred to as adult-onset or noninsulin dependent diabetes.

Issues

The occurrence of diabetes, especially type 2 diabetes, as well as associated diabetes complications, is increasing in the United States.[1, 2, 3] The number of persons with diabetes has increased steadily over the past decade; presently, 10.5 million persons have been diagnosed with diabetes, while 5.5 million persons are estimated to have the disease but are undiagnosed. This increase in the number of cases of diabetes has occurred particularly within certain racial and ethnic groups.[4] Over the past decade, diabetes has remained the seventh leading cause of death in the United States, primarily from diabetes-associated cardiovascular disease. While premenopausal nondiabetic women usually are at less risk of cardiovascular disease than men, the presence of diabetes in women is associated with a three- to four-fold increase in coronary heart disease compared to nondiabetic females.[5] In the United States, diabetes is the leading cause of nontraumatic amputations (approximately 57,000 per year or 150 per day); blindness among working-age adults (approximately 20,000 per year or 60 per day); and end-stage renal disease (ESRD) (approximately 28,000 per year or 70 per day).[6] (See Focus Area 28. Vision and Hearing and Focus Area 4. Chronic Kidney Disease.)

These and other health problems associated with diabetes contribute to an impaired quality of life and substantial disability among people with diabetes.[7]

Diabetes is a costly disease; estimates of the total attributable cost of diabetes are around $100 billion ($43 billion direct; $45 billion indirect).[8, 9] Hospitalizations for diabetes-associated cardiovascular disease account for the largest component of the direct costs. However, diabetes management is occurring increasingly in the outpatient setting, and more people with diabetes are using nursing home facilities.[8, 9]

Diabetes is a major clinical and public health challenge within certain racial and ethnic groups where both new cases of diabetes and the risk of associated complications are great.[4, 10]

These realities are especially disturbing given the validated efficacy and economic benefits of secondary prevention (controlling glucose, lipid, and blood pressure levels) and tertiary prevention (screening for early diabetes complications [eye, foot, and kidney abnormalities], followed by appropriate treatment and prevention strategies).[11, 12, 13, 14, 15, 16, 17] For many reasons, however, these scientifically and economically justified prevention programs are not used routinely in daily clinical management of persons with diabetes.[18, 19, 20] Diabetes is thus a "wasteful" disease. Strategies that would lessen the burden of this disease are not used regularly, resulting in unnecessary illness, disability, death, and expense.

Trends

The toll of diabetes on the health status of people in the United States is expected to worsen before it improves, especially in vulnerable, high-risk populations— African Americans, Hispanics, American Indians or Alaska Natives, Asians or other Pacific Islanders, elderly persons, and economically disadvantaged persons. Several factors account for this chronic disease epidemic, including behavioral elements (improper nutrition, for example, increased fat consumption; decreased physical activity; obesity); demographic changes (aging, increased growth of "at-risk populations"); improved ascertainment and surveillance systems that more completely capture the actual burden of diabetes; and the relative weakness of interventions to change individual, community, or organizational behaviors.[1, 3, 7, 21] Several other interrelated factors influence the present and future burden of diabetes, including genetics, cultural and community traditions, and socioeconomic status. In addition, unanticipated scientific breakthroughs, the characteristics of the health care system, and the level of patient knowledge and empowerment all have a great impact on the amount of disease burden associated with diabetes.

Personal behaviors. "Westernization," which includes a diet high in fat and processed foods as well as total calories, has been associated with a greater number of overweight persons in the United States when compared to a decade ago, especially within certain racial and ethnic groups, for example, African-American females.[22, 23] Obesity, improper nutrition (including increased ingestion of fats and processed foods), and lack of physical activity are occurring in persons under age 15 years. These behaviors and conditions may explain the increasing diagnosis of type 2 diabetes in teenagers.[24, 25] Increased television watching associated with diminished physical activity also may contribute to the emergence of type 2 diabetes in youth.[24, 25, 26, 27]

Demographics. Diabetes is most common in persons over age 60 years.[28] Increased insulin resistance and gradual deterioration in the function of insulin-producing cells may account for this phenomenon. As the population in the United States ages, especially as the number of persons who are 60 years and

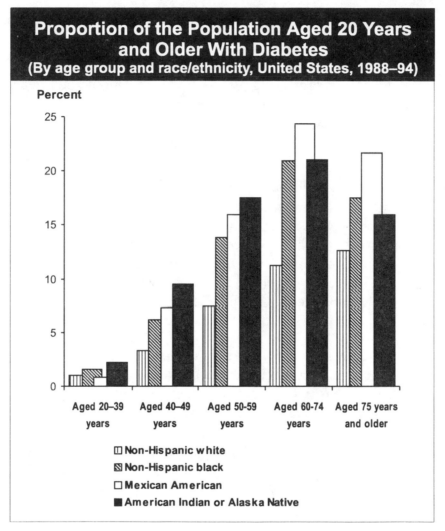

Sources: Harris et al. *Diabetes Care* 21(4):518–24, 1998; Indian Health Service national outpatient database.

older grows, an increase in the number of people with diabetes is expected. While studies indicate that aging itself may not be a major factor in the substantial increase in the number of persons with diabetes,[21] present and future prevention strategies for diabetes will be associated with a greater lifespan for persons with diabetes.[29]

Other changes in the U.S. population can be expected to affect the number of persons with diabetes. By 2050, almost half of the population will be other than white

(53 percent white; 24 percent Hispanic; 14 percent African American; and 8 percent Asian).[30] Because these racial and ethnic groups are at greater risk for diabetes and associated complications, and because of rising levels of obesity and physical inactivity in the general population, the number of persons with diabetes is expected to increase into the first few decades of the 21st century.[31]

Ascertainment. Known as the "hidden" disease, diabetes is undiagnosed in an estimated 5 million persons.[32, 33] In addition, complications and health services associated with diabetes frequently are not recorded on death certificates,[34, 35] hospital discharge forms,[36] emergency department paperwork, and other documents. Much of this "missing" burden of diabetes now is being captured due to improved surveillance and data systems,[37] including boxes on data forms to indicate the presence of diabetes and screening programs for undiagnosed diabetes in high-risk persons.[32] Thus, the real—but previously undocumented—burden of diabetes is becoming better recognized.

Limitations in programs to change behaviors. Scientific evidence indicates that secondary and tertiary prevention programs are effective in reducing the burden of diabetes. Yet changing the behaviors of persons with diabetes, health care providers, or other individuals or organizations involved in diabetes health care (for example, health maintenance organizations and employers), is difficult. Although many factors account for these challenges,[37] more effective interventions will need to be developed and implemented to improve the practice of diabetes care. Several other factors influence the present and future burden of diabetes, including genetics, culture, socioeconomic status (SES), scientific discoveries, and the characteristics of both chronic diseases and the health care system.

Both type 1 and type 2 diabetes have a significant genetic component.[38, 39] For type 1 diabetes, genetic markers that indicate a greater risk for this condition have been identified; they are sensitive but not specific. Type 2 diabetes, especially in vulnerable racial and ethnic groups, may be associated with a "thrifty gene."[40, 41] Family and twin studies demonstrate considerable influence of genetics for type 2 diabetes, but a specific genetic marker for the common variety of type 2 diabetes has not been identified. The degree to which such genetic indicators can be both validated and clinically available will determine effectiveness of primary prevention trials.[42, 43]

Patient behaviors are influenced by beliefs and attitudes, and these are greatly affected by community and cultural traditions.[44, 45] In many racial and ethnic communities, fatalism, use of alternative medicine, desirability of rural living conditions, lack of economic resources, and other factors will influence significantly both availability of health care and the capabilities of persons with diabetes in handling their own care. Thirteen percent of the total U.S. population speak a language at home other than English. Cultural and linguistic factors affect interactions with health care providers and the system. The degree to which diabetes prevention strategies recognize and incorporate these traditions will largely determine program effectiveness.[46, 47]

The public health and medical communities are increasingly recognizing the influence of SES in the occurrence of new cases and progression of chronic diseases.[48, 49, 50] Chronic diseases, such as diabetes, reflect the social fabric of our society, and the degree to which employment, financial security, feelings of safety, education, and the availability of health care are addressed and improved within the United States will influence the likelihood of developing type 2 diabetes, as well as effectively managing both types of diabetes.[51] For example, unemployment without access to health insurance will substantially limit attention to and expenditures for preventive health practices.

Because acute infectious diseases were the dominant health threats during the first half of the 20th century, a dichotomous view of health existed, for example, people were either alive or dead, vaccinated or not vaccinated, etc. Death and length of life were the most important markers of disease burden and program effectiveness during those years. Chronic diseases such as diabetes pose different challenges because qualitative terms such as "doing better" are valid indicators of health improvement, as are measures of quality of life and disability. Further, a variety of nonphysician health professionals (for example, nurses or pharmacists) and nonhealth care professionals (for example, faith or community leaders, employers) can be involved in critical decisions affecting chronic diseases. Diabetes, like other chronic conditions, is long term and is affected by the environment where people live, work, and play. For diseases like diabetes, the accurate measurement of quality of life as an indicator of program effectiveness and the incorporation of nonhealth professionals at work or worship on the health team will influence the successes of preventive treatment programs.[37, 45, 46]

The rapidity and utility of scientific discoveries also will influence the control of the diabetes burden. In all aspects of scientific investigation, important observations about diabetes will continue to occur. These scientific results will greatly influence diabetes prevention and management,[54] but any scientific study that is not translated and used in daily practice is ultimately "wasted."[10, 55]

The availability of a responsive and effective health care system will determine access to quality care, especially in secondary and tertiary prevention.[56, 57] With the emergence of managed care, a person with diabetes theoretically could receive effective, economical, and planned preventive care that would minimize the diabetes burden.[58] Several additional changes need to occur within the managed care setting, however, to maximize fully this theoretical opportunity for persons with diabetes, including managed care (1) not denying access to potentially expensive patients, (2) allowing adequate time for health professionals to interact with patients, and (3) ensuring patient protection rights.

In addition, the apparent movement toward primary care will affect diabetes management and outcomes. At present, about 90 percent of all persons with diabetes receive continuous care from the primary care community. This is highly unlikely to change. Thus, the degree that improved relationships can be established be-

Data as of November 30, 1999

tween diabetes specialists and primary care health providers will determine the quality of diabetes care.[59]

People with diabetes spend a small percentage of their time in contact with health professionals. In addition to family, friends, and work colleagues, individual patient knowledge, beliefs, and attitudes affect diabetes management and outcomes. The ability to understand and influence individual, community, and organizational behaviors will influence significantly the success of preventive programs in diabetes.[60, 61, 62]

Disparities

Gaps exist among racial and ethnic groups in the rate of diabetes and its associated complications in the United States. Racial and ethnic communities, including African Americans, Hispanics, American Indians, and certain Pacific Islander and Asian American populations as well as economically disadvantaged or older Americans, suffer disproportionately compared to white populations. For example, the relative number of persons with diabetes in African American, Hispanic, and American Indian communities is one to five times greater than in white communities.[4] When compared to their white counterparts, death from diabetes is two times as great in African-American persons, and diabetes-associated renal failure is two and a half times that in Hispanic individuals with diabetes.[1, 6, 7]

Particularly within certain racial and ethnic groups, there are four potential individual reasons for the greater burden of diabetes:

Greater number of cases of diabetes. If diabetes is more common, then more amputations, death, and other complications from diabetes would be expected.

Greater seriousness of diabetes. If hyperglycemia or other serious comorbid conditions, such as high blood pressure or elevated blood lipids, are present in certain racial and ethnic groups, a greater diabetes-related disease burden would occur. Many other factors could be involved, including genetics and excess weight. "Greater seriousness" of diabetes can be determined by comparing, for example, death or amputation rates for specific racial and ethnic diabetic groups with those rates in the general diabetes population.

Inadequate access to proper diabetes prevention and control programs. If diabetes services, such as self-management training programs or eye-retina examinations, are not a part of routine diabetes care, then effective programs to reduce the burden of diabetes will not be accessed and used. These essential diabetes services often are provided by specialists. Unfortunately, many diabetes "at-risk" groups reside in medically undeserved areas or are without adequate insurance, and thus do not receive these types of preventive services.

Improper quality of care. If diabetes management services are available, but the quality of that service is inadequate, prevention programs would not be effective in reducing the burden of diabetes.

Identifying the reasons for disparities in diabetes health outcomes is important in tailoring programs to those specific areas where deficiencies exist. Collection of racial and ethnic health services data for all health activities is critical to designate the reason for the greater disease burden.

Opportunities

Opportunities to meet the challenges of diabetes lie in four "transition points" in the natural history of this disease and the preventive interventions which target them: primary prevention, screening and early diagnosis, access, and quality of care (secondary and tertiary prevention).[63]

The transition points and associated public health intervention are as follows:

- Transition Point 1: From No Diabetes to Diabetes Present (although not recognized). Intervention, *Primary Prevention.*

- Transition Point 2: From Diabetes Not Recognized to Diabetes Recognized (but preventive diabetes care not provided). Intervention, *Screening/Early Diagnosis.*

- Transition Point 3: From No Care to Diabetes Care Applied. Intervention, *Access.*

- Transition Point 4: From Improper Care to Proper Care. Intervention, *Quality of Care.* (Secondary and Tertiary Prevention—for example, glucose control and decreasing diabetes complications.)

Each transition point represents a diabetes prevention and control opportunity that is contained in the diabetes objectives of Healthy People 2010. Objectives are categorized as: (1) diabetes education; (2) burden of disease (new cases, existing cases, undiagnosed diabetes, death, pregnancy complications); (3) macrovascular, microvascular, and metabolic complications; (4) laboratory services (lipids, glycosylated hemoglobin, microalbumin measurements); (5) health provider services (eye, foot, and dental examinations); and (6) patient protection behaviors (aspirin, self-glucose monitoring). These objectives measure both the processes and outcomes of preventive diabetes programs.

To improve the quality of diabetes care, the Diabetes Quality Improvement Project (DQIP)—a joint public/private effort—has identified a set of measures to track critical performance measures of diabetes management. Through the Quality Interagency Coordination (QuIC) task force, Federal agencies with health care responsibilities are collaborating to use DQIP to better focus efforts to improve diabetes care.

Interim Progress Toward Year 2000 Objectives

In Healthy People 2000, five diabetes-related objectives were included in a group of objectives addressing chronic conditions linked by their potential impact on quality of life and disability. Of these five objectives, eye examinations is moving toward the 2000 target. Death from diabetes, nonretinal diabetes complications, new cases of diabetes, and the number of existing cases are all moving away from the 2000 targets. Diabetes education is increasing in frequency among persons with diabetes.

These changes in direction need to be considered carefully with regard to significance, causes, and implications. The greater number of new cases of ESRD among persons with diabetes may in part be due to "ascertainment," that is persons with diabetes were not in the past but now are allowed access to ESRD treatment programs. Similarly, while new cases of type 2 diabetes truly may be increasing in association with obesity and inactivity, a higher number of cases of diabetes also may reflect increased efforts to screen for previously undiagnosed diabetes as well as decreased deaths from such conditions as diabetic acidosis or amputations. Thus, an increased number of existing cases of type 2 diabetes may in part reflect successes in other types of diabetes prevention programs.

Note: Unless otherwise noted, data are from Centers for Disease Control and Prevention, National Center for Health Statistics, *Healthy People 2000 Review, 1998-99.*

Diabetes

Goal: Through prevention programs, reduce the disease and economic burden of diabetes, and improve the quality of life for all persons who have or are at risk for diabetes.

Number	Objective
5-1	Diabetes education
5-2	Prevent diabetes
5-3	Reduce diabetes
5-4	Diagnosis of diabetes
5-5	Diabetes deaths
5-6	Diabetes-related deaths
5-7	Cardiovascular deaths in persons with diabetes
5-8	Gestational diabetes
5-9	Foot ulcers
5-10	Lower extremity amputations
5-11	Annual urinary microalbumin measurement
5-12	Annual glycosylated hemoglobin measurement
5-13	Annual dilated eye examinations
5-14	Annual foot examinations
5-15	Annual dental examinations
5-16	Aspirin therapy
5-17	Self-blood glucose monitoring

5-1. **Increase the proportion of persons with diabetes who receive formal diabetes education.**

Target: 60 percent.

Baseline: 40 percent of persons with diabetes received formal diabetes education in 1998 (age adjusted to the year 2000 standard population).

Target setting method: Better than the best.

Data source: National Health Interview Survey (NHIS), CDC, NCHS.

Persons With Diabetes, 1993*	Diabetes Education Percent
TOTAL	45
Race and ethnicity	
American Indian or Alaska Native	DSU
Asian or Pacific Islander	DSU
Asian	DSU
Native Hawaiian and other Pacific Islander	DSU
Black or African American	55
White	42
Hispanic or Latino	DSU
Not Hispanic or Latino	48
Black or African American	45
White	57
Gender	
Female	49
Male	41
Age	
Under 18 years	DNC
18 to 44 years	48
45 to 64 years	44
65 to 74 years	41
75 years and older	36

Persons With Diabetes, 1993*	Diabetes Education Percent
Education level (aged 25 years and older)	
Less than high school	46
High school graduate	39
At least some college	51
Disability status	
Persons with activity limitation	48
Persons without activity limitations	43
Geographic location	
Urban	47
Rural	42

DNA = Data have not been analyzed. DNC = Data are not collected. DSU = Data are statistically unreliable.

Note: Age adjusted to the year 2000 standard population.

*New data for population groups will be added when available.

Diabetes patient education is uniformly viewed as effective and economical in the ultimate prevention of long term complications from diabetes. An individual with diabetes spends less than one percent of his or her time in contact with the health care system and on a daily basis must make a variety of critical decisions about diabetes. An informed and motivated patient is essential in managing the disease and reducing the risk of complications (for example, foot ulcers, hypoglycemia, and hypertension).[64, 65]

5-2.   Prevent diabetes.

Target: 2.5 new cases per 1,000 persons per year.

Baseline: 3.1 new cases of diabetes per 1,000 persons (3-year average) in 1994-96.

Target setting method: Better than the best (retain year 2000 target).

Data source: National Health Interview Survey (NHIS), CDC, NCHS.

Total Population, 1994–96	New Cases of Diabetes Rate per 1,000
TOTAL	3.1
Race and ethnicity	
American Indian or Alaska Native	8.7
Asian or Pacific Islander	2.9

Total Population, 1994–96	New Cases of Diabetes
	Rate per 1,000
Asian	DSU
Native Hawaiian and other Pacific Islander	DSU
Black or African American	3.7
White	3.0
Hispanic or Latino	3.5
Not Hispanic or Latino	3.1
Black or African American	3.8
White	2.9
Gender	
Female	3.7
Male	2.6
Age	
Under 18 years	DNA
18 to 44 years	DNA
45 to 64 years	6.5
65 to 74 years	DNA
75 years and older	DNA
Education level (aged 25 years and older)	
Less than high school	7.7
High school graduate	4.0
At least some college	3.8
Geographic location	
Urban	DNA
Rural	DNA
Disability status	
Persons with activity limitations	DNA
Persons without activity limitations	DNA

DNA = Data have not been analyzed. DNC = Data are not collected. DSU = Data are statistically unreliable.

5-3. Reduce the overall rate of diabetes that is clinically diagnosed.

Target: 25 overall cases per 1,000 population.

Baseline: 40 overall cases (including new and existing cases) of diabetes per 1,000 population in 1997 (age adjusted to the year 2000 standard population).

Target setting method: Better than the best (retain year 2000 target).

Data source: National Health Interview Survey (NHIS), CDC, NCHS.

Total Population, 1997	Cases of Diagnosed Diabetes Rate per 1,000
TOTAL	40
Race and ethnicity	
American Indian or Alaska Native	DSU
Asian or Pacific Islander	DSU
Asian	DSU
Native Hawaiian and other Pacific Islander	DSU
Black or African American	74
White	36
Hispanic or Latino	61
Not Hispanic or Latino	38
Black or African American	74
White	34
Gender	
Female	40
Male	39
Age	
Under 18 years	DSU
18 to 44 years	15
45 to 64 years	76
65 to 74 years	143
75 years and older	117
Education level (aged 25 years and older)	
Less than high school	95
High school graduate	58
At least some college	44

Total Population, 1997	Cases of Diagnosed Diabetes Rate per 1,000
Geographic location	
Urban	40
Rural	38
Disability status	
Persons with disabilities	87
Persons without disabilities	28

DNA = Data have not been analyzed. DNC = Data are not collected. DSU = Data are statistically unreliable.

Note: Age adjusted to the year 2000 standard population.

5-4. Increase the proportion of adults with diabetes whose condition has been diagnosed.

Target: 80 percent.

Baseline: 65 percent of adults aged 20 years and older with diabetes had been diagnosed in 1988-94.

Target setting method: Better than the best.

Data source: National Health and Nutrition Examination Survey (NHANES), CDC, NCHS.

Adults Aged 20 Years and Older With Diabetes, 1988–94	Persons Whose Diabetes Has Been Diagnosed Percent
TOTAL	65
Race and ethnicity	
American Indian or Alaska Native	DSU
Asian or Pacific Islander	DSU
Asian	DNC
Native Hawaiian and other Pacific Islander	DNC
Black or African American	DNA
White	DNA
Hispanic or Latino	DNA
Mexican American	62

Adults Aged 20 Years and Older With Diabetes, 1988–94	Persons Whose Diabetes Has Been Diagnosed
	Percent
Not Hispanic or Latino	DNA
Black or African American	66
White	67
Gender	
Female	68
Male	61
Age	
20 to 44 years	67
45 to 64 years	61
65 to 74 years	69
75 years and older	69
Education level (aged 25 years and older)	
Less than high school	DNA
High school graduate	DNA
At least some college	DNA
Geographic location	
Urban	DNA
Rural	DNA
Disability status	
Persons with disabilities	DNA
Persons without disabilities	DNA

DNA = Data have not been analyzed. DNC = Data are not collected. DSU = Data are statistically unreliable.

Diabetes is increasingly common in the United States and the world. Many factors could be contributing to this "chronic disease epidemic," including an increase in new cases, a decrease in deaths, and improvements in detection.[1, 2, 3, 21, 63] Given the seriousness and cost associated with diabetes and the complexities of the disease, factors that account for the increasing frequency of diabetes should be identified.[66, 67, 68, 69]

5-5. Reduce the diabetes death rate.

Target: 45 deaths per 100,000 persons.

Baseline: 75 deaths per 100,000 persons were related to diabetes in 1997 (age adjusted to the year 2000 standard population).

Target setting method: 43 percent improvement.

Data source: National Vital Statistics System (NVSS), CDC, NCHS.

Total Population, 1997	Diabetes Deaths Rate per 100,000
TOTAL	75
Race and ethnicity	
American Indian or Alaska Native	107
Asian or Pacific Islander	62
Asian	DNC
Native Hawaiian and other Pacific Islander	DNC
Black or African American	130
White	70
Hispanic or Latino	86
Mexican American	115
Puerto Rican	87
Cuban	39
Not Hispanic or Latino	74
Black or African American	133
White	68
Gender	
Female	67
Male	87
Age	
Under 45 years	3
45 to 64 years	64
65 to 74 years	281
75 years and older	673
Education level (aged 25 to 64 years)	
Less than high school	48
High school graduate	38
At least some college	17

DNA = Data have not been analyzed. DNC = Data are not collected. DSU = Data are statistically unreliable.
Note: Age adjusted to the year 2000 standard population.

5-6. Reduce diabetes-related deaths among persons with diabetes.

Target: 7.8 deaths per 1,000 persons with diabetes.

Baseline: 8.8 deaths per 1,000 persons with diabetes listed anywhere on the death certificate in 1997 (age adjusted to the year 2000 standard population).

Target setting method: 11 percent improvement.

Data sources: National Vital Statistics System (NVSS), CDC, NCHS; National Health Interview Survey (NHIS), CDC, NCHS.

Persons With Diabetes, 1997	Diabetes-Related Deaths Rate per 1,000
TOTAL	8.8
Race and ethnicity	
American Indian or Alaska Native	3.3
Asian or Pacific Islander	5.4
Asian	6.3
Native Hawaiian and other Pacific Islander	2.5
Black or African American	8.1
White	8.9
Hispanic or Latino	7.4
Not Hispanic or Latino	8.9
Black or African American	8.1
White	9.0
Gender	
Female	8.6
Male	9.5
Age	
Under 45 years	2.0
45 to 64 years	7.7
65 to 74 years	20.1
75 years and older	73.4

Persons With Diabetes, 1997	Diabetes-Related Deaths Rate per 1,000
Education level (aged 25 to 64 years)	
Less than high school	4.7
High school graduate	7.3
At least some college	3.4

DNA = Data have not been analyzed. DNC = Data are not collected. DSU = Data are statistically unreliable.
Note: Age adjusted to the year 2000 standard population.

5-7. Reduce deaths from cardiovascular disease in persons with diabetes.

Target: 309 deaths per 100,000 persons with diabetes.

Baseline: 343 deaths from cardiovascular disease per 100,000 persons with diabetes in 1997 (age adjusted to the year 2000 standard population).

Target setting method: 10 percent improvement.

Data sources: National Vital Statistics System (NVSS), CDC, NCHS; National Health Interview Survey (NHIS), CDC, NCHS.

Persons With Diabetes, 1997	Cardiovascular Disease Deaths Rate per 100,000
TOTAL	343
Race and ethnicity	
American Indian or Alaska Native	93
Asian or Pacific Islander	223
Asian	263
Native Hawaiian and other Pacific Islander	113
Black or African American	283
White	359
Hispanic or Latino	270
Not Hispanic or Latino	351
Black or African American	284
White	367

Persons With Diabetes, 1997	Cardiovascular Disease Deaths Rate per 100,000
Gender	
Female	339
Male	363
Age	
Under age 45 years	38
45 to 64 years	306
65 to 74 years	850
75 years and older	3,222
Education level (aged 25 to 64 years)	
Less than high school	145
High school graduate	247
At least some college	125

DNA = Data have not been analyzed. DNC = Data are not collected. DSU = Data are statistically unreliable.
Note: Age adjusted to the year 2000 standard population.

Persons with diabetes experience death rates two to four times greater than nondiabetic persons, especially from cardiovascular disease. Other causes of death include renal failure, diabetic acidosis, and infection. Studies have clearly indicated that secondary prevention[70, 71, 72, 73] and tertiary prevention[74, 75, 76, 77] can reduce overall cardiac-related illness, disability, and death. Death rates and their significance, however, are complicated by how accurately and completely diabetes is recorded on death certificates.[34, 35] Thus, attention to both prevention behaviors to delay or prevent death, as well as death rates themselves, should be examined carefully.[70, 71, 72, 73, 74, 75, 76, 77, 78, 79, 80, 81]

5-8. (Developmental) Decrease the proportion of pregnant women with gestational diabetes.

Potential data source: National Vital Statistics System (NVSS), CDC, NCHS.

Studies of diabetes and pregnancy are consistent in their conclusions that proper prepregnancy and pregnancy glycemia control and careful perinatal obstetrical monitoring are associated with reduction in perinatal death and congenital abnormalities. More recently, the importance of good fetal and neonatal nutrition in general, as well as in persons with diabetes, has been emphasized.[82, 83, 84, 85, 86, 87]

5-9. (Developmental) Reduce the frequency of foot ulcers in persons with diabetes.

Potential data source: National Health and Nutrition Examination Survey (NHANES), CDC, NCHS.

5-10. Reduce the rate of lower extremity amputations in persons with diabetes.

Target: 5 per 1,000 persons with diabetes per year.

Baseline: 11 lower extremity amputations per 1,000 persons with diabetes in 1996.

Target setting method: 55 percent improvement.

Data sources: National Hospital Discharge Survey (NHDS), CDC, NCHS; National Health Interview Survey (NHIS), CDC, NCHS.

Persons With Diabetes, 1996	Lower Extremity Amputation Rate per 1,000
TOTAL	11
Race and ethnicity	
American Indian or Alaska Native	DSU
Asian or Pacific Islander	DSU
Asian	DNC
Native Hawaiian and other Pacific Islander	DNC
Black or African American	10
White	DNA
Hispanic or Latino	DSU
Not Hispanic or Latino	DSU
Black or African American	DSU
White	DSU
Gender	
Female	DNA
Male	DNA
Age	
Under 65 years	DNA
65 to 74 years	DNA
75 years and older	DNA

Persons With Diabetes, 1996	Lower Extremity Amputation Rate per 1,000
Education level (aged 25 years and older)	
Less than high school	DNC
High school graduate	DNC
At least some college	DNC

DNA = Data have not been analyzed. DNC = Data are not collected. DSU = Data are statistically unreliable.

5-11. (Developmental) Increase the proportion of persons with diabetes who obtain an annual urinary microalbumin measurement.

Potential data source: Behavioral Risk Factor Surveillance System (BRFSS), CDC, NCCDPHP.

Scientific evidence documents that with secondary and tertiary prevention, microvascular complications of diabetes can be substantially reduced. Improved quality of life, decreased death rates, and reduced costs all can result from improved clinical and public health diabetes prevention strategies directed at microvascular and metabolic complications from diabetes. Monitoring the consequences of these strategies through reductions in mid- and end-stage microvascular complications needs to be an important component in determining the effectiveness of national diabetes activities. In both type 1 and 2 diabetes, evidence is now firmly established that microvascular and metabolic complications of diabetes can be prevented through secondary (glucose[88, 89]) and tertiary (screening and early treatment of complications[90]) prevention strategies.[91, 92, 93, 94]

Improper nutrition, obesity, and inactivity appear to be significant risk factors for the development of type 2 diabetes. (See Focus Area 22. Physical Activity and Fitness, and Focus Area 19. Nutrition and Overweight.) In addition, nutrition, weight, and physical activity components are particularly critical in both glucose management and blood pressure and lipid control in persons with diabetes. These components are closely related to abilities to control both micro- and macrovascular diabetic complications. Given the discouraging trends in obesity and physical inactivity, these elements should be particularly and carefully monitored in persons with diabetes.[95, 96, 97]

Data as of November 30, 1999

5-12. Increase the proportion of adults with diabetes who have a glycosylated hemoglobin measurement at least once a year.

Target: 50 percent.

Baseline: 24 percent of adults aged 18 years and older with diabetes had a glycosylated hemoglobin measurement at least once a year (mean of data from 39 States in 1998; age adjusted to the year 2000 standard population).

Target setting method: Better than the best.

Data source: Behavioral Risk Factor Surveillance System (BRFSS), CDC, NCCDPHP.

Adults Aged 18 Years and Older With Diabetes, 1998	Annual Glycosylated Hemoglobin Assessment
	Percent
TOTAL	24
Race and ethnicity	
American Indian or Alaska Native	29
Asian or Pacific Islander	48
Asian	DNC
Native Hawaiian and other Pacific Islander	DNC
Black or African American	21
White	25
Hispanic or Latino	22
Not Hispanic or Latino	25
Black or African American	21
White	24
Gender	
Female	24
Male	25
Education level (aged 25 years and older)	
Less than high school	13
High school graduate	19
At least some college	31

Data as of November 30, 1999

Adults Aged 18 Years and Older With Diabetes, 1998	Annual Glycosylated Hemoglobin Assessment Percent
Age	
18 to 44 years	29
45 to 64 years	23
65 to 74 years	13
75 years and older	11

DNA = Data have not been analyzed. DNC = Data are not collected. DSU = Data are statistically unreliable.

Note: Age adjusted to the year 2000 standard population.

During the past decade, scientific investigations have established that controlling certain macrovascular risk factors, such as elevated blood lipids and blood pressure, as well as microvascular factors, such as elevated blood glucose, will result in fewer diabetes-related complications. Further, identification of early indicators of organ damage, for example, microalbuminuria, and proper treatment with angiotensin-converting enzyme-inhibitors, will reduce progression to renal failure. Diabetes-associated complications can be detected with available laboratory and clinical measures, thus indicating the need for prevention programs. Monitoring these clinical and laboratory measures can serve to identify targets for intervention programs.[98, 99, 100, 101, 102]

5-13. Increase the proportion of adults with diabetes who have an annual dilated eye examination.

Target: 75 percent.

Baseline: 56 percent of adults aged 18 years and older with diabetes had an annual dilated eye examination (mean of data from 39 States in 1998; age adjusted to the year 2000 standard population).

Target setting method: Better than the best.

Data source: Behavioral Risk Factor Surveillance System (BRFSS), CDC, NCCDPHP.

Adults Aged 18 Years and Older With Diabetes, 1998	Annual Dilated Eye Examination Percent
TOTAL	56
Race and ethnicity	
American Indian or Alaska Native	60
Asian or Pacific Islander	69
Asian	DNC
Native Hawaiian and other Pacific Islander	DNC
Black or African American	59
White	55
Hispanic or Latino	53
Not Hispanic or Latino	57
Black or African American	59
White	56
Gender	
Female	55
Male	58
Education level (aged 25 years and older)	
Less than high school	48
High school graduate	60
At least some college	58
Age	
18 to 44 years	51
45 to 64 years	61
65 to 74 years	65
75 years and older	65

DNA = Data have not been analyzed. DNC = Data are not collected. DSU = Data are statistically unreliable.

Note: Age adjusted to the year 2000 standard population.

5-14. Increase the proportion of adults with diabetes who have at least an annual foot examination.

Target: 75 percent.

Baseline: 55 percent of adults aged 18 years and older with diabetes had at least an annual foot examination (mean value of data from 39 States in 1998; age adjusted to the year 2000 standard population).

Data as of November 30, 1999

Target setting method: Better than the best.

Data source: Behavioral Risk Factor Surveillance System (BRFSS), CDC, NCCDPHP.

Adults Aged 18 Years and Older With Diabetes, 1998	Annual Foot Examination Percent
TOTAL	55
Race and ethnicity	
American Indian or Alaska Native	40
Asian or Pacific Islander	57
Asian	DNC
Native Hawaiian and other Pacific Islander	DNC
Black or African American	55
White	55
Hispanic or Latino	56
Not Hispanic or Latino	54
Black or African American	54
White	54
Gender	
Female	51
Male	59
Age	
18 to 44 years	53
45 to 64 years	59
65 to 74 years	56
75 years and older	51
Education level (aged 25 years and older)	
Less than high school	46
High school graduate	56
At least some college	59

DNA = Data have not been analyzed. DNC = Data are not collected. DSU = Data are statistically unreliable.
Note: Age adjusted to the year 2000 standard population.

Health practitioner behaviors, such as blood pressure monitoring or eye and foot examinations, are associated with greater identification of early indicators of end-organ damage from diabetes. These screening behaviors are necessary to initiate secondary and tertiary prevention programs, and should be monitored.[103, 104, 105]

5-15. Increase the proportion of persons with diabetes who have at least an annual dental examination.

Target: 75 percent.

Baseline: 58 percent of persons aged 2 years and older with diagnosed diabetes saw a dentist at least once within the preceding 12 months in 1997 (age adjusted to the year 2000 standard population).

Target setting method: Better than the best.

Data source: National Health Interview Survey (NHIS), CDC, NCHS.

Persons with Diabetes Aged 2 Years and Older, 1997	Annual Dental Examination Percent
TOTAL	58
Race and ethnicity	
American Indian or Alaska Native	DSU
Asian or Pacific Islander	56
Asian	DSU
Native Hawaiian or Pacific Islander	DSU
Black or African American	63
White	58
Hispanic or Latino	32
Not Hispanic or Latino	61
Black or African American	63
White	61
Gender	
Female	59
Male	57
Age	
18 to 44 years	64
45 to 64 years	68
65 to 74 years	68
75 years and older	65
Education level (aged 25 years and older)	
Less than high school	40
High school graduate	52
At least some college	65

Data as of November 30, 1999

Persons with Diabetes Aged 2 Years and Older, 1997	Annual Dental Examination Percent
Disability status	
Persons with disabilities	42
Persons without disabilities	66

DNA = Data have not been analyzed. DNC = Data are not collected. DSU = Data are statistically unreliable.
Note: Age adjusted to the year 2000 standard population.

Persons with diabetes are at increased risk for destructive periodontitis and subsequent tooth loss. [106, 107] In addition, untreated periodontitis in persons with diabetes may complicate glycemic control.[108] Regular dental visits provide opportunities for prevention, early detection, and treatment of periodontal problems in persons with diabetes.

5-16. Increase the proportion of adults with diabetes who take aspirin at least 15 times per month.

Target: 30 percent.

Baseline: 20 percent of adults with diabetes aged 40 years and older took aspirin at least 15 times per month in 1988-94.

Target setting method: Better than the best.

Data source: National Health and Nutrition Examination Survey (NHANES), CDC, NCHS.

Adults Aged 40 Years and Older With Diabetes, 1988–94	Take Aspirin at Least 15 Times per Month Percent
TOTAL	20
Race and ethnicity	
American Indian or Alaska Native	DSU
Asian or Pacific Islander	DSU
Asian	DNC
Native Hawaiian and other Pacific Islander	DNC
Black or African American	9
White	24
Hispanic or Latino	DSU
Mexican American	8

Adults Aged 40 Years and Older With Diabetes, 1988–94	Take Aspirin at Least 15 Times per Month Percent
Not Hispanic or Latino	DNA
Black or African American	DNA
White	DNA
Gender	
Female	19
Male	21
Education level	
Less than high school	18
High school graduate	23
At least some college	19

DNA = Data have not been analyzed. DNC = Data are not collected. DSU = Data are statistically unreliable.

5-17. Increase the proportion of adults with diabetes who perform self-blood glucose monitoring at least once daily.

Target: 60 percent.

Baseline: 42 percent of adults aged 18 years and older with diabetes performed self-blood glucose monitoring at least once daily (mean of data from 39 States in 1998; age adjusted to the year 2000 standard population).

Target setting method: Better than the best.

Data source: Behavioral Risk Factor Surveillance System (BRFSS), CDC, NCCDPHP.

Adults Aged 18 Years and Older With Diabetes, 1998	Daily Self-Blood Glucose Monitoring Percent
TOTAL	42
Race and ethnicity	
American Indian or Alaska Native	53
Asian or Pacific Islander	30
Asian	DNC
Native Hawaiian and other Pacific Islander	DNC
Black or African American	40
White	43

Adults Aged 18 Years and Older With Diabetes, 1998	Daily Self-Blood Glucose Monitoring Percent
Hispanic or Latino	36
Not Hispanic or Latino	43
Black or African American	37
White	45
Gender	
Female	43
Male	41
Age	
25 to 44 years	43
45 to 64 years	41
65 to 74 years	44
75 years and older	38
Education level (aged 25 years and older)	
Less than high school	38
High school graduate	41
At least some college	44

DNA = Data have not been analyzed. DNC = Data are not collected. DSU = Data are statistically unreliable.

Note: Age adjusted to the year 2000 standard population.

Certain activities, ultimately chosen by the patients themselves, are essential in the proper preventive management of diabetes. Smoking cessation, use of aspirin, and self-blood glucose monitoring are representative of individual behaviors that should be periodically monitored because each behavior is associated with a decreased likelihood of microvascular and macrovascular complications.[109, 110, 111, 112, 113] Aspirin therapy in persons with diabetes mellitus—especially in the presence of other cardiovascular risk factors, such as high blood pressure, elevated blood lipids, etc.—has been demonstrated to reduce the likelihood of a future heart attack or stroke.[113]

Related Objectives From Other Focus Areas

1. Access to Quality Health Services

1-1.   Persons with health insurance

1-2.   Health insurance coverage for clinical preventive services

1-3.   Counseling about health behaviors

4. Chronic Kidney Disease

4-1.   End-stage renal disease

Data as of November 30, 1999

4-2. Cardiovascular disease deaths in persons with chronic kidney failure

4-7. Kidney failure due to diabetes

4-8. Medical therapy for persons with diabetes and proteinuria

9. Family Planning

9-3. Contraceptive use

9-11. Pregnancy prevention education

12. Heart Disease and Stroke

12-1. Coronary heart disease (CHD) deaths

12-2. Knowledge of symptoms of heart attack and importance of dialing 911

12-7. Stroke deaths

12-8. Knowledge of early warning symptoms of stroke

12-9. High blood pressure

12-10. High blood pressure control

12-11. Action to help control blood pressure

12-12. Blood pressure monitoring

12-13. Mean total cholesterol levels

12-14. High blood cholesterol levels

12-15. Blood cholesterol screening

12-16. LDL-cholesterol level in CHD patients

14. Immunization and Infectious Diseases

14-5. Invasive pneumococcal infections

14-29. Flu and pneumococcal vaccination of high-risk adults

16. Maternal, Infant, and Child Health

16-6. Prenatal care

16-10. Low birth weight and very low birth weight

16-19. Breastfeeding

19. Nutrition and Overweight

19-1. Healthy weight in adults

19-2. Obesity in adults

19-3. Overweight or obesity in children and adolescents

19-16. Worksite promotion of nutrition education and weight management

19-17. Nutrition counseling for medical conditions

22. Physical Activity and Fitness

22-1. No leisure-time physical activity

22-2. Moderate physical activity

22-3. Vigorous physical activity

22-6. Moderate physical activity in adolescents

22-7. Vigorous physical activity in adolescents

28. Vision and Hearing

28-1. Dilated eye exam

28-5. Impairment due to diabetic retinopathy

28-10. Vision rehabilitation services and devices

Terminology

(A listing of all abbreviations and acronyms used in this publication appears in Appendix K.)

Ascertainment: The processes and systems used to collect information and data about a particular health condition, for example, written surveys, telephone calls, electronic records, etc.

Co-morbidity: The presence of serious health conditions in addition to the one being examined, for example, high blood pressure in people with diabetes mellitus.

Diabetes mellitus (diabetes): A chronic disease due to either or both insulin deficiency and resistance to insulin action, and associated with hyperglycemia (elevated blood glucose levels). Over time, without proper preventive treatment, organ complications related to diabetes develop, including heart, nerve, foot, eye, and kidney damage; problems with pregnancy also occur. Diabetes is classified into four major categories:

Type 1 diabetes: (previously called insulin-dependent diabetes mellitus [IDDM] or juvenile-onset diabetes [JODM]) represents clinically about 5 percent of all persons with diagnosed diabetes. Its clinical onset is typically at ages under 30 years. Most often this type of diabetes represents an autoimmune destructive disease in beta (insulin-producing) cells of the pancreas in genetically susceptible individuals. Insulin therapy always is required to sustain life and maintain diabetes control.

Type 2 diabetes: (previously called non-insulin-dependent diabetes mellitus [NIDDM] or adult-onset diabetes [AODM]) is the most common form of diabetes in the United States and the world, especially in certain racial and ethnic groups and in elderly persons. In the United States, approximately 95 percent of all persons with diagnosed diabetes (10.5 million) and almost 100 percent of all persons with undiagnosed (5.5 million) diabetes probably have type 2 diabetes.

Gestational diabetes mellitus (GDM): refers to the development of hyperglycemia during pregnancy in an individual not previously known to have diabetes. Approximately 3 percent of all pregnancies are associated with GDM. GDM identifies health risks to the fetus and newborn and future diabetes in the mother and offspring.

Other types: include genetic abnormalities, pancreatic diseases, and medication use.

Complications: Microvascular—small vessel abnormalities in the eyes and kidneys; macrovascular—large vessel abnormalities in the heart, brain, and legs; and metabolic—abnormalities in nerves and during pregnancy.

Diabetic acidosis: A severe condition of diabetes. Due to a lack of insulin, the body breaks down fat tissue and converts the fat to very strong acids. The condition most often is associated with a very high blood sugar and happens most often in poorly controlled or newly diagnosed type 1 diabetes.

Direct costs: Costs associated with an illness that can be attributed to a medical service, procedure, medication, etc. Examples include payment for an x-ray; pharmaceutical drugs, for example, insulin; surgery; or a clinic visit.

Formal diabetes education: Self-management training that includes a process of initial individual patient assessment; instruction provided or supervised by a qualified health professional; evaluation of accumulation by the diabetic patient of appropriate knowledge, skills, and attitudes; and ongoing reassessment and training.

Indirect costs: Those costs associated with an illness that occur because an individual cannot work at his or her usual job due to premature death, sickness, or disability (for example, amputation).

Prevention: Primary: stopping or delaying onset of diabetes; secondary: early identification and stopping or delaying onset of complications; tertiary: stopping disability from disease and its complications.

Thrifty gene: An idea which suggests that in people likely to develop type 2 diabetes, a "thrifty gene" is present. It is speculated that thousands of years ago, people with "thrifty gene" could store food very efficiently and thus survive long periods of starvation. Now when starvation is unusual, this thrifty gene tends to make people overweight and thus prone to diabetes.

Urinary microalbumin measurement: A laboratory procedure to detect very small quantities of protein in the urine, indicating early kidney damage.

References

1. Clark, C. How should we respond to the worldwide diabetes epidemic? *Diabetes Care* 21:475-476, 1998.

2. Burke, J.; Williams, K.; Gaskill, S.; Hazuda, H.; Haffner, S.; and Stern, M. Rapid rise in the incidence of type 2 diabetes from 1987 to 1996: results from the San Antonio Heart Study. *Archives of Internal Medicine* 159:1450-1457, 1999.

3. King, H.; Aubert, R.; and Herman, H. Global burden of diabetes, 1995-2025: Prevalence, numerical estimates and projections. *Diabetes Care* 21:1414-1431, 1997.

4. Flegal, K.; Ezzati, T.; Harris, M.; Haynes, S.; Juarex, R.; Knowler, W.; Perez-Stable, E.; and Stern, M. Prevalence of diabetes in Mexican Americans, Cubans and Puerto Ricans from the Hispanic Health and Nutritional Examination Survey, 1982-1984. *Diabetes Care* 14:628-638, 1991.

5. American Diabetes Association. *Diabetes 1996: Vital Statistics.* Alexandria, VA: American Diabetes Association, 1996.

6. Centers for Disease Control and Prevention (CDC). *National Diabetes Fact Sheet: National Estimates and General Information on Diabetes in the United States.* Atlanta, GA: U.S. Department of Health and Human Services, Centers for Disease Control and Prevention, 1999.

7. Centers for Disease Control and Prevention. *Diabetes Surveillance, 1997.* Atlanta, GA: U.S. Department of Health and Human Services, 1997.

8. American Diabetes Association. Economic consequences of diabetes mellitus in the U.S. in 1997. *Diabetes Care* 21:296-306, 1998.

9. Hodgson, T., and Cohen, A. Medical care expenditures for diabetes, its chronic complications and its comorbidities. *Preventive Medicine* 29:173-186, 1999.

10. Vinicor, F. Is diabetes a public health disorder? *Diabetes Care* 17(S1):22-27, 1994.

11. Diabetes Control and Complications Trial Research Group. The effects of intensive treatment of diabetes on the development and progression of long-term complications in insulin-dependent diabetes mellitus. *New England Journal of Medicine* 329:977-986, 1993.

12. Gotto, A. Cholesterol management in theory and practice. *Circulation* 96:4424-4430, 1997.

13. American College of Physicians, American Diabetes Association, and Academy of Ophthalmology. Screening guidelines for diabetic retinopathy. *Annals of Internal Medicine* 116:683-685, 1992.

14. Levin, M. Diabetes and peripheral neuropathy. *Diabetes Care* 21:1, 1998.

15. Steffes, M. Diabetic nephropathy: Incidence, prevalence, and treatment. *Diabetes Care* 20:1059-1060, 1997.

16. Diabetes Control and Complications Trial Research Group. Lifetime benefits and costs of intensive therapy as practiced in the Diabetes Control and Complications Trial. *Journal of the American Medical Association* 276:1409-1415, 1996.

17. Eastman, R.; Javitt, J.; Herman, W.; Dasbach, J.; and Harris, M. Prevention strategies for non-insulin dependent diabetes mellitus: An economic perspective. In: LeRoith, D.; Taylor, S., and Olefsky, J. (eds.). *Diabetes Mellitus.* Philadelphia, PA: Lippincott-Raven Publishers, 1996, 621-630.

18. Vinicor, F. Challenges to the translation of the Diabetes Control and Complications Trial. *Diabetes Review* 2:371-383, 1994.

19. Brechner, R.; Cowie, C.; Howie, L.; Herman, W.; Will, J.; and Harris, M. Ophthalmic examination among adults with diagnosed diabetes mellitus. *Journal of the American Medical Association* 270:1714-1718, 1993.

20. Kraft, S.; Marrero, D.; Lazaridis, E.; Fineberg, N.; Qui, C.; and Clark, C. Primary care physicians' practice patterns and diabetic

retinopathy. *Archives of Family Medicine* 6:29-37, 1997.

21. CDC. Trends in the prevalence and incidence of self-reported diabetes mellitus—United States, 1980-1994. *Morbidity and Mortality Weekly Report* 46:1014-1018, 1997.

22. Kuckzmarski, R. Increasing prevalence of overweight among U.S. adults: National Health and Nutrition Examination Survey 1960-1994. *Journal of the American Medical Association* 272:205-211, 1994.

23. Christoffel, K., and Ariza, A. The epidemiology of overweight in children: Relevance for clinical care. *Pediatrics* 101:103-105, 1998.

24. Fagot-Campagna, A.; Rios Burrows, N.; and Williamson, D. The public health epidemiology of type 2 diabetes in children and adolescents: a case study of American Indian adolescents in the Southwestern United States. *Clinica Chimica Acta* 286:81-95, 1999.

25. Rosenbloom, A.; Joe, J.; Young, R.; and Winter, W. Emerging epidemic of type 2 diabetes in youth. *Diabetes Care* 22:345-354, 1999.

26. U.S. Department of Health and Human Services. *Physical Activity and Health: A Report of the Surgeon General*. Atlanta, GA: the Department, Centers for Disease Control and Prevention, National Center for Chronic Disease Prevention and Health Promotion, 1996.

27. Dietz, W. Critical periods in childhood for the development of obesity. *American Journal of Clinical Nutrition* 59:955-959, 1994.

28. Vita, A.; Terry, R.; Hubert, H.; and Fries, J. Aging, health risk and cumulative disability. *New England Journal of Medicine* 338:1035-1041, 1998.

29. Herman, W.; Thompson, T.; Visscher, W.; Aubert, R.; Engelgau, M.; Liburd, L.; Watson, D.; and Hartwell, T. Diabetes mellitus and its complications in an African American community: Project DIRECT. *Journal of the National Medical Association* 90:147-156, 1998.

30. Pollard, K., and O'Hare, W. American's racial and ethnic minorities. *Population Bulletin* 54:1-48, 1999.

31. Pearce, D.; Griffin, T.; Kelly, J.; and Mikkelsen, L. An overview of the population in Europe and North America. *Population Trends* 89:24-36, 1997.

32. Expert Committee on the Diagnosis and Classification of Diabetes Mellitus. Report of the expert committee on the diagnosis and classification of diabetes mellitus. *Diabetes Care* 20:1183-1197, 1997.

33. Eastman, R., and Vinicor, F. Science: Moving us in the right direction. *Diabetes Care* 20(7):1057-1058, 1997.

34. Bild, D., and Stevenson, J. Frequency of recording of diabetes on U.S. death certificates: Analysis of the 1986 National Mortality Follow Back Survey. *Journal of Clinical Epidemiology* 454:275-281, 1992.

35. Vinicor, F., and Will, J. The grim reaper and diabetes mellitus (DM): do we know how often (s)he strikes? *Diabetes* 48:A170, 1999.

36. Levatan, C.; Passaro, M.; Jablonski, K.; Kass, M.; and Ratner, R. Unrecognized diabetes among hospitalized patients. *Diabetes Care* 21:246-249, 1998.

37. Glasgow, R.; Wagner, E.; Kaplan, R.; Vinicor, F.; Smith, L.; and Norman, J. If diabetes is a public health problem, who not treat it as one? A population-based approach to chronic illness. *Annals of Behavioral Medicine* 21:159-170, 1999.

38. Pozzilli, P. Prevention of insulin-dependent diabetes. *Diabetes Metabolism Review* 12:27-136, 1996.

39. O'Rahilly, S. Diabetes in midlife: Planting genetic time bombs. *Nature Medicine* 3:1080-1081, 1997.

40. Neel, J. At mid-point in the molecular revolution. *Bioessays* 18:943-944, 1996.

41. Swinburn, B. The thrifty genotype hypothesis: how does it look after 30 years? *Diabetes Medicine* 13:695-699, 1996.

42. DPT I Study Group. The diabetes prevention trial: Type 1 diabetes (DPT1): Implementation of screening and staging of relatives. *Transplant Process* 27:3377, 1995.

43. National Institutes of Health. Non-insulin dependent diabetes primary prevention trial. *NIH Guide to Grants and Contracts* 22:1-20, 1993.

44. Sussman, L. Sociocultural concerns of diabetes mellitus. In: Haire-Joshua, D. (ed.). *Management of Diabetes Mellitus: Perspectives of Care Across the Life Span*, 2nd Edition. St. Louis, MO: Mosby, 1996, 473-512.

45. Hahn, R. *Sickness and Healing: An Anthropologic Perspective*. New Haven, CT: Yale University Press, 1995.

46. Resnicow, K.; Baranowski, T.; Ahluwalia, J.; and Braithwaite, R. Cultural sensitivity in public health: defined and demystified. *Ethnicity & Disease* 9(1):10-21, 1999.

47. Yen, I., and Syme, S. The social environment and health: a discussion of the

epidemiologic literature. *Annual Review of Public Health* 20:287-308, 1999.

48. Robinson, N.; Lloyd, C.; and Stevens, L. Social deprivation and mortality in adults with diabetes mellitus. *Diabetes Medicine* 15:205-212, 1998.

49. Williamson, D., and Fast, J. Poverty and medical treatment: When public policy compromises accessibility. *Canadian Journal of Public Health* 89:120-124, 1998.

50. Editorial. The medical cost of social deprivation—whose job is it anyways? *Diabetes Medicine* 15:187, 1998.

51. Marmot, M. Improvement of social environment to improve health. *Lancet* 351:57-60, 1998.

52. Erickson, P.; Wilson, R.; and Shannon, I. *Years of Healthy Life.* Hyattsville, MD: National Center for Health Statistics, 1995.

53. Murray, C., and Lopez, A. Alternative projections of mortality and disability by cause, 1990-2020: Global burden of disease study. *Lancet* 349:1498-1504, 1997.

54. Weathererall, D. Science and the quiet art: The role of medical research in health care. New York: W.W. Norton, 1995.

55. Detsky, A., and Naglie, I. A clinician's guide to cost-effectiveness analysis. *Annals of Internal Medicine* 113:147-154, 1990.

56. Wagner, E.; Austin, B.; and von Korff, M. Organizing care for patients with chronic illness. *Milbank Quarterly* 4:511-544, 1996.

57. Etzweiler, D. Chronic care: A need in search of a system. *Diabetes Educator* 23:569-573, 1997.

58. McDonald, R. The evolving care of diabetes: Models, managed care and public health. *Annals of Internal Medicine* 20:685-686, 1997.

59. Smith, D. Toward common ground. *Diabetes Care* 20:467-468, 1997.

60. Glasgow, R.; Strycker, L.; Hampson, S.; and Ruggiero, L. Personal-model beliefs and social-environmental barriers related to diabetes self-care management. *Diabetes Care* 20:556-561, 1997.

61. Golden, M. Incorporation of quality-of-life considerations into intensive diabetes management protocols in adolescents. *Diabetes Care* 21:885-886, 1998.

62. Weed, D. Towards a philosophy of public health. *Journal of Epidemiology and Community Health* 53:99-104, 1999.

63. Vinicor, F. The public health burden of diabetes and the reality of limits. *Diabetes Care* 21(S3):C15-18, 1998.

64. Glasgow, R., and Osteen, V. Evaluating diabetes education—are we measuring the most important outcomes? *Diabetes Care* 15:1423-1432, 1992.

65. Brown, S. Studies of educational interventions and outcomes in diabetic adults: A meta-analysis revisited. *Patient Education Counseling* 16:189-215, 1990.

66. Harris, M. NIDDM: Epidemiology and scope of the problem. *Diabetes Spectrum* 9:26-29, 1996.

67. Harris, M.; Eastman, R.; Cowie, C.; Flegal, K.; and Eberhardt, M. Comparison of diabetes diagnostic categories in the U.S. population according to 1997 American Diabetes Association and 1980-1985 World Health Organization Diagnostic Criteria. *Diabetes Care* 20:1859-1862, 1997.

68. Nathan, D.; Meigs, J.; and Singer, D. The epidemiology of cardiovascular disease in type 2 diabetes mellitus: How sweet it is...or is it? *Lancet* 350:4-9, 1997.

69. Harris, M.; Flegal, K.; Cowie, C.; Eberhardt, M.; Goldstein, D.; Little, R., Wiediabeteseyer, H.; and Byrd-Holt, D. Prevalence of diabetes, impaired fasting glucose, and impaired glucose tolerance in U.S. adults: The Third National Health and Nutrition Examination Survey, 1988-1994. *Diabetes Care* 21:518-524, 1998.

70. Hansson, L.; Zanchetti, A.; George-Carruthers, S.; Daholf, B.; Elmfeldt, D.; Julius, S.; Menard, J.; Heinz-Rahn, K.; Wedel, H.; and Westerling, S. Effects of intensive blood-pressure lowering and low-dose aspirin in patients with hypertension: principal results of the Hypertension Optimal Treatment (HOT) randomized trial. *Lancet* 351:1755-1762, 1998.

71. UKPDS Group. Tight blood pressure control and risk of macrovascular and microvascular complications in type 2 diabetes: UKPDS 38. *British Medical Journal* 317: 703-713, 1998.

72. Lyons, T., and Jenkins, A. Lipoprotein glycation and its metabolic consequences. *Curr Opin Lipidol* 8:174-180, 1997

73. Kannel, W. The worth of controlling plasma lipids. *American Journal of Cardiology* 81:1047-1049, 1998.

74. Malmberg, K. Diabetes Mellitus, Insulin-Glucose infusion in Acute Myocardial Infarction (DIGAMI) Study Group. Prospective randomized study of intensive insulin treatment on long term survival after acute myocardial

infarction in patients with diabetes mellitus. *British Medical Journal* 14:1512-1515, 1997.

75. Vinicor, F. Features of macrovascular disease of diabetes. In: Haire-Joshu (ed.). *Management of Diabetes Mellitus: Perspectives of Care Across the Life Span,* 2nd Edition. St. Louis, MO: Mosby, 1996, 281-308.

76. Depre, C.; Vanoverschelde, J.; and Taegtmeyer, H. Glucose for the heart. *Circulation* 99: 578-588, 1999.

77. Shotliff, K.; Kaushal, R.; Dove, D.; and Nussey, S. Withholding thrombolysis in patients with diabetes mellitus and acute myocardial infarction. *Diabetic Medicine* 15:1028-1030, 1998.

78. Ochi, J.; Melton, L.; Palumbo, P.; and Chu-Pin, C. A population based study of diabetes mortality. *Diabetes Care* 8:224-229, 1985.

79. Stern, M. Diabetes and cardiovascular disease: The "common soil" hypothesis. *Diabetes* 44:369-374, 1995.

80. Haffner, S. Management of dyslipidemia in adults with diabetes. *Diabetes Care* 21:160-178, 1998.

81. Califf, R., and Granger, C. Hypertension and diabetes and the Fosinopril vs. Amlodipine Cardiovascular Events Trial (FACET). *Diabetes Care* 21:655-657, 1998.

82. Lesser, K., and Carpenter, M. Metabolic changes associated with normal pregnancy and pregnancy associated with diabetes mellitus. *Seminars in Perinatalogy* 18:399-406, 1994.

83. Kitzmiller, J.; Buchanan, T.; Kjos, S.; Combs, C.; and Ratner, R. Preconception care of diabetes, congenital malformations, and spontaneous abortions.

Diabetes Care 514-541, 1996.

84. American Diabetes Association. Preconception care of women with diabetes. *Diabetes Care* 20(S1):40-43, 1997.

85. Jovanovic, L. American Diabetes Association's Fourth International Workshop-Conference on Gestational Diabetes Mellitus: summary and discussion. *Diabetes Care* 21(S2):131-137, 1998.

86. Gold, A.; Reilly, R.; Little, J.; and Walker, J. The effect of glycemic control in the pre-conception period and early pregnancy on birth weight in women with IDDM. *Diabetes Care* 21:535-538, 1998.

87. American Diabetes Association. Preconception care of women with diabetes. *Diabetes Care* 22(S1):56-59, 1999.

88. Reichard, P.; Nilsson, B.; and Rosenqvist, U. The effect of long-term intensified insulin treatment on the development of microvascular complications of diabetes mellitus. *New England Journal of Medicine* 329:304-309, 1993.

89. UKPDS Group. Intensive blood-glucose control with sulphonylureas or insulin compared with conventional treatment and risk of complications in patients with type 2 diabetes (UKPDS 33). *Lancet* 352:837-853, 1998.

90. Reichard, P.; Pihl, M.; Rosenqvist, U.; and Sule J. Complications in IDDM are caused by elevated blood glucose levels: the Stockhom Diabetes Intervention Study (SDIS) at 10-year follow-up. *Diabetologia* 39:1483-1488, 1996.

91. Frank, R. Etiologic mechanisms in diabetic retinopathy. In: Ryan, S.J. (ed.). *Retina, Volume II*. St.

Louis, MO: C.V. Mosby, 1989, 301-326.

92. Defronzo, R. Nephropathy. In: Lebovitz, H.; et al. *Therapy for Diabetes Mellitus and Related Disorders,* 2nd Edition. Alexandria, VA: American Diabetes Association, 1994, 257-269.

93. Clark, C., and Lee, D. Prevention and treatment of the complications of diabetes mellitus. *New England Journal of Medicine* 332:1210-1217, 1995.

94. Nathans, D. The pathophysiology of diabetic complications: How much does the glucose hypothesis explain? *Annals of Internal Medicine* 124:86-89, 1996.

95. Wylie-Rosett, J. Efficacy of diet and exercise in reducing body weight and conversion to overt diabetes. *Diabetes Care* 21:334-335, 1998.

96. Wheeler, M. A brave new world for nutrition and diabetes. *Diabetes Care* 20:109-110, 1997.

97. Clark, D. Physical activity efficacy and effectiveness among older adults and minorities. *Diabetes Care* 20:1176-1182, 1997.

98. Haffner, S. The Scandinavian Simvastatin Survival Study (4S) Subgroup Analysis of Diabetic Subjects: Implications for the prevention of coronary heart disease. *Diabetes Care* 20:469-471, 1997.

99. Braatvedt, G.; Drury, P.; and Cundy, T. Assessing glycemic control in diabetes: Relationships between fructosamine and HbA1C. *New Zealand Journal of Medicine* 110:459-462, 1997.

100. Dinneen, S., and Gertstein H. The association of microalbuminuria and mortality in non-insulin dependent diabetes mellitus. *Archives of Internal Medicine* 14:1413-1418, 1997.

101. Durrington, P. Prevention of macrovascular disease: absolute proof or absolute risk? *Diabetic Medicine* 12:561-562, 1995.

102. Eckel, R. Natural history of macrovascular disease and classic risk factors for athersclerosis: session summary. *Diabetes Care* 22(S3):21-24, 1999.

103. Peters, A.; Legerreta, A.; Ossorio, R.; and Davidson, M. Quality of outpatient care provided to diabetic patients: A health maintenance organization experience. *Diabetes Care* 19:601-606, 1996.

104. Weiner, J.; Parente, S.; Garnick, D.; Fowles, J.; and Lawthers, A. Variation in office-based quality: Claims-based profile of care provided to Medicare patients with diabetes. *Journal of the American Medical Association* 273:1503-1508, 1995.

105. Clark, C. Where do we go from here? *Annals of Internal Medicine* 124:184-186, 1995.

106. Loe, H. Periodontal disease: the sixth complication of diabetes mellitus. *Diabetes Care* 16(S1):329-334, 1993.

107. Papapanou, P. Periodontal diseases: epidemiology. *Annals of Periodontology* 1:1-36, 1996.

108. Taylor, G. Periodontal treatment and its effects on glycemic control. *Oral Surgery, Oral Medicine, Oral Pathology, Oral Radiology, and Endodontics* 87:311-316, 1999.

109. Miller, C.; Probait, C.; and Acterbaerg, C. Knowledge and misconceptions about food labels among women with NIDDM. *Diabetes Educator* 23:425-432, 1997.

110. Rubin R. and Peyrot, M. Psychosocial problems and interventions in diabetes. *Diabetes Care* 15:1640-1657, 1992.

111. CDC. Diabetes-specific preventive-care practices among adults in a managed care population—Colorado Behavioral Risk Factor Surveillance System. *Morbidity and Mortality Weekly Report* 46:1018-1023, 1997.

112. CDC. Preventive-care knowledge and practices among persons with diabetes mellitus—North Carolina Behavioral Risk Factor Surveillance System, 1994-1995. *MMWR* 46:1023-1026, 1997.

113. American Diabetes Association. Aspirin therapy in diabetes. *Diabetes Care* 22(S1):45-46, 1999.

6
Disability and Secondary Conditions

Co-Lead Agencies: Centers for Disease Control and Prevention;
National Institute on Disability and Rehabilitation
Research, U.S. Department of Education

Contents

Goal

Promote the health of people with disabilities, prevent secondary conditions, and eliminate disparities between people with and without disabilities in the U.S. population.

Overview

Because disability status has been traditionally equated with health status, the health and well-being of people with disabilities has been addressed primarily in a medical care, rehabilitation, and long-term care financing context. Four main issues emerge from this contextual approach: the belief that all people with disabilities automatically have poor health; the belief that preventing disabling conditions should be the major focus of public health; the lack of a crosscutting, standard definition of "disability" or "people with disabilities" for public health; and the absence of discussion about the role of the environment in the disabling process. Underemphasis of health promotion and disease prevention activities targeting people with disabilities has increased the occurrence of secondary conditions (medical, social, emotional, family, or community problems that a person with a primary disabling condition likely experiences).

Issues

Understanding these issues will help to clarify the health status of people with disabilities and address the environmental barriers that undermine their health, well-being, and participation in life activities. A broad array of health promotion activities are relevant to all people experiencing a disability, whether they are categorized by racial or ethnic group, gender, and primary conditions or diagnoses, such as major depression, cerebral palsy, diabetes, spinal cord injury, or fetal alcohol syndrome. The activities in themselves, however, do not address the prevention of specific primary conditions. The similarities among people with disabilities are as important as or more important than the differences among clinical diagnostic groups. Caregiver issues have also been considered, as well as environmental barriers. Environmental factors affect the health and well-being of people with disabilities in many ways. For example, weather can hamper wheelchair maneuvers, medical offices and equipment may not be accessible, and shelters or fitness centers may not be staffed or equipped for people with disabilities. Compliance with the Americans with Disabilities Act (ADA) would help overcome some of these barriers. A cross-cutting goal is to eliminate disparities with the nondisabled population.

The *International Classification of Functioning and Disability* (ICIDH-2), developed by the World Health Organization (WHO) with the input of several

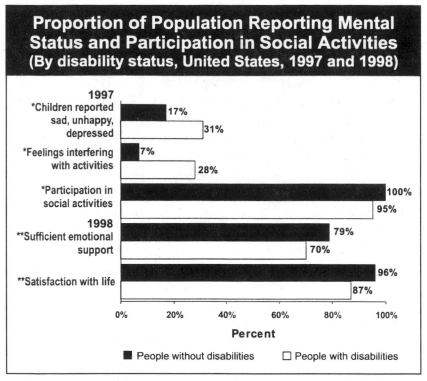

Proportion of Population Reporting Mental Status and Participation in Social Activities
(By disability status, United States, 1997 and 1998)

1997
- *Children reported sad, unhappy, depressed: 17% / 31%
- *Feelings interfering with activities: 7% / 28%
- *Participation in social activities: 100% / 95%

1998
- **Sufficient emotional support: 79% / 70%
- **Satisfaction with life: 96% / 87%

Percent

■ People without disabilities   □ People with disabilities

Sources: *1997 National Health Interview Survey (NHIS), CDC, NCHS;
**1998 Behavioral Risk Factor Surveillance System (BRFSS), CDC, NCEH.

nations—including the United States—provides uniform language and a framework for describing functioning, health, and disability status among all people.[1] This framework will clarify definitional issues and include environmental factors.

Trends

It is estimated that 54 million Americans, or nearly 20 percent of the population, currently live with disabilites.[2] Data for the period 1970 to 1994 suggest that the proportion is increasing.[3] The increase in disability among all age groups indicates a growing need for public health programs serving people with disabilities.

Among youth under age 18 years, disability rates increased from 1990 to 1994.[3] There was a 33 percent increase in activity limitations among girls, from 4.2 percent to 5.6 percent, and a 40 percent increase in activity limitations among boys, from 5.6 percent to 7.9 percent.

Among adults aged 18 to 44 years, there was a 16 percent increase in activity limitations, from 8.8 percent in 1990 to 10.3 percent in 1994.[3] This increase suggests that 3.1 million more people aged 18 to 44 years were limited in 1994 than in 1990.

The absolute number of adults aged 65 years and older with disabilities increased from 26.9 million in 1982 to 34.1 million in 1996. Because the total number of

Data as of November 30, 1999

adults aged 65 years and older increased even faster, the proportion of those with disabilities declined from 24.9 percent in 1982 to 21.3 percent in 1994.[3] However, the rise in numbers indicates a growing need for programs and services to serve this older population.

The direct medical and indirect annual costs associated with disability are more than $300 billion, or 4 percent of the gross domestic product.[4] This total cost includes $160 billion in medical care expenditures (1994 dollars) and lost productivity costs approaching $155 billion.

The health promotion and disease prevention needs of people with disabilities are not nullified because they are born with an impairing condition or have experienced a disease or injury that has long-term consequences.[5] People with disabilities have increased health concerns and susceptibility to secondary conditions. Having a long-term condition increases the need for health promotion that can be medical, physical, social, emotional, or societal.

People who have activity limitations report having had more days of pain, depression, anxiety, and sleeplessness and fewer days of vitality during the previous month than people not reporting activity limitations.[6] Increased emotional distress, however, does not arise directly from the person's limitations. The distress is likely to stem from encounters with environmental barriers that reduce the individual's ability to participate in life activities and that undermine physical and emotional health. In view of the increased rates of disability among youth, it is particularly important to target activities and services that address all aspects of health and well-being, including health promotion, preventing secondary conditions, and removing environmental barriers, as well as providing access to medical care. For an older person with a disability, it is important to target worsening coexisting conditions that may intensify and thus threaten general well-being. For example, declining vision combined with declining hearing can greatly impair mobility, nutrition, and fitness.[7]

Disparities

Disability can be viewed as a universal phenomenon everyone experiences at some time.[8] Disability can also be viewed as nonuniversal or confined to a minority of the population, in that people with disabilities may be less visible, undercounted, and underserved.[9] As a potentially underserved minority group, people with disabilities would be expected to experience disadvantages in health and well-being compared with the general population. People with disabilities may experience lack of access to health services and medical care and may be considered at increased risk for various conditions.

Few data systems identify people with disabilities as a subpopulation. Disparities need to be identified to plan appropriate public health programs. Despite the paucity of data, some disparities between people with and without disabilities have been noted. These disparities include excess weight, reduced physical activity, increased stress, and less frequent mammograms for women over age 55 with disabilities.[10]

Opportunities

Health promotion programs that focus on improving functioning across a spectrum of diagnoses and a range of age groups are effective in reducing secondary conditions and outpatient physician visits among people with disabilities.[11, 12, 13] For example, a focus on improving muscle tone, flexibility, and strength can accrue benefits for mobility-impaired people in wheelchairs and mobility-impaired people with arthritis.[14] For people with communication disabilities and disorders, interventions can improve access to health-enhancement programs. People with sight impairments can have access to readable job applications, food labels, and medications. People with hearing impairments can have access to televised or videotaped exercise programs that are captioned or signed by interpreters depicted within an inset of a video screen. Often, the most effective interventions may be environmental rather than medical.

Many health promotion interventions already in place for the population at large may be easily adapted to the needs of people with disabilities. New strategies can be influenced by results from studies that describe risk factors for secondary conditions or protective factors against additional impairments. For example, the number of cases of secondary osteoporosis among able-bodied women and their range of bone mineral density deficits can be estimated using existing Federal data sets. The degree to which women exercise and ingest calcium or estrogen supplements also can be estimated, leading to measurements of the influence of both risk and protective factors associated with osteoporosis in the able-bodied population. Because women with mobility impairments experience an elevated risk for secondary osteoporosis at earlier ages, their risk factors, including diminished bone mineral density, and their potential protective factors, including optimal calcium or estrogen supplementation and types of exercise, become critically important epidemiologic parameters.[15, 16] The results of investigations of secondary osteoporosis already influence health promotion strategies among able-bodied women. Similar investigations can augment the development of health promotion strategies among women with disabilities.

Current guidelines provide opportunity to design health promotion interventions targeting people with disabilities that accommodate ongoing evidence-based evaluation[17] and demonstrate cost-effectiveness.[18, 19] For example, clinical interventions that focus on appropriate and timely medical care can be equally accessible for people with and without disabilities. Mammography screening is recommended every 1 to 2 years, with or without annual clinical breast examination, for able-bodied women aged 50 to 69 years.[18] This recommendation can also be adapted for women with disabilities. Clinical providers, however, must first recognize the reasons women with disabilities often refrain from seeking mammography services, such as the lack of adaptive equipment on mammography screening machines or unfamiliarity with needs of people with disabilities expressed by clinicians. Counseling to prevent injuries among all adults also is recommended. For example, men and women with disabilities, especially those with skeletal insufficiencies or calcium deficits, are at increased risk for fractures. Adding bone mineral screening and fitness counseling during clinical encounters may be beneficial in preventing injuries. In these ways, evidence-based health promotion and disease prevention programs can be developed, implemented, and evaluated to target the health and injury disparities between people with and without disabilities.

Health promotion interventions for people with disabilities, in the community, clinical settings, or elsewhere, should include culturally and linguistically appropriate elements.

Interim Progress Toward Year 2000 Objectives

Healthy People 2000 did not have a chapter specifically establishing health objectives for people with disabilities. However, there were some objectives targeting people with disabilities, including leisure-time physical activity, use of community support programs by people with severe mental disorders, treatment for depression, activity limitations associated with chronic conditions and back conditions, and receipt of recommended clinical preventive services. A progress review held in January 1997 showed that none of these specific objectives relevant to people with disabilities had been met,[10] and parity with the nondisabled population will continue to be monitored.

People with disabilities reporting no leisure-time physical activity declined from the 1985 baseline of 35 percent to 29 percent in 1995, short of the target of 20 percent for 2000. In addition, the review noted several disparities. Forty percent of people with disabilities aged 20 years and older reported being overweight when compared with 35 percent of the general population and short of the goal of 25 percent; 49 percent of people aged 18 years and older with disabilities reported adverse health effects from stress compared with 34 percent of the general population; and clinical preventive services showed disparities for data on tetanus boosters (56 percent versus 59 percent for the general population), Pap tests (69 percent versus 77 percent of women aged 18 years and over in 1994), and breast exams and mammograms (50 percent versus 56 percent for women aged 50 years and over).

Note: Unless otherwise noted, data are from Centers for Disease Control and Prevention, National Center for Health Statistics, *Healthy People 2000 Review, 1998-99.*

Disability and Secondary Conditions

Goal: Promote the health of people with disabilities, prevent secondary conditions, and eliminate disparities between people with and without disabilities in the U.S. population.

Number	Objective
6-1	Standard definition of people with disabilities in data sets
6-2	Feelings and depression among children with disabilities
6-3	Feelings and depression interfering with activities among adults with disabilities
6-4	Social participation among adults with disabilities
6-5	Sufficient emotional support among adults with disabilities
6-6	Satisfaction with life among adults with disabilities
6-7	Congregate care of children and adults with disabilities
6-8	Employment parity
6-9	Children and youth with disabilities included in regular education programs
6-10	Accessibility of health and wellness programs
6-11	Assistive devices and technology
6-12	Environmental barriers affecting participation
6-13	Surveillance and health promotion programs

6-1. **Include in the core of all relevant Healthy People 2010 surveillance instruments a standardized set of questions that identify "people with disabilities."**

Target: 100 percent.

Baseline: No Healthy People 2010 surveillance instruments include a standard set of questions that identify people with disabilities.

Target setting method: Total coverage.

Data source: CDC, NCEH.

The call for statistics on people with disabilities is longstanding and increasing. Various Federal agencies have attempted to collect these data in several research areas.[20] Two separate issues exist regarding data collection: the use of different operational survey definitions of disability and not collecting information from people with disabilities during surveys. None of the federally funded surveys attempting data collection is using the same definition of disability. This lack of standardization has made it difficult to (1) identify and include all individuals with a disability, (2) measure the nature and extent of disability in the United States, (3) assess the impact of various disabilities on the person's ability to participate in society, (4) assess the extent of secondary conditions among people with disabilities, and (5) identify environmental barriers to participation and risk factors for poor health in this population. The issue of not including people with disabilities is reflected in the initial survey design. Some studies are not designed to target and analyze data on people with disabilities. People with disabilities could be included as a select population if, for example, the data collection method ensured appropriate access and outreach.

To remedy these gaps, a set of survey questions has been developed and tested to identify individuals with varying degrees of disability in terms of activity limitations.[21] This short set of questions may be placed in the core of all Healthy People surveillance instruments that collect demographic data to include and standardize information on people with disabilities. On the basis of standardization and inclusion in the Nation's disability data collection activities, the call for disability statistics may be satisfied. Once collected, these data will help government policymakers, consumers and advocates, researchers, and clinicians make better informed choices to promote the health status and well-being of people with disabilities.

6-2. Reduce the proportion of children and adolescents with disabilities who are reported to be sad, unhappy, or depressed.

Target: 17 percent.

Baseline: 31 percent of children and adolescents with disabilities were reported to be sad, unhappy, or depressed in 1997.

Target setting method: 45 percent improvement (parity with children and adolescents without disabilities in 1997).

Data source: National Health Interview Survey (NHIS), CDC, NCHS.

Children and Adolescents Under Age 18 Years, 1997	Reported To Be Sad, Unhappy, or Depressed	
	With Disabilities	Without Disabilities*
	Percent	
TOTAL	31	17
Race and ethnicity		
American Indian or Alaska Native	DSU	DSU
Asian or Pacific Islander	DSU	13
Asian	DSU	16
Native Hawaiian and other Pacific Islander	DSU	DSU
Black or African American	DSU	16
White	31	17
Hispanic or Latino	32	16
Not Hispanic or Latino	30	17
Black or African American	DSU	17
White	31	18
Gender		
Female	32	16
Male	30	18
Family income level		
Poor	DSU	20
Near poor	31	17
Middle/high income	27	17

Children and Adolescents Under Age 18 Years, 1997	Reported To Be Sad, Unhappy, or Depressed	
	With Disabilities	Without Disabilities*
	Percent	
Geographic location		
Urban	27	17
Rural	39	16

DNA = Data have not been analyzed. DNC = Data are not collected. DSU = Data are statistically unreliable.

*The total represents the target. Data for population groups by race, ethnicity, gender, socioeconomic status, and geographic location are displayed to further characterize the issue.

6-3. Reduce the proportion of adults with disabilities who report feelings such as sadness, unhappiness, or depression that prevent them from being active.

Target: 7 percent.

Baseline: 28 percent of adults aged 18 years and older with disabilities reported feelings that prevented them from being active, 1997 (age-adjusted to the year 2000 standard population).

Target setting method: 75 percent improvement (parity with adults without disabilities in 1997).

Data source: National Health Interview Survey (NHIS), CDC, NCHS.

Adults Aged 18 Years and Older, 1997	Reported Feelings That Prevent Activity	
	With Disabilities	Without Disabilities*
	Percent	
TOTAL	28	7
Race and ethnicity		
American Indian or Alaska Native	22	15
Asian or Pacific Islander	30	7
Asian	DSU	6
Native Hawaiian and other Pacific Islander	DSU	14
Black or African American	31	8
White	28	7

Adults Aged 18 Years and Older, 1997	Reported Feelings That Prevent Activity	
	With Disabilities	Without Disabilities*
	Percent	
Hispanic or Latino	40	9
Not Hispanic or Latino	27	7
Black or African American	31	8
White	27	6
Gender		
Female	30	8
Male	26	6
Family income level		
Poor	38	13
Near poor	30	10
Middle/high income	21	6
Education level (aged 25 years and older)		
Less than high school	34	10
High school graduate	29	7
At least some college	25	5
Geographical location		
Urban	29	7
Rural	26	6

DNA = Data have not been analyzed. DNC = Data are not collected. DSU = Data are statistically unreliable.

Note: Age adjusted to the year 2000 standard population.

*The total represents the target. Data for population groups by race, ethnicity, gender, socioeconomic status, and geographic location are displayed to further characterize the issue.

Children and adults with disabilities and their families face issues of coping, adapting, adjusting, and learning to live well with the disability—a dynamic, ongoing process. Good mental health, including refusal to internalize the social stigma of disability and developing a positive attitude and strong self-esteem, is a key ingredient to overcoming these issues.[22] Improving mental health status among people with disabilities and their families will help address psychological barriers and enhance their ability to participate fully in society.[23]

6-4. Increase the proportion of adults with disabilities who participate in social activities.

Target: 100 percent.

Baseline: 95.4 percent of adults aged 18 years and older with disabilities participated in social activities in 1997 (age adjusted to the year 2000 standard population).

Target setting method: Total participation (parity with adults without disabilities in 1997).

Data source: National Health Interview Survey (NHIS), CDC, NCHS.

Adults Aged 18 Years and Older, 1997	Participation In Social Activity	
	With Disabilities	Without Disabilities*
	Percent	
TOTAL	95.4	100.0
Race and ethnicity		
American Indian or Alaska Native	87.4	100.0
Asian or Pacific Islander	99.6	100.0
Asian	99.5	100.0
Native Hawaiian and other Pacific Islander	100.0	100.0
Black or African American	95.0	99.8
White	95.6	100.0
Hispanic or Latino	93.9	100.0
Not Hispanic or Latino	95.5	100.0
Black or African American	95.0	99.8
White	95.7	100.0
Gender		
Female	95.2	99.9
Male	95.7	100.0
Family income level		
Poor	93.1	99.9
Near poor	95.8	99.9
Middle/high income	96.5	100.0

| Adults Aged 18 Years and Older, 1997 | Participation In Social Activity | |
| | With Disabilities | Without Disabilities* |
	Percent	
Education level (aged 25 years and older)		
Less than high school	94.1	99.9
High school graduate	94.8	99.9
At least some college	96.0	100.0
Geographic location		
Urban	95.3	100.0
Rural	95.6	99.9

DNA = Data have not been analyzed. DNC = Data are not collected. DSU = Data are statistically unreliable.

Note: Age adjusted to the year 2000 standard population.

*The total represents the target. Data for population groups by race, ethnicity, gender, socioeconomic status, and geographic location are displayed to further characterize the issue.

People with disabilities report significantly lower levels of social participation compared with people without disabilities.[24] Participating in social activities routinely requires personal interaction with the environment, a component of life that is vital to the well-being of all humanity. ICIDH-2, the *International Classification of Functioning and Disability,* highlights the importance of participating in social activities as a measurable outcome of living well with a disability.[1] The ICIDH-2 framework indicates that the environment should be examined as a barrier to participation.

Social participation can include activities such as volunteering, shopping, going to the movies, or attending sporting events. Targeting increased participation in regular social activities such as traveling, socializing with friends and family, attending church or community events, and voting can result in improved functional status and well-being.

6-5. Increase the proportion of adults with disabilities reporting sufficient emotional support.

Target: 79 percent.

Baseline: 70 percent of adults aged 18 years and older with disabilities reported sufficient emotional support in 1998 (data from 10 States and the District of Columbia).

Target setting method: 13 percent improvement (parity with adults without disabilities in 1998).

Data source: Behavioral Risk Factor Surveillance System (BRFSS), CDC, NCCDPHP.

Adults Aged 18 Years and Older, 1998*	Reported Sufficient Emotional Support	
	With Disabilities	Without Disabilities
	Percent	
TOTAL	70	79
Race and ethnicity		
American Indian or Alaska Native	56	73
Asian or Pacific Islander	44	70
Asian	DSU	DSU
Native Hawaiian and other Pacific Islander	DSU	DSU
Black or African American	53	68
White	74	82
Hispanic or Latino	43	69
Not Hispanic or Latino	72	80
Black or African American	DNA	DNA
White	DNA	DNA
Gender		
Female	70	79
Male	70	79
Family income level		
Poor	60	69
Near poor	59	69
Middle/high income	76	81
Education level (aged 25 years and older)		
Less than high school	57	70
High school graduate	74	76
At least some college	72	80

DNA = Data have not been analyzed. DNC = Data are not collected. DSU = Data are statistically unreliable.

*Data are from 10 states and the District of Columbia.

The total represents the target. Data for population groups by race, ethnicity, gender, socioeconomic status, and geographic location are displayed to further characterize the issue.

Emotional support often is derived from a person's social supports. Two hypotheses suggest that social supports help a person cope with stress and that supportive relationships help reduce a person's level of disease in various life situations.[25] With the information gained by monitoring the personal perspective, the United States may better meet the needs of people with disabilities.

6-6. Increase the proportion of adults with disabilities reporting satisfaction with life.

Target: 96 percent.

Baseline: 87 percent of adults aged 18 years and older with disabilities reported satisfaction with life in 1998 (data from 10 States and the District of Columbia).

Target setting method: 10 percent improvement (parity with adults without disabilities in 1998).

Data source: Behavioral Risk Factor Surveillance System (BRFSS), CDC, NCCDPHP.

Adults Aged 18 Years and Older, 1998*	Reported Satisfaction With Life	
	With Disabilities	Without Disabilities
	Percent	
TOTAL	87	96
Race and ethnicity		
American Indian or Alaska Native	81	94
Asian or Pacific Islander	82	97
Asian	DSU	DSU
Native Hawaiian and other Pacific Islander	DSU	DSU
Black or African American	83	92
White	88	96
Hispanic or Latino	81	94
Not Hispanic or Latino	88	86
Black or African American	DNA	DNA
White	DNA	DNA
Gender		
Female	88	95
Male	87	96

Data as of November 30, 1999

Adults Aged 18 Years and Older, 1998*	Reported Satisfaction With Life	
	With Disabilities	Without Disabilities
	Percent	
Family income level		
Poor	78	90
Near poor	81	93
Middle/high income	93	96
Education level (aged 25 years and older)		
Less than high school	83	94
High school graduate	87	95
At least some college	88	95

DNA = Data have not been analyzed. DNC = Data are not collected. DSU = Data are statistically unreliable.

*Data are from 10 states and the District of Columbia.

The total represents the target. Data for population groups by race, ethnicity, gender, socioeconomic status, and geographic location are displayed to further characterize the issue.

Satisfaction with life is associated with the more general term quality of life, which is a personal evaluation of one's own position in numerous dimensions of life, including physical, emotional, social, spiritual, level of independence, and environmental support.[26] Monitoring the life satisfaction of people with disabilities, as well as that of the broader population, allows an opportunity to evaluate society's progress in accommodating the needs of people with disabilities.

6-7. **Reduce the number of people with disabilities in congregate care facilities, consistent with permanency planning principles.**

Objective	Reduction in People With Disabilities in Congregate Care Facilities	1997 Baseline	2010 Target
6-7a.	Adults aged 22 years and older in 16 or more bed congregate facilities	93,362	46,681
6-7b.	Persons aged 21 years and under in congregate care facilities	24,300	0

Target setting method: For adults, 50 percent improvement; for persons aged 21 years and under, total elimination.

Data source: Survey of Residential Facilities, University of Minnesota.

> **Data for population groups currently are not collected.**

Many people with activity limitations or cognitive impairments need ongoing and long-term assistance, yet some do not require institutional care.[27] From the 1970s through the 1990s, States began reducing the size of and closing State institutions that served people with mental retardation or developmental disabilities. This social, political, and economic movement resulted in dramatic growth in the total number of individuals served in community residential settings—from 5,000 in 1960 to 255,117 in 1996.[28, 29] This movement, coupled with increases in life expectancy and an expanding elderly population, resulted in the development of several community-based and in-home assistance programs, such as home-delivered meals, hospice, and homemaker and home-health services. The goal to increase home and community-based care will broaden health and lifestyle choices for people with disabilities and their families.[30]

Much of this expansion in community services is funded through Medicaid Home and Community-Based Services (HCBS) Waiver Program, a Federal-State partnership authorized in 1981 under Title XIX of the Social Security Act. Between 1990 and 1997, the HCBS Program demonstrated a 25.8 percent increase in benefits per person.[29] Despite this dramatic growth to support home and community-based care, in 1993, only 11 percent of long-term Medicaid expenditures and 5.3 percent of total Medicaid expenditures went toward community-based care.[31] The other sources of support for community-based long-term care are Medicare, Title III of the Older Americans Act, and the Social Services Block Grant.[31]

6-8. Eliminate disparities in employment rates between working-aged adults with and without disabilities.

Target: 82 percent.

Baseline: 52 percent of adults with disabilities aged 21 through 64 years were employed in 1994-95.

Target setting method: 58 percent improvement (parity with adults without disabilities in 1994-95).

Data source: Survey of Income and Program Participation (SIPP), U.S. Department of Commerce, Bureau of the Census.

Adults Aged 21 through 64 Years, 1994-95	Employment of People With Disabilities	Employment of People Without Disabilities*
	Percent	
TOTAL	52	82
Race and ethnicity		
American Indian or Alaska Native	41	77
Asian or Pacific Islander	48	78
Asian	DNC	DNC
Native Hawaiian and other Pacific Islander	DNC	DNC
Black or African American	37	77
White	DNA	DNA
Hispanic or Latino	45	76
Not Hispanic or Latino	DNA	DNA
Black or African American	DNA	DNA
White	57	84
Gender		
Female	46	75
Male	60	90
Education level		
Less than high school	34	69
High school graduate	54	81
At least some college	63	83

DNA = Data have not been analyzed. DNC = Data are not collected. DSU = Data are statistically unreliable.

*The total represents the target. Data for population groups by race, ethnicity, gender, and socioeconomic status are displayed to further characterize the issue.

The ability to work has implications for economic and social self-sufficiency, for full inclusion and integration into society, and for personal self-esteem. Work and disability are understood best within the context of a person's abilities and the role of accommodation, accessibility, and legal mandates. The Presidential Task Force on Employment of Adults with Disabilities emphasized the need for a coordinated and aggressive national policy to address the many components of work and disability.[32] Changes in economic policies and benefits underscore the need to continue to examine and address the structural, social, and psychological deterrents to work for some persons with disabilities.

In 1994-95, SIPP employment rates varied depending on degree of disability. For persons aged 21 through 64 years with no disability, the rate was 82.1 percent, whereas those with a nonsevere disability had a rate of 76.9 percent, and those with a severe disability had a rate of 26.1 percent. Analyses of rates by gender indicate similar patterns.[2] Moreover, employment patterns for persons with disabilities mirror general social patterns of employment rates for age, race, and ethnicity.[33] Education has a positive association with employment for all people, although the association is strongest for adolescents and adults with a "work disability."

6-9. Increase the proportion of children and youth with disabilities who spend at least 80 percent of their time in regular education programs.

Target: 60 percent.

Baseline: 45 percent of children and youth with disabilities aged 6 to 21 years spent at least 80 percent of their time in regular education programs in 1995-96 school year.

Target setting method: 33 percent improvement. (Better than the best will be used when data are available.)

Data source: Data Analysis System (DANS), U.S. Department of Education, Office of Special Education.

> **Data for population groups currently are not analyzed.**

This objective aims to improve the well-being of students with disabilities by encouraging academic and learning opportunities and nonacademic social and emotional experiences that can facilitate normal growth and development, postsecondary educational attainment, independent living skills, and economic participation as adults. Serving students with disabilities in regular nonspecial education classrooms is a concern that cuts across the goals of many Federal agencies. The current target of the Office of Special Education and Rehabilitative Services is that 60 percent of children and youth with disabilities aged 6 through

21 years will be reported by the States as being served in the regular education classroom at least 80 percent of the time. In support of the target, the 1997 Amendments to the Individuals with Disabilities Education Act states that "to the maximum extent appropriate, children and youth with disabilities, including children in public or private institutions or other care facilities, are educated with children who are not disabled."[34]

6-10. (Developmental) Increase the proportion of health and wellness and treatment programs and facilities that provide full access for people with disabilities.

Potential data source: National Independent Living Centers Network.

For people with disabilities to have the opportunity for healthy lives, both physically and emotionally, programs and facilities that offer wellness and treatment services must be fully accessible. Effective enforcement of the Americans with Disabilities Act can improve services for people with disabilities and help prevent secondary disabilities.

6-11. (Developmental) Reduce the proportion of people with disabilities who report not having the assistive devices and technology needed.

Potential data source: National Health Interview Survey (NHIS), CDC, NCHS.

In 1990, a one-time survey showed that 2.5 million people said they needed assistive technology that they did not have.[35] The inability to pay for such technology was the main reason given for the unmet need. Assistive technology can be critical in the lives of people with disabilities; thus, technology need, availability, and use must be studied.[36] Technology can aid the independence and self-sufficiency of people with disabilities and can enable people to work, attend school, and participate in community life. Without assistive technology, people with disabilities may become dependent and isolated.

6-12. (Developmental) Reduce the proportion of people with disabilities reporting environmental barriers to participation in home, school, work, or community activities.

Potential data source: Behavioral Risk Factor Surveillance System (BRFSS), CDC, NCCDPHP.

The focus on measuring the environmental impact on people with disabilities echoes the underlying theme of the disability rights movement and the ADA.[37] Both argue that the most important outcome for persons with disabilities—in fact, for all persons in the United States—is their full participation as active, involved, and productive members of society. Indeed, this participation is the implicit outcome for the overarching Healthy People themes to achieve a healthier life and eliminate disparities.

Full participation cannot be achieved without eliminating environmental barriers such as architectural barriers, organizational policies and practices, discrimination, and social attitudes. Thus, public health agencies need to measure not only the nature and extent of disability in the United States, but also the extent to which environmental factors enhance or impede that participation.

6-13. Increase the number of Tribes, States, and the District of Columbia that have public health surveillance and health promotion programs for people with disabilities and caregivers.

Target and baseline:

Objective	Increase in Public Health Surveillance and Health Promotion Programs for People With Disabilities and Caregivers	1999 Baseline	2010 Target
		Number	
6-13a.	States and the District of Columbia	14	51
6-13b.	Tribes	**Developmental**	

Target setting method: Total coverage.

Data sources: Tribal, State, and District of Columbia reports, Office on Disability and Health, CDC.

The needs of people with disabilities and caregivers should be addressed by public health activities. In a telephone survey, 23 percent of all U.S. households included at least one caregiver.[38] While not all people with disabilities are dependent on the services of a nonpaid (usually a family member) or paid caregiver, meeting the needs of those who benefit from personal assistance cannot be easily separated from the needs of people who provide assistance.[39] Whether caring for infants, children, or adults with disabilities or for the increasing number of people who become activity-limited as they grow older, the caregiver is an important health component.[40]

Related Objectives From Other Focus Areas

1. Access to Quality Health Services

1-1.   People with health insurance

1-4.   Source of ongoing care

1-5.   Usual primary care provider

Data as of November 30, 1999

1-6.   Difficulties or delays in obtaining health care

1-16.   Pressure ulcers among nursing home residents

2. Arthritis, Osteoporosis, and Chronic Back Conditions

2-3.   Personal care limitations

2-5.   Employment rates

2-8.   Arthritis education

2-11.   Activity limitations due to chronic back conditions

3. Cancer

3-9.   Sun exposure

3-11.   Pap tests

3-13.   Mammograms

5. Diabetes

5-1.   Diabetes education

5-2.   Prevent diabetes

5-3.   Reduce diabetes

5-4.   Diagnosis of diabetes

5-9.   Foot ulcers

5-10.   Lower extremity amputations

7. Educational and Community-Based Programs

7-1.   High school completion

7-3.   Health-risk behavior information for college and university students

7-6.   Participation in employer-sponsored health promotion activities

7-11   Culturally appropriate community health promotion programs

7-12.   Older adult participation in community health promotion activities

9. Family Planning

9-2.   Birth spacing

9-4.   Contraceptive failure

9-7.   Adolescent pregnancy

12. Heart Disease and Stroke

12-1.   Coronary heart disease (CHD) deaths

12-7.   Stroke deaths

12-9.   High blood pressure

12-10. High blood pressure control

12-11. Action to help control blood pressure

12-12. Blood pressure monitoring

12-13. Mean total cholesterol levels

12-14. High blood cholesterol levels

12-15. Blood cholesterol screening

Data as of November 30, 1999

14. Immunization and Infectious Diseases

14-22. Universally recommended vaccination among children aged 19 to 35 months

14-24. Fully immunized children aged 19 to 35 months

14-26. State/community population-based immunization registries for children

14-29. Flu and pneumococcal vaccination of high-risk adults

16. Maternal, Infant, and Child Health

16-1. Fetal and infant deaths

16-2. Child deaths

16-4. Maternal deaths

16-6. Prenatal care

16-9. Cesarean deliveries

16-10. Low birth weight and very low birth weight

16-11. Preterm birth

16-13. Infants put to sleep on their backs

16-16. Optimum folic acid

16-17. Prenatal substance exposure

16-19. Breastfeeding

16-21. Sepsis among infants with sickle cell disease

16-23. Service systems for children with special health care needs

17. Medical Product Safety

17-3. Provider review of medications taken by patients

17-4. Receipt of useful information from pharmacies

17-5. Receipt of counseling from prescribers and dispensers

18. Mental Health and Mental Disorders

18-4. Employment of persons with serious mental illness

18-5. Treatment for adults with mental disorders

19. Nutrition and Overweight

19-1. Healthy weight in adults

19-2. Obesity in adults

19-3. Overweight or obesity in children and adolescents

19-4. Growth retardation in children

19-5. Fruit intake

19-6. Vegetable intake

19-7. Grain product intake

19-8. Saturated fat intake

19-9. Total fat intake

19-10. Sodium intake

19-11. Calcium intake

19-12. Iron deficiency in young children and in females of childbearing age

19-13. Anemia in low-income pregnant females

19-17. Nutrition counseling for medical conditions

19-18. Food security

20. Occupational Safety and Health

20-1.   Work-related injury deaths

20-2.   Work-related injuries

20-3.   Overexertion or repetitive motion

20-4.   Pneumoconiosis deaths

20-6.   Work-related assault

21. Oral Health

21-1.   Dental caries experience

21-2.   Untreated dental decay

21-3.   No permanent tooth loss

21-4.   Complete tooth loss

21-5.   Periodontal disease

21-6.   Early detection of oral and pharyngeal cancer

21-8.   Dental sealants

21-10. Use of the oral health care system

21-13. Use of the oral health care system by residents of long-term care facilities

22. Physical Activity and Fitness

22-1.   No leisure-time physical activity

22-2.   Moderate physical activity

22-3.   Vigorous physical activity

22-4.   Muscular strength and endurance

22-5.   Flexibility

23. Public Health Infrastructure

23-4.   Data for all population groups

23-5.   Data for Leading Health Indicators, Health Status Indicators, and Priority Data
        Needs at Tribal, State, and local levels

24. Respiratory Diseases

24-1.   Deaths from asthma

24-5.   School or work days missed

24-6.   Patient education

26. Substance Abuse

26-5.   Alcohol-related emergency department visits

27. Tobacco Use

27-1.   Adult tobacco use

27-5.   Smoking cessation by adults

28. Vison and Hearing

28-10. Vision rehabilitation services and devices

28-12. Otitis media

28-13. Rehabilitation hearing impairment

Terminology

(A listing of all abbreviations and acronyms used in this publication appears in Appendix K.)

Assistive devices and technology: Under the Assistive Technology Act of 1998 (P.L.105-394), "any item, piece of equipment, or product system, whether acquired commercially, modified or customized, that is used to increase, maintain, or improve the functional capabilities of individuals with disabilities."

Activity limitations: Problems in a person's performance of everyday functions such as communication, self-care, mobility, learning, and behavior.

Congregate care facilities: An out-of-home facility that provides housing for people with disabilities in which rotating staff members provide care—16 or more beds when referring to adults and any number of beds when referring to children and youth under age 21 years. Congregate care excludes foster care, adoptive homes,

residential schools, correctional facilities, and nursing facilities.

Disability: The general term used to represent the interactions between individuals with a health condition and barriers in their environment.

Environmental factors: The policies, systems, social contexts, and physical barriers or facilitators that affect a person's participation in activities, including work, school, leisure, and community events.

Health promotion: Efforts to create healthy lifestyles and a healthy environment to prevent medical and other secondary conditions, such as teaching people how to address their health care needs and increasing opportunities to participate in usual life activities.

ICIDH-2: *International Classification of Functioning and Disability*, the World Health Organization's conceptual and coding framework for describing a person's functioning and disability associ-

ated with his or her health condition.

People with disabilities: People identified as having an activity limitation or who use assistance or who perceive themselves as having a disability.

Permanency planning: A planning process undertaken by public and private agencies on behalf of a child with developmental disabilities and their families with the explicit goal of securing a permanent living arrangement that enhances the child's growth and development.[41]

Secondary conditions: Medical, social, emotional, family, or community problems that a person with a primary disabling condition likely experiences.

References

1. World Health Organization. *International Classification of Functioning and Disability (ICIDH-2): Beta-1 Draft for Field Trials*. Geneva: the Organization, 1997, 11-21, 206-215, 221-225.

2. McNeil, J.M. Americans with Disabilities 1994-95. *Current Populations Report* P7061:3-6, August 1997.

3. National Institute on Disability and Rehabilitation Research. Trends in Disability Prevalence and Their Causes: Proceedings of the Fourth National Disability Statistics and Policy Forum, May 16, 1997, Washington, DC. San Francisco, CA: The Disability Statistics Rehabilitation Research and Training Center, 1998.

4. Institute of Medicine. *Enabling America: Assessing the Role of Rehabilitation Science and Engineering*. Washington, DC: National Academy Press, 1997.

5. U.S. Department of Health and Human Services (HHS). *Healthy People 2000, National Health Promotion and Disease Prevention Objectives*. Pub. No. (PHS)

91-50213, Washington, DC: the Department, 1991, 39-42.

6. Centers for Disease Control and Prevention. Health Related Quality of Life and Activity Limitation: Eight States, 1995. *Morbidity and Mortality Weekly Report* (47):134-140, 1998.

7. Manton, K.; Corder, L.; and Stallard, E. *Chronic Disability Trends in Elderly in United States Populations 1982-1994.* Washington, DC: National Academy of Sciences, 1997, 2593-2598.

8. Zola, I. Disability Statistics, What We Count and What It Tells Us, A Personal and Political Analysis. *Journal of Disability Policy Studies* 4(2):10-39, 1993.

9. Hahn, H. The Political Implications of Disability Definitions and Data. *Journal of Disability Policy Studies* 4(2):42-52, 1993.

10. Office of Disease Prevention and Health Promotion (ODPHP). *Healthy People 2000 Progress Review, People with Disabilities.* Washington, DC: The Department, ODPHP, January 1997, 1-3.

11. Seekins, T.; White, G.; Ravesloot, C.; Norris, K.; Szalda-Petree, A.; Lopez, J.C.; Golden, K.; and Young, Q. Developing and Evaluating Community-Based Health Promotion Programs for People with Disabilities. In: *Secondary Conditions Among People With Disabilities: Current Research and Trends.* Pacific Grove, CA: Brookes-Cole Publisher, in press.

12. Lorig, K. A Workplace Health Education Program that Reduces Outpatient Visits. *Medical Care* 9:1044-1054, 1995.

13. Research and Training Center on Rural Rehabilitation. Cost containment

Through Disability Prevention: Preliminary Results of a Health Promotion Workshop for People with Physical Disabilities. Missoula, MT: University of Montana, Research and Training Center on Rural Rehabilitation, 1996.

14. Lorig, K.; Lubeck, D.; Kraines, R.; Seleznick, M.; and Holman, H. Outcomes of Self-Help Education for Patients with Arthritis. *Arthritis Rheumatism* 28(6):680-685, 1985.

15. National Osteoporosis Foundation. Physician Guide to Prevention and Treatment of Osteoporosis. Washington, DC: National Osteoporosis Foundation, 1998.

16. Melnikova, N.; Hough, J.; and Lollar, D. "Osteoporosis Among Women with Physical Disabilities: Risk factors and protective factors." Presentation at the 126th Annual Meeting of the American Public Health Association, Disability Forum Special Interest Group, Washington, DC, November 17, 1998.

17. DHHS. *Healthy People in Healthy Communities: A Guide for Community Leaders.* Washington, DC: the Department, Public Health Service, Office of Public Health and Science, ODPHP, June 1998.

18. DHHS. *Preventive Services Task Force: Guide to Clinical Preventive Services, 2nd Edition.* Washington, DC, the Department of Health and Human Services, Office of Disease Prevention and Health Promotion, 1995, Chapter V.

19. DHHS. *Task Force on Community Preventive Services: Guide to Community Preventive Services.* Washington, DC: the Department, in press.

20. National Council on Disability. *Reorienting Disability Research: letter to the United States President.* Washington, DC: the Council, April 1998, 1-17.

21. Office on Disability and Health. *1999 Behavioral Risk Factor Surveillance System Disability Module.* Atlanta, GA: Center for Disease Control and Prevention, 1999.

22. Tuttle, D. Self Esteem and Adjusting with Blindness: The process of responding to life demands. Springfield, IL: Charles C. Thomas Publisher, 1984, 61, 145-158.

23. Sowers, J., and Powers, L. Enhancing the Participation and Independence of Students with Severe and Multiple Disabilities in Performing Community Activities. *Mental Retardation* 33(4):209-220, August 1995.

24. Kaye, S. Is the Status of People with Disabilities Improving? *Disability Status Abstract (21):3-4,* May 1998.

25. Novack, T., and Gage, R. Assessment of Family Functioning and Social Support. In: Cushman, L., Scherer, M. (eds.). *Psychological Assessment in Medical Rehabilitation.* Washington, DC: American Psychological Association, 1995, 286-297.

26. Patrick, D. Rethinking Prevention for People with Disabilities Part I: A Conceptual Model for Promoting Health. *American Journal of Health Promotion* 11(4):25-260, 1997.

27. Swain, P. Helping Disabled People: The users view. *British Medical Journal* 306(6883):990-992, April 1993.

28. Braddock, D.; Hemp, R.; Parish, S.; and Westrich, J. *The State of the States in Developmental Disabilities,* 5th Edition. Washington, DC:

Data as of November 30, 1999

Conference Edition 6-27

American Association on Mental Retardation, 1998, 9-10.

29. Prouty, R., and Lakin, K. Residential Services for Persons with Developmental Disabilities: Status and trends through 1997. Minneapolis. MN: University of Minnesota, Research Training Center on Community Living, Institute on Community Integration, 1998, xii, 47, 53, 58, 60, 65-67, 76, 88, 101.

30. Kane, R. Expanding the Home Care Concept: Blurring distinctions among home care, institutional care and other long-term care facilities. *Milbank Quarterly* 73(2):161-186, 1995.

31. Hardwick, S.; Pack, J.; Donohoe, E.; and Aleksa, K. *Across the States 1994: Profiles of Long-Term Care Systems*. Washington, DC: American Association of Retired Persons, Center on Elderly People Living Alone, Public Policy Institute, 1994, 5-7.

32. Presidential Task Force on Employment of Adults with Disabilities. *Recharting the Course: First Report.*

Washington, DC: Presidential Task Force on Employment of Adults with Disabilities, 1998.

33. Stoddard, S.; Jans, L.; Ripple, J.; and Kraus, L. *Chartbook on Work and Disabilities in the United States, 1998. An Info Use Report.* Washington, DC: U.S. National Institute on Disability and Rehabilitation, 1998.

34. U.S. Department of Education. *To Assure the Free Appropriate Public Education of all Children with Disabilities: Nineteenth Annual Report to Congress on the Implementation of the Individuals with Disabilities Education Act, Section 618.* Washington, DC: the Department, 1997.

35. Laplante, M.; Hendershot, G.; and Moss, A. Assistive Technology Devices and Home Accessibility Features: Prevalence, payment, need, and trends. In: *Advance Data from Vital and Health Statistics: No. 217.* Hyattsville, MD: National Center for Health Statistics, 1992.

36. National Council on Disability. *Study on Financ-*

ing of Assistive Technology Devices and Services for Individuals with Disabilities. Washington, DC: the Council, 1993.

37. National Council on Disability. *Equality of Opportunity: The Making of the Americans with Disabilities Act.* Washington, DC: the Council, July 1997, 9-21.

38. National Alliance for Caregiving and the American Association of Retired Persons. *Family Caregiving in the U.S.: Findings from a national survey.* Bethesda, MD: The American Association of Retired Persons, Washington, DC, June 1997, 8.

39. Singer, G., and Irvin L. *Support for Caregiving Families: Enabling positive adaptation to disability.* Baltimore, MD: Paul H. Brooks Publishing Company, 1989, 44.

40. Pugliese, J.M.; Ingram, T.O.; and Edwards, G. *Stability of Employment Status of Caregivers Who Have a Child with a Disability.* Birmingham, AL: United Cerebral Palsy of Greater Birmingham, Inc., February 1, 1998.

7

Educational and Community-Based Programs

Co-Lead Agencies: Centers for Disease Control and Prevention;
Health Resources and Services Administration

Contents

Goal

Increase the quality, availability, and effectiveness of educational and community-based programs designed to prevent disease and improve health and quality of life.

Overview

Educational and community-based programs have played an integral role in the attainment of Healthy People 2000 objectives and will continue to contribute to the improvement of health outcomes in the United States by the year 2010. These programs, developed to reach people outside traditional health care settings, are fundamental for health promotion and quality of life.

Issues and Trends

People working together can improve individual health and create healthier communities. Although more research is needed in community health improvement, clearly, the health of communities not only depends on the health of individuals, but also on whether the physical and social aspects of communities enable people to live healthy lives.[1] Health and quality of life rely on many community systems and factors, not simply on a well-functioning health and medical care system. Making changes within existing systems, such as the school system, can effectively and efficiently improve the health of a large segment of the community. Also, environmental and policy approaches, such as better street lighting and policies to fortify foods, tend to have a greater impact on the whole community than do individual-oriented approaches.[2] An increasing number of communities are using community health planning processes, such as Assessment Protocol for Excellence in Public Health (APEX/PH); Healthy Cities, Healthy Communities; and Planned Approach to Community Health (PATCH), to take ownership of their health and quality-of-life improvement process.[3]

Communities experiencing the most success in addressing health and quality-of-life issues have involved many components of their community: public health, health care, business, local governments, schools, civic organizations, voluntary health organizations, faith organizations, park and recreation departments, and other interested groups and private citizens. Communities that are eager to improve the health of specific at-risk groups have found that they are more likely to be successful if they work collaboratively within their community and if the social and physical environments also are conducive to supporting healthy changes.

Because many health problems relate to more than one behavioral risk factor, as well as to social and environmental factors, communities with effective programs also work to improve health by addressing the multiple determinants of a health problem. Among the more effective community health promotion programs are those that implement comprehensive intervention plans with multiple intervention strategies, such as educational, policy, and environmental, within various settings, such as the community, health care facilities, schools (including colleges and universities), and worksites.[1,4,5,6]

Educational strategies may include efforts to increase health awareness, communication, and skill building. Policy strategies are those laws, regulations, formal and informal rules, and understandings adopted on a collective basis to guide individual and collective behavior.[2,7,8,9] These include health-friendly policies designed to encourage healthful actions (for example, flex-time at worksites that enables employees to engage in physical activity, clinic hours that meet the needs of working people) and policies to discourage or limit unhealthy actions (for example, restrictions on the sale of tobacco products to minors as a way to discourage youth tobacco use). Environmental strategies are measures that alter or control the legal, social, economic, and physical environment.[10] They make the environment more supportive of health and well-being (for example, increasing the accessibility of low-fat foods in grocery stores to encourage a low-fat diet). Environmental measures also are used to discourage actions that are not supportive of health (for example, the removal of cigarette vending machines from public buildings to discourage smoking).

These educational, policy, and environmental strategies are effective when used in as many settings as appropriate.[5] Settings—schools, worksites, health care facilities, and the community—serve as channels to reach desired audiences as well as apply strategies in as wide a population as possible. These settings also provide major social structures for intervening at the policy level to facilitate healthful choices.[10]

The school setting. The importance of including health instruction in education curricula has been recognized since the early 1900s.[11] In 1997, the Institute of Medicine advised that students should receive the health-related education and services necessary for them to derive maximum benefit from their education and enable them to become healthy, productive adults.[12]

The school setting, ranging from preschool to university, is an important avenue to reach the entire population and specifically to educate children and youth. Schools have more influence on the lives of youth than any other social institution except the family, and provide a setting in which friendship networks develop, socialization occurs, and norms that govern behavior are developed and reinforced. Each school day about 48 million youth in the United States attend almost 110,000 elementary and secondary schools for about 6 hours of classroom time. More than 95 percent of all youth aged 5 to 17 years are enrolled in school.

Schools are second only to homes among the primary places that children spend their time and thus are one of the significant places where children may be exposed to potentially harmful environmental conditions. (See Focus Area 8. Environmental Health.) During high school, national dropout rates average 12 percent. Prior to high school, dropout is almost nonexistent.[13, 14, 15] Because healthy children learn better than children with health problems, schools also have an interest in addressing the health needs of students. Although schools alone cannot be expected to address the health and related social problems of youth, they can provide, through their climate and curriculum, a focal point for efforts to reduce health-risk behaviors and improve the health status of youth.[16]

In 1990, the key elements of school health education were identified: a documented, planned, and sequential program of health education for students in kindergarten through grade 12; a curriculum that addresses and integrates education about a range of categorical health problems and issues at developmentally appropriate ages; activities to help young persons develop the skills they will need to avoid risky behaviors; instruction provided for a prescribed amount of time at each grade level; management and coordination in each school by an education professional trained to implement the program; instruction from teachers who have been trained to teach the subject; involvement of parents, health professionals, and other concerned community members; and periodic evaluation, updating, and improvement.[17]

More than 12 million students currently are enrolled in the Nation's 3,600 colleges and universities.[18] Thus, colleges and universities are important settings for reducing health-risk behaviors among many young adults. Health clinics at the postsecondary level can help empower students to take responsibility for their own health through education, prevention, early detection, and treatment. In addition, colleges and universities can play an important role in eliminating racial and ethnic disparities and other inequalities in health outcomes by influencing how people think about these issues and providing a place where opinions and behaviors contributing to these factors can be addressed.

The worksite setting. The growing cost of health care combined with the increase of preventable acute and chronic illnesses drive the continuing need for comprehensive worksite health promotion programs. (See Focus Area 20. Occupational Safety and Health.) The worksite setting provides an opportunity to implement educational programs and policy and environmental actions that support health, which benefit managers, employees and, ultimately, the community as a whole. These programs have become an integral part of corporate plans to reduce health care costs, improve worker morale, decrease absenteeism, and improve behaviors associated with increased worker productivity.[19]
Although reductions in health risks have been achieved through many worksite

health promotion programs, risk reduction for hourly and part-time workers and companies with fewer than 50 employees has lagged.[20]

The health care setting. In health care facilities, including hospitals, medical and dental clinics, and offices, health care providers often see their patients at a "teachable moment." Individualized education and counseling by health care providers at these "moments" in these settings have been shown to have positive and clinically significant effects on behavior in persons with chronic and acute conditions.[10] (See Focus Area 1. Access to Quality Health Services.) Providers must be cognizant of these opportunities and prepared to provide appropriate patient education. Institutions that employ providers also must be cognizant and allow sufficient time and training for patient education and counseling to occur.

The health care setting is critical to the delivery of health education and health promotion because of the dramatic change it has undergone in the past 10 years. In 1989, 18 percent[21] of the population reported they were covered by some form of managed care; in 1996 that number had risen to 29 percent, an increase of 57 percent. As of June 1999, the number had jumped to 70 percent. As of January 1, 1997, more than 4.9 million Medicare beneficiaries were enrolled in managed care plans, accounting for 13 percent of the total Medicare program and representing a 108 percent increase in managed care enrollment since 1993. As of June 30, 1998, over 16 million or 54 percent of Medicaid beneficiaries were enrolled in managed care programs.

This growth in enrollment in managed care plans has been accompanied by the development of the Health Plan Employer Data and Information Set (HEDIS) and a set of common data indicators to examine MCO performance by the National Committee on Quality Assurance (NCQA). The latest version of HEDIS requires MCOs to report on more than 50 prevention-oriented indicators.[22] With the increasing marketing importance of HEDIS to MCOs, there will be greater demands for MCO health promotion programs to address HEDIS-related issues.[23] As a result, increased attention must be devoted to examining patient satisfaction with health promotion programs in health care organizations.

The community setting. While health promotion in schools, health care centers, and worksites provides targeted interventions for specific population groups, community-based programs can reach the entire population. Broad public concern and support are vital to the functioning of a healthy community and to ensure the conditions in which people can be healthy.[24] Included in the community setting are public facilities; local government and agencies; and social service, faith, and civic organizations that provide channels to reach people where they live, work, and play. Places of worship may be a particularly important setting for health promotion initiatives and they may effectively reach some underserved populations. These groups and organizations also can be strong advocates for educational, policy, and environmental changes throughout the community. Approaches to prevention must account for the character of the community and ensure community participation in the process.[3] Valuable and effective health benefits of community-based approaches have been demonstrated by community interventions that have served a variety of ethnic and socioeconomic population groups.[3, 7, 25] Community-based approaches in conjunction with targeted approaches in schools, health care, and worksites increase the likelihood for success to improve personal and community health.

A community health promotion program should include the following:

- Involved community participation with representation from at least three of the following community sectors: government, education, business, faith organizations, health care, media, voluntary agencies, and the public.

- Community assessment to determine community health problems, resources, and perceptions and priorities for action.

- Measurable objectives that address at least one of the following: health outcomes, risk factors, public awareness, or services and protection.

- Monitoring and evaluation processes to determine whether the objectives are reached.

- Comprehensive, multifaceted, culturally relevant interventions that have multiple targets for change—individuals (for example, racial and ethnic, age, and socioeconomic groups), organizations (for example, worksites, schools, faith), and environments (for example, local policies and regulations)—and multiple approaches to change, including education, community organization, and regulatory and environmental reforms.

Schools are natural settings for reaching children and youth while worksites reach the majority of adults. Efforts to reach older adults necessarily must involve the community at large. Senior centers have been established in most communities and provide a range of services, including health promotion programs for adults aged 60 years and older. Several types of housing arrangements designed specifically for older adults also can be found in many communities, including congregate housing, life care facilities, and retirement villages. These usually offer some mix of health care, recreational programs, and other types of activities and services. Health promotion strategies, policies, and educational approaches have been developed for aging populations.[26]

Disparities

The U.S. population is composed of many diverse groups. Evidence indicates a persistent disparity in the health status of racially and culturally diverse populations as compared with the overall health status of the U.S. population. Over the next decade, the composition of the Nation will become more racially and ethnically diverse, thereby increasing the need for effective prevention programs tailored to specific community needs. Poverty, lack of adequate access to quality health services, lack of culturally and linguistically competent health services, and lack of preventive health care also are underlying factors that must be addressed. (See Focus Area 1. Access to Quality Health Services.) Given these disparities, the need for appropriate interventions is clear.

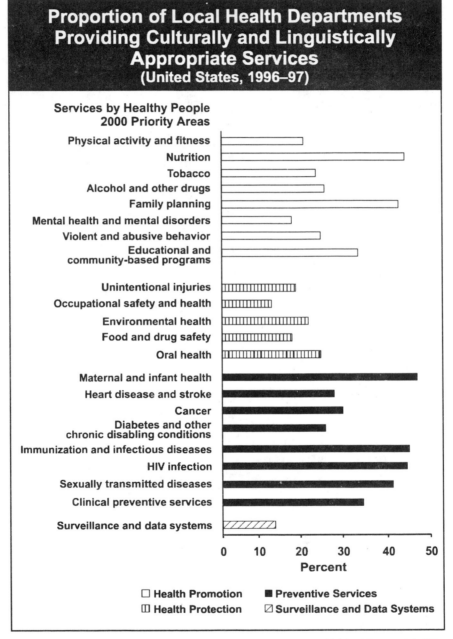

Proportion of Local Health Departments Providing Culturally and Linguistically Appropriate Services
(United States, 1996–97)

Source: CDC, NCHS. *Healthy People 2000 Review 1998–99*, pp. 96-97.

Effective prevention programs in diverse communities must be tailored to community needs and take into consideration factors concerning individuals, such as

Data as of November 30, 1999

disability status, sexual orientation, and gender appropriateness, which also play a significant role in determining health outcomes, behaviors, use patterns, and attitudes across age, racial, and ethnic groups. For example, women often are the health care decisionmakers and caregivers in their families and in their communities. When provided with enabling services and health promotion and prevention information, they can make better health choices and better navigate the health care system to get the information and services they and their families need.

Opportunities

Health promotion programs need to be sensitive to the diverse cultural norms and beliefs of the people for whom the programs are intended. This is a continuing challenge as the Nation's population becomes increasingly diverse. To ensure that interventions are culturally appropriate, linguistically competent, and appropriate for the needs of racial, ethnic, gender, sexual orientation, disability status, and age groups within the community, members of the populations served and their gatekeepers must be involved in the community assessment and planning process.

Community assessment helps to identify the cultural traditions and beliefs of the community and the education, literacy level, and language preferences necessary for the development of appropriate materials and programs. In addition, a community assessment can help identify levels of social capital and community capacity. Such assessments help identify the skills, resources, and abilities needed to manage health improvement programs in communities.[5, 27]

Educational and community-based programs must be supported by accurate, appropriate, and accessible information derived from a science base. Increasing evidence supports the efficacy and effectiveness of health education and health promotion in schools, worksites, health care facilities, and community-based programming.[8] Gaps in research include the dissemination and diffusion of effective programs, new technologies, policies, relationships between settings, and approaches to disadvantaged and special populations.[10]

Communities need to be involved as partners in conducting research ensuring that the content of the prevention efforts developed are tailored to meet the needs of the communities and populations being served. Communities also need to be involved as equal partners in research, to enhance the appropriateness and sustainability of science-based interventions and prevention programs and ensure that the lessons of research are transferred back to the community. Sustainability is necessary for successful research to be translated into programs of lasting benefit to communities.

The importance of social ecology on behavior and the successes of environmental and policy approaches to health promotion and disease prevention need further documentation. Techniques to evaluate community processes and community health improvement methods and models need to be refined and disseminated so that other communities can learn from and duplicate successful strategies. Issues of partnering and the role of collaborative efforts to increase the capacity of individuals and communities to achieve long-term outcomes and improvements in health status are not fully understood[27] and should be evaluated. Mechanisms need to be developed to share what is learned in an appropriate and timely manner with communities.

Interim Progress Toward Year 2000 Objectives

Progress toward the 14 educational and community-based program objectives in Healthy People 2000 is mixed. Improvements have been made in the number of worksites that offer health promotion activities and in the proportion of hospitals that offer patient education programs. New information from the National College Health Risk Behavior Survey shows that college students are receiving information on health topics such as human immunodeficiency virus (HIV) and sexually transmitted disease prevention. High school completion rates have not changed from their baseline. Participation in health promotion activities by hourly workers over age 18 exceeds the target. Baseline data are available for older adults participating in health promotion activities and on counties with programs for certain racial and ethnic populations.

Note: Unless otherwise noted, data are from Centers for Disease Control and Prevention, National Center for Health Statistics, *Healthy People 2000 Review, 1998-99.*

Educational and Community-Based Programs

Goal: Increase the quality, availability, and effectiveness of educational and community-based programs designed to prevent disease and improve health and quality of life.

Number **Objective**

School Setting

7-1   High school completion

7-2   School health education

7-3   Health-risk behavior information for college and university students

7-4   School nurse-to-student ratio

Worksite Setting

7-5   Worksite health promotion programs

7-6   Older adult participation in employer-sponsored health promotion activities

Health Care Setting

7-7   Patient and family education

7-8   Satisfaction with patient education

7-9   Health care organization sponsorship of community health promotion activities

Community Setting and Select Populations

7-10   Community health promotion programs

7-11   Culturally appropriate community health promotion programs

7-12   Older adult participation in community health promotion activities

School Setting

7-1.   Increase high school completion.

Target: 90 percent.

Baseline: 85 percent of persons aged 18 to 24 years had completed high school in 1998.

Target setting method: Consistent with National Education Goals Panel–Goals 2000.

Data sources: Current Population Survey, U.S. Department of Commerce, Bureau of the Census.

Persons Aged 18 to 24 Years, 1998 (unless noted)	Completed High School
	Percent
TOTAL	85
Race and ethnicity	
American Indian or Alaska Native	85
Asian or Pacific Islander	94
Asian	94
Native Hawaiian and other Pacific Islander	DSU
Black or African American	81
White	85
Hispanic or Latino	63
Not Hispanic or Latino	DNA
Black or African American	81
White	90
Gender	
Female	87
Male	83
Family income level	
Poor	DNA
Near poor	DNA
Middle/high income	DNA

Data as of November 30, 1999

Persons Aged 18 to 24 Years, 1998 (unless noted)	Completed High School Percent
Disability status	
Persons with disabilities	79 (1995)
Persons without disabilities	86 (1995)

DNA = Data have not been analyzed. DNC = Data are not collected. DSU = Data are statistically unreliable.

Dropping out of school is associated with delayed employment opportunities, poverty, and poor health. During adolescence, dropping out of school is associated with multiple social and health problems, including substance abuse, delinquency, intentional and unintentional injury, and unintended pregnancy. Some researchers suggest that the antecedents of drug and alcohol problems, school dropout, delinquency, and a host of other problems can be identified in the early elementary grades, long before the actual problems manifest themselves. These antecedents include low academic achievement and low attachment to school, adverse peer influence, inadequate family management and parental supervision, parental substance abuse, sensation-seeking behavior, and diminished personal capabilities. Children who perform poorly in school, are more than a year behind their modal grade, and are chronically truant are more likely to exhibit risk behaviors and experience serious problems in adolescence. Finally, risk of these outcomes is increased if children fail to form meaningful social bonds to positive adult and peer role models with whom they interact at school or in the community. If high school dropout rates are addressed as part of the Nation's health promotion and disease prevention agenda, unwarranted risks of problem behavior may be reduced and the health of young people improved.

The target of 90 percent set for this objective is consistent with the National Education Goal to increase the high school graduation rate to at least 90 percent. A National Education Objective under that goal is to eliminate the gap in high school graduation rates between racial and ethnic minority and nonminority students. In 1998, only 63 percent of Hispanic or Latino and 81 percent of African American youth aged 18 to 24 years had completed high school, compared to a completion rate of 90 percent for white, non-Hispanic youth.

7-2. Increase the proportion of middle, junior high, and senior high schools that provide comprehensive school health education to prevent health problems in the following areas: unintentional injury; violence; suicide; tobacco use and addiction; alcohol or other drug use; unintended pregnancy, HIV/AIDS, and STD infection; unhealthy dietary patterns; inadequate physical activity; and environmental health.

Objective	Schools Providing Comprehensive School Health Education in Priority Areas	1994 Baseline	2010 Target
		Percent	
7-2a.	Summary objective (all components)	28	70
	Specific objectives (components to prevent health problems in the following areas):		
7-2b.	Unintentional injury	66	90
7-2c.	Violence	58	80
7-2d.	Suicide	58	80
7-2e.	Tobacco use and addiction	86	95
7-2f.	Alcohol and other drug use	90	95
7-2g.	Unintended pregnancy, HIV/AIDS, and STD infection	65	90
7-2h.	Unhealthy dietary patterns	84	95
7-2i.	Inadequate physical activity	78	90
7-2j.	Environmental health	60	80

Target setting method: 150 percent improvement.

Data source: School Health Policies and Programs Study (SHPPS), CDC, NCCDPHP.

7-3. Increase the proportion of college and university students who receive information from their institution on each of the six priority health-risk behavior areas.

Target: 25 percent.

Baseline: 6 percent of undergraduate students received information from their college or university on all six topics in 1995: injuries (intentional and unintentional), tobacco use, alcohol and illicit drug use, sexual behaviors that cause unintended pregnancies and sexually transmitted diseases, dietary patterns that cause disease, and inadequate physical activity.

Target setting method: Better than the best.

Data source: National College Health Risk Behavior Survey, CDC, NCCDPHP.

Undergraduates, 1995	Received Information on Six Priority Health-Risk Behavior Areas
	Percent
TOTAL	6
Race and ethnicity	
American Indian or Alaska Native	DSU
Asian or Pacific Islander	DSU
Asian	DSU
Native Hawaiian and other Pacific Islander	DSU
Black or African American	8
White	6
Hispanic or Latino	5
Not Hispanic or Latino	DNA
Black or African American	8
White	6
Gender	
Female	6
Male	6
Family income level	
Poor	DNC
Near poor	DNC
Middle/high income	DNC
Disability status	
Persons with disabilities	DNC
Persons without disabilities	DNC
Select populations	
Sexual orientation	DNC

DNA = Data have not been analyzed. DNC = Data are not collected. DSU = Data are statistically unreliable.

The School Health Education Study[28] conducted during the 1960s identified 10 conceptual areas that have traditionally served as the basis of health education curricula. Subsequently, six categories of behaviors have been identified as responsible for more than 70 percent of illness, disability, and death among adolescents and young adults. These categories, which should be the primary focus of school health education, are injuries (unintentional and intentional); tobacco use; alcohol and illicit drug use; sexual behaviors that cause unintended pregnancies and sexually transmitted diseases; dietary patterns that cause disease; and inadequate physical activity.[29] While unintentional and intentional injuries are grouped together, the prevention program and policy implications for each are distinct, given the differences in the risk behaviors and related health outcomes. In addition to the 6 behavior categories, environmental health (recognized influence on personal and community health), mental and emotional health, personal health, and consumer health are among the 10 conceptual areas being added to track the influence of these factors over the next 10 years.

The overall goal of the National Health Education Standards[30] for youth is to achieve health literacy—the capacity to obtain, interpret, and understand basic health information and services and the competence to use such information and services to enhance health. Research has shown that for health education curricula to affect priority health-risk behaviors among adolescents, effective strategies, considerable instructional time, and well-prepared teachers are required. To attain this objective, States and school districts need to support effective health education with appropriate policies, teacher training, effective curricula, and regular progress assessment. In addition, the support of families, peers, and the community at large is critical to long-term behavior change among adolescents. Text about the contributions comprehensive school health education can make in achieving objectives can be found in the appropriate priority area chapters.

Health education and health promotion activities also can be conducted in postsecondary settings and reach the Nation's future leaders, teachers, corporate executives, health professionals, and public health personnel. Personal involvement in a health promotion program can educate future leaders about the importance of health and engender a commitment to prevention.

In 1995, 23 percent of undergraduate students reported receiving information on unintentional injuries, 38 percent on intentional injuries, 49 percent on alcohol and other drug use, 55 percent on unintended pregnancy, HIV/AIDS, and STD infection; 30 percent on unhealthy dietary patterns; and 36 percent on inadequate physical activity.[31]

7-4. **Increase the proportion of the Nation's elementary, middle, junior high, and senior high schools that have a nurse-to-student ratio of at least 1:750.**

Target and baseline:

Objective	Increase in Schools With Nurse-to-Student Ratio of at Least 1:750	1994 Baseline	2010 Target
		Percent	
7-4a.	All middle, junior high, and senior high schools	28	50
7-4b.	Senior high schools	26	50
7-4c.	Middle and junior high schools	32	50
7-4d.	Elementary schools	**Developmental**	

Target setting method: 79 percent improvement for all schools combined.

Data source: School Health Policies and Programs Study (SHPPS), CDC, NCCDPHP. Data for elementary schools are developmental.

The importance of providing health services to students in schools is widely accepted.[12] Such services began over 100 years ago to control communicable disease and reduce absenteeism. Over the years, school health services have evolved to keep pace with changes in the health care, social, and educational systems in the United States.[32] Current models of school health services reflect an understanding that children's physical and mental health are linked to their abilities to succeed academically and socially in the school environment.[15]

School nurses serve 48 million youth in the Nation's schools. School nurses assess student health and development, help families determine when medical services are needed, and serve as a professional link with physicians and community resources. Nurses manage care and provide services to support and sustain school attendance and academic achievement. An LPN or RN is an essential component of a healthy school. The ratio of 1 school nurse per 750 students should be improved if many students with special needs are enrolled.[33] For children with disabilities, the nurse is an essential resource. These children are dependent on daily medication, nursing procedures, or special diets for normal function.

Data as of November 30, 1999

Worksite Setting

7-5. Increase the proportion of worksites that offer a comprehensive employee health promotion program to their employees.

Objective	Increase in Worksites Offering a Comprehensive Employer-Sponsored Health Promotion Program	1999 Baseline	2010 Target
		Percent	
7-5a.	Worksites with fewer than 50 employees	Developmental	
7-5b.	Worksites with 50+ employees	95	100
7-5c.	Worksites with 50 to 99 employees	94	100
7-5d.	Worksites with 100 to 249 employees	96	100
7-5e.	Worksites with 250 to 749 employees	98	100
7-5f.	Worksites with 750+ employees	99	100

Target setting method: Better than the best.

Data source: 1999 National Worksite Health Promotion Survey, Association for Worksite Health Promotion (AWHP). Note: Data do not reflect complete definition for comprehensive worksite health promotion program; for explanation, see *Tracking Healthy People 2010*.

7-6. Increase the proportion of employees who participate in employer-sponsored health promotion activities.

Target: 50 percent.

Baseline: 28 percent of employees aged 18 years and older participated in employer-sponsored health promotion activities in 1994.

Target setting method: Better than the best.

Data source: National Health Interview Survey (NHIS), CDC, NCHS.

Employees Aged 18 Years and Older, 1994	Participation in Employer-Sponsored Health Promotion Activities
	Percent
TOTAL	28
Race and ethnicity	
American Indian or Alaska Native	DSU
Asian or Pacific Islander	DSU
Asian	DNC
Native Hawaiian and other Pacific Islander	DNC
Black or African American	33
White	28
Hispanic or Latino	16
Not Hispanic or Latino	30
Black or African American	33
White	30
Gender	
Female	34
Male	27
Family income level	
Poor	10
Near poor	22
Middle/high income	35
Education level (aged 25 years and older)	
Less than high school	17
High school graduate	33
At least some college	37
Disability status	
Persons with activity limitations	24
Persons without activity limitations	29
Select populations	
Employees at worksites with 50 plus employees	DNA
Employees at worksites with <50 employees	DNC

Data as of November 30, 1999

Employees Aged 18 Years and Older, 1994	Participation in Employer-Sponsored Health Promotion Activities Percent
Geographic	
Urban	27
Rural	30
Insurance status	DNA

DNA = Data have not been analyzed. DNC = Data are not collected. DSU = Data are statistically unreliable.

By 1999, 95 percent of employers with more than 50 employees reported that they offered at least one health promotion activity.[20] While the growth in worksite health promotion programming since 1985 has been remarkable, many programs lack comprehensive design or sufficient duration and therefore are potentially limited in their impact on employee health and well-being.[34] Participation rates in worksite health promotion programs are generally low. Most worksite statistics indicate that enrollees in worksite health promotion programs tend to be salaried employees whose general health is better than average. Employees working in administrative support, service, crafts, and trades often have greater health risks and higher rates of illness and injury than professional and administrative workers do. Contributing factors include differences in socioeconomic status, in the nature of the work, and in access to and extent of health insurance coverage, as well as exclusion of those workers from worksite health promotion programs. This exclusion may be an unintentional result of failing to market the program effectively to them.[35] Optimally, worksite health promotion efforts should be part of a comprehensive occupational health and safety program.

More than 80 percent of private-sector employees work in organizations of fewer than 50 people.[36] Over the next decade, strategies need to be developed to provide workers in these settings access to health promotion programs.[37, 38] Limited purchasing power can make the provision of health promotion services difficult for worksites with only a few employees. Employers can take advantage of community agency programs and services through outsourcing and by collaborating with other small worksites to purchase services, such as employee assistance programs and health insurance for preventive health services, to increase their purchasing power and benefits offered to their employees.[38]

Collaboration between trade and professional organizations is needed to identify new opportunities for worksite health promotion. Employee involvement to define and manage worksite health promotion activities can be especially valuable to address resource constraints among smaller employers while simultaneously enhancing program success.[38]

Data as of November 30, 1999

Health Care Setting

7-7. **(Developmental) Increase the proportion of health care organizations that provide patient and family education.**

Potential data source: Joint Commission on Accreditation of Healthcare Organizations (JCAHO) Survey.

7-8. **(Developmental) Increase the proportion of patients who report that they are satisfied with the patient education they receive from their health care organization.**

Potential data source: Press Ganey.

7-9. **(Developmental) Increase the proportion of hospitals and managed care organizations that provide community disease prevention and health promotion activities that address the priority health needs identified by their community.**

Potential data source: Annual Survey, American Hospital Association.

The concept of increased consumer protection in the health care industry, particularly in the form of a Consumers' Bill of Rights and Responsibilities, is gaining support. These protections include consumers' rights to accurate, easily understood information related to choice of a health plan, its benefits, availability of specialty care, and confidentiality of medical records. However, the right to comprehensive patient and family education is missing from this list. Two distinctive characteristics of health care settings underscore their importance to promote patient and family education: improved health is a primary objective; and health care providers generally are considered credible sources of information.[10] The interaction between these two factors helps create an environment conducive to effective patient and family education programs and activities. The positive and clinically significant effects of patient education and counseling of persons with chronic and acute conditions are well-documented; however, the amount and types of health promotion and disease prevention activities offered by MCOs to their participating employers vary widely.[23]

On the national level, about 70 percent of employees are covered by some form of managed care. The growth of MCOs is expected to increase. For example, as of January 1, 1997, more than 4.9 million Medicare beneficiaries were enrolled in managed care plans, accounting for 13 percent of the total Medicare program and representing a 108 percent increase in managed care enrollment since 1993.[39] Another important factor is the emerging role of the National Committee on Quality Assurance (NCQA) and its development of the Health Plan Employer Data and

Information Set (HEDIS) and set of common data indicators for examining performance of MCOs. The latest version requires MCOs to report on more than 50 prevention-oriented indicators, largely secondary and tertiary prevention-related issues.[22] With the increasing marketing importance of HEDIS to MCOs, there will be greater demands for health promotion to address HEDIS-related issues, potentially leaving critical programming gaps.[23] As a result, increased public attention must be devoted to examining patient satisfaction in health care organizations.

Community health promotion services provided by hospitals and MCOs are growing. This is illustrated by the expansion of Federal and State managed care reform legislation directed at the creation of a core set of prevention activities across MCOs.[23] Despite the different motivations and strategic objectives of public health and managed care, they share a mutual interest to improve the health of communities and specific populations within communities. Collaboration between managed care plans and public health agencies is a logical consequence of the health promotion objectives shared by these organizations.[40] Additionally, a number of Federal public health agencies are developing collaborative relationships with the managed care community on issues of clinical preventive services and prevention surveillance and research.[41]

Community Setting and Select Populations

7-10. **(Developmental) Increase the proportion of Tribal and local health service areas or jurisdictions that have established a community health promotion program that addresses multiple Healthy People 2010 focus areas.**

Potential data sources: Special Survey, Association of State and Territorial Directors of Health Promotion and Public Health Education (ASTDHPPHE) Survey; IHS.

This objective reflects the need for comprehensive and multifaceted health promotion and community health improvement activities at the State and local levels. A 1996 review of the literature on 135 urban health promotion programs conducted between 1980 and 1995 found that only 41 percent identified a specific model for program planning and implementation.[42] In addition, community members constituted the smallest percentage of those involved in the local effort, and very little tailoring to the population and population groups served was noted. These efforts also had a strong focus on the individual rather than the population.[42]

This objective includes activities conducted through local health departments as well as those conducted by other community-based organizations, particularly in those communities not served by a local health department. Activities such as Assessment Protocol for Excellence in Public Health (APEX/PH); Healthy Cities, Healthy Communities; and Planned Approach to Community Health (PATCH) recognize the need for community involvement and mobilization as basic methods for planning, implementing, and evaluating educational and community-based programs. Public health departments, community health centers, faith communities, civic organizations, voluntary health organizations, businesses, worksites, schools, universities, Area Health Education Centers (AHECs), and healthy city or community groups are a few of the organizations that plan and deliver such programs in the United States.

Identifying the use of established health promotion planning and identification models provides more information on strategically planned and implemented programs as opposed to single-method or noncomprehensive approaches considered less productive.

7-11. Increase the proportion of local health departments that have established culturally appropriate and linguistically competent community health promotion and disease prevention programs for racial and ethnic minority populations.

Target and baseline:

Objective	Local Health Department Community Health Promotion and Disease Prevention Programs That Are Culturally and Linguistically Competent	1996–97 Baseline	2010 Target
		Percent	
7-11a.	Access to quality health services	Developmental	
	Clinical preventive services	35	*
7-11b.	Arthritis, osteoporosis, and chronic back conditions	Developmental	
7-11c.	Cancer	30	50
	Diabetes and chronic disabling conditions	26	*
7-11d.	Chronic kidney disease	Developmental	
7-11e.	Diabetes	Developmental	
7-11f.	Disability and secondary conditions	Developmental	
7-11g.	Educational and community-based programs	33	50
7-11h.	Environmental health	22	50
7-11i.	Family planning	42	50
	Food and drug safety	18	*
7-11j.	Food safety	Developmental	
7-11k.	Medical product safety	Developmental	
7-11l.	Health communication	Developmental	
7-11m.	Heart disease and stroke	28	50

Objective	Local Health Department Community Health Promotion and Disease Prevention Programs That Are Culturally and Linguistically Competent	1996–97 Baseline	2010 Target
		Percent	
7-11n.	HIV	45	50
7-11o.	Immunizations and infectious diseases	48	50
7-11p.	Injury and violence prevention	**Developmental**	
	Unintentional injuries	19	*
	Violent and abusive behavior	25	*
7-11q.	Maternal, infant (and child) health	47	50
7-11r.	Mental health (and mental disorders)	18	50
7-11s.	Nutrition and overweight	44	50
7-11t.	Occupational safety and health	13	50
7-11u.	Oral health	25	50
7-11v.	Physical activity and fitness	21	50
7-11w.	Public health infrastructure	**Developmental**	
	Surveillance and data systems	14	*
7-11x.	Respiratory diseases	**Developmental**	
7-11y.	Sexually transmitted diseases	41	50
7-11z.	Substance abuse (alcohol and other drugs)	26	50
7-11aa.	Tobacco use	24	50
7-11bb.	Vision and hearing	**Developmental**	

*These are Healthy People 2000 priority areas that are not applicable to Healthy People 2010.

Target setting method: Percentage improvement varies by program.

Data source: National Profile of Local Health Departments, National Association of City and County Health Organization (NACCHO).

Over the next decade, the Nation's population will become even more diverse. Mainstream health education activities often fail to reach select populations.[43] This may contribute to select and disadvantaged communities lagging behind the overall U.S. population on virtually all health status indicators. In 1991, an estimated 78,643 excess deaths occurred among African Americans and an additional 4,485 among Hispanics or Latinos.[44] Approximately 75 percent of these excess deaths occurred in seven categories, all of which had contributing factors that can be controlled or prevented: cancer, cardiovascular disease, cirrhosis, diabetes, HIV or AIDS, homicide, and unintentional injuries. Special efforts are needed to develop and disseminate culturally and linguistically appropriate health information to overcome the cultural differences and meet the special language needs of these population groups.

Data as of November 30, 1999

7-12. **Increase the proportion of older adults who have partici-pated during the preceding year in at least one organized health promotion activity.**

Target: 90 percent.

Baseline: 12 percent of adults aged 65 years and older participated during the preceding year in at least one organized health promotion activity in 1998 (preliminary data; age adjusted to the year 2000 standard population).

Target setting method: Better than the best.

Data source: National Health Interview Survey (NHIS), CDC, NCHS.

Adults Aged 65 Years and Older, 1995*	One or More Health Promotion Activity Past Year Percent
TOTAL	12
Race and ethnicity	
American Indian or Alaska Native	DSU
Asian or Pacific Islander	DSU
Asian	DNC
Native Hawaiian and other Pacific Islander	DNC
Black or African American	DSU
White	12
Hispanic or Latino	DSU
Not Hispanic or Latino	12
Black or African American	DSU
White	12
Gender	
Female	14
Male	9
Family income level	
Poor	DSU
Near poor	9
Middle/high income	15

Data as of November 30, 1999

Adults Aged 65 Years and Older, 1995*	One or More Health Promotion Activity Past Year
	Percent
Education level	
Less than high school	7
High school	11
At least some college	19
Disability status	
Persons with activity limitations	10
Persons without activity limitations	12

DNA = Data have not been analyzed. DNC = Data are not collected. DSU = Data are statistically unreliable.

Note: Age adjusted to the year 2000 standard population.

*New data for population groups will be added when available.

Adults aged 65 years or older numbered 33.9 million in 1996. They represented 12.8 percent of the U.S. population, about one in every eight Americans. More than any other age group, older adults are seeking health information and are willing to make changes to maintain their health and independence. Prevention efforts should focus on modifiable risk behaviors and early diagnosis and match the leading problems by age (for example, aged 60 or 65 to 74 years, 75 to 84 years, and 85 years and older) and functional status. Programs should address these health issues through multiple strategies, including education, counseling, screening/chemoprophylaxis, environmental enhancements, and protective services. As with any successful program, those for older adults need to be tailored to the audience.

Related Objectives From Other Focus Areas

1. Access to Quality Health Services

1-3.   Counseling about health behaviors

Arthritis, Osteoporosis, and Chronic Back Conditions

2-8.   Arthritis education

3. Cancer

3-10.   Provider counseling about preventive measures

5. Diabetes

5-1.   Diabetes education

6. Disability and Secondary Conditions

6-9.   Children and youth with disabilities included in regular education programs

6-13.   Surveillance and health promotion programs

9. Family Planning

9-11.   Pregnancy prevention education

11. Health Communication

11-6.   Satisfaction with providers' communication skills

16. Maternal, Infant, and Child Health

16-7.   Childbirth classes

17. Medical Product Safety

17-3.   Provider review of medications taken by patients

17-5.   Receipt of useful counseling from prescribers and dispensers

18. Mental Health and Mental Disorders

18-12.   State tracking of consumer satisfaction

19. Nutrition and Overweight

19-16.   Worksite promotion of nutrition education and weight management

19-17.   Nutrition counseling for medical conditions

20. Occupational Safety and Health

20-9.   Worksite stress reduction programs

22. Physical Activity and Fitness

22-8.   Physical education requirement in schools

22-9.   Daily physical education in schools

22-10.   Physical activity in physical education class

22-12.   School physical activity facilities

22-13.   Worksite physical activity and fitness

24. Respiratory Diseases

24-6.   Patient education

26. Substance Abuse

26-23.   Community partnerships and coalitions

27. Tobacco Use

27-11.   Smoke-free and tobacco-free schools

27-12.   Worksite smoking policies

Terminology

(A listing of all abbreviations and acronyms used in this publication appears in Appendix K.)

Community: A specific group of people, often living in a defined geographical area, who share a common culture, values, and norms and who are arranged in a social structure according to relationships the community has developed over a period of time.[45]

Community-based program: A planned, coordinated, ongoing effort operated by a community that characteristically includes multiple interventions intended to improve the health status of members of the community.

Community capacity: The characteristics of communities that affect their ability to identify, mobilize, and address social and public health problems.[46, 47]

Community health planning or community health improvement process: Helps a community mobilize to collect and use local data; set health priorities; and design, implement, and evaluate comprehensive programs that address community health and quality of life issues.[1]

Community health promotion program: Includes all of the following: (1) involved community participation with representatives from at least three of the following community sectors: government, education, business, faith organizations, health care, media, voluntary agencies, and the public; (2) community assessment, guided by a community assessment and planning model, to determine community health problems, resources, perceptions, and priorities for action; (3) targeted and measurable objectives to address any of the following: health outcomes, risk factors, public awareness, services, and protection; (4) comprehensive, multifaceted, culturally relevant interventions that have multiple targets for change; and (5) monitoring and evaluation processes to determine whether the objectives are reached.

Comprehensive worksite health promotion programs: Refers to programs that contain the following elements: (1) health education that focuses on skill development and lifestyle behavior change in addition to information dissemination and awareness building, preferably tailored to employees' interests and needs; (2) supportive social and physical work environments, including established norms for healthy behavior and policies that promote health and reduce the risk of disease, such as worksite smoking policies, healthy nutrition alternatives in the cafeteria and vending services, and opportunities for obtaining regular physical activity; (3) integration of the worksite program into the organization's administrative structure; (4) related programs, such as employee assistance programs; and (5) screening programs, preferably linked to medical care service delivery to ensure followup and appropriate treatment as necessary and to encourage adherence. Optimally, these efforts should be part of a comprehensive occupational health and safety program.[37, 48]

Culturally appropriate: Refers to an unbiased attitude and organizational policy that values cultural diversity in the population served. Reflects an understanding of diverse attitudes, beliefs, behaviors, practices, and communication patterns that could be attributed to race, ethnicity, religion, socioeconomic status, historical and social context, physical or mental ability, age, gender, sexual orientation, or generational and acculturation status. Includes an awareness that cultural differences may affect health and the effectiveness of health care delivery. Knowledge of disease prevalence in specific cultural populations, whether defined by race, ethnicity, socioeconomic status, physical or mental ability, gender, sexual orientation, age, disability, or habits.

Excess deaths: The statistically significant difference between the number of deaths expected and the number that actually occurred.

Health: A state of physical, mental, and social well-being and not merely the absence of disease and infirmity.

Health care organizations: Included are hospitals, managed care organizations, home health organizations, long-term care facilities, and community-based health care providers.

Health education: Any planned combination of learning experiences designed to predispose, enable, and reinforce voluntary behavior conducive to health in individuals, groups, or communities.[49]

Health literacy: The capacity to obtain, interpret, and understand basic health information and services and the competence to use such information and services to enhance health.[49]

Health promotion: Any planned combination of educational, political, regulatory, and organizational supports for actions and conditions of living conducive to the health of individuals, groups, or communities.[49]

Health promotion activity: Broadly defined to include any activity that is part of a planned health promotion program, such as implementing a policy to create a smoke-free workplace, developing walking trails in communities, or teaching the skills needed to prepare healthy meals and snacks.

Healthy community: A community that is continuously creating and improving those physical and social environments and expanding those community resources that enable people to mutually support each other in performing all the functions of life and in developing to their maximum potential.[50]

Healthy public policy: Characterized by an explicit concern for health and equity in all areas of policy and by an accountability for health impact. The main aim of healthy public policy is to create a supportive environment to enable people to lead healthy lives by making healthy choices possible and easier for citizens. It makes social and physical environments health enhancing.[45]

High school completion rate: Refers to the percentage of persons aged 18 to 24 years who are not currently enrolled in high school and who report that they have received a high school diploma or the equivalent, such as a General Education Development certificate.

Linguistically competent: Refers to skills for communicating effectively in the native language or dialect of the targeted population, taking into account general educational levels, literacy, and language preferences.

Local health service areas: Refers to local health jurisdictions and local health unit catchment areas.

Managed care organizations (MCOs): Refers to systems that integrate the financing and delivery of health care services to covered individuals by means of arrangements with selected providers to furnish health care services to members. Managed care includes health maintenance organizations, preferred provider organizations, and point-of-service plans.

Patient and family education: Refers to a planned learning experience using a combination of methods, such as teaching, counseling, skill building, and behavior modification, to promote patient self-management and patient and family empowerment regarding their health.

Postsecondary institutions: Includes 2- and 4-year community colleges, private colleges, and universities.

Quality of life: An expression that, in general, connotes an overall sense of well-being when applied to an individual and a pleasant and supportive environment when applied to a community. On the individual level, health-related quality of life (HRQOL) has a strong relationship to a person's health perceptions and ability to function. On the community level, HRQOL can be viewed as including all aspects of community life that have a direct and quantifiable influence on the physical and mental health of its members.[51]

School health education: Any combination of learning experiences organized in the school setting to predispose, enable, and reinforce behavior conducive to health or to prepare schoolaged children to be able to cope with the challenges to their health in the years ahead.[49]

Settings (worksites, schools, health care sites, and the community): Major social structures that provide channels and mechanisms of influence for reaching defined populations and for intervening at the policy level to facilitate healthful choices and address quality of life issues. Conceptually, the overall community, worksites, schools, and health care sites are contained under the broad umbrella of "community." Health promotion and health education may occur within these individual settings or across settings in a comprehensive, communitywide approach.[10]

Social capital: The process and conditions among people and organizations that lead to accomplishing a goal of mutual social benefit, usually characterized by four interrelated constructs: trust, cooperation, civic engagement, and reciprocity.[49]

Social ecology: Refers to the complex interactions among people and their physical and social environments and the effects of these interactions on the emotional, physical, and social well-being of individuals and groups.[52]

References

1. Centers for Disease Control and Prevention (CDC). *Planned Approach to Community Health: Guide for the Local Coordinator.* Atlanta, GA: U.S. Department of Health and Human Services, Public Health Service, CDC, National Center for Chronic Disease Prevention and Health Promotion, 1995.

2. Brownson, R.C.; Koffman, D.M.; Novotny, T.E.; et al. Environmental and policy interventions to control tobacco use and prevent cardiovascular disease. *Health Education Quarterly* 22:478-498, 1995.

3. Katz, M.F., and Kreuter, M.W. Community assessment and empowerment. In: Scutchfield, F.D., and Keck, C.W. (eds.). *Principles of Public Health Practice.* Washington DC: International Thomson Publishing, 1997, 147-156.

4. Goodman, R.M.; Speers, M.A.; McLeroy, K.; et al. An initial attempt to identify and define the dimensions of community capacity to provide a basis for measurement. *Health Education & Behavior* 25(3), 1998.

5. Steckler, A.; et al. Health education intervention strategies: Recommendations for future research. *Health Education Quarterly* 22:307-328, 1995.

6. Rootman, I.; Goodstadt, M.; Hyndman, B.; McQueen, D. et al. *Evaluation in Health Promotion Principles and Perspectives.* Copenhagen: World Health Organization, 1999.

7.   Glanz, K.; et al. Environmental and policy approaches to cardiovascular disease prevention through nutrition: Opportunities for state and local action. *Health Education Quarterly* 22:512-527, 1995.

8.   King, A.C.; et al. Environmental and policy approaches to cardiovascular disease prevention through physical activity: Issues and opportunities. *Health Education Quarterly* 22:499-511, 1995.

9.   Speers, M.A., and Schmid, T.L. Policy and environmental interventions for the prevention and control of cardiovascular diseases. *Health Education Quarterly* 22:476-477, 1995.

10.   Mullen, P.D.; Evans, D.; Forster, J.; et al. Settings as an important dimension in health education/promotion policy, programs, and research. *Health Education Quarterly* 22:329-345, 1995.

11.   Commission on the Reorganization of Secondary Education. *Cardinal Principles of Secondary Education.* Bulletin 35. Washington, DC: Bureau of Education, 1918.

12.   Institute of Medicine. *Schools and Health: Our Nation's Investment.* Washington, DC: National Academy Press, 1997.

13.   National Center for Education Statistics. *Digest of Education Statistics, 1993.* Washington, DC: U.S. Department of Education, Office of Educational Research and Improvement, 1993.

14.   National Center for Education Statistics. *Dropout Rates in the United States: 1993.* Washington, DC: U.S. Department of Education, Office of Educational Research and Improvement, 1994.

15.   National Health Education Consortium. The relationship to learning: Healthy brain development. Principles and practices of student health. *School Health* 2:262-272, 1992.

16.   Kann, L.; et al. The School Health Policies and Programs Study (SHPPS): Rationale for a nationwide status report on school health programs. *Journal of School Health* 65(8):291-294, 1995.

17.   Marx, E.; Wooley, S.F.; and Northrop, D. (eds.). *Health is Academic: A Guide to Coordinated School Health.* New York: Teachers College Press, 1998.

18.   Kominski, R., and Adams, A. *Educational Attainment in the United States: March 1993 and 1992.* Washington, DC: U.S. Bureau of the Census, 1994.

19.   Gebhardt, D.L., and Crump, C.E. Employee fitness and wellness programs in the workplace. *American Psychologist* 45:262-271, 1990.

20.   Association for Worksite Health Promotion, *1999 National Worksite Health Promotion Survey.* Northbrook, IL: the Association, 1999.

21.   National Center for Health Statistics. Health U.S. 1999. With health and aging chartbook. Hyattsville, MD: the Center 1999.

22.   National Committee for Quality Assurance. Retrieved December 15, 1999 http://www.NCQA.org/policy/HEDIS/HEDIS.com.

23.   Chapman, L.S. Worksite health promotion in the managed care era. *The Art of Health Promotion* 1:1-7, 1998.

24.   Institute of Health Promotion Research, University of British Columbia, and British Columbia Consortium for Health Promotion Research. *Study of Participatory Research in Health Promotion. Review and Recommendations for the Development of Participatory Research in Health Promotion in Canada.* Vancouver, British Columbia: The Royal Society of Canada, 1995.

25.   Lacey, L.P.; et al. An urban, community-based cancer prevention screen and health education intervention in Chicago. *Public Health Reports* 104(6):536-541, 1989.

26.   Hickey, T.; Speers, M.A.; and Prohaska, T.R. *Public Health and Aging.* Baltimore, MD: Johns Hopkins University Press, 1997.

27.   Kreuter, M.W.; Lezin, N.A.; and Young, L.A. Community-based collaborative mechanisms: Implications for practitioners. *Health Promotion Practice,* 1(1):in press.

28.   Sliepcevich, E. *School Health Education Study: A Summary Report.* Washington, DC: School Health Education Study, 1964.

29.   Kann, L.; Kolbe, L.; and Collins, J. eds. Measuring the health behavior of adolescents: the Youth Risk Behavior Surveillance System. *Public Health Reports* 108(suppl):1-67, 1993.

30.   Joint Committee on National Health Education Standards. *National Health Education Standards: Achieving Health Literacy.* Atlanta, GA: American Cancer Society, 1995.

31.   CDC. Youth risk behavior surveillance: National college health risk behavior survey/United States. *Morbidity and Mortality Weekly Report* 46(55-6), 1997.

32.   Lear, J.G. School-based services and adolescent health: Past, present, and future. *Adolescent Medicine: State of the Art Reviews* 7(2):163-180, 1996.

33. Proctor, S.; Lordi, S.; and Saiger, D. *School Nursing Practice: Roles and Standards*. Scarborough, ME: National Association of School Nurses, 1993.

34. Pelletier, K.R. A review and analysis of the health and cost-effective outcome studies of comprehensive health promotion and disease prevention programs at the worksite: 1993-95 update. *American Journal of Health Promotion* 10:380-388, 1996.

35. U.S. Department of Health and Human Services. *Healthy People 2000: National Health Promotion and Disease Prevention Objectives*. Washington DC: the Department, Public Health Service, Office of Health Promotion and Disease Prevention, 1991.

36. National Center for Health Statistics. *Employer-Sponsored Health Insurance: State and National Estimates*. Hyattsville, MD: U.S. Department of Health and Human Services, 1997.

37. Glasgow, R.E.; McCaul, K.D.; and Fisher, K.J. Participation in worksite health promotion: A critique of the literature and recommendations for future practice. *Health Education Quarterly* 20:391-408, 1993.

38. National Resource Center on Worksite Health Promotion. *Working for Good Health: Health Promotion and Small Business*. Washington, DC: Washington Business Group on Health, 1991.

39. Health Care Financing Administration (HCFA). *Managed Care in Medicare and Medicaid* [fact sheet].

Washington, DC: the Administration, 1997.

40. Halverson, P.K.; Mays, G.P.; Kaluzny, A.D.; and Richards, T.B. Not-so-strange bedfellows: Models of interactions between managed care plans and public health agencies. *The Milbank Quarterly* 75(1):113-138, 1997.

41. CDC. Prevention and managed care: Opportunities for managed care organizations, purchasers of health care, and public health agencies. *Morbidity and Mortality Weekly Report* 42(Rr-14):1-12, 1995.

42. Freudenberg, N. Health promotion in the city: A review of current practice and recommendations for new directions to improve the health of urban populations in the United States. Report to the Centers for Disease Control and Prevention, Center on AIDS, Drugs, and Community Health. New York: Hunter College, City University of New York, 1997.

43. National Heart, Lung, and Blood Institute. *Strategies for Diffusing Health Information to Minority Populations: A Profile of a Community-Based Diffusion Model*. Executive Summary. Washington, DC: U.S. Department of Health and Human Services, 1987.

44. National Center for Health Statistics. *Excess Deaths and Other Mortality Measures for Hispanic and Black Populations*. Washington, DC: U.S. Department of Health and Human Services, 1995.

45. World Health Organization (WHO), Division of

Health Promotion, Education and Communication. *Health Promotion Glossary*. Geneva: the Organization, 1998.

46. McLeroy, K. Community Capacity: What Is It? How Do We Measure It? What Is the Role of the Prevention Centers and CDC? Presented at Sixth Annual Prevention Centers Conference, Centers for Disease Control and Prevention, National Center for Chronic Disease Prevention and Health Promotion, Atlanta, GA.

47. Green, L.W., and Ottoson, J.M. *Community and Population Health*, 8th ed. New York, NY: McGraw Hill, 1999.

48. Heaney, C.A., and Goetzel, R.Z. A review of health-related outcomes of multi-component worksite health promotion programs. *American Journal of Health Promotion* 11:290-307, 1997.

49. Green, L.W., and Kreuter, M.W. *Health Promotion Planning: An Educational and Ecological Approach*, 3rd ed. Mountain View, CA: Mayfield Publishing Company, 1999.

50. Duhl, L., and Hancock, T. Assessing Healthy Cities. World Health Organization Healthy Cities papers.

51. Moriarty, D. CDC studies community quality of life. *NACCHO NEWS* 12(3):10,13, 1996.

52. Stokols, D. Establishing and maintaining healthy environments: Toward a social ecology of health promotion. *American Psychologist* 47(1):6-22, 1992.

8

Environmental Health

Co-Lead Agencies: Agency for Toxic Substances and Disease
Registry; Centers for Disease Control and
Prevention; National Institutes of Health

Contents

Goal

Promote health for all through a healthy environment.

Overview

According to the World Health Organization, "In its broadest sense, environmental health comprises those aspects of human health, disease, and injury that are determined or influenced by factors in the environment. This includes the study of both the direct pathological effects of various chemical, physical, and biological agents, as well as the effects on health of the broad physical and social environment, which includes housing, urban development, land-use and transportation, industry, and agriculture."[1] The term "environment" may also be used to refer to air, water, and soil. This more narrow definition ignores the man-made environment created by a society. Where and how a society chooses to grow and develop affects the quality of life by determining how long people spend traveling to work, shopping, or going to school. Where and how a society builds its houses, schools, parks, and roadways can also limit the ability of some people to move about and lead a normal life.

Because the impact of the environment on human health is so great, protecting the environment has long been a mainstay of public health practice. National, State, and local efforts to ensure clean air and safe supplies of food and water, to manage sewage and municipal wastes, and to control or eliminate vector-borne illnesses have contributed a great deal to improvements in public health in the United States. Unfortunately, in spite of the billions of dollars spent to manage and clean up hazardous waste sites in the Nation each year, little money has been spent evaluating the health risks associated with chronic, low-level exposures to hazardous substances. This imbalance results in an inadequate amount of useful information to evaluate and manage these sites effectively and to evaluate the health status of people who live near the sites.[2] In the past, research in environmental epidemiology and toxicology has often been based on limited information. New knowledge about the interactions between specific genetic variations among individuals and specific environmental factors provides enormous opportunity for further developing modifications in environmental exposures that contribute to disease. Further research is needed to address these and other problems and to improve the science and management of health effects on people exposed to environmental hazards.[3]

Issues

Environmental factors play a central role in human development, health, and disease. Broadly defined, the environment, including infectious agents, is one of three primary factors that affect human health. The other two are genetic factors and personal behavior.

Human exposures to hazardous agents in the air, water, soil, and food, and to physical hazards in the environment are major contributors to illness, disability, and death worldwide. Furthermore, deterioration of environmental conditions in many parts of the world slow sustainable development. Poor environmental quality is estimated to be directly responsible for approximately 25 percent of all preventable ill health in the world, with diarrheal diseases and respiratory infections heading the list.[4] Ill health resulting from poor environmental quality varies considerably among countries. Poor environmental quality has its greatest impact on people whose health status already may be at risk.

Because the effect of the environment on human health is so great, protecting the environment has been a mainstay of public health practice since 1878.[5] National, Tribal, State, and local efforts to ensure clean air and safe supplies of food and water, to manage sewage and municipal wastes, and to control or eliminate vector-borne illnesses have contributed significantly to improvements in public health in the United States. However, the public's awareness of the environment's role in health is more recent. Publication of Rachel Carson's *Silent Spring* in the early 1960s, followed by the well-publicized poor health of residents of Love Canal, New York, the site of a significant toxic waste site, awakened public consciousness to environmental issues. The result of these and other similar events is the so-called "environmental movement" which has led to the introduction into everyday life of such terms as Superfund sites, water quality, clean air, ozone, urban sprawl, and agricultural runoff.

In 1993 alone, over $109 billion was spent on pollution abatement and control in the United States.[6] However, many hazardous sites still remain. Minimal research has been done to evaluate the health risks associated with chronic low-level exposures to hazardous substances, resulting in an inability to evaluate and manage such sites effectively and to evaluate the health status of residents living near such sites. Further environmental epidemiology and toxicology research is needed to address such problems and to improve the science and public health management of the health effects on people exposed to environmental hazards.

To address the broad range of human health issues affected by the environment, this chapter discusses six topics that cover environmental health: outdoor air quality, water quality, toxics and waste, healthy homes and healthy communities, infrastructure and surveillance, and global environmental health issues.

Outdoor air quality. Air pollution continues to be a widespread public health and environmental problem in the United States, causing premature death, cancer, and long-term damage to respiratory and cardiovascular systems. Air pollution also reduces visibility, damages crops and buildings, and deposits pollutants on the soil and in bodies of water where they affect the chemistry of the water and the organisms living there. Approximately 113 million people live in U.S. areas designated as nonattainment areas by EPA for one or more of the six commonly found air pollutants for which the Federal Government has established health-based standards.[7] The problem of air pollution is national—even international—in scope. Most of the U.S. population lives in expanding urban areas where air pollution crosses local and State lines and, in some cases, crosses U.S. borders with Canada and Mexico.

Although some progress toward reducing unhealthy air emissions has been made, a substantial air pollution problem remains, with millions of tons of toxic air pollutants released into the air each year.[8] The presence of unacceptable levels of ground-level ozone is the largest problem, as determined by the number of people affected and the number of areas not meeting Federal standards.

Motor vehicles account for approximately one-fourth of emissions that produce ozone and one-third of nitrogen oxide emissions. Particulate and sulfur dioxide emissions from motor vehicles represent approximately 20 percent and 4 percent, respectively. Some 76.6 percent of carbon monoxide emissions are produced each year by transportation sources (for example, motor vehicles, etc.).[9]

Unhealthy air is expensive. The estimated annual health costs of human exposure to all outdoor air pollutants from all sources range from $40 billion to $50 billion, with an associated 50,000 premature deaths.[10]

Water quality. Providing drinking water free of disease-causing agents, whether biological or chemical, is the primary goal of all water supply systems. During the first half of the 20th century the causes for most waterborne disease outbreaks were bacteria; protozoa and chemicals became the dominate causes beginning in the 1970s.[11] Most outbreaks involve only a few individuals.[12, 13,14] In 1993, however, more than 403,000 people became sick during a single episode of waterborne cryptosporidiosis.[14]

One problem in evaluating the relationship between drinking water and infectious diseases is the lack of adequate technology to detect parasitic contamination and to determine whether the organisms detected are alive and infectious. The development of new molecular technologies to detect and monitor water contamination will enhance water quality monitoring and surveillance.

Contamination of water can come from both point (for example, industrial sites) and nonpoint (for example, agricultural runoff) sources. Biological and chemical contamination significantly reduce the value of surface waters (streams, lakes, and estuaries) for fishing, swimming, and other recreational activities. For example, during the summer of 1997, blooms of *Pfiesteria piscicida* were implicated as the likely cause of fish kills in North Carolina and Maryland. The development of intensive animal feeding operations has worsened the discharge of improperly or inadequately treated wastes,[15] which presents an increased health threat in waters used either for recreation or for producing fish and shellfish.

Toxics and waste. Critical information on the levels of exposure to hazardous substances in the environment and their associated health effects often is lacking. As a result, efficient health-outcome measures of progress in eliminating health hazards in the environment are unavailable. The identification of toxic substances and waste, whether hazardous, industrial, or municipal, that pose an environmental health risk represents a significant achievement in itself. Public health strategies are aimed at tracking the Nation's success in eliminating these substances or minimizing their effects.

Toxic and hazardous substances, including low-level radioactive wastes, deposited on land often are carried far from their sources by air, groundwater, and surface water runoff into streams, lakes, and rivers where they can accumulate in the sediments beneath the waters. Ultimate decisions about the cleanup and management of these sites must be made keeping public health concerns in mind.

The introduction and widespread use of pesticides in the American landscape continues in agricultural, commercial, recreational, and home settings. As a result, these often very toxic substances pose a potential threat to people using them, especially if they are handled, mixed, or applied inappropriately or excessively. Furthermore, children are at increased risk for pesticide poisoning because of their smaller size and because pesticides may be stored improperly or applied to surfaces that are more readily accessible by children.

Healthy homes and communities. The public's health, particularly its environmental health, depends on the interaction of many factors. To provide a healthy environment within the Nation's communities, the places people spend the most time—their homes, schools, and offices—must be considered. Potential risks

Data as of November 30, 1999

include indoor air pollution, inadequate heating, cooling, and sanitation, structural problems, electrical and fire hazards, and lead-based paint hazards. More than 6 million housing units across the country meet the Federal Government's definition of substandard housing.[16]

Many factors—including air quality, lead-based paint on walls, trim, floors, ceilings, etc., and hazardous household substances such as cleaning products and pesticides—can affect health and safety. In 1996, the American Association of Poison Control Centers reported more than 2 million poison exposures from 67 participating poison control centers. The site of exposure was a residence in 91 percent of cases.[17]

Infrastructure and surveillance. Preventing health problems caused by environmental hazards requires: (1) having enough personnel and resources to investigate and respond to diseases and injuries potentially caused by environmental hazards; (2) monitoring the population and its environment to detect hazards, exposure of the public and individuals to hazards, and diseases potentially caused by these hazards; (3) monitoring the population and its environment to assess the effectiveness of prevention programs; (4) educating the public and select populations on the relationship between health and the environment; (5) ensuring that laws, regulations, and practices protect the public and the environment from hazardous agents; (6) providing public access to understandable and useful information on hazards and their sources, distribution, and health effects; (7) coordinating the efforts of all government agencies and nongovernmental groups responsible for environmental health; and (8) providing adequate resources to accomplish these tasks. Development of additional methods to measure environmental hazards in people will permit more careful assessments of exposures and health effects.

Global environmental health. Increased international travel and improvements in telecommunications and computer technology are making the world a smaller place. The term "global community" has real significance, as shared resources—air, water, and soil—draw people together. Actions in every country affect the environment and influence events around the world. Undoubtedly, the environment affects everyone's health. Sometimes benefits in one area inadvertently create worse conditions for people in different areas of the world. For example, in 1996, the United States exported more than $2.5 billion worth of pesticides.[18] Exported pesticides that are not registered, or pesticides that are restricted for use in the United States, are often used by developing countries. Their use not only endangers populations in those countries but also can contaminate food being exported from those countries to the United States. Sensitive populations, such as children and pregnant women, may be at risk from these environmental exposures. The United States can contribute to improving the health of people internationally, not only as part of a shared goal for humanity, but also because a healthy global population has positive social and economic benefits throughout the world.

Additionally, a number of countries have resources available to protect their populations from adverse health impacts but because of inadequate information they are unable to do so. Lead abatement technology, for example, is one area that the United States can provide information to other countries. Likewise, consultation and assistance on numerous environmental health issues from lead poisoning to disaster preparedness will help reduce illness, disability, and death in countries with these problems which leads to a healthier global community.

The Nation should expand its efforts to improve environmental conditions to enhance the health of developing countries and should also increase collaboration, coordination, and outreach efforts with the rest of the world to help close the gap between existing and attainable health status.

Trends

During the 1990s, progress in improving environmental health was mixed. The decline in childhood lead poisoning in the United States represents a public health success. In 1984, between 2 and 3 million children aged 6 months to 5 years had blood lead levels (BLLs) greater than 15 µg/dL, and almost a quarter of a million had BLLs above 25 µg/dL,[19] a level which can damage vital organs and the brain. (Blood levels are measured in micrograms of lead found in a deciliter of blood.) By the early 1990s, fewer than 900,000 children had BLLs above 10µg/dL, the current standard for identifying children at risk.[20] This dramatic reduction is the result of research to identify persons at risk, professional and public education campaigns to "spread the word," broad-based screening measures to find those at risk, and effective community efforts to clean up problem areas, namely substandard housing units. However, despite the success achieved, more remains to be done before childhood lead poisoning becomes a disease of the past. Although childhood lead poisoning occurred in all population groups, the risk was higher for persons having low income, living in older housing, and belonging to certain racial and ethic groups. For example, among non-Hispanic black children living in homes built before 1946, 22 percent had elevated BBLs. Because the risk for lead poisoning is not spread evenly throughout the population, efforts are continuing to identify children at risk and assure that they receive preventive interventions.

Unfortunately, not all trends for environmental health issues are as encouraging. Since the mid-1980s, asthma rates in the United States have risen to the level of an epidemic.[21] Asthma and other respiratory conditions often are triggered or worsened by substances found in the air, such as tobacco smoke, ozone, and other particles or chemicals. Based on existing data, an estimated 17.3 million people in the United States had asthma in 1998,[22] including more than 5 million children aged 18 years and under. Between 1980 and 1993, the overall death rate for asthma increased 52 percent, from 12.8 to 19.5 per million population; for people aged 18 years and under, the death rate increased 67 percent, from 1.8 to 3.0 per million population. The direct economic and health care costs of asthma and other respiratory conditions can be large. In 1990, the estimated total cost of asthma was

Data as of November 30, 1999

$6.2 billion; the total cost was projected to rise to $14.5 billion by the year 2000. The indirect costs of asthma, measured in reduced quality of life and lost productivity, include the estimated 10 million school days each year that children miss. Lost productivity from missed work days of parents caring for children with asthma is estimated to be $1 billion—not including the cost of lost productivity from adults with asthma who miss work.[23] (See Focus Area 24. Respiratory Diseases.)

Although successes in environmental public health are possible, they are difficult to achieve. Infectious and chemical agents still contaminate food and water. Animals continue to carry diseases to human populations, and outbreaks of once-common intestinal diseases (for example, typhoid fever) although less frequent, still occur. (See Focus Area 10. Food Safety.) These outbreaks underscore the need to maintain and improve programs developed in the first half of the 20th century to ensure the safety of food and water. The challenge is to retain these basic capacities in the 21st century, with the added responsibilities for dealing with emerging hazards. The control of well-known hazards must coexist with ongoing research and the development of strategies and methods to understand and control new hazards. Another challenge is the need to help the public understand the link between human activity and the destruction of the environment.

Within the United States, significant strides toward a reduction in harmful air emissions can be achieved by individuals choosing not to drive their cars. People need to use public transit, walk, or bicycle more often. Laws can help improve street and highway design to facilitate pedestrians and bicyclists, and employers can embrace telecommuting, but the choice remains with the individual. Encouraging individuals to walk or bike also reduces the problem of overweight people and obesity, which have risen to alarming levels in the U.S. population.

Urban sprawl has become an increasingly important concern in the United States for several reasons: increased outdoor air pollution in major urban areas, reduced quality of life due to the loss of free time and the stress of increased commuting time, and less green space in our major metropolitan areas. Between 1983 and 1995, the average annual vehicle miles traveled increased 80 percent.[24] These conditions lead to negative health conditions, such as asthma and injuries from road rage due to traffic-related stress. In addition, sprawl diminishes the amount of land available for prime recreational and agricultural uses and can bring two land uses together that do not coexist well. Examples include when new residential development in an area that was previously agricultural exposes new residents to sounds, smells, and substances, such as pesticides, which can pose a possible hazard to their health.

On a global scale, the U.S.-Mexico border area illustrates how human activity can contribute to damaging the environment, affecting generations to come. Over the past 30 years, this region has experienced a dramatic surge in population and industrialization. The region has had great difficulty in supporting this growth and suffers from a lack of resources and expertise to properly manage solid waste, handle and store pesticides and other hazardous materials, supply sufficient drinking water, and support other sustainable development efforts.[25] Nations need to make choices about how to deal with such regions; offering technical assistance is an option to speed knowledge transfer and reduce environmental harm.

Disparities

Studies have linked race and socioeconomic status to increased exposure to environmental hazards and information about gene-environment interactions improve the ability to determine who has increased risk of disease from these exposures. Table 8-A and Table 8-B summarize some inequities in the United States regarding exposure to selected potential environmental hazards.

Table 8-A. Percentage of African American, Hispanic, and white populations living in air-quality nonattainment areas, 1992.[26]

Pollutant	African American	Hispanic	White
		Percent	
Particulates	16.5	34.0	14.7
Carbon Monoxide	46.0	57.1	33.6
Ozone	62.2	71.2	52.5
Sulfur Dioxide	12.1	5.7	7.0
Lead	9.2	18.5	6.0

Table 8-B. Proportions of certain racial and ethnic and lower socioeconomic populations in census tracts surrounding waste treatment, storage, and disposal facilities (TSDF) vs. the proportion of these groups in other census tracts, 1994.[26]

Location of TSDFs	Demographic Breakdowns		
	African Americans	Hispanics	Persons Living Below the Poverty Line
		Percent	
Census tracts with either TSDFs or at least 50 percent of their area within 2.5 miles of a tract with TSDF.	24.7	10.7	19.0
Census Tracts without TSDFs	13.6	7.3	13.1

Disparities exist in the environmental exposures certain populations face and in the health status of these populations. For example, in New York City, African American, Hispanic, and low-income populations have been found to have

Data as of November 30, 1999

hospitalization and death rates from asthma 3 to 5 times higher than those for all New York City residents. African American children have been found to be 3 times more likely than white children to be hospitalized for asthma and asthma-related conditions and 4 to 6 times more likely to die from asthma.[25] (See Focus Area 24. Respiratory Diseases.) With respect to BLL, children from certain racial and ethnic groups are disproportionately affected. While there are no studies to show rural/frontier dwellers are at increased risk to exposure to contaminated drinking water, the preponderace of this population depends on unregulated private wells for their drinking water. The U.S. Geological Survey (USGS) reports that 42.8 million persons in the United States (17 percent of the total population) were served by their own (self-supplied) water systems in 1990.[27]

Opportunities

An increase in public awareness of environmental health issues is key to achieving this chapter's goal and objectives. Education—at all levels—is a cornerstone of broad prevention efforts.

Improving the availability of environmental health data also will help meet the objectives. The Internet has increased dramatically access to environmental information. Databases, such as Toxnet® (at http://sis.nlm.nih.gov/sisl),[28] Internet Grateful Med® (at http://igm.nlm.nih.gov),[29] and TRI (the Toxic Release Inventory www.epa.gov/ceisweb1/ceishome/ceisdata/xplor-tri/explorer.htm), may provide useful information about environmental hazards or other environmental problems in communities to health care providers, policymakers, and the public. Moreover, better dissemination of global environmental health information may reduce the occurrence of disease or exposure to harmful environmental agents for U.S. citizens traveling abroad.

To be successful, programs to improve environmental health must be based on scientific evidence. The complex relationship between human health and the acute and long-term effects of environmental exposures must be studied so prevention measures can be developed. Surveillance systems to track exposures to toxic substances such as commonly used pesticides and heavy metals must be developed and maintained. To the extent possible, these systems should use biomonitoring data, which provide measurements of toxic substances in the human body. A mechanism is needed for tracking the export of pesticides restricted or not registered for use in the United States.

Environmental hazards are not limited by political boundaries. Through the year 2010, the scope of public and environmental health must be global if the Nation is to achieve good health for all Americans. A global scope will help develop and achieve effective ways to prevent disease worldwide as well. The United States must work with other governments, nongovernmental organizations, and international organizations to help improve human health on a global scale.

Healthy People 2000 targets have been met for objectives dealing with outbreaks of waterborne diseases, with solid wastes, and with toxic substances released through industrial processes. Substantial progress has been made in objectives involving the proportion of people who live in counties that meet EPA air standards for air pollution, the number of States that require radon disclosures with real estate transactions, and with the recycling of household hazardous waste. More moderate progress has taken place for the objectives involving radon and lead-based paint testing in homes, asthma hospitalizations, and States with laws to track environmental diseases. Mixed progress or movement away from the targets is being seen in objectives dealing with mental retardation and impaired surface waters (rivers, lakes, and estuaries). Data have been mixed or difficult to assess for the objective centered around cleanup of hazardous waste sites. The target for blood lead levels in children has not been met, though some progress has been made.

Note: Unless otherwise noted, data are from Centers for Disease Control and Prevention, National Center for Health Statistics, *Healthy People 2000 Review, 1998-99.*

Environmental Health

Goal: Promote health for all through a healthy environment.

Number   Objective

Outdoor Air Quality

8-1	Harmful air pollutants
8-2	Alternative modes of transportation
8-3	Cleaner alternative fuels
8-4	Airborne toxins

Water Quality

8-5	Safe drinking water
8-6	Waterborne disease outbreaks
8-7	Water conservation
8-8	Surface water health risks
8-9	Beach closings
8-10	Fish contamination

Toxics and Waste

8-11	Elevated blood lead levels in children
8-12	Cleanup of hazardous sites
8-13	Pesticide exposures
8-14	Toxic pollutants
8-15	Recycled municipal solid waste

Healthy Homes and Healthy Communities

8-16	Indoor allergens
8-17	Office building air quality
8-18	Homes tested for radon
8-19	Radon resistant new home construction
8-20	School policies to protect against environmental hazards
8-21	Disaster preparedness plans and protocols
8-22	Lead-based paint testing
8-23	Substandard housing

Number   Objective

Infrastructure and Surveillance

8-24   Exposure to pesticides

8-25   Exposure to heavy metals and other toxic chemicals

8-26   Information systems used for environmental health

8-27   Monitoring environmentally related diseases

8-28   Local agencies using surveillance data for vector control

Global Environmental Health

8-29   Global burden of disease

8-30   Water quality in the U.S.-Mexico border region

Outdoor Air Quality

8-1. **Reduce the proportion of persons exposed to air that does not meet the U.S. Environmental Protection Agency's (EPA's) health-based standards for harmful air pollutants.**

Target and baseline:

Objective	Reduction in Air Pollutants	1997 Baseline	2010 Target
		Percent	
8-1a.	Ozone*	43	0
8-1b.	Particulate matter, 10 μm or less in diameter (PM_{10})*	12	0
8-1c.	Carbon monoxide	19	0
8-1d.	Nitrogen dioxide	5	0
8-1e.	Sulfur dioxide	2	0
8-1f.	Lead	<1	0
		Number	
8-1g.	Total number of people	119,803,000	0

*The targets of zero people for ozone and PM_{10} will be met in 2012 and 2018, respectively.

Target setting method: Consistent with the Clean Air Act (Public Law 101-549).

Data source: National Air Quality and Emissions Trends Report, EPA.

Note: For the purpose of this objective, EPA is counting persons living in nonattainment areas only.

Historically, EPA's air quality monitoring and National Ambient Air Quality Standards data collection have taken place in large urban centers and other areas generally considered to have the Nation's poorest air quality. As nonattainment areas become attainment areas, EPA will continue its monitoring efforts. (See Focus Area 24. Respiratory Diseases.)

8-2. Increase use of alternative modes of transportation to reduce motor vehicle emissions and improve the Nation's air quality.

Target and baseline:

Objective	Increase in Use of Alternative Modes of Transportation	1995 Baseline	2010 Target
		Percent	
8-2a.	Trips made by bicycling	0.9	1.8
8-2b.	Trips made by walking	5.4	10.8
8-2c.	Trips made by transit	1.8	3.6
8-2d.	Persons who telecommute	Developmental	

Target setting method: Consistent with the goal of the National Bicycling and Walking Study, U.S. Department of Transportation (DOT).

Data sources: DOT, Federal Highway Administration (FHA); Nationwide Personal Transportation Survey (NPTS), U.S. Department of Commerce, Bureau of the Census; Youth Risk Behavior Survey (YRBS), CDC, NCHS; Behavioral Risk Factor Surveillance System (BRFSS), CDC, NCHS; National Center for Bicycling and Walking; local government databases; FHA TEA-21 implementation.

For many communities in the United States, motor vehicle emissions are the primary cause of air pollution. Increasing use of alternative modes of transportation is a comprehensive approach that each citizen can take to affect local levels of air pollution. An increase in neighborhood streets with ways to slow traffic and with more sidewalks and bike lanes, offroad pedestrian or bike routes, and bicycle and pedestrian plans and programs will aid in reaching the targets for biking, walking, and transit objectives. (See Focus Area 22. Physical Activity and Fitness.) As technology improves, telecommuting will play an increasing role in U.S. business. Many people will be able to do some or all of their work from home, thus reducing peak-period demand.

8-3. Improve the Nation's air quality by increasing the use of cleaner alternative fuels.

Target: 30 percent of U.S. motor fuel consumption.

Baseline: Cleaner alternative fuels represented 2.7 percent of U.S. motor fuel consumption in 1997.

Target setting method: 10-fold improvement.

Data source: Alternatives to Traditional Transportation Fuels, U.S. Department of Energy, Energy Information Administration.

Privately owned cars, vans, and trucks; commercial fleets, trucks, and busses; and power plants are the major users of alternative fuels. Ethanol-blended fuels have been used in small engines and other nonautomotive gasoline engines since they first came into the marketplace over 25 years ago. Today, all mainstream manufacturers of power equipment, motorcycles, snowmobiles, and outboard motors permit the use of ethanol blends in their products.

The primary force behind development of an alternative fuels infrastructure is the Department of Energy Clean Cities Program—a voluntary program and locally based government and industry partnership designed to promote the use of alternative fuels and alternative fuel vehicles; cleaner air in major U.S. cities; reduced dependence on imported oil; and stimulate local economic activity.[30]

Infrastructure building also is aided by development of alternative fuel vehicles by the major automobile manufacturers. Also, ethanol blends of up to 10 percent are approved under the warranties of all major auto manufacturers, domestic and foreign, marketing vehicles in the United States. In fact, some recommend the use of cleaner-burning fuels such as ethanol in their vehicle owner manuals because of ethanol's clean air benefits. Ethanol actually can enhance engine performance by increasing octane and raising oxygen, cleaning and preventing engine deposits, and acting as a gas-line antifreeze.[31]

More than a trillion miles have been driven on ethanol-blended gasolines, and ethanol-blended fuels represent more than 12 percent of United States motor gasoline sales. Congress established the Federal ethanol program in 1979 to stimulate rural economies and reduce the Nation's alarming dependence on imported oil through the production of a domestic, renewable energy source. The program has helped build a strong domestic energy industry. From just over 10 million gallons of production in 1979, the U.S. fuel ethanol industry has grown to more than 1.8 billion gallons of annual production capacity. Ethanol is widely marketed across the country as a high-quality octane enhancer and as an oxygenate capable of reducing air pollution and improving automobile performance.

8-4.   Reduce air toxic emissions to decrease the risk of adverse health effects caused by airborne toxics.

Target: 2.0 tons.

Baseline: 8.1 million tons of air toxics were released into the air in 1993.

Target setting method: 75 percent improvement.

Data source: U.S National Toxics Inventory, EPA.

Toxic air pollutants are those pollutants known or suspected to cause cancer or other serious health effects, such as reproductive effects or birth defects, or to cause adverse environmental effects. The degree to which a toxic air pollutant affects a person's health depends on many factors, including the quantity of pollutant the person is exposed to, the duration and frequency of exposures, the toxicity of the chemical, and the person's state of health and susceptibility. Examples of toxic air pollutants include benzene, which is found in gasoline; perchloroethylene, which is emitted from some dry cleaning facilities; and methylene chloride, which is used as a solvent and paint stripper by a number of industries. Examples of other listed air toxics include dioxin, asbestos, toluene, and metals such as cadmium, mercury, chromium, and lead compounds.

Scientists estimate that millions of tons of toxic pollutants are released into the air each year. Some air toxics are released from natural sources such as volcanic eruptions and forest fires. Most, however, originate from manmade sources, including both mobile sources (for example, cars, buses, trucks) and stationary sources (for example, factories, refineries, power plants). Emissions from stationary sources constitute almost two-thirds of all manmade air toxics emissions. (See Focus Area 24. Respiratory Diseases.)

Water Quality

8-5. **Increase the proportion of persons served by community water systems who receive a supply of drinking water that meets the regulations of the Safe Drinking Water Act.**

Target: 95 percent.

Baseline: 73 percent of persons served by community water systems received drinking water that met SDWA (Public Law 93-523) regulations in 1995.

Target setting method: Consistent with EPA's strategic plan.

Data sources: Potable Water Surveillance System (PWSS) and Safe Drinking Water Information System (SDWIS), EPA.

Most people in the United States obtain their drinking water from public water supply systems. The Environmental Protection Agency (EPA) has established regulations intended to ensure that community water systems supply safe drinking water to their customers. Compliance with the established regulations is one measure of the public's receipt of a safe water supply, free from disease-causing agents. In 1997, small systems (serving 25 to 3,300 people) accounted for more than 85 percent of the community water systems in the United States but served only about 10 percent of the population. These systems accounted for 91 percent of the violations of the EPA drinking water regulations.[32] According to USGS, 17 percent of the Nation's total population were served by their own water-supply systems in 1990, compared with 18 percent in 1985.[27]

8-6. Reduce waterborne disease outbreaks arising from water intended for drinking among persons served by community water systems.

Target: 2 outbreaks per year.

Baseline: 6 outbreaks per year originated from community water systems (1987-96 average).

Target setting method: 67 percent improvement.

Data source: State Reporting Systems, CDC, NCID.

CDC compiles the results of State investigations into waterborne disease outbreaks arising from water intended for drinking. Between 1987 and 1996, the States reported an average of 15.5 outbreaks per year, of which 6 outbreaks were identified as originating from community water supplies.[12, 13, 14] Limited existing data suggest that State and CDC surveillance systems for detecting waterborne disease outbreaks are able to detect most waterborne disease outbreaks.

8-7. Reduce per capita domestic water withdrawals.

Target: 90.9 gallons per day.

Baseline: 101 gallons of water per day in 1995.

Target setting method: 10 percent improvement.

Data source: U.S. Department of Interior, U.S. Geological Survey (USGS).

Historically, water management in the United States has focused on directing the country's abundant supplies of fresh water to meet the needs of users. This approach has resulted in the building of large storage reservoirs and conveyance systems, especially in the West. Increasing development costs, capital shortages, government fiscal restraint, diminishing sources of water supply, polluted water, and a growing concern for the environment have forced water managers and planners to begin to rethink traditional approaches to management and to experiment with new ones. Experts on the subject of water supply and demand agree that the West is in transition from the era of water-supply development to an era of water-demand management and conservation. As the population increases in the eastern United States, the water quantity problems already facing the West will become apparent there as well. Estimates place the amount of water withdrawn for public supply during 1990 at about 5 percent more than during 1985.[27] Public-supply domestic deliveries averaged 105 gallons per day for each person served, the same as during 1985.[27] The per capita use remained about the same for the past decade as the result of active conservation programs that include the installation of additional meters and water-conserving plumbing fixtures.[27] Information about water use is available from USGS at http://water.usgs.gov/watuse/wudo.html.[33]

8-8.   (Developmental) Increase the proportion of assessed rivers, lakes, and estuaries that are safe for fishing and recreational purposes.

Potential data source: Clean Water Act (Public Law 92-500), Section 305-b Report, EPA.

EPA reported that about 40 percent of the Nation's surface waters (streams, lakes, and estuaries) are too polluted for fishing, swimming, or other uses designated for them by States and Tribes.[34] Water quality in lakes, streams, and estuaries of the United States affects both the recreational and food production use of these waters. States and Tribes have water-quality management programs that address recreational use and fish and shellfish harvesting. EPA establishes water-quality objectives for these waters and monitors progress toward these goals. Discharging inadequately treated or inappropriate quantities of human, industrial, or agriculture wastes reduces the ability of water to provide conditions that support the growth and harvesting of fish and shellfish for human consumption. Such discharging also prevents water's use as a recreational resource.

8-9.   (Developmental) Reduce the number of beach closings that result from the presence of harmful bacteria.

Potential data source: EPA.

During the first half of the decade (2001-2010), EPA plans to focus on conserving and enhancing the Nation's waters and aquatic ecosystems so that 75 percent of waters will support healthy aquatic communities.[35] Part of this effort will include developing a national beach-closing survey to monitor efforts to improve the quality of water used for recreational purposes. Although small streams, private lakes, and ponds will not be addressed by the EPA beach-closing survey (available at http://www.epa.gov/ost/beaches),[36] this program will provide a method to evaluate progress toward improving water quality on U.S. swimming beaches. Information from the 1997 and 1998 EPA surveys has been expanded on by the Natural Resources Defense Council (NRDC) and published in its annual beach closing report. The latest version, providing data for 1998, entitled *Testing the Waters IX: A Guide to Water Quality at Vacation Beaches* is available from NRDC and on its web site (www.nrdc.org).[37]

8-10.   (Developmental) Reduce the potential human exposure to persistent chemicals by decreasing fish contaminant levels.

Potential data sources: U.S. Department of the Interior, U.S. Fish and Wildlife Service and USGS.

The Biomonitoring of Environmental Status and Trends (BEST) program (www.best.usgs.gov) is a cooperative activity of the USGS and the U.S. Fish and

Wildlife Service. Designed to assess and monitor the effects of environmental contaminants on biological resources, the program measures 51 organochlorine persistent chemicals, organophosphate and carbamate insecticides, and 21 metals.

Toxics and Waste

8-11. Eliminate elevated blood lead levels in children.

Target: Zero children.

Baseline: 4.4 percent of children aged 1 to 5 years had blood lead levels exceeding 10 µg/dL during 1991-94.

Target setting method: Total elimination.

Data source: National Health and Nutrition Examination Survey (NHANES), CDC, NCHS.

Proportion of Children Aged 1 to 5 Years With Blood Lead Levels Greater Than or Equal to 10 µg/dL, 1991-94	All Houses	Resided in House Built:		
		Before 1946*	1946 to 1973*	After 1973*
		Percent		
TOTAL	4.4	8.6	4.6	1.6
Race and ethnicity				
American Indian or Alaska Native	DSU	DSU	DSU	DSU
Asian or Pacific Islander	DSU	DSU	DSU	DSU
Asian	DNC	DNC	DNC	DNC
Native Hawaiian and other Pacific Islander	DNC	DNC	DNC	DNC
Black or African American	11.5	22.7	13.2	3.3
White	2.6	6.6	1.9	1.4
Hispanic or Latino	DSU	DSU	DSU	DSU
Mexican American	4.0	13.0	2.3	1.6
Not Hispanic or Latino	DNA	DNA	DNA	DNA
Black or African American	11.2	21.9	13.7	3.4
White	2.3	5.6	1.4	1.5
Gender				
Female	3.3	7.1	2.8	1.5
Male	5.5	9.6	6.6	1.7

Proportion of Children Aged 1 to 5 Years With Blood Lead Levels Greater Than or Equal to 10 µg/dL, 1991-94	All Houses	Resided in House Built:		
		Before 1946*	1946 to 1973*	After 1973*
		Percent		
Family income level†				
Low	1.9	4.1	2.0	0.4
High	1.0	0.9	2.7	0
Geographic location				
Population ≥ 1 million	5.4	11.5	5.8	0.8
Population ≤ 1 million	3.3	5.8	3.1	2.5

DNA = Data have not been analyzed. DNC = Data are not collected. DSU = Data are statistically unreliable.

*Data for "all houses" are from a separate analysis of NHANES data; data for specific periods of time provided for information purposes.

†Income categories defined using poverty-income ratio (PIR) (the ratio of total family income to the poverty threshold for the year). Low equals PIR ≤ 1.300; middle equals PIR 1.301 - 3.500; high equals PIR ≥ 3.501.

Although considerable progress has been made in reducing BLLs in the Nation's children, lead poisoning remains a preventable environmental problem in the United States. Culturally and linguistically appropriate information is needed alerting persons to the dangers of lead poisonings.

8-12. Minimize the risks to human health and the environment posed by hazardous sites.

Target: 98 percent of sites on the following lists:

8-12a. National Priority List sites

8-12b. Resource Conservation and Recovery Act facilities

8-12c. Leaking underground storage facilities

8-12d. Brownfield properties

Baseline: 1,200 National Priority List sites; 2,475 Resource Conservation Recovery Act facilities; 370,000 leaking underground storage facilities; 1,500 brownfield properties in 1998.

Target setting method: Consistent with EPA's 1997 Strategic Plan.

Data source: EPA and HazDat data system, Agency for Toxic Substances and Disease Registry.

The National Priorities List (NPL) is a published list of the most hazardous waste sites in the country eligible for extensive, long-term cleanup under the Superfund program. Sites listed on the NPL often are initially discovered by local or State agencies, businesses, EPA, the Coast Guard, or the public. If a site poses a significant risk to human health, as determined by the number and toxicity of substances discovered at the site and its capacity to affect surrounding populations, then the site is placed on the NPL. The Agency for Toxic Substances and Disease Registry (ATSDR) is the Federal health agency that issues recommendations to EPA, State health and environmental agencies, and the public concerning the elimination of public health threats at these sites. This advice often also includes recommendations to the public and the health care community concerning practices to identify and prevent exposures and adverse health effects. The Resource Conservation and Recovery Act (RCRA) was enacted by Congress in 1976 to find a safe way to manage and dispose of the huge volumes of municipal and industrial waste generated nationwide. RCRA facilities are authorized and regulated by this Act. With several amendments, the Act and its subsequent regulations govern the management of nonhazardous (solid) waste, hazardous waste, and underground storage tanks (USTs). The Leaking Underground Storage Tanks Program attempts to identify and eliminate the threat to human health posed by groundwater or soil contamination from petroleum released from these tanks. The term "brownfields" denotes abandoned, idle, or underused industrial or commercial sites where expansion or redevelopment is complicated by real or perceived environmental contamination.

8-13. Reduce pesticide exposures that result in visits to a health care facility.

Target: 13,500 visits to a health care facility per year.

Baseline: Out of 129,592 total pesticide exposures, 27,156 required management in health care facilities in 1997.

Target setting method: 50 percent improvement.

Data source: Toxic Exposure Surveillance System (TESS), American Association of Poison Control Centers.

Pesticide exposures include those involving disinfectants, fungicides, herbicides, insecticides, moth repellants, and rodenticides, as defined by EPA. The American Association of Poison Control Centers surveillance covers approximately 93 percent of the U.S. population.

8-14. (Developmental) Reduce the amount of toxic pollutants released, disposed of, treated, or used for energy recovery.

Potential data source: Toxic Release Inventory (TRI), EPA.

Reductions in toxic pollutants released, disposed of, treated, or used for energy recovery can be measured by industry's success in reducing pollution at the source—that is, not producing pollutants at all, through manufacturing process changes, shifting to less polluting ingredients, packaging changes, and other source reduction methods. For that reason, all pollutants, those released and those treated or disposed of in some manner, should be measured.

8-15. Increase recycling of municipal solid waste.

Target: 38 percent of municipal solid waste generated.

Baseline: 27 percent of total municipal solid waste generated was recycled in 1996 (includes composting).

Target setting method: Consistent with the EPA's 1997 Strategic Plan.

Data source: Characterization of Municipal Solid Waste, EPA.

Healthy Homes and Healthy Communities

8-16. Reduce indoor allergen levels.

Target and baseline:

Objective	Allergen	1998-99 Baseline	2010 Target
		Number of Homes (in millions)	
8-16a.	Group I dust mite allergens that exceed 2µ/gram of dust in bed	36.3	29.0
8-16b.	Group I dust mite allergens that exceed 10 µ/gram of dust in the bed	18.6	14.9
8-16c.	German cockroach allergens that exceed 0.1 unit/gram of dust in the bed	4.7	3.8

Indoor allergens—such as from house dust mites, cockroaches, mold, rodents, and pets—can worsen symptoms of respiratory conditions, such as asthma and allergies. These allergies are an important public health issue because most people spend the majority of their time indoors, both at home and at work. In addition, effective methods to reduce exposure to some of these allergens exist (for example, placement of impermeable covers on mattresses and pillows reduces dust mite allergen exposures in beds). (See Focus Area 24. Respiratory Diseases.)

Target setting method: 20 percent improvement.

Data source: National Survey of Lead and Allergens in Housing, CDC, NIEHS, and U.S. Department of Housing and Urban Development.

8-17. (Developmental) Increase the number of office buildings that are managed using good indoor air quality practices.

Potential data source: Indoor Environment Division, EPA.

The air quality inside a building impacts both the comfort and health of its occupants. Pollutants are found at higher levels in indoor air as compared to outdoor air. In addition, most people spend over 90 percent of their time indoors.[38]

8-18. Increase the proportion of persons who live in homes tested for radon concentrations.

Target: 20 percent.

Baseline: 17 percent of the population lived in homes in 1998 that had been tested for radon (preliminary data; age adjusted to the year 2000 standard population).

Target setting method: Better than the best.

Data source: National Health Interview Survey (NHIS), CDC, NCHS.

Total Population, 1994*	Persons Living in Homes Tested for Radon
	Percent
TOTAL	11
Race and ethnicity	
American Indian or Alaska Native	DSU
Asian or Pacific Islander	12
Asian	13
Native Hawaiian and other Pacific Islander	DSU
Black or African American	10
White	11
Hispanic or Latino	7
Not Hispanic or Latino	11
Black or African American	10
White	11
Gender	
Female	11
Male	11
Family income level	
Poor	8
Near poor	6
Middle/high income	13

DNA = Data have not been analyzed. DNC = Data are not collected. DSU = Data are statistically unreliable.

Note: Age adjusted to the year 2000 standard population.

*New data for population groups will be added when available.

8-19. **Increase the number of new homes constructed to be radon resistant.**

Target: 2.1 million additional new homes.

Baseline: 1.4 million new homes as of 1997.

Target setting method: 50 percent improvement.

Data source: National Association of New Home Builders.

8-20. **(Developmental) Increase the proportion of the Nation's primary and secondary schools that have official school policies ensuring the safety of students and staff from environmental hazards, such as chemicals in special classrooms, poor indoor air quality, asbestos, and exposure to pesticides.**

Potential data source: School Health Policies and Programs Study (SHPPS), CDC, DASH.

8-21. **(Developmental) Ensure that State health departments establish training, plans, and protocols and conduct annual multi-institutional exercises to prepare for response to natural and technological disasters.**

Potential data sources: Association of State and Territorial Health Officials; Public Health Foundation.

8-22. **Increase the proportion of persons living in pre-1950s housing that have tested for the presence of lead-based paint.**

Target: 50 percent.

Baseline: 16 percent of persons living in 1998 in homes built before 1950 had tested for the presence of lead-based paint (preliminary data; age adjusted to the year 2000 standard population).

Target setting method: Better than the best.

Data source: National Health Interview Survey (NHIS), CDC, NCHS.

Persons Living in Homes Built Before 1950, 1993*	Persons Living in Homes Tested for Lead-Based Paint
	Percent
TOTAL	10
Race and ethnicity	
American Indian or Alaska Native	DSU
Asian or Pacific Islander	17
Asian	18
Native Hawaiian and other Pacific Islander	DSU
Black or African American	18
White	8
Hispanic or Latino	11
Not Hispanic or Latino	10
Black or African American	18
White	8
Gender	
Female	10
Male	9
Family income level	
Poor	15
Near poor	10
Middle/high income	9

DNA = Data have not been analyzed. DNC = Data are not collected. DSU = Data are statistically unreliable.

Note: Age adjusted to the year 2000 standard population.

*New data for population groups will be added when available.

8-23. Reduce the proportion of occupied housing units that are substandard.

Target: 3 percent.

Baseline: 6.2 percent of occupied U.S. housing units had moderate or severe physical problems in 1995.

Target setting method: 52 percent improvement.

Data source: American Housing Survey, U.S. Department of Commerce, Bureau of the Census.

Residents of substandard housing are at increased risk for fire, electrical injuries, lead poisoning, falls, rat bites, and other illnesses and injuries.

Infrastructure and Surveillance

8-24. Reduce exposure to pesticides as measured by blood and urine concentrations of metabolites.

Target and baseline:

Objective	Reduction in Pesticide Exposure as Measured by Metabolites (Pesticide)	1988–94 Baseline*	2010 Target
		Blood/Urine Concentration	
8-24a.	1-naphthol (carbaryl)	36.0 µg/g creatinine	25.2 µg/g creatinine
8-24b.	Paranitrophenol (methyl parathion and parathion)	3.8 µg/g creatinine	2.7 µg/g creatinine
8-24c.	3, 5, 6-trichloro-2-pyridinol (chlorpyrifos)	8.3 µg/g creatinine	5.8 µg/g creatinine
8-24d.	Isopropoxyphenol (propoxur)	1.6 µg/g creatinine	1.1 µg/g creatinine

*95 percent of the population had concentrations below this level.

Target setting method: 30 percent improvement.

Data source: National Health and Nutrition Examination Survey (NHANES), CDC, NCHS.

Note: Data are from a subset of NHANES data and are not nationally representative. Therefore, a population data template is not available.

Pesticides included in the table inhibit cholinesterase, an enzyme found in the human body. These pesticides are among those commonly used in the home and garden, agriculture, and industry.[39] Metabolites (or breakdown products) of pesticides are measured in urine samples obtained from persons aged 6 years and older. Urinary measurements of pesticide metabolites are an accurate way to measure recent exposure to pesticides that inhibit cholinesterase. Concentrations of pesticide metabolites in urine are corrected for kidney function and expressed in µg/g creatinine, a measure of kidney function.

Data as of November 30, 1999

8-25. **(Developmental) Reduce exposure of the population to pesticides, heavy metals, and other toxic chemicals, as measured by blood and urine concentrations of the substances or their metabolites.**

Objective	Exposure Item
	Heavy metals
8-25a.	Arsenic
8-25b.	Cadmium
8-25c.	Lead
8-25d.	Manganese
8-25e.	Mercury
	Pesticides
8-25f.	2, 4-D, o-phenylphenol
8-25g.	Permethrins
8-25h.	Diazinon
	Persistent chemicals
8-25i.	Polychlorinated biphenyls
8-25j.	Dioxins
8-25k.	Furans
	Organochlorine compounds
8-25l.	Chlordane
8-25m.	Dieldrin
8-25n.	DDT
8-25o.	Lindane

Potential data source: National Health and Nutrition Examination Survey (NHANES), CDC, NCHS.

Heavy metals, PCBs, dioxins, furans, and organochlorines are in use or have been used in the past. These compounds are known or suspected to cause cancer, birth defects, or other diseases in people.

8-26. **(Developmental) Improve the quality, utility, awareness, and use of existing information systems for environmental health.**

Potential data sources: Toxic Release Inventory, EPA; Environmental Defense Fund.

Other environmental health information systems include Toxline®, IRIS, RTECS®, HazDat, TRI, and AIRS. They can be accessed via the Internet.

8-27. **Increase or maintain the number of Territories, Tribes, and States, and the District of Columbia that monitor diseases or conditions that can be caused by exposure to environmental hazards.**

Target and baseline:

Objective	Disease	1999 Baseline	2010 Target
		Number of Jurisdictions	
8-27a.	Lead poisoning	41	51
8-27b.	Pesticide poisoning	20	25
8-27c.	Mercury poisoning	14	15
8-27d.	Arsenic poisoning	10	10
8-27e.	Cadmium poisoning	10	10
8-27f.	Methemoglobinemia	9	10
8-27g.	Acute chemical poisoning*	8	15
8-27h.	Carbon monoxide poisoning	7	51
8-27i.	Asthma	6	51
8-27j.	Hyperthermia	4	10
8-27k.	Hypothermia	Developmental	
8-27l.	Skin cancer	Developmental	
8-27m.	Malignant melanoma	Developmental	
8-27n.	Other skin cancer	Developmental	
8-27o.	Birth defects	Developmental	

*Includes chemicals not covered elsewhere in the table.

Note: Target and baseline data are for States and the District of Columbia. The targets will be adjusted as data for Tribes and Territories become available.

Target setting method: Total coverage or expert opinion.

Data sources: Periodic surveys, Public Health Foundation and Council of State and Territorial Epidemiologists.

8-28. **(Developmental) Increase the number of local health departments or agencies that use data from surveillance of environmental risk factors as part of their vector control programs.**

Potential data source: Profile of local health departments, National Association of County and City Health Officials (NACCHO).

8-29. Reduce the global burden of disease due to poor water quality, sanitation, and personal and domestic hygiene.

Target: 2,130,000 deaths worldwide attributable to these factors.

Baseline: 2,668,200 deaths worldwide attributable to these factors in 1990.

Target setting method: 20 percent improvement.

Data source: Global Burden of Disease, World Health Organization.

Improving access to clean water and sanitation has been cited as the single most effective means of alleviating human distress.[40] Better water supply and sanitation may increase the average life expectancy in developing countries by 15 years. Furthermore, poor sanitation ranks as one of the highest contributing factors to the global burden of disease and injury. Diarrheal diseases, which kill nearly 3 million persons a year in developing countries, typically result from poor sanitation practices and the consumption of substandard drinking water. These diseases are mostly preventable by improving environmental services.

8-30. Increase the proportion of the population in the U.S.-Mexico border region that have adequate drinking water and sanitation facilities.

Target and baseline:

Objective	Type of Drinking Water and Sanitation Service	1997 Baseline	2010 Target
		Percent of Population Receiving Water Service or Treatment	
	Wastewater sewer service provided		
8-30a.	Ciudad Acuna	39	49
8-30b.	Matamoros	47	57
8-30c.	Mexicali	80	90
8-30d.	Nogales, Sonora	81	91
8-30e.	Piedras Negras	80	90
8-30f.	Reynosa	57	67
	Wastewater receiving treatment		
8-30g.	Ciudad Acuna	0	10
8-30h.	Matamoros	0	10
8-30i.	Mexicali	72	82
8-30j.	Nogales, Sonora	100	100

Data as of November 30, 1999

| 8-30k. | Piedras Negras | 0 | 10 |
| 8-30l. | Reynosa | 100 | 100 |

Target setting method: 10 percentage point improvement.

Data sources: EPA; Mexico's Comisión Nacional de Agua; State and local health departments; American Water Works Association; Rural Water Association; U.S.-Mexican Border Health Association.

Water pollution is one of the principal environmental and public health problems facing the U.S.-Mexico border area. Deficiencies in the treatment of wastewater, the disposal of untreated sewage, and inadequate operation and maintenance of treatment plants result in health risks. Better environmental services such as sewer service, wastewater treatment service, and safe drinking water may help achieve a balance among social and economic factors and protecting the environment in border communities and natural areas.

Related Objectives From Other Focus Areas

1. Access to Quality Health Services

1-7. Core competencies in health provider training

1-12. Single toll-free number for poison control centers

3. Cancer

3-1. Cancer deaths

3-2. Lung cancer deaths

3-8. Melanoma cancer deaths

3.9. Sun exposure

3-10. Provider counseling about preventive measures

3-14. Statewide cancer registries

4. Chronic Kidney Disease

4-1. End-stage renal disease

6. Disability and Secondary Conditions

6-12. Environmental barriers affecting participation

7. Educational and Community-Based Programs

7-2. School health education

7-10. Community health promotion programs

10. Food Safety

10-1. Foodborne Infections

10-2. Outbreaks of foodborne infections

10-5. Consumer food safety practices

11. Health Communication

11-1. Households with Internet access

11-2. Health literacy

11-4. Quality of Internet health information sources

12. Heart Disease and Stroke

12-1. Coronary heart disease deaths

14. Immunization and Infectious Diseases

14-31. Active surveillance for vaccine safety

15. Injury and Violence Prevention

15-7. Nonfatal poisonings

15-8. Deaths from poisoning

15-10. Emergency department surveillance systems

15-11. Hospital discharge surveillance systems

15-12. Emergency department visits

15-13. Deaths from unintentional injuries

15-14. Nonfatal unintentional injuries

16. Maternal, Infant, and Child Health

16-10. Low birth weight and very low birth weight

16-11. Preterm birth

16-14. Developmental disabilities

20. Occupational Safety and Health

20-1. Work-related injury deaths

20-2. Work-related injuries

20-7. Elevated blood lead levels from work exposure

20-8. Occupational skin diseases or disorders

22. Physical Activity and Fitness

22-14. Community walking

22-15. Community bicycling

23. Public Health Infrastructure

23-1. Public health employee access to Internet

23-2. Public access to information and surveillance systems

23-3. Use of geocoding in health data systems

23-4. Data for all population groups

23-5. Data for Leading Health Indicators, Health Status Indicators, and Priority Data Needs at State, Tribal, and local level

23-6. National tracking of Healthy People 2010 objectives

23-7. Timely release of data on objectives

23-8. Competencies for public health workers

23-9. Training in essential public health services

23-10. Continuing education and training by public health agencies

Terminology

(A listing of all abbreviations and acronyms used in this publication appears in Appendix K.)

Acute chemical poisoning: Unintentional poisonings caused by chemicals that are not medicines.

Aerometric Information Retrieval System (AIRS): This system, administered by EPA, contains information about air pollution in the United States and other countries.

Algae: Small one- or many-celled plants that live in the water and do not have roots, stem, or leaves but usually contain chlorophyll.

Annual vehicle miles: The distance traveled by a passenger vehicle over a given interval of time.

Bloom: Populations of algae that have grown so large that they can be seen in water with the naked eye.

Brownfields: Abandoned, idle, or underused industrial or commercial sites that raise concern in nearby communities that any expansion or redevelopment could contaminate the environment.

Chlorophyll: The green photosynthetic pigment found chiefly in plants.

Community water system: A public water system that provides water to at least 15 service connections used by year-round residents or that regularly serves at least 25 year-round residents.

Disaster: Any event, either natural (such as hurricanes, wind storms, earthquakes, volcanic eruptions, or floods) or technological (such as the release of radiation or chemical or biologic substances), that, because of its scope or severity, overwhelms a population's ability to respond.

Domestic water use: Using water for household purposes, such as drinking, preparing food, bathing, washing clothes and dishes, flushing toilets, or watering lawns and gardens. Also called residential water use. The water may be obtained from a public supply or may be self-supplied by a homeowner (such as by a well).

Environmental epidemiology: The study of the effect on human health of physical, biological, and chemical factors in the external environment. Can include examining specific populations or communities exposed to different ambient environments to clarify the relationship between physical, biological, or chemical factors and human health.

Environmental hazards: Situations or conditions in which something in the environment, such as radiation, a chemical, or other pollutant, can cause human illness or injury.

Environmental tobacco smoke: Smoke given off by cigarettes, pipes, or cigars to which nonsmokers can be exposed.

Environmental toxicology: Scientific analysis of the relationship between exposure to hazardous substances found in the environment and adverse health effects in people.

Epidemic: The occurrence in a community or region of cases of an illness, specific health-related behavior, or other health-related events

clearly in excess of normal expectancy.

Evidence based: Empirical proof that accurately validates professional guidance or recommendations, or illustrates how an approach has been used successfully in the past.

Good indoor air quality practices: Operation and maintenance procedures designed to provide air quality inside a building to increase comfort and productivity and to reduce health risks for people in the building.

Greenhouse gas (GHG): A gas that absorbs radiation of specific wave lengths within the infrared spectrum of radiation released by the earth's surface and clouds so that part of the absorbed energy is trapped and the earth's surface warms up. Water vapor, carbon dioxide, nitrous oxide, methane, and ozone are the primary greenhouse gases in the earth's atmosphere.

Hazard Ranking System (HRS): The principal screening tool used by EPA to evaluate risks to public health and the environment associated with abandoned or uncontrolled hazardous waste sites. HRS calculates a score based on the potential of hazardous substances spreading from the site through the air, surface water, or ground water and on other factors, such as density and proximity of human population. This score is the primary factor in deciding whether the site should be on the National Priorities List and, if so, what ranking it should have compared to other sites on the list.

Hazardous substances: Any substance which possesses properties that can cause harm to human health and ecologic systems. A subset of these substances,

toxics or toxicants are substances not produced by a living organism that can cause harm to human health and ecologic systems.

HazDat: A scientific database maintained by the Agency for Toxic Substances and Disease Registry. Provides access to information on the release of hazardous substances from Superfund sites or from emergency events and on the effects of hazardous substances on health.

Household lead dust: Very fine particles containing lead that are usually caused by the deterioration of lead paint.

Humanitarian emergencies: Emergencies that occur as a result of disasters that destroy or have a negative effect on basic human needs, such as food, shelter, and water.

Indoor air quality (IAQ): The overall state of the air inside a building as reflected by the presence of pollutants, such as dust, fungi, animal dander, volatile organic compounds, carbon monoxide, and lead.

Indoor allergens: Fine particles in indoor air that can cause allergic reactions and respiratory problems, including dust mites and animal dander.

Infectious agents: Any organism, such as a virus, parasite, or bacterium, that is capable of invading the body, multiplying, and causing disease.

Integrated Risk Information System (IRIS): This database, maintained by EPA, contains information on health hazards from over 5,000 substances.

Metabolites: Any substance produced by biological processes in the human body. In some cases, it is not possible to measure certain substances (for example, pesticides) in the human body to determine exposure to those substances, but instead it is possible to measure the secondary substance or metabolite which is created when the human body breaks down the primary substance.

National Ambient Air Quality Standards (NAAQS): Standards set by EPA for the level of common air pollutants allowed by the Clean Air Act.

National Priorities List (NPL): EPA's list of the most serious uncontrolled or abandoned hazardous waste sites identified for possible long-term cleanup under Superfund. The list is based primarily on the score a site receives from the Hazard Ranking System. EPA updates the NPL at least yearly. A site must be on the NPL to receive funds from the Superfund Trust Fund for remedial action.

Nonattainment area: A locality where air pollution levels persistently exceed EPA's National Ambient Air Quality Standards.

Nonpoint source: The source of runoff water coming from an area such as a yard, parking lot, pasture, or other urban or agricultural area.

Ozone: Ozone occurs naturally in the stratosphere and provides a protective layer high above the earth. At ground-level, however, ambient ozone is the prime ingredient of smog. Ambient ozone refers to ozone in the troposphere—the air that people breathe—which is different from ozone in the stratosphere, the hole in the ozone layer. Ozone is not emitted directly into the air but is formed readily in the atmosphere, usually during hot summer weather, from

volatile organic compounds emitted by motor vehicles, chemical plants, refineries, factories, consumer and commercial products, other industrial sources, and trees—and from nitrogen oxides emitted by motor vehicles, power plants, and other sources of combustion. Changing weather patterns contribute to yearly differences in ozone concentrations from city to city.

Particulate matter: General term used for a mixture of solid particles and liquid droplets found in the air. These particles, which come in a wide range of sizes, originate from "built" and natural sources. Fine particles (PM2.5) result from fuel combustion from motor vehicles, power generation, and industrial facilities, as well as from residential fireplaces and wood stoves. Coarse particles (PM10) generally are emitted from other sources, such as vehicles traveling on unpaved roads, materials handling, and crushing and grinding operations, as well as windblown dust.

Per capita water use: The average amount of water used per person during a standard period, generally per day. In the United States, this measure usually is reported in gallons per day.

Persistent chemicals: Chemicals, such as organochlorine compounds, that remain in the environment for a long time and can accumulate in the fat of people and animals exposed to them.

Photosynthesis: Formation of carbohydrates from carbon dioxide and a source of hydrogen (as water) in the chlorophyll-containing tissues of plants exposed to light.

Point source: The source of water coming from a specific

location, such as a drain pipe from a wastewater treatment plant or an industrial plant.

Poisoning: An exposure to a toxic substance that produces negative signs or symptoms.

Premature death: A death that occurs earlier than the life expectancy expected for most members of the population.

Protozoa: A subkingdom of the animal kingdom, including all of the so-called acellular or unicellular forms (for example, Amoeba, Giardia, and Cryptosporidium).

Radon: A colorless, naturally occurring radioactive gas found in some soils or rocks.

Radon-resistant construction: Affordable and simple techniques that, when incorporated during construction of a new home, reduce indoor radon levels by preventing radon entry and providing a means for venting radon to the outdoors.

Registry of Toxic Effects of Chemical Substances (RTECS®): Maintained by the National Institute for Occupational Safety and Health, this database contains information on the toxic effects of chemical substances. The list of substances includes drugs, food additives, preservatives, ores, pesticides, dyes, detergents, lubricants, soaps, plastics, extracts from plant and animal sources, plants or animals that are toxic by contact or consumption, and industrial intermediates and waste products from production processes.

Service connection: The point at which a customer's water supply attaches to a water utilities distribution system.

Special classrooms: Classrooms with special characteristics, such as laboratories or art rooms, in

Data as of November 30, 1999

or art rooms, in which particular environ-mental hazards may be found.

Substandard housing: Housing with moderate or severe physical problems in plumbing, heating, or electrical systems, upkeep and sanitation, hallways, or kitchens.

Superfund: The program operated under the legislative authority of Comprehensive Environmental Response, Compensation, and Liability Act (CERCLA) and Superfund Amendments and Reauthorization Act (SARA) that funds and carries out EPA solid waste emergency and long-term removal or remedial activites. These activities include establishing the National Priorities List, investigating sites for inclusion on the list, determining their priority, and conducting or supervising cleanup and other remedial actions or both.

Sustainable development: Growth and development within a society that is intended to meet the needs of the present without compromising the ability of future generations to meet their own needs.

Toxic Release Inventory (TRI): EPA's list of more that 600 designated chemicals that threaten health and the environment. Authorized under the Emergency Planning and Community Right-To-Know Act (EPCRA) of 1986, this system requires manufacturers to report releases of these chemicals to EPA and State governments. EPA compiles the data in an online, publicly accessible national computerized database.

Toxline®: A collection of online information on drugs and other chemicals maintained by the National Library of Medicine.

Transit: Represents what used to be called "mass transit." The 1990 Nationwide Personal Transportation Survey (NPTS/U.S. Department of Transportation) included the following modes in its transit count: bus, subway or elevated rail, commuter rail, streetcar, and trolley. The 1995 NPTS characterizes a "trip" as travel to a destination (for example, worksite). Travel to work, for instance, that includes two stops along the way (trip chains) would constitute three "trips."

µg/dL: Micrograms per deciliter.

Urban sprawl: Unplanned and inefficient development of open land.

Vector-borne diseases: Illnesses that are transmitted to people by organisms, such as insects.

Vector control: Control of any object, organism, or thing that transmits disease from one host to another.

Waterborne disease outbreaks: Includes only outbreaks from infectious agents and chemical poisoning incidents in which two or more people experience a similar illness after consumption or use of water intended for drinking and epidemiologic evidence implicates water as the source of illness. The stipulation that at least two people be ill is waived for single cases of laboratory-confirmed, primary amebic meningoencephalitis and for single cases of chemical poisoning if water-quality data indicate contamination by the chemical.

References

1.   World Health Organization (WHO). Indicators for Policy and Decision Making in Environmental Health (draft). Geneva, Switzerland: the Organization, June 1997.

2.   National Research Council. *Environmental Epidemiology: Public Health and Hazardous Wastes,* Vol. 1. Washington, DC: National Academy Press, 1991.

3.   Agency for Toxic Substances and Disease Registry: Priority Health Conditions—An Integrated Strategy to Evaluate the Relationship Between Illness and Exposure to Hazardous Substances. Atlanta, GA: U.S. Department of Health and Human Services, 1993.

4.   WHO Fact Sheet 170, June 1997.

5.   The Commissioned Corps of the United States Public Health Service, U.S. Department of Health and Human Services Website. http://www.os.dhhs.gov/phs/corps/direct1.html#history.

6.   U.S. Bureau of Economic Analysis. Survey of Current Business. May 1995.

7.   National Air Quality and Trends Report, EPA, Office of Air and Radiation, Washington, DC, 1997.

8.   National Toxics Inventory, EPA, 1997 Report.

9.   National Air Quality and Trends Report, EPA, Washington, DC, 1997.

10.   Health Costs of Air Pollution, American Lung Association, 1990.

11. Craun, G.F. In: Craun, G.F., ed. *Waterborne disease outbreaks in the United States.* Boca Raton, FL: CRC Press, 1986.

12. CDC, Waterborne disease outbreaks, 1991-1992. *Morbidity and Mortality Weekly Report* 42 (no. SS-5):1-22, 1993.

13. CDC, Waterborne disease outbreaks, 1989-1990. *Morbidity and Mortality Weekly Report* 40 (no. SS-3):1-21, 1991.

14. CDC, Waterborne disease outbreaks, 1993-1994. *Morbidity and Mortality Weekly Report* 45 (no. SS-1):1-33, 1995.

15. Minority Staff Report for Senator Tom Harkin, (D-IA) Ranking Member, United States Senate Committee on Agriculture, Nutrition, & Forestry, "ANIMAL WASTE POLLUTION IN AMERICA: AN EMERGING NATIONAL PROBLEM, Environmental Risks Of Livestock & Poultry Production," December 1997.

16. Bureau of the Census. American Housing Survey for the United States in 1995. Current Housing Reports H150/95RV. Washington, DC: U.S. Government Printing Office. 1997.

17. Litovitz, T.L.; Smilkstein, M.; Felberg, L.; et al. 1996 annual report of the American Association of Poison Control Centers: Toxic Exposure Surveillance System. *American Journal of Emergency Medicine* 15:447-500, 1997.

18. Chemical Economics Handbook [Online] (1997, September). SRF International. Available: DIALOG File 359 [1998, April 10].

19. Agency for Toxic Substances and Disease Registry. *The Nature and Extent of Childhood Lead Poisoning in Children in the United States: A Report to Con-* *gress.* Washington, DC: U.S. Department of Health and Human Services, July 1988.

20. Centers for Disease Control and Prevention (CDC). Screening Young Children for Lead Poisoning: Guidance for State and Local Public Health Officials. Atlanta, GA: the Agency, November 1997.

21. Last, J.M. (ed.). *A Dictionary of Epidemiology.* p.42, 1998.

22. CDC. Forecasted state-specific estimates of self-reported asthma prevalence—United States, 1998. *Morbidity and Mortality Weekly Report*, 47:1022-1025, 1998.

23. Weiss, K.B.; Gergen, P.J.; Hodgson, T.A. An economic evaluation of asthma in the United States. *New England Journal of Medicine* 326:862-866, 1992.

24. Summary of Travel Trends 1995 Nationwide Personal Transportation Survey, Oak Ridge National Library, Oak Ridge, TN, January 8, 1999, p. 13.

25. EPA. U.S.-Mexico Border XXI Program: Framework Document. No. 160-R-96-003. Washington, DC. October 1996.

26. Institute of Medicine. Toward Environmental Justice—Research, Education, and Health Policy Needs. Washington, DC: National Academy Press, 1999.

27. United States Geological Survey (1993), United States Geological Survey, Estimated use of water in the United States in 1990, USGS National Circular 1081, Washington, DC: Government Printing Office, 1993.

28. Toxnet7, National Library of Medicine, Toxicology and Environmental Health Information Program, Bethesda, MD.

29. Internet Grateful Med, National Library of Medicine, Bethesda, MD 20894, USA.

30. Department of Energy Clean Cities Program

31. Renewable Fuels Association <www.etanolRFA.Org>

32. Description of FY 1993BFY 1997 PWS Statistics, Safe Drinking Water Information System (SDWIS/FED), 1997 data frozen April 1, 1998, Environmental Protection Agency, Office of Enforcement and Compliance Assurance.

33. The National Water Use Program. U.S. Geological Survey. Washington, DC.

34. EPA, National Water Quality Inventory 1994 Report to Congress, 1994.

35. Environmental Protection Agency. Strategic Plan. Washington, DC: EPA, September, 1997.

36. EPA, Office of Water's Office of Science and Technology, Washington, DC.

37. NRCD Headquarters-Water Program, New York, NY.

38. Spengler, J.D., and K. Sexton. 1983. Indoor air pollution: a public health perspective. Science 221:9-17.

39. EPA. Pesticides Industry Sales and Usage; 1994 and 1995 Market estimates, 1997.

40. World Resources Institute, World Resources: A guide to the global environment. 1996-1997. Oxford: Oxford University Press.

9
Family Planning

Lead Agency: Office of Population Affairs

Contents

Goal

Improve pregnancy planning and spacing and prevent unintended pregnancy.

Overview

In an era when technology should enable couples to have considerable control over their fertility, half of all pregnancies in the United States are unintended.[1] Although between 1987 and 1994, the proportion of pregnancies that were unintended declined in the United States from 57 to 49 percent,[2] other industrialized nations report fewer unintended pregnancies,[3] suggesting that the number of unintended pregnancies can be reduced further. Family planning remains a keystone in attaining a national goal aimed at achieving planned, wanted pregnancies and preventing unintended pregnancies. Family planning services provide opportunities for individuals to receive medical advice and assistance in controlling if and when they get pregnant and for health providers to offer health education and related medical care.

The family planning objectives for Healthy People 2010 echo the recommendations contained in the 1995 Institute of Medicine report *Best Intentions: Unintended Pregnancy and the Well-Being of Children and Families.*[4] The foremost recommendation of the report calls for the Nation to adopt a social norm in which all pregnancies are intended—that is, clearly and consciously desired at the time of conception. Emphasizing personal choice and intent, this norm speaks to planning for pregnancy, as well as to avoiding unintended pregnancy.

Unintended pregnancy rates in the United States show a decline, probably as a result of higher contraceptive use and use of more effective contraceptive methods.[2] Despite this improvement, unintended pregnancy remains a common problem, and further progress is needed.

Issues and Trends

One important determinant of pregnancy and birth rates is contraceptive use. The proportion of all females aged 15 to 44 years who currently are practicing contraception (including females who have been sterilized for contraceptive reasons and husbands or partners who have had vasectomies) rose from about 56 percent in 1982 to 60 percent in 1988 and 64 percent in 1995.[5] However, 5.2 percent of all females aged 15 to 44 years had intercourse in the past 3 months and did not use contraceptives.[5]

No one method of contraception is likely to be consistently and continuously suitable for each woman, man, or couple. Total abstinence is the only fool-proof method of contraception. Sterilization, the most common method of contraception

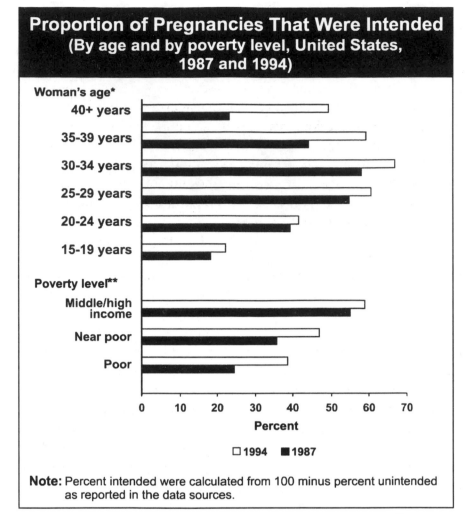

Proportion of Pregnancies That Were Intended
(By age and by poverty level, United States, 1987 and 1994)

Woman's age*
- 40+ years
- 35-39 years
- 30-34 years
- 25-29 years
- 20-24 years
- 15-19 years

Poverty level**
- Middle/high income
- Near poor
- Poor

Percent

□ 1994 ■ 1987

Note: Percent intended were calculated from 100 minus percent unintended as reported in the data sources.

Sources: *Henshaw, S.K. Unintended Pregnancy in the United States. *Family Planning Perspectives* 30(1)24–29, 46; 1998. **Brown, S.S., and Eisenberg, L. *The Best Intentions: Unintended Pregnancy and the Well-Being of Children and Families.* Washington, DC: National Academy Press, 1995.

in the United States, has near-perfect effectiveness and differs from other methods because it is usually permanent.[5]

Used by an estimated 10 million females, combination oral contraceptives are the most popular method of reversible contraception in the United States. Other hormonal contraceptives, such as injectables and implants, and intrauterine devices (IUDs) have the appeal of providing effective contraception without the need for daily compliance. For barrier methods, such as the condom and diaphragm, the average effectiveness is more variable. Used correctly and consistently, condoms can prevent both pregnancy and disease. Other barrier methods include the diaphragm, cervical cap, and female condom, which may reduce the risk but do not prevent sexually transmitted diseases (STDs) that primarily affect the cervix. Spermicides used alone (foams, creams, and jellies), coitus interruptus (withdrawal), and periodic abstinence (rhythm) are other options; however, their effectiveness in actual use is lower than that for other methods.

Contraceptive method choices are far from ideal. Even with all financial and knowledge barriers removed, effective and consistent contraceptive use is difficult. Contraceptive research and development efforts must be expanded to bring new methods to the market, methods that combine high contraceptive efficacy and ease of use with protection against STDs and HIV. Increased attention also must be given to bringing new methods to the United States, including male methods of contraception, spermicide, and microbicide alternatives. Improving the range of contraceptive choices increases the likelihood that individuals and couples will be able to find a contraceptive method that suits them. Greater choice enhances individuals' control over their fertility and reduces the risk of unintended pregnancy.

Reducing unintended pregnancies is possible and necessary. Unintended pregnancy in the United States is serious and costly and occurs frequently. Socially, the costs can be measured in unintended births, reduced educational attainment and employment opportunity, greater welfare dependency, and increased potential for child abuse and neglect. Economically, health care costs are increased. An unintended pregnancy, once it occurs, is expensive no matter what the outcome. Medically, unintended pregnancies are serious in terms of the lost opportunity to prepare for an optimal pregnancy, the increased likelihood of infant and maternal illness, and the likelihood of abortion.[4] The consequences of unintended pregnancy are not confined to those occurring in teenagers or unmarried couples. In fact, unintended pregnancy can carry serious consequences at all ages and life stages.[4]

With an unintended pregnancy, the mother is less likely to seek prenatal care in the first trimester and more likely not to obtain prenatal care at all.[6,7] She is less likely to breastfeed[8] and more likely to expose the fetus to harmful substances, such as tobacco or alcohol.[4] The child of such a pregnancy is at greater risk of low birth weight, dying in its first year, being abused, and not receiving sufficient resources for healthy development.[9] A disproportionate share of the women bearing children whose conception was unintended are unmarried or at either end of the reproductive age span—factors that, in themselves, carry increased medical and social burdens for children and their parents. Pregnancy begun without some degree of planning often prevents individual women and men from participating in preconception risk identification and management.

For teenagers, the problems associated with unintended pregnancy are compounded, and the consequences are well documented. Teenaged mothers are less likely to get or stay married, less likely to complete high school or college, and more likely to require public assistance and to live in poverty than their peers who are not mothers. Infants born to teenaged mothers, especially mothers under age 15 years, are more likely to suffer from low birth weight, neonatal death, and sudden infant death syndrome. The infants may be at greater risk of child abuse, neglect, and behavioral and educational problems at later stages.[10] Nearly 1 million teenage pregnancies occur each year in the United States.[11] Clearly, the solution to the problem needs to be found.

Unintended pregnancy is expensive, and contraceptives save health care resources by preventing unintended pregnancy.[12] The pregnancy care cost for one woman who does not intend to be pregnant, yet is sexually active and uses no contraception, is estimated at about $3,200 annually in a managed care setting.[12, 13] Estimates of the overall cost to U.S. taxpayers for teenage childbearing range between $7 billion and $15 billion a year, mainly attributed to higher public assistance costs, foregone tax revenues resulting from changes in productivity of the teen parents, increased child welfare, and higher criminal justice costs.[14] Unintended births to teenagers, which account for about 40 percent of teenaged pregnancies, cost more than $1.3 billion in direct health expenditures each year.[15]

Induced abortion is another consequence of unintended pregnancy. Although the numbers of abortions in this country have been declining over the past 15 years,[16] approximately one abortion occurs for every three live births annually in the United States, a ratio 2 to 4 times higher than in many other Western democracies. Just as unintended pregnancy occurs across the spectrum of age and socioeconomic status, women of all reproductive ages, married or unmarried, and in all income categories obtain abortions.

Abortion results when women have unintended pregnancies, and adequate access to family planning services reduces the number of unintended pregnancies. Each year, publicly subsidized family planning services prevent an estimated 1.3 million unintended pregnancies.[17] For every $1 spent on publicly funded contraceptive services, $3 is saved in Medicaid bills for pregnancy-related health care and medical care for newborns.[17]

Disparities

Unintended pregnancies occur among females of all socioeconomic levels and all marital status and age groups, but females under age 20 years, and poor and African American women are especially likely to become pregnant unintentionally.[4] More than 4 in 10 pregnancies to white and Hispanic females are unintended; 7 in 10 pregnancies to African American females are unintended. Unintended pregnancies during contraceptive use are most common among African American and Hispanic females. Poverty is strongly related to greater difficulty in using reversible contraceptive methods successfully, with these females also the least likely to have the resources necessary to access family planning services and the most likely to be affected negatively by an unintended pregnancy. For this reason, publicly subsidized family planning services are important. Yet, half of all females who are at risk for an unintended pregnancy and need publicly subsidized family planning services are not getting them.[18] Clearly, while these programs have con-

Data as of November 30, 1999

tributed substantially to preventing unintended pregnancy, the need for services continues to outstrip resources available.

Difficulty in obtaining and paying for care is, of course, exacerbated for poor and low-income people. Several Federal programs support family planning services, with most targeting poor or low-income females. The Medicaid program is the largest, but reimbursement for family planning services is typically not available to adolescents, women without children, women who are married, and working poor women whose income may just exceed the eligibility level.

An estimated 6.6 million females receive services from subsidized family planning providers annually, slightly less than one-half of those considered to be in need of subsidized family planning services (those at risk of unintended pregnancy and with a family income less than 250 percent of the poverty level).[19] Family planning programs consisting of some 3,000 agencies with over 7,000 clinic locations provide nearly 40 percent of family planning services in the United States. Health departments represent nearly half of these locations, along with hospitals, community health centers, and other public and nonprofit organizations. Nearly two-thirds of all females served (4.2 million) obtained care at 1 of 4,200 clinics receiving funds from the Federal Title X Family Planning Program.[19]

Opportunities

A 1995 survey of the Nation's family planning agencies estimated that almost 70 percent of agencies have at least one special program of outreach education or service to meet the needs of teenagers. Fewer have special programs for hard-to-serve populations, such as homeless persons, persons with disabilities, or substance abusers.[20] Furthermore, whether those agencies target their services or simply provide care to those who happened to seek it is not known.[21] The need for family planning services among all these groups is undeniably great. In the case of substance abuse, the link between illegal drug use and infection with HIV has meant more Federal and State funding for programs designed to reach these groups. Thus, substance abusers may be more likely to be targeted by family planning agencies than other hard-to-reach populations. Some programs focus specifically on HIV prevention, whereas others offer comprehensive family planning services and related education and counseling.[21]

Language and cultural differences are significant barriers to serving non-English-speaking population groups. Providers report that they often have difficulty finding staff with appropriate language skills who also have adequate family planning skills and experience. Furthermore, simply speaking the language of the client is not sufficient; the provider also must be able to relate on a cultural level.[21] Persons of various ethnic backgrounds often are uncomfortable talking to strangers about intimate topics, such as sex and birth control, let alone undergoing a pelvic or breast exam. Some racial and ethnic groups tend to visit a doctor only when they are sick and not to seek preventive services, including family planning. Reaching such populations can be difficult.

Providing outreach, education, and clinical services to hard-to-reach populations is expensive. Frequently, these groups have more health problems than less disadvantaged family planning clients, and these health problems are not necessarily confined to family planning. One study estimated that the cost of providing services to homeless women is twice that of other women, with homeless women at such high risk of gynecological problems that they must undergo a complete exam and diagnostic workup at every visit.[21] Disabled individuals often require extra staff, equipment, and time (especially if they are clients with developmental disabilities) to ensure contraceptive compliance and to deal with side-effect issues.[21] The extra time, effort, and expense required to reach hard-to-serve groups undoubtedly discourage some family planning agencies from implementing programs for these populations.[20] Clearly, there is a need to expand services to hard-to-reach populations and to find effective strategies to overcome barriers to services experienced by individuals in these populations.

Finally, public education and information about family planning need to be expanded. Public education efforts and the media could help persons to better understand the benefits of sexual abstinence. Numerous studies and polls indicate a disturbing degree of misinformation about contraceptive methods. The modest health risks of oral contraceptives frequently are exaggerated, whereas the more considerable benefits are underestimated. Knowledge about emergency contraception is not widespread, and the relative effectiveness of various contraceptive methods often is not well understood. Moreover, the risk of unintended pregnancy in the absence of contraceptive use is underestimated, and many population groups lack accurate information on STDs and reproductive health in general.[22] The media—print, broadcast, and video—must be encouraged to help in the task of conveying accurate and balanced information on contraception, highlighting the benefits as well as the risks of contraceptives.

Access to quality contraceptive services continues to be an important factor in promoting healthy pregnancies and preventing unintended pregnancies. Although people in the United States view contraception as basic to their lives, and their health care, health insurance plans traditionally have not covered family planning services. Three-fourths of U.S. women of childbearing age rely on private insurance; the extent to which they are covered for contraception can differ dramatically depending on the type of insurance.[23] Traditional plans provide the least comprehensive coverage for family planning services, while health maintenance organizations and newer managed care plans provide more comprehensive contraceptive coverage. Increased access through insurance coverage for family planning is important since in the absence of comprehensive coverage, many women may opt for whatever method may be covered by their health plan rather than the method most appropriate for their individual needs and circumstances. Other women may opt not to use contraception if it is not covered under their insurance plan.

Interim Progress Toward Year 2000 Objectives

Of the 12 family planning Healthy People 2000 objectives, progress has been made for 9 objectives. Substantial decreases have occurred in unintended pregnancy. The use of contraceptives among females aged 15 to 44 years at risk for unintended pregnancy has increased. The pregnancy rate for females using a contraceptive method has declined. Increases in adolescents' abstinence from sexual intercourse have occurred, as well as in their use of contraceptives. Although short of the year 2000 targets, decreases in adolescent pregnancy have been reported. Data are not available to update objectives on family planning counseling and age-appropriate preconception care counseling.

Note: Unless otherwise noted, data are from Centers for Disease Control and Prevention, National Center for Health Statistics, *Healthy People 2000 Review, 1998-99.*

Family Planning

Goal: Improve pregnancy planning and spacing and prevent unintended pregnancy.

Number	Objective
9-1	Intended pregnancy
9-2	Birth spacing
9-3	Contraceptive use
9-4	Contraceptive failure
9-5	Emergency contraception
9-6	Male involvement
9-7	Adolescent pregnancy
9-8	Abstinence before age 15 years
9-9	Abstinence among adolescents aged 15 to 17 years
9-10	Pregnancy prevention and sexually transmitted disease (STD) protection
9-11	Pregnancy prevention education
9-12	Problems in becoming pregnant and maintaining a pregnancy
9-13	Insurance coverage for contraceptive supplies and services

9-1. Increase the proportion of pregnancies that are intended.

Target: 70 percent.

Baseline: 51 percent of all pregnancies among females aged 15 to 44 years were intended in 1995.

Target setting method: Better than the best.

Data source: National Survey of Family Growth (NSFG), CDC, NCHS.

Pregnancies Among Females Aged 15 to 44 Years, 1995	Pregnancy Intended Percent
TOTAL	51
Race and ethnicity	
American Indian or Alaska Native	DSU
Asian or Pacific Islander	DSU
Asian	DNC
Native Hawaiian and other Pacific Islander	DNC
Black or African American	28
White	57
Hispanic or Latino	51
Not Hispanic or Latino	DNA
Black or African American	DNA
White	DNA
Age	
15 to 19 years	22
20 to 24 years	42
25 to 29 years	60
30 to 34 years	67
35 to 39 years	59
40 to 44 years	49
Family income level	
Poor	39
Near poor	47
Middle/high income	59

Pregnancies Among Females Aged 15 to 44 Years, 1995	Pregnancy Intended Percent
Select populations	
Marital status	
Currently married	69
Formerly married	38
Never married	22

DNA = Data have not been analyzed. DNC = Data are not collected. DSU = Data are statistically unreliable.

A significant decline in the rates of unintended pregnancy has occurred, indicating that progress toward a goal of increased intended pregnancy is possible. Between 1987 and 1994, the proportion of pregnancies that were unintended declined from 57 to 49 percent.[2] By comparison, the percentage of unintended pregnancy is much lower in some other countries—in 1994-95, it was 39 percent in Canada and 6 percent in the Netherlands.[3] Overall, females in the United States spend three-fourths of their reproductive years trying to avoid pregnancy.[17] Unintended pregnancy often is mistakenly perceived as predominantly an adolescent problem; however, unintended pregnancy is a problem among all age groups. In 1994, nearly one-half (48 percent) of American females aged 15 to 44 years had at least one unintended pregnancy in their lifetime, more than one-fourth (28 percent) had one or more unplanned births, nearly one-third (30 percent) had one or more abortions, and 1 in 10 (11 percent) had both an unintended birth and an induced abortion.[2] A goal of 70 percent is ambitious and will require strategies to reduce the gaps among population groups.

9-2. Reduce the proportion of births occurring within 24 months of a previous birth.

Target: 6 percent.

Baseline: 11 percent of females aged 15 to 44 years gave birth within 24 months of a previous birth in 1995.

Target setting method: Better than the best.

Data source: National Survey of Family Growth (NSFG), CDC, NCHS.

Females Aged 15 to 44 Years, 1995	New Birth Occurred Within 24 Months of Previous Birth
	Percent
TOTAL	11
Race and ethnicity	
American Indian or Alaska Native	DSU
Asian or Pacific Islander	DSU
Asian	DNC
Native Hawaiian and other Pacific Islander	DNC
Black or African American	DNA
White	DNA
Hispanic or Latino	14
Not Hispanic or Latino	DNA
Black or African American	14
White	10
Age	
15 to 19 years	9
20 to 24 years	14
25 to 29 years	10
30 to 34 years	11
35 to 39 years	10
40 to 44 years	DSU
Family income level	
Poor	19
Near poor	11
Middle/high income	7
Disability status	
Persons with disabilities	DNC
Persons without disabilities	DNC
Select populations	
Marital status	
Currently married	11
Formerly married	13
Never married	11

DNA = Data have not been analyzed. DNC = Data are not collected. DSU = Data are statistically unreliable.

Encouraging females of all ages to space their pregnancies adequately can help lower their risk of adverse perinatal outcomes. To the extent that very closely spaced pregnancies are unplanned, unintended pregnancy may increase the risk of low birth weight.[4] A recent study indicates that females who wait 18 to 23 months after delivery before conceiving their next child lower their risk of adverse perinatal outcomes, including low birth weight, preterm birth, and small-for-size gestational age.[24] Health care providers can help all new mothers understand that they can become pregnant again soon after delivery and should assist them with contraceptive education and supplies.

For adolescents, bearing a child is associated with poor outcomes for young females and their children. Giving birth to a second child while still a teen further increases these risks. The prevention of second and subsequent births to very young females is of great interest to public health. Research has shown that such births are associated with physical and mental health problems for the mother and the child.[25] Yet, analysis indicates that in the 2 years following the first birth, teenaged mothers have a second birth at about the same rate as other mothers. In 1997, nearly one in every five births to teenaged mothers was a birth of second order or higher.[26]

9-3. Increase the proportion of females at risk of unintended pregnancy (and their partners) who use contraception.

Target: 100 percent.

Baseline: 93 percent of females aged 15 to 44 years at risk of unintended pregnancies used contraception in 1995.

Target setting method: Total coverage.

Data source: National Survey of Family Growth (NSFG), CDC, NCHS.

Females Aged 15 to 44 Years at Risk of Unintended Pregnancy, 1995	Used Contraception Percent
TOTAL	93
Race and ethnicity	
American Indian or Alaska Native	DSU
Asian or Pacific Islander	DSU
Asian	DNC
Native Hawaiian and other Pacific Islander	DNC
Black or African American	90
White	93

Data as of November 30, 1999

Females Aged 15 to 44 Years at Risk of Unintended Pregnancy, 1995	Used Contraception Percent
Hispanic or Latino	91
Not Hispanic or Latino	DNA
Black or African American	90
White	93
Age	
15 to 19 years	81
20 to 24 years	91
25 to 29 years	94
30 to 34 years	94
35 to 39 years	95
40 to 44 years	93
Family income level	
Poor	92
Near poor	91
Middle/high income	93
Select populations	
Marital status	
Currently married	95
Formerly married	92
Never married	88

DNA = Data have not been analyzed. DNC = Data are not collected. DSU = Data are statistically unreliable.

The percentage of at-risk females using any form of contraception rose from 88 in 1982 to 93 in 1995.[27] Increasing the target to 100 percent by 2010 will be challenging and could reduce dramatically occurrences of unintended pregnancy. Poor or nonexistent contraceptive use is one of the main causes of unintended pregnancy, with unintended pregnancy occurring among two groups: females using no contraception and females whose contraceptives fail or are used improperly. In the United States, the small proportion of females who are at risk of unintended pregnancy and use no method of contraception account for over half of all unintended pregnancies. Reducing the proportion of sexually active persons using no birth control method and increasing the effectiveness (correct and consistent use) with which persons use contraceptive methods would do much to lower the unintended pregnancy rate.[28] Just reducing the proportion of females not using contraception by half could prevent as many as one-third of all unintended pregnancies and 500,000 abortions per year.[29]

9-4. Reduce the proportion of females experiencing pregnancy despite use of a reversible contraceptive method.

Target: 7 percent.

Baseline: 13 percent of females aged 15 to 44 years experienced pregnancy despite use of a reversible contraceptive method in 1995.

Target setting method: Better than the best (retain year 2000 target).

Data sources: National Survey of Family Growth (NSFG), CDC, NCHS; Abortion Patient Survey, Alan Guttmacher Institute.

Females Aged 15 to 44 Years Using Reversible Contraception, 1995	Experienced Pregnancy Percent
TOTAL	13
Race and ethnicity	
American Indian or Alaska Native	DSU
Asian or Pacific Islander	DSU
Asian	DNC
Native Hawaiian and other Pacific Islander	DNC
Black or African American	DNC
White	DNC
Hispanic or Latino	16
Not Hispanic or Latino	DNA
Black or African American	20
White	11
Family income level	
Poor	DSU
Near poor	18
Middle/high income	10
Disability status	
Persons with disabilities	DNC
Persons without disabilities	DNC

Data as of November 30, 1999

Females Aged 15 to 44 Years Using Reversible Contraception, 1995	Experienced Pregnancy Percent
Select populations	
Marital/cohabiting status	
Married	10
Cohabiting	22
Unmarried, not cohabiting	14

DNA = Data have not been analyzed. DNC = Data are not collected. DSU = Data are statistically unreliable.

The public health benefits of improved contraceptive practices are potentially enormous. Whether fertile females who are sexually active and do not want to get pregnant experience an unintended pregnancy is a function of their choice—and their partners' choice—of contraceptive methods and how effectively they use them. The efficacy of reversible contraceptive methods depends on consistent and appropriate usage. Unintended pregnancies experienced by females using reversible methods are primarily a result of inconsistent and/or inappropriate use.[30] Ideally, an objective would focus on consistent and correct use of a particular method. The data, however, cannot address the role that method switching may play in unintended pregnancy.

9-5. (Developmental) Increase the proportion of health care providers who provide emergency contraception.

Potential data source: Alan Guttmacher Institute.

The *U.S. Guide to Clinical Preventive Services*[6] identifies postcoital administration of emergency contraceptive pills (ECP) after unprotected intercourse as an effective means of reducing subsequent pregnancy. ECP is estimated to reduce the risk of subsequent pregnancy by 75 percent. Yet, this method, which has the public health potential of significantly reducing unintended pregnancy, is not well known and not yet widely available to the public. Surveys indicate that knowledge and use of postcoital contraception remains low among patients and clinicians alike.[29] In 1995, less than 1 percent of females in the United States reported ever having used ECP.[31]

Several developments, however, have formalized recognition within the medical community of ECP as an effective means of preventing pregnancy, including the American College of Obstetrics and Gynecology issuance of practice guidelines for emergency oral contraception. Barriers to the more frequent use of ECP include a lack of physician awareness of the method, a lack of public awareness of the method's availability, and a lack of access by patients to a physician who will prescribe the method.[32] Increased public awareness, including culturally and linguistically competent education about ECP, as well as direct access to and insurance reimbursement for ECP, would contribute significantly toward attainment of this objective.

In February 1997, the Food and Drug Administration (FDA) announced that certain regimens of combined oral contraceptives are safe and effective for ECP when initiated within 72 hours after unprotected intercourse.[33] The FDA notice was intended to encourage manufacturers to make this additional contraceptive option available.[33] One product, an emergency contraceptive kit, has been approved by FDA and is being marketed. On July 28, 1999, FDA approved the first progestin-only emergency contraceptive.

9-6. (Developmental) Increase male involvement in pregnancy prevention and family planning efforts.

Potential data source: National Survey of Family Growth (NSFG), CDC, NCHS.

There is increasing recognition of the value of male involvement in pregnancy prevention and family planning. Several related developments in public health and welfare demonstrate that male involvement is key, including culturally and linguistically appropriate programs promoting condom use and addressing HIV and STD prevention, culturally and linguistically competent services targeting men as part of managed care marketing strategies, emphasis on male responsibility in welfare, child support enforcement, and pregnancy prevention efforts. Concern about the spread of HIV and other STDs and the recognition of condoms as the most effective way of preventing transmission during intercourse have accentuated the need to change the sexual behavior of males. The need for rapid treatment of male partners of females testing positive for bacterial STDs is a critical element in slowing not only STD spread but also that of HIV.

Yet, information about how males could and should participate in pregnancy prevention programs is lacking. For many years, reproductive policy in the United States concentrated almost entirely on females. The National Survey of Adolescent Males (NSAM), begun in 1988 by the Urban Institute and repeated again in 1995, collected the first national trend data on the reproductive behavior of male teens. An Urban Institute survey of publicly funded family planning clinics found that males make up more than 10 percent of the total clientele in only 13 percent of clinics. An average of 6 percent of clients are males. Males represent an even smaller share of clients who receive family planning services subsidized by the Title X program (2 percent in 1991) or by Medicaid (2 percent in 1990).[34] Even though males do not actually get pregnant, integrating them in prevention programs makes sense. Males must be included in any efforts to address unintended pregnancy.[35]

The next National Survey of Family Growth (NSFG) is being expanded to include males, providing an avenue for institutionalizing data collection about male fertility that will be reflected in the Healthy People 2010 objectives. Over the course of

Healthy People 2010, male measures for family planning objectives will shift from NSAM to NSFG. NSFG will be able to collect information from males about sexual activity, contraceptive use, pregnancies to which they contribute, and the outcomes of these pregnancies, as well as male perceptions of their and their partners' views on the intendedness of pregnancies and births. NSFG will cover a broader range of male age groups than had been covered under the NSAM, which included only males aged 15 to 19 years.

9-7.   Reduce pregnancies among adolescent females.

Target: 46 pregnancies per 1,000.

Baseline: 72 pregnancies per 1,000 females aged 15 to 17 years in 1995.

Target setting method: Better than the best.

Data sources: Abortion Provider Survey, Alan Guttmacher Institute; National Vital Statistics System (NVSS), CDC, NCHS; National Survey of Family Growth (NSFG), CDC, NCHS.

Females Aged 15 to 17 Years, 1995	Pregnancy Rate per 1,000
TOTAL	72
Race and ethnicity	
American Indian or Alaska Native	DNC
Asian or Pacific Islander	DNC
Asian	DNC
Native Hawaiian and other Pacific Islander	DNC
Black or African American	133
White	61
Hispanic or Latino	110
Not Hispanic or Latino	62
Black or African American	137
White	47
Family income level	
Poor	DNC
Near poor	DNC
Middle/high income	DNC

Data as of November 30, 1999

Females Aged 15 to 17 Years, 1995	Pregnancy Rate per 1,000
Disability status	
Persons with disabilities	DNC
Persons without disabilities	DNC

DNA = Data have not been analyzed. DNC = Data are not collected. DSU = Data are statistically unreliable.

The teenage pregnancy rate in the United States is much higher than in many other developed countries—twice as high as in England and Wales, France, and Canada and nine times as high as in the Netherlands or Japan.[10] Teenage pregnancy remains an intense national issue, within the context of public health and welfare reform, concerning the optimum potential of the Nation's youth and the growth and development of newborns. Most adolescent childbearing occurs outside marriage, a trend that has increased markedly during the past two decades. In 1997, 78 percent of births to adolescent females (under age 20 years) were out of wedlock, compared to 44 percent two decades earlier (1977).[26]

Females under age 15 years experience about 30,000 pregnancies each year.[36] Consensus is widespread that all pregnancies in this age group are inappropriate and that ideally the target number should be zero. Nearly two-thirds of pregnancies in this age group end in induced abortion or fetal loss. Because of the relatively small numbers of events (and small sample sizes for fetal losses) involved, the resulting rates are not as stable as for older females. Almost no discernible decline in pregnancy rates for this age group occurs on an annual basis. Therefore, baseline and target data for pregnancies among adolescents under age 15 years are not included in this objective.[36]

9-8. Increase the proportion of adolescents who have never engaged in sexual intercourse before age 15 years.

Target and baseline:

Objective	Increase in Adolescents Aged 15 to 19 Years Never Engaging in Sexual Intercourse Before Age 15 Years	1995 Baseline	2010 Target
		Percent	
9-8a.	Females	81	88
9-8b.	Males	79	88

Data as of November 30, 1999

Target setting method: Better than the best.

Data sources: Females—National Survey of Family Growth (NSFG), CDC, NCHS; Males—National Survey of Adolescent Males (NSAM), Urban Institute.

Adolescents Aged 15 to 19 Years, 1995	No Intercourse Before Age 15 Years	
	9-8a. Females	9-8b. Males
	Percent	
TOTAL	81	79
Race and ethnicity		
American Indian or Alaska Native	DSU	DSU
Asian or Pacific Islander	DSU	DSU
Asian	DNC	DNC
Native Hawaiian and other Pacific Islander	DNC	DNC
Black or African American	70	50
White	83	84
Hispanic or Latino	76	73
Not Hispanic or Latino	81	79
Black or African American	69	51
White	83	86
Family income level		
Poor	DNA	DNC
Near poor	DNA	DNC
Middle/high income	DNA	DNC

DNA = Data have not been analyzed. DNC = Data are not collected. DSU = Data are statistically unreliable.

9-9. Increase the proportion of adolescents who have never engaged in sexual intercourse.

Objective	Increase in Adolescents Aged 15 to 17 Years Never Engaging in Sexual Intercourse	1995 Baseline	2010 Target
		Percent	
9-9a.	Females	62	75
9-9b.	Males	57	75

Target setting method: Better than the best.

Data sources: Females—National Survey of Family Growth (NSFG), CDC, NCHS; Males—National Survey of Adolescent Males (NSAM), Urban Institute.

Adolescents Aged 15 to 17 Years, 1995	Never Engaged in Sexual Intercourse	
	9-9a. Females	9-9b. Males
	Percent	
TOTAL	62	57
Race and ethnicity		
American Indian or Alaska Native	DSU	DSU
Asian or Pacific Islander	DSU	DSU
Asian	DNC	DNC
Native Hawaiian and other Pacific Islander	DNC	DNC
Black or African American	51	24
White	63	64
Hispanic or Latino	49	50
Not Hispanic or Latino	64	57
Black or African American	52	24
White	65	65
Family income level		
Poor	DSU	DNC
Near poor	DSU	DNC
Middle/high income	DSU	DNC

DNA = Data have not been analyzed. DNC = Data are not collected. DSU = Data are statistically unreliable.

Sexual experience, and particularly age at first intercourse, represents a critical indicator of the risk of pregnancy and STDs. Although all forms of intercourse (vaginal, oral, and anal) involve risk of disease transmission, this chapter focuses on avoiding unintended pregnancy and not on sexual behavior per se. Therefore, the relevant objectives reference heterosexual, vaginal intercourse only. Youth who begin having sex at younger ages are exposed to these risks over a longer period of time. Research has shown that youth who have early sexual experiences are more likely at later ages to have more sexual partners and more frequent intercourse.[37] Adolescents should be encouraged to delay sexual intercourse until they are physically, cognitively, and emotionally ready for mature sexual relationships and their consequences. They should receive education about intimacy; setting limits; resistance to social, media, peer, and partner pressure; the benefits of abstinence from intercourse; and prevention of pregnancy and STDs. Since many adolescents are or will be sexually active, they should receive support and assistance in developing the skills to evaluate their readiness for mature sexual relationships. Culturally and linguistically appropriate materials are needed that can capture the attention and affect the behaviors of these youth.

9-10. **Increase the proportion of sexually active, unmarried adolescents aged 15 to 17 years who use contraception that both effectively prevents pregnancy and provides barrier protection against disease.**

Target and baseline:

Objective	Increase in Contraceptive Use at First Intercourse by Unmarried Adolescents Aged 15 to 17 Years	1995 Baseline	2010 Target
		Percent	
	Condom		
9-10a.	Females*	68	75
9-10b.	Males	72	83
	Condom plus hormonal method		
9-10c.	Females*	6	9
9-10d.	Males	8	11

Target setting method: Better than the best.

Data sources: Females—National Survey of Family Growth (NSFG), CDC, NCHS; Males—National Survey of Adolescent Males (NSAM), Urban Institute.

*Data currently are collected for females aged 15 to 19 years. Data for females aged 15 to 17 years will be used when available.

Sexually Active, Unmarried Adolescents Aged 15 to 17 Years, 1995	Used Condom at First Intercourse		Used Condom Plus Hormonal at First Intercourse	
	9-10a. Females (15 to 19 years)*	9-10b. Males	9-10c. Females (15 to 19 years)*	9-10d. Males
	Percent			
TOTAL	68	72	6	8
Race and ethnicity				
American Indian or Alaska Native	DSU	DSU	DSU	DSU
Asian or Pacific Islander	DSU	DSU	DSU	DSU
Asian	DNC	DNC	DNC	DNC

Sexually Active, Unmarried Adolescents Aged 15 to 17 Years, 1995	Used Condom at First Intercourse		Used Condom Plus Hormonal at First Intercourse	
	9-10a. Females (15 to 19 years)*	9-10b. Males	9-10c. Females (15 to 19 years)*	9-10d. Males
	Percent			
Native Hawaiian and other Pacific Islander	DNC	DNC	DNC	DNC
Black or African American	60	60	8	12
White	70	77	5	8
Hispanic or Latino	48	64	DSU	7
Not Hispanic or Latino	71	DNA	6	DNA
Black or African American	60	61	8	11
White	74	79	6	8
Family income level				
Poor	DSU	DNC	DSU	DNC
Near poor	DSU	DNC	DSU	DNC
Middle/high income	DSU	DNC	DSU	DNC

DNA = Data have not been analyzed. DNC = Data are not collected. DSU = Data are statistically unreliable.

*Data currently are collected for females aged 15 to 19 years. Data for females aged 15 to 17 years will be used when available.

Target and baseline:

Objective	Increase in Contraceptive Use at Last Intercourse by Unmarried Adolescents Aged 15 to 17 Years	1995 Baseline	2010 Target
		Percent	
	Condom		
9-10e.	Females*	38	41
9-10f.	Males	70	72
	Condom plus hormonal method		
9-10g.	Females*	8	11
9-10h.	Males	16	20

Target setting method: Better than the best.

Data sources: Females—National Survey of Family Growth (NSFG), CDC, NCHS; Males—National Survey of Adolescent Males (NSAM), Urban Institute.

*Data currently are collected for females aged 15 to 19 years. Data for females aged 15 to 17 years will be used when available.

Sexually Active, Unmarried Adolescents Aged 15 to 17 Years, 1995	Used Condom at Last Intercourse		Used Condom Plus Hormonal at Last Intercourse	
	9-10e. Females (15 to 19 years)*	9-10f. Males	9-10g. Females (15 to 19 years)*	9-10h. Males
	Percent			
TOTAL	38	70	8	16
Race and ethnicity				
American Indian or Alaska Native	DSU	DSU	DSU	DSU
Asian or Pacific Islander	DSU	DSU	DSU	DSU
Asian	DNC	DSU	DNC	DSU
Native Hawaiian and other Pacific Islander	DNC	DSU	DNC	DSU
Black or African American	39	78	8	19
White	37	67	9	15
Hispanic or Latino	22	59	DSU	10
Not Hispanic or Latino	40	DNA	10	DNA
Black or African American	39	78	8	18
White	40	69	10	16
Family income level				
Poor	DSU	DNC	DSU	DNC
Near poor	DSU	DNC	DSU	DNC
Middle/high income	DSU	DNC	DSU	DNC

DNA = Data have not been analyzed. DNC = Data are not collected. DSU = Data are statistically unreliable.

*Data currently are collected for females aged 15 to 19 years. Data for females aged 15 to 17 years will be used when available.

There are two major health consequences of unprotected intercourse among youth—STDs, including HIV infection, and unintended pregnancy. Although abstinence is the most effective way for adolescents to avoid STDs and pregnancy and should be stressed as the certain way to prevent STDs and pregnancy, sexually active teens must be taught to use condoms properly, effectively, and consistently. Teenaged females and males who depend upon hormonal methods of contraception must be educated about the inability of these methods to prevent STDs. (See Focus Area 13. HIV and Focus Area 25. Sexually Transmitted Diseases.) Condom use must be promoted in conjunction with other contraceptive methods.[38]

Public health messages encourage individuals whose behavior places them at risk of exposure to STDs, HIV, and unintended pregnancy to use condoms, as well as effective pregnancy prevention methods, consistently and correctly.[39] Sexual intercourse in the teen years, especially first intercourse, often is unplanned and unprotected by contraception. Condom use at last intercourse has risen substantially and significantly among both male and female teenagers, suggesting more protection from STD transmission. Condom use at first intercourse also has risen—an important indicator of how well teenagers anticipate and plan for protection at the initiation of sexual activity. Culturally and linguistically appropriate materials are needed that can capture the attention and affect the behaviors of these youth.

While condom use has risen among most teenagers, the use of oral contraceptives has dropped dramatically, suggesting greater vulnerability to unintended pregnancy if other hormonal methods or consistent use of condoms is not practiced. Among currently sexually active females, the use of oral contraceptives at last intercourse fell from 43 percent to 25 percent between 1988 and 1995. The reductions in the use of oral contraception are evident across African American, Hispanic, and white teenagers. Some of the reduction in oral contraceptive use is counteracted by the adoption of new hormonal methods of contraception, such as hormonal implants and injectables. In 1995, 7 percent of sexually active teenaged females overall used these methods at last intercourse. They were used most widely among sexually active African American teenaged females: 16 percent reported using either a hormonal implant or an injectable at last intercourse.[40]

9-11. **Increase the proportion of young adults who have received formal instruction before turning age 18 years on reproductive health issues, including all of the following topics: birth control methods, safer sex to prevent HIV, prevention of sexually transmitted diseases, and abstinence.**

Target: 90 percent.

Baseline: 64 percent of females aged 18 through 24 years reported having received formal instruction on all of these reproductive health issues before turning age 18 years in 1995. (Data on males will be available in the future.)

Target setting method: Better than the best.

Data source: National Survey of Family Growth, (NSFG), CDC, NCHS.

Females Aged 18 to 24 Years, 1995	Received Reproductive Health Instruction Prior to Age 18 Years		
	9-11a. Aged 18 to 24 Years	Aged 18 to 19 Years*	Aged 20 to 24 Years*
	Percent		
TOTAL	64	80	57
Race and ethnicity			
American Indian or Alaska Native	DSU	DSU	DSU
Asian or Pacific Islander	DSU	DSU	DSU
Asian	DNC	DNC	DNC
Native Hawaiian and other Pacific Islander	DNC	DNC	DNC
Black or African American	65	81	59
White	64	81	57
Hispanic or Latino	56	69	51
Not Hispanic or Latino	65	DNA	DNA
Black or African American	66	80	60
White	65	83	58
Family income level			
Poor	63	82	56
Near poor	58	76	52
Middle/high income	66	81	60

DNA = Data have not been analyzed. DNC = Data are not collected. DSU = Data are statistically unreliable.

*Data for females aged 18 to 19 years and 20 to 24 years are displayed to further characterize the issue.

All adolescents need education that teaches the interpersonal skills they will need to withstand pressure to have sex until they are ready and that includes up-to-date information about methods to prevent pregnancy and STDs. More important, they need to receive this education before they start having sex. Ideally, such education would be developmentally appropriate, include special education students, be culturally and linguistically appropriate, be medically accurate, involve parents, and be linked into a broader context of avoiding risky health behaviors and promoting improved health. Education and knowledge, however, are not enough. Adolescents need strong reinforcement from parents, schools, the media, and other sources about the importance of making conscious, informed, responsible decisions regarding whether to have intercourse; the necessity of consistent, correct condom use to protect themselves and their partners against STDs and HIV; and the use of effective contraception to prevent unintended pregnancy. (See Focus Area 13. HIV and Focus Area 25. Sexually Transmitted Diseases.)

Becoming a sexually healthy adult is a key developmental task of adolescence. Adults can encourage adolescent sexual health by providing accurate information and education about sexuality, fostering responsible decisionmaking skills, offering support and guidance in exploring and affirming personal values, and modeling healthy sexual attitudes and behaviors. Discussions between parents and their children about sexuality and their family value system related to sexual behavior are crucial. Yet, many parents of adolescents aged 10 to 15 years in families today do not talk enough about such important topics as relationships and becoming sexually active.[41]

9-12. Reduce the proportion of married couples whose ability to conceive or maintain a pregnancy is impaired.

Target: 10 percent.

Baseline: 13 percent of married couples with wives aged 15 to 44 years had impaired ability to conceive or maintain a pregnancy in 1995.

Target setting method: 23 percent improvement.

Data source: National Survey of Family Growth (NSFG), CDC, NCHS.

Married Couples With Wives Aged 15 to 44 Years, 1995	Impaired Fecundity Percent
TOTAL	13
Race and ethnicity	
American Indian or Alaska Native	DSU
Asian or Pacific Islander	DSU
Asian	DNC
Native Hawaiian and other Pacific Islander	DNC
Black or African American	14
White	13
Hispanic or Latino	13
Not Hispanic or Latino	13
Black or African American	14
White	13
Parity status	
Parity 0	25
Parity 1 or more	10

Data as of November 30, 1999

Married Couples With Wives Aged 15 to 44 Years, 1995	Impaired Fecundity Percent
Family income level	
Poor	15
Near poor	12
Middle/high income	13

DNA = Data have not been analyzed. DNC = Data are not collected. DSU = Data are statistically unreliable.

A woman is classified as having impaired fecundity if it is impossible for her (or her husband or cohabiting partner) to have a baby for any reason other than a sterilizing operation, it is difficult or dangerous to carry a baby to term, or she and her partner have not used contraception and have not had a pregnancy for 3 years or longer. Impaired fecundity includes problems carrying pregnancies to term in addition to problems conceiving, whereas infertility includes only problems conceiving. By 1995, there had been a small overall decline in infertility, which was more marked in Hispanic couples.

Although infertility itself does not represent a serious public health threat, it carries significant personal, societal, and economic consequences that call for data surveillance and action. Infertility due to STDs is a preventable condition. Diagnosis and treatment of infertility are very costly, time-consuming, and invasive, and they can place immense stress on marital and family relations. Furthermore, those costs are likely to rise. The trend to delay childbearing (fecundity becomes increasingly impaired with age), the availability of fewer infants for adoption, and the development of new drugs and treatment procedures will mean that more and more couples seek expensive infertility services.

9-13. (Developmental) Increase the proportion of health insurance policies that cover contraceptive supplies and services.

Potential data source: Alan Guttmacher Institute.

In a 1995 report, the Institute of Medicine concluded that among the reasons for high rates of unintended pregnancy in the United States was lack of contraceptive coverage by private health insurance.[4] The report noted that many privately insured females who need contraceptive care must go out of plan and pay for it themselves, use over-the-counter methods that may be less effective, or not use any method at all. It recommended increasing the proportion of health insurance policies that cover contraceptive services and supplies.

The issue of private insurance coverage for reversible contraceptive methods affects most women and their families. Both newer managed care insurance plans and traditional fee-for-service insurance plans are more likely to pay for general gynecological services than they are to cover contraceptive services or supplies.[42] Many insurance plans do not cover reversible contraceptive methods. A 1993 survey conducted by the Alan Guttmacher Institute found that half of indemnity plans and 7 percent of health maintenance organizations (HMOs) do not cover nonpermanent contraception. The survey also found that plans that do cover contraceptive services and/or supplies are often inconsistent in which methods they cover and have a pronounced bias toward covering permanent surgical methods.[43]

Related Objectives From Other Focus Areas

1. Access to Quality Health Services

1-2.   Health insurance coverage for clinical preventive services

1-3.   Counseling about health behaviors

1-7.   Core competencies in health provider training

3. Cancer

3-3.   Breast cancer deaths

3-4.   Cervical cancer deaths

3-10.   Provider counseling about preventive measures

3-11.   Pap tests

3-13.   Mammograms

7. Educational and Community-Based Programs

7-2.   School health education

7-3.   Health-risk behavior information for college and university students

7-9.   Health care organization sponsorship of community health promotion activities

7-11.   Culturally appropriate community health promotion programs

11. Health Communication

11-3.   Research and evaluation of communication programs

11-6.   Satisfaction with providers' communication skills

13. HIV

13-1.   New AIDS cases

13-5.   New HIV cases

13-6.   Condom use

13-7.   Knowledge of serostatus

13-9.   HIV/AIDS, STD, and TB education in State prisons

13-10.   HIV counseling and testing in State prisons

13-12.   Screening for STDs and immunization for hepatitis B

13-14.   HIV-infection deaths

13-15.   Interval between HIV infection and AIDS diagnosis

13-17.   Perinatally acquired HIV infection

14. Immunization and Infectious Diseases

14-3. Hepatitis B in adults and high-risk groups

14-9. Hepatitis C

14-28. Hepatitis B vaccination among high-risk groups

15. Injury and Violence Prevention

15-34. Physical assault by intimate partners

15-35. Rape or attempted rape

15-36. Sexual assault other than rape

16. Maternal, Infant, and Child Health

16-3. Adolescent and young adult deaths

16-4. Maternal deaths

16-5. Maternal illness and complications due to pregnancy

16-6. Prenatal care

16-15. Prenatal substance exposure

16-18. Optimum folic acid

19. Nutrition and Overweight

19-12. Iron deficiency in young children and in females of childbearing age

19-13. Anemia in low-income pregnant females

19-14. Iron deficiency in pregnant females

25. Sexually Transmitted Diseases

25-1. Chlamydia

25-2. Gonorrhea

25-3. Primary and secondary syphilis

25-4. Genital herpes

25-5. Human papillomavirus infection

25-6. Pelvic inflammatory disease (PID)

25-7. Fertility problems

25-8. Heterosexually transmitted HIV infection in women

25-9. Congenital syphilis

25-10. Neonatal STDs

25-11. Responsible adolescent sexual behavior

25-12. Responsible sexual behavior messages on television

25-13. Hepatitis B vaccine services in STD clinics

25-14. Screening in youth detention facilities and jails

25-15. Contracts to treat nonplan partners of STD patients

25-16. Annual screening for genital chlamydia

25-17. Screening of pregnant women

25-18. Compliance with recognized STD treatment standards

25-19. Provider referral services for sex partners

26. Substance Abuse

26-19.   Treatment in correctional institutions

Terminology

(A listing of all abbreviations and acronyms used in this publication appears in Appendix K.)

Contraception (birth control): The means of pregnancy prevention. Methods include permanent methods (vasectomy for men and tubal ligation for women) and temporary methods (for example, hormonal implant, injectable, birth control pill, emergency contraceptive pills, intrauterine device, diaphragm, female condom, male condom, spermicidal foam/cream/jelly, sponge, cervical cap, abstinence, natural family planning, calendar rhythm, and withdrawal).

Emergency contraceptive pills (ECPs): The use of prescribed doses of birth control pills to prevent pregnancy following unprotected vaginal intercourse. The pills must be taken within 72 hours of having unprotected sex.

Family planning: The process of establishing the preferred number and spacing of one's children, selecting the means to achieve the goals, and effectively using that means.

Federal Title X Family Planning Program: A program created in 1970 as Title X at the Public Health Service Act. The program provides grants for the provision of family planning information and services.

Impaired fecundity: A broad term used to describe problems with pregnancy loss as well as problems conceiving a pregnancy.

Infertility: Failure to conceive a pregnancy after 12 months of unprotected intercourse.

Intended pregnancy: A pregnancy that a woman states was wanted at the time of conception.

Parity: The number of live births a woman has had.

Unintended pregnancy: A general term that includes pregnancies a woman reports as either mistimed or unwanted at the time of conception. If an unintended pregnancy occurs and is carried to term, the birth may be a wanted one, but the pregnancy would be classified as unintended.

Mistimed conception: Those that were wanted by the woman at some time in the future but occurred sooner than they were wanted. For example, a woman became pregnant at age 18 years but actually wanted to have her first child at age 21 years.

Unwanted conception: Those that occurred when the woman did not want any pregnancy then or in the future. For example, a woman wanted only two children but became pregnant with her third.

References

1.   National Center for Health Statistics. *Healthy People 2000 Review.* Hyattsville, MD: Public Health Service, 1997.

2.   Henshaw, S.K. Unintended Pregnancy in the United States. *Family Planning Perspectives* 30(1):24-29, 46, 1998.

3.   Delbanco, S.; Lundy, J.; Hoff, T.; Parke, M.; and Smith, M.D. Public Knowledge and Perceptions about Unplanned Pregnancy and Contraception in Three Countries. *Family Planning Perspectives* 29(2):70-75, April 1997.

4.   Brown, S.S., and Eisenberg, L., eds. *The Best Intentions: Unintended Pregnancy and the Well-Being of Children and Families.* Washington, DC: National Academy Press, 1995.

5.   Piccinino, L.J., and Mosher, W.D. Trends in Contraceptive Use in the United States: 1982–1995. *Family Planning Perspectives* 30(1):4-10, 46, 1998.

6.   Kost, K.; Landry, D.; and Darroch, J. Predicting Maternal Behaviors During Pregnancy: Does Intention Status Matter? *Family Planning Perspectives* 30(2):79-88, March/April 1998.

7.   Piccinino, L.J. Unintended Pregnancy and Childbearing. Reproductive Health of Women. In: L.S.

Wilcox, and J.S. Marks, (eds.). *From Data to Action: CDC's Public Health Surveillance for Women, Infants and Children.* Atlanta, GA: U.S. Department of Health and Human Services, Public Health Service, Centers for Disease Control and Prevention, 1994.

8. Dye, T.D.; Wojtowycz, M.A.; Aubry, R.H.; Quade, J.; and Kilburn, H. Unintended Pregnancy and Breast-Feeding Behavior. *American Journal of Public Health* 87(10):1709-1711, 1997.

9. Kost, K.; Landry, D.; and Darroch, J. The Effects of Pregnancy Planning Status on Birth Outcomes and Infant Care. *Family Planning Perspectives* 30(5):223-230, September/October 1998.

10. The Alan Guttmacher Institute. Sex and America's Teenagers. New York, NY: The Institute, 1994.

11. Henshaw, S.K. U.S. Teenage Pregnancy Statistics. New York: The Alan Guttmacher Institute, 1998.

12. Trussell, J.; Levengue, J.; Koenig, J.; London, R.; Borden, S.; Henneberry, J.; LaGuardia, K.; Stewart, F.; Wilson, G.; Wysocki, S.; and Strauss, M. The Economic Value of Contraception: A Comparison of 15 Methods. *American Journal of Public Health* 85(4):494-503, April 1995.

13. Lee, L.R., and Stewart, F.H. Editorial: Failing to Prevent Unintended Pregnancy is Costly. *American Journal of Public Health* 85(4):479-480, April 1995.

14. Maynard, R.A., ed. Kids Have Kids: The Economic and Social Consequences of Teen Pregnancy. *The Costs of Adolescent Childbearing* 10:285-323, 1997.

15. Trussell, J.; Koenig, J.; Stewart, F.; and Darroch, J.E. Medical Care Cost Savings from Adolescents Contraceptive Use. *Family Planning Perspectives* 29(6):248-255, 295, November/December 1997.

16. U.S. Department of Health and Human Services. *Guide to Clinical Preventive Services*, 2nd ed. Washington, DC: the Department, 1995.

17. Forrest, J.D. and Samara, R. Impact of Publicly Funded Contraceptive Services on Unintended Pregnancies and Implications for Medicaid Expenditures. *Family Planning Perspectives* 28(5):188-195, September/October 1996.

18. The Alan Guttmacher Institute. *Contraceptive Needs and Services, 1995.* New York, NY: The Institute, 1997, page 7 (table A).

19. Frost, J. Family Planning Clinic Services in the United States, 1994. *Family Planning Perspectives* 28(3):92-100, May/June 1996.

20. Frost, J., and Bolzan, M. The Provision of Public-Sector Services by Family Planning Agencies in 1995. *Family Planning Perspectives* 29(1):6-14, January/February 1997.

21. Donovan, P. Taking Family Planning Services to Hard-to-Reach Populations. *Family Planning Perspectives* 28(3):120-126, June 1996.

22. Mauldon, J., and Delbanco, S. Public Perceptions About Unplanned Pregnancy. *Family Planning Perspectives* 29(1):25-29, 40, January/February 1997.

23. The Guttmacher Report on Public Policy. The need for and cost of mandating private insurance coverage of contraception. Vol. 1, No. 4. New York, NY: The Alan Guttmacher Institute, August 1998.

24. Zhu, B.; Rolfs, R.; Nangle, B.; and Horan, J. Effect of the Interval Between Pregnancies on Perinatal Outcomes. *New England Journal of Medicine* 340(8):589-594, February 25, 1999.

25. Klerman, L. "Can Intervention Programs Prevent Subsequent Births to Teenage Mothers? Reactions to Reviews of Recent Research." Prepared for Program on Preventing Second Births to Teenage Mothers: Demonstration Findings. Sponsored by the American Enterprise Institute for Public Policy Research. March 6, 1998.

26. Ventura, S.J.; Martin, J.A.; Curtin, S.C.; and Mathews, T.J. Births: Final Data for 1997. *National Vital Statistics Reports*, 47(18), April 19, 1999.

27. National Center for Health Statistics. Healthy People 2000 Review, 1998-99. Hyattsville, MD: Public Health Service, 1999.

28. Westoff, C.D. Contraceptive Paths Toward the Reduction of Unintended Pregnancy and Abortion. *Family Planning Perspectives* 20(1):4-13, 1988.

29. Yuzpe, A.A.; Thurlow, H.J.; Ramzy, I.; and Leyshon, J.I. Post Coital Contraception—A Pilot Study. *Journal of Reproductive Medicine*, 13:53-58, 1974.

30. Haishan, F.; Darroch, J.E.; Hass, T.; and Ranjit, N. Contraceptive Failure Rates: New Estimates from the 1995 National Survey of Family Growth. *Family Planning Perspectives*, 31(2):56-63, March/April 1999.

31. Unpublished tabulation from the 1995 National Survey of Family Growth.

32. American College of Obstetricians and Gynecologists. Practice Patterns. Evidence-Based Guidelines

for Clinical Issues in Obstetrics and Gynecology. Number 3, December 1996.

33. 62 Federal Register 8610. Prescription Drug Products; Certain Combined Oral Contraceptives for Use in Postcoital Emergency Contraception, February 25, 1997.

34. Schulte, M.M., and Sonenstein, F.L. Special Report. Men at Family Planning Clinics: The New Patients? *Family Planning Perspectives* 27(5):212-216, 225, September/October 1995.

35. Sonenstein, F.L.; Stewart, K.; Lindberg, L.D.; Pernas, M.; and Williams, S. Involving Males in Preventing Teen Pregnancy: A Guide for Program Planners. The Urban Institute. December 1997.

36. Ventura, S.J.; Mosher, W.D.; Curtin, S.C.; Abma, J.C.; and Henshaw, S.K. Trends in Pregnancies and Pregnancy Rates by Outcome: Estimates for the United States, 1976-96.

National Vital Statistic Reports 47(29) Hyattsville, Maryland: National Center for Health Statistics, 1999.

37. Office of the Assistant Secretary for Planning and Evaluation. Trends in the Well-Being of America's Children and Youth: 1998. Washington, DC: U.S. Department of Health and Human Services, Office of the Assistant Secretary for Planning and Evaluation, 1996, 324.

38. American College of Obstetricians and Gynecologists, Committee on Adolescent Health Care Condom Availability for Adolescents, Opinion Number 154, April 1995. Internal Journal of Gynecology & Obstetrics 49(3):347-351, June 1995.

39. Santelli, J.; Warren, C.; Lowry, R.; Sogolow, E.; Collins, J.; Kann, L.; Kaufman, R.; and Celentano, D. The Use of Condoms with Other Contraceptive Methods Among Young Men and Women. *Family Planning*

Perspectives 29(6):261-267, November/December 1997.

40. Abma, J., and Sonenstein, F. "Teenage Sexual Behavior and Contraceptive Use: An Update." Paper presented at the American Enterprise Institute Sexuality and American Social Policy Seminar Series, April 28, 1998.

41. Kaiser Family Foundation and Children Now National Survey. Talking with Kids about Tough Issues. March 1, 1999 News Release.

42. Landry, D.J., and Forrest, J.D. Private Physicians' Provision of Contraceptive Services. *Family Planning Perspectives* 28(5):203-209, September/October 1996.

43. The Alan Guttmacher Institute. Uneven & Unequal: Insurance Coverage and Reproductive Health Services. New York: The Institute, July 1994.

10
Food Safety

Co-Lead Agencies: Food and Drug Administration; Food Safety and Inspection Service, U.S. Department of Agriculture

Contents

Goal

Reduce foodborne illnesses.

Overview

Foodborne illness imposes a burden on public health. It contributes significantly to the cost of health care.

Between 1988-92, outbreaks of foodborne illness caused an annual average of more than 15,000 cases of illness in the United States, as reported to the Centers for Disease Control and Prevention (CDC).[1] The actual illness rate may be higher because a count is taken only when the microorganism that caused the illness is identified by a laboratory and reported by a physician.

When unreported cases are taken into account, an estimated 76 million illnesses, 325,000 hospitalizations, and 5,000 deaths each year may be associated with microorganisms in food.[2] Hospitalizations due to foodborne illnesses are estimated to cost over $3 billion each year.[3] The cost of lost productivity is estimated at between $20 billion and $40 billion each year.[3] In addition to acute illness, some microorganisms can cause delayed or chronic illness. Foodborne chemical contaminants may cause chronic rather than acute problems and specific estimates of their impact on health and the economy are not available.

Since 1996, selected State and local health departments, CDC, the Food and Drug Administration (FDA), and the Food Safety and Inspection Service (FSIS) have been cooperating in FoodNet to produce better national estimates of foodborne disease. The focus is on organisms that cause the highest number of foodborne illnesses and on new or emerging foodborne pathogens. Active surveillance, based on laboratory data, is being conducted at FoodNet sites.

The success of improvements in food production, processing, preparation, and storage practices can be measured through the reduction in "outbreaks" of disease caused by foodborne pathogens. An outbreak occurs when two or more cases of a similar illness result from eating the same food.[1] Smaller outbreaks, those with fewer cases, may be a direct result of improved food preparation practices and better epidemiological followup once cases are identified.

Issues and Trends

Underlying forces may make foodborne illnesses more of a problem in the years to come. These include emerging pathogens; improper food preparation, storage, and distribution practices; insufficient training of retail employees; an increasingly

Data as of November 30, 1999

global food supply, and an increase in the number of people at risk because of aging and compromised capacity to fight these diseases.[4]

Emerging pathogens. Microorganisms continue to adapt and evolve, sometimes increasing in their ability to make an individual sick. Microorganisms previously not recognized as human pathogens or pathogens unexpectedly found in particular foods have caused outbreaks of illness. Examples are *Listeria monocytogenes, Escherichia coli* O157:H7, and *Cyclospora cayetanensis*. Known pathogens also may become resistant to drugs. For example, some strains of *Salmonella* species now are resistant to multiple important antimicrobial drugs.

The general trend toward increased resistance by microorganisms to multiple antimicrobial agents heightens public health concerns about treatment options and health care costs associated with foodborne illness. Of particular concern is the potential for transmission of antimicrobial-resistant pathogens to humans through the food supply. For these reasons, increased testing is planned to identify and monitor changes in patterns and trends of antimicrobial resistance in both human and animal populations.

Food preparation and storage practices. Most meals (71 percent) and snacks (78 percent) are prepared at home.[5] For these meals, the food-preparing consumer needs to protect against foodborne illness. Surveys show that consumers should improve the way they prepare, thaw, and store food.[6, 7]

Training of retail employees. The retail food industry has a large employee population with high rates of turnover. Language and literacy barriers and nonuniform systems for training and certifying workers pose additional challenges. Improper holding temperatures, inadequate cooking, poor personal hygiene, contaminated equipment, and foods from unsafe sources have been associated with foodborne outbreaks in retail food establishments. Retail food employees' use of safe food preparation and storage practices, along with use of recommended practices spelled out in the U.S. Public Health Service's *Food Code*, should reduce outbreaks.

Global food supply. An increasing amount of the food eaten in most countries originates in other countries. Diverse methods of and standards for growing and processing agricultural products and different frequencies and types of gastrointestinal infections in food workers in different regions increase the possibility of food contamination and the range of pathogens expected.

Protecting the safety of the Nation's food supply involves safeguarding against both biological and chemical contaminants in food. Chemical contaminants in food can include pesticides, toxic elements, naturally occurring toxins (for example, mycotoxins and phytotoxins), antibiotic residues in animal products, endocrine disruptor compounds, and other trace substances in food. Many questions remain unanswered about the chronic effects of exposure to these types of substances. (See Focus Area 8. Environmental Health.)

The U.S. Environmental Protection Agency (EPA) has set safety standards (tolerances) to limit the amount of pesticide residues that legally may remain in or on food or animal feed sold in the United States. Consumers and others have been concerned about the potential risk to children from pesticides. The Food Quality Protection Act of 1996 requires EPA to reassess all existing standards for pesticides by the year 2006. Under this act, EPA considers the risk from dietary exposures from all food uses of pesticides and drinking water; nonoccupational exposure, such as the use of the pesticides for lawn care; and any special sensitivities for children. FDA monitors domestic and imported foods to ensure compliance with these pesticide safety standards.[8] Under the Pesticide Data Program, the Agricultural Marketing Service of the U.S. Department of Agriculture measures how much of certain pesticides remains in or on food.[9]

Naturally occurring toxins present a different issue. Mycotoxins cannot be avoided entirely or eliminated from human foods or animal feeds because the molds that create them occur naturally in grains and other food commodities. Risk reduction strategies, such as adherence to specific good manufacturing practices (GMPs), have been developed for aflatoxins. For other mycotoxins, FDA is using a science-based risk assessment procedure to help identify appropriate risk reduction measures.

Because representative national data systems may not be available in the first half of the decade for tracking progress on mycotoxins in foods, this subject is not covered in this focus area's objectives. Research on risk reduction and efforts to collect representative national data on mycotoxins in foods will be addressed in the coming decade.

Allergen risk. Although most foodborne illness results from a microbial or chemical contaminant in food, a food itself also can cause severe adverse reactions. In the United States food allergy is an important problem: 2 to 4 percent of children under the age of 6 years[10, 11] and 1 to 2 percent of adults are allergic to specific foods.[12] The foods most likely to cause allergic reactions are milk and milk products, eggs and egg products, peanuts and peanut products, tree nuts and tree nut products, soybeans and soybean products, fish and fish products, shellfish and shellfish products, cereals containing gluten, and seeds. Allergic reactions to natural rubber latex from food handlers' gloves also occur.[13, 14]

Based on a 3-year study of anaphylaxis cases treated at an emergency department, an estimated 2,500 individuals per year in the United States experience food-induced anaphylaxis.[15, 16] Food allergy is the most frequent cause of anaphylaxis occurring outside of the hospital and the most common cause for emergency department visits for anaphylaxis.[17] Because potentially allergenic foods are present as ingredients in a variety of food products, and because even trace amounts of these allergenic foods can induce anaphylaxis, research, education, and clear food ingredient labeling information are critical for managing food allergies.

The Food, Drug, and Cosmetic Act requires manufacturers to list all ingredients of a packaged food, with two exemptions. Spices, flavorings, and colorings may be declared collectively without each one named.[18] Incidental additives, such as processing aids present in a food at insignificant levels and not having a technical or functional effect in the finished food, do not have to be listed individually.[19] However, the presence of a substance that may cause an adverse reaction is considered significant and so it must be listed on the food label. FDA has advised manufacturers that, because adhering to GMPs is essential for effective reduction of adverse reactions, precautionary labeling, such as "may contain (insert name of allergenic ingredient)," should not be used in lieu of adherence to GMPs.[20]

Disparities

More than 30 million people in the United States are likely to be particularly susceptible to foodborne disease.[21] Very young, elderly, and immunocompromised persons experience the most serious foodborne illnesses. They may become ill from smaller doses of organisms and may be more likely to die of foodborne

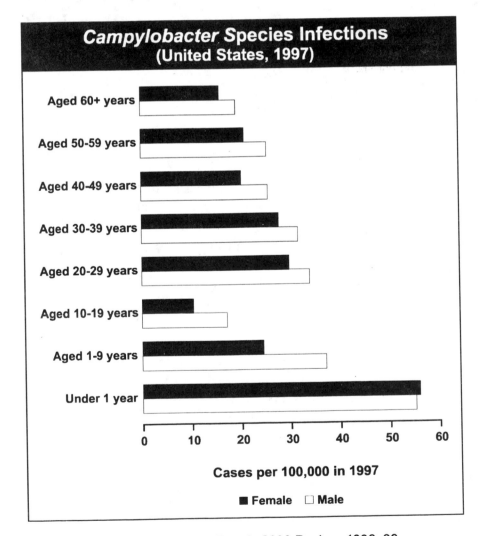

Source: CDC, NCHS. *Healthy People 2000 Review, 1998–99.*

disease than other persons. For example, children under age 1 have the highest rate of *Campylobacter* species infections (see figure). Other high-risk populations include residents in nursing homes or chronic care facilities; hospitalized, cancer, and organ transplant patients; and individuals with AIDS, with cirrhosis, on anti-microbial treatment, or with reduced stomach acid such as due to anti-acid medications. In cases of listeriosis and toxoplasmosis, pregnant women and their fetuses or newborns are at higher risk than other groups.

Representative data on specific U.S. populations, such as racial and ethnic groups or socioeconomic groups, are not available from FoodNet. Efforts are underway to improve reporting of this information. A report from the United Kingdom indicates a relationship between socioeconomic status and foodborne illness that may apply to the United States. It found that hospital admissions for gastrointestinal infections increased with increasing socioeconomic deprivation.[22]

Opportunities

The opportunities to reduce the burden of foodborne illness involve risk reduction and control interventions targeted at various steps from production to consumption. These strategies include Hazard Analysis and Critical Control Points programs (required starting in 1997 for seafood and in 1998 for meat and poultry processing); improved adherence to GMPs; education of food processors, preparers, and servers at all levels in the food industry and in the home; and improved investigation of outbreaks and sporadic cases of foodborne illness.

The Partnership for Food Safety Education was formed in 1997 as a part of the National Food Safety Initiative. The Partnership—composed of industry, State, and consumer organizations and government liaisons from FDA, FSIS, Cooperative State Research, Education, and Extension Service (CSREES), CDC, and EPA—cooperatively developed the FightBAC!™ Campaign with messages to reach all consumers. The messages are based on four key food safety practices:

- Clean: Wash hands and surfaces often.

- Separate: Don't cross-contaminate.

- Cook: Cook to proper temperatures.

- Chill: Refrigerate promptly.

Increased surveillance, planned as a result of the 1997 initiative and improvements to the FoodNet program, will inform the public health community, veterinary and producer groups, and regulatory agencies of the extent of the problem of human pathogens that come from the intestines of animals. These organisms might resist drug therapy when human illness occurs. Public health experts anticipate an initial increase in the number of resistant pathogens detected due to improved surveillance. Over time, as control and educational programs are enacted,

Data as of November 30, 1999

decreases should follow. Wider and more representative testing will give a better picture of the nature and extent to which antimicrobial-resistant foodborne pathogens are transmitted from animals to humans.

Interim Progress Toward Year 2000 Objectives

Of the four Healthy People 2000 food safety objectives targeted to reducing foodborne illness, only one has been met—reducing the incidence of disease caused by four key pathogens (*Salmonella* species, *Campylobacter* species, *Escherichia coli* O157:H7, and *Listeria monocytogenes*). Two objectives show solid progress—decreasing the number of outbreaks of *Salmonella* serotype Enteritidis from 77 to 44 outbreaks per year and State agency adoption (16 States) and review (23 States plus Puerto Rico and the District of Columbia) of the *Food Code* for retail-level food establishments (1999 *Food Code* data). The consumer food safety practices objective shows improvement. In fact, the target for washing cutting boards with soap has been surpassed (79 percent) if all safe practices, such as washing with bleach or using a different cutting board following use with raw meat or poultry, are considered.

Note: Some data are from Centers for Disease Control and Prevention, National Center for Health Statistics, *Healthy People 2000 Review, 1998-99.*

Food Safety

Goal: Reduce foodborne illnesses.

Number	Objective
10-1	Foodborne infections
10-2	Outbreaks of foodborne infections
10-3	Antimicrobial resistance of *Salmonella* species
10-4	Food allergy deaths
10-5	Consumer food safety practices
10-6	Safe food preparation practices in retail establishments
10-7	Organophosphate pesticide exposure

10-1. Reduce infections caused by key foodborne pathogens.

Target and baseline:

Objective	Reduction in Infections Caused by Microorganisms	1997 Baseline	2010 Target
		Cases per 100,000 Population	
10-1a.	*Campylobacter* species	24.6	12.3
10-1b.	*Escherichia coli* O157:H7	2.1	1.0
10-1c.	*Listeria monocytogenes*	0.5	0.25
10-1d.	*Salmonella* species	13.7	6.8
10-1e.	*Cyclospora cayetanensis*	**Developmental**	
10-1f.	Postdiarrheal hemolytic uremic syndrome	**Developmental**	
10-1g.	Congenital *Toxoplasma gondii*	**Developmental**	

Target setting method: 50 percent improvement.

Data sources: Foodborne Disease Active Surveillance Network (FoodNet), CDC, NCID; FDA, CFSAN; FSIS, OPHS; and State agencies.

Potential data source: Toxoplasmosis data—National Notifiable Diseases Surveillance System (NNDSS), CDC, NCID.

Total Population, 1997	10-1a. *Campylobacter* species	10-1b. *Escherichia coli* O157:H7	10-1c. *Listeria monocytogenes*	10-1d. *Salmonella* species
	Cases per 100,000			
TOTAL	24.6	2.1	0.5	13.7
Race and ethnicity				
American Indian or Alaska Native	DSU	DSU	DSU	DSU
Native Hawaiian and other Pacific Islander	DSU	DSU	DSU	DSU
Black or African American	DSU	DSU	DSU	DSU
White	DSU	DSU	DSU	DSU

Total Population, 1997	10-1a. Campylo-bacter species	10-1b. Escherichia coli O157:H7	10-1c. Listeria monocyto-genes	10-1d. Salmonella species
	Cases per 100,000			
	DSU	DSU	DSU	DSU
Hispanic or Latino	DSU	DSU	DSU	DSU
Not Hispanic or Latino	DSU	DSU	DSU	DSU
Black or African American	DSU	DSU	DSU	DSU
White	DSU	DSU	DSU	DSU
Gender				
Female	21.7	2.2	0.4	13.3
Male	27.5	2.0	0.5	14.0
Age				
Under 1 year	55.5	4.6	2.3	111.4
1 to 19 years	21.9	4.9	0.1	17.5
20 to 59 years	27.2	0.9	0.3	10.7
60 years and older	17.1	1.6	1.7	9.1
Family income level				
Poor	DNC	DNC	DNC	DNC
Near poor	DNC	DNC	DNC	DNC
Middle/high income	DNC	DNC	DNC	DNC

DNA = Data have not been analyzed. DNC = Data are not collected. DSU = Data are statistically unreliable.

Campylobacteriosis and salmonellosis are the most frequently reported foodborne illnesses in the United States.[2] The emerging pathogens *E. coli* O157:H7 and *L. monocytogenes* cause infections that are less often reported but commonly more severe. *L. monocytogenes* is rare; however, septicemia and meningitis may result from infection with this organism, and up to 20 percent of patients may die.[2] Persons with altered or deficient immune response, such as infants and young children, older adults, pregnant women and their fetuses, and immunosuppressed persons, are at highest risk. Listeriosis in pregnant women may lead to miscarriage, stillbirth, or septicemia and meningitis in newborns.

Cyclospora cayetanensis, a parasite, was made a nationally notifiable disease (States report all cases to CDC) and added to FoodNet in 1998. Information about this emerging pathogen, such as the proportion of infections that are foodborne, is needed. Examination for *C. cayetanensis* is not universal in clinical laboratories; thus, data for this organism may be less reliable than for the other organisms.

The parasite *Toxoplasma gondii* causes toxoplasmosis and may cause miscarriage, stillbirth, or fetal abnormality. Although results of *Toxoplasma gondii* testing are

Data as of November 30, 1999

not generally reported by clinicians, results from national surveys that include blood testing suggest that toxoplasmosis may be one of the most common infections associated with food. Blood tests reveal toxoplasmosis infections at a rate of 7.2 percent for children aged 6 to 10 years.[23] Preliminary data from a European study showed that a majority of toxoplasmosis cases were foodborne.[24] Another study found that food consumption and preparation practices accounted for five of the top six practices by pregnant women that were significantly associated with congenital toxoplasmosis.[25] The food practices were eating raw or undercooked minced meat products, eating raw or undercooked mutton, eating raw or undercooked pork or lamb, eating unwashed raw vegetables, and washing kitchen knives infrequently after preparation of raw meat and prior to handling another food item.[25] Changing the cat litter, although often thought to be the major cause of toxoplasmosis, ranked fifth in importance of the six practices. As with other parasitic diseases, diagnostic laboratory testing for toxoplasmosis often is not available or is done infrequently. Efforts are underway in the United States to make congenital toxoplasmosis a nationally notifiable disease, with serological data collection beginning in 2000.

10-2. Reduce outbreaks of infections caused by key foodborne bacteria.

Target and baseline:

Objective	Reduction in Infections Caused by Foodborne Bacteria	1997 Baseline	2010 Target
		Number of Outbreaks per Year	
10-2a.	*Escherichia coli* O157: H7	22	11
10-2b.	*Salmonella* serotype Enteritidis	44	22

Target setting method: 50 percent improvement.

Data source: Foodborne Disease Outbreak Surveillance System, CDC, NCID.

Outbreaks of *E. coli* O157:H7 have been associated with undercooked or raw ground beef, unpasteurized apple juice, and some types of fresh (raw) produce. The most frequent known cause of outbreaks of *Salmonella* Enteritidis is the consumption of food that contains undercooked or raw eggs.

10-3. Prevent an increase in the proportion of isolates of *Salmonella* species from humans and from animals at slaughter, that are resistant to antimicrobial drugs.

Target and baseline:

Objective	Prevention of Increase in Proportion of *Salmonella* Species Resistant to Antimicrobial Drugs	1997 Baseline	2010 Target
		Percent of Isolates	
	***Salmonella* from humans that are resistant to:**		
10-3a.	Fluoroquinolones	0	0
10-3b.	Third-generation cephalosporins	0	0
10-3c.	Gentamicin	3	3
10-3d.	Ampicillin	18	18
	***Salmonella* from cattle at slaughter that are resistant to:**		
10-3e.	Fluoroquinolones	Developmental	
10-3f.	Third-generation cephalosporins	Developmental	
10-3g.	Gentamicin	Developmental	
10-3h.	Ampicillin	Developmental	
	***Salmonella* from broilers at slaughter that are resistant to:**		
10-3i.	Fluoroquinolones	Developmental	
10-3j.	Third-generation cephalosporins	Developmental	
10-3k.	Gentamicin	Developmental	
10-3l.	Ampicillin	Developmental	
	***Salmonella* from swine at slaughter that are resistant to:**		
10-3m.	Fluoroquinolones	Developmental	
10-3n.	Third-generation cephalosporins	Developmental	
10-3o.	Gentamicin	Developmental	
10-3p.	Ampicillin	Developmental	

Target setting method: No increase.

Data sources: National Antimicrobial Resistance Monitoring System, CDC, NCID; FDA, CVM; FSIS, APHIS, and ARS; Foodborne Disease Active Surveillance Network (FoodNet), CDC, NCID.

10-4. (Developmental) Reduce deaths from anaphylaxis caused by food allergies.

Potential data source: National Vital Statistics System (NVSS), CDC, NCHS.

10-5. Increase the proportion of consumers who follow key food safety practices.

Target: 79 percent.

Baseline: 72 percent of consumers followed key food safety practices in 1998.

Target setting method: 10 percent improvement.

Data source: Food Safety Survey (FSS), FDA and FSIS, USDA.

Key food safety practices are based on the four FightBAC!™ Campaign messages. They are clean, wash hands and surfaces often; separate, don't cross-contaminate; cook, cook to proper temperatures; and chill, refrigerate promptly.

10-6. (Developmental) Improve food employee behaviors and food preparation practices that directly relate to foodborne illnesses in retail food establishments.

Potential data sources: GPRA (Government Performance and Results Act) Baseline Data Collection Project (on Retail Food Establishments), FDA. Followup data from the Retail Food Database of Foodborne Illness Risk Factors, FDA, CFSAN.

Five food safety risk factors related to employee behaviors and preparation practices have been identified by CDC as contributing to foodborne illness: improper holding temperatures, inadequate cooking, contaminated equipment, food from an unsafe source, and poor personal hygiene. For each year from 1988 through 1992, the most commonly reported food preparation practice that contributed to foodborne disease concerned improper holding temperature; the second concerned poor personal hygiene of food handlers. Food obtained from an unsafe source was the least commonly reported factor for all 5 years. In most outbreaks caused by bacterial pathogens, the food was stored at improper holding temperatures.[1]

To help control the risk factors, the *Food Code* provides key public health interventions: use of time-temperature control, prevention of hand contact with foods as a vehicle of contamination, employee health, demonstration of knowledge by the manager, and a consumer advisory to inform consumers of their risk when eating raw or undercooked animal foods. Proper application and implementation of these interventions are crucial to combat foodborne disease.

10-7. (Developmental) Reduce human exposure to organophosphate pesticides from food.

Potential data source: Total Diet Study, FDA, CFSAN.

The Food Quality Protection Act of 1996 mandated that EPA reassess existing standards for pesticides used on food crops. Organophosphates, a group of approximately 40 closely related pesticides, have been designated as first priority in the standards reassessment. These pesticides are used on fruits and vegetables important in the diet of children.

Related Objectives From Other Focus Areas

8. Environmental Health

8-5.	Safe drinking water
8-6.	Waterborne disease outbreaks
8-8.	Surface water health risks
8-10.	Fish contamination
8-24.	Exposure to pesticides
8-25.	Exposure to heavy metals and other toxic chemicals
8-29.	Global burden of disease
8-30.	Water quality in the U.S.-Mexico border region

14. Immunization and Infectious Diseases

14-21.	Antimicrobial use in intensive care units

20. Occupational Safety and Health

20-8.	Occupational skin diseases or disorders

23. Public Health Infrastructure

23-2.	Public access to information and surveillance data

Terminology

(A listing of all abbreviations and acronyms used in this publication appears in Appendix K.)

Anaphylaxis: A severe allergic reaction commonly caused by certain foods. It occurs within minutes of exposure and may include hives, itching, skin swelling, blood vessel collapse, shock, and often life-threatening respiratory distress.[26]

Cephalosporins, third generation: Potent antimicrobial drugs capable of fighting a wide variety of bacterial infections. *Salmonella* species infections in certain high-risk and severely ill patients, particularly children, often are treated with such drugs.

Emerging pathogen: An illness-causing microorganism previously unknown to be a human pathogen, a foodborne pathogen not expected to occur in particular foods, or a pathogen that has caused a dramatic increase in new cases of illness.

Food Code: A book of recommendations of the U.S. Public Health Service that FDA first published in 1993 and revises every 2 years. It consists of model requirements for safeguarding public health and ensuring food is unadulterated and honestly presented to the consumer. FDA offers the *Food Code* for adoption by local, State, Tribal, and Federal government jurisdictions for administration by the units that have compliance responsibilities for food service, retail food stores, or food vending operations.

Foodborne disease or **foodborne illness:** Infection or intoxication caused by

Data as of November 30, 1999

microbial or chemical contaminants in foods. Some foodborne illnesses, such as salmonellosis and staphylococcal food poisoning, can be caused by a single helping or less of a food that contains sufficient microorganisms or toxin to cause illness. Other foodborne illnesses result from eating compounds, such as naturally occurring aflatoxin, in foods over long periods of time.

Foodborne disease outbreak: When two or more cases of a similar illness result from eating the same food.[1]

Food industry: Food producers (farmers, fishers, ranchers), food processors, food storers, food warehousers and transporters, and retail food operators.

FoodNet: The Foodborne Diseases Active Surveillance Network, a collaborative project conducted by CDC, participating States, FSIS, and FDA that began in 1996. FoodNet produces national estimates of the burden and sources of specific diseases in the United States through active surveillance and other studies. California, Connecticut, Georgia, Maryland, Minnesota, New York, Ore-gon, and Tennessee, representing a total population of 28 million people (approximately 10 percent of the U.S. population), are the eight FoodNet sites.[27]

Good manufacturing practices (GMPs): Criteria, including regulations, that ensure that food is fit for consumption and is manufactured under sanitary conditions. These criteria address factors that affect production of safe food, including disease control, cleanliness (personal hygiene and dress codes), education, and training.

Hazard Analysis and Critical Control Points (HACCP): A science-based and systematic approach to prevent potential food safety problems by anticipating how biological, chemical, or physical hazards are most likely to occur and by installing appropriate measures to prevent them from occurring. The seven principles of HACCP are hazard analysis, determination of critical control points, specification of critical limits, monitoring, corrective actions, verification, and documentation (recordkeeping).

Hemolytic uremic syndrome (HUS), postdiarrheal: A serious, sometimes fatal complication often associated with illness caused by *Escherichia coli* O157:H7 and other shiga toxin-producing *E. coli*.[28] HUS occurs mainly in children under the age of 10 years. Renal failure, hemolytic anemia, and a severe decrease in the number of blood platelets characterize HUS.

Mycotoxins: Naturally occurring toxins formed by fungi (molds) in food and in animal feed (for example, aflatoxins, fumonisins, deoxynivalenol, and patulin).

Outbreak: See foodborne disease outbreak above.

Pathogen: A microorganism that causes illness.

Retail food industry: As covered by the *Food Code*, a level within the food industry that includes but is not limited to the following establishments: vending operations, grocery stores, other retail food outlets, and food service in restaurants and institutions.

References

1. Centers for Disease Control and Prevention (CDC). Surveillance for Foodborne-Disease. Outbreaks—United States, 1988-92. *Morbidity and Mortality Weekly Report* 45(SS-5):1-55, 1996.

2. Mead, P.S.; Slutsker, L.; Dietz, V.; McCaig, L.F.; Bresee, J.S.; Shapiro, C.; Griffin, P.M.; and Tauxe, R.V. Food-related illness and death in the United States. *Emerging Infectious Diseases* 5(5), 607-625, 1999.

3. Food and Drug Administration (FDA), U.S. Department of Agriculture (USDA), U.S. Environmental Protection Agency (EPA). *Food Safety From Farm to Table: A National Food Safety Initiative. Report to the President, May 1997.* Washington, DC: FDA, USDA, EPA, 1997.

4. U.S. Department of Health and Human Services (DHHS). Healthy People 2000 Progress Review. Washington, DC: DHHS, Public Health Service, Office of Disease Prevention and Health Promotion, 1995.

5. Lin, B.H.; Guthrie, J.; and Frazão, E. Away-from-home foods increasingly important to quality of American diet. *Agriculture Information Bulletin* No. 749, 22, 1999.

6. Altekruse, S.F.; Street, D.A.; Fein, S.B.; and Levy, A.S. Consumer knowledge of foodborne microbial hazards and food-handling practices. *Journal of Food Protection* 59:287-294, 1996.

7. National Center for Health Statistics. Healthy People 2000 Review, 1998-99. Hyattsville, MD: DHHS, Public Health Service, Office of Disease Prevention and Health Promotion, 126-127, 1999.

8. FDA. *Pesticide Program Residue Monitoring, 1997.* Washington, DC: Food and Drug Administration, 1998.

9. Agricultural Marketing Service. *Pesticide Data Program—Annual Summary, Calendar Year 1997.* Washington, DC: U.S. Department of Agriculture, 1997.

10. Kayosaari, M. Food allergy in Finnish children aged 1-6 years. *Acta Paediatrica Scandinavica* 71(5):815-819, 1982.

11. Bock, S.A. Prospective appraisal of complaints of adverse reactions to foods in children during the first three years of life. *Pediatrics* 79(5):683-688, 1987.

12. Sampson, H.A., and Metcalf, D.D. Food allergies. *Journal of the American Medical Association* 268(20):2840-2844, 1992.

13. Schwartz, H.J. Latex: A potential hidden "food" allergen in fast food restaurants. *Journal of Allergy and Clinical Immunology* 95(1, part 1):139-40, 1995.

14. Tomazic, V.J.; Shampaine, E.L.; Lamanna, A.; Withrow, T.J.; Adkinson, Jr., N.F.; and Hamilton, R.G. Cornstarch powder on latex products is an allergen carrier. *Journal of Allergy and Clinical Immunology* 93(4):751-758, 1994.

15. Yocum, M.W., and Khan, D.A. Assessment of patients who have experienced anaphylaxis: a 3-year survey. *Mayo Clinic Proceedings* 69(1):16-23, 1994.

16. Sampson, H.A. Fatal food-induced anaphylaxis. *Allergy* 53(suppl. 46):125-130, 1998.

17. Kemp, S.F.; Lockey, R.F.; Wolf, B.L.; and Lieberman, P. Anaphylaxis. *Archives of Internal Medicine* 155(16):1749-1754, 1995.

18. Anonymous. *Federal Food, Drug, and Cosmetic Act, As Amended July 1993.* Washington, DC: U.S. Government Printing Office, 1993, Section 403 (i).

19. Anonymous. *Code of Federal Regulations*, title 21, part 101, section 100 (a)(3). Washington, DC: U.S. Government Printing Office, 1998.

20. Shank, F.A. Notice to Manufacturers: Label Declaration of Allergenic Substances in Foods, 1996. Letter from FDA, Center for Food Safety and Applied Nutrition, June 10, 1996.

21. Council for Agricultural Science and Technology. *Foodborne Pathogens: Risks and Consequences.* Task Force Report No. 122, 1994.

22. Olowokure, B.; Hawker, J.; Weinberg, J.; Gill, N.; and Sufi, F. Deprivation and hospital admission for infectious intestinal diseases. *The Lancet* 353(9155):807-808, 1999.

23. National Center for Health Statistics. *National Health and Nutrition Examination Survey III, 1988-94.* Washington, DC: CDC, National Center for Infectious Diseases, unpublished data.

24. CDC. National Workshop on Toxoplasmosis: Preventing Congenital Toxoplasmosis in Atlanta, GA, September 9-10, 1998.

25. Kapperud, G.; Jenum, P.A.; Stray-Pederson, B.; Melby, K.K.; Eskild, A.; and Eng. J. Risk factors for *Toxoplasma gondii* infection in pregnancy. Results of a prospective case-control study in Norway. *American Journal of Epidemiology* 144(4):405-412, 1996.

26. W.B. Saunders Dictionary Staff. *Dorland's Illustrated Medical Dictionary*, 28th ed. Philadelphia, PA: Saunders Co., 1994, 68-69.

27. CDC. *FoodNet 1998 Surveillance Results: Preliminary Report, March 1999.* Washington, DC: the Centers, 1999.

28. Lindsay, J.A. Chronic sequelae of foodborne disease. *Emerging Infectious Diseases* 3(4):443-452, 1997.

11

Health Communication

Lead Agency: Office of Disease Prevention and Health Promotion

Contents

Goal

Use communication strategically to improve health.

Overview

Health communication links the domains of communication and health and is increasingly recognized as a necessary element of efforts to improve personal and public health.[1, 2, 3] Health communication can contribute to all aspects of disease prevention and health promotion and is relevant in a number of contexts, including (1) health professional-patient relations; (2) individuals' exposure to, search for, and use of health information; (3) individuals' adherence to clinical recommendations and regimens; (4) the construction of public health messages and campaigns; (5) the dissemination of individual and population health risk information, that is, risk communication; (6) images of health in the mass media and the culture at large; (7) the education of consumers about how to gain access to the public health and health care systems; and (8) the development of telehealth applications. [3, 4, 5, 6, 7, 8, 9, 10, 11]

For individuals, effective health communication can help raise awareness of health risks and solutions, provide the motivation and skills needed to reduce these risks, help them to find support from other people in similar situations, and affect or reinforce attitudes.[1] Health communication also can increase demand for appropriate health services and decrease demand for inappropriate health services. It can make available information to assist in making complex choices, such as selecting health plans, care providers, and treatments.[1] For the community, health communication can be used to influence the public agenda, advocate for policies and programs, promote positive changes in the socioeconomic and physical environments, improve the delivery of public health and health care services, and encourage social norms that benefit health and quality of life.[2]

The practice of health communication has contributed to health promotion and disease prevention in several areas. One is the improvement of interpersonal and group interactions in clinical situations (for example, provider-patient, provider-provider, and among members of a health care team) through the training of health professionals and patients in effective communication skills.[3, 4] Collaborative and partnership relationships are enhanced when all parties are capable of good communications.

Another is the dissemination of health messages through public education campaigns that seek to change the social climate to encourage healthy behaviors, create awareness, change attitudes, and motivate individuals to adopt recommended behaviors.[6, 9, 10] Campaigns traditionally have relied on mass communication (such as public service announcements on billboards, radio, and television) and

Attributes of Effective Health Communication

- **Accuracy**: The content is valid and presented accurately.
- **Availability**: The content (whether targeted message or other information) is delivered or placed where the audience can access it. Placement varies according to audience, message complexity, and purpose, ranging from interpersonal and social networks to billboards and mass transit signs to prime-time TV or radio, to public kiosks (print or electronic), to the Internet.
- **Balance**: Where appropriate, the content presents the benefits and risks of potential actions or recognizes different but valid perspectives on the issue.
- **Consistency**: The content remains internally consistent over time and also is consistent with information from other sources (the latter is a problem when other widely available content is not accurate or reliable).
- **Culturally competent**: The design, implementation, and evaluation process addresses special issues for select population groups (for example, ethnic, racial, and linguistic) and also educational levels and disability.
- **Evidence-based**: The content and strategies are based on formative research with the intended audience and on applicable findings from other communication research.
- **Reach**: The content gets to or is available to the largest possible number of people in the target population.
- **Reliability**: The source of the content is credible, and the content itself is kept up to date.
- **Repetition**: The delivery of/access to the content is continued or repeated over time, both to reinforce the impact with a given audience and to reach new generations.
- **Timeliness**: The content is provided or available when the audience is most receptive to, or in need of, the specific information.
- **Understandable**: The reading or language level and format (including multimedia) are appropriate for the specific audience.

educational messages in printed materials (such as pamphlets) to deliver health messages. Other campaigns have integrated mass media with community-based programs. Many campaigns have used social marketing techniques.

Increasingly, health improvement activities are taking advantage of computer-based technologies, such as CD-ROM and the World Wide Web, that can target audiences, tailor messages, and engage people in interactive, ongoing exchanges about health.[4, 11, 12] An emerging area is health communication to support community-centered prevention.[13] Community-centered prevention shifts attention from individual to group-level change and emphasizes the empowerment of individuals and communities to effect change on multiple levels.

A set of Leading Health Indicators, which focus on key health improvement activities and are described in the first section of *Healthy People 2010*, all depend to some extent on effective health communication. The promotion of regular physical activity, healthy weight, good nutrition, and responsible sexual behavior will require a range of information, education, and advocacy efforts, as will the reduction of tobacco use, substance abuse, injuries, and violence. For example, advocacy efforts to change prices and availability of tobacco and alcohol products have resulted in lower consumption levels. (See Focus Area 26. Substance Abuse and Focus Area 27. Tobacco Use.) Effective counseling and patient education for behavior change require health care providers and patients to have good communication skills. Public information campaigns are used to promote increased fruit and vegetable consumption (5-A-Day for Better Health!), higher rates of preventive screening (mammogram and colonoscopy), higher rates of clinical preventive services (immunization), and greater rates of adoption of risk-reducing behaviors (Back to Sleep and Buckle Up for Safety).

Health communication alone, however, cannot change systemic problems related to health, such as poverty, environmental degradation, or lack of access to health care, but comprehensive health communication programs should include a systematic exploration of all the factors that contribute to health and the strategies that could be used to influence these factors. Well-designed health communication activities help individuals better understand their own and their communities' needs so that they can take appropriate actions to maximize health.

Issues and Trends

The environment for communicating about health has changed significantly. These changes include dramatic increases in the number of communication channels and the number of health issues vying for public attention as well as consumer demands for more and better quality health information, and the increased sophistication of marketing and sales techniques, such as direct-to-consumer advertising of prescription drugs and sales of medical devices and medications over the Internet. The expansion of communication channels and health issues on the public agenda increases competition for people's time and attention; at the same time, people have more opportunities to select information based on their personal interests and preferences. The trend toward commercialization of the Internet suggests that the marketing model of other mass media will be applied to emerging media, which has important consequences for the ability of noncommercial and public health-oriented health communications to stand out in a cluttered health information environment.

Communication occurs in a variety of contexts (for example, school, home, and work); through a variety of channels (for example, interpersonal, small group, organizational, community, and mass media) with a variety of messages; and for a variety of reasons. In such an environment, people do not pay attention to all communications they receive but selectively attend to and purposefully seek out information.[8] One of the main challenges in the design of effective health communication programs is to identify the optimal contexts, channels, content, and reasons that will motivate people to pay attention to and use health information.

The diversity of the U.S. population suggests that a one-dimensional approach to health promotion, such as reliance on mass media campaigns or other single-component communication activities, is insufficient to achieve program goals. Successful health promotion efforts increasingly rely on multidimensional interventions to reach diverse audiences about complex health concerns, and communication is integrated from the beginning with other components, such as community-based programs, policy changes, and improvements in services and the health delivery system.[10, 14] Research shows that health communication best supports health promotion when multiple communication channels are used to reach specific audience segments with information that is appropriate and relevant to them.[6] An important factor in the design of multidimensional programs is to allot sufficient time for planning, implementation, and evaluation and sufficient money to support the many elements of the program. Public-private partnerships and collaborations can leverage resources to strengthen the impact of multidimensional efforts. Collaboration can have the added benefit of reducing message clutter and targeting health concerns that cannot be fully addressed by public resources or market incentives alone.

Research indicates that effective health promotion and communication initiatives adopt an audience-centered perspective, which means that promotion and communication activities reflect audiences' preferred formats, channels, and contexts.[6] An audience-centered perspective also reflects the realities of people's everyday lives and their current practices, attitudes and beliefs, and lifestyles. Some specific audience characteristics that are relevant include gender, age, education and income levels, ethnicity, cultural beliefs and values, primary language(s), and physical and mental functioning. Additional considerations include their experience with the health care system, attitudes toward different types of health problems, and willingness to use certain types of health services. Particular attention should be paid to the needs of underserved audience members.

Targeting specific segments of a population and tailoring messages for individual use are two methods to make health promotion activities relevant to audiences.[15] Examples include the targeted use of mass media messages for adolescent girls at increased risk of smoking;[16] the tailoring of computer-generated nutritional information to help individuals reduce their fat intake and increase fruit and vegetable consumption;[17] and a national telephone service for Spanish speakers to obtain AIDS information as well as counseling and referrals.[18]

Interventions that account for the cultural practices and needs of specific populations have shown some success. For example, a breastfeeding promotion program among Navajo women that was based on investigations of their cultural beliefs about infant feeding practices showed increased rates of breastfeeding.[19] Similarly, an intervention that used the novela, a popular form of Latino mass media, to reach young people and their parents sought to improve parent-youth communication in Hispanic families and to influence the adolescents' attitudes about alcohol.[20]

Advances in medical and consumer health informatics are changing the delivery of health information and services and are likely to have a growing impact on individual and community health.[4, 11, 21, 3] The convergence of media (computers, telephones, television, radio, video, print, and audio) and the emergence of the Internet create a nearly ubiquitous networked communication infrastructure. This infrastructure facilitates access to an increasing array of health information and health-related support services and extends the reach of health communication efforts. Delivery channels such as the Internet expand the choices available for health professionals to reach patients and consumers and for patients and consumers to interact with health professionals and with each other (for example, in online support groups).

Compared to traditional mass media, interactive media may have several advantages for health communication efforts. These advantages include (1) improved access to personalized health information; (2) increased confidentiality because of the opportunity to seek sensitive information anonymously; (3) access to health information, support, and services on demand; (4) enhanced ability to distribute materials widely and update content or functions rapidly; (5) just-in-time expert decision support; and (6) more choices for consumers.[4, 21] The health impact of interactivity, customization, and enhanced multimedia is just beginning to be explored, and already interactive health communication technologies are being used to exchange information, facilitate informed decisionmaking, promote healthy behaviors, enhance peer and emotional support, promote self-care, manage demand for health services, and support clinical care.

Widespread availability and use of interactive health communication and telehealth applications create at least two serious challenges. One is related to the risks associated with consumers' use of poor quality health information to make decisions. Concerns are growing about the Web making available large amounts of information that may be misleading, inaccurate, or inappropriate, which may put consumers at unnecessary risk. Although many health professionals agree that the Internet is a boon for consumers because they have easier access to much more information than before, these professionals are concerned that poor quality of a lot of information on the Web will undermine informed decisionmaking. These concerns are driving the development of a quality standards agenda to help health professionals and consumers find reliable Web sites and health information on the Internet. An expert panel convened by the Department of Health and Human Services describes high quality health information as accurate, current, valid, appropriate, intelligible, and free of bias.[4]

The other challenge is related to the privacy and confidentiality concerns raised by the collection, transformation, and distribution of personal health information through electronic means. The privacy and confidentiality of personal health information are major issues for consumers, and these concerns are magnified when information is collected, stored, and made available online.[4] As the availability and variety of interactive health applications grow, consumer confidence about

Data as of November 30, 1999

developers' ability or intent to ensure privacy will be challenged. In the near future, personal health information will be collected during both clinical and non-clinical encounters in disparate settings, such as schools, mobile clinics, public places, and homes, and will be made available for administrative, financial, clinical, and research purposes. Although public health and health services research may require de-identified personal health information, policies and procedures to protect privacy will need to ensure a balance between confidentiality and appropriate access to personal health information.

The trend of rapidly expanding opportunities in health communication intersects with recent demands for more rigorous evaluation of all aspects of the health care and public health delivery systems and for evidence-based practices.[22] Numerous studies of provider-patient communication support the connection among the quality of the provider-patient interaction, patient behavior, and health outcomes.[23] As the knowledge base about provider-patient interactions increases, a need becomes apparent for the development of practice guidelines to promote better provider-patient communication. Additional evidence about the process of health information-seeking and the role of health information in decisionmaking also is needed. Health communication campaigns could benefit as well from more rigorous formative research and evaluation of outcomes. Expected outcomes should be an important consideration and central element of campaign design. As health communication increasingly involves electronic media, new evaluation approaches are emerging.[4, 24, 25, 26] Given the critical role that communication plays in all aspects of public health and health care, health communication and outcomes research should become more tightly linked across all health communication domains.

Because national data systems will not be available in the first half of the decade for tracking progress, one subject of interest concerning health communication is not addressed in this focus area's objectives. Representing a research and data collection agenda for the coming decade, the topic covers persons who report being satisfied with the health information they received during their most recent search for such information. Health-conscious consumers are increasingly proactive in seeking out health information. Individuals want information about prevention and wellness as much as about medical problems. Public health and the medical community share an interest in promoting—and sustaining—"informed decisions" for better health. Surveys suggest that people want to get health information from a professional and that counseling by health professionals can be effective both in reducing lifestyle risks and supporting self-management of chronic diseases like diabetes. (See Focus Area 1. Access to Quality Health Services and Focus Area 7. Educational and Community-Based Programs.) However, diminished time in clinical visits and some clinicians' discomfort with open communication work against optimum information exchange. In addition, many people want information to be available when and where they need it most. Health information should be not only easily accessible but also of good quality and relevant for the needs of the person. The increasing use of the Internet as a source for health information will require greater awareness of the importance of the quality of information.

Disparities

Often people with the greatest health burdens have the least access to information, communication technologies, health care, and supporting social services. Even the most carefully designed health communication programs will have limited impact if underserved communities lack access to crucial health professionals, services, and communication channels that are part of a health improvement project.

Research indicates that even after targeted health communication interventions, low education and income groups remain less knowledgeable and less likely to change behavior than higher education and income groups, which creates a "knowledge gap" and leaves some people "chronically uninformed."[27] With communication technologies, the disparity in access to electronic information resources is commonly referred to as the "digital divide."[28] The digital divide becomes more critical as the amount and variety of health resources available over the Internet increase and as people need more sophisticated skills to use electronic resources.[29] Equitably distributed health communication resources and skills, and a robust communication infrastructure can contribute to the closing of the digital divide and the national goal of Healthy People 2010 to eliminate health disparities.

Even with access to information and services, however, disparities may still exist because many people lack health literacy.[30] Health literacy is increasingly vital to help people navigate a complex health system and better manage their own health. Differences in the ability to read and understand materials related to personal health as well as navigate the health system appear to contribute to health disparities. People with low health literacy are more likely to report poor health, have an incomplete understanding of their health problems and treatment, and be at greater risk of hospitalization.[31] The average annual health care costs of persons with very low literacy (reading at grade two or below) may be four times greater than for the general population.[32] An estimated 75 percent of persons in the United States with chronic physical or mental health problems are in the limited literacy category.[33] People with chronic conditions, such as asthma, hypertension, and diabetes, and low reading skills have been found to have less knowledge of their conditions than people with higher reading skills.[34, 35]

Although the majority of people with marginal or low literacy are white native-born Americans,[36] changing demographics suggest that low literacy is an increasing problem among certain racial and ethnic groups, non-English-speaking populations, and persons over the age of 65 years. One study of Medicare enrollees found that 34 percent of English speakers and 54 percent of Spanish speakers had inadequate or marginal health literacy.[37] As the U.S. population ages, low health literacy among elderly people is potentially a large problem. Nearly half of the people in the elderly population have low reading skills, and reading ability appears to decline with age. A study of patients 60 years and older at a public hospital found that 81 percent could not read and understand basic materials such as prescription labels and appointments.[38]

Opportunities

For health communication to contribute to the improvement of personal and community health during the first decade of the 21st century, stakeholders, including health professionals, researchers, public officials, and the lay public, must collaborate on a range of activities. These activities include (1) initiatives to build a robust health information system that provides equitable access; (2) development of high-quality, audience-appropriate information and support services for specific health problems and health-related decisions for all segments of the population, especially underserved persons; (3) training of health professionals in the science of communication and the use of communication technologies; (4) evaluation of interventions; and (5) promotion of a critical understanding and practice of effective health communication.

A national health information infrastructure (NHII) provides a framework that stakeholders can use to communicate with each other and to transform data into useful information on multiple levels. Efforts are underway throughout the world to develop integrated national and global health information infrastructures to support health improvements. In the United States, the National Committee on Vital and Health Statistics (NCVHS) is advising the Secretary of Health and Human Services on the data and infrastructure needs of the country. The NCVHS defines NHII as all of the technologies, standards, applications, systems, values, and laws that support individual health, health care, and public health. Issues related to technical standards, privacy and confidentiality, and regulatory guidelines are being addressed by the public and private sectors.

The infrastructure makes it possible for people not only to use health information designed by others, but also to create resources to manage their own health and to influence the health of their communities. For example, community groups could use computers to gain access to survey information about the quality of life in their neighborhoods and apply this information to create an action plan to present to local elected and public health officials. Information is a critical element of informed participation and decisionmaking, and appropriate, quality information and support services for all are empowering and democratic.

As patients and consumers become more knowledgeable about health information, services, and technologies, health professionals will need to meet the challenge of becoming better communicators and users of information technologies. Health professionals need a high level of interpersonal skills to interact with diverse populations and patients who may have different cultural, linguistic, educational, and socioeconomic backgrounds. Health professionals also need more direct training in and experience with all forms of computer and telecommunication technologies. In addition to searching for information, patients and consumers want to use technology to discuss health concerns, and health professionals need to be ready to respond. To support an increase in health communication activities, research and evaluation of all forms of health communication will be necessary to build the scientific base of the field and the practice of evidence-based health communication. Collectively, these opportunities represent important areas to make significant improvements in personal and community health.

Interim Progress Toward Year 2000 Objectives

Health Communication is a new focus area for Healthy People 2010.

Health Communication

Goal: Use communication strategically to improve health.

Number Objective

11-1   Households with Internet access

11-2   Health literacy

11-3   Research and evaluation of communication programs

11-4   Quality of Internet health information sources

11-5   Centers for excellence

11-6   Satisfaction with providers' communication skills

11-1. Increase the proportion of households with access to the Internet at home.

Target: 80 percent.

Baseline: 26 percent of households in 1998.

Target setting method: Better than the best.

Data source: School Enrollment Supplement to the Current Population Survey, U.S. Department of Commerce, Bureau of the Census.

Households, 1998	Internet Access at Home Percent
TOTAL	26
Race and ethnicity	
American Indian or Alaska Native	19
Asian or Pacific Islander	36
Asian	DNC
Native Hawaiian and other Pacific Islander	DNC
Black or African American	DNA
White	DNA
Hispanic or Latino	13
Not Hispanic or Latino	DNA
Black or African American	11
White	30
Gender (head of household)	
Female	DNC
Male	DNC
Family income level	
Poor	DNC
Near poor	DNC
Middle/high income	DNC
Education level (head of household)	
Less than high school	DNC
High school	DNC

Households, 1998	Internet Access at Home
	Percent
At least some college	DNC
Geographic location	
Urban	28
Rural	22

DNA = Data have not been analyzed. DNC = Data are not collected. DSU = Data are statistically unreliable.

Many health care organizations and public service agencies use the Internet as one of their main channels for information delivery. Access to the Internet and subsequent technologies is likely to become essential to gain access to health information, contact health care organizations and health professionals, receive services at a distance, and participate in efforts to improve local and national health.[4, 11] The integration of communication media means electronic access to health information not only via computers, but also with Web-enabled televisions and telephones, handheld devices, and other emerging technologies. Technical literacy, or the ability to use electronic technologies and applications, will be essential to gain access to this information.

Internet availability in the home is an important indicator of equitable access among population groups. An increasing number of people have access to the Internet at work and public facilities, such as libraries and community centers, but several limitations affect the use of online health information and support in these settings. Some employers monitor electronic mail and the types of sites visited by employees. Access in public settings may be problematic because of privacy and confidentiality concerns, and access may be needed during times when these facilities are unavailable. Because of the potentially sensitive nature of health-related uses of the Internet, access at home is essential.

Although the proportion of people with access to the Internet has risen dramatically since 1995, many segments of the population lack access, such as low-income and rural households; persons with less education; and certain racial and ethnic groups, such as African Americans and Hispanics.[28] Internet access rates vary considerably according to income. Only 11 percent of households earning less than $24,999 have access, whereas 19 percent are connected among those earning $25,000 to $34,999; 30 percent access among those earning $35,000 to $49,999; and 52 percent of households with $50,000 or greater in income have an Internet connection.[28] Barriers to Internet access include cost, lack of services in certain communities, limited literacy, lack of familiarity with different technologies, and, especially for people with disabilities, inaccessible formats that limit appropriate and effective technology use. Initiatives to promote universal access to the Internet will involve public and private sector stakeholders, particularly government agencies and technology corporations.

11-2. (Developmental) Improve the health literacy of persons with inadequate or marginal literacy skills.

Potential data source: National Adult Literacy Survey, 2002, U.S. Department of Education.

Responses from the National Adult Literacy Survey indicate that approximately 90 million adults in the United States have inadequate or marginal literacy skills.[36] Health literacy is a "constellation of skills, including the ability to perform basic reading and numerical tasks required to function in the health care environment. Patients with adequate health literacy can read, understand, and act on health care information."[30] Written information is not the only way to communicate about health, but a great deal of health education and promotion are organized around the use of print materials, usually written at the 10th grade level and above. These materials are of little use to people who have limited literacy skills.[39] The result is that a very large segment of the population is denied the full benefits of health information and services.

Closing the gap in health literacy is an issue of fundamental fairness and equity and is essential to reduce health disparities. Public and private efforts need to occur in two areas: the development of appropriate written materials and improvement in skills of those persons with limited literacy. The knowledge exists to create effective, culturally and linguistically appropriate, plain language health communications. Professional publications and Federal documents provide the criteria to integrate and apply the principles of organization, writing style, layout, and design for effective communication.[39, 40] These criteria should be widely distributed and used. Many organizations such as public and medical libraries, voluntary, professional, and community groups, and schools could offer health literacy programs that target skill improvement for low-literacy and limited English proficient individuals. If appropriate materials exist and people receive the training to use them, then measurable improvements in health literacy for the least literate can occur.

11-3. (Developmental) Increase the proportion of health communication activities that include research and evaluation.

Potential data sources: Sponsored survey of *Federal Register* notices; Grant-makers in Health; National Health Council.

Effective health communication programs are built on sound research and evaluation. Meaningful research and evaluation are not afterthoughts but integral parts of initial program design. Research provides the ideas and tools to design and carry out formative, process, and outcome evaluations to improve health communication efforts, certify the degree of change that has occurred, and identify programs, or elements of programs, that are not working.[1, 10] Research and evaluation systematically obtain information that can be used to refine the design, development, implementation, adoption, redesign, and overall quality of a communication intervention.[41, 42]

Programs funded by Federal, philanthropic, and not-for-profit organizations could be strengthened with requirements for a minimum set of evaluation activities and specific measurements. The level of research and evaluation required should reflect the costs, scope, and potential impact (in terms of benefit or harm) of the communication activity proposed. At a minimum, programs should be expected to conduct appropriate audience testing for need, cultural and linguistic competence, comprehension, and receptivity. Requirements and specifications for evaluation could be set for grant-funded communication programs and included in requests for funding proposals and grant program guidelines as well as for programs directly funded and implemented by public or private sector organizations by including research and evaluation activities in their work plans.

11-4. (Developmental) Increase the proportion of health-related World Wide Web sites that disclose information that can be used to assess the quality of the site.

Potential data sources: Health on the Net Foundation; Internet Healthcare Coalition.

With the rapidly growing volume of health information, advertising, products, and services available on the Internet, serious concerns arise regarding the accuracy, appropriateness, and potential health impact of these sites.[4, 21] People are using the Internet to look up information, purchase medications, consult remotely with providers, and maintain their personal health records. Approximately 70 million persons in the United States use the Internet for health-related reasons,[43] and the potential for harm from inaccurate information, inferior quality goods, and inappropriate services is significant. Many initiatives are under way to identify appropriate and feasible approaches to evaluate online health sites.[26] Professional associations are issuing guidelines and recommendations,[44] Federal agencies such as the Federal Trade Commission are actively monitoring and sanctioning owners of Web sites that are false or misleading,[45] and developers and purchasers of online health resources are being urged to adopt standards for quality assurance.[4]

To allow users to evaluate the quality and appropriateness of Internet health resources, health-related Web sites should publicly disclose the following essential information about their site:[4] (1) the identity of the developers and sponsors of the site (and how to contact them) and information about any potential conflicts of interest or biases; (2) the explicit purpose of the site, including any commercial purposes and advertising; (3) the original sources of the content on the site; (4)

how the privacy and confidentiality of any personal information collected from users is protected; and (5) how the site is evaluated and updated. An additional mark of quality which should be present in a Web site relates to the site's accessibility by all users. Contents of the site should be presented in a way that it can be used by people with disabilities and with low-end technology.

11-5. (Developmental) Increase the number of centers for excellence that seek to advance the research and practice of health communication.

Potential data sources: Health Communication Interest Group, American Public Health Association; Society for Social Marketing; Association of Schools of Public Health; Health Communication Divisions, International Communication Association and National Communication Association.

To enlarge the knowledge base of health communication and incorporate it into health promotion practice, a research and training infrastructure is needed to develop, model, and coordinate activities. For this purpose, centers for excellence located in academic institutions, national organizations, or research centers would be instrumental to meet scientific and practical needs. The centers would be responsible for an array of activities, such as (1) promoting the adoption of health communication theories and practices in health care, disease prevention, and health promotion initiatives; (2) developing and disseminating quality standards; (3) coordinating initiatives to develop a consensus research agenda; (4) developing systems to identify and assess health communication research; (5) evaluating communication strategies, messages, materials, and resources; (6) fostering networking and collaboration among health communicators, health educators, and other health professionals; (7) promoting health communication skills training for health professionals; and (8) promoting research and dissemination activities among specific population groups.

These centers should provide expert staff, model curricula with core competencies in health communication and media technologies, equipped media labs, research seminars, continuing education and distance learning courses, and training and placement programs to expand the pool of health communication professionals and health professionals with communication skills. The centers also could create databases that would catalog items such as formative and outcomes research studies and reports and partner with existing governmental dissemination networks to make data publicly available. Centers for excellence in health communication could be funded through Federal grants, foundations, or private sector health care organizations.

11-6. (Developmental) Increase the proportion of persons who report that their health care providers have satisfactory communication skills.

Potential data sources: National Committee for Quality Assurance; Behavioral Risk Factor Surveillance System (BRFSS), CDC, NCCDPHP; National Health Interview Survey (NHIS), CDC, NCHS; industry surveys (FIND/SVP, Nielsen, Jupiter Communications).

Good provider-patient communication contributes to quality care and improved health status. Patients' assessment of their providers' communication skills is important for individuals with a usual source of care as well as for those without, who may have less frequent contact with the medical care system. Studies indicate that patients find communicating with their health care providers difficult[23, 46] and report that providers do not give them enough information, even though they highly value the information and want to know more.[47] Clear, candid, accurate, culturally and linguistically competent provider-patient communication is essential for the prevention, diagnosis, treatment, and management of health concerns.[23]

Effective communication underpins prevention and screening efforts at the clinical level, when providers have the opportunity to engage in one-on-one counseling and supply information that is culturally and linguistically appropriate and delivered at the person's health literacy level. Diagnoses and treatments require doctors to negotiate a common understanding with patients about what is to be done. The quality of provider-patient communication can affect numerous outcomes, including patient adherence to recommendations and health status.[48] Appropriate information and communication with a provider not only can relieve patients' anxieties, but also can help patients understand their choices, allow them to participate in informed decisionmaking, and better manage their own health concerns.

Related Objectives From Other Focus Areas

1. Access

1-3.   Counseling about health behaviors

1-12.   Single toll-free number for poison control centers

2. Arthritis, Osteoporosis, and Chronic Back Conditions

2-8.   Arthritis education

3. Cancer

3-10.   Provider counseling about preventive measures

4. Chronic Kidney Disease

4-3.   Counseling for chronic kidney failure care

5. Diabetes

5-1.   Diabetes education

7. Educational and Community-Based Programs

7-2.   School health education

7-3.   Health-risk behavior information for college and university students

7-5.   Worksite health promotion programs

7-7.   Patient and family education

7-8.   Satisfaction with patient education

7-9.   Health care organization sponsorship of community health promotion activities

7-10.   Community health promotion programs

7-11.   Culturally appropriate community health promotion programs

9. Family Planning

9-11.   Pregnancy prevention education

10. Food Safety

10-5.   Consumer food safety practices

12. Heart Disease and Stroke

12-2.   Knowledge of symptoms of heart attack and importance of dialing 911

12-4.   Bystander response to cardiac arrest

12-8.   Knowledge of early warning symptoms of stroke

13. HIV

13-8.   HIV counseling and education for persons in substance abuse treatment

13-9.   HIV/AIDS, STD, and TB education in State prisons

13-10. HIV counseling and testing in State prisons

16. Maternal, Infant, and Child Health

16-7.   Childbirth classes

16-13. Infants put to sleep on their back

17. Medical Product Safety

17-3.   Provider review of medications taken by patients

17-4.   Receipt of useful information from pharmacies

17-5.   Receipt of oral counseling from prescribers and dispensers

17-6.   Blood donations

19. Nutrition and Overweight

19-16. Worksite promotion of nutrition education and weight management

19-17. Nutrition counseling for medical conditions

23. Public Health Infrastructure

23-2.   Public access to information and surveillance data

24. Respiratory Diseases

24-6.   Patient education

25. Sexually Transmitted Diseases

25-15. Sexual behavior messages on television

26. Substance Abuse

26-17. Perception of risk associated with substance abuse

27. Tobacco Use

27-15. Tobacco advertising and promotion targeting adolescents and young adults

Terminology

(A listing of all abbreviations and acronyms used in this publication appears in Appendix K.)

Accuracy: Content that is valid and without errors of fact, interpretation, or judgment.

Advocacy: Communication directed at policymakers and decisionmakers to promote policies, regulations, and programs to bring about change.

Availability: Content (whether targeted message or other information) that is delivered or placed where the audience can access it. Placement varies according to audience, message complexity, and purpose—from interpersonal and social networks to billboards, mass transit signs, prime-time TV, and radio and from public kiosks (print or electronic) to the Internet.

Balance: Where appropriate, content that fairly and accurately presents the benefits and risks of potential actions or recognizes different but valid perspectives on an issue.

Consistency: Content that remains internally consistent over time and also is consistent with information from other sources.

Consumer health informatics: Interactive health communication (see below) focusing on consumers.

Consumer health information: Information designed to help individuals understand their health and make health-related decisions for themselves and their families.

Culturally competent: The design, implementation, and evaluation process that accounts for special issues of select population groups (ethnic and racial, linguistic) as well as differing educational levels and physical abilities.

Decision support systems: Computer software programs designed to assist diagnostic and treatment decisions. Examples include drug alert notification systems, prompts to implement practice guidelines, and health risk appraisals.

Evidence based: Comprehensive review and rigorous analysis of relevant scientific evidence to formulate practice guidelines, performance measures, review criteria, performance measures, and technology assessments[22] for telehealth applications.[4, 24]

Formative research: Assesses the nature of the problem, the needs of the target audience, and the implementation process to inform and improve program design. Formative research is conducted both prior to and during program development to adapt the program to audience needs. Common methods include literature reviews, reviews of existing programs, and surveys, interviews, and focus group discussions with members of the target audience.

Health communication: The art and technique of informing, influencing, and motivating individual, institutional, and public audiences about important health issues. The scope of health communication includes disease prevention, health promotion, health care policy, and the business of health care, as well as enhancement of the quality of life and health of individuals within the community.[49]

Health education: Any planned combination of learning experiences designed to predispose, enable, and reinforce voluntary behavior conducive to health in individuals, groups, or communities.[50]

Health literacy: The capacity to obtain, interpret, and understand basic health information and services and the competence to use such information and services to enhance health. (See also *Literacy*.)

Health promotion: Any planned combination of educational, political, regulatory, and organizational supports for actions and conditions of living conducive to the health of individuals, groups, or communities.

Interactive health communication: The interaction of an individual with an electronic device or communication technology to access or transmit health information or to receive guidance on a health-related issue.[21]

Internet: A worldwide interconnection of computer networks operated by government, commercial, and academic organizations and private citizens.

Literacy: The ability to read, write, and speak in English and to compute and solve problems at levels of proficiency necessary to function on the job and in society, to achieve one's goals, and develop one's knowledge and potential.[51]

Medical informatics: A field of study concerned with the broad range of issues in the management and use of biomedical information, including medical computing and the study of the nature of medical information itself.[52]

Outcome evaluation (sometimes called "impact evaluation"): Examines the results of a communication intervention, including changes in awareness, attitudes, beliefs, actions, professional practices, policies, costs, and institutional or social systems.

Patient communication: Information for individuals with health conditions to help them maximize recovery, maintain therapeutic regimens, and understand alternative approaches. Patient communication includes educational resources, provider-patient communication, and, increasingly, peer-to-peer communication.

Process evaluation: Monitors the administrative, organizational, or other operational characteristics of an intervention. Process evaluation includes monitoring the dissemination of communication products to intended users (whether gatekeepers or audiences) and audience members' exposure to a message. For an interactive health communication application, process evaluation may include testing how the application functions.

Reach: Information that gets to or is available to the largest possible number of people in the target population.

Reliability: Content that is credible, in terms of its source and is kept up to date.

Repetition: Delivery of and access to content continued or repeated over time, both to reinforce the impact with a given audience and to reach new generations.

Risk communication: Engaging communities in discussions about environmental and other health risks and about approaches to deal with them. Risk communication also includes individual counseling about genetic risks and consequent choices.

Social marketing: The application of marketing principles and techniques to program development, implementation, and evaluation to promote healthy behaviors or reduce risky ones.[53, 54]

Tailoring: Creating messages and materials to reach one specific person, based on characteristics unique to that person, related to the outcome of interest, and derived from an assessment of that individual.[15]

Targeting: Creating messages and materials intended to reach a specific segment of a population, usually based on one or more demographic or other characteristics shared by its members.[15]

Telehealth: The application of telecommunication and computer technologies to the broad spectrum of public health and medicine.

Telemedicine: The use of electronic information and communication technologies to provide clinical care across distance.[24]

Timelessness: Content that is provided or available when the audience is most receptive to, or in need of, the specific information.

Underserved: Individuals or groups who lack access to health services or information relative to the national average. The underserved population may include residents of rural, remote, or inner-city areas; members of certain racial and ethnic groups; socioeconomically disadvantaged persons; or people with disabilities.

Understandable: Reading or language level and format (including multimedia) that are appropriate for a specific audience.

World Wide Web (Web): An international virtual network composed of Internet host computers that can be accessed by graphical browsers.

References

1. National Cancer Institute. *Making Health Communications Work.* Pub. No. NIH 89-1493. Washington, DC: U.S. Department of Health and Human Services, 1989.

2. Piotrow, P.T.; Kincaid, D.L.; Rimon, II, J.G.; et al. *Health Communication.* Westport, CT: Praeger, 1997.

3. Jackson, L.D., and Duffy, B.K., eds. *Health Communication Research.* Westport, CT: Greenwood, 1998.

4. Science Panel on Interactive Communication and Health. *Wired for Health and Well-Being: the Emergence of Interactive Health Communication.* Eng, T.R., and Gustafson, D.H. (eds.). Washington DC: U.S.

Department of Health and Human Services, April 1999.

5.   Northouse, L.L., and Northouse, P.G. *Health Communication: Strategies for Health Professionals*, 3rd ed. Stamford, CT: Appleton & Lange, 1998.

6.   Maibach, E., and Parrott, R.L. *Designing Health Messages*. Thousand Oaks, CA: Sage Publications, 1995.

7.   Ray, E.B., and Donohew, L., eds. *Communication and Health: Systems and Applications*. Hillsdale, NJ: Lawrence Erlbaum Associates, 1990.

8.   Freimuth, V.S.; Stein, J.A.; and Kean, T.J. *Searching for Health Information: the Cancer Information Service Model*. Philadelphia: University of Pennsylvania Press, 1989.

9.   Atkin, C., and Wallack, L., eds. *Mass Communication and Public Health*. Newbury Park, CA: Sage Publications, 1990.

10.   Backer, T.E.; Rogers, E.M.; and Sopory, P. *Designing Health Communication Campaigns: What Works?* Newbury Park, CA: Sage Publications, 1992.

11.   Harris, L.M., ed. Health and the New Media. *Technologies Transforming Personal and Public Health*. Mahwah, NJ: Lawrence Erlbaum Associates, 1995.

12.   Street, R.L.; Gold, W.R.; and Manning, T., eds. *Health Promotion and Interactive Technology: Theoretical Applications and Future Directions*. Mahwah, NJ: Lawrence Erlbaum Associates, 1997.

13.   Finnegan, Jr., J.R., and Viswanath, K. Health and Communication: Medical and Public Health Influences on the Research Agenda. In: Ray, E.B., and Donohew, L. *Communication and Health:*

Systems and Applications. Hillsdale, NJ: Lawrence Erlbaum Associates, 1990.

14.   Simons-Morton, B.G.; Donohew, L.; and Crump, A.D. Health communication in the prevention of alcohol, tobacco, and drug use. *Health Education & Behavior* 24:544-554, 1997.

15.   Kreuter, M.W.; Strecher, V.J.; and Glassman, B. One size does not fit all: The case for tailoring cancer prevention materials. *Annals of Behavioral Medicine*, in press, 1999.

16.   Worden, J.K.; Flynn, B.S.; Solomon, L.J.; et al. Using mass media to prevent cigarette smoking among adolescent girls. *Health Education Quarterly* 23:453-468, 1996.

17.   Brug, J.; Glanz, K.; Van Assema, P.; et al. The impact of computer-tailored feedback and iterative feedback on fat, fruit, and vegetable intake. *Health Education & Behavior* 25:517-531, 1998.

18.   Scott, S.A.; Jorgensen, C.M.; and Suarez, L. Concerns and dilemmas of Hispanic AIDS information seekers: Spanish-speaking callers to the CDC National AIDS hotline. *Health Education & Behavior* 25(4):501-516, 1998.

19.   Wright, A.L.; Naylor, A.; Wester, R.; et al. Using cultural knowledge in health promotion: Breastfeeding among the Navajo. *Health Education & Behavior* 24:625-639, 1997.

20.   Lalonde, B.; Rabinowitz, P.; Shefsky, M.L.; et al. La Esperanza del Valle: Alcohol prevention novelas for Hispanic youth and their families. *Health Education & Behavior* 24:587-602, 1997.

21.   Robinson, T.N.; Patrick, K.; Eng, T.R.; et al., for the Science Panel on Interactive Communication and Health.

An evidence-based approach to interactive health communication: A challenge to medicine in the Information Age. *Journal of the American Medical Association* 280:1264-1269, 1998.

22.   Agency for Health Care Policy and Research. *Evidence-based Practice Centers*. RFP No. AHCPR-97-0001. Washington, DC: U.S. Department of Health and Human Services, 1997.

23.   Roter, D.L., and Hall, J.A. Doctors Talking with Patients/Patients Talking with Doctors: Improving Communication in Medical Visits. Westport, CT: Auburn House, 1992.

24.   Committee on Evaluating Clinical Applications of Telemedicine. *Telemedicine: A Guide to Assessing Telecommunications for Health Care*. Field, M.J. (ed.). Washington, DC: National Academy Press, 1996.

25.   Anderson, J.G.; Aydin, C.E.; and Jay, S.J., eds. *Evaluating Health Care Information Systems*. Thousand Oaks, CA: Sage Publications, 1994.

26.   Kim, P.; Eng, T.R.; Deering, M.J.; et al. Published criteria for evaluating health-related Web sites: Review. *British Medical Journal* 318:647-649, 1999.

27.   Freimuth, V.S. The Chronically Uninformed: Closing the Knowledge Gap in Health. In: Ray, E.B., and Donohew, L. *Communication and Health: Systems and Applications*. Hillsdale, NJ: Lawrence Erlbaum Associates, 1990.

28.   U.S. Department of Commerce. *Falling Through the Net: Defining the Digital Divide*. Washington, DC: National Telecommunications and Information Administration, 1999. Retrieved July 29, 1999

<www.ntia.doc.gov/ntiahome/digitaldivide/>

29.   Eng, T.R.; Maxfield, A.; Patrick, K.; et al. Access to health information and support: A public highway or a private road? *Journal of the American Medical Association* 280:1371-1375, 1998.

30.   American Medical Association, Ad Hoc Committee on Health Literacy for the Council on Scientific Affairs. Health literacy: Report of the Council on Scientific Affairs. *Journal of the American Medical Association* 281:552-557, 1998.

31.   Baker, D.W.; Parker, R.M.; Williams, M.V.; et al. The relationship of patient reading ability to self-reported health and use of health services. *American Journal of Public Health* 87:1027-1030, 1997.

32.   Weiss, B.D.; Blanchard, J.S.; McGee, D.L;. et al. Illiteracy among Medicaid recipients and its relationship to health care costs. *Journal of Health Care for the Poor and Under served* 5:99-111, 1994.

33.   Davis, T.C.; Meldrum, H.; Tippy, P.K.P.; et al. How poor literacy leads to poor healthcare. *Patient Care* 94-108, October 15, 1996.

34.   Williams, M.V.; Baker, D.W.; Parker, R.M.; et al. Relationship of functional health literacy to patients' knowledge of their chronic disease. A study of patients with hypertension and diabetes. *Archives of Internal Medicine* 158:166-172, 1998.

35.   Williams, M.V.; Baker, D.W.; Honig, E.G.; et al. Inadequate literacy is a barrier to asthma knowledge and self-care. *Chest* 114:1008-1015, 1998.

36.   Kirsch, I.; Jungeblut, A.; Jenkins, L.; et al. Adult Literacy in America: A First Look at the Findings of the National Adult Literacy Survey.

Washington, DC: National Center for Education Statistics, U.S. Department of Education, 1993.

37.   Gazmararian, J.A.; Baker, D.W.; Williams, M.V.; et al. Health literacy among Medicare enrollees in a managed care organization. *Journal of the American Medical Association* 281:545-551, 1999.

38.   Williams, M.V.; Parker, R.M.; Baker, D.W.; et al. Inadequate functional health literacy among patients at two public hospitals. *Journal of the American Medical Association* 274:1677-1682, 1995.

39.   National Cancer Institute. *Clear & Simple: Developing Effective Print Materials for Low-literate Readers.* Pub. No. NIH 95-3594. Washington, DC: U.S. Department of Health and Human Services, 1995.

40.   Doak, C.C.; Doak, L.G.; and Root, J.H. *Teaching Patients with Low Literacy Skills,* 2nd ed. Philadelphia: J.B. Lippincott Company, 1996.

41.   Rossi, P.H. Twelve Laws of Evaluation Research. In: Fisher, A.; Pavlova, M.; and Covello, V. (eds.). *Evaluation and Effective Risk Communications, Workshop Proceedings.* Interagency Task Force on Environmental Cancer and Heart and Lung Disease, Committee on Public Education and Communication. EPA/600/9-90/054. Washington, DC: U.S. Environmental Protection Agency (EPA), 1991.

42.   Rossi, P.H., and Freeman, H.E. *Evaluation: A Systematic Approach,* 5th ed. Newbury Park, CA: Sage Publications, 1993.

43.   ReutersHealth. Americans seek health information on-line. Retrieved August 6,

1999. <www.reutershealth. Com>

44.   American Telemedicine Association. American Telemedicine Association issues advisory on use of medical Web sites. Retrieved August 10, 1999 www.atmeda.org

45.   U.S. Federal Trade Commission. "Operation Cure All" targets Internet health fraud. Press release, June 24, 1999. Washington, DC.

46.   Rosenberg, E.E.; Lussier, M.T.; and Beaudoin, C. Lessons for clinicians from physician-patient communication literature. *Archives of Family Medicine* 6:279-283, 1997.

47.   Laine, C.; Davidoff, F.; Lewis, C.E.; et al. Important elements of outpatient care: a comparison of patients' and physicians' opinions. *Annals of Internal Medicine* 125:640-645, 1996.

48.   Ong, L.M.L.; de Haes, J.C.J.M.; Hoos, A.M.; et al. Doctor-patient communication: A review of the literature. *Social Science and Medicine* 40:903-918, 1995.

49.   Ratzan, S.C., ed. Health communication, challenges for the 21st century. Special issue. *American Behavioral Scientist* 38(2), 1994.

50.   Green, L.W., and Kreuter, M.W. *Health Promotion Planning, an Educational and Ecological Approach,* 3rd ed. Mountain View, CA: Mayfield Publishing Company, 1999.

51.   U.S. Congress. National Literacy Act of 1991. Public Law 102-73, 1991.

52.   Shortliffe, E.H., and Perreault, L.E., eds. *Medical Informatics.* New York: Addison-Wesley, 1990.

53. Lefebvre, R.C., and Rochlin, L. Social Marketing. In: Glanz, K.; Lewis, F.M.; and Rimer, B.K. *Health Behavior and Health Education: Theory, Research, and Practice,* 2nd ed. San Francisco: Jossey-Bass Publishers, 1997, 384-401.

54. Ling, J.C.; Franklin, B.A.; Lindsteadt, J.F.; et al. Social Marketing, Its Place in Public Health. *Annual Reviews of Public Health* 13:341-62, 1992.

12

Heart Disease and Stroke

Co-Lead Agencies: Centers for Disease Control and Prevention;
National Institutes of Health

Contents

Goal

Improve cardiovascular health and quality of life through the prevention, detection, and treatment of risk factors; early identification and treatment of heart attacks and strokes; and prevention of recurrent cardiovascular events.

Overview

Heart disease is the leading cause of death for all Americans. Stroke is the third leading cause of death. Heart disease and stroke continue to be a major cause of disability and a significant contributor to increases in health care costs in the United States.[1]

Epidemiologic and statistical studies have identified a number of factors that increase the risk of heart disease and stroke. In addition, clinical trials and prevention research studies have demonstrated effective strategies to prevent and control these risk factors and thereby reduce illnesses, disabilities, and deaths caused by heart disease and stroke.

Issues and Trends

Coronary heart disease (CHD) accounts for the largest proportion of heart disease. About 12 million Americans have CHD.[1] The CHD death rate peaked in the mid-1960s and has declined in the general population over the past 35 years. This decline began in females in the 1950s and in males in the 1960s. Although absolute declines (reduction in the total number of cases) have been much greater in males than in females, rates of decline (the speed at which the number of cases had decreased) also have been greater in males, but in recent years they have been greater in females.

Since 1950, there has been a clear rise and fall in CHD death rates for each racial and gender group. Although the age-adjusted death rate for CHD continues to decline each year, declines in the unadjusted death rate and in the number of deaths have slowed because of an increase in the number of older Americans, who have higher rates of CHD.

High blood cholesterol is a major risk factor for CHD that can be modified. More than 50 million American adults have blood cholesterol levels that require medical advice and treatment.[2] More than 90 million adults have cholesterol levels that are higher than desirable. All adults aged 20 years and older should have their cholesterol levels checked at least once every 5 years to help them take action to prevent or lower their risk of CHD.[3] Lifestyle changes that prevent or lower high blood cholesterol include eating a diet low in saturated fat and cholesterol, increasing physical activity, and reducing excess weight.[3]

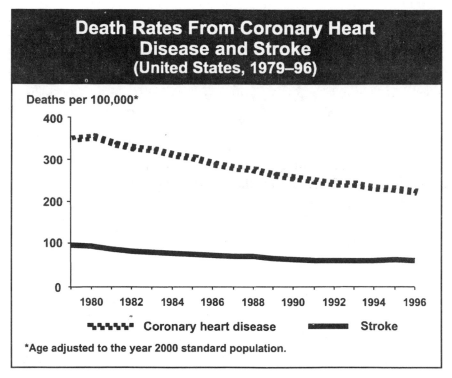

Death Rates From Coronary Heart Disease and Stroke
(United States, 1979–96)

Deaths per 100,000*

*Age adjusted to the year 2000 standard population.

■ ■ ■ ■ ■ ■ Coronary heart disease　　━━━━━ Stroke

Source: National Vital Statistics System (NVSS), CDC, NCHS, 1979–96.

About 4 million persons have cerebrovascular disease,[1] a major form of which is stroke. About 600,000 strokes occur each year in the United States, resulting in about 158,000 deaths. Death rates for stroke are highest in the southeastern United States. Like CHD death rates, stroke death rates have declined over the past 30 years. The decline accelerated in the 1970s for whites and African Americans. The rate of decline, however, has slowed in recent years. The overall decline has occurred mainly because of improvements in the detection and treatment of high blood pressure (hypertension).

High blood pressure is known as the "silent killer" and remains a major risk factor for CHD, stroke, and heart failure. About 50 million adult Americans have high blood pressure. High blood pressure also is more common in older persons. Comparing the 1976–80 National Health and Nutrition Examination Survey (NHANES II) and the 1988–91 survey (NHANES III, phase 1) reveals an increase from 51 to 73 percent in the proportion of Americans who were aware that they had high blood pressure.[4,5] Nevertheless, a large proportion of Americans with high blood pressure still are unaware that they have this disorder.[4,5]

The age composition of the U.S. population has changed dramatically during the 20th century and will continue to change during the 21st century. By the end of the 1990s, one in every four persons was aged 50 years or older. By 2030, about one in three will be aged 50 years or older. Most significant has been the increase in the size of the population aged 65 years and older. In addition, the percentage of persons aged 85 years and older has increased significantly. Heart disease and stroke deaths rise significantly after age 65 years, accounting for more than 40 percent of all deaths among persons aged 65 to 74 years and almost 60 percent of those aged 85 years and older. In the 1980s and 1990s, heart failure emerged as a major chronic disease for older adults. [6, 7, 8, 9] Almost 75 percent of the nearly 5 million patients with heart failure in the United States are older than 65 years.[8] Hospitalization rates for heart failure continue to increase significantly in those aged 65 years and older.[9]

Atrial fibrillation (AF) affects close to 2 million people. The number of existing cases of AF increases with age and is more common in males than in females.[1] The rate of AF is 0.5 percent for the group aged 50 to 59 years and rises to 8.8 percent in the group aged 80 to 89 years.[6] Because females have a longer life expectancy than males, the actual number of cases in elderly females (older than 75 years) is greater than in elderly males. Cases of AF may continue to rise as persons live longer and as more persons survive a first heart attack.

Because national data systems will not be available in the first half of the decade for tracking progress, two subjects of interest are not addressed in this focus area's objectives. Representing a research and data collection agenda for the coming decade, the topics are related to provider counseling and increasing awareness of cardiovascular disease (CVD) as the leading cause of death for all females. The first topic covers instruction of high-risk patients and family members or significant others in preparing appropriate heart attack and stroke action plans for seeking rapid emergency care, including when to call 911 or the local emergency number. The second topic deals with increasing awareness among all females that CVD is their leading cause of death.

Disparities

In general, the heart disease death rate has been consistently higher in males than in females and higher in the African American population than in the white population. In addition, over the past 30 years the CHD death rate has declined differentially by gender and race. In the 1970s, African American females experienced the greatest decline in CHD. This steep decline disappeared in the 1980s, when rates of decline for white males and females exceeded those for African American males and females, and African American females had the lowest rate of decline.[10] In the 1980s, males had a steeper rate of decline than females. Between 1980 and 1995, the percentage declines were greater in males than in females and greater in whites than in African Americans. In 1995, the age-adjusted death rate for heart disease was 42 percent higher in African American males than in white males, 65 percent higher in African American females than in white females, and almost twice as high in males as in females.

Disparities also exist in treatment outcomes for patients who have a heart attack. Females, in general, have poorer outcomes following a heart attack than do males: 44 percent of females who have a heart attack die within a year, compared with 27 percent of males. At older ages, females who have heart attacks are twice as likely as males to die within a few weeks.[11] These differences are explained, in part, by the presence of coexisting conditions, such as high blood pressure, diabetes, and congestive heart failure. After controlling for such factors, however, studies indicate an association remains between female gender and death following a heart attack. Complications are more frequent in females than in males after coronary intervention procedures, such as angioplasty or bypass surgery, are performed. Additional studies are needed to evaluate specific interventions and determine whether gender-specific interventions may be beneficial. In general, factors such as age (older), gender (female), race or ethnicity, low socioeconomic status, and prior medical conditions (previous heart attack, history of angina or diabetes) have been associated with longer prehospital delays in seeking care for symptoms of a heart attack.[12]

The male-female disparity in stroke deaths widened until the 1980s and then narrowed. Although stroke death rates have been decreasing, the decline among African Americans has not been as substantial as the decline in the total population. The racial differences in the number of new cases of stroke and deaths due to stroke are even greater than those found in CHD. Stroke deaths are highest in African American females born before 1950 and in African American males born after 1950. Among the racial and gender groups, declines in the stroke death rate are smallest in African American males. When adjusted for age, stroke deaths are almost 80 percent higher in African Americans than in whites and about 17 percent higher in males than in females. Moreover, age-specific stroke deaths are higher in African Americans than in whites in all age groups up to age 84 years and higher in males than in females throughout all adult age groups.

The number of existing cases of high blood pressure is nearly 40 percent higher in African Americans than in whites (an estimated 6.4 million African Americans have high blood pressure),[13] and its effects are more frequent and severe in the African American population.

Opportunities

Primary prevention. Heart disease and stroke share several risk factors, including high blood pressure, cigarette smoking, high blood cholesterol, and overweight. Physical inactivity and diabetes are additional risk factors for heart disease. (See Focus Area 5. Diabetes.) The lifetime risk for developing CHD is very high in the United States: one of every two males and one of every three females aged 40 years and under will develop CHD sometime in their life. Primary prevention, specifically through lifestyle interventions which promote heart-healthy behaviors, is a major strategy to reduce the development of heart disease or stroke.

A number of studies have shown that lifestyle interventions can help prevent high blood pressure and reduce blood cholesterol levels. For high blood pressure, these changes include increasing the level of aerobic physical activity, maintaining a healthy weight, limiting the consumption of alcohol to moderate levels for those who drink, reducing salt and sodium intake, and eating a reduced fat diet high in fruits, vegetables, and low-fat dairy food. Moreover, studies show that a diet low in total fat, saturated fat, and dietary cholesterol—with physical activity and weight control—can lower blood cholesterol levels.

Overweight and obesity are growing public health problems, affecting adults, adolescents, and children. Some 97 million adults are obese or overweight and thus are at increased risk of illness from high blood pressure, high blood cholesterol and other lipid disorders, type 2 diabetes, CHD, stroke, and other diseases. Efforts to prevent overweight and obesity by promoting heart-healthy behaviors—beginning in childhood—are needed to help reverse the trend. Balancing calorie intake with physical activity is critical. Research in the 1990s showed that a wide range of physical activities are beneficial to health and that everyone can benefit from physical activity. Even when physical activity is less than vigorous, it can still produce health benefits, including a decreased risk of CHD.[14, 15, 16, 17]

Nonetheless, increasing the level of physical activity remains a challenge. Furthermore, according to the 1996 *Surgeon General's Report on Physical Activity and Health*,[18] the percentage of people who say they engage in no leisure-time physical activity is higher among females than males, among African Americans and Hispanics than whites, among older adults than younger adults, and among the less affluent than the more affluent persons.

Progress on smoking cessation will play a critical role in achieving the national goal for heart disease reduction. Smoking cessation has major and immediate health benefits for men and women of all ages. For example, people who quit smoking before aged 50 years have half the risk of dying in the next 15 years, compared with continuing smokers.[19]

Studies have shown that risk factors for heart disease and stroke develop early in life: atherosclerosis already is present in late adolescence, diabetes in overweight children is on the rise, and hypertension can begin in the early teens.[20, 21] Tobacco use also begins in adolescence, therefore, primary prevention efforts should be expanded in elementary and secondary schools and at the college level. Nationwide mass media campaigns, community-based programs, and other communication efforts should be expanded to give groups better access to information and programs. These programs should promote heart-healthy behaviors at the community level as well as detect and treat existing risk factors.

Risk factor detection and treatment. Screening for risk factors, particularly for high blood pressure and high blood cholesterol, is an important step in identifying individuals whose risk factors may be undiagnosed and to refer them to ongoing care. A host of studies have shown that dietary and pharmacologic therapy can reduce CHD and stroke risk factors, especially high blood pressure and high blood cholesterol. These interventions, coupled with other lifestyle changes, such as stopping smoking, increasing physical activity, and maintaining a healthy weight, can be even more effective in lowering the risk of a heart attack or stroke.[22, 23, 24, 25]

Research showing the importance of blood pressure for health led to the introduction by the National Heart, Lung, and Blood Institute (NHLBI) of the National High Blood Pressure Education Program (NHBPEP) in 1972.[26] NHBPEP is the first large-scale public outreach and education campaign to reduce high blood pressure. Its promotion of the detection, treatment, and control of high blood pressure has been credited with influencing the dramatic increase in the public's understanding of hypertension and its role in heart attacks and strokes, as well as related declines in deaths. The percentage of people who were able to control their high blood pressure through lifestyle changes and through antihypertensive drug therapy rose from about 16 percent in 1971–72 to about 65 percent in 1988–94.[1, 6] About 90 percent of all adults now have their blood pressure measured at least once every 2 years. Average blood pressure levels have fallen by 10 to 12 mmHg since the advent of NHBPEP.[27] A slowly changing issue has been the recognition of systolic blood pressure as a more important predictor of CHD than diastolic blood pressure, especially in older adults.[28, 29]

Research reported in the 1980s showed for the first time that lowering high blood cholesterol significantly reduces the risk for heart attacks and heart attack deaths. This research led to the creation of the National Cholesterol Education Program (NCEP) in 1985.[30] Clinical trials have proved that lowering cholesterol in persons with and without existing CHD reduces illness and death from CHD and even reduces overall death rates. Since NCEP was launched, the percentage of persons who have had their cholesterol checked has more than doubled, from 35 percent in 1983 to 75 percent in 1995.[31] Consumption of saturated fat, total fat, and cholesterol declined during the 1980s and 1990s, average blood cholesterol levels in adults dropped from 213 mg/dL in 1978 to 203 mg/dL in 1988–94, and the prevalence of high blood cholesterol requiring medical advice and treatment fell from 36 percent to 29 percent.[30] These results reflect the impact of NCEP's population and high-risk strategies for lowering cholesterol.

The NHLBI Obesity Education Initiative, in cooperation with the National Institute of Diabetes and Digestive and Kidney Diseases, released in 1998 the first Federal guidelines on the identification, evaluation, and treatment of overweight and obesity in adults.[32] These clinical practice guidelines are designed to help physicians in their identification and treatment of overweight and obesity, a growing public health problem. Persons who are overweight or obese are at increased risk of illness from high blood pressure, lipid disorders, type 2 diabetes, CHD, stroke, gallbladder disease, osteoarthritis, sleep apnea and other respiratory problems, and certain cancers. The total cost attributable to obesity-related diseases in the United States is nearly $100 billion annually. The guidelines present a new approach to the assessment of overweight and obesity and establish principles of safe and effective weight loss. According to the guidelines, the assessment of overweight involves three key measures—body mass index (BMI), waist circumference, and

Data as of November 30, 1999

risk factors for diseases and conditions associated with obesity. The definitions in the guidelines are based on research that relates body mass index to the risk of death and illness, with overweight defined as a BMI of 25 to 29.9 and obesity as a BMI of 30 and above.[32]

As BMI levels rise, the average blood pressure and total cholesterol levels increase, and average HDL (good cholesterol) levels decrease. Males in the highest obesity category have more than twice the risk of high blood pressure, high blood cholesterol, or both, compared to males of normal weight. Females in the highest obesity category have four times the risk of either or both of these risk factors, compared to normal weight females. Therefore, the guidelines recommend weight loss to reduce high total cholesterol, raise low levels of HDL, reduce high blood pressure, and reduce elevated blood glucose in overweight persons who have two or more risk factors and in obese persons. Overweight persons without other risk factors are advised to prevent further weight gain.

The Agency for Healthcare Research and Quality's evidence-based guideline on smoking cessation interventions clearly shows that a variety of interventions are effective and concludes that improvements in cessation will require active participation of health care systems.[33]

These national education efforts have changed the way people think about their health. More persons than ever are having their blood pressure and their cholesterol levels checked and are taking action to keep them under control. Persons are aware of preventive measures and health promotion behaviors that can reduce their risk of developing CHD- and stroke-related illnesses. In addition, improved pharmacologic therapies are available to treat and control major CHD risk factors, such as high blood pressure, high blood cholesterol, and obesity. These therapies however, may be underutilized by health care providers.

Early identification and treatment. Each year in the United States, about 1.1 million persons experience a heart attack (myocardial infarction). In 1996, 476,000 persons died from heart attacks—about 51 percent were males and 49 percent were females. More than half of these deaths occurred suddenly, within 1 hour of symptom onset, outside the hospital.[1, 34] For those patients who survive, delay in treatment can mean increased damage to the heart muscle and poorer outcomes.

The benefits of rapid identification and treatment of heart attacks are clear. Early treatment of heart attack patients reduces heart-muscle damage, improves heart muscle function, and lowers the heart attack death rate.[35, 36]

Controlled trials of clot-dissolving (thrombolytic) agents used during the acute phase of a heart attack have demonstrated the benefits of opening the affected coronary artery and reestablishing blood flow. The results from these trials have been incorporated into the current treatment model for early intervention during the acute phase of a heart attack.[35] Patients who receive clot-dissolving agents in the first and second hours after the onset of heart attack symptoms experience significant reductions in disability and death when compared to patients who are treated in the third to sixth hours.[37] Even patients who are treated between 6 and 12 hours after the onset of symptoms show modest but significant benefits when compared to patients whose treatment is delayed more than 12 hours.[38] Other acute interventions for heart attack patients include balloon angioplasty, coronary stenting, and coronary artery bypass surgery.[36, 39] The importance of early treatment has generated a growing interest in detecting the earliest warning, or "prodromal," symptoms of a heart attack, thus providing the lead time needed to treat heart attack patients as quickly and effectively as possible.[40]

As with heart attacks, deaths from stroke can be reduced or delayed by preventing and controlling risk factors and using the most effective therapies in a timely manner. Functional limitations can be minimized when patients are treated with clot-dissolving therapy within 3 hours of a thrombotic stroke.[41] As therapies have become increasingly more effective, delays in treatment initiation and lack of implementation of therapies pose major barriers to improving outcomes. Thus far, efforts to provide appropriate access to timely and optimal care to patients with acute coronary syndromes and thrombotic stroke generally are not organized into a unified, cohesive system in communities across the United States.[42]

Early access to emergency health care services is also a critical determinant of outcome for victims of out-of-hospital cardiac arrest. For out-of-hospital cardiac arrest where bystanders are present, a key factor is minimizing the time from the moment the collapse is recognized to the delivery of a short burst of electrical current. Collapse recognition occurs when a bystander notices that the affected individual is unresponsive, has slowed or stopped breathing, or lacks a detectable pulse.[42] As soon as the emergency is recognized, the bystander should call 911 or the local emergency number. Cardiopulmonary resuscitation (CPR) is critical and should begin immediately. The sooner CPR is given to a person in cardiac arrest or ventilation is given for respiratory arrest, the greater the chances of survival.[43]

Despite evidence that effective treatment depends on rapid response to the patient, only a minority of individuals who can benefit from defibrillatory shock or thrombolytic agents are treated early enough for them to work.[44] The public health challenge is to develop and maintain programs for easier identification and treatment of individuals with acute myocardinal infarction (AMI) and out-of-hospital cardiac arrest.

Counseling by health care providers could help to increase awareness of the symptoms and signs of a heart attack or stroke and the appropriate actions to take, such as accessing emergency medical services. It also can help reduce and control factors that increase the risk of a heart attack or a stroke. To focus resources where they might derive the greatest benefit, education should be, at a minimum, aimed at reducing delays in seeking treatment for those individuals who are at high risk for a future cardiovascular events—for example, those with existing CHD and multiple CHD risk factors.

Cardiovascular disease recurrence. Patients with CHD, atherosclerotic disease of the aorta or peripheral arteries, or carotid artery disease are at high risk for heart attack and CHD death.[45, 46] About 50 percent of all heart attacks and at least 70 percent of CHD deaths occur in individuals with prior symptoms of CVD.[47, 48] The risk for heart attack and death among persons with established CHD (or other atherosclerotic disease) is five to seven times higher than among the general population.[3]

Risk factor control can greatly reduce the risk of subsequent cardiovascular problems in patients with CHD. For example, clinical trials have proved that lowering LDL-cholesterol levels in CHD patients dramatically reduces heart attacks, CHD and CVD deaths, and total deaths.[49, 50, 51] Clinical trials have also demonstrated that lowering blood pressure in such patients reduces CVD endpoints and deaths from all causes.[52, 53, 54] Adequate control of risk factors in the 12 million adults with CHD could reduce the overall rate of heart attacks and CHD deaths in the United States by over 20 percent. Many CHD patients, however, are not getting the aggressive risk factor management they need.

Clinical trials also show that therapeutic interventions can relieve symptoms, reduce deaths, reduce the number of rehospitalizations, and improve the quality of life for older adults with heart failure. Despite the development and promotion of clinical practice guidelines, physicians are continuing to underutilize recommended therapies. As the number of older adults who experience heart failure rises (expected to double by about 2040), these guidelines will need to be incorporated into clinical practice.

Adherence and compliance. There currently exist a number of well-established recommendations for preventing and treating cardiovascular disease and its associated risk factors. However, the potential benefits to be gained from applying these science-based recommendations often are not realized because of the multiple factors involved in adherence to such recommendations. The ability or willingness of the patient to carry out a treatment program successfully is of critical importance. Experience with the long-term management of asymptomatic CHD risk factors, such as hypertension, indicates that a sizable number of patients do not successfully carry out their prescribed treatment regimen. The reasons vary: the patient may choose not to have the initial prescription filled, may successfully initiate therapy only to abandon it after a few weeks or months, or may comply with only part of the regimen and thus fail to achieve optimal control. Continued efforts are needed to better understand the determinants of adherence to ensure that patients stay with their prescribed therapy. Also, health care providers and the health care systems in which they work are critical factors in determining whether established interventions are prescribed and patients adequately educated and monitored for therapeutic response. Finally, support from the patient's community and greater use of technology such as the Internet also have an increasingly greater role in promoting long-term adherence to lifestyle and pharmacologic regimens. Achieving long-term control of CHD risk factors requires that the same interest and attention given to initial evaluation and treatment decisions also be given to long-term management issues.

Future efforts. Population studies and public outreach are two of the most important areas of future research. Advanced technology allows researchers to screen persons noninvasively and painlessly for signs of developing atherosclerosis. Eventually, when their role in medical practice has been better delineated, noninvasive methods (such as magnetic resonance imaging, ultrasound, and others) may be used to determine the number of persons in the population who have heart disease or are at risk of developing heart disease.

Many people know what a desirable cholesterol level is, what their blood pressure should be, and that these factors relate to a risk of heart disease and stroke. The average person can expect to live 5½ years longer today than he or she did 30 years ago and nearly 4 years of that gain in life expectancy can be attributed to progress against CVD, including CHD and stroke. However, much remains to be done to ensure that all segments of the population share in these benefits. Although national health data on African Americans and Hispanics have been collected since the early 1980s, data on heart disease and stroke risk factors are sparse for other minority groups, including American Indians, Alaska Natives, Native Hawaiians, Asians, and Pacific Islanders. Adequate national data on all these populations will enable researchers to examine racial and ethnic differences more fully.

Public outreach and community health intervention efforts, such as those that encourage persons to lower their high blood pressure or to get their cholesterol checked or to help people stop smoking, are important parts of health care in the United States. Culturally and linguistically appropriate counseling by health care providers is important to those efforts. New coalitions between health care providers and individual communities are forming to focus on the prevention and management of chronic CVD throughout all stages of life. Emerging areas of research include the effect of socioeconomic status on health and access to care; health status in rural populations, which often have low income and education levels; and quality of life as a criterion for evaluating treatment. With the knowledge gained through these efforts, communities will be able to use well-tested health promotion, disease prevention, and early management strategies to lower their costs and begin to extend the benefits of improved health to all Americans.[55]

Extensive progress has been made in reducing deaths from and risk factors for heart disease and stroke, but significant challenges remain. Between 1987 and 1996, the age-adjusted death rate for CHD declined by 22.2 percent, and for stroke, it declined by 13.2 percent. Despite these achievements, the Healthy People 2000 objectives on CHD and stroke did not reach the year 2000 targets, and the disparities between African Americans and whites were not reduced.

However, progress occurred in reducing high blood cholesterol and controlling high blood pressure. Average total cholesterol declined from 213 mg/dL in 1976–80 to 203 mg/dL in 1988–94, and the prevalence of high blood cholesterol declined from 26 percent to 19 percent, thereby achieving the year 2000 target. In the same time period, control rates among persons who have high blood pressure increased from 11 to 29 percent. However, levels fell short of year 2000 targets. The age-adjusted prevalence of overweight or obesity increased from 26 percent in 1976–80 to 35 percent in 1988–94. The percentage of the population who engaged in light to moderate physical activity remained stable at around 22 percent between 1985 and 1995. Caloric intake from fat as a percentage of total calories consumed declined from 36 percent in 1976–80 to 34 percent in 1988–94, but fell short of the target of 30 percent. Smoking among adults declined steadily from the mid-1960s through the late 1980s, and has leveled off in the 1990s. In 1998, median adult smoking prevalence for all 50 States and the District of Columbia was 22.9 percent—25.3 percent for men and 21.0 percent for women.[55]

Note: Unless otherwise noted, data are from Centers for Disease Control and Prevention, National Center for Health Statistics, *Healthy People 2000 Review, 1998-99.*

Heart Disease and Stroke

Goal: Improve cardiovascular health and quality of life through the prevention, detection, and treatment of risk factors; early identification and treatment of heart attacks and strokes; and prevention of recurrent cardiovascular events.

Number	Objective
Heart Disease	
12-1	Coronary heart disease (CHD) deaths
12-2	Knowledge of symptoms of heart attack and importance of dialing 911
12-3	Artery-opening therapy
12-4	Bystander response to cardiac arrest
12-5	Out-of-hospital emergency care
12-6	Heart failure hospitalizations
Stroke	
12-7	Stroke deaths
12-8	Knowledge of early warning symptoms of stroke
Blood Pressure	
12-9	High blood pressure
12-10	High blood pressure control
12-11	Action to help control blood pressure
12-12	Blood pressure monitoring
Cholesterol	
12-13	Mean total blood cholesterol levels
12-14	High blood cholesterol levels
12-15	Blood cholesterol screening
12-16	LDL-cholesterol level in CHD patients

Heart Disease

12-1.   Reduce coronary heart disease deaths.

Target: 166 deaths per 100,000 population.

Baseline: 208 coronary heart disease deaths per 100,000 population in 1998 (preliminary data; age adjusted to the year 2000 standard population).

Target setting method: 20 percent improvement.

Data source: National Vital Statistics System (NVSS), CDC, NCHS.

Total Population, 1997*	Coronary Heart Disease Deaths Rate per 100,000
TOTAL	216
Race and ethnicity	
American Indian or Alaska Native	134
Asian or Pacific Islander	125
Asian	DNC
Native Hawaiian and other Pacific Islander	DNC
Black or African American	257
White	214
Hispanic or Latino	151
Not Hispanic or Latino	219
Black or African American	262
White	216
Gender	
Female	170
Male	276
Education level (aged 25 to 64 years)	
Less than high school	95
High school graduate	84
At least some college	40

Total Population, 1997*	Coronary Heart Disease Deaths
	Rate per 100,000
Disability status	
Persons with disabilities	DNC
Persons without disabilities	DNC

DNA = Data have not been analyzed. DNC = Data are not collected. DSU = Data are statistically unreliable.

Note: Age adjusted to the year 2000 standard population.

*New data for population groups will be added when available.

12-2. **(Developmental) Increase the proportion of adults aged 20 years and older who are aware of the early warning symptoms and signs of a heart attack and the importance of accessing rapid emergency care by calling 911.**

Potential data source: National Health Interview Survey (NHIS), CDC, NCHS.

12-3. **(Developmental) Increase the proportion of eligible patients with heart attacks who receive artery-opening therapy within an hour of symptom onset.**

Potential data source: National Registry of Myocardial Infarction, National Acute Myocardial Infarction Project, HCFA.

12-4. **(Developmental) Increase the proportion of adults aged 20 years and older who call 911 and administer cardiopulmonary resuscitation (CPR) when they witness an out-of-hospital cardiac arrest.**

Potential data source: National Health Interview Survey (NHIS), CDC, NCHS.

12-5. **(Developmental) Increase the proportion of persons with witnessed out-of-hospital cardiac arrest who are eligible and receive their first therapeutic electrical shock within 6 minutes after collapse recognition.**

Potential data sources: National Health Interview Survey (NHIS), CDC, NCHS; Medical Expenditure Panel Survey (MEPS), AHCPR and CDC.

12-6. Reduce hospitalizations of older adults with heart failure as the principal diagnosis.

Target and baseline:

Objective	Hospitalizations of Older Adults With Heart Failure as the Principal Diagnosis	1997 Baseline	2010 Target
		Per 1,000 Population	
12-6a.	65 to 74 years	13.4	6.5
12-6b.	75 to 84 years	26.9	13.5
12-6c.	85 years and older	53.1	26.5

Target setting method: Better than the best.

Data source: National Hospital Discharge Survey (NHDS), CDC, NCHS.

Adults With Heart Failure as Principal Diagnosis, 1997	Heart Failure Hospitalization		
	12-6a. Aged 65 to 74 Years	12-6b. Aged 75 to 84 Years	12-6c. Aged 85 Years and Older
	Rate per 1,000		
TOTAL	13.4	26.9	53.1
Race and ethnicity			
American Indian or Alaska Native	DSU	DSU	DSU
Asian or Pacific Islander	DSU	DSU	DSU
Asian	DNC	DNC	DNC
Native Hawaiian and other Pacific Islander	DNC	DNC	DNC
Black or African American	20.0	21.9	47.6
White	10.1	21.6	42.1
Hispanic or Latino	DSU	DSU	DSU
Not Hispanic or Latino	DSU	DSU	DSU
Black or African American	DSU	DSU	DSU
White	DSU	DSU	DSU
Gender			
Female	11.5	25.2	50.6
Male	15.6	29.5	59.3

Data as of November 30, 1999

Adults With Heart Failure as Principal Diagnosis, 1997	Heart Failure Hospitalization		
	12-6a. Aged 65 to 74 Years	12-6b. Aged 75 to 84 Years	12-6c. Aged 85 Years and Older
	Rate per 1,000		
Education level			
Less than high school	DNC	DNC	DNC
High school graduate	DNC	DNC	DNC
At least some college	DNC	DNC	DNC
Disability status			
People with disabilities	DNC	DNC	DNC
People without disabilities	DNC	DNC	DNC

DNA = Data have not been analyzed. DNC = Data are not collected. DSU = Data are statistically unreliable.

Stroke

12-7. Reduce stroke deaths.

Target: 48 deaths per 100,000 population.

Baseline: 60 deaths from stroke per 100,000 population in 1998 (preliminary data; age adjusted to the year 2000 standard population).

Target setting method: 20 percent improvement.

Data source: National Vital Statistics System (NVSS), CDC, NCHS.

Total Population, 1997*	Stroke Deaths Rate per 100,000
TOTAL	62
Race and ethnicity	
American Indian or Alaska Native	39
Asian or Pacific Islander	55
Asian	DNC
Native Hawaiian and other Pacific Islander	DNC
Black or African American	82
White	60
Hispanic or Latino	40
Not Hispanic or Latino	63

Total Population, 1997*	Stroke Deaths Rate per 100,000
Black or African American	84
White	60
Gender	
Female	60
Male	64
Education level (aged 25 to 64 years)	
Less than high school	22
High school graduate	17
At least some college	8
Disability status	
Persons with disabilities	DNC
Persons without disabilities	DNC

DNA = Data have not been analyzed. DNC = Data are not collected. DSU = Data are statistically unreliable.

Note: Age adjusted to the year 2000 standard population.

*New data for population groups will be added when available.

12-8. **(Developmental) Increase the proportion of adults who are aware of the early warning symptoms and signs of a stroke.**

Potential data source: National Health Interview Survey (NHIS), CDC, NCHS.

Blood Pressure

12-9. Reduce the proportion of adults with high blood pressure.

Target: 16 percent.

Baseline: 28 percent of adults aged 20 years and older had high blood pressure in 1988–94 (age adjusted to the year 2000 standard population).

Target setting method: Better than the best.

Data source: National Health and Nutrition Examination Survey (NHANES), CDC, NCHS.

Adults Aged 20 Years and Older, 1988–94 (unless noted)	High Blood Pressure Percent
TOTAL	28
Race and ethnicity	
American Indian or Alaska Native	DSU
Asian or Pacific Islander	DSU
Asian	DNC
Native Hawaiian and other Pacific Islander	DNC
Black or African American	40
White	27
Hispanic or Latino	DNC
Mexican American	29
Not Hispanic or Latino	DNA
Black or African American	40
White	27
Gender	
Female	26
Male	30
Family income level	
Poor	32
Near poor	30
Middle/high income	27
Disability status	
Persons with disabilities	32 (1991-94)
Persons without disabilities	27 (1991-94)
Select populations	
Persons with diabetes	DNA
Persons without diabetes	DNA

DNA = Data have not been analyzed. DNC = Data are not collected. DSU = Data are statistically unreliable.
Note: Age adjusted to the year 2000 standard population.

12-10. Increase the proportion of adults with high blood pressure whose blood pressure is under control.

Target: 50 percent.

Baseline: 18 percent of adults aged 18 years and older with high blood pressure had it under control in 1988–94 (age adjusted to the year 2000 standard population).

Target setting method: Better than the best.

Data source: National Health and Nutrition Examination Survey (NHANES), CDC, NCHS.

Adults Aged 18 Years and Older With High Blood Pressure, 1988-91* (unless noted)	Blood Pressure Controlled Percent
TOTAL	18
Race and ethnicity	
American Indian or Alaska Native	DSU
Asian or Pacific Islander	DSU
Asian	DNC
Native Hawaiian and other Pacific Islander	DNC
Black or African American	19
White	18
Hispanic or Latino	DNC
Mexican American	12
Not Hispanic or Latino	DNA
Black or African American	19
White	18
Gender	
Female	28
Male	12
Family income level	
Poor	24
Near poor	20
Middle/high income	16
Disability status	
Persons with disabilities	20 (1991-94)
Persons without disabilities	18 (1991-94)

Data as of November 30, 1999

Adults Aged 18 Years and Older With High Blood Pressure, 1988-91* (unless noted)	Blood Pressure Controlled Percent
Select populations	
Persons with diabetes	DNA
Persons without diabetes	DNA

DNA = Data have not been analyzed. DNC = Data are not collected. DSU = Data are statistically unreliable.

Note: Age adjusted to the year 2000 standard population.

*New data for population groups will be added when available.

12-11. Increase the proportion of adults with high blood pressure who are taking action (for example, losing weight, increasing physical activity, and reducing sodium intake) to help control their blood pressure.

Target: 95 percent.

Baseline: 72 percent of adults aged 18 years and older with high blood pressure were taking action to control it in 1998 (preliminary data; age adjusted to the year 2000 standard population).

Target setting method: Better than the best.

Data source: National Health Interview Survey (NHIS), CDC, NCHS.

Adults Aged 18 Years and Older With High Blood Pressure, 1994*	Taking Action To Control Blood Pressure Percent
TOTAL	79
Race and ethnicity	
American Indian or Alaska Native	DSU
Asian or Pacific Islander	DSU
Asian	DNC
Native Hawaiian and other Pacific Islander	DNC
Black or African American	84
White	78
Hispanic or Latino	79
Not Hispanic or Latino	79
Black or African American	84
White	78

Adults Aged 18 Years and Older With High Blood Pressure, 1994*	Taking Action To Control Blood Pressure Percent
Gender	
Female	81
Male	77
Family income level	
Poor	78
Near poor	80
Middle/high income	79
Disability status	
Persons with activity limitations	84
Persons without activity limitations	76
Geographic variation	
Urban	80
Rural	78
Select populations	
Persons with diabetes	DNA
Persons without diabetes	DNA

DNA = Data have not been analyzed. DNC = Data are not collected. DSU = Data are statistically unreliable.

Note: Crude rates. Data not currently age adjusted.

*New data for population groups will be added when available.

12-12. Increase the proportion of adults who have had their blood pressure measured within the preceding 2 years and can state whether their blood pressure was normal or high.

Target: 95 percent.

Baseline: 90 percent of adults aged 18 years and older had their blood pressure measured in the past 2 years and could state whether it was high or low in 1998 (preliminary data; age adjusted to the year 2000 standard population).

Target setting method: Better than the best.

Data source: National Health Interview Survey (NHIS), CDC, NCHS.

Adults Aged 18 Years and Older, 1994*	Had Blood Pressure Measured in Past 2 Years and Knew Whether It Was Normal or High
	Percent
TOTAL	85
Race and ethnicity	
American Indian or Alaska Native	85
Asian or Pacific Islander	80
Asian	DNC
Native Hawaiian and other Pacific Islander	DNC
Black or African American	88
White	85
Hispanic or Latino	80
Not Hispanic or Latino	86
Black or African American	88
White	86
Gender	
Female	89
Male	81
Education level (aged 25 years and older)	
Less than high school	80
High school graduate	85
At least some college	88
Disability status	
Persons with activity limitations	90
Persons without activity limitations	84

DNA = Data have not been analyzed. DNC = Data are not collected. DSU = Data are statistically unreliable.

Note: Age adjusted to the year 2000 standard population.

*New data for population groups will be added when available.

Cholesterol

12-13. Reduce the mean total blood cholesterol levels among adults.

Target: 199 mg/dL.

Baseline: 206 mg/dL was the mean total blood cholesterol level for adults aged 20 years and older in 1988–94 (age adjusted to the year 2000 standard population).

Target setting method: Better than the best.

Data source: National Health and Nutrition Examination Survey (NHANES), CDC, NCHS.

Adults Aged 20 Years and Older, 1988–94 (unless noted)	Cholesterol Level mg/dL
TOTAL	206
Race and ethnicity	
American Indian or Alaska Native	DSU
Asian or Pacific Islander	DSU
Asian	DNC
Native Hawaiian and other Pacific Islander	DNC
Black or African American	204
White	206
Hispanic or Latino	DNC
Mexican American	205
Not Hispanic or Latino	DNA
Black or African American	204
White	206
Gender	
Female	207
Male	204
Family income level	
Poor	205
Near poor	204
Middle/high income	206

Adults Aged 20 Years and Older, 1988–94 (unless noted)	Cholesterol Level mg/dL
Disability status	
Persons with disabilities	208 (1991-94)
Persons without disabilities	204 (1991-94)

DNA = Data have not been analyzed. DNC = Data are not collected. DSU = Data are statistically unreliable.
Note: Age adjusted to the year 2000 standard population.

12-14. Reduce the proportion of adults with high total blood cholesterol levels.

Target: 17 percent.

Baseline: 21 percent of adults aged 20 years and older had total blood cholesterol levels of 240 mg/dL or greater in 1988–94 (age adjusted to the year 2000 standard population).

Target setting method: Better than the best.

Data source: National Health and Nutrition Examination Survey (NHANES), CDC, NCHS.

Adults Aged 20 Years and Older, 1988–94 (unless noted)	Cholesterol, 240 mg/dL or Greater Percent
TOTAL	21
Race and ethnicity	
American Indian or Alaska Native	DSU
Asian or Pacific Islander	DSU
Asian	DNC
Native Hawaiian and other Pacific Islander	DNC
Black or African American	19
White	21
Hispanic or Latino	DNC
Mexican American	18
Not Hispanic or Latino	DNA
Black or African American	19
White	21

Adults Aged 20 Years and Older, 1988–94 (unless noted)	Cholesterol, 240 mg/dL or Greater Percent
Gender	
Female	22
Male	19
Education level	
Less than high school	22
High school graduate	22
At least some college	19
Disability status	
Persons with disabilities	24 (1991-94)
Persons without disabilities	19 (1991-94)

DNA = Data have not been analyzed. DNC = Data are not collected. DSU = Data are statistically unreliable.
Note: Age adjusted to the year 2000 standard population.

12-15. Increase the proportion of adults who have had their blood cholesterol checked within the preceding 5 years.

Target: 80 percent.

Baseline: 68 percent of adults aged 18 years and older had their blood cholesterol checked within the preceding 5 years in 1998 (preliminary data; age adjusted to the year 2000 standard population).

Target setting method: Better than the best.

Data source: National Health Interview Survey (NHIS), CDC, NCHS.

Adults Aged 18 Years and Older, 1993*	Cholesterol Checked in Past 5 Years Percent
TOTAL	67
Race and ethnicity	
American Indian or Alaska Native	57
Asian or Pacific Islander	58
Asian	DNC
Native Hawaiian and other Pacific Islander	DNC
Black or African American	66
White	67

| Adults Aged 18 Years and Older, 1993* | Cholesterol Checked in Past 5 Years

Percent |
|---|---|
| Hispanic or Latino | 62 |
| Not Hispanic or Latino | 67 |
| Black or African American | 65 |
| White | 68 |
| **Gender** | |
| Female | 69 |
| Male | 64 |
| **Education level** (aged 25 years and older) | |
| Less than high school | 56 |
| High school graduate | 69 |
| At least some college | 78 |
| **Disability status** | |
| Persons with activity limitations | 72 |
| Persons without activity limitations | 66 |
| **Geographic variation** | |
| Urban | 68 |
| Rural | 63 |

DNA = Data have not been analyzed. DNC = Data are not collected. DSU = Data are statistically unreliable.

Note: Age adjusted to the year 2000 standard population.

*New data for population groups will be added when available.

12-16. (Developmental) Increase the proportions of persons with coronary heart disease who have their LDL-cholesterol level treated to a goal of less than or equal to 100 mg/dL.

Potential data source: National Health and Nutrition Examination Survey, CDC, NCHS.

Related Objectives From Other Focus Areas

Access to Quality Health Services

1-3.   Counseling about health behaviors

1-7.   Core competencies in health provider training

1-10.   Delay or difficulty in getting emergency care

1-11.   Rapid prehospital emergency care

Chronic Kidney Disease

4-2.   Cardiovascular disease deaths in persons with chronic kidney failure

Educational and Community-Based Programs

7-2.   School health education

7-5.   Worksite health promotion programs

7-8.   Satisfaction with patient education

7-10.   Community health promotion programs

7-11.   Culturally appropriate community health promotion

7-12.   Older adult participation in community health promotion activities

Health Communication

11-1.   Households with Internet access

11-2.   Health literacy

11-4.   Quality of Internet health information sources

11-6.   Satisfaction with providers' communication skills

Nutrition and Overweight

19-1.   Healthy weight in adults

19-2.   Obesity in adults

19-3.   Overweight or obesity in children and adolescents

19-5.   Fruit intake

19-6.   Vegetable intake

19-8.   Saturated fat intake

19-9.   Total fat intake

19-11. Calcium intake

19-16. Worksite promotion of nutrition education and weight management

Physical Activity and Fitness

22-1.   No leisure-time physical activity

22-2.   Moderate physical activity

22-3.   Vigorous physical activity

22-6.   Moderate physical activity in adolescents

22-7.   Vigorous physical activity in adolescents

22-11. Television viewing

22-13. Worksite physical activity and fitness

22-14. Community walking

22-15. Community bicycling

Public Health Infrastructure

23-1.   Public health employees access to Internet

23-3.   Use of geocoding in health data systems

23-10. Continuing education and training by public health agencies

23-15. Data on public health expenditures

Tobacco Use

27-1.   Adult tobacco use

27-2.   Adolescent tobacco use

27-3.   Initiation of tobacco use

27-4.   Age at first use of tobacco

27-5.   Smoking cessation by adults

27-10.   Exposure to environmental tobacco smoke

27-16.   Tobacco advertising and promotion targeting adolescents and young adults

27-17.   Adolescent disapproval of smoking

Terminology

(A listing of all acronyms and abbreviations used in this publication appears in Appendix K.)

Angina (angina pectoris): A pain or discomfort in the chest that occurs when some part of the heart does not receive enough blood. It is a common symptom of coronary heart disease. Angina often recurs in a regular or characteristic pattern. However, it may first appear as a very severe episode or as frequently recurring bouts. When an established stable pattern of angina changes sharply—for example, it may be provoked by far less exercise than in the past, or it may appear at rest—it is referred to as unstable angina.

Angioplasty: A nonsurgical procedure used to treat blockages in blood vessels, particularly the coronary arteries that feed the heart. Also known as percutaneous transluminal coronary angioplasty (PTCA). A thin tube (catheter), fed through blood vessels to the point of blockage, is used to open the artery.

Anticoagulants: Drugs that delay the clotting (coagulation) of blood. When a blood vessel is plugged up by a clot and an anticoagulant is given, it tends to prevent new clots from forming or the existing clot from enlarging. An anticoagulant does not dissolve an existing blood clot.

Arrhythmia: A change in the regular beat or rhythm of the heart. The heart may seem to skip a beat, or beat irregularly, or beat very fast or very slowly.

Atherosclerosis: A type of hardening of the arteries in which cholesterol and other substances in the blood are deposited in the walls of arteries, including the coronary arteries that supply blood to the heart. In time, narrowing of the coronary arteries by atherosclerosis may reduce the flow of oxygen-rich blood to the heart.

Atrial fibrillation (AF): The most common sustained irregular heart rhythm encountered in clinical practice. AF occurs when the two small upper chambers of the heart (the atria) quiver instead of beating effectively, and blood cannot be pumped completely out of them when the heart beats, allowing the blood to pool and clot. If a piece of the blood clot in the atria becomes lodged in an artery in the brain, a stroke may result. AF is a risk factor for stroke and heart failure.

Blood pressure: The force of the blood pushing against the walls of arteries. Blood pressure is given as two numbers that measure systolic pressure (the first number, which measures the pressure while the heart is contracting) and diastolic pressure (the second number, which measures the pressure when the heart is resting between beats). Blood pressures 140/90 mmHg or above are considered high, while blood pressures in the range of 130-139/85-89 are high normal. Less than 130/85 mmHg is normal.

Body mass index (BMI): A number that indicates a person's body weight relative to height. BMI is a useful indirect measure of body composition, because it correlates highly with body fat in most people.

Cardiovascular disease (CVD): Includes a variety of diseases of the heart and blood vessels, coronary heart disease (coronary artery disease, ischemic heart disease), stroke (brain attack), high blood pressure (hypertension), rheumatic heart disease, congestive heart failure, and peripheral artery disease.

Cerebrovascular disease: Affects the blood vessels supplying blood to the brain. Stroke occurs when a blood vessel bringing oxygen and nutrients to the brain bursts or is clogged by a blood clot. Because of this rupture or blockage, part of the brain does not get the flow of blood it needs and nerve cells in the affected area die. Small stoke-like events like transient ischemic attacks (ITAs), which resolve in a day or less, are symptoms of cerebrovascular disease.

Cholesterol: A waxy substance that circulates in the bloodstream. When the level of cholesterol in the blood is too high, some of the cholesterol is deposited in the walls of the blood vessels. Over time, these deposits can build up until they narrow the blood vessels, causing atherosclerosis, which reduces the blood flow. The higher the blood cholesterol level, the greater is the risk of getting heart disease. Blood cholesterol levels of less than 200 mg/dL are considered desirable. Levels of 240 mg/dL or above are considered high and require further testing and possible intervention. Levels of 200-239 mg/dL are considered borderline. Lowering blood cholesterol reduces the risk of heart disease.

Congestive heart failure (or heart failure): A condition in which the heart cannot pump enough blood to meet the needs of the body's other organs. Heart failure can result from narrowed arteries that supply blood to the heart muscle and other factors. As the flow of blood out of the heart slows, blood returning to the heart through the veins backs up, causing congestion in the tissues. Often swelling (edema) re- sults, most commonly in the legs and ankles, but possibly in other parts of the body as well. Sometimes fluid col- lects in the lungs and inter- feres with breathing, causing shortness of breath, espe-

cially when a person is lying down.

Coronary heart disease (CHD): A condition in which the flow of blood to the heart muscle is reduced. Like any muscle, the heart needs a constant supply of oxygen and nutrients that are carried to it by the blood in the coro- nary arteries. When the coronary arteries become narrowed or clogged, they cannot supply enough blood to the heart. If not enough oxygen-carrying blood reaches the heart, the heart may respond with pain called angina. The pain usually is felt in the chest or some- times in the left arm or shoulder. When the blood supply is cut off completely, the result is a heart attack. The part of the heart muscle that does not receive oxygen begins to die, and some of the heart muscle is perma- nently damaged.

Coronary stenting: A procedure that uses a wire mesh tube (a stent) to prop open an artery that recently has been cleared using angioplasty. The stent remains in the artery permanently, holding it open to improve blood flow to the heart muscle and relieve symptoms, such as chest pain.

HDL (high-density lipoprotein) cholesterol: The so-called good cholesterol. Cholesterol travels in the blood combined with protein in packages called lipoproteins. HDL is thought to carry cholesterol away from other parts of the body back to the liver for removal from the body. A low level of HDL increases the risk for CHD, whereas a high HDL level helps protect against CHD.

Heart attack (also called acute myocardial infarc- tion): Occurs when a coro- nary artery becomes completely blocked, usually

by a blood clot (thrombus), resulting in lack of blood flow to the heart muscle and therefore a loss of needed oxygen. As a result, part of the heart muscle dies (in- farcts). The blood clot usu- ally forms over the site of a cholesterol-rich narrowing (or plaque) that has burst or ruptured.

Heart disease: The leading cause of death and a common cause of illness and disability in the United States. Coronary heart disease and ischemic heart disease are specific names for the principal form of heart disease, which is the result of atherosclerosis, or the buildup of cholesterol deposits in the coronary arteries that feed the heart.

High blood pressure: A systolic blood pressure of 140 mmHg or greater or a diastolic pressure of 90 mmHg or greater. With high blood pressure, the heart has to work harder, resulting in an increased risk of a heart attack, stroke, heart failure, kidney and eye problems, and peripheral vascular disease.

Ischemic heart disease: Includes heart attack and related heart problems caused by narrowing of the coronary arteries and therefore a decreased supply of blood and oxygen to the heart. Also called coronary artery disease and coronary heart disease.

LDL (low-density lipoprotein): The so-called bad cholesterol. LDL contains most of the cholesterol in the blood and carries it to the tissues and organs of the body, including the arteries. Cholesterol from LDL is the main source of damaging buildup and blockage in the arteries. The higher the level of LDL in the blood, the greater is the risk for CHD.

Lipid: Fat and fat-like substances, such as cholesterol, that are present in blood and body tissues.

Peripheral vascular disease: Refers to diseases of any blood vessels outside the heart and to diseases of the lymph vessels. It is often a narrowing of the blood vessels that carry blood to leg and arm muscles. Symptoms include leg pain (for example, in the calves) when walking and ulcers or sore on the legs and feet.

Stroke: A form of cerebrovascular disease that affects the arteries of the central nervous system. A stroke occurs when blood vessels bringing oxygen and nutrients to the brain burst or become clogged by a blood clot or some other particle. Because of this rupture or blockage, part of the brain does not get the flow of blood it needs. Deprived of oxygen, nerve cells in the affected area of the brain cannot function and die within minutes. When nerve cells cannot function, the part of the body controlled by these cells cannot function either.

References

1. National Heart, Lung, and Blood Institute. *Morbidity and Mortality: 1998 Chartbook on Cardiovascular, Lung, and Blood Diseases*. Bethesda, MD: National Institutes of Health, Public Health Service, National Heart, Lung, and Blood Institute, October 1998.

2. Sempos, C.T.; Cleeman, J.I.; Carroll, M.K.; et al. Prevalence of high blood cholesterol among U.S. adults: An update based on guidelines from the second report of the National Cholesterol Education Program Adult Treatment Panel. *Journal of the American Medical Association*, 269:3009-3014, 1993.

3. Expert Panel on Detection, Evaluation, and Treatment of High Blood Cholesterol in Adults. National Cholesterol Education Program: Second Report of the Expert Panel on Detection, Evaluation, and Treatment of High Blood Cholesterol in Adults (Adult Treatment Panel II). *Circulation* 89:1329-1445, 1994.

4. The Sixth Report of the Joint National Committee on Prevention, Detection, Evaluation, and Treatment of High Blood Pressure. *Archives of Internal Medicine* 157:2413-2446, 1997.

5. Burt, V.L.; Culter, J.A.; Higgins, M.; et al. Trends in the prevalence, awareness, treatment, and control of hypertension in the adult U.S. population. *Hypertension* 26:60-69, 1995.

6. Centers for Disease Control and Prevention. Mortality from congestive heart failure—United States, 1980-1990. *Morbidity and Mortality Weekly Report* 43:77-78, 1994.

7. Gillum, R.F. Epidemiology of heart failure in the United States. *American Heart Journal* 126:1042-1047, 1993.

8. Lenfant, C. Fixing the failing heart. *Circulation* 95:771-772, 1997.

9. Croft, J.B.; Giles, W.H.; Pollard, R.A.; Casper, M.L.; and Livengood, Jr., R.F. National trends in the initial hospitalizations for heart failure. *Journal of the American Geriatrics Society* 45:270-275. 1997.

10.. Huston, S.L.; Lengerich, E.J.; Conlisk, E.; and Passaro, K. Trends in ischemic heart disease death rates for blacks and whites— United States, 1981-1995. *Morbidity and Mortality Weekly Review* 47:945-949, 1998.

11. Gillum, R.F.; Muscolino, M.F.; and Madans, J.A. Fatal MI among black men and women. *Annals of Internal Medicine* 127:111-118, 1997.

12. National Heart Attack Alert Program Coordination Committee. Working Group Report on Educational Strategies to Prevent Prehospital Delay in Patients at High Risk for Acute Myocardial Infarction. NIH Publication No. 97-3787. Bethesda, MD: National Heart, Lung, and Blood Institute, National Institutes of Health, 1997.

13. Burt, V.; Whelton, P.; and Roccella, E.J. Prevalence of hypertension in the U.S. adult population. *Hypertension* 25:305-313, 1995.

14. Pate, R.R.; Pratt, M.; Blair, S.N.; et al. Physical Activity and Public Health: A Recommendation from the Centers for Disease Control and Prevention and the American College of Sports Medicine. *Journal of the American Medical Association* 273:402-407, 1995.

15. Physical Activity and Cardiovascular Health. NIH Consensus Development Panel on Physical Activity and Cardiovascular Health. *Journal of the American Medical Association* 276(3):241-246, 1996.

16. Dunn, A.L.; Marcus, B.H.; Kampert, J.B.; Garcia,

M.E.; Kohl, H.W.; and Blair, S.N. Comparison of lifestyle and structured interventions to increase physical activity and cardiorespiratory fitness: a randomized trial. *Journal of the American Medical Association* 281:327-334, 1999.

17. Manson, J.A.; Hu, F.; Rich-Edwards, J.W.; Colditz, G.; Stampfer, M.J.; Willett, W.H.; Speizer, F.; and Hennekens, C. A prospective study of walking as compared with vigorous exercise in the prevention of coronary heart disease in women. *New England Journal of Medicine* 341:650-658, 1999.

18. U.S. Department of Health and Human Services (HHS). *Physical Activity and Health: A Report of the Surgeon General.* Atlanta, GA: The Department, Centers for Disease Control (CDC) and Prevention, National Center for Chronic Disease Prevention and Health Promotion, 1996.

19. HHS. *The Health Benefits of Smoking Cessation. A Report of the Surgeon General.* HHS Publ. No. CDC 90-8416. Atlanta, GA: HHS, Public Health Services, Centers for Disease Control, NCCDPHP. Office on Smoking and Health, 1990.

20. Freedman, D.S.; Dietz, W.H.; Srinivasan, S.R.; and Berenson, G.S. The relation of overweight to cardiovascular risk factors among children and adolescents: the Bogalusa Heart Study. *Pediatrics* 103:1175-1182, 1999.

21. Winkleby, M.; Robinson, T.; Sundquist, J.; and Kraemer, H. Ethnic variations in cardiovascular disease risk factors among children and young adults: Findings from the Third National Health and Nutrition Examination Survey 1998-1994. *Journal of the Ameri-* can Medical Association 281:1006-1013, 1999.

22. Leon, A.S.; Cornett, J.; Jacobs, Jr., D.R.; and Rauramaa, R. Leisure time physical activity and risk of coronary heart disease and death: The Multiple Risk Factor Intervention Trial. *Journal of the American Medical Association* 258:2388-2395, 1987.

23. O'Connor, G.T.; Hennekens, C.H.; Willett, W.H.; Goldhaber, S.Z.; Paffenbarger, Jr., R.S.; Breslow, J.L.; and Buring, J.E. Physical exercise and reduced risk of nonfatal myocardial infarction. *American Journal of Epidemiology* 142:1147-1156, 1995.

24. Blair, S.N.; Kohl, III, H.W.; Barlow, C.E.; Paffenbarger, Jr., R.S.; Gibbons, L.W.; and Macera, C.A. Changes in physical fitness and all cause mortality: A prospective study of healthy and unhealthy men. *Journal of the American Medical Association* 273:1093-1098, 1995.

25. Willett, W.H.; Dietz, W.H.; and Colditz, G.A. Primary care: Guidelines for healthy weight. *New England Journal of Medicine* 341:427-434, 1999.

26. Roccella, E.J., and Horan, M.J. The National High Blood Pressure Education Program: measuring progress and assessing its impact. *Health Psychology* (7 suppl.):237-303, 1998.

27. HHS. *Health, United States, 1998.* Hyattsville, MD: the Department, Centers for Disease Control and Prevention, National Center for Health Statistics, 1998.

28. Kannel, W.B.; Dawber, T.R.; and McGee, D.L. Perspectives on systolic hyper- tension, the Framingham Study. *Circulation* 61:1179-82, 1980.

29. The Systolic Hypertension in the Elderly Program (SHEP) Cooperative Research Group. Prevention of stroke by antihypertensive drug treatment in older persons with isolated systolic hypertension. Final results of the SHEP. *Journal of the American Medical Association* 265:3255-3264, 1991.

30. Cleeman, J.I., and Lenfant, C. The National Cholesterol Education Program: Progress and Prospects. *Journal of the American Medical Association* 280:2099-2104, 1998.

31. National Heart, Lung, and Blood Institute. Cholesterol Awareness Surveys. Press conference (December 4, 1995). Bethesda, MD: the Institute.

32. Clinical Guidelines on the Identification, Evaluation, and Treatment of Overweight and Obesity in Adults: Evidence Report. *Journal of Obesity Research* (Suppl 2); September, 1998.

33. *Smoking Cessation: Clinical Practice Guidelines, No. 18.* HHS Pub. No. (AHCPR) 96-06920. Washington, DC: HHS, Public Health Service, Agency for Health Care Policy and Research, 1996.

34. Marano, M.A. Current estimates from the National Health Interview Survey, 1995. National Center for Health Statistics. *Vital Health Statistics* 10(199):1-428, 1998.

35. National Heart Attack Alert Program Coordinating Committee 60 Minutes to Treatment Working Group. Emergency Department: Rapid identification and treatment of patients with

acute myocardial infarction. *Annals of Emergency Medicine* 23:311-329, 1994.

36. Ryan, T.J.; Antman, E.M.; Brooks, N.H.; et al. 1999 update: ACC/AHA guidelines for the management of patients with acute myocardial infarction: a report of the American College of Cardiology/American Heart Association Task Force on Practice Guidelines (Committee on Management of Acute Myocardial Infarction). *Journal of the American College of Cardiology* 34:890-911, 1999.

37. Boersma, E.; Maas, A.C.P.; Deckers, J.W.; and Simoons, M.L. Early thrombolytic treatment in acute myocardial infarction: Reappraisal of the golden hour. *Lancet* 348:771-775, 1996.

38. Betts, J.H. Late assessment of thrombolytic efficacy with altiplase (rt-PA) 6-24 hours after onset of acute myocardial infarction. *Australian New Zealand Journal of Medicine* 23:745-748, 1993.

39. The Global Use of Strategies to Open Occluded Coronary Arteries in Acute Coronary Syndrome's (GUSTO IIb) Angioplasty Substudy Investigators. A clinical trial comparing primary coronary angioplasty with tissue plasminogen activator for acute myocardial infarction. *New England Journal of Medicine* 336:1621-1628, 1997.

40. Bahr, R.D.; Introduction: community message in acute myocardial ischemia. *Clinician* 14:1, 1996.

41. National Institute of Stroke and Neurological Diseases and T-PA Working Group. Tissue Plasminogen Activator for Acute Ischemic Stroke. *New England Journal of Medicine* 333(24):1581-1587, 1995.

42. American Heart Association. Emergency Cardiovascular Care Programs. Chain of Survival. Links in the Chain. Retrieval June 1999 <http://www.proed.net/ecc/chain/links.htm>.

43. National Heart Attack Alert Program Coordinating Committee, Access to Care Subcommittee. Access to timely and optimal care of patients with acute coronary syndromes—community planning considerations: Report by the National Heart Attack Alert Program. *Journal of Thrombosis and Thrombolysis* 6:19-46, 1998.

44. National Heart Attack Alert Program. *Patient/Bystander Recognition and Action: Rapid Identification and Treatment of Acute Myocardial Infarction.* NIH Pub. No. 93-3303 Bethesda, MD: National Heart, Lung, and Blood Institute, National Institutes of Health, 1993.

45. Criqui, M.H.; Langer, R.D.; Fronek, A.; Feigelson, H.S.; Klauber, M.R.; McCann, T.J.; et al. Mortality over a period of 10 years in patients with peripheral arterial disease. *New England Journal of Medicine* 326(6):381-386, 1992.

46. Salonen, J.T., and Salonen, R. Ultrasonographically assessed carotid morphology and the risk of coronary heart disease. *Arteriosclerosis and Thrombosis* 11(5):1245-1249, 1991.

47. Kannel, W.B., and Schatzkin, A. Sudden death: Lessons from subsets in population studies. *Journal of the American College of Cardiology* 5(6 suppl.):141-149B, 1985.

48. Kuller, L.; Perper, J.; and Cooper, M. Demographic characteristics and trends in arteriosclerotic heart disease mortality: Sudden death and myocardial infarction. *Circulation* 51(1 suppl.):III-1-III-15, 1975.

49. Scandinavian Simvastatin Survival Study Group. Randomized trial of cholesterol lowering in 4444 patients with coronary heart disease: the Scandinavian Simvastatin Survival Study (4S). *Lancet* 334:1383-1389, 1994.

50. Sacks, F.M.; Pfeffer, M.A.; Moye, L.A.; et al., for the Cholesterol and Recurrent Events Trial Investigators. The effect of pravastatin on coronary events after myocardial infarction in patients with average cholesterol levels. *New England Journal of Medicine* 335:1001-1009, 1996.

51. The Long-Term Intervention with Pravastatin in Ischaemic Disease (LIPID) Study Group. Prevention of cardiovascular events and death with pravastatin in patients with coronary heart disease and a broad range of initial cholesterol levels. *New England Journal of Medicine* 339:1349-1357, 1998.

52. Joint National Committee on Detection, Evaluation, and Treatment of High Blood Pressure. *The Sixth Report of the Joint National Committee on Detection, Evaluation, and Treatment of High Blood Pressure.* NIH Pub. No. 98-4080. Bethesda, MD: National High Blood Pressure Education Program, National Institutes of Health, National Heart, Lung, and Blood Institute, November 1998, 24-25.

53. Psaty, B.M.; Smith, N.L.; Siscovick, D.S.; et al. Health outcomes associated

with antihypertensive therapies used as first-line agents: a systematic review and meta-analysis. *Journal of the American Medical Association* 277:739-745, 1997.

54. MacMahon, S., and Rodgers, A. The effect of blood pressure reduction in older patients: an overview of five randomized controlled trials in elderly hypertensives. *Clinical and Experimental Hypertension* 15967-15978, 1993.

55. CDC. State-specific Prevalence of Current Cigarette and Cigar Smoking Adults—United States, 1998. *Morbidity and Mortality Weekly Report* 48(45), 1999.

13
HIV

Co-Lead Agencies: Centers for Disease Control and Prevention;
Health Resources and Services Administration

Contents

Goal

Prevent HIV infection and its related illness and death.

Overview

Beginning in 1981, a new infectious disease, AIDS, or acquired immunodeficiency syndrome, was identified in the United States.[1] Several years later, the causative agent of AIDS—human immunodeficiency virus (HIV)—was discovered. This discovery coincided with the growing recognition of AIDS in the United States as part of a global infectious disease pandemic.

Currently, HIV/AIDS has been reported in virtually every racial and ethnic population, every age group, and every socioeconomic group in every State and most large cities in the United States. Initially identified among men who have sex with men on the East and West Coasts,[2] the AIDS epidemic is composed of diverse multiple subepidemics that vary by region and community. By the end of 1998, more than 680,000 cases of AIDS had been reported, and nearly 410,800 people had died from HIV disease or AIDS.[3]

Issues

Estimates of the number of people infected with HIV in the United States range from 650,000 to 900,000.[4] The HIV/AIDS subepidemics not only vary by region and community, but also may vary by population, risk behavior, and geography. Disparities in the rate of infection among certain racial and ethnic groups, particularly African American and Hispanic populations, remain a challenge. Recently introduced therapies for HIV/AIDS have reduced illness, disability, and death due to HIV/AIDS; however, access to culturally and linguistically appropriate testing and care may limit progress in this area.

In the United States, HIV/AIDS remains a significant cause of illness, disability, and death, despite declines in 1996 and 1997.[5] Current surveillance provides population-based HIV/AIDS data for tracking trends in the epidemic, targeting and allocating resources for prevention and treatment services, and planning and conducting program evaluation activities. Since the early 1980s, surveillance studies have identified four distinct populations and issues that have affected the epidemic in these populations:

- Men who have sex with men, facilitated by frequent changes of sex partners in highly infected sexual networks and by high-risk sexual practices.

- Injection drug users, facilitated by the shared use of needles and syringes contaminated with HIV-infected blood.

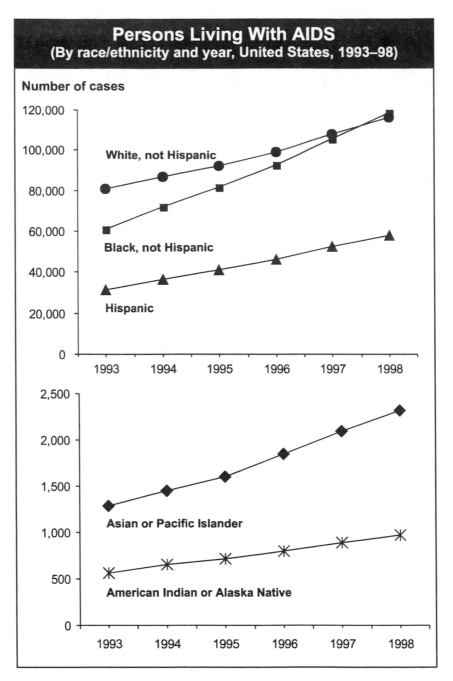

Persons Living With AIDS
(By race/ethnicity and year, United States, 1993–98)

Number of cases

White, not Hispanic

Black, not Hispanic

Hispanic

Asian or Pacific Islander

American Indian or Alaska Native

Source: CDC. *HIV/AIDS Surveillance Report*, Vol. 11, No. 1, 1999.

- Heterosexual persons (principally in certain racial and ethnic populations), facilitated by (1) a high rate of HIV among drug-using populations that resulted in heterosexual transmission to some partners, (2) high rates of other sexually transmitted diseases (STDs) that can increase both susceptibility to transmissibility of HIV infection, (3) high-risk sexual practices (mainly unprotected sex) associated with certain addictive substances, such as crack cocaine, and (4) sex in exchange for drugs.

- Perinatal transmission among infants, caused by undetected or untreated HIV infection in pregnant females (although the number of perinatally infected infants has declined dramatically since the mid 1990s to a point where elimination of perinatal transmission in the United States may be possible).

The proportion of different populations affected by HIV/AIDS has changed over time. By 1998, 83 percent of the cumulative AIDS cases had occurred in males, 16 percent in females, and 1 percent in children.[3] The response to the epidemic reflects these changes:

- Comparing the 1980s to the 1990s, the proportion of AIDS cases in white men who have sex with men declined, whereas the proportion in females and males in other racial and ethnic populations increased, particularly among African Americans and Hispanics (see Disparities section). AIDS cases also appeared to be increasing among injection drug users and their sexual partners.[5]

- Increases among women have occurred over time. By the mid 1980s, a majority of AIDS cases had been reported among males, with only 7 percent reported among females in 1983.[6] Reported AIDS cases in females have increased steadily since then and accounted for nearly 23 percent of the cases reported in 1998.[3]

- Monitoring and tracking of the current HIV/AIDS epidemic remains a challenge. Even though AIDS may occur much later than infection with HIV, only AIDS cases are currently reported by all State health departments. Because tracking HIV is more accurate for tracking the status of the epidemic and because States are making progress in reporting HIV infection, it is anticipated that key baseline data about HIV will be available by the early 2000s.[7]

- Even though a test for HIV was developed and made widely available in the early to mid-1980s, the lack of available treatment until 1995, negative implications of treatment (including concerns about lack of confidentiality), and possible discrimination and stigmatization resulted in barriers to the reporting of HIV infection.

The lifetime costs of health care associated with HIV, in light of recent advances in diagnostics and therapeutics, have grown from $55,000 to $155,000 or more per person.[8] These costs mean that HIV prevention efforts may be even more cost-effective and even cost-saving to society. Prevention efforts include availability of culturally and linguistically appropriate HIV counseling and testing, partner counseling, and referral systems for individuals at high risk for HIV infection; needle and syringe exchange programs; and information, education, treatment and counseling for injection drug users.

The true extent of the epidemic remains difficult to assess for several reasons, including the following:

Data as of November 30, 1999

- Because of the long period of time from initial HIV infection to AIDS and because highly active antiretroviral therapy (HAART) has slowed the progression to AIDS, new cases of AIDS no longer provide accurate information about the current HIV epidemic in the United States.

- Because of a lack of awareness of HIV serostatus as well as delays in accessing counseling, testing, and care services by individuals who may be infected or are at risk of infection, some populations do not perceive themselves to be at risk. As a result, some HIV-infected persons are not identified and provided care until late in the course of their infection.

Trends

HIV infection rates appear to have stabilized since the early 1990s at about 40,000 new infections per year, which represents a slowing from growth rates experienced in the mid-1980s.[4] About 750,000 to 900,000 persons are estimated to be infected with HIV, with over 200,000 to 250,000 persons who are not aware of their infection. About 250,000 persons are estimated to be in treatment with new antiretroviral treatment therapies, and another 250,000 are not currently in treatment.[5, 9]

Significant changes in the epidemic have occurred over time. In 1992, AIDS became a leading cause of death among persons aged 25 to 44 years, but by 1997 had dropped to the eighth leading cause of death in this age group. In 1997, HIV/AIDS remained the leading cause of death only for African Americans among persons in this age group.[10, 11] Between 1992 and 1997, the number of persons reported living with AIDS increased in all groups as a result of the 1993 expanded AIDS case definition and, more recently, improved survival rates due to new HAART treatment.

Some of these changes are reflected in the following:

- Women accounted for just under 14 percent of persons over age 13 years living with AIDS in 1992, compared with 20 percent in 1998.[3, 12]

- By the end of 1998, the number of African Americans living with AIDS, which increased from 33 percent of the AIDS population in 1992 to 40 percent in 1998, was almost identical to the number of whites living with AIDS.[3]

- Persons living in the South accounted for 34 percent of AIDS cases in 1992 and 38.5 percent in 1998. Persons living in the Northeast accounted for 28.3 percent in 1992 and 31.0 percent in 1998. The proportion living in the West declined from 23.8 percent to 20.8 percent.[3, 13]

- By December 1998, approximately 297,136 persons were reported to be living with AIDS, compared with 269,775 in 1997.[3, 14]

In late 1982, cases of AIDS attributed to blood transfusions were first reported in the United States.[15, 16] The publication, dissemination, and implementation of specific guidelines and recommendations to prevent HIV infection among health care workers and to test donated blood for HIV[17, 18, 19, 20] have resulted in a reduction in transfusion-related AIDS and increases in safety among health workers.

Another prevention success has been the 66 percent decline in perinatal transmission from 1992 to 1997. With the finding that perinatal HIV transmission rates could be reduced substantially with zidovudine therapy during pregnancy, the U.S. Public Health Service issued guidelines recommending that HIV counseling and voluntary testing become a part of routine prenatal care for all pregnant women.[21] This policy ensures that HIV-infected pregnant women have access to important health care for themselves and also have the opportunity to reduce the risk of HIV transmission to their infants. Subsequent declines in new cases of AIDS among children demonstrate that these strategies are showing success in reducing mother-to-infant HIV transmission.[22]

However, initial declines in deaths from AIDS after the availability of treatments have slowed. Deaths from AIDS continued to decline throughout 1997 and 1998 (down 42 percent and 20 percent, respectively, compared to 1996), and the number of persons living with AIDS (AIDS prevalence) in 1997 and 1998 increased by 12 percent and 10 percent, respectively.[3, 13] If declines continue in newly diagnosed AIDS cases in the coming years, an increasing number of persons will be living with HIV infection. As HIV surveillance extends to additional States, so will the ability to monitor HIV cases and to direct prevention and treatment services to people with asymptomatic infection or mild illness.

Principal health determinants. Behaviors (sexual practices, substance abuse, and accessing prenatal care) and biomedical status (having other STDs) are major determinants of HIV transmission. Unprotected sexual contact, whether homosexual or heterosexual, with a person infected with HIV and sharing drug-injection equipment with an HIV-infected individual account for most HIV transmission in the United States.[23, 24] Increasing the number of people who know their HIV serostatus is an important component of a national program to slow or halt the transmission of HIV in the United States.

For persons infected with HIV, behavioral determinants also play an important role in health maintenance. Although drugs are available specifically to prevent and treat a number of opportunistic infections, HIV-infected individuals also need to make lifestyle-related behavioral changes to avoid many of these infections. The new HIV antiretroviral drug therapies for HIV infection bring with them difficulties in adhering to complex, expensive, and demanding medication schedules, posing a significant challenge for many persons infected with HIV.

Because HIV infection weakens the immune system, people with tuberculosis (TB) infection and HIV infection are at very high risk of developing active TB disease.[25]

Interventions. Interventions for combating HIV are behavioral as well as bio-medical. Recent advances in antiretroviral therapy have been credited with dramatic declines in deaths associated with HIV/AIDS. However, declines in overall AIDS cases, particularly in the early epicenters of the epidemic such as San Francisco and New York, predate the advent of antiretroviral therapies and support the belief that behavior-based prevention programs are effective. In San Francisco, for example, new cases of AIDS among men who have sex with men began dropping in 1992, suggesting that sustained, comprehensive prevention activities begun in the 1980s succeeded in reducing HIV transmission in this group.[26]

Behavioral interventions to prevent HIV vary depending on the audience for whom the program is designed, who designed it, and funds available. Effective community-level prevention strategies in the United States have included social marketing interventions to increase condom use and messages about safer sex and needle-sharing that rely on popular opinion leaders and role model stories. Effective small and large group interventions have aimed at increasing safer sex practices for high-risk HIV-infected men and women and have tended to employ cognitive behavioral and skill-building methods.[26]

Several effective individual counseling or education interventions have focused on increasing condom use and other safer sex practices for HIV-infected persons. For example, at the individual level, client-centered HIV counseling and testing appear to be effective in preventing high-risk uninfected persons from becoming infected and in helping HIV-infected persons prevent transmission to uninfected partners. Intervention venues vary and include STD clinic waiting rooms, drug treatment centers, schools, community agencies, street settings, and community settings where HIV-infected and high-risk uninfected persons congregate.[26]

While HIV testing in STD clinics is an important intervention, detection, and treatment of other STDs are also an important biomedical component of an HIV prevention program that should include both behavioral and biomedical interventions. STD prevention programs must address STD concerns and their cofactor role in HIV transmission. Early STD detection and treatment are a biomedical tool for lowering the risk for sexual transmission of HIV infection. Behavioral interventions emphasize reducing the number of sex partners, knowing the serostatus of one's partner, using condoms consistently and correctly, and avoiding risky sexual behaviors.[23, 27, 28]

Disparities

In the United States, African Americans and Hispanics have been affected disproportionately by HIV and AIDS, compared to other racial and ethnic groups. Through December 1998, 688,200 cases of AIDS had been reported among persons of all ages and racial and ethnic groups, including 304,094 cases among whites, 251,408 cases among African Americans, and 124,841 cases among Hispanics. Although 55 percent of the reported AIDS cases occurred among African

Americans and Hispanics, these two population groups represent an estimated 13 percent and 12 percent, respectively, of the total U.S. population.[3]

In 1997, AIDS remained the leading cause of death for all African Americans aged 25 to 44 years—the second leading cause among African American females and the leading cause among African American males.[10] In 1996, for the first time, African Americans accounted for a larger proportion of AIDS cases than whites, and this trend has continued. The AIDS case rate among African Americans in calendar year 1998 was 66.4 per 100,000 persons, or eight times the rate for whites (8.2 per 100,000) and over twice the rate for Hispanics (28.1 per 100,000).[3]

Among women with AIDS, African Americans and Hispanics have been especially affected, accounting for nearly 77 percent of cumulative cases reported among women by 1998. Of the 109,311 AIDS cases in women reported through December 1998, 61,874 cases occurred in African American women and 21,937 occurred in Hispanic women.[3]

For young adults aged 20 to 24 years, 24,437 cumulative AIDS cases were reported through December 1998. Of this total, 10,107 (41 percent) occurred among African Americans, 8,804 (36 percent) among whites, and 5,203 (21 percent) among Hispanics. Overall, 73 percent of the AIDS cases in this age group occurred among males and 27 percent among females. Among African Americans in this age group, 63 percent were male, and 37 percent were female. Among Hispanics, 74 percent were male, and 26 percent were female. Because the time from initial infection with HIV to the development of AIDS is long and variable (often 8 to 10 years or more), many of these young adults likely acquired their infections while in their teens.[3]

Among teenagers aged 13 to 19 years, 3,423 cumulative AIDS cases had been reported through December 1998.[3] In this age group, 1,047 cases (31 percent) occurred among whites, 1,654 (48 percent) among African Americans, and 668 (20 percent) among Hispanics. Overall, males accounted for 61 percent of the AIDS cases in this age group, and females accounted for 39 percent. Among African American teenagers with AIDS, 46 percent were male, and 54 percent were female. Among Hispanic teens, 67 percent of those with AIDS were male, and 33 percent were female. Among white teenagers with AIDS, 79 percent were male, and 21 percent were female.[3]

The disproportionate impact of HIV/AIDS on African Americans and Hispanics underscores the importance of implementing and sustaining effective prevention efforts for these racial and ethnic populations. HIV prevention efforts must take into account not only the multiracial and multicultural nature of society, but also other social and economic factors—such as poverty, underemployment, and poor access to the health care system. These factors affect health status and disproportionately affect African American, Hispanic, Alaska Native, and American Indian populations.

Opportunities

In the 21st century, strategies for reducing HIV/AIDS transmission will continue to evolve and will require shifts from current efforts.[29] Future strategies should focus on:

- Continuing to address the disproportionate impact of HIV/AIDS among certain racial and ethnic groups.

- Enhancing prevention strategies for populations that are particularly high risk, such as injection drug users, homeless persons, runaway youth, mentally ill persons, and incarcerated persons. Some of these populations are also difficult to reach.

- Increasing the number of people who learn their HIV status in order to detect HIV infection when the potential for transmission is greatest and the need for prevention, care, and treatment, including HAART, is greatest.

- Reaching high-risk seronegative people to help them to stay uninfected.

- Improving access to HAART, thereby reducing deaths and HIV-associated illness and, possibly, infection of others.

- Detecting and treating ulcerative and inflammatory STDs, especially in groups at risk for HIV infection.

- Setting the discovery of a safe and effective HIV vaccine as a reachable goal, as a result of ongoing HIV vaccine testing. The development and testing of candidate microbicides may be important in enhancing prevention efforts until a vaccine is available.

Interim Progress Toward Year 2000 Objectives

Data to assess progress are available for 13 of the 17 Healthy People 2000 objectives. Two objectives have met or exceeded the year 2000 targets. The objective to lower the risk of transfusion-transmitted HIV infection exceeded its target, and the objective to protect workers from exposure to bloodborne infections was met with the Occupational Safety and Health Administration's bloodborne pathogens standard in December 1991. Data show progress toward the year 2000 targets for objectives to slow the rise in the rate of new AIDS cases, contain the rate of HIV infection, and increase the proportion of sexually active females whose partners used condoms at last sexual intercourse. The objective to increase the proportion of HIV-positive people who know their serostatus is moving away from its target, as are objectives for counseling, outreach, and school-based AIDS education.

Note: Unless otherwise noted, data are from Centers for Disease Control and Prevention, National Center for Health Statistics, *Healthy People 2000 Review, 1998-99.*

13. HIV

Goal: Prevent HIV infection and its related illness and death.

Number	Objective
13-1	New AIDS cases
13-2	AIDS among men who have sex with men
13-3	AIDS among persons who inject drugs
13-4	AIDS among men who have sex with men and who inject drugs
13-5	New HIV cases
13-6	Condom use
13-7	Knowledge of serostatus
13-8	HIV counseling and education for persons in substance abuse treatment
13-9	HIV/AIDS, STD, and TB education in State prisons
13-10	HIV counseling and testing in State prisons
13-11	HIV testing in TB patients
13-12	Screening for STDs and immunization for hepatitis B
13-13	Treatment according to guidelines
13-14	HIV-infection deaths
13-15	Interval between HIV infection and AIDS diagnosis
13-16	Interval between AIDS diagnosis and death from AIDS
13-17	Perinatally acquired HIV infection

13-1. Reduce AIDS among adolescents and adults.

Target: 1.0 new case per 100,000 persons.

Baseline: 19.5 cases of AIDS per 100,000 persons aged 13 years and older in 1998. Data are estimated; adjusted for delays of AIDS in reporting.

Target setting method: Better than the best.

Data source: HIV/AIDS Surveillance System, CDC, NCHSTP.

| Persons Aged 13 Years and Older, 1998 | New AIDS Cases | | |
| | 13-1. Both Sexes | Females* | Males* |
	Rate per 100,000		
TOTAL	19.5	8.8	30.8
Race and ethnicity			
American Indian or Alaska Native	9.4	4.5	14.5
Asian or Pacific Islander	4.3	1.2	7.8
Asian	DNC	DNC	DNC
Native Hawaiian and other Pacific Islander	DNC	DNC	DNC
Black or African American	DNC	DNC	DNC
White	DNC	DNC	DNC
Hispanic or Latino	33.0	13.8	52.2
Not Hispanic or Latino	DNC	DNC	DNC
Black or African American	82.9	48.5	122.9
White	8.5	2.2	15.2
Family income level			
Poor	DNC	DNC	DNC
Near poor	DNC	DNC	DNC
Middle/high income	DNC	DNC	DNC

DNA = Data have not been analyzed. DNC = Data are not collected. DSU = Data are statistically unreliable.

*Data for females and males are displayed to further characterize the issue.

Historically, AIDS incidence data have served as the basis for assessing needs for prevention and treatment programs. However, because of the effect of potent anti-retroviral therapies, AIDS incidence no longer can provide unbiased information on HIV incidence patterns; it is hoped that AIDS will not develop in the growing number of HIV-infected persons as they benefit from these new therapies. Persons reported with AIDS will increasingly represent persons who were diagnosed too late for them to benefit from treatments, persons who either did not seek or had no access to care, or persons who failed treatment. This objective will be modified to track HIV cases as additional States implement HIV surveillance as an extension of their current AIDS case surveillance systems.

13-2. Reduce the number of new AIDS cases among adolescent and adult men who have sex with men.

Target: 13,385 new cases.

Baseline: 17,847 new cases of AIDS in 1998 among males aged 13 years and older. Data are estimated; risk is redistributed; adjusted for delays in reporting.

Target setting method: 25 percent improvement.

Data source: HIV/AIDS Surveillance System, CDC, NCHSTP.

In 1998, an estimated 17,847 AIDS cases were diagnosed among men having sex with men. This was a decrease from 1997 and part of a continuing trend. The decline is a result of prevention activities and the impact of and access to potent antiretroviral therapies which are delaying progression to AIDS in many HIV-infected individuals. This objective will be modified when additional States implement HIV infection surveillance as an extension of their current AIDS case surveillance systems.

13-3. Reduce the number of new AIDS cases among females and males who inject drugs.

Target: 9,075 cases.

Baseline: 12,099 new cases of AIDS among injection drug users aged 13 years and older (females, 3,667; males, 8,432) in 1998. Data are point estimates; risk redistributed; adjusted for delays in reporting.

Target setting method: 25 percent improvement.

Data source: HIV/AIDS Surveillance System, CDC, NCHSTP.

In 1998, an estimated 12,099 cases were diagnosed among adult men and women who injected drugs. This was a decrease from the previous year and part of a continuing trend. The decline is a result of prevention activities and the impact of potent antiretroviral therapies which are delaying progression to AIDS in many HIV-infected individuals.

Data as of November 30, 1999

13-4. Reduce the number of new AIDS cases among adolescent and adult men who have sex with men and inject drugs.

Target: 1,592 cases.

Baseline: 2,122 new cases of AIDS among males aged 13 years and older in 1998. Data are point estimates; risk redistributed; adjusted for delays in reporting.

Target setting method: 25 percent improvement.

Data source: HIV/AIDS Surveillance System, CDC, NCHSTP.

In 1998, an estimated 2,122 AIDS cases were diagnosed among adult and adolescent men who have sex with men and inject drugs. This was a decrease from 1997 and part of a continuing trend. The decline is a result of prevention activities and the impact of potent antiretroviral therapies which are delaying progression to AIDS in many HIV-infected individuals. This objective will be modified when additional States implement HIV infection surveillance as an extension of their current AIDS case surveillance systems.

13-5. (Developmental) Reduce the number of cases of HIV infection among adolescents and adults.

Potential data source: HIV/AIDS Surveillance System, CDC, NCHSTP.

Recent advances in HIV treatment have slowed the progression of HIV disease for infected persons on treatment and contributed to a decline in AIDS incidence These advances in treatment have diminished the ability of AIDS surveillance data to represent trends in HIV incidence or to represent the impact of the epidemic on the health care system. Once HIV case surveillance is implemented nationwide by 2001, CDC will be able to report baseline and progress toward the objective of "reducing the annual incidence of HIV infection."

13-6. Increase the proportion of sexually active persons who use condoms.

Target: 50 percent.

Baseline: 23 percent of unmarried females aged 18 to 44 years reported condoms used by partners in 1995. Data on males aged 18 to 49 years will be collected and reported by 2003.

Target setting method: Better than the best.

Data source: National Survey of Family Growth (NSFG), CDC, NCHS.

Unmarried Females 18 to 44 years, 1995	Condom Use Females, Aged 18 to 44 Years Reporting Condom Use by Partners* Percent
TOTAL	23
Race and ethnicity	
American Indian or Alaska Native	DSU
Asian or Pacific Islander	DSU
Asian	DNC
Native Hawaiian and other Pacific Islander	DNC
Black or African American	22
White	23
Hispanic or Latino	17
Aged 18 to 19 years	16
Aged 20 to 24 years	18
Aged 25 to 29 years	19
Aged 30 to 34 years	22
Aged 35 to 44 years	9
Not Hispanic or Latino	24
Black or African American	22
Aged 18 to 19 years	31
Aged 20 to 24 years	35
Aged 25 to 29 years	23
Aged 30 to 34 years	17
Aged 35 to 44 years	12
White	24
Aged 18 to 19 years	39
Aged 20 to 24 years	29
Aged 25 to 29 years	24
Aged 30 to 34 years	14
Aged 35 to 44 years	18
Family income level	
Poor	16
Near poor	21
Middle/high income	27

Unmarried Females 18 to 44 years, 1995	Condom Use Females, Aged 18 to 44 Years Reporting Condom Use by Partners* Percent
Education level (aged 25 to 44 years)	
Less than high school	7
High school	15
At least some college	25
Geographic location	
Urban	24
Rural	18

DNA = Data have not been analyzed. DNC = Data are not collected. DSU = Data are statistically unreliable.
*Data for both genders and for males currently are not collected.

When used consistently and correctly, latex condoms are highly effective in preventing HIV transmission. Increased use of latex condoms is essential for slowing the spread of HIV infection. Carefully designed studies among heterosexual couples in which one partner is HIV positive and the other is not demonstrate that latex condoms provide a high level of protection against HIV. [9, 23]

Persons in some populations, especially sexually active young persons, may experience problems in obtaining access to condoms because of several factors, including cost, convenience, and embarrassment. The lack of readily accessible condoms may also be a significant barrier to consistent use. To eliminate this barrier, many local communities actively support programs that make condoms available to populations most vulnerable to HIV infection, including sexually active young persons. Research shows that providing access to condoms can increase their use among sexually active young persons. Research also clearly demonstrates that—despite fears to the contrary—young persons who participate in comprehensive HIV prevention programs which include approaches to ensure access to condoms are no more likely to initiate or increase sexual activity than other young persons.

In addition to access, the correct and consistent use of condoms is an issue for many young females, some of whom are having intercourse with older males. Young females often are limited by intimidation or threats of mistrust by their partners if they suggest condom use. Knowledge of effective negotiating skills is another critical element of increased condom use.

13-7. (Developmental) Increase the number of HIV-positive persons who know their serostatus.

Potential data source: HIV/AIDS Surveillance System, CDC, NCHSTP.

Advances in HIV prevention and treatment increase the importance of persons learning their HIV status. Estimates are that approximately 250,000 persons in the United States are unaware they were infected with HIV in 1998. HIV testing provides a critical avenue to reach persons at risk with prevention counseling and services as well as to link infected individuals with needed care and treatment services. Clearly, infected persons should be counseled about ways they can protect their own health and keep from infecting others. New treatments offer infected persons the promise of a longer, healthier life. For HIV-infected pregnant females, therapy is available to reduce the chance of transmitting HIV to their babies. Although the evidence still is not entirely clear, persons who are being treated successfully for HIV may be less likely to transmit the virus. Because the science is evolving, communicating the continuing need for infected persons, even those in treatment, to take steps to protect their partners is essential.[23]

13-8. Increase the proportion of substance abuse treatment facilities that offer HIV/AIDS education, counseling, and support.

Target: 70 percent.

Baseline: 58 percent of substance abuse treatment facilities offered HIV/AIDS education, counseling, and support in 1997.

Target setting method: 21 percent improvement.

Data source: Uniform Facility Data Set (UFDS), SAMHSA.

To date, more than one-third of all reported AIDS cases in the United States have occurred among injection drug users, their heterosexual sex partners, and children whose mothers were injection drug users or sex partners of injection drug users.[3]

Preventing drug use and providing treatment to stop drug use among persons already using drugs are the best ways to prevent drug-associated transmission of HIV. Among persons who inject drugs, reusing or sharing blood-contaminated injection equipment (particularly syringes) continues to play a substantial role in HIV transmission, as well as the transmission of hepatitis B and C and other bloodborne infections.

Needle and syringe exchange programs (NSEPs) can be an effective component of comprehensive community-based HIV prevention efforts.[24] Additionally, NSEPs can provide a pathway for linking injection drug users to other important services, such as risk-reduction counseling, drug treatment, and support services.

13-9. **(Developmental) Increase the number of State prison systems that provide comprehensive HIV/AIDS, sexually transmitted diseases, and tuberculosis (TB) education.**

Potential data source: Survey of HIV, STD, and TB Prevention in Correctional Facilities, CDC/National Institute of Justice.

Incarceration provides an environment in which early interventions and risk-reduction behaviors can be taught and reinforced over time. It also represents an opportunity to provide the education, support, and continuity of care needed when incarcerated persons are released and return to their home communities.

13-10. **(Developmental) Increase the proportion of inmates in State prison systems who receive voluntary HIV counseling and testing during incarceration.**

Potential data source: Survey of HIV, STD, and TB Prevention in Correctional Facilities, CDC and National Institute of Justice.

Although not standardized, State prison systems can provide access to treatment and care for persons infected with HIV. Early access to care reduces both immediate and long-term health care costs for correctional institutions and the community. This objective focuses on State systems because, in accordance with the Federal Bureau of Prisons guidance, all Federal correctional facilities are required to provide HIV testing to all inmates at some time prior to discharge. Continuing this practice is important. It is also important to provide HIV testing to inmates upon intake to allow for sufficient medical care and necessary followup. In addition, discharge planning and formal linkages with community-based HIV care should be offered to all HIV-positive inmates just prior to or upon release.

13-11. **Increase the proportion of adults with tuberculosis (TB) who have been tested for HIV.**

Target: 85 percent.

Baseline: 55 percent of adults aged 25 to 44 years with TB were tested for HIV in 1998.

Target setting method: Better than the best.

Data source: National TB Surveillance System, CDC, DTBE.

Adults Aged 25 to 44 Years With TB, 1998	Tested for HIV Percent
TOTAL	55
Race and ethnicity	
American Indian or Alaska Native	39
Asian or Pacific Islander	29
Asian	DNC
Native Hawaiian and other Pacific Islander	DNC
Black or African American	76
White	50
Hispanic or Latino	46
Not Hispanic or Latino	58
Black or African American	76
White	58
Gender	
Female	51
Male	58
Family income level	
Poor	DNC
Near poor	DNC
Middle/high income	DNC

DNA = Data have not been analyzed. DNC = Data are not collected. DSU = Data are statistically unreliable.

The rapid rate of progression from infection with TB bacteria to active TB disease among HIV-positive patients with *Mycobacterium tuberculosis* has been well documented. When State health departments compared their TB and AIDS registries, 27 percent of the TB cases reported in 1993-94 in adults aged 25 to 44 years had a match in the AIDS registry. However, estimates based on registry matches provide only a minimum estimate of coinfection.[25]

Early detection of HIV in TB patients also allows for early intervention and treatment that may prevent or delay the development of other HIV-related illnesses and AIDS. In fact, many persons diagnosed with TB who have immune system problems caused by HIV are unaware of their HIV status. TB patients receive HIV testing only after counseling and informed consent from the patient. Because testing is voluntary, some patients may decline HIV testing.

13-12. (Developmental) Increase the proportion of adults in publicly funded HIV counseling and testing sites who are screened for common bacterial sexually transmitted diseases (STDs) (chlamydia, gonorrhea, and syphilis) and are immunized against hepatitis B virus.

Potential data source: HIV Counseling and Testing Data Summary, CDC, NCHSTP.

Data indicate that the presence of other STDs substantially increases the risk of HIV transmission by making it easier both to get and to give HIV infection.[28, 30] Treating other STDs reduces the spread of HIV. U.S. STD rates are high, and STD clinical services are inadequate in the face of a changing HIV epidemic.[31]

STD vaccines can minimize the probability of infection. While vaccines for some STDs are in various stages of development, an effective vaccine for hepatitis B is widely available. Unfortunately, hepatitis B vaccine coverage remains low, especially in high-risk groups. The main reasons are a lack of awareness among health care providers, limited opportunity to reach high-risk youth in traditional health care settings, and limited financial support for widescale implementation of this intervention. Many persons requesting HIV counseling and testing, although not HIV infected, are nonetheless at high risk for acquiring sexually transmitted infections. Offering hepatitis B vaccine at sites screening for common STDs would take advantage of reaching high-risk persons who otherwise may not have access to immunization services.

13-13. Increase the proportion of HIV-infected adolescents and adults who receive testing, treatment, and prophylaxis consistent with current Public Health Service treatment guidelines.

Target and baseline:

Objective	Increase in HIV-Infected Persons Aged 13 Years and Older Receiving Testing, Treatment, and Prophylaxis Consistent With Current Public Health Service Guidelines	1997 Baseline	2010 Target
		Percent	
	Testing		
13-13a.	Viral load testing	76	95
13-13b.	Tuberculin skin testing (TST)	Developmental	
	Treatment		
13-13c.	Any antiretroviral therapy	92	95
13-13d.	Highly active antiretroviral therapy (HAART)	54	95

Data as of November 30, 1999

Prophylaxis

13-13e.	*Pneumocystis carinii* pneumonia (PCP) prophylaxis	95	95
13-13f.	*Mycobacterium avium* complex (MAC) prophylaxis	61	95
13-13g.	Pneumococcal vaccination	43	95

Note: Data from 11 cities and 9 States.

Target setting method: An improvement to the same percentage as that of the highest service (*Pneumocystis carinii* pneumonia prophylaxis at 95 percent).

Data source: Adult Spectrum of Disease (ASD) Surveillance Project, CDC, NCHSTP.

Estimated new cases of AIDS in adults and adolescents declined by 15 percent from 1996 to 1997. As new therapies continue to be developed and as people with HIV/AIDS live longer, HIV-infected persons need access to these life-enhancing treatments. Once individuals access care, they need to receive the most beneficial treatment possible. The survival benefits of antiretroviral therapy, PCP and MAC prophylaxis, and TB prophylaxis have been demonstrated for persons with HIV/AIDS who meet the criteria for these preventive therapies. (CD4+ testing is included as a standard of care in the Public Health Service treatment guidelines but is not included here because it already is provided to nearly 100 percent of individuals measured by this objective.)

Data from HIV and AIDS case surveillance continue to reflect the disproportionate impact of the epidemic on select populations, especially females, youth, and children. Everyone needs equal access to appropriate care and treatment services necessary to maintain a healthy life.

13-14. Reduce deaths from HIV infection.

Target: 0.8 death per 100,000 persons.

Baseline: 4.9 deaths from HIV infection per 100,000 persons in 1998 (preliminary data; age adjusted to the year 2000 population).

Target setting method: Better than the best.

Data source: National Vital Statistics System, CDC, NCHS.

Total Population, 1997*	Deaths Due to HIV Infection		
	13-14. Both Sexes	Females†	Males†
	Rate per 100,000		
TOTAL	6.1	2.7	9.7
Race and ethnicity			
American Indian or Alaska Native	2.5	DSU	3.8
Asian or Pacific Islander	0.9	DSU	1.7
Asian	DNC	DNC	DNC
Native Hawaiian and other Pacific Islander	DNC	DNC	DNC
Black or African American	26.6	13.9	41.7
White	3.5	1.0	6.0
Hispanic or Latino	8.9	3.5	14.2
Not Hispanic or Latino	5.9	2.6	9.3
Black or African American	27.3	14.3	42.9
White	2.8	0.7	4.9
Education level (aged 25 to 64 years)			
Less than high school	19.4	11.8	26.3
High school graduate	14.3	6.2	23.0
At least some college	5.8	1.6	10.1

DNA = Data have not been analyzed. DNC = Data are not collected. DSU = Data are statistically unreliable.

Note: Age adjusted to the year 2000 standard population.

*New data for population groups will be added when available.

†Data for females and males are displayed to further characterize the issue.

The impact of new combination drug therapies first was reported in 1997 when deaths attributable to HIV infection were down 44 percent from the first 6 months of 1996, compared with the first 6 months of 1997. These surveillance data suggest that not only are new therapies delaying progression from AIDS to death, but, with early diagnosis and treatment, these therapies also are helping to delay the progression from HIV infection to an AIDS diagnosis for many persons.

13-15. (Developmental) Extend the interval of time between an initial diagnosis of HIV infection and AIDS diagnosis in order to increase years of life of an individual infected with HIV.

Potential data source: HIV/AIDS Surveillance System, CDC, NCHSTP.

This objective is meant to indicate which populations arc not benefiting from current treatment therapies and where to direct resources. HIV-infected persons should be identified at the earliest possible opportunity and referred to appropriate medical, social, and preventive services that may preserve their health, help them avoid opportunistic illnesses, reduce sexual and drug-use behaviors that may spread HIV, and generally extend the quality of their lives. For HIV-infected persons to benefit from treatment advances, HIV counseling and testing programs must facilitate an early diagnosis of HIV infection. All persons should have equal access to appropriate care and treatment services necessary for maintaining a healthy life.

13-16. (Developmental) Increase years of life of an HIV-infected person by extending the interval of time between an AIDS diagnosis and death.

Potential data source: HIV/AIDS Surveillance System, CDC, NCHSTP.

This objective provides insight into which population groups lack or fail to respond to treatment. To sustain reductions in deaths due to HIV infection, access to treatment and care is necessary. Targeting prevention efforts at groups disproportionately affected also is important.

13-17. (Developmental) Reduce new cases of perinatally acquired HIV infection.

Potential data source: HIV/AIDS Surveillance System, CDC, NCHSTP.

Perinatal transmission of HIV accounts for virtually all new HIV infections in children. Through 1993, an estimated 15,000 HIV-infected children were born to HIV-positive women in the United States. As of June 1998, 8,280 AIDS cases had been reported in children under age 13 years in the United States. Perinatally acquired AIDS cases have been reported from 48 States, the District of Columbia, Puerto Rico, and the U.S. Virgin Islands.[3, 22]

The National Institutes of Health sponsored an AIDS clinical trial, ACTG-076, after demonstrating that the risk of perinatal HIV transmission could be reduced by as much as two-thirds with the use of zidovudine therapy. This therapy was given to HIV-positive pregnant females during pregnancy and childbirth and for their newborns for 6 weeks after birth.[21] Additional research confirmed that routine and universal counseling and voluntary testing, combined with zidovudine therapy, are highly effective in preventing HIV.[21] In addition, recently completed and ongoing research suggests that other antiretroviral agents also can reduce significantly maternal-infant HIV transmission. These additional therapeutic options should increase the opportunity to intervene to reduce perinatal HIV transmission. Substantial declines in perinatal AIDS cases have been reported. Estimated new cases of pediatric AIDS declined from 947 in 1992 to 225 in 1998.[3]

Even though these prevention efforts are proving to be effective in reducing peri-natal HIV transmission, the continued number of new cases of perinatally acquired HIV infection among infants indicates an ongoing risk of perinatal transmission and underscores the need for strategies to ensure that HIV-infected females have access to and receive adequate prenatal care and timely HIV counseling and voluntary testing, gain access to HIV-related care and services, receive chemoprophylaxis to reduce perinatal transmission, and avoid breastfeeding. This objective will remain developmental until all States extend their surveillance systems to include HIV.

Related Objectives From Other Focus Areas

7. Educational and Community-Based Programs

7-2.   School health education

9. Family Planning

9-10.   Pregnancy prevention and sexually transmitted disease protection

14. Immunization and Infectious Diseases

14-11.   Tuberculosis

14-13.   Treatment for high-risk persons with latent tuberculosis infection

20. Occupational Safety and Health

20-10.   Needlestick injuries

25. Sexually Transmitted Diseases

25-8.   Heterosexually transmitted HIV infection in women

25-11.   Responsible adolescent sexual behavior

25-17.   Screening of pregnant women

Terminology

(A listing of all acronyms and abbreviations used in this publication appears Appendix K.)

AIDS: Acquired immunodeficiency syndrome, the most severe phase of infection with the human immunodeficiency virus (HIV). Persons infected with HIV are said to have AIDS when they get certain opportunistic infections or when their CD4+ cell count drops below 200.

CD4+ cell (also known as T helper cell): A type of T cell found in the blood that is involved in protecting the body against infections.

CD4+ cells normally orchestrate the immune response, signaling other cells in the immune system to perform their special disease-fighting functions.

CD4+ cell count: A measure of the number of CD4+ cells present in the blood. Because HIV infection kills CD4+ cells, CD4+ cell count is used to track the progress of HIV infection.

Cost-effective: Indicates that the cost of a particular intervention compares favorably to life-saving interventions associated with other diseases.

Cost-saving: Indicates that a particular intervention averts health care costs in excess of the cost of the intervention.

HIV (human immunodeficiency virus): A virus that infects and takes over certain cells of the immune system that are important in fighting disease.

HIV antiretrovirals: Drugs, such as zidovudine (AZT) and saquinavir, designed to attack HIV and prevent it from multiplying.

HAART (highly active antiretroviral therapy): Aggressive anti-HIV treatment usually including a combination of drugs called protease inhibitors and reverse transcriptase inhibitors whose purpose is to reduce viral load infection to undetectable levels.

***Mycobacterium avium* complex (MAC):** Bacteria that cause disease in individuals who have weakened immune systems and one of the opportunistic infections that define AIDS.

Opportunistic infections: Infections that take advantage of the opportunity offered when a person's immune system has been weakened by HIV infection. At least 25 medical conditions, including bacterial, fungal, and viral infections and certain types of cancer, are associated with HIV infection.

***Pneumocystis carinii* pneumonia (PCP):** A type of pneumonia that strikes indi-

viduals who have weakened immune systems.

Prevalence: A proportion of persons in a population who are infected, at a specified point in time or over a specified period of time, with HIV.

Prophylaxis: Measures designed to prevent the spread of disease and preserve health; protective or preventive treatment.

Prophylactic: Something that guards against or prevents disease.

Protease: An enzyme that triggers the breakdown of proteins in the body. HIV's protease enzyme breaks apart long strands of viral protein into the separate proteins constituting the viral core and the enzymes it contains. HIV protease acts as new virus particles are budding off a cell membrane.

Protease inhibitor: A drug that binds to and blocks HIV

protease from working, thus preventing the production of new functional viral particles.

Seronegative: Indicates that a person's blood lacks antibodies to a specific infectious agent, such as HIV.

Seropositive: Indicates that a person's blood contains antibodies to infections, such as HIV.

Serostatus: The result of a blood test for the antibodies that the immune system creates to fight specific diseases.

Universal infection control precautions: Guidelines and procedures to protect health care workers from exposure to infection from blood and other body fluids.

References

1. Centers for Disease Control and Prevention (CDC). Kaposi's sarcoma and pneumocystis pneumonia among homosexual men—New York City and California. *Morbidity and Mortality Weekly Report* 30(25):305-308, 1981.

2. CDC. Update on acquired immune deficiency syndrome (AIDS)—United States. *Morbidity and Mortality Weekly Report*, 31(37):507-514, 1982.

3. CDC. *HIV/AIDS Surveillance Report*, Year end 1998. Vol. 10, No. 2, 1999.

4. Karon, J.M.; Rosenberg, P.S.; McQuillan, G.; Khare, M.; Gwinn, M.; and Petersen, L.R. Prevalence of HIV infection in the United States, 1984-1992. *Journal of the*

American Medical Association 276(2):126-131, 1996.

5. CDC. Update: Trends in AIDS incidence, deaths, and prevention—United States, 1996. *Morbidity and Mortality Weekly Report* 46(8):165-173, 1997.

6. CDC. Current Trends Update: Acquired Immunodeficiency Syndrome (AIDS)—United States. *Morbidity and Mortality Weekly Report* 32(52):688-691, 1984.

7. CDC. CDC guidelines for national human immundeficiency virus case surveillance, including monitoring for human immunodeficiency virus infection and acquired immunodeficiency syndrome. *Morbidity and Mortality Weekly Report* 48(RR-13), 1999.

8. Holtgrave, D.R., and Pinkerton, S.D. Updates of Cost of Illness and Quality of Life Estimates for Use in Economic Evaluations of HIV Prevention Programs. *Journal of Acquired Immune Syndrome and Human Retrovirology* 16(1):54-62, 1997.

9. Sweeney, D.A.; Fleming, P.L.; Karon, J.M.; and Ward, J.W. A minimum estimate of the number of living HIV-infected persons confidentially tested in the United States. [Abstract 1-16] Presented at the Interscience Conference on Antimicrobial Agents and Chemotherapy in Toronto, Canada.

10. Hoyert, D.L.; Kochanek, K.D.; and Murphy, S.L. Births and deaths: final data for 1997. *National Vital Statistics Report*, 47(19). Hyattsville,

MD: National Center for Health Statistics, 1999.

11. CDC. Update: Trends in AIDS incidence—United States, 1996. *Morbidity and Mortality Weekly Report* 46(37):861-867, 1997.

12. CDC. *HIV/AIDS Surveillance Report. 2nd quarter 1993*, Vol. 5, No. 4, 1994.

13. CDC. *HIV/AIDS Surveillance Report Mid Year 1999.* Vol. 11, No. 1, 1999.

14. CDC. *HIV/AIDS Surveillance Report, Year End 1997.* Vol. 9, No. 2, 1997.

15. CDC. Update on acquired immune deficiency syndrome (AIDS) among patients with hemophilia A. *Morbidity and Mortality Weekly Report* 31(48):644-652, 1982.

16. CDC. Possible transfusion-associated acquired immune deficiency syndrome (AIDS)—California. *Morbidity and Mortality Weekly Report* 31(48):652-654, 1982.

17. CDC. Prevention of acquired immune deficiency syndrome (AIDS): Report of inter-agency recommendations. *Morbidity and Mortality Weekly Report* 32 (8):101-104, 1983.

18. CDC. Acquired immunodeficiency syndrome (AIDS): Precautions for health-care workers and allied professionals. *Morbidity and Mortality Weekly Report* 32(30):450-452, 1983.

19. CDC. Provisional public health service inter-agency recommendations for screening donated blood and plasma for antibody to the virus causing acquired immunodeficiency syndrome. *Morbidity and Mortality Weekly Report* 34(1):1-5, 1985.

20. CDC. Recommendations for preventing transmission of infection with human T-lymphotropic virus III/lymphadenopathy-

associated virus in the workplace. *Morbidity and Mortality Weekly Report* 34(45):681-686, 691-696, 1985.

21. CDC, Public Health Service Task Force. Recommendations for the use of antiretroviral drugs in pregnant women infected with HIV-1 for maternal health and for reducing perinatal HIV-1 transmission in the United States. *Morbidity and Mortality Weekly Report* 47(RR-2), 1998.

22. CDC. Update: Perinatally acquired HIV/AIDS—United States, 1997. *Morbidity and Mortality Weekly Report* 46(46):1086-1092, 1997.

23. CDC. Update: Barrier Protection Against HIV Infection and Other Sexually Transmitted Diseases. *Morbidity and Mortality Weekly Report* 42(30):589-591, 1993.

24. Institute of Medicine. The Effects of Needle Exchange Programs. In: Norman, J.; Vlahov, D.; Moses, L. (eds.). *Preventing HIV Transmission: The Role of Sterile Needles and Bleach*. Washington, DC: National Academy Press, 1995.

25. CDC. Prevention and treatment of tuberculosis among persons with human immunodeficiency virus: Principles of therapy and revised recommendations. *Morbidity and Mortality Weekly Report* 47(RR-20), 1998.

26. Kamb, M.L.; Fishbein, M.; Douglas, Jr., J.M.; Rhodes, F.; Rogers, J.; Bolan, G.; Zenilman, J.; Hoxworth, T.; Malotte, C.K.; Iatesta, M.; Kent, C.; Lentz, A.; Graziano, S.; Byers, R.H.; and Peterman,T.A. Efficacy of risk-reduction counseling to prevent human immunodeficiency virus and sexually transmitted diseases: a randomized controlled trial. Project RESPECT Study Group. *Journal of the Ameri-

can Medical Association* 280(13):1161-1167, 1998.

27. CDC. HIV prevention through early detection and treatment of other sexually transmitted diseases. United States: Recommendations of the advisory committee for HIV and STD prevention. *Morbidity and Mortality Weekly Report* 47(RR-12):175-219, 1998.

28. Wasserheit, J. Epidemiological Synergy. Interrelationships between human immunodeficiency virus infection and other sexually transmitted diseases. *Sexually Transmitted Diseases* 19(2):61-77, 1992.

29. Joint United Nations Programme on HIV/AIDS. *The UNAIDS Report.*, 1999.

30. Fleming, D.T., and Wasserheit, J.N. From epidemiological synergy to public health policy and practice: the contribution of other sexually transmitted diseases to sexual transmission of HIV infection. *Sexually Transmitted Infections* 75(1):3-17, 1999.

31. Institute of Medicine. Current STD Related Services. In: *The Hidden Epidemic: Confronting Sexually Transmitted Diseases*. Washington, DC: National Academy Press, 175-219, 1997.

14

Immunization and Infectious Diseases

Lead Agency: Centers for Disease Control and Prevention

Contents

Goal

Prevent disease, disability, and death from infectious diseases, including vaccine-preventable diseases.

Overview

Infectious diseases remain major causes of illness, disability, and death. Moreover, new infectious agents and diseases are being detected, and some diseases considered under control have reemerged in recent years. In addition, antimicrobial resistance is evolving rapidly in a variety of hospital- and community-acquired infections. These trends suggest that many challenges still exist in the prevention and control of infectious diseases.

Issues

Between 1980 and 1992, the number of deaths from infectious diseases rose 58 percent in the United States. Even when human immunodeficiency virus (HIV)-associated diagnoses are removed, deaths from infectious diseases still increased 22 percent during this period. (See Focus Area 13. HIV.) Considered as a group, three infectious diseases—pneumonia, influenza, and HIV infection—constituted the fifth leading cause of death in the United States in 1997.

The direct and indirect costs of infectious diseases are significant. Every hospital-acquired infection adds an average of $2,100 to a hospital bill. Bloodstream infections result in an average of $3,517 in additional hospital charges per infected patient because the patient stay averages an additional 7 days. A typical case of Lyme disease diagnosed in the early stages incurs about $174 in direct medical treatment costs. Delayed diagnosis and treatment, however, can result in complications that cost from $2,228 to $6,724 per patient in direct medical costs in the first year alone.[1]

Infectious diseases also must be considered in a global context. Increases in international travel, importation of foods, inappropriate use of antibiotics on humans and animals, and environmental changes multiply the potential for worldwide epidemics of all types of infectious diseases. International cooperation and collaboration on disease surveillance, response, research, and training are essential to prevent or control these epidemics. Actions taken to improve health in one country affect the health of people worldwide.

Vaccines. Vaccines are biological substances that interact with the person's immune system to produce an immune response identical to that produced by the natural infection.

Vaccines can prevent the debilitating and, in some cases, fatal effects of infectious diseases. Vaccines help to eliminate the illness and disability of polio,[2] measles, and rubella.[3] However, the organisms that cause these diseases have not disappeared. Rather, they have receded and will reemerge if the vaccination coverage drops. The serious health burden of vaccine-preventable diseases (VPDs) is evident from the measles resurgence of 1989 to 1991, resulting in more than 55,000 cases, 11,000 hospitalizations, 120 deaths, and $100 million in direct medical care costs.[4, 5, 6, 7]

Vaccines protect more than the vaccinated individual. They also protect society. When vaccination levels in a community are high, the few who cannot be vaccinated—such as young children and persons with contraindications to vaccination—often are indirectly protected because of group immunity (in other words, they live among vaccinated persons who may offer protection from exposure to disease).

Vaccines provide significant cost benefits. Three childhood vaccines—diphtheria, tetanus toxoids, and acellular pertussis vaccine (DTaP); measles, mumps, and rubella vaccine (MMR); and *Haemophilus influenzae* type b (Hib) vaccine—result in substantial direct medical savings for each dollar spent to vaccinate children against these diseases. Varicella vaccine saves roughly 90 cents in direct medical costs for every dollar invested. Consideration of indirect savings—prevention of work loss by parents to care for ill children, prevention of death and therefore lost earnings from disability—shows that vaccines routinely recommended for children are highly cost saving. Savings range from $24 for every dollar spent on DTaP to $2 for the more recently approved Hib vaccine.[8]

Trends

Significant progress has been made in reducing indigenous (not imported) cases of VPDs. The occurrence of many VPDs is at or near record-low levels. Most diseases have been reduced by more than 95 percent from peak prevaccine levels.[9]

In 1998, overall vaccination coverage for children aged 19 to 35 months was at record-high levels.[10] Antigen-specific rates have shown striking progress since 1992.[11] For example, coverage for three or more doses of polio vaccine increased from 72 percent to 91 percent, and coverage for three or more doses of Hib vaccine increased from 28 percent to 93 percent. Significant achievements also were made among racial and ethnic groups in that most of the 1996 goals for the Childhood Immunization Initiative were met for individual vaccines.[12] Since 1989, vaccination requirements have been expanded for schools and day care settings.[11] As of the 1998-99 school year, all States required vaccination against diphtheria, measles, and polio. Similarly, all States and the District of Columbia now require vaccination for day care.[13]

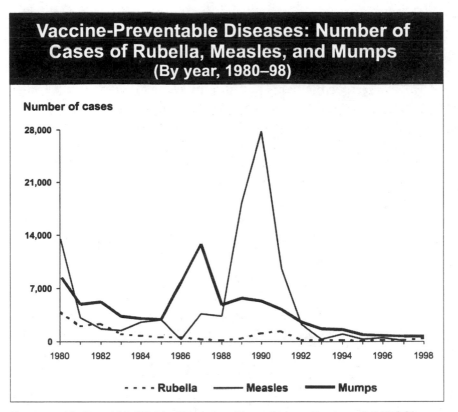

Vaccine-Preventable Diseases: Number of Cases of Rubella, Measles, and Mumps (By year, 1980–98)

Number of cases

- - - - Rubella   ——— Measles   ▬▬▬ Mumps

Source: National Notifiable Diseases Surveillance System (NNDSS), CDC, EPO, 1980–98.

In 1996, a vaccine against hepatitis A virus (HAV) was licensed that has the potential to reduce the health burden of this disease as well. The vaccine is now recommended primarily for high-risk groups. To decrease hepatitis A virus transmission, universal vaccination was recommended in 1999 for children who lived in States where the rate of new cases was greater than two times the national average.[14]

Financing for childhood vaccinations has improved significantly as a result of two initiatives—Vaccines for Children and the Children's Health Insurance Program that cover children on Medicaid, uninsured children, and Native American and Alaskan Native children. Underinsured children who receive vaccinations at Federal and rural health clinics also are covered. Because they promote free vaccines for children, these programs eliminate vaccine cost as a barrier to childhood vaccination. Also, the Public Health Service Act, Section 317 immunization grant program and State funds provide free vaccines for children not covered by other programs.

Adult vaccination rates continued to increase over the decade. Influenza vaccine coverage rates were up from 33 percent in 1989 to 63 percent in 1997, and pneumococcal vaccine coverage rates were up from 15 percent to 43 percent. Despite these increases, coverage rates for certain racial and ethnic groups remain substantially below the general population.[15]

Invasive diseases invade the bloodstream and cause distant infection. The most common types of invasive disease caused by *Haemophilyus influenzae* type b (Hib) are meningitis, epiglottitis, pneumonia, certain types of arthritis, and cellulitis. Conjugate vaccines—licensed in 1990 for use beginning at age 2 months—are highly effective in protecting against Hib meningitis and other invasive diseases caused by Hib. These vaccines also interrupt spread of the disease-causing organism by affecting the organism's nasopharyngeal colonization. New cases of Hib meningitis declined by 96 percent from 1987 to 1995.[16] During that period, bacterial meningitis caused by one of the five leading agents (*Haemophilus influenzae*, *Streptococcus pneumoniae*, *Neisseria meningitidis*, group B *Streptococcus* [GBS], and *Listeria monocytogenes*) fell by 55 percent. Bacterial meningitis was traditionally a disease of childhood, infecting children with a median age of 15 months in 1986.[17] Following the dramatic reduction in Hib meningitis, which primarily occurs among children under age 2 years, the median age of persons with the disease shifted to 25 years in 1995.[17] The success of conjugate vaccines against Hib disease has stimulated efforts to develop conjugate vaccines for other pathogens, including *Streptococcus pneumoniae*, *Neisseria meningitidis*, and GBS. Conjugate vaccines against these three agents are being tested in clinical trials. The success of bacterial meningitis vaccines suggests comparable results may be achieved for other causes of meningitis, sepsis, and pneumonia as their conjugate vaccines become used more routinely in target populations.

Disparities

The updated *Preventing Emerging Infectious Diseases: A Strategy for the 21st Century* focuses on certain emerging infectious disease issues and on particular groups of people at risk.[18] Historically, childhood vaccination rates have been lower in certain racial and ethnic populations, compared to the white population. Vaccination rates for preschool children in racial and ethnic groups with lower vaccination rates, however, have been increasing at a more rapid rate, significantly narrowing the gap.

Efforts need to be intensified, particularly to increase vaccination coverage for children living in poverty. Substantial numbers of undervaccinated children remain in some areas, particularly the large urban areas with traditionally underserved populations, creating great concern because of the potential for outbreaks of disease.

In addition to very young children, many adults are at increased risk for VPDs. Vaccination against pneumococcal infections and influenza among persons aged 65 years and over has increased slightly for African Americans and Hispanics. The coverage in these groups, however, remains substantially below the general population. For example, influenza vaccination rates for whites were 66 percent in

Data as of November 30, 1999

1997, while for African Americans and Hispanics, rates were only 45 and 53 percent, respectively. In September 1997, the Department of Health and Human Services approved a plan to improve adult vaccination rates and reduce disparities among racial and ethnic groups.[19] The elimination of disparities, however, may require further interventions in particular geographic, cultural, or racial and ethnic populations.

Opportunities

A coordinated strategy is necessary to understand, detect, control, and prevent infectious diseases. Such a strategy will protect the gains achieved in life expectancy in the 20th century resulting from control and prevention of infectious diseases and ensure further improvements in the 21st century.

Priority issues include antimicrobial resistance, foodborne and waterborne diseases, vector-borne and zoonotic diseases, diseases transmitted through transfusion of blood or blood products, and vaccine development and use. Some of these diseases and pathogens were unknown 20 years ago. Others are reemergent problems once thought under control. At-risk populations include persons with impaired host defenses; pregnant women and newborns; travelers, immigrants, and refugees; older adults; or other persons identified by the Advisory Committee on Immunization Practices (ACIP).

The major strategies to protect people from VPDs are the following:[20]

- Improving the quality and quantity of vaccination delivery services.

- Minimizing financial burdens for needy persons.

- Increasing community participation, education, and partnership.

- Improving monitoring of disease and vaccination coverage.

- Developing new or improved vaccines and improving vaccine use.

These strategies include a broad range of interventions for children, such as entry requirements for school and promoting the Vaccines for Children and Children's Health Insurance Program, in which eligible children are vaccinated in their medical home. Assessment of vaccination coverage of persons served at individual clinics and provider offices with feedback of the results to the individual providers to guide them in improving performance also is important. The exchange of information on coverage assessment among colleagues stimulates a friendly competition to achieve better vaccination levels.[21] Populations at risk of undervaccination can be reached through linkages with other programs, including Women, Infants, and Children (WIC) services.[22] State and local registries that enroll children and record their vaccinations are valuable tools for helping parents and providers to identify immunization needs of individual children, assessing coverage in individual practices, and generating communitywide estimates.[23]

In the United States, most VPDs occur among adults. Pneumococcal disease and influenza account for more than 30,000 deaths annually, most of which occur in elderly persons. Studies have consistently shown that focusing efforts to improve coverage on health care providers, as well as health care systems, is the most effective means of raising vaccine coverage in adults. For example, all health care providers should assess routinely the vaccination status of their patients. Likewise, health plans should develop mechanisms for assessing the vaccination status of their participants. Also, nursing home facilities and hospitals should ensure that policies exist to promote vaccination.

Since no vaccine is completely safe, vaccine safety research and monitoring are necessary to identify and minimize vaccine-related injuries. As programs continue to reduce the new cases of VPDs, concerns about vaccine adverse events have emerged, posing a threat to public acceptance of vaccines. Knowing the safety profile of vaccines is essential to assess accurately the risks and benefits, to formulate appropriate vaccine recommendations, and to address public concerns.

Interim Progress Toward Year 2000 Objectives

Significant progress has been made in reaching the Healthy People 2000 objectives. Reductions in indigenous cases of VPDs have been dramatic. For example, measles was reduced from a 1988 baseline of 3,396 indigenous cases to a total of only 100 in 1998. Substantial progress also has been made in reducing hepatitis B virus (HBV) transmission. The vaccine against hepatitis A provides the opportunity to reduce the burden of this disease. Achieving the year 2000 objective to reduce new cases of bacterial meningitis was entirely due to the introduction of Hib conjugate vaccines for infants.[24] In 1998, individual coverage levels for children aged 19 to 35 months were at record high levels. For example, individual coverage levels for three or more doses of polio, three or more doses of diphtheria/tetanus/acellular pertussis, one or more doses of measles/mumps/rubella, and three or more does of Hib vaccines were each at or above 91 percent. Progress has also been made in expanding immunization requirements for schools and day care settings. Data for viral hepatitis indicate that targets for hepatitis B and C were met in the early 1990s.

Note: Unless otherwise noted, data are from Centers for Disease Control and Prevention, National Center for Health Statistics, *Healthy People 2000 Review, 1998-99.*

Immunization and Infectious Diseases

Goal: Prevent disease, disability, and death from infectious diseases, including vaccine-preventable diseases.

Number   **Objective**

Diseases Preventable Through Universal Vaccination

14-1	Vaccine-preventable diseases
14-2	Hepatitis B in infants and young children
14-3	Hepatitis B in adults and high-risk groups
14-4	Bacterial meningitis in young children
14-5	Invasive pneumococcal infections

Diseases Preventable Through Targeted Vaccination

14-6	Hepatitis A
14-7	Meningococcal disease
14-8	Lyme disease

Infectious Diseases and Emerging Antimicrobial Resistance

14-9	Hepatitis C
14-10	Identification of persons with chronic hepatitis C
14-11	Tuberculosis
14-12	Curative therapy for tuberculosis
14-13	Treatment for high-risk persons with latent tuberculosis infection
14-14	Timely laboratory confirmation of tuberculosis cases
14-15	Prevention services for international travelers
14-16	Invasive early-onset group B streptococcal disease
14-17	Peptic ulcer hospitalizations
14-18	Antibiotics prescribed for ear infections
14-19	Antibiotics prescribed for colds
14-20	Hospital-acquired infections
14-21	Antimicrobial use in intensive care units

Vaccination Coverage and Strategies

Vaccine Safety

Diseases Preventable Through Universal Vaccination

14-1. Reduce or eliminate indigenous cases of vaccine-preventable disease.

Target and baseline:

Objective	Reduction in Vaccine-Preventable Diseases	1998 Baseline	2010 Target
		Number of Cases	
14-1a.	Congenital rubella syndrome	7	0
14-1b.	Diphtheria (persons under age 35 years)	1	0
14-1c.	*Haemophilus influenzae* type b* (children under age 5 years)	253	0
14-1d.	Hepatitis B (persons aged 2 to 18 years)	945[†]	9
14-1e.	Measles	74	0
14-1f.	Mumps	666	0
14-1g.	Pertussis (children under age 7 years)	3,417	2,000
14-1h.	Polio (wild-type virus)	0	0
14-1i.	Rubella	364	0
14-1j.	Tetanus (persons under age 35 years)	14	0
14-1k.	Varicella (chicken pox)	4 million[‡]	400,000

*Includes cases with type b and unknown serotype.
†Estimated hepatitis B cases for 1997.[25]
‡Data based on average from 1990-94.

Target setting method: Total elimination for congenital rubella syndrome, diphtheria, *Haemophilus influenzae* type b, measles, mumps, polio, rubella, and tetanus; 41 percent improvement for pertussis; 99 percent improvement for hepatitis B; and 99 percent improvement for varicella.

Data sources: National Notifiable Disease Surveillance System (NNDSS), CDC, EPO; National Congenital Rubella Syndrome Registry (NCRSR), CDC, NIP—congenital rubella syndrome; National Health Interview Survey (NHIS), CDC, NCHS—varicella.

Highly effective vaccines are used routinely in childhood for prevention of measles, mumps, rubella, varicella, diphtheria, tetanus, pertussis, polio, hepatitis B, and Hib invasive disease.[26] Vaccinations for these diseases have reduced reported cases of most VPDs common in childhood to record-low levels.[10, 25, 27] Measles transmission probably was interrupted multiple times in the United States since 1993.[28, 29, 30] With a high level of coverage of two doses of measles, mumps, and rubella vaccine, interruption of the spread of both rubella and mumps is feasible.[31, 32] Recent outbreaks of rubella and a number of cases of congenital rubella syndrome, however, highlight the importance of ensuring rubella immunity particularly in women of child-bearing age and foreign-born adults.[33] Polio has been eliminated in the United States due to high vaccination coverage. Although polio is expected to be eradicated globally, surveillance for cases of the disease will continue. Because of widespread vaccination, reported cases of diphtheria are near zero.[34, 35] Tetanus toxoid is highly effective, but with the absence of group immunity, all persons must be vaccinated to achieve the goal of zero cases.[36] Pertussis among children will be reduced by increasing vaccination coverage, but the disease will continue to occur because the organism circulates among older age groups, and the vaccine is not 100 percent effective.[37, 38]

Hepatitis B virus (HBV) infection will be reduced greatly as the age groups covered by universal infant and adolescent vaccination efforts enter young adulthood, a period when the risk of HBV infection increases.

Conjugate vaccines for prevention of *Haemophilus influenzae* type b are highly effective and have led to near elimination of invasive Hib disease.[16, 39] Further reductions in new cases are anticipated as Hib vaccine coverage increases.

The licensure of new vaccines against common diseases that are not reportable diseases, such as varicella, has created new challenges for surveillance and evaluation. Without national reporting, documenting the impact of national and State vaccination programs and measuring progress for reducing indigenous cases of disease are difficult.[40] However, with an increase in vaccination coverage and a decline in the number of new cases, varicella is expected to become a reportable condition.

14-2.   Reduce chronic hepatitis B virus infections in infants and young children (perinatal infections).

Target: 400 infections.

Baseline: 1,682 chronic hepatitis B virus infections in children under age 2 years in 1995.

Target setting method: 76 percent improvement.

Data source: Perinatal Hepatitis B Prevention Program, CDC, NCID.

Each year, 16,000 to 18,000 children in the United States are born to mothers infected with HBV.[41] Without prevention programs, about 8,000 of these infants would become infected with HBV. Ninety-five percent of the infections, however, are preventable through appropriate maternal screening and infant care.[42]

Screening pregnant women during an early prenatal visit is essential to identify those who are infected. Women at high risk should be retested late in pregnancy. In 1997, 14 States had laws or regulations to ensure such screening.

To be maximally effective, steps to prevent transmission of HBV to infants born to mothers who are infected must begin as soon as the child is born. Such infants should receive a first dose of hepatitis B vaccine within 12 hours of birth, along with hepatitis B immune globulin (HBIG), and two more doses of vaccine by age 6 months. Children need to be tested between the ages of 12 and 15 months to ensure that they are not infected and have developed immunity to the virus.

14-3.   Reduce hepatitis B.

Target and baseline:

Objective	Reduction in Hepatitis B	1997 Baseline	2010 Target
		Rate per 100,000	
	Adults		
14-3a.	19 to 24 years	24.0	2.4
14-3b.	25 to 39 years	20.2	5.1
14-3c.	40 years and older	15.0	3.8
	High-risk groups	Number of Cases	
14-3d.	Injection drug users	7,232	1,808
14-3e.	Heterosexually active persons	15,225	1,240
14-3f.	Men who have sex with men	7,232	1,808
14-3g.	Occupationally exposed workers	249	62

Target setting method: Better than the best for 14-3a, 14-3b, and 14-3c; 75 percent improvement for 14-3d, 14-3f, and 14-3g; 92 percent improvement for 14-3e.

Data sources: National Notifiable Disease Surveillance System (NNDSS), CDC, EPO; Sentinel Counties Study of Viral Hepatitis, CDC, NCID.

Select Age Groups, 1997	Hepatitis B Cases		
	14-3a. Aged 19 to 24 Years	14-3b. Aged 25 to 39 Years	14-3c. Aged 40 Years and Older
	Rate per 100,000		
TOTAL	24.0	20.2	15.0
Race and ethnicity			
American Indian or Alaska Native	16.0	20.1	10.9
Asian or Pacific Islander	42.2	30.4	33.2
Asian	DNC	DNC	DNC
Native Hawaiian and other Pacific Islander	DNC	DNC	DNC
Black or African American	48.3	32.5	27.6
White	10.4	10.2	7.4
Hispanic or Latino	16.9	16.0	18.1
Not Hispanic or Latino	25.2	20.7	14.8
Black or African American	50.6	34.1	28.4
White	10.3	10.2	7.1
Gender			
Female	24.1	15.4	9.4
Male	22.5	24.1	20.8
Family income level			
Poor	DNC	DNC	DNC
Near poor	DNC	DNC	DNC
Middle/high income	DNC	DNC	DNC

DNA = Data have not been analyzed. DNC = Data are not collected. DSU = Data are statistically unreliable.

To reduce HBV transmission in the United States by 2010, vaccination programs must be targeted to adolescents and adults in high-risk groups. The primary means of achieving high levels of vaccination coverage in groups with behavioral risk factors for HBV infection is to identify settings where these individuals can be vaccinated. Such sites include clinics that treat sexually transmitted diseases, correctional facilities (juvenile detention facilities, prisons, jails), drug treatment clinics, and community-based HIV prevention sites. The primary means of achieving high levels of vaccine coverage among household and sex contacts of the estimated 1.25 million persons in the United States with chronic HBV infection are programs that offer followup for all HbsAg-positive persons reported to State and local health departments.

Routine infant vaccination eventually will produce a highly immune population sufficient to eliminate HBV transmission in the United States. However, high rates of acute hepatitis B continue to occur, with an estimated 65,000 cases in 1996. Most cases occur in young adult risk groups, including persons with a history of multiple sex partners, men who have sex with men, injection drug users, incarcerated persons, and household and sex contacts of persons with HBV infection. Investigation of reported cases of acute hepatitis B indicates that as many as 70 percent of these individuals previously had been seen in settings such as drug treatment clinics, correctional facilities, or clinics for the treatment of STD where they could have received vaccine.

14-4.   Reduce bacterial meningitis in young children.

Target: 8.6 new cases per 100,000 children aged 1 through 23 months.

Baseline: 13.0 new cases of bacterial meningitis per 100,000 children aged 1 through 23 months in 1998.

Target setting method: 34 percent improvement. (Better than the best will be used when data are available.)

Data source: Active Bacterial Core Surveillance (ABCs), CDC, NCID.

Children Aged 1 Through 23 Months, 1998	New Cases of Bacterial Meningitis Rate per 100,000
TOTAL	13.0
Race and ethnicity	
American Indian or Alaska Native	DSU
Asian or Pacific Islander	DSU
Asian	DNC
Native Hawaiian and other Pacific Islander	DNC
Black or African American	25.9
White	11.0

Children Aged 1 Through 23 Months, 1998	New Cases of Bacterial Meningitis Rate per 100,000
Hispanic or Latino	DSU
Not Hispanic or Latino	DSU
Black or African American	DSU
White	DSU
Gender	
Female	13.0
Male	13.1
Family income level	
Poor	DNC
Near poor	DNC
Middle/high income	DNC

DNA = Data have not been analyzed. DNC = Data are not collected. DSU = Data are statistically unreliable.

Children aged 1 month to 2 years have higher rates of meningitis than older children. New vaccines for pneumococcal disease, including pneumococcal meningitis, may help protect young children. Meningococcal conjugate vaccines are in clinical trials and may become available for widespread use before 2010, although it is not yet known whether they will target young children. Pneumococcal conjugate vaccines, modeled after the successful construction of Hib conjugate vaccines, are also in clinical trials. Before 2010, licensure and widespread use of these new products are expected.

14-5. Reduce invasive pneumococcal infections.

Target and baseline:

Objective	Reduction in Invasive Pneumococcal Infections	1997 Baseline	2010 Target
		Rate per 100,000	
	New invasive pneumococcal infections		
14-5a.	Children under age 5 years	76	46
14-5b.	Adults aged 65 years and older	62	42
	Invasive penicillin-resistant pneumococcal infections		
14-5c.	Children under age 5 years	16	6
14-5d.	Adults aged 65 years and older	9	7

Target setting method: Better than the best.

Data source: Active Bacterial Core Surveillance (ABCs), CDC, NCID; Arctic Investigations Program (for data on pneumococcal disease rates among Alaska Natives), CDC.

Select Age Groups, 1997	New Cases of Invasive Pneumococcal Infections		New Cases of Invasive Penicillin-Resistant Pneumococcal Infections	
	14-5a. Under Age 5 Years	14-5b. Aged 65 Years and Older	14-5c. Under Age 5 Years	14-5d. Aged 65 Years and Older
	Rate per 100,000			
TOTAL	76	62	16	9
Race and ethnicity				
American Indian or Alaska Native	DSU	DSU	DSU	DSU
Asian or Pacific Islander	58	DSU	DSU	DSU
Asian	DSU	DSU	DSU	DSU
Native Hawaiian and other Pacific Islander	DSU	DSU	DSU	DSU
Black or African American	154	83	20	9
White	63	61	17	9
Hispanic or Latino	59	43	7	DSU
Not Hispanic or Latino	DSU	DSU	DSU	DSU
Black or African American	DSU	DSU	DSU	DSU
White	DNC	DNC	DNC	DNC
Gender				
Female	69	61	14	9
Male	84	62	17	9
Family income level				
Poor	DNC	DNC	DNC	DNC
Near poor	DNC	DNC	DNC	DNC
Middle/high income	DNC	DNC	DNC	DNC

DNA = Data have not been analyzed. DNC = Data are not collected. DSU = Data are statistically unreliable.

The number of invasive penicillin-resistant pneumococcal infections can be reduced by lowering the proportion of invasive pneumococcal infections due to drug-resistant strains or by decreasing invasive pneumococcal infections in general. The objectives for specific age groups address the key age groups at risk for invasive pneumococcal infections. Among children under age 5 years, promoting judicious antibiotic use may reverse the current trends toward increasing proportions of infections being caused by drug-resistant strains. For adults aged 65 years and older, licensure and widespread use of pneumococcal conjugate vaccines by 2010 could reduce dramatically all invasive pneumococcal infections, and judicious antibiotic use may have some impact on the proportion of pneumococcal infections caused by drug-resistant strains. In this age group, a much greater impact potentially is achievable through improved use of licensed 23-valent pneumococcal polysaccharide vaccine for the prevention of invasive pneumococcal disease. Increasing the use of this vaccine for elderly persons could have a beneficial impact on the rate of drug-resistant invasive pneumococcal infections.

Diseases Preventable Through Targeted Vaccination

14-6.   Reduce hepatitis A.

Target: 4.5 new cases per 100,000 population.

Baseline: 11.3 new cases of hepatitis A per 100,000 population in 1997.

Target setting method: Better than the best.

Data source: National Notifiable Disease Surveillance System (NNDSS), CDC, EPO.

Total Population, 1997	New Hepatitis A Cases Rate per 100,000
TOTAL	11.3
Race and ethnicity	
American Indian or Alaska Native	23.1
Asian or Pacific Islander	4.6
Asian	DNC
Native Hawaiian and other Pacific Islander	DNC
Black or African American	6.0
White	8.1

Total Population, 1997	New Hepatitis A Cases Rate per 100,000
Hispanic or Latino	24.2
Not Hispanic or Latino	9.8
Black or African American	6.3
White	7.3
Gender	
Female	8.1
Male	12.8
Family income level	
Poor	DNC
Near poor	DNC
Middle/high income	DNC

DNA = Data have not been analyzed. DNC = Data are not collected. DSU = Data are statistically unreliable.

The health status objectives for HAV will not be achieved until a vaccination strategy is implemented that produces high levels of immunity in children. Children have the highest rates of hepatitis A and are a primary source for new infections in the community. In 1999, the Advisory Committee on Immunization Practices (ACIP) recommended routine hepatitis A vaccination for children living in States with consistently elevated rates of hepatitis A as the approach most likely to prevent and control transmission of HAV.[14] Hepatitis A vaccine is included in the Vaccines for Children Program. Incorporation of hepatitis A vaccine into the routine childhood vaccination schedule would facilitate implementation of these recommendations, but data are needed to determine the appropriate dose and timing of vaccination in the first or second year of life. Implementation of the recommendations also would be enhanced by the development of vaccines that combine HAV antigen with other antigens.

Although routine immunization of children is the approach most likely to decrease significantly the overall rates of hepatitis A in a community, it may take some time before the impact of implementing these programs is measurable. In the interim, persons in groups at high risk of HAV infection should be vaccinated routinely. These groups include:

- Illicit drug users.

- Men who have sex with men.

- Persons traveling to HAV-endemic countries (see objective 14-15).

- Persons with occupational risk of infection—that is, persons who work with HAV-infected primates or with HAV in a research laboratory. No other occupational groups have been shown to be at increased risk of exposure.

- Persons with chronic liver disease.

14-7. Reduce meningococcal disease.

Target: 1.0 new cases per 100,000 population.

Baseline: 1.3 new cases of meningococcal disease per 100,000 population in 1997.

Target setting method: Better than the best.

Data sources: Active Bacterial Core Surveillance (ABCs), Emerging Infection Program, CDC, NCID; National Notifiable Diseases Surveillance System (NNDSS), CDC, EPO.

Total Population, 1997	New Cases of Meningococcal Disease
	Rate per 100,000
TOTAL	1.3
Race and ethnicity	
American Indian or Alaska Native	DSU
Asian or Pacific Islander	DSU
Asian	DNC
Native Hawaiian and other Pacific Islander	DNC
Black or African American	1.9
White	1.2
Hispanic or Latino	DSU
Not Hispanic or Latino	DNC
Black or African American	DNC
White	DNC
Gender	
Female	1.2
Male	1.3

Total Population, 1997	New Cases of Meningococcal Disease
	Rate per 100,000
Family income level	
Poor	DNC
Near poor	DNC
Middle/high income	DNC

DNA = Data have not been analyzed. DNC = Data are not collected. DSU = Data are statistically unreliable.

The polysaccharide meningococcal vaccine currently available in the United States is recommended for certain high-risk groups (people with asplenia), for laboratory personnel routinely exposed to *Neisseria meningitidis*, and for travelers to regions where meningococcal disease is hyperendemic or epidemic (the African "meningitis belt"). Routine vaccination of civilians is not recommended because of its relative ineffectiveness in children under age 2 years (among whom risk of endemic disease is highest) and its relatively short duration of protection. The vaccine is useful for controlling serogroup C meningococcal epidemics; these account, however, for less than 5 percent of the cases of meningococcal disease that occur each year in the United States. The vaccine provides no protection against serogroup B meningococci, which account for approximately one-third of the disease overall in the United States.

New meningococcal conjugate vaccines against serogroups C and Y, which account for two-thirds of current disease, are now undergoing clinical trials. Soon they should be available for incorporation into routine childhood immunization as well as for vaccination of high-risk groups, possibly including college students. Similar to Hib conjugate vaccines, new meningococcal conjugate vaccines are expected to be effective in children.

Development and licensing of new serogroup B meningococcal vaccines will also help reduce meningococcal disease.

14-8.   Reduce Lyme disease.

Target: 9.7 new cases per 100,000 population in endemic States.

Baseline: 17.4 new cases of Lyme disease per 100,000 population in 1992-96 (in endemic States of Connecticut, Delaware, Maryland, Massachusetts, Minnesota, New Jersey, New York, Pennsylvania, Rhode Island, and Wisconsin).

Target setting method: 44 percent improvement. (Better than the best will be used when data are available.)

Data source: National Notifiable Disease Surveillance System (NNDSS), CDC, EPO.

Total Population, 1992-96	New Cases of Lyme Disease Rate per 100,000
TOTAL	17.4
Race and ethnicity	
American Indian or Alaska Native	DSU
Asian or Pacific Islander	DSU
Asian	DNC
Native Hawaiian and other Pacific Islander	DSU
Black or African American	DSU
White	DSU
Hispanic or Latino	DSU
Not Hispanic or Latino	DSU
Black or African American	DSU
White	DSU
Gender	
Female	DNA
Male	DNA
Family income level	
Poor	DNC
Near poor	DNC
Middle/high income	DNC

DNA = Data have not been analyzed. DNC = Data are not collected. DSU = Data are statistically unreliable.

In 1991 a standardized case definition for Lyme disease was adopted by the Council of State and Territorial Epidemiologists. Since then, the number of reported cases of Lyme disease has increased from 8,257 in 1993 to 16,455 in 1996 because of increased surveillance as well as a true increase in new cases. From 1992 through 1996, 92 percent of cases were reported from 10 endemic States. New initiatives to prevent Lyme disease include the implementation of community-based prevention programs, host-targeted acaricides to reduce the numbers of vector ticks, and appropriate use of Lyme disease vaccine.

Infectious Diseases and Emerging Antimicrobial Resistance

14-9. Reduce hepatitis C.

Target: 1 new case per 100,000 population.

Baseline: 2.4 new cases of hepatitis C per 100,000 population in selected counties in 1996.

Target setting method: Better than the best.

Data source: Sentinel Counties Study of Viral Hepatitis, CDC, NCID.

Total Population, 1996	New Hepatitis C Cases Rate per 100,000
TOTAL	2.4
Race and ethnicity	
American Indian or Alaska Native	DNC
Asian or Pacific Islander	DSU
Asian	DNC
Native Hawaiian and other Pacific Islander	DNC
Black or African American	DSU
White	3.0
Hispanic or Latino	DSU
Not Hispanic or Latino	DSU
Black or African American	DSU
White	DSU
Gender	
Female	2.0
Male	2.8

Total Population, 1996	New Hepatitis C Cases
	Rate per 100,000
Family income level	
Poor	DNC
Near poor	DNC
Middle/high income	DNC

DNA = Data have not been analyzed. DNC = Data are not collected. DSU = Data are statistically unreliable.

Note: Data represent rates based on estimates from selected counties.

Hepatitis C virus (HCV) is the most common chronic bloodborne viral infection in the United States.[43] This virus is usually transmitted through large or repeated percutaneous exposures to blood—for example, through sharing of equipment between injection drug users. HCV infects persons of all ages, but most new cases are among young adults aged 20 to 39 years. The highest proportion of new cases is among whites, but the highest rates of new cases are among nonwhite racial and ethnic groups.

14-10. (Developmental) Increase the proportion of persons with chronic hepatitis C infection identified by State and local health departments.

Potential data sources: State health department databases of persons with HCV infection; National Health and Nutrition Examination Survey (NHANES), CDC, NCHS.

An estimated 4 million persons in the United States are infected chronically with HCV. Although the annual number of newly acquired HCV infections has declined from an estimated 180,000 in the mid-1980s to an estimated 28,000 in 1995, this reservoir of chronically infected persons can transmit the virus to others, and all of them are at risk for the severe consequences of chronic liver disease. Because of the large number of people with chronic HCV infection, identification of these persons must be a major focus of a comprehensive prevention strategy. Identification of HCV-infected persons allows (1) counseling to prevent further HCV transmission, (2) vaccination against HAV and HBV to prevent additional liver damage, (3) evaluation for chronic liver disease, (4) possible antiviral therapy, and (5) counseling to avoid potential hepatotoxins, such as alcohol, that may increase the severity of HCV-related liver disease.

14-11. Reduce tuberculosis.

Target: 1.0 new case per 100,000 population.

Baseline: 6.8 new cases of tuberculosis per 100,000 population in 1998.

Target setting method: Better than the best.

Data source: National TB Surveillance System, CDC, NCHSTP.

Total Population, 1998	New Tuberculosis Cases Rate per 100,000
TOTAL	6.8
Race and ethnicity	
American Indian or Alaska Native	11.2
Asian or Pacific Islander	34.9
Asian	DNC
Native Hawaiian and other Pacific Islander	DNC
Black or African American	17.4
White	3.8
Hispanic or Latino	13.6
Not Hispanic or Latino	5.9
Black or African American	17.8
White	2.3
Gender	
Female	5.0
Male	8.6
Family income level	
Poor	DNC
Near poor	DNC
Middle/high income	DNC

DNA = Data have not been analyzed. DNC = Data are not collected. DSU = Data are statistically unreliable.

The 1989 *Strategic Plan for the Elimination of TB in the United States*[44] set a tuberculosis elimination goal of reducing TB to 1 per million by 2010, with an interim goal of 3.5 cases per 100,000 population by 2000. However, in the mid-1980s the trend toward TB elimination was reversed, and drug-resistant strains emerged that were even more deadly. TB cases increased by 20 percent between 1985 and 1992. Renewed efforts to combat the resurgence included improving laboratories, strengthening surveillance and expanding directly observed therapy, and expediting investigation of close contacts of TB patients. From 1993 through 1998, new cases of TB again declined, although the resurgence and related outbreaks set back TB elimination efforts by about a decade. This effort depends on significant effort and cooperation between public and private health care providers and agencies at the Federal, State, and local levels.

14-12. Increase the proportion of all tuberculosis patients who complete curative therapy within 12 months.

Target: 90 percent of patients.

Baseline: 74 percent of tuberculosis patients completed curative therapy within 12 months in 1996.

Target setting method: Better than the best.

Data source: National TB Surveillance System, CDC, NCHSTP.

Tuberculosis Patients, 1996	Completed Curative Therapy Within 12 Months Percent
TOTAL	74
Race and ethnicity	
American Indian or Alaska Native	82
Asian or Pacific Islander	75
Asian	DNC
Native Hawaiian and other Pacific Islander	DNC
Black or African American	72
White	74
Hispanic or Latino	73
Not Hispanic or Latino	74
Black or African American	72
White	75
Gender	
Female	75
Male	73

DNA = Data have not been analyzed. DNC = Data are not collected. DSU = Data are statistically unreliable.

Data for socioeconomic status currently are not collected.

The highest priority for TB control is to ensure that persons with the disease complete curative therapy. If treatment is not continued for a sufficient length of time, such persons often become ill and contagious again. Completion of therapy is essential to prevent transmission of the disease as well as to prevent outbreaks and the development and spread of drug-resistant TB.

Current therapy guidelines recommend that patients with drug-susceptible TB should complete a successful regimen within 12 months.[45] Multidrug-resistant TB presents difficult treatment problems, often requiring consultation with a TB specialist and longer treatment regimens. The measurement of completion of therapy is a long-accepted indicator of the effectiveness of community TB control efforts. Health departments traditionally have reported completion-of-therapy results to CDC and used this information locally and statewide as an evaluation measure.

14-13. Increase the proportion of contacts and other high-risk persons with latent tuberculosis infection who complete a course of treatment.

Target: 85 percent.

Baseline: 62.2 percent of tuberculosis contacts and other high-risk persons completed treatment for latent TB infection in 1997.

Target setting method: 27 percent improvement. (Better than the best will be used when data are available.)

Data source: Completion of Preventive Therapy Report forms submitted by State and local health departments, CDC, NCHSTP.

Data for population groups currently are not collected.

Treatment for latent TB infection substantially reduces the risk that TB infection will progress to disease. Certain groups are at very high risk of developing TB disease once infected. Identifiable population groups at high risk for TB vary in time and geographic area depending on unique and changing TB-related demographics.[46]

14-14. Reduce the average time for a laboratory to confirm and report tuberculosis cases.

Target: 2 days for 75 percent of cases.

Baseline: 21 days were needed for a laboratory to confirm and report 75 percent of TB cases in 1996.

Target setting method: 90 percent improvement.

Data source: Survey of State Public Health Laboratories, CDC, NCHSTP.

Commercially available nucleic acid amplification tests are capable of detecting *Mycobacterium tuberculosis* in a specimen within 48 hours of receipt. Concerns regarding sensitivity, cost, quality control, and special expertise requirements prevent widespread use of such tests. Upgrading TB laboratory capabilities and facilities, improving training in state-of-the-art mycobacteriology, and evaluating proficiency should better enable State public health laboratories to apply these new rapid tests to the diagnosis of TB.

14-15. (Developmental) Increase the proportion of international travelers who receive recommended preventive services when traveling in areas of risk for select infectious diseases: hepatitis A, malaria, typhoid.

Potential data source: Abstract of International Travel To and From the United States, U.S. Department of Commerce.

The number of international travelers from the United States has increased an average of 3 percent a year for the past decade. The three diseases highlighted in this objective—hepatitis A, malaria, and typhoid—account for a large proportion of illness and disability for international travelers. Before embarking, some travelers go to a travel clinic, some visit primary care providers, and some receive no pretravel care.

An appropriate prescription of antimalarial prophylaxis medications constitutes recommended preventive services for this disease. Risk areas can be identified by referencing the malaria section in the most recent edition of *Health Information for International Travel*.

14-16. Reduce invasive early onset group B streptococcal disease.

Target: 0.5 new cases per 1,000 live births.

Baseline: 1.0 new case of invasive early onset group B streptococcal disease per 1,000 live births in 1996.

Target setting method: Better than the best.

Data source: Active Bacterial Core Surveillance (ABCs), Emerging Infections Program Network, CDC, NCID.

Live Births, 1996	New Cases of Group B Streptococcal Disease Rate per 1,000
TOTAL	1.0
Race and ethnicity	
American Indian or Alaska Native	DSU
Asian or Pacific Islander	DSU
Asian	DNC
Native Hawaiian and other Pacific Islander	DNC
Black or African American	1.5
White	1.0
Hispanic or Latino	DSU
Not Hispanic or Latino	DSU
Black or African American	DSU
White	DSU
Gender	
Female	DNA
Male	DNA
Family income level	
Poor	DNC
Near poor	DNC
Middle/high income	DNC

DNA = Data have not been analyzed. DNC = Data are not collected. DSU = Data are statistically unreliable.

The number of new cases of early onset group B streptococcal (GBS) disease in 1996 reflected a substantial decline from earlier years, before intervention became common practice. GBS causes bloodstream infections and meningitis in babies. Additional prevention is possible, since occurrence of the disease is more likely to reflect ineffective prevention efforts than antibiotic failures. In certain areas, rates approximating 0.5 per 1,000 births already have been achieved. Although these data may represent the background rate of nonpreventable cases, most geographic areas should be able to achieve the same low rates. The racial disparity in rates will be eliminated with more aggressive use of prevention protocols.

African Americans have consistently had higher rates of GBS diseases than other races. Implementation of GBS prevention policies is expected to eliminate the disparity. Thus, the target of 0.5 cases per 1,000 births is one that can be obtained in all geographic areas and all racial and ethnic groups. By the year 2010, reductions in early-onset disease might be the result of both improved use of intrapartum antibiotic prophylaxis and implementation of GBS conjugate vaccines currently in clinical trials.

14-17. Reduce hospitalizations caused by peptic ulcer disease in the United States.

Target: 46 hospitalizations per 100,000 population.

Baseline: 71 hospitalizations per 100,000 population in 1997.

Target setting method: Better than the best.

Data source: National Hospital Discharge Survey (NHDS), CDC, NCHS.

Total Population, 1997	Peptic Ulcer Hospitalizations Rate per 100,000
TOTAL	71
Race and ethnicity	
American Indian or Alaska Native	DSU
Asian or Pacific Islander	DSU
Asian	DNC
Native Hawaiian and other Pacific Islander	DNC
Black or African American	79
White	53
Hispanic or Latino	DSU
Not Hispanic or Latino	DSU
Black or African American	DSU
White	DSU
Gender	
Female	65
Male	78
Family income level	
Poor	DNC
Near poor	DNC
Middle/high income	DNC

DNA = Data have not been analyzed. DNC = Data are not collected. DSU = Data are statistically unreliable.
Note: Age adjusted to the year 2000 standard population.

Peptic ulcer disease affects up to 25 million persons in the United States and causes up to 6,500 deaths each year. Until recently, peptic ulcers were thought to be caused by stress, spicy foods, and excess stomach acid. Most patients were treated with antacids or acid-reducing medications, and recurrences were the rule after therapy was discontinued. The discovery in the 1980s that a bacterial organism, *Helicobacter pylori (H. pylori)*, causes up to 90 percent of peptic ulcers has changed the way ulcers are evaluated and managed.[47, 48] Now appropriate antibiotic regimens successfully eradicate the infection and prevent recurrence and complications such as bleeding or perforation.

Despite extensive scientific data linking peptic ulcer disease to *H. pylori*, studies indicate that many health care providers and consumers are unaware of the relationship, and many persons with ulcers do not receive appropriate therapy.[49, 50] A campaign to educate health care providers and consumers about *H. pylori* and its link to peptic ulcer disease was initiated in 1997. The CDC and Partnership H. pylori Educational Campaign includes partners from academic institutions, government agencies, and industry.[51] The increased awareness of the link between *H. pylori* and ulcers among health care providers and consumers is expected to lead to the increased use of appropriate antibiotics. This improved treatment, if available to those who need it, should decrease hospitalization rates—an indicator for severe illness and disability—due to peptic ulcer disease and its complications.

14-18. Reduce the number of courses of antibiotics for ear infections for young children.

Target: 88 antibiotic courses per 100 children under age 5 years.

Baseline: 108 antibiotic courses for otitis media per 100 children under age 5 years were prescribed during 1996-97 (2-year average).

Target setting method: 19 percent improvement.

Data sources: National Ambulatory Medical Care Survey (NAMCS), CDC, NCHS; National Hospital Ambulatory Medical Care Survey (NHAMCS), CDC, NCHS.

Children Under Age 5 Years, 1996-97	Courses of Antibiotics for Ear Infections
	Rate per 100
TOTAL	108
Race and ethnicity	
American Indian or Alaska Native	DSU
Asian or Pacific Islander	DSU
Asian	DNC
Native Hawaiian and other Pacific Islander	DNC
Black or African American	84
White	116
Hispanic or Latino	DSU
Not Hispanic or Latino	DSU
Black or African American	DSU
White	DSU
Gender	
Female	107
Male	109

DNA = Data have not been analyzed. DNC = Data are not collected. DSU = Data are statistically unreliable.

Data for socioeconomic status currently are not collected.

Antibiotic courses for otitis media, commonly called ear infection, can be reduced through two methods. A portion of otitis media cases—otitis media with effusion, rather than acute otitis media—do not require antimicrobial treatment. A national campaign for judicious antibiotic use aims to reduce inappropriate antibiotic treatment for this portion of otitis media.[52] The leading cause of otitis media is pneumococcus. Preventing pneumococcal otitis media is expected to be possible following licensure of pneumococcal conjugate vaccines. (See Focus Area 28. Vision and Hearing.)

14-19. Reduce the number of courses of antibiotics prescribed for the sole diagnosis of the common cold.

Target: 1,268 antibiotic courses per 100,000 population.

Baseline: 2,535 antibiotic courses per 100,000 population were prescribed for the sole diagnosis of the common cold, 1996-97.

Target setting method: 50 percent improvement.

Data sources: National Ambulatory Medical Care Survey (NAMCS), CDC, NCHS; National Hospital Ambulatory Medical Care Survey (NHAMCS), CDC, NCHS.

Total Population, 1996-97	Courses of Antibiotics for Common Cold
	Rate per 100,000
TOTAL	2,535
Race and ethnicity	
American Indian or Alaska Native	DSU
Asian or Pacific Islander	DSU
Asian	DNC
Native Hawaiian and other Pacific Islander	DNC
Black or African American	DSU
White	2,431
Hispanic or Latino	DSU
Not Hispanic or Latino	DSU
Black or African American	DSU
White	DSU
Gender	
Female	2,644
Male	2,421
Family income level	
Poor	DNC
Near poor	DNC
Middle/high income	DNC

DNA = Data have not been analyzed. DNC = Data are not collected. DSU = Data are statistically unreliable.

The common cold does not require antimicrobial therapy. Inappropriate therapy for the common cold can be reduced by 50 percent by promoting judicious antimicrobial use, provided that care givers and patients accept that antibiotics are ineffective in treating colds. Effective programs for the judicious use of antibiotics could help reduce the prescription of antibiotics for the common cold.

14-20. Reduce hospital-acquired infections in intensive care unit patients.

Target and baseline:

Objective	Reduction in Hospital-Acquired Infections in Intensive Care Units	1998 Baseline	2010 Target
		Infections per 1,000 Days' Use	
	Intensive care patients		
14-20a.	Catheter-associated urinary tract infection	5.9	5.3
14-20b.	Central line-associated blood-stream infection	5.3	4.8
14-20c.	Ventilator-associated pneumonia	11.1	10.0
	Infants weighing 1,000 grams or less in intensive care		
14-20d.	Central line-associated blood-stream infection	12.2	11.0
14-20e.	Ventilator-associated pneumonia	4.9	4.4

Target setting method: 10 percent improvement. (Better than the best will be used when data are available.)

Data source: National Nosocomial Infections Surveillance System (NNIS), CDC, NCID.

> **Data for population groups currently are not collected.**

Hospital-acquired infections are a leading cause of illness and death in the United States. Each year, 36 million patients are admitted to U.S. hospitals. Annually, more than 500,000 of the nearly 2 million patients stricken with a hospital-acquired infection are intensive care patients. Of the total, nearly 90,000 die. The annual cost of hospital-acquired infections is approximately $4.5 billion a year. In the last 20 years, the rate of hospital-acquired infections has increased 36 percent.

The rate of hospital-acquired infections has increased largely because hospital patients of the late 1990s on average were older and sicker than those of 20 years earlier and thus more susceptible to infection, and also because medical advances that can save or prolong lives may carry risks for infections. Because both trends are expected to continue, only a modest reduction in the number of new cases of infections can be expected; however, a small reduction will save thousands of lives.

14-21. Reduce antimicrobial use among intensive care unit patients.

Target: 120 daily doses per 1,000 patient days.

Baseline: 150 daily doses of antimicrobials per 1,000 patient days were used among intensive care unit patients in 1995.

Target setting method: 20 percent improvement.

Data source: National Nosocomial Infections Surveillance System (NNIS), CDC, NCID.

Hospital-acquired infections caused by antimicrobial-resistant pathogens can be virtually untreatable. Further, antimicrobial resistance that develops in the hospital can spread into the community and has the potential to cause a public health disaster. Excessive or inappropriate use of antimicrobials or both, which occur most frequently in intensive care units (ICUs), is the major cause of antimicrobial resistance. Research indicates that antibiotics are being used more often than hospital prescription guidelines recommend. For example, one study in the late 1990s indicated that as much as 60 percent of the hospital prescriptions for vancomycin are not in accordance with the guidelines. Decreasing the use of antimicrobials, especially in intensive care units, is the critical step in reducing the public threat of antimicrobial resistance. Studies have shown that interventions in individual hospitals have achieved reductions of 20 percent or more in antimicrobial use.

Vaccination Coverage and Strategies

14-22. Achieve and maintain effective vaccination coverage levels for universally recommended vaccines among young children.

Target and baseline:

Objective	Increase and Maintenance of Vaccination Coverage Levels Among Children Aged 19 Through 35 Months	1998 Baseline	2010 Target
		Percent	
14-22a.	4 doses diphtheria-tetanus-pertussis (DtaP) vaccine	84	90
14-22b.	3 doses *Haemophilus influenzae* type b (Hib) vaccine	93	90
14-22c.	3 doses hepatis B vaccine (hep B)	87	90
14-22d.	1 dose measles-mumps-rubella (MMR) vaccine	92	90
14-22e.	3 doses polio vaccine	91	90
14-22f.	1 dose varicella vaccine	43	90

Data as of November 30, 1999

Target setting method: Consistent with the Childhood Immunization Initiative.

Data source: National Immunization Survey (NIS), CDC, NCHS and NIP.

Children Aged 19 Through 35 Months, 1998	Vaccination Coverage					
	14-22a. 4 Doses DTaP	14-22b 3 Doses Hib	14-22c. 3 Doses Hep B	14-22d. 1 Dose MMR	14-22e. 3 Doses Polio	14-22f. 1 Dose Varicella
	Percent					
TOTAL	84	93	87	92	91	43
Race and ethnicity						
American Indian or Alaska Native	78	92	80	86	83	33
Asian or Pacific Islander	87	93	90	93	94	57
Asian	DNC	DNC	DNC	DNC	DNC	DNC
Native Hawaiian and other Pacific Islander	DNC	DNC	DNC	DNC	DNC	DNC
Black or African American	77	90	84	89	88	43
White	86	94	88	93	92	43
Hispanic or Latino	80	92	86	91	89	47
Not Hispanic or Latino	85	94	87	92	91	42
Black or African American	77	90	84	89	88	42
White	87	95	88	93	92	42
Gender						
Female	84	94	87	92	91	43
Male	84	93	87	92	90	43
Family income level						
Poor	81	92	86	91	90	46
Near poor	83	92	87	91	91	42
Middle/high income	89	96	89	94	92	49

Data as of November 30, 1999

Children Aged 19 Through 35 Months, 1998	Vaccination Coverage					
	14-22a. 4 Doses DTaP	14-22b 3 Doses Hib	14-22c. 3 Doses Hep B	14-22d. 1 Dose MMR	14-22e. 3 Doses Polio	14-22f. 1 Dose Varicella
	Percent					
Disability status						
Persons with disabilities	DNC	DNC	DNC	DNC	DNC	DNC
Persons without disabilities	DNC	DNC	DNC	DNC	DNC	DNC

DNA = Data have not been analyzed. DNC = Data are not collected. DSU = Data are statistically unreliable.

Vaccination coverage levels of 90 percent are, in general, sufficient to prevent circulation of viruses and bacteria causing vaccine-preventable diseases.[53, 54] Maintenance of high vaccination coverage levels in early childhood is the best way to prevent the spread of VPDs in childhood and to provide the foundation for controlling VPDs among adults. Diseases that affect humans only may eventually be eradicated or at least eliminated through high vaccination coverage levels.[55] These diseases include polio and measles in the near future and possibly hepatitis B later on. Although polio is expected to be eradicated by the year 2000, vaccine coverage levels will continue to be assessed until vaccination is no longer recommended. The measles epidemic of 1989-91 demonstrated that achievement of high coverage levels at the time of school entry was insufficient to control VPD outbreaks. Although coverage levels are currently the highest ever recorded, the United States must continue to assure that each new cohort of children is fully vaccinated with all required vaccine doses; as of November 1, 1999, 16 to 20 vaccine doses are required through age 16 years with 12 to 16 doses by age 2 years. Any new universally recommended vaccine should be at a 90 percent coverage level within 5 years of the recommendation.

Although national coverage levels may exceed 90 percent, variation in the level of coverage among smaller areas may include subgroups of the population at substantially lower levels of protection. These subgroups or pockets of undervaccinated persons make the population vulnerable to major outbreaks of VPDs. Monitoring of coverage at smaller geographic levels within the United States helps ensure that these potential pockets of children are identified to target interventions and reduce the risk of future disease outbreaks. In addition, each State and major urban area should aim to achieve 90 percent coverage to ensure uniformly high vaccination coverage.

14-23. Maintain vaccination coverage levels for children in licensed day care facilities and children in kindergarten through the first grade.

Target and baseline:

Objective	Maintain Vaccination Coverage Levels for Children	1997–98 Baseline	2010 Target
		Percent	
	Children in day care		
14-23a.	Diphtheria-tetanus-acellular pertussis (DTaP) vaccine	96	95
14-23b.	Measles-mumps-rubella (MMR) vaccine	93	95
14-23c.	Polio vaccine	95	95
14-23d.	Hepatitis B vaccine	Developmental	
14-23e.	Varicella vaccine	Developmental	
	Children in K-1st grade		
14-23f.	Diphtheria-tetanus-acellular pertussis (DtaP) vaccine	97	95
14-23g.	Measles-mumps-rubella (MMR) vaccine	96	95
14-23h.	Polio vaccine	97	95
14-23i.	Hepatitis B vaccine	Developmental	
14-23j.	Varicella vaccine	Developmental	

Target setting method: Consistent with year 2000 target. (Better than the best will be used when data are available.)

Data source: Immunization Program Annual Reports, CDC, NIP.

Data for population groups currently are not collected.

Uniformly high coverage levels are required to prevent circulation of the viruses and bacteria that cause VPDs. The target level was set to be consistent with the Healthy People 2000 objective because the achievement of that objective has been successful at preventing disease spread, and this objective seeks to maintain the high coverage achieved in these settings.

Entry requirements for school and day care are one of the most effective interventions the States have at their disposal to ensure that children are appropriately vaccinated. The impact of entry requirements for school and day care has been profound—more than 95 percent of children are vaccinated. Several studies support the role of entry requirements in increasing vaccination rates and decreasing the rate of new cases of measles. Strict enforcement of school vaccination requirements has been shown to play a determining role in lowering new cases of measles.[56]

14-24. Increase the proportion of young children who receive all vaccines that have been recommended for universal administration for at least 5 years.

Target: 80 percent of children aged 19 through 35 months.

Baseline: 73 percent of children aged 19 through 35 months received the recommended vaccines (4 DTaP, 3 polio, 1 MMR, 3 Hib, 3 hepatitis B) in 1998.

Target setting method: Better than the best.

Data source: National Immunization Survey (NIS), CDC, NCHS and NIP.

Children Aged 19 Through 35 Months, 1998	Vaccinations	
	14-24. 4 DTaP, 3 polio, 1 MMR, 3 Hib, 3 Hepatitis B	4 DTaP, 3 polio, 1 MMR*
	Percent	
TOTAL	73	81
Race and ethnicity		
American Indian or Alaska Native	65	75
Asian or Pacific Islander	73	82
Asian	DNC	DNC
Native Hawaiian and other Pacific Islander	DNC	DNC
Black or African American	66	74
White	74	82
Hispanic or Latino	69	77
Not Hispanic or Latino	74	81
Black or African American	67	74
White	76	83
Gender		
Female	72	81
Male	73	81

Children Aged 19 Through 35 Months, 1998	Vaccinations	
	14-24. 4 DTaP, 3 polio, 1 MMR, 3 Hib, 3 Hepatitis B	4 DTaP, 3 polio, 1 MMR*
	Percent	
Family income level		
Poor	70	78
Near poor	72	80
Middle/high income	77	85
Disability status		
Persons with disabilities	DNC	DNC
Persons without disabilities	DNC	DNC

DNA = Data have not been analyzed. DNC = Data are not collected. DSU = Data are statistically unreliable.
*Data for 4 DTaP, 3 polio, and 1 MMR are displayed to further characterize the issue.

Determining whether the population is protected against a VPD is best evaluated by examining the immunization coverage of individual vaccines (see objective 14-22). It is also important to assure that the health care system fully vaccinates individual children, providing vaccines that have been universally recommended for at least 5 years and that are currently recommended. Changes in the immunization schedule will occur as new vaccines are added to the list of recommended vaccines and as vaccines for eradicated diseases are removed from the list.[57] For example, polio virus vaccine is not expected to be recommended by the year 2010. Although monitoring the proportion of children who have received the combination of four DTaP, three polio, and one MMR will continue for historical comparison, attention should be focused on the combination of all universally recommended vaccines.

14-25. Increase the proportion of providers who have measured the vaccination coverage levels among children in their practice population within the past 2 years.

Target and baseline:

Objective	Increase in Providers Measuring Vaccination Levels	1997 Baseline	2010 Target
		Percent	
14-25a.	Public health providers	66	90
14-25b.	Private providers	6	90

Target setting method: 36 percent improvement for public health providers; 1,400 percent improvement for private providers.

Data source: Immunization Program Annual Reports, CDC, NIP.

In 1997, 66 percent of public health department providers assessed their vaccination levels.[58] State immunization programs are collaborating with private providers to extend provider-based assessments to the private sector. With the increasing role of managed care and Health Plan and Employer Data and Information Set (HEDIS) measures, private providers should have additional occasions to examine their coverage levels.

Most providers (public and private) overestimate the vaccination coverage level they are achieving with their clients.[59] Assessment of practice-based coverage levels and feedback of those data to the providers have been an effective strategy for increasing vaccination of children served by a given practice.[60, 61] Managed care organizations have begun reporting vaccination coverage levels using the HEDIS criteria as a way of evaluating quality of care.[62] Practice-based assessment also has been recommended by the Advisory Committee on Immunization Practices,[63] the National Vaccine Advisory Committee, the American Academy of Pediatrics, and the American Academy of Family Physicians.[64] The Clinic Assessment Software Application provides a mechanism for assessing levels of vaccination coverage as well as for tracking patients; the system reminds patients of upcoming vaccinations and sends notices for children who are overdue.

14-26. Increase the proportion of children who participate in fully operational population-based immunization registries.

Target: 95 percent of children under age 6 years.

Baseline: 32 percent of children under age 6 years participated in a fully operational population-based immunization registry in 1998.

Target setting method: 197 percent improvement. (Better than the best will be used when data are available.)

Data source: Immunization Program Annual Reports, CDC, NIP.

Data for population groups currently are not collected.

A fully operational population-based registry includes capabilities to (1) protect confidential information, (2) enroll all children at the State or community level automatically at birth, (3) give providers access to complete vaccination history, (4) recommend needed vaccinations, (5) notify children who are due and overdue for vaccinations, (6) assess practice and geographic-level coverage, and (7) produce authorized immunization records. Registries may provide other important functions such as automatic reporting of adverse events. Registries may serve other purposes as well, including VPD surveillance, vaccine efficacy monitoring, and vaccine inventory management.

Population-based immunization registries will be a cornerstone of the Nation's immunization system by 2010. Responsibility for registry development rests with State and local communities, with assistance from Federal agencies and private partners. Registries facilitate the timely vaccination of children by ensuring that the child's complete vaccination history is available to the health care provider. Registries are valuable given the mobile nature of today's population and that many persons do not see the same provider consistently. Registries also can be used to monitor the vaccination status of populations that are low income, uninsured, and at greater risk for incomplete vaccination.

Few population-based immunization registries existed at the State or community level before 1992, and limited data are available regarding their implementation. A 1999 CDC survey shows immunization registries are being developed in all States.[65] Additional efforts are underway to establish registry links between private providers and immunization partners such as managed care organizations and WIC programs. Issues such as privacy, confidentiality, and access of registry data are being addressed as registries are developed.

Participation in immunization registries will continue to increase. The development of childhood immunization registries has widespread support among parents and providers[66] and the required technology is becoming less expensive and simpler. Registries are part of the current trend to computerize medical data in the United States. To be successful, registries must be seamlessly integrated into the current provider environment and create no additional burdens.

14-27. (Developmental) Increase routine vaccination coverage levels of adolescents.

Potential data source: National Health Interview Survey (NHIS), CDC, NCHS.

Illness and disability caused by vaccine-preventable diseases, such as hepatitis B, measles, and varicella, continue among adolescents.[25] While primary health care providers are vital to ensuring that infants and younger children are up to date on their vaccinations, they have an equally important role in ensuring comprehensive vaccination for adolescents.[67] Any new universally recommended vaccine for adolescents should be at a 90 percent coverage level within 5 years of the recommendation. An estimated 79 percent of adolescents and children visit a health care provider annually.[68] Providers such as nurses, nurse practitioners, pediatricians, family physicians, general practitioners, and emergency medicine specialists deliver most of the primary health care received by adolescents.[69] Strategies should specifically target these providers to increase vaccination among adolescents, especially hard-to-reach and at-risk adolescents in urban and rural areas.

School entry laws and regulations ensure high vaccination levels. Much of the experience to date in implementing adolescent vaccination comes from school-based hepatitis B demonstration projects.[70] To encourage school participation in an adolescent vaccination program, a partnership between schools and local health departments is essential.

Managed care organizations also have an increasingly important role in the delivery of health care services, including vaccinations, to adolescents. Measures for assessing immunization recommendations for adolescents have been incorporated into HEDIS 3.0.[62] Such standards should greatly assist in implementing immunization recommendations for adolescents in the managed care setting.

14-28. Increase hepatitis B vaccine coverage among high-risk groups.

Target and baseline:

Objective	Increase Hepatitis B Vaccine Coverage in High-Risk Groups	1995 Baseline	2010 Target
		Percent	
14-28a.	Long-term hemodialysis patients	35	90
14-28b.	Men who have sex with men	9	60
14-28c.	Occupationally exposed workers	71	98

Target setting method: 157 percent improvement for long-term hemodialysis patients; 567 percent improvement for men who have sex with men; 38 percent improvement for occupationally exposed workers.

Data sources: Young Men's Survey, CDC, NCHSTP; Annual Survey of Chronic Hemodialysis Centers, CDC, NCID, and HCFA; Periodic vaccine coverage surveys, CDC, NCID.

Hepatitis B vaccination has been recommended for persons with risk factors for hepatitis B virus infection since the vaccine was first licensed in 1981. These risk groups include the following: hemodialysis patients, men who have sex with men, incarcerated persons, health care and public safety workers who have exposure to blood in the workplace, persons with a history of sexually transmitted diseases or multiple sex partners, injection drug users, and household and sex contacts of HBV-infected persons. While data currently are not collected for inmates in long-term correctional facilities, it is recommended that prison officials should consider undertaking screening and vaccination programs directed at inmates with histories of high-risk behaviors.

14-29. Increase the proportion of adults who are vaccinated annually against influenza and ever vaccinated against pneumococcal disease.

Target and baseline:

Objective	Increase in Adult Vaccinations	1997 Baseline	2010 Target
		Percent	
	Noninstitutionalized adults aged 65 years and older*		
14-29a.	Influenza vaccine	63	90
14-29b.	Pneumococcal vaccine	43	90
	Noninstitutionalized high-risk adults aged 18 to 64 years*		
14-29c.	Influenza vaccine	25	60
14-29d.	Pneumococcal vaccine	11	60
	Institutionalized adults (persons in long-term or nursing homes)†		
14-29e.	Influenza vaccine	64	90
14-29f.	Pneumococcal vaccine	28	90

*Data on noninstitutionalized population age adjusted to the year 2000 standard population.

†Data on institutionalized population age adjusted to the year 2000 nursing home population. National Nursing Home Survey estimates include a significant number of residents who have an unknown vaccination status. See *Tracking Healthy People 2010* for further discussion of the data issues.

Target setting method: Better than the best.

Data sources: National Health Interview Survey (NHIS), CDC, NCHS–noninstitutionalized populations; National Nursing Home Survey (NNHS), CDC, NCHS—institutionalized populations.

Select Age Groups, 1997	Annual Influenza and One-Time Pneumococcal Vaccinations					
	Noninstitutionalized Adults Aged 65 Years and Older*		Noninstitutionalized High-Risk Adults Aged 18 to 64 Years*		Institutionalized Adults Aged 18 Years and Older†	
	14-29a. Influenza	14-29b. Pneumococcal Disease	14-29c. Influenza	14-29d. Pneumococcal Disease	14-29e. Influenza	14-29f. Pneumococcal Disease
	Percent					
TOTAL	63	43	25	11	64	28
Race and ethnicity						
American Indian/ Alaska Native	DSU	DSU	29	22	DSU	DSU
Asian or Pacific Islander	50	24	22	DSU	DSU	DSU
Asian	50	DSU	DSU	DSU	DNC	DNC
Native Hawaiian and other Pacific Islander	DSU	DSU	DSU	DSU	DNC	DNC
Black or African American	45	22	21	13	DNA	DNA
White	65	45	25	11	DNA	DNA
Hispanic or Latino	53	24	18	7	52	17
Not Hispanic or Latino	64	44	25	11	DNA	DNA
Black or African American	45	22	21	13	60	24
White	66	46	26	11	65	29
Gender						
Female	62	42	26	11	DNA	DNA
Male	65	44	23	11	DNA	DNA
Education level						
Less than high school	58	37	18	10	DNA	DNA
High school graduate	65	45	24	12	DNA	DNA
Some college	69	48	27	11	DNA	DNA

Data as of November 30, 1999

Select Age Groups, 1997	Annual Influenza and One-Time Pneumococcal Vaccinations					
	Noninstitutionalized Adults Aged 65 Years and Older*		Noninstitutionalized High-Risk Adults Aged 18 to 64 Years*		Institutionalized Adults Aged 18 Years and Older†	
	14-29a. Influenza	14-29b. Pneumococcal Disease	14-29c. Influenza	14-29d. Pneumococcal Disease	14-29e. Influenza	14-29f. Pneumococcal Disease
	Percent					
Disability status						
Persons with disabilities	66	47	28	16	DNA	DNA
Persons without disabilities	62	40	23	9	DNA	DNA
Select populations						
Age Groups						
18 to 49 years	NA	NA	19	8	59	26
50 to 64 years	NA	NA	40	19	62	23
65 to 74 years	61	40	NA	NA	62	28
75 to 84 years	66	46	NA	NA	61	26
85 years and older	67	42	NA	NA	66	30
Persons with diabetes	68	44	27	15	DNA	DNA
Persons with heart disease	71	51	25	11	DNA	DNA
Persons with lung disease	73	65	25	13	DNA	DNA
Persons with lung disease (excluding asthma)	74	66	26	14	DNA	DNA
Persons with kidney disease	71	46	21	13	DNA	DNA
Persons with liver disease	71	43	26	10	DNA	DNA
Persons with cancer	71	51	25	10	DNA	DNA

DNA = Data have not been analyzed. DNC = Data are not collected. DSU = Data are statistically unreliable.

*Data on noninstitutionalized population age adjusted to the year 2000 standard population.

†Data on institutionalized population age adjusted to the year 2000 nursing home population.

Federal initiatives have highlighted the need to focus vaccination resources on adults.[71] Vaccination is an effective strategy to reduce illness and deaths due to pneumococcal disease and influenza. Current levels of coverage among adults vary widely among age, risk, and racial and ethnic groups. Any new universally recommended vaccine should be at a 60 percent coverage level within 5 years of recommendation. Influenza and pneumococcal vaccines are covered by Medicare; thus vaccinating greater numbers of adults aged 65 years and older is feasible. High-risk adults aged 18 to 64 years may not have insurance coverage for influenza and pneumococcal vaccines.

With the aging of the U.S. population, increasing numbers of adults will be at risk for these major causes of illness and death. Persons with high-risk conditions (that is, heart disease, diabetes, and chronic respiratory disease[72, 73]) remain at increased risk for these diseases, as do persons living in institutional settings.

Continuing education of providers and the community is needed to increase awareness of and demand for adult vaccination services. Interventions, such as standing orders for vaccination, provider reminders and feedback, and patient notifications and reminders have been effective in increasing adult vaccination levels.[21, 74] Guidelines and tools for implementing these interventions are available through *Put Prevention Into Practice*, a national campaign to improve delivery of clinical preventive services.[75] Measurement and feedback about vaccination providers' performance in delivering vaccines enhance coverage rates. Providers should be given feedback on their performance in a timely manner. Measurement and feedback can result in improvements in vaccine coverage either by changing provider knowledge, attitudes, and behavior or by stimulating changes in the vaccine delivery system—for example, reminders and standing orders—or some combination.

In addition, opportunities for vaccination outside of primary care and other traditional health care settings could be increased to reach elderly persons who do not routinely access primary care. For example, over 90 million emergency department visits are made in the United States annually. Emergency department vaccination is likely to increase vaccination rates among select populations difficult to vaccinate through office-based programs. In any nontraditional site, a method for tracking and communicating vaccinations is needed so that vaccination information may be shared with patients' primary care providers.

Vaccine Safety

14-30. Reduce vaccine-associated adverse events.

14-30a. Eliminate vaccine-associated paralytic polio (VAPP).

Target: Zero cases.

Baseline: 5 VAPP cases in 1997.

Target setting method: Total elimination.

Data source: National Notifiable Disease Surveillance System (NNDSS), CDC, EPO.

14-30b. Reduce febrile seizures caused by pertussis vaccines.

Target: 75 febrile seizures.

Baseline: 152 febrile seizures were caused by pertussis vaccines in 1998.

Target setting method: 50 percent improvement.

Data sources: Vaccine Adverse Event Reporting System (VAERS) and Vaccine Safety Datalink (VSD), CDC, NIP.

Because no natural reservoirs for wild poliomyelitis exist, VAPP is caused by the oral polio vaccine (OPV). With global polio eradication targeted for 2000, use of OPV should decrease and then stop, resulting in zero cases of VAPP. From 1980 to 1998, no indigeneous cases of paralytic poliomyelitis caused by wild polio virus transmission have occurred in the United States. However, 141 cases of VAPP have been reported in this same period, averaging 8 or 9 cases per year. Persons with VAPP experience the full range of illness and disability as well as loss of social function associated with being partially or fully paralyzed. Due to the progress in global poliomyelitis eradication and to the reduction of the burden of VAPP in the United States, ACIP recommended that beginning in 2000, only IPV will be used for routine immunization.[76] In general, IPV is as effective as OPV and should be sufficient at preventing polio in the United States.

Controlled clinical trials indicate that whole cell pertussis (wP) vaccines cause seizures at a frequency of 1 per 1,750 doses.[37, 77, 78] The majority of these seizures are febrile seizures without any residual deficit. Nevertheless, such seizures—frightening patients and parents alike—frequently result in emergency department or other medical visits as well as costly diagnostic evaluations to rule out possible neurologic disorders. Recently licensed acellular pertussis (aP) vaccines are less likely to cause fever or seizures; data show seizure frequency of up to 1 per 14,280 doses.[37] With the increasing use of aP vaccines, the number of pertussis vaccine-associated febrile seizures should be reduced by 50 percent.

14-31. Increase the number of persons under active surveillance for vaccine safety via large linked databases.

Target: 13 million persons.

Baseline: 6 million persons were under active surveillance for vaccine safety via large linked databases in 1999.

Target setting method: 117 percent improvement.

Data source: Vaccine-Safety Datalink, CDC, NIP.

A high standard of safety is expected of vaccines since they are recommended for millions of healthy people, including infants. Vaccine safety monitoring to identify and minimize vaccine-related reactions is necessary to help ensure safety because no vaccine is completely safe. Knowledge of vaccine safety is essential to accurately assess the risks and benefits in formulating vaccine use recommendations. For example, the Institute of Medicine has reported that of 76 adverse events assessed, 66 percent had inadequate or no evidence available to accept or reject vaccine as a cause of the adverse reactions.[79, 80]

In collaboration with several health maintenance organizations, CDC has linked anonymous vaccination and medical records in a large database.[81] This system is used to study vaccine safety, especially for evaluating new concerns arising from the Vaccine Adverse Event reporting System (VAERS) and other sources. These databases also are used for monitoring vaccine safety, conducting active surveillance of VPDs, carrying out vaccine safety and immunogenicity trials, evaluating vaccine economics, and assessing vaccine coverage.

Related Objectives From Other Focus Areas

1. Access to Quality Health Services

1-1.	Persons with health insurance
1-2.	Health insurance coverage for clinical preventive services
1-3.	Counseling about health behaviors
1-4.	Source of ongoing care
1-5.	Usual primary care provider
1-6.	Difficulties or delays in obtaining needed health care
1-7.	Core competencies in health provider training
1-8.	Racial and ethnic representation in health professions
1-9.	Hospitalization for ambulatory-care-sensitive conditions
1-14.	Special needs of children
1-15.	Long-term care services

7. Educational and Community-Based Programs

7-2.	School health education
7-4.	School nurse-to-student ratio
7-5.	Worksite health promotion programs
7-6.	Participation in employer-sponsored health promotion activities
7-7.	Patient and family education
7-8.	Satisfaction with patient education
7-9.	Health care organization sponsorship of community health promotion activities
7-10.	Community health promotion programs
7-11.	Culturally appropriate community health promotion programs
7-12.	Older adult participation in community health promotion activities

8. Environmental Health

8-5.	Safe drinking water
8-6.	Waterborne disease outbreaks
8-29.	Global burden of disease
8-30.	Water quality in the U.S.-Mexico border region

10. Food Safety

10-1.	Foodborne infections
10-2.	Outbreaks of foodborne infections
10-3.	Antimicrobial resistance of *Salmonella* species
10-5.	Consumer food safety practices
10-6.	Safe food preparation practices in retail establishments

11. Health Communication

11-1.	Households with Internet access
11-2.	Health literacy
11-3.	Research and evaluation of communication programs
11-4.	Quality of Internet health information sources
11-5.	Centers for excellence
11-6.	Satisfaction with providers' communication skills

13. HIV

13-9.	HIV/AIDS, STD, and TB education in State prisons
13-11.	HIV testing in TB patients
13-12.	Screening for STDs and immunization for hepatitis B

16. Maternal, Infant, and Child Health

16-22.	Medical home for children with special health care needs

23. Public Health Infrastructure

23-1.	Public health employee access to Internet
23-2.	Public access to information and surveillance data
23-3.	Use of geocoding in health data systems
23-4.	Data for population groups
23-5.	Data for Leading Health Indicators, Health Status Indicators, and Priority Data Needs at State, Tribal, and local levels
23-6.	National tracking of Healthy People 2010 objectives
23-7.	Timely release of data on objectives
23-8.	Competencies for public health workers

Terminology

(A list of all acronyms used in this publication appears in Appendix K.)

Advisory Committee on Immunization Practices (ACIP): Federally chartered advisory committee with the goals of providing advice to the CDC Director on decreasing disease through the use of vaccines and other biological products and on improving the safety of their use.

Common cold: Defined based on International Classification of Disease (ICD)-9 diagnostic codes 460.0, 461.0, 465.0, 465.8, 465.9, 472.0.

Complete curative therapy: Full course of recommended treatment.

Comprehensive primary care: All aspects of routine health care (preventive, diagnostic, and therapeutic) delivered by a trained health care provider.

Conjugate vaccines: A type of inactivated vaccine composed of fractions of bacteria linked to a protein. This linkage makes the vaccine more potent.

Emerging infectious diseases: Diseases of infectious origin whose occurrence in humans has increased within the past two decades or threatens to increase in the near future. Recognition of an emerging disease occurs because the disease is present in the population for the first time, the disease has been detected for the first time, or links between an infectious agent and a chronic disease or syndrome have only recently been identified.

Group B Streptococcus (GBS): A normal germ found in the intestines and on the genitals of about one out of five pregnant women. GBS is usually not harmful to the woman carrying the germ. But it can cause dangerous infections in the blood, spinal fluid, and lungs of babies born to these women.

Early onset of group B streptococcal disease: Illness onset at less than 7 days of age.

Invasive group B streptococcal disease: Isolation of group B streptococcus from a normally sterile site, such as blood or cerebrospinal fluid.

Group immunity: The immunity of a group or community. Immunity based on the resistance to infection among a high proportion of individual members of the group.

Hospital-acquired infection: Any infection that a patient acquires as a result of medical treatment while in the hospital.

Invasive pneumococcal infection: Isolating the bacteria Streptococcus pneumoniae from a normally sterile site, including blood, cerebrospinal fluid, or pleural fluid.

Latent TB infection: The state of being infected with the organism Mycobacterium tuberculosis but without signs or symptoms of active TB disease.

Multiple sex partners: More than one partner in the prior 6 months.

National Notifiable Disease Surveillance System (NNDSS): Tracking system that State health departments use to report cases of selected diseases to CDC. (See Reportable disease).

Patient day: A day or part of a day for which a patient was hospitalized.

Penicillin resistant: Having a minimum inhibitory concentration (MIC) equal to or greater than 2 µg/ml. Strains with "intermediate" susceptibility are not included in this category.

Reemerging infectious diseases: Reappearance of a known infection after a decline in occurrence. Reemergence of "old" infectious agents can be the result of lapses in public health measures, changes in human behavior that increase person-to-person transmission of infectious agents, changes in food handling or eating habits, or changes in the way humans interact with their environment.

Reportable disease: A disease for which there are legal requirements for reporting and notification to public health authorities. In the United States, requirements for reporting diseases are mandated by State laws or regulations, and the list of reportable diseases in each State differs.

Surveillance regions: The nine regions of the United States used for influenza surveillance purposes.

Vaccine Adverse Events Reporting System (VAERS). A passive surveillance system that monitors vaccine safety by collecting and analyzing reports of adverse events following immunization from vaccine manufacturers, private practitioners, State and local public health clinics, parents, and individuals who receive vaccines. CDC and the Food and Drug Administration work together to implement VAERS.

Vaccines: Biological substances used to stimulate the development of antibodies and thus confer active immunity against a specific disease or number of diseases.

Vector-borne disease: Viral and bacterial diseases transmitted to humans by arthropods, primarily mosquitoes, ticks, and fleas.

Zoonotic disease: Viral and bacterial diseases transmitted to humans by arthropods, primarily mosquitoes, ticks, and fleas.

References

1. Meltzer, M.I.; Dennis, D.T.; and Orloski, K.A. The Cost Effectiveness of Vaccinating Against Lyme Disease. *Emerging and Infectious Diseases* 5(3):321-328, May-June 1999. Retrieved December 14, 1999 <http://www.cdc.gov/ncidod/eid/vol5no3/meltzer.htm>.

2. Centers for Disease Control and Prevention (CDC). Summary of notifiable disease—United States, 1994. *Morbidity and Mortality Weekly Report* 43(53), 1995.

3. Rubella Surveillance National Communicable Disease Center, United States Department of Health, Education and Welfare (No. 1), June 1969.

4. Atkinson, W.; Humiston, S.G.; and Pollard., B., eds. Epidemiology and prevention of vaccine-preventable diseases. Atlanta, GA: U.S. Department of Health and Human Services, CDC, 1997.

5. Atkinson, W.L.; Orenstein, W.A.; and Krugman, S. The resurgence of measles in the United States, 1989-90. *Annual Review of Medicine* 43:451-463, 1992.

6. Gindler, J.S.; Atkinson, W.L.; Markowitz, L.E.; and Hutchins, S.S. The epidemiology of measles in the United States in 1989-1990. *Pediatric Infectious Disease Journal* 11:841-846, 1992.

7. National Vaccine Advisory Committee. The measles epidemic: The problems, barriers and recommendations. *Journal of the American Medical Association* 266:1547-1552, 1991.

8. CDC. National Immunization Program. Atlanta, GA: CDC, Immunization Services Division, Health Services Research and Evaluation Branch, unpublished data, 1999.

9. CDC. Achievements in Public Health, 1900-1999/Impact of Vaccines Universally Recommended for Children—United States, 1990-1998. *Morbidity and Mortality Weekly Report* 48(12):243-248, 1999.

10. CDC. Notice to readers: National Vaccination Coverage Levels Among Children Aged 19 to 35 Months—United States, 1998. *Morbidity and Mortality Weekly Report* 48(37):829-830, 1999.

11. National Center for Health Statistics. *Healthy People 2000 Review, 1998-99.* Hyattsville, MD: Public Health Service, 1999, 195-205.

12. CDC. Vaccination Coverage by Race/Ethnicity and Poverty Level Among Children Aged 19 to 35 Months—United States, 1996. *Morbidity and Mortality Weekly Report* 46(41):963-968, 1997.

13. CDC. *State Immunization Requirements, 1998-1999.* Washington, DC: U.S. Government Printing Office, 1999, 1-27.

14. CDC. Prevention of Hepatitis A Through Active or Passive Immunization: Recommendations of the Advisory Committee on Immunization Practices (ACIP). *Morbidity and Mortality Weekly Report* 48(RR-12):1-37, 1999.

15. CDC. Pneumococcal and influenza vaccination levels among adults aged >

65 years—United States, 1995. *Morbidity and Mortality Weekly Report* 46(39):913-919, 1997.

16. CDC. Progress towards elimination of *Haemophilus influenzae* type b disease among infants and children—United States, 1987-1995. *Morbidity and Mortality Weekly Report* 45(42):901-906, 1996.

17. Schuchat, A.; Robinson, A.K.; and Wenger, J.D. Bacterial Meningitis in the United States in 1995. *New England Journal of Medicine* 337:970-976,1997.

18. CDC. Preventing emerging infectious disease threats: A strategy for the 21st century. Atlanta, GA: U.S. Department of Health and Human Services, Public Health Service, 1998. Retrieved October 12, 1999 <http://www.cdc.gov/ncidod/emergplan>.

19. U.S. Department of Health and Human Services (DHHS). *Adult Immunization Action Plan, Report of the Workgroup on Adult Immunization.* Washington, DC: the Department, 1997. Retrieved November 23, 1999 <http://www.cdc.gov/od/nvpo/adult.htm>.

20. CDC. Reported vaccine-preventable disease—United States, 1993, and the childhood immunization initiative. *Morbidity and Mortality Weekly Report* 43(4):57-60, 1994.

21. Shefer, A.; Briss, P.; Rodewald, L.; et al. Improving immunization coverage rates: An evidence-based review of the literature. *Epidemiologic Reviews,* 21(1), 1999.

22. Hoekstra, E.J.; LeBaron, C.W.; Megaloeconomou, Y.; et al. Impact of a large-scale immunization initiative in the special supplemental nutrition program for women, infants, and children (WIC). *Journal of the American Medical Association* 280(13):1143-1147, 1998.

23. Abramson, J.S.; O'Shea, T.M.; Ratledge, D.L.; et al. Development of a vaccine tracking system to improve the rate of age-appropriate primary immunization in children of lower socioeconomic status. *Journal of Pediatrics* 126(4):583-586, 1995.

24. CDC. Progress towards elimination of *Haemophilus influenzae* type b disease among infants and children—United States, 1987-1997. *Morbidity and Mortality Weekly Report* 47(46):993-998,1998.

25. CDC. Summary of notifiable disease—United States 1997. *Morbidity and Mortality Weekly Report* 46(54):1-87, 1998.

26. CDC. Prevention of varicella: Recommendations of the advisory committee on immunization practices (ACIP). *Morbidity and Mortality Weekly Report* 45(RR-11):1-36, 1996.

27. CDC. National, State and urban area vaccination coverage levels among children aged 19-35 months—United States, 1997. *Morbidity and Mortality Weekly Report* 47(26):547-554, 1998.

28. Rota, J.S.; Heath, J.L.; Rota, R.A.; et al. Molecular epidemiology of measles virus: Identification of pathways of transmission and implications for measles elimination. *Journal of Infectious Diseases* 173:32-37, 1996.

29. CDC. Measles—United States, 1996 and the interruption of indigenous transmission. *Morbidity and Mortality Weekly Report* 46(11):242-246, 1997.

30. CDC. Epidemiology of Measles–United States, 1998. *Morbidity and Mortality Weekly Report* 48(34):749-753, 1999.

31. Wharton, M. Mumps. In: Wallace, R.B.; Duebbeling, B.N.; Last, J.M.; et al. (eds.). Maxcy-Rosenau-Last. Public Health and Preventive Medicine. 14th ed. Stamford, CT: Appleton & Lange, 1998, 93-95.

32. CDC. Measles, mumps and rubella—vaccine use and strategies for elimination of measles, rubella—and congenital rubella syndrome and control of mumps: Recommendations of the Advisory Committee on Immunization Practices (ACIP). *Morbidity and Mortality Weekly Report* 47(RR-8):1-57, 1998.

33. CDC. Rubella and congenital rubella syndrome—United States, 1994-1997. *Morbidity and Mortality Weekly Report* 46(16):350-354, 1997.

34. Bisgard, K.M.; Hardy, I.R.B.; Popovic, T.; et al. Respiratory diphtheria in the United States, 1980-1995. *American Journal of Public Health* 88:787-791, 1998.

35. CDC. Toxigenic *Corynebacterium diphtheriae*—Northern Plains Indian Community, August-October 1996. *Morbidity and Mortality Weekly Report* 46(22):506-510, 1997.

36. Bardenheier, B.; Prevots, D.R.; Khetsuriani, N.; et al. Tetanus—United States, 1995-1997. *Morbidity and Mortality Weekly Report* 47(SS-2):1-13, 1998.

37. CDC. Pertussis vaccination: Use of acellular pertussis vaccines among infants and young children. *Morbidity and Mortality Weekly Report* 46(RR-7):1-25, 1997.

38. Guris, D.; Strebel, P.M.; Tachdjian, R.; et al. Effec-

tiveness of the pertussis vaccination program as determined by use of the screening method—United States, 1992-1994. *Journal of Infectious Diseases* 176:456-463, 1997.

39. Bisgard, K.M.; Kao, A.; Leake, J.; et al. The epidemiology of *Haemophilus influenzae* invasive disease in the United States, 1994-1995: Near disappearance of a child vaccine preventable disease. *Emerging Infectious Diseases* 4(2):229-237, 1998.

40. CDC. Varicella-related deaths among adults—United States, 1997. *Morbidity and Mortality Weekly Report* 46(19):409-412, 1997.

41. CDC. *Hepatitis Surveillance Report,* No. 56. Atlanta, GA: Centers for Disease Control and Prevention, 1996.

42. CDC. Hepatitis B Virus: A Comprehensive Strategy for Eliminating Transmission in the United States Through Universal Childhood Vaccination: Recommendations of the Immunization Practices Advisory Committee (ACIP). *Morbidity and Mortality Weekly Report* 40(RR-13):1-19, 1991.

43. CDC. Recommendations for Prevention and Control of Hepatitis C Virus (HCV) Infection and HCV-Related Chronic Disease. *Morbidity and Mortality Weekly Report* 47(RR-19):1-39, 1998.

44. CDC. A strategic plan for the elimination of tuberculosis in the United States. *Morbidity and Mortality Weekly Report* 38(S-3):1-25, 1989.

45. American Thoracic Society/CDC. Treatment of Tuberculosis and Tuberculosis Infection in Adults and Children. *American Journal of Respiratory Care Medicine* 149:1359-1374, 1994.

46. CDC. Screening for tuberculosis and tuberculosis infection in high-risk populations. *Morbidity and Mortality Weekly Report,* 44 (RR-11):9-13, 1995.

47. Marshall, B., and Warren, J.R. Unidentified curved bacilli on gastic epithelium in active chronic gastritis. *Lancet* 1:1273-1275, 1983.

48. CDC. Knowledge about causes of peptic ulcer disease–United States. *Morbidity and Mortality Weekly Report* 45(42):985-987, 1997.

49. American Digestive Health Foundation and Opinion Research Corporation. Familiarity with *H. pylori* among adults with digestive disorders and their views toward diagnostic and treatment options. Bethesda, MD: American Digestive Health Foundation and Opinion Research Corporation, 1995.

50. Breuer, T.; Malaty, H.M.; Goodman, K.; et al. Has the scientific evidence about Heliobacter pylori infection in gastrointestinal diseases reached the practicing physicians in the U.S.? *American Journal of Gastroenterology* 91:1905, 1996.

51. CDC. National Center for Infectious Diseases, Division of Bacterial and Mycotic Diseases, Atlanta, GA, 1999.

52. Powell, S.E.; Marcy, S.M.; Phillips, W.R.; et al. Otitis Media–principles of Judicious Use of Antimicrobial Agents. *Pediatrics* 101:165-171, 1998.

53. Redd, S.C.; Markowitz, L.E.; and Katz, S.L. Measles Vaccine. In: Plotkin, S.A. and Orenstein, W.A. (eds.). Vaccines. 3rd ed. Philadelphia, PA: W.B. Saunders Company, 1999, 222-226.

54. Orenstein, W.H.; Hinman, A.R.; and Rodewald, L.E. Public Health Considerations in the United States. In: Plotkin, S.A. and Orenstein, W.A. (eds.). Vaccines. 3rd ed. Philadelphia, PA: W.B. Saunders Company, 1999, 1006-1032.

55. Dowdle, W.R.; Hopkins, D.R., eds. The Eradication of Infectious Diseases. Dahlem Workshop Report. Chichester, NY: John Wiley and Sons, 1997, 1-218.

56. CDC. School Immunization Requirements for Measles—United States, 1981. *Morbidity and Mortality Weekly Report* 30:158-160, 1981.

57. CDC. Notice to readers: Recommended childhood immunization schedule—United States, 1999. *Morbidity and Mortality Weekly Report* 48(1):8-16, 1999.

58. CDC, National Immunization Program, Immunization Services Division. Annual Immunization Assessment Progress—Percentage of Sites Assessed Nationwide in 1997 [chart]. Atlanta, GA: the Center, 1997. Retrieved November 23, 1999 <http://www.cdc.gov/nip/afix/pres/prog/97perc.gif>.

59. Watt, J.; Kahane, S.; Smith, N.; et al. The difference between measured and estimated vaccination coverage among private physicians in California. Presented before the Ambulatory Pediatric Association in New Orleans, LA, May 1998.

60. LeBaron, C.W.; Chaney, M.; Baughman, A.L., et al. Impact of measurement and feedback on vaccination coverage in public clinics, 1988-1994. *Journal of the American Medical Association* 277:631-635, 1997.

61. Dini, E.F.; Chaney, M.; Moolenaar, R.L.; et al. Information as intervention: How

Data as of November 30, 1999

Georgia used vaccination coverage data to double public sector vaccination coverage in seven years. *Journal of Public Health Management Practice* 2(1):45-49, 1996.

62. National Committee for Quality Assurance. The Health Plan Employer Data and Information Set (HEDIS) 3.0/1998, Vol. 2, Technical Specifications. Washington, DC: the Committee, 1997, 38-48.

63. Advisory Committee on Immunization Practices, CDC. Programmatic strategies to increase vaccination rates—assessment and feedback of provider-based vaccination coverage information. *Morbidity and Mortality Weekly Report* 45(10):219-220, 1996.

64. CDC. *Standards for Pediatric Immunization Practices*. Washington, DC: U.S. Government Printing Office, 1993.

65. CDC. National Immunization Program. Atlanta, GA: CDC, Data Management Division, Systems Development Branch, unpublished data, 1999.

66. Sharp, K.; Edgar, T.; and Fowler, K. Findings of Focus Group Research on Immunization Registries. Rockville, MD: Westat, December 1998. Retrieved October 1999 <http://www.cdc.gov/nip/registry/i_fgmenu.htm>.

67. CDC. Immunization of Adolescents: Recommendations of the Advisory Committee on Immunization Practices, the American Academy of Pediatrics, the American Academy of Family Physicians, and the American Medical Association. *Morbidity and Mortality Weekly Report* 45(RR-13):1-16, 1996.

68. Benson, V., and Marano, M.A. Current estimates from the National Health Interview Survey, 1995. National Center for Health Statistics. *Vital Health Statistics* 10(199). 1998.

69. National Center for Health Statistics. *Health—United States, 1994.* Hyattsville, MD: Public Health Service. 1995.

70. Unti, L., and Woodruff, B.A. A review of adolescent school-based hepatitis B vaccination projects: A report prepared for the Centers for Disease Control and Prevention, Hepatitis Branch. Washington, DC: U.S. Department of Health and Human Services, Public Health Service, October 1996.

71. Fedson, D.S. Adult immunization: Summary of the National Vaccine Advisory Committee report. *Journal of the American Medical Association* 272:1133, 1994.

72. CDC. Prevention and control of influenza: Recommendations of the Advisory Committee on Immunization Practices (ACIP). *Morbidity and Mortality Weekly Report* 47(RR-6):1-26, 1998.

73. CDC. Prevention of Pneumococcal Disease: Recommendations of the Advisory Committee on Immunization Practices. *Morbidity and Mortality Weekly Report* 46(RR-8):1-24, 1997.

74. Gyorkos, T.W.; Tannenbaum, T.N.; Abrahamowicz, M.; et al. Evaluation of the effectiveness of immunization delivery methods. *Canadian Journal of Public Health* 85:S14-S30, 1994.

75. Agency for Health Care Policy and Research. *Implementing preventive care.* Retrieved January 6, 1999 <http://www.ahcpr.gov/ppip/handbkiv.htm>.

76. CDC. Notice to Readers: Recommendations of the Advisory Committee on Immunization Practices: Revised Recommendations for Routine Poliomyelitis Vaccination. *Morbidity and Mortality Weekly Report* 48(27):590, 1999.

77. Cody, C.L.; Baraff, L.J.; Cherry, J.D.; et al. Nature and rates of adverse reactions associated with DTP and DT immunizations in infants and children. *Pediatrics* 68:650-660, 1981.

78. CDC. Diphtheria, tetanus, and pertussis: Recommendations for vaccine use and other preventive measures. Recommendations of the Advisory Committee on Immunization Practices. *Morbidity and Mortality Weekly Report* 40(RR-10):1-28, 1991.

79. Stratton, K.R.; Howe, C.J.; and Johnston, Jr., R.B. *Adverse Events Associated with Childhood Vaccines—Evidence Bearing on Causality.* Washington, DC: National Academy Press, 1994.

80. Howson, C.P.; Howe, C.J.; and Fineberg, F.V. *Adverse Effects of Pertussis and Rubella Vaccines.* Washington, DC: National Academy Press, 1991.

81. Chen, R.T.; Glasser, J.W.; Rhodes, P.H.; et al. The Vaccine Safety Datalink Project: A new tool for improving vaccine safety monitoring in the United States. *Pediatrics* 99:765-773, 1997

15

Injury and Violence Prevention

Lead Agency: Centers for Disease Control and Prevention

Contents

Goal

Reduce injuries, disabilities, and deaths due to unintentional injuries and violence.

Overview

The risk of injury is so great that most persons sustain a significant injury at some time during their lives.[1] Nevertheless, this widespread human damage too often is taken for granted, in the erroneous belief that injuries happen by chance and are the result of unpreventable "accidents." In fact, many injuries are not "accidents," or random, uncontrollable acts of fate; rather, most injuries are predictable and preventable.[2]

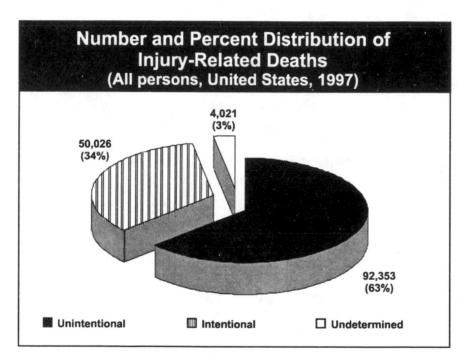

Number and Percent Distribution of Injury-Related Deaths (All persons, United States, 1997)

4,021 (3%)
50,026 (34%)
92,353 (63%)

- ■ Unintentional
- ▥ Intentional
- ☐ Undetermined

Source: National Vital Statistics System (NVSS), CDC, NCHS, 1997.

Issues and Trends

Injury Prevention

In 1997, 149,691 Americans died from injuries due to a variety of causes such as motor vehicle crashes, firearms, poisonings, suffocation, falls, fires, and drownings. About 400 persons die from injuries each day, including 55 children and teenagers. One death out of every 17 in the United States results from injury.[3] Of these deaths, 67 percent are classified as unintentional and 33 percent as intentional. Unintentional injury deaths include approximately 42,000 resulting from motor vehicle crashes per year. In 1997, of approximately 50,000 intentional injury deaths, almost 31,000 were classified as suicide and nearly 20,000 as homicide.[1] In 1997, injuries accounted for 20 percent more years of potential life lost (YPPL) than cancer did (1,990/100,000 compared to 1,500/100,000).[4]

For ages 1 through 44 years, deaths from injuries far surpass those from cancer—the overall leading natural cause of death at these ages—by about 3 to 1. Injuries cause more than two out of five deaths (43 percent) of children aged 1 through 4 years and result in 4 times the number of deaths due to birth defects, the second leading cause of death for this age group. For ages 15 to 24 years, injury deaths exceed deaths from all other causes combined from ages 5 through 44 years. For ages 15 to 24 years, injuries are the cause of nearly four out of five deaths. After age 44 years, injuries account for fewer deaths than other health problems, such as heart disease, cancer, and stroke. However, despite the decrease in the proportion of deaths due to injury, the death rate from injuries is actually higher among older persons than among younger persons.

Injuries are often classified on the basis of events and behaviors that preceded them, as well as the intent of the persons involved. For example, many injuries are preceded by alcohol consumption in amounts or circumstances that increase risk of injury.[5] Although the events leading to an intentional and unintentional injury differ, the outcomes and extent of the injury are similar.

Unintentional Injury Prevention

More persons aged 1 to 34 years die as a result of unintentional injuries than any other cause of death. Across all ages, 95,644 persons died in 1997 as a result of unintentional injuries. Motor vehicle crashes account for approximately half the deaths from unintentional injuries; other unintentional injuries rank second, and falls rank third, followed by poisonings, suffocations, and drownings.[6]

Additional millions of persons are incapacitated by unintentional injuries, with many suffering lifelong disabilities. These events occur disproportionately among the young and the elderly. In 1995, 29 million persons visited emergency departments (EDs) as a result of unintentional injuries.[7]

Although the greatest impact of injury is in human suffering and loss of life, the financial cost is staggering. Included in the costs associated with injuries are the costs of direct medical care and rehabilitation as well as lost income and productivity. By the late 1990s, injury costs were estimated at more than $224 billion annually, an increase of 42 percent over the 1980s.[8] As with other health problems, it costs far less to prevent injuries than to treat them. For example:

- Every child safety seat saves $85 in direct medical costs and an additional $1,275 in other costs.

- Every bicycle helmet saves $395 in direct medical costs and other costs.

- Every smoke detector saves $35 in direct medical costs and an additional $865 in other costs.

- Every dollar spent on poison control centers saves $6.50 in medical costs.[9]

Several themes become evident when examining reports on injury prevention and control, including acute care, treatment, and rehabilitation. First, unintentional injury comprises a group of complex problems involving many different sectors of society. No single force working alone can accomplish everything needed to reduce the number of injuries. Improved outcomes require the combined efforts of many fields, including health, education, transportation, law, engineering, and safety sciences. Second, many of the factors that cause unintentional injuries are closely associated with violent and abusive behavior. Injury prevention and control addresses both unintentional and intentional injuries.

Violence and Abuse Prevention

Violence in the United States is pervasive and can change quality of life. Reports of children killing children in schools are shocking and cause parents to worry about the safety of their children at school. Reports of gang violence make persons fearful for their safety. Although suicide rates began decreasing in the mid 1990s, prior increases among youth aged 10 to 19 years and adults aged 65 years and older have raised concerns about the vulnerability of these population groups. Intimate partner violence and sexual assault threaten people in all walks of life.

Violence claims the lives of many of the Nation's young persons and threatens the health and well-being of many persons of all ages in the United States. On an average day in America, 53 persons die from homicide and a minimum of 18,000 persons survive interpersonal assaults, 84 persons complete suicide, and as many as 3,000 persons attempt suicide. (See Focus Area 18. Mental Health and Mental Disorders.)[10]

Youth continue to be involved as both perpetrators and victims of violence. The elderly, females, and children continue to be targets of both physical and sexual assaults, which are frequently perpetrated by individuals they know. Examples of general issues that impede the public health response to progress in this area include the lack of comparable data sources, lack of standardized definitions and definitional issues, lack of resources to adequately establish consistent tracking systems, and lack of resources to fund promising prevention programs.

Because national data systems will not be available in the first half of the decade for tracking progress, one subject of interest, maltreatment of elders, is not addressed in this focus area's objectives. The maltreatment of persons aged 60 years and older is a topic for research and data collection for the coming decade.

Disparities

While every person is at risk for injury, certain types of injuries appear to affect some groups more frequently. American Indians or Alaska Natives have disproportionately higher death rates from motor vehicle crashes, residential fires, and drownings. In addition, their death rates are about 1.75 times higher than the death rate for the overall U.S. population. Higher death rates from unintentional injury also occur among African Americans.[1]

Certain racial and ethnic groups have more new cases of unintentional injuries and deaths than whites. Unintentional injuries are the second leading cause of death for American Indian males and the third leading cause of death for American Indian females. More than 1,000 American Indians die from injuries, and 10,000 more are hospitalized for injuries each year. The age-adjusted injury death rate for American Indians is 3 times higher than that of all other Americans. Among American Indians, 46 percent of the YPLL is a result of injury, which is 5 times greater than the YPLL due to a next highest cause, heart disease (8 percent). Among the factors that contribute to these increased rates for American Indians are rural or isolated living, minimal emergency medical services, and great distances to sophisticated trauma care.[11]

African American, Hispanic, and American Indian children are at higher risk than white children for home fire deaths.[12] Adults aged 65 years and older are at increased risk of death from fire because they are more vulnerable to smoke inhalation and burns and are less likely to recover. Sense impairment (such as blindness or hearing loss) may prevent older adults from noticing a fire, and mobility impairment may prevent them from escaping its consequences. Older adults also are less likely to have learned fire safety behavior and prevention information, since they grew up at a time when little fire safety was taught in schools, and most current educational programs target children.

In every age group, drowning rates are almost 2 to 4 times greater for males than for females.[13] In 1997, the overall drowning rate for African Americans was 50 percent greater than that for whites; however, the rate was not higher for all age groups. For example, among children aged 1 through 4 years, the drowning rate for whites was slightly higher than the rate for African Americans. For children aged 5 to 19 years, African American children are twice as likely to drown as white children.[14]

Homicide victimization is especially high among African American and Hispanic youths. In 1995, African American males and females aged 15 to 24 years had homicide rates (74.4/100,000) that were more than twice the rate of their Hispanic counterparts (34.1/100,000) and nearly 14 times the rate of their white non-Hispanic counterparts (5.4/100,000).[15]

Data as of November 30, 1999

Trends in suicide among blacks aged 10 to 19 years in the United States during 1980-95 indicate that suicidal behavior among all youth has increased; however, rates for black youth have shown a greater increase.[1]

Although black youth historically have lower suicide rates than have whites, during 1980-95, the suicide rate for black youths aged 10 to 19 years increased from 2.1 to 4.5 per 100,000 population. As of 1995, suicide was the third leading cause of death among blacks aged 15 to 19 years.[17]

Opportunities

To reduce the number and severity of injuries, prevention activities must focus on the type of injury—drowning, fall, fire or burn, firearm, or motor vehicle.[18] For example, a nonfatal spinal cord injury produces the same outcome whether it was caused by an unintentional motor vehicle crash or an attempted suicide.

Understanding injuries allows for development and implementation of effective prevention interventions. Some interventions can reduce injuries from both unintentional and violence-related episodes. For instance, efforts to promote proper storage of firearms in homes can help reduce the risk of assaultive, intentional self-inflicted, and unintentional shootings in the home.[19] Higher taxes on alcoholic beverages are associated with lower death rates from motor vehicle crashes and lower rates for some categories of violent crime, including rape.[20, 21]

Many injuries and injury-related deaths occur in some population groups (such as younger children from birth to 4 years) where the intentionality of the injury is unknown and requires more detailed investigation. As these cases are examined, interventions can be developed to address ways injuries occur—for instance, unintentional poisonings in children or hangings among teenagers—that are emerging in society as growing public health concerns.

Poverty, discrimination, lack of education, and lack of employment opportunities are important risk factors for violence and must be addressed as part of any comprehensive solution to the epidemic of violence. Strategies for reducing violence should begin early in life, before violent beliefs and behavioral patterns can be adopted.

Many potentially effective culturally and linguistically competent intervention strategies for violence prevention exist, such as parent training, mentoring, home visitation, and education.[22] Evaluation of ongoing programs is a major component to help identify effective approaches for violence prevention. The public health approach to violence prevention is multidisciplinary, encouraging experts varying from scientific disciplines, organizations, and communities to work together to find solutions to violence in our Nation.

Many school-aged children suffer disabling and fatal injuries each year. As educational programs for school children are developed and proven effective in preventing injuries, these programs should be included in quality health education curricula at the appropriate grade level. Education should aim at reducing risks of injury directly and at preparing children to be knowledgeable adults. (See Focus Area 7. Educational and Community-Based Programs.)

Interim Progress Toward Year 2000 Objectives

A total of 45 objectives addressed injury prevention in Healthy People 2000. Twenty-six objectives were specific for unintentional injuries and 19 objectives were specific for violence prevention. By the end of the decade, targets had been met for 11 objectives. Unintentional injury objectives showing achievement were unintentional injury hospitalizations, residential fire deaths, nonfatal head injuries, spinal cord injuries, nonfatal poisonings, and pedestrian deaths. Violence prevention objectives which met their targets were homicide, suicide, weapon carrying by adolescents, conflict resolution in schools, and child death review systems.

Progress was made for 13 objectives. Much of the progress made in unintentional injury objectives were with motor vehicle fatalities and use of vehicle occupant restraints. Those unintentional injury objectives showing progress were unintentional injury deaths, motor vehicle deaths, motor vehicle crash deaths, motor vehicle occupant protection systems, helmet use by motorcyclists and bicyclists, safety belt use laws, alcohol-related motor vehicle deaths, and drownings. Violence prevention objectives showing progress were firearm-related deaths, partner abuse, rape and attempted rape, physical fighting among adolescents 14 to 17 years of age, and the number of States with firearm storage laws.

There were six objectives with no progress or movement away from the Healthy People 2000 targets. In unintentional injury, the hospitalization rate for hip fractures remains above baseline levels, indicating no progress toward the year 2000 target. Data from five violence prevention objectives also show movement away from the year 2000 target. Those objectives relate to child abuse and neglect, assault injuries, suicide attempts among adolescents aged 14 to 17 years, battered women turned away from shelters, and suicide prevention protocols in jails.

Note: Unless otherwise noted, data are from Centers for Disease Control and Prevention, National Center for Health Statistics, *Healthy People 2000 Review, 1998-99.*

Injury and Violence Prevention

Goal: Reduce disabilities, injuries, and deaths due to unintentional injuries and violence.

Number	Objective
Injury Prevention	
15-1	Nonfatal head injuries
15-2	Nonfatal spinal cord injuries
15-3	Firearm-related deaths
15-4	Proper firearm storage in homes
15-5	Nonfatal firearm-related injuries
15-6	Child fatality review
15-7	Nonfatal poisonings
15-8	Deaths from poisoning
15-9	Deaths from suffocation
15-10	Emergency department surveillance systems
15-11	Hospital discharge surveillance systems
15-12	Emergency department visits
Unintentional Injury Prevention	
15-13	Deaths from unintentional injuries
15-14	Nonfatal unintentional injuries
15-15	Deaths from motor vehicle crashes
15-16	Pedestrian deaths
15-17	Nonfatal motor vehicle injuries
15-18	Nonfatal pedestrian injuries
15-19	Safety belts
15-20	Child restraints
15-21	Motorcycle helmet use
15-22	Graduated driver licensing
15-23	Bicycle helmet use
15-24	Bicycle helmet laws
15-25	Residential fire deaths

Injury Prevention

15-1. Reduce hospitalization for nonfatal head injuries.

Target: 54 hospitalizations per 100,000 population.

Baseline: 75.5 hospitalizations for nonfatal head injuries per 100,000 population in 1997 (age adjusted to the year 2000 standard population).

Target setting method: Better than the best.

Data source: National Hospital Discharge Survey (NHDS), CDC, NCHS.

Total Population, 1997	Hospitalizations for Nonfatal Head Injuries Rate per 100,000
TOTAL	75.5
Race and ethnicity	
American Indian or Alaska Native	DSU
Asian or Pacific Islander	DSU
Asian	DNC
Native Hawaiian and other Pacific Islander	DNC
Black or African American	88.5
White	55.3
Hispanic or Latino	DSU
Not Hispanic or Latino	DSU
Black or African American	DSU
White	DSU
Gender	
Female	51.8
Male	98.5
Education level	
Less than high school	DNC
High school graduate	DNC
At least some college	DNC

Total Population, 1997	Hospitalizations for Nonfatal Head Injuries Rate per 100,000
Select populations	
Males aged 15 to 25 years	157.3
Persons aged 75 years and older	225.4

DNA = Data have not been analyzed. DNC = Data are not collected. DSU = Data are statistically unreliable.
Note: Age adjusted to the year 2000 standard population.

15-2. Reduce hospitalization for nonfatal spinal cord injuries.

Target: 2.6 hospitalizations per 100,000 population.

Baseline: 4.8 hospitalizations for nonfatal spinal cord injuries per 100,000 population in 1997 (age adjusted to the year 2000 standard population).

Target setting method: 46 percent improvement. (Better than the best will be used when data are available.)

Data source: National Hospital Discharge Survey (NHDS), CDC, NCHS.

Total Population, 1997	Hospitalizations for Nonfatal Spinal Cord Injuries Rate per 100,000
TOTAL	4.8
Race and ethnicity	
American Indian or Alaska Native	DSU
Asian or Pacific Islander	DSU
Asian	DNC
Native Hawaiian and other Pacific Islander	DNC
Black or African American	DSU
White	2.7
Hispanic or Latino	DSU
Not Hispanic or Latino	DSU
Black or African American	DSU
White	DSU
Gender	
Female	DSU
Male	6.1

Total Population, 1997	Hospitalizations for Nonfatal Spinal Cord Injuries
	Rate per 100,000
Education level	
Less than high school	DNC
High school graduate	DNC
At least some college	DNC

DNA = Data have not been analyzed. DNC = Data are not collected. DSU = Data are statistically unreliable.
Note: Age adjusted to the year 2000 standard population.

The physical and emotional toll associated with head and spinal cord injuries can be significant for the survivors and their families. Persons with existing disabilities from head and spinal cord injuries are at high risk for further secondary disabilities. Prevention efforts should target motor vehicle crashes, falls, firearm injury, diving, and water safety.

Approximately 5 percent of the persons who sustained a brain injury each year and who do not experience a good recovery were injured with a firearm. About 12 percent of the new cases of quadriplegia and paraplegia each year are attributable to spinal cord injuries related to firearms.[23]

Motor vehicle crashes cause 44 percent of all spinal cord injuries.

Among pedalcyclists killed, most died from head injuries. Similarly, the common cause of death among motorcyclists is catastrophic head injury. Death rates from head injuries have been shown to be twice as high among cyclists in States lacking helmet laws or laws that apply only to young riders, compared with States where laws apply to all riders.

Falls account for 87 percent of all fractures among adults aged 65 years and older and are the second leading cause of both spinal cord injury and brain injury for this age group.[24, 25] Falls also cause the majority of deaths and severe injuries from head trauma among children under age 14 years. Falls account for 90 percent of the most severe playground-related injuries treated in hospital emergency departments (mostly head injuries and fractures) and one-third of reported fatalities. Head injuries are involved in about 75 percent of all reported fall-related deaths associated with playground equipment.

Many diving-related incidents also result in spinal cord injury. Diving-related injury first becomes an issue during adolescence. Injuries to males outnumber injuries to females. Diving injuries account for one of eight spinal cord injuries, with half of those injuries resulting in quadriplegia.[55]

15-3. Reduce firearm-related deaths.

Target: 4.9 deaths per 100,000 population.

Baseline: 11.0 deaths per 100,000 population were related to firearm injuries in 1998 (preliminary data; age adjusted to the year 2000 standard population).

Target setting method: Better than the best.

Data source: National Vital Statistics System (NVSS), CDC, NCHS.

Total Population, 1997*	Firearm-Related Deaths Rate per 100,000
TOTAL	12.1
Race and ethnicity	
American Indian or Alaska Native	11.4
Asian or Pacific Islander	5.0
Asian	DNC
Native Hawaiian and other Pacific Islander	DNC
Black or African American	22.9
White	10.4
Hispanic or Latino	10.7
Cuban	13.1
Mexican	11.1
Puerto Rican	8.5
Not Hispanic or Latino	12.1
Black or African American	23.7
White	10.0
Gender	
Female	3.4
Male	21.4
Education level (aged 25 to 64 years)	
Less than high school	22.9
High school graduate	18.3
At least some college	7.4

Data as of November 30, 1999

Total Population, 1997*	Firearm-Related Deaths
	Rate per 100,000
Select firearm-related deaths	
Homicides	4.9
Suicides	6.6
Unintentional	0.4

DNA = Data have not been analyzed. DNC = Data are not collected. DSU = Data are statistically unreliable.

Note: Age adjusted to the year 2000 standard population.

*New data for population groups will be added when available.

15-4. Reduce the proportion of persons living in homes with firearms that are loaded and unlocked.

Target: 16 percent.

Baseline: 19 percent of the population lived in homes with loaded and unlocked firearms in 1998 (preliminary data; age adjusted to the year 2000 standard population).

Target setting method: Better than the best.

Data source: National Health Interview Survey (NHIS), CDC, NCHS.

Total Population, 1994*	Loaded, Unlocked Firearms in Home
	Percent
TOTAL	20
Race and ethnicity	
American Indian or Alaska Native	DSU
Asian or Pacific Islander	DSU
Asian	DSU
Native Hawaiian and other Pacific Islander	DSU
Black or African American	24
White	20
Hispanic or Latino	DSU
Not Hispanic or Latino	20
Black or African American	25
White	20

Total Population, 1994*	Loaded, Unlocked Firearms in Home
	Percent
Gender	
Female	18
Male	22
Education level (aged 25 years and older)	
Less than high school	23
High school graduate	19
At least some college	20

DNA = Data have not been analyzed. DNC = Data are not collected. DSU = Data are statistically unreliable.

Note: Age adjusted to the year 2000 standard population.

*New data for population groups will be added when available.

15-5. Reduce nonfatal firearm-related injuries.

Target: 10.9 injuries per 100,000 population.

Baseline: 26 nonfatal firearm-related injuries per 100,000 population in 1996.

Target setting method: Better than the best.

Data source: National Electronic Injury Surveillance System (NEISS), Consumer Product Safety Commission (CPSC).

Total Population, 1996	Nonfatal Firearm-Related Injuries
	Rate per 100,000
TOTAL	26
Race and ethnicity	
American Indian or Alaska Native	DSU
Asian or Pacific Islander	DSU
Asian	DSU
Native Hawaiian and other Pacific Islander	DSU
Black or African American	DNA
White	DNA
Hispanic or Latino	35
Not Hispanic or Latino	DNA
Black or African American	93
White	11

Total Population, 1996	Nonfatal Firearm-Related Injuries
	Rate per 100,000
Gender	
Female	6
Male	47
Education level	
Less than high school	DNC
High school graduate	DNC
At least some college	DNC
Select populations	
Males aged 15 to 24 years	152

DNA =Data have not been analyzed. DNC = Data are not collected. DSU =Data are statistically unreliable.

The United States has the highest rates of lethal childhood violence than every other industrialized country.[27] The increase in the total homicide rate from 1979 through 1993 resulted solely from increases in firearms homicides.[28] Fatalities, however, are only part of the problem. For each of the 35,957 persons killed by a gunshot wound in the United States in 1995, approximately 3 more received non-fatal wounds.[29]

15-6. (Developmental) Extend State-level child fatality review of deaths due to external causes for children aged 14 years and under.

Potential data sources: National Vital Statistics System (NVSS), CDC, NCHS; Inter-Agency Council on Child Abuse and Neglect (ICAN) National Database, FBI Uniform Crime Report, U.S. Department of Justice.

Death resulting from injury is one of the most profound public health issues facing children in the United States today. In 1997, nearly 19,000 children aged 19 years and under were victims of injury—33 percent from violence and 67 percent from unintentional injury.[30]

In examination of these trends in childhood injury-related cause of death, information has typically come from one of several sources (vital statistics, protective service records, and the FBI Uniform Crime Report), each with specific limitations. In response to the increasing trend of violence against children and the lack of a comprehensive data source on violent childhood deaths, the Child Fatality Review Team (CFRT) process was developed in 1978 in California.

The goal of the CFR teams is the prevention of childhood fatalities. Their responsibility is to review so-called "suspicious" or "preventable" childhood fatalities.

Minimal or core standards for CFR teams must include representatives from criminal justice, health, and social services. After integrating information from multiple sources, review teams strive to determine if the cause and manner of death were recorded accurately and suggest prevention initiatives for all relevant agencies. Simply reviewing fatalities is not helpful unless recommendations for prevention also are included and plans are made for periodic followup to ensure that recommendations are being acted on.

Focusing on children aged 14 years and under will include most "unexplained" childhood deaths and is considered a more reasonable goal to achieve. However, States should continue to improve their CFRT systems. Teams with adequate resources are encouraged to extend their review to all causes of death for all children aged 18 years and under as their ultimate goal. CFR teams also should include culturally appropriate members.

15-7. Reduce nonfatal poisonings.

Target: 292 nonfatal poisonings per 100,000 population.

Baseline: 348.4 nonfatal poisonings per 100,000 population in 1997 (age adjusted to the year 2000 standard population).

Target setting method: Better than the best.

Data sources: National Hospital Ambulatory Medical Care System (NHAMCS), CDC, NCHS; NEISS, CPSC.

Total Population, 1997 (unless noted)	Nonfatal Poisonings Rate per 100,000
TOTAL	348.4
Race and ethnicity	
American Indian or Alaska Native	DSU
Asian or Pacific Islander	DSU
Asian	DSU
Native Hawaiian and other Pacific Islander	DSU
Black or African American	464.5
White	340.6
Hispanic or Latino	DSU
Not Hispanic or Latino	DSU
Black or African American	DSU
White	DSU

Total Population, 1997 (unless noted)	Nonfatal Poisonings Rate per 100,000
Gender	
Female	410.9
Male	281.6
Education level	
Less than high school	DNC
High school graduate	DNC
At least some college	DNC
Select populations of poisonings	
Assault or attempted homicide	6 (1996)
Intentional suicide attempts	63 (1996)
Unintentional poisonings	268 (1996)
Children aged 4 years and under	460

DNA =Data have not been analyzed. DNC =Data are not collected. DSU =Data are statistically unreliable.
Note: Age adjusted to the year 2000 standard population.

15-8. Reduce deaths caused by poisonings.

Target: 1.8 death per 100,000 population.

Baseline: 5.8 deaths per 100,000 population were caused by poisonings in 1998 (preliminary data; age adjusted to the year 2000 standard population).

Target setting method: Better than the best.

Data sources: National Vital Statistics System (NVSS), CDC, NCHS; NEISS, CPSC.

Total Population, 1997* (unless noted)	Poisoning Deaths Rate per 100,000
TOTAL	6.6
Race and ethnicity	
American Indian or Alaska Native	8.0
Asian or Pacific Islander	2.0
Asian	DNC
Native Hawaiian and other Pacific Islander	DNC
Black or African American	8.1
White	6.6

Total Population, 1997* (unless noted)	Poisoning Deaths Rate per 100,000
Hispanic or Latino	5.7
Cuban	3.1
Mexican	4.6
Puerto Rican	12.7
Not Hispanic or Latino	6.7
Black or African American	8.3
White	6.6
Gender	
Female	3.9
Male	9.4
Education level (aged 25 to 64 years)	
Less than high school	16.2
High school graduate	13.8
At least some college	5.7
Select populations	
Unintentional poisoning	3.3 (1996)
Suicide	2.0 (1996)
Homicide	DSU (1996)

DNA =Data have not been analyzed. DNC =Data are not collected. DSU =Data are statistically unreliable.

Note: Age adjusted to the year 2000 standard population.

*New data for population groups will be added when available.

Children are at significantly greater risk from poisoning death and exposure than adults because children are more likely to ingest potentially harmful chemicals. In 1995, 80 children aged 14 years and under died from poisoning. Children aged 4 years and under accounted for nearly half of these deaths. In 1996, more than 1.1 million unintentional poisonings among children aged 5 years and under were reported to U.S. poison control centers. Approximately 90 percent of all poison exposures occur at a residence.[31]

In 1996, 29 children aged 5 years and under died from exposure to medicines and household products. Among children aged 5 years and under, 60 percent of poisoning exposures come from nonpharmaceutical products such as cosmetics, cleaning substances, plants, foreign bodies, toys, pesticides and art supplies; 40 percent come from pharmaceuticals. Immediately calling a poison control center can reduce the likelihood of severe poisoning, decrease the cost of a poisoning incident, and prevent the need for a hospital emergency department (ED) visit.

The total annual cost of poisoning-related injury and death exceeds $7.6 billion among children aged 14 years and under. Children aged 4 years and under account for $5.1 billion, or two-thirds, of these costs. Medical expenses associated with a poisoning exposure average $925 per case. The average cost of hospital treatment for a poisoning exposure is $8,700.[32]

15-9.   Reduce deaths caused by suffocation.

Target: 2.9 death per 100,000 population.

Baseline: 4.0 deaths per 100,000 population were caused by suffocation in 1998 (preliminary data; age adjusted to the year 2000 standard population).

Target setting method: Better than the best.

Data source: National Vital Statistics System (NVSS), CDC, NCHS.

Total Population, 1997*	Suffocation Deaths Rate per 100,000
TOTAL	4.0
Race and ethnicity	
American Indian or Alaska Native	6.2
Asian or Pacific Islander	3.8
Asian	DNC
Native Hawaiian and other Pacific Islander	DNC
Black or African American	4.5
White	3.9
Hispanic or Latino	3.0
Not Hispanic or Latino	4.1
Black or African American	4.6
White	4.0
Gender	
Female	2.3
Male	5.9
Education level (aged 25 to 64 years)	
Less than high school	6.1
High school graduate	4.8
At least some college	2.1

Total Population, 1997*	Suffocation Deaths
	Rate per 100,000
Select Populations	
Homicide	DNA
Suicide	DNA
Unintentional	DNA

DNA =Data have not been analyzed. DNC = Data are not collected. DSU =Data are statistically unreliable.

Note: Age adjusted to the year 2000 standard population.

*New data for population groups will be added when available.

In 1997, 10,650 persons died from suffocation. In the same year, 934 children aged 14 years and under died from suffocation. Of these children, 64 percent were aged 4 years and under.[33] Approximately 5,000 children aged 14 years and under are treated in hospital EDs for aspirating and ingesting toys and toy parts each year. The majority of childhood suffocations, strangulations, and chokings occur in the home. The total annual cost of airway obstruction injury among children aged 14 and under exceeds $1.5 billion. Children aged 4 years and under account for more than 60 percent of these costs. It is estimated that as many as 30 percent of the infants whose deaths are attributed to Sudden Infant Death Syndrome (SIDS) each year are found in potentially suffocating environments, frequently on their stomachs, with their noses and mouths covered by soft bedding.[34]

15-10. Increase the number of States and the District of Columbia with statewide emergency department surveillance systems that collect data on external causes of injury.

Target: All States and the District of Columbia.

Baseline: 12 States had statewide ED surveillance systems that collected data on external causes of injury in 1998.

Target setting method: Total coverage.

Data source: External Cause of Injury Survey, American Public Health Association (APHA), September 1998.

15-11. Increase the number of States and the District of Columbia that collect data on external causes of injury through hospital discharge data systems.

Target: All States and the District of Columbia.

Baseline: 23 States collected data on external causes of injury through hospital discharge data systems in 1998.

Target setting method: Total coverage.

Data source: External Cause of Injury Survey, American Public Health Association (APHA).

15-12. Reduce hospital emergency department visits caused by injuries.

Target: 112 hospital emergency department visits per 1,000 population.

Baseline: 130 hospital emergency department visits per 1,000 population were caused by injury in 1997.

Target setting method: Better than the best.

Data source: National Hospital Ambulatory Medical Care Survey (NHAMCS), CDC, NCHS.

Total Population, 1997	Injury-Related Hospital Emergency Department Visits
	Rate per 1,000
TOTAL	130
Race and ethnicity	
American Indian or Alaska Native	DSU
Asian or Pacific Islander	DSU
Asian	DSU
Native Hawaiian and other Pacific Islander	DSU
Black or African American	180
White	125
Hispanic or Latino	DSU
Not Hispanic or Latino	DSU
Black or African American	DSU
White	DSU

Gender	
Female	115
Male	145
Education level	
Less than high school	DNC
High school graduate	DNC
At least some college	DNC

DNA = Data have not been analyzed. DNC = Data are not collected. DSU = Data are statistically unreliable.

Emergency department (ED) patient records and hospital discharge systems are an important source of public health surveillance and an integral part of the vision of electronically linked health information systems that can serve multiple purposes. Because of the volume and case mix of patients they treat, EDs are well positioned to provide data on cause and severity of injuries. Access to such data can help with the development of population-based public health interventions.

Unintentional Injury Prevention

15-13. Reduce deaths caused by unintentional injuries.

Target: 20.8 deaths per 100,000 population.

Baseline: 33.3 deaths per 100,000 population were caused by unintentional injuries in 1998 (preliminary data; age adjusted to the year 2000 standard population).

Target setting method: Better than the best.

Data source: National Vital Statistics System (NVSS), CDC, NCHS.

Total Population, 1997*	Unintentional Injury Deaths Rate per 100,000
TOTAL	34.8
Race and ethnicity	
American Indian or Alaska Native	62.7
Asian or Pacific Islander	20.9
Asian	DNC
Native Hawaiian and other Pacific Islander	DNC
Black or African American	40.9
White	34.3

Data as of November 30, 1999

Total Population, 1997*	Unintentional Injury Deaths
	Rate per 100,000
Hispanic or Latino	30.1
Cuban	23.2
Mexican	32.1
Puerto Rican	27.7
Not Hispanic or Latino	35.1
Black or African American	40.9
White	34.2
Gender	
Female	21.8
Male	49.2
Education level (aged 25 to 64 years)	
Less than high school	51.6
High school graduate	39.9
At least some college	17.2
Select populations	
Black or African American male	60.3
American Indian or Alaska Native male	89.6
Hispanic male	45.4
White male	48.4

DNA =Data have not been analyzed. DNC = Data are not collected. DSU =Data are statistically unreliable.

Note: Age adjusted to the year 2000 standard population.

*New data for population groups will be added when available.

15-14. (Developmental) Reduce nonfatal unintentional injuries.

Potential data source: National Hospital Discharge Survey (NHDS), CDC, NCHS.

15-15. Reduce deaths caused by motor vehicle crashes.

Target: 9.0 deaths per 100,000 population for 15-15a and 1 death per 100 million vehicle miles traveled (VMT) for 15-15b.

Baseline: 15.0 deaths per 100,000 population were caused by motor vehicle crashes in 1998 (preliminary data; age adjusted to the year 2000 standard population) for 15-15a and 2 deaths per 100 million VMT were caused by motor vehicle crashes in 1997 for 15-15b.

Target setting method: Better than the best for 15-15a; 50 percent improvement for 15-15b. (Better than the best will be used when data are available.)

Data sources: National Vital Statistics System (NVSS), CDC, NCHS; Federal Highway Administration (FHWA).

Total Population, 1997* (unless noted)	Motor Vehicle Crash Deaths	
	15-15a. Rate per 100,000	15-15b. Rate per 100 Million VMT
TOTAL	15.8	2
Race and ethnicity		
American Indian or Alaska Native	31.5	DNC
Asian or Pacific Islander	10.6	DNC
Asian	DNC	DNC
Native Hawaiian and other Pacific Islander	DNC	DNC
Black or African American	17.0	DNC
White	15.8	DNC
Hispanic or Latino	15.2	DNC
Cuban	13.9	DNC
Mexican	17.1	DNC
Puerto Rican	9.1	DNC
Not Hispanic or Latino	16.3	DNC
Black or African American	17.8	DNC
White	16.1	DNC
Gender		
Female	10.4	DNA
Male	21.7	DNA
Education level (aged 25 to 64 years)		
Less than high school	25.0	DNC
High school graduate	20.7	DNC

| Total Population, 1997* (unless noted) | Motor Vehicle Crash Deaths | |
	15-15a. Rate per 100,000	15-15b. Rate per 100 Million VMT
Select populations		
Children aged 14 years and under	4.2 (1998)	DNA
Persons aged 15 to 24 years	25.4 (1998)	DNA
Persons aged 70 years and older	24.3 (1998)	DNA
Motorcyclists	NA	21.3

DNA =Data have not been analyzed. DNC =Data are not collected. DSU =Data are statistically unreliable. NA; Not applicable.

Note: Age adjusted to the year 2000 standard population; 1998 data are preliminary.

*New data for population groups will be added when available.

15-16. Reduce pedestrian deaths on public roads.

Target: 1 pedestrian death per 100,000 population.

Baseline: 2 pedestrian deaths per 100,000 population occurred on public roads in 1997.

Target setting method: 50 percent improvement. (Better than the best will be used when data are available.)

Data source: Fatality Analysis Reporting System (FARS), DOT, NHTSA.

Total Population, 1997	Pedestrian Deaths on Public Roads Rate per 100,000
TOTAL	2
Gender	
Female	1
Male	3
Select populations	
Persons aged 70 years and older	4

Data for other population groups currently are not collected.

15-17. Reduce nonfatal injuries caused by motor vehicle crashes.

Target: 1,000 nonfatal injuries per 100,000 population.

Baseline: 1,270 nonfatal injuries per 100,000 population were caused by motor vehicle crashes in 1997.

Target setting method: 21 percent improvement. (Better than the best will be used when data are available.)

Data source: General Estimates System (GES), DOT, NHTSA.

Total Population, 1997	Nonfatal Motor Vehicle Crash Injuries
	Rate per 100,000
TOTAL	1,270
Select populations	
Persons aged 16 to 20 years	3,116
Persons aged 21 to 24 years	2,496

> **Data for other population groups currently are either not collected or not analyzed.**

15-18. Reduce nonfatal pedestrian injuries on public roads.

Target: 21 nonfatal injuries per 100,000 population.

Baseline: 29 nonfatal pedestrian injuries per 100,000 population occurred on public roads in 1997.

Target setting method: 28 percent improvement. (Better than the best will be used when data are available.)

Data source: General Estimates System (GES), DOT, NHTSA.

| Total Population, 1997 | Nonfatal Pedestrian Injuries on Public Roads |
	Rate per 100,000
TOTAL	29
Select populations	
Persons aged 5 to 9 years	56
Persons aged 10 to 15 years	46
Persons aged 16 to 20 years	36

> **Data for other population groups currently are either not collected or not analyzed.**

15-19. Increase use of safety belts.

Target: 92 percent.

Baseline: 69 percent of the total population used safety belts in 1998.

Target setting method: 33 percent improvement. (Better than the best will be used when data are available.)

Data sources: National Occupant Protection Use Survey (NOPUS), DOT, NHTSA; Youth Risk Behavior Survey (YRBS), NCCDPHP.

| Total Population, 1998 | Safety Belt Use |
	Percent
TOTAL	69
Select populations	
9th through 12th grade students	81

> **Data for other population groups currently are not collected.**

15-20. Increase use of child restraints.

Target: 100 percent.

Baseline: 92 percent of motor vehicle occupants aged 4 years and under used child restraints in 1998 (preliminary data).

Target setting method: Total coverage.

Data source: National Occupant Protection Use Survey (NOPUS), Controlled Intersection Study, DOT, NHTSA.

Data for population groups currently are not collected.

15-21. Increase the proportion of motorcyclists using helmets.

Target: 79 percent.

Baseline: 67 percent of motorcycle operators and passengers used helmets in 1997.

Target setting method: 18 percent improvement. (Better than the best will be used when data are available.)

Data sources: National Occupant Protection Use Survey (NOPUS), DOT, NHTSA; Youth Risk Behavior Survey (YRBS), CDC, NCCDPHP.

Motorcyclists, 1997	Helmet Use Percent
TOTAL	67
Select populations	
9th through 12th grade students	64

Data for other population groups currently are not collected.

15-22. Increase the number of States and the District of Columbia that have adopted a graduated driver licensing model law.

Target: All States and the District of Columbia.

Baseline: 23 States had a graduated driver licensing model law in 1999.

Target setting method: Total coverage.

Data source: U.S. Licensing Systems for Young Drivers, Insurance Institute for Highway Safety.

Motor vehicle crashes remain a major public health problem. They are the leading cause of death for persons in the United States aged 5 to 29 years. In 1998, 41,471 persons died in motor vehicle crashes.[35] Thirty-eight percent of these deaths occurred in alcohol-related crashes.[35] The motor vehicle death rate per 100,000 persons is especially high among persons aged 16 to 24 years and persons aged 75 years and older. Safety belts, when worn correctly, are the most effective way for occupants to reduce the risk of death and serious injury in a motor vehicle crash on public roads (including those on Indian Reservations). As of December 1998, the national safety belt use rate was 69 percent.

In 1998, 69,000 pedestrians were injured and 5,220 were killed in traffic crashes in the United States. On average, a pedestrian is killed in a motor vehicle crash every 101 minutes, and one is injured every 8 minutes.[36]

In 1998, persons aged 70 years and older made up 9 percent of the population but accounted for 14 percent of all traffic fatalities and 18 percent of all pedestrian fatalities. Compared with the fatality rate for drivers aged 25 through 69 years, the rate for drivers in the oldest group is 9 times higher.[37]

Older persons also are more susceptible than younger persons to medical complications following motor vehicle crash injuries. Thus, they are more likely to die from their injuries.[37]

Fewer persons aged 70 years and older are licensed to drive, compared to younger persons, and they drive fewer miles per licensed driver. Persons in this older age group, however, have higher rates of fatal crashes per mile driven, per 100,000 persons, and per licensed driver than any other group except young drivers (aged 16 to 24 years).

Pedestrians account for about 13 percent of motor vehicle deaths. The problem of pedestrian deaths and injuries is worse among young children and older adults. Children are more likely to be injured, while older adults are more likely to die in pedestrian crashes.[36]

As of December 1997, 49 States had safety belt laws. Eleven States had primary enforcement laws, and the remaining 38 States had secondary enforcement laws.[38] In 1998, the average observed belt use rate by States with secondary enforcement laws was 62 percent, compared to 79 percent in States with primary enforcement laws.[38]

Among children aged 1 to 14 years, crash injuries are the leading cause of death. In 1998, 2,549 children aged 14 years and under died in motor vehicle crashes.[35] The use of age-appropriate restraint systems can reduce this problem. Because all States have child restraint laws, more children now ride restrained. But loopholes in the laws exempt many children from coverage under either safety belt or child restraint use laws. Another problem is the persistence of incorrectly used child restraints and safety belts.[39]

Motorcycles are less stable and less visible than cars, and they have high-performance capabilities. When motorcycles crash, their riders lack the protection of an enclosed vehicle, so they are more likely to be injured or killed. The number of deaths on motorcycles per mile traveled is about 16 times the number of deaths in cars. Wearing a motorcycle helmet reduces the chances of dying in a motorcycle crash by 29 percent and reduces the chances of brain injury by 67 percent. An unhelmeted rider is 40 percent more likely to suffer a fatal head injury, compared with a helmeted rider. In 1998, 2,284 motorcyclists died in crashes.[40]

Teenagers accounted for 10 percent of the U.S. population in 1997 and 15 percent of the motor vehicle deaths. In 1998, 3,427 drivers aged 15 to 20 years were killed, and an additional 348,000 were injured in motor vehicle crashes.[41] Graduated licensing laws allow a young driver to gain driving experience at incremental levels. Graduated licensing is a system for phasing in on-road driving that allows beginners to obtain their initial experience under lower risk conditions.

The National Committee on Uniform Traffic Laws and Ordinances (NCUTLO) has developed a model law that calls for a minimum of 6 months in the learner stage and a minimum of 6 months in the intermediate license stage with night driving restrictions. Twenty-three States have all the core provisions of the model graduated licensing model law developed by NCUTLO. The NCUTLO model also requires applicants for intermediate and full licenses to have no safety belt or zero tolerance violations and to be conviction-free during the mandatory holding periods.

15-23. (Developmental) Increase use of helmets by bicyclists.

Potential data sources: Consumer Product Safety Commission; Behavioral Risk Factor Surveillance System (BRFSS), CDC; World Health Organization Study of Health Behavior in School Children.

15-24. Increase the number of States and the District of Columbia with laws requiring bicycle helmets for bicycle riders.

Target: All States and the District of Columbia.

Baseline: 11 States had laws requiring bicycle helmets for bicycle riders under age 15 years in 1999.

Target setting method: Total coverage.

Data source: Bicycle Helmet Safety Institute.

Head injuries are the most serious type of injury sustained by pedalcyclists of all ages. In 1998, 761 bicyclists were killed in crashes involving motor vehicles, and an additional 53,000 were injured in traffic crashes. Almost one-third (30 percent) of the pedalcyclists killed in traffic crashes in 1998 were between age 5 and 15 years. The proportion of pedalcyclist fatalities among persons aged 25 to 64 years was 1.7 times higher in 1997 than in 1987 (46 percent and 27 percent, respectively).[42] More bicyclists were killed on major roads than on local roads (59 percent compared with 36 percent) in 1997.[43]

Bicycle helmets reduce the risk of bicycle-related head injury by 85 percent.[44] Although no States have bicycle laws that apply to all riders, 15 States have laws that apply to young bicyclists under age 18 years.[45] In addition, several localities have ordinances that require some or all bicyclists to wear helmets. Helmets are important for riders of all ages, especially because older bicyclists represent two-thirds of bicycle deaths.[44]

15-25. Reduce residential fire deaths.

Target: 0.6 deaths per 100,000 population.

Baseline: 1.2 deaths per 100,000 population were caused by residential fires in 1998 (preliminary data; age adjusted to the year 2000 standard population).

Target setting method: Better than the best.

Data source: National Vital Statistics System (NVSS), CDC, NCHS.

Total Population, 1997*	Residential Fire Deaths Rate per 100,000
TOTAL	1.3
Race and ethnicity	
American Indian or Alaska Native	2.2
Asian or Pacific Islander	0.8
Asian	DNC
Native Hawaiian and other Pacific Islander	DNC
Black or African American	3.4
White	1.1
Hispanic or Latino	0.8
Cuban	DSU
Mexican	0.7
Puerto Rican	1.4
Not Hispanic or Latino	1.4
Black or African American	3.5
White	1.1
Gender	
Female	1.0
Male	1.7
Education level (aged 25 to 64 years)	
Less than high school	2.0
High school graduate	1.3
At least some college	0.5

Total Population, 1997*	Residential Fire Deaths Rate per 100,000
Select populations	
Persons aged 4 years and younger	2.1
Persons aged 65 years and older	3.5
Black or African American	3.4
Females	2.6
Males	4.5

DNA = Data have not been analyzed. DNC = Data are not collected. DSU = Data are statistically unreliable.

Note: Age adjusted to the year 2000 standard population.

*New data for population groups will be added when available.

15-26. Increase functioning residential smoke alarms.

Target and baseline:

Objective	Increase in Function- ing Residential Smoke Alarm on Every Floor	Baseline Percent	2010 Target
15-26a.	Total population living in residences with functioning smoke alarm on every floor	87 (1994)	100
15-26b.	Residences with a functioning smoke alarm on every floor	87 (1998)	100

Age adjusted to the year 2000 standard population.

Target setting method: Total coverage.

Data source: National Health Interview Survey (NHIS), CDC, NCHS.

Total Population, 1994	15-26a. Live in Residences With Functioning Smoke Alarm on Every Floor
	Percent
TOTAL	87
Race and ethnicity	
American Indian or Alaska Native	89
Asian or Pacific Islander	86
Asian	DSU
Native Hawaiian and other Pacific Islander	DSU
Black or African American	88
White	86
Hispanic or Latino	90
Not Hispanic or Latino	87
Black or African American	88
White	86
Gender	
Female	87
Male	86
Education level (aged 25 years and older)	
Less than high school	87
High school graduate	87
At least some college	87

DNA = Data have not been analyzed. DNC = Data are not collected. DSU = Data are statistically unreliable.
Note: Age adjusted to the year 2000 standard population.

In 1997, 3,220 deaths occurred as a result of residential fires. Residential property loss caused by these fires was roughly $4.4 billion. In 1995, the cost of all fire-related deaths and injuries, including deaths and injuries to firefighters, was estimated at $15.8 billion.[46]

Fires are the second leading cause of unintentional injury death among children. Compared to the total population, children aged 4 years and under have a fire death rate more than twice the national average. About 800 children aged 14 years and under die by fire each year, and 65 percent of these children are under age 5 years. Children are disproportionately affected because they react less effectively to fire than adults, and they also generally sustain more severe burns at lower temperatures than adults. Two-thirds of fire-related deaths and injuries among children under age 5 years occur in homes without working smoke alarms.[47]

Working smoke alarms on every level and in every sleeping area of a home can provide residents with sufficient warning to escape from nearly all types of fires. Therefore, working smoke alarms can be highly effective in preventing fire-related deaths. If a fire occurs, homes with smoke alarms are roughly half as likely to have a death occur as homes without smoke alarms.[47]

15-27. Reduce deaths from falls.

Target: 2.3 deaths per 100,000 population.

Baseline: 4.5 deaths per 100,000 population were caused by falls in 1998 (preliminary data; age adjusted to the year 2000 standard population).

Target setting method: Better than the best.

Data source: National Vital Statistics System (NVSS), CDC, NCHS.

Total Population, 1997*	Deaths From Falls Rate per 100,000
TOTAL	4.6
Race and ethnicity	
American Indian or Alaska Native	5.6
Asian or Pacific Islander	3.5
Asian	DNC
Native Hawaiian and other Pacific Islander	DNC
Black or African American	3.1
White	4.7
Hispanic or Latino	3.3
Cuban	2.4
Mexican	3.4
Puerto Rican	2.7
Not Hispanic or Latino	4.6
Black or African American	3.1
White	4.7
Gender	
Female	3.3
Male	6.3

Total Population, 1997*	Deaths From Falls Rate per 100,000
Education level (aged 25 to 64 years)	
Less than high school	3.0
High school graduate	2.2
At least some college	1.1
Select populations	
Persons aged 65 to 84 years	16.4
Persons aged 85 years and older	104.9

DNA = Data have not been analyzed. DNC = Data are not collected. DSU = Data are statistically unreliable.

Note: Age adjusted to the year 2000 standard population.

*New data for population groups will be added when available.

15-28. Reduce hip fractures among older adults.

Target and baseline:

Objective	Reduction in Hip Fractures	1997 Baseline	2010 Target
		Rate per 100,000	
15-28a.	Females aged 65 years and older	1,120.9	491.0
15-28b.	Males aged 65 years and older	563.1	450.5

Target setting method: Better than the best for 15-28a; 20 percent improvement for 15-28b. (Better than the best will be used when data are available.)

Data source: National Hospital Discharge Survey (NHDS), CDC, NCHS.

Adults Aged 65 Years and Older, 1997	Hip Fracture	
	15-28a. Females	15-28b. Males
	Rate per 100,000	
TOTAL	1,120.9	563.1
Race and ethnicity		
American Indian or Alaska Native	DSU	DSU
Asian or Pacific Islander	DSU	DSU
Asian	DNC	DNC
Native Hawaiian and other Pacific Islander	DNC	DNC

Adults Aged 65 Years and Older, 1997	Hip Fracture	
	15-28a. Females	15-28b. Males
	Rate per 100,000	
Black or African American	492.0	DSU
White	932.1	469.4
Hispanic or Latino	DSU	DSU
Not Hispanic or Latino	DSU	DSU
Black or African American	DSU	DSU
White	DSU	DSU
Gender		
Female	DNA	DNA
Male	DNA	DNA
Education level (aged 25 to 64 years)		
Less than high school	DNC	DNC
High school graduate	DNC	DNC
At least some college	DNC	DNC

DNA = Data have not been analyzed. DNC = Data are not collected. DSU = Data are statistically unreliable.

In 1996, falls became the second leading cause of injury deaths among adults aged 65 years and older. In 1997, 9,023 adults over age 65 years died as a result of falls.[48] Falls are the most common cause of injuries and hospital admissions for trauma among elderly persons. Since most fractures are the result of falls, understanding factors that contribute to falling is essential to designing effective intervention strategies. Alcohol use has been implicated in 35 to 63 percent of deaths from falls.[48a] For persons aged 65 years and older, 60 percent of fatal falls occur in the home, 30 percent occur in public places, and 10 percent occur in health care institutions.

The most serious fall-related injury is hip fracture. Approximately 212,000 hip fractures occur each year in the United States among adults aged 65 years and older; 75 to 80 percent of all hip fractures are sustained by females.[49] The impact of these injuries on the quality of life is enormous. Half of all elderly adults hospitalized for hip fracture cannot return home or live independently after the fracture. The total direct cost of all fall injuries for adults aged 65 years and older in 1994 was $20.2 billion.[50] Factors that contribute to falls include difficulties in gait and balance, neurological and musculoskeletal disabilities, psychoactive medications, dementia, and visual impairment.[51] Environmental hazards such as slippery surfaces, uneven floors, poor lighting on stairs, loose rugs, unstable furniture, grab bars in bathrooms, and objects on floors also may play a role.

15-29. Reduce drownings.

Target: 0.9 drownings per 100,000 population.

Baseline: 1.6 drownings per 100,000 population in 1998 (preliminary data; age adjusted to the year 2000 standard population).

Target setting method: Better than the best.

Data source: National Vital Statistics System (NVSS), CDC, NCHS, CPSC.

Total Population, 1997* (unless noted)	Drownings Rate per 100,000
TOTAL	1.5
Race and ethnicity	
American Indian or Alaska Native	3.7
Asian or Pacific Islander	1.6
Asian	DNC
Native Hawaiian and other Pacific Islander	DNC
Black or African American	1.9
White	1.4
Hispanic or Latino	1.4
Cuban	DSU
Mexican	1.5
Puerto Rican	1.0
Not Hispanic or Latino	1.5
Black or African American	2.0
White	1.4
Gender	
Female	0.6
Male	2.4
Education level (aged 25 to 64 years)	
Less than high school	2.4
High school graduate	1.7
At least some college	0.8
Geographic location	
Urban	DNA
Rural	DNA

Total Population, 1997* (unless noted)	Drownings Rate per 100,000
Select populations	
Black or African American males	3.4
Children aged 4 years and younger	1.5
Males aged 15 to 34 years	1.8 (1998)

DNA = Data have not been analyzed. DNC = Data are not collected. DSU = Data are statistically unreliable.

Note: Age adjusted to the year 2000 standard population; 1998 data are preliminary.

*New data for population groups will be added when available.

In 1997, drownings accounted for over 4,000 deaths in the United States.[52] In 1992, 6,000 crashes involving recreational boats resulted in 3,700 injuries and 816 deaths.[53] Drowning is the second leading cause of injury-related death for children and adolescents aged 1 to 19 years, accounting for 1,502 deaths in 1995.[54]

Most deaths involving diving occur among persons aged 15 to 39 years, with the largest proportion (14.8 percent) occurring among persons aged 30 to 39 years. Many diving-related incidents result in spinal cord injury. Alcohol use is involved in about 50 percent of deaths associated with water recreation.[13]

Backyard swimming pools and spas represent the greatest risk to preschoolers, particularly those 18 to 30 months of age. Of the 600 annual downing deaths of children from birth to 5 years of age, more than 300 occur in residential swimming pools. Annually, approximately 2,300 nonfatal injuries sustained in residential swimming pools occur in this age group.[55]

15-30. Reduce hospital emergency department visits for nonfatal dog bite injuries.

Target: 114 hospital emergency department visits per 100,000 population.

Baseline: 151.4 hospital emergency department visits per 100,000 population were for nonfatal dog bite injuries in 1997 (age adjusted to the year 2000 standard population).

Target setting method: Better than the best.

Data source: National Hospital Ambulatory Medical Care Survey (NHAMCS), CDC, NCHS.

Total Population, 1997	Hospital Emergency Department Visits for Nonfatal Dog Bite Injuries
	Rate per 100,000
TOTAL	151.4
Race and ethnicity	
American Indian or Alaska Native	DSU
Asian or Pacific Islander	DSU
Asian	DNC
Native Hawaiian and other Pacific Islander	DNC
Black or African American	115.1
White	164.2
Hispanic or Latino	DSU
Not Hispanic or Latino	DSU
Black or African American	DSU
White	DSU
Gender	
Female	150.8
Male	152.0
Education level	
Less than high school	DNC
High school graduate	DNC
At least some college	DNC

DNA = Data have not been analyzed. DNC = Data are not collected. DSU = Data are statistically unreliable.
Note: Age adjusted to the year 2000 standard population.

Between 500,000 and 4 million persons in the United States are bitten by dogs every year.[56] Children are among the most vulnerable, and almost half of all people are estimated to have been bitten by a dog during childhood. Among children, more than half of bites have been to the head, face, or neck.

Because of the risk to large parts of the population, especially children, effective prevention strategies are needed to reduce the painful and costly burden of dog bites. More knowledge is needed through a combination of enhanced and coordinated dog bite reporting systems, expanded population-based surveys, and implementation and evaluation of prevention trials. Particularly for the more severe episodes, information needs to be obtained regarding high-risk situations, high-risk dogs, and elements of successful interventions.

15-31. (Developmental) Increase the proportion of public and private schools that require use of appropriate head, face, eye, and mouth protection for students participating in school-sponsored physical activities.

Potential data source: School Health Policies and Programs Study (SHPPS), CDC, NCCDPHP.

Trauma to the head, face, eyes, and mouth occurs frequently during school-sponsored physical activities. Schools with recreation and sports programs can reduce traumas by requiring students to use appropriate protective gear.

Violence and Abuse Prevention

15-32. Reduce homicides.

Target: 3.2 homicides per 100,000 population.

Baseline: 6.2 homicides per 100,000 population in 1998 (preliminary data; age adjusted to the year 2000 standard population).

Target setting method: Better than the best.

Data sources: National Vital Statistics System (NVSS), CDC, NCHS; Uniform Crime Reports, U.S. Department of Justice, Federal Bureau of Investigation.

Total Population, 1997*	Homicides Rate per 100,000
TOTAL	7.2
Race and ethnicity	
American Indian or Alaska Native	10.4
Asian or Pacific Islander	4.1
Asian	DNC
Native Hawaiian and other Pacific Islander	DNC
Black or African American	25.2
White	4.3
Hispanic or Latino	9.9
Cuban	11.4
Mexican	10.3
Puerto Rican	9.4

Data as of November 30, 1999

Total Population, 1997*	Homicides Rate per 100,000
Not Hispanic or Latino	6.8
Black or African American	26.1
White	3.3
Gender	
Female	3.2
Male	11.2
Education level (aged 25 to 64 years)	
Less than high school	18.3
High school graduate	10.5
At least some college	3.1
Select populations	
Children under 1 year	8.3
Children aged 1 to 4 years	2.4
Children aged 10 to 14 years	1.5
Adolescents aged 15 to 19 years	13.6
Persons aged 15 to 34 years	14.5
Intimate partners aged 14 to 45 years (spouse, ex-spouse, boyfriend, girlfriend)	DNC
Black or African Americans aged 15 to 34 years	55.0
Females	14.4
Males	97.6
Hispanic males aged 15 to 34 years	34.9

DNA = Data have not been analyzed. DNC = Data are not collected. DSU = Data are statistically unreliable.

Note: Age adjusted to the year 2000 standard population.

*New data for population groups will be added when available.

Homicide was the cause of death for 19,491 Americans (7.2 per 100,000 population) in 1997.[58] Homicide is the second leading cause of death for young persons aged 15 to 24 years and the leading cause of death for African Americans in this age group.[59] Homicide rates are dropping among all groups, but the decreases are not as dramatic among youth, who already exhibit the highest rates. In 1997, 6,146 young persons aged 15 to 24 years were victims of homicide, amounting to almost 17 youth homicide victims per day in the United States.[60] Of all homicide victims in 1994, 38 percent were under age 24 years.[61] The homicide rate among males aged 15 to 24 years in the United States is 10 times higher than in Canada, 15 times higher than in Australia, and 28 times higher than in France or Germany.[62]

15-33. Reduce maltreatment and maltreatment fatalities of children.

15-33a. Reduce maltreatment of children.

Target: 11.1 per 1,000 children under age 18 years.

Baseline: 13.9 child victims of maltreatment per 1,000 children under age 18 years in 1997.

Target setting method: 20 percent improvement. (Better than the best will be used when data are available.)

Data source: National Child Abuse and Neglect Data System (NCANDS), Administration on Children, Youth and Families, Administration for Children and Families (ACF), Children's Bureau.

Data for population groups currently are not analyzed.

15-33b. Reduce child maltreatment fatalities.

Target: 1.5 per 100,000 of children under age 18 years.

Baseline: 1.7 per 100,000 child maltreatment fatalities in 1997.

Target setting method: 12 percent improvement. (Better than the best will be used when data are available.)

Data source: National Child Abuse and Neglect Data System (NCANDS), Children's Bureau, Administration on Children, Youth, and Families, Administration for Children and Families (ACF).

Data for population groups currently are not analyzed.

The 1997 Child Maltreatment report from the States to the National Child Abuse and Neglect Data System found there were approximately 984,000 victims of maltreatment, a decrease from more than 1 million victims in 1996 in the 50 States, the District of Columbia, Puerto Rico, the Virgin Islands, and Guam. The rate of child victims was 13.9 per 1,000 children in the general population in 1997, which is slightly higher than the rate of 13.4 victims per 1,000 children in 1990. There were an estimated 1,196 fatalities due to child maltreatment in the 50 States and the District of Columbia. The findings regarding the types of maltreatment were as follows: 55.9 percent neglect, 24.6 percent physical abuse, 12.5 percent sexual abuse, and 6.1 percent emotional abuse. It is also important to note that 58.8 percent of the substantiated or indicated reports of maltreatment were from professional sources, legal, medical, social service, or education professionals. Based on data from 39 States, 75.4 percent of the perpetrators were the victim's parents, 10.2 percent were relatives, and 1.9 percent were individuals in other caretaking relationships.[63]

Information needs to be collected about new cases and causes of maltreatment. National surveys of new cases are needed to describe the magnitude of the problem. In addition, existing interventions and their impact need to be evaluated. Some long-term studies on home-visitation programs for young mothers have shown potential for preventing child abuse and neglect.

15-34. Reduce the rate of physical assault by current or former intimate partners.

Target: 3.6 physical assaults per 1,000 persons aged 12 years and older.

Baseline: 4.5 physical assaults per 1,000 persons aged 12 years and older by current or former intimate partners in 1994.

Target setting method: 20 percent improvement. (Better than the best will be used when data are available.)

Data source: National Crime Victimization Survey (NCVS), U.S. Department of Justice, Bureau of Justice Statistics.

Persons Aged 12 Years and Older, 1994*	Physical Assault by Current and/or Former Intimate Partners Rate per 1,000
TOTAL	4.5
Race and ethnicity	
American Indian or Alaska Native	DSU
Asian or Pacific Islander	DSU
Asian	DNC
Native Hawaiian and other Pacific Islander	DSU
Black or African American	DNA
White	DNA
Hispanic or Latino	DNC
Not Hispanic or Latino	DNA
Black or African American	DNA
White	DNA
Gender	
Female	7.6
Male	1.4

Persons Aged 12 Years and Older, 1994*	Physical Assault by Current and/or Former Intimate Partners Rate per 1,000
Education level	
Less than high school	DNA
High school graduate	DNA
At least some college	DNA

DNA = Data have not been analyzed. DNC = Data are not collected. DSU = Data are statistically unreliable.

15-35. Reduce the annual rate of rape or attempted rape.

Target: 0.7 rapes or attempted rapes per 1,000 persons.

Baseline: 0.9 rapes or attempted rapes per 1,000 persons aged 12 years and older in 1998.

Target setting method: Better than the best.

Data sources: National Crime Victimization Survey (NCVS), U.S. Department of Justice, Bureau of Justice Statistics.

Persons Aged 12 Years and Older, 1994*	Rape or Attempted Rape Rate per 1,000
TOTAL	1.5
Race and ethnicity	
Other (Asian/Pacific Islander and American Indian/Alaska Native)	1.9
Native Hawaiian and other Pacific Islander	DNC
Black or African American	2.4
White	1.3
Hispanic or Latino	1.6
Not Hispanic or Latino	1.5
Black or African American	DSU
White	DSU
Gender	
Female	2.7
Male	DSU

Persons Aged 12 Years and Older, 1994*	Rape or Attempted Rape Rate per 1,000
Education level	
Less than high school	DNA
High school graduate	DNA
At least some college	DNA

DNA = Data have not been analyzed. DNC = Data are not collected. DSU = Data are statistically unreliable.

*New data for population groups will be added when available.

15-36. Reduce sexual assault other than rape.

Target: 0.2 sexual assaults other than rape per 1,000 persons aged 12 years and older.

Baseline: 0.6 sexual assaults other than rape per 1,000 persons aged 12 years and older in 1998.

Target setting method: Better than the best.

Data sources: Criminal Victimization in the United States, 1994; National Crime Victimization Survey (NCVS), U.S. Department of Justice, Bureau of Justice Statistics.

Persons Aged 12 Years and Older, 1994*	Sexual Assault Other Than Rape Rate per 1,000
TOTAL	0.5
Race and ethnicity	
Other (Asian/Pacific Islander and American Indian/Alaska Native)	0.6
Native Hawaiian and other Pacific Islander	DSU
Black or African American	0.3
White	0.6
Hispanic or Latino	0.9
Not Hispanic or Latino	0.5
Black or African American	DSU
White	DSU

Persons Aged 12 Years and Older, 1994*	Sexual Assault Other Than Rape Rate per 1,000
Gender	
Female	1.0
Male	0.1
Education level	
Less than high school	DNC
High school graduate	DNC
At least some college	DNC

DNA = Data have not been analyzed. DNC = Data are not collected. DSU = Data are statistically unreliable.
*New data for population groups will be added when available.

Both females and males experience family and intimate violence and sexual assault. Perpetrators can be the same or opposite sex. Male victimization of females is more common in intimate partner violence and sexual assault.

In 1995, almost 5,000 females in the United States were murdered. In those cases for which the Federal Bureau of Investigation has data on the relationship between the offender and the victim, 85 percent were killed by someone they knew. Nearly half of the females who knew the perpetrators were murdered by a husband, ex-husband, or boyfriend.[64] In 1994, more than 500,000 females were seen in hospital EDs for violence-related injuries, and 37 percent of those females were there for injuries inflicted by spouses, ex-spouses, or nonmarital partners.[65] Although most assault victims survive, they suffer physically and emotionally.

In 1985, a minimum of 16 percent of couples in the United States experienced an assault, and about 40 percent of these assaults involved severe violence, such as kicking, biting, punching, choking, and attacking with weapons.[66] In these families, nearly one out of eight of the husbands had carried out one or more acts of physical aggression against his wife during the preceding 12 months.[67]

Estimates of abuse rates during pregnancy also are a concern. A 1996 literature review indicted that estimated proportions of women experiencing intimate partner violence (IPV) during pregnancy ranged between 0.9 percent and 20.1 percent. The proportion of pregnant women who had experienced IPV at any time in the past ranged between 9.7 percent and 29.7 percent.[68]

Males who are physically violent toward their partners are more likely to be sexually violent toward them and are more likely to use violence toward children.[69] The perpetration of intimate partner violence is most common in adults who, as children or adolescents, witnessed intimate partner violence or became the targets of violence from their caregivers.[69]

Survey data from 1994 indicate that 407,190 females aged 12 years and older were victims of rape, attempted rape, or sexual assault.[70] Other surveys indicate that the problem is underestimated.[71] For example, the National Women's Study, in conjunction with estimates based on the U.S. Census, suggests that 12.1 million females in the United States have been victims of forcible rape sometime in their lives. According to this study, 0.7 percent or approximately 683,000 of adult females experienced a forcible rape in the last year.[72]

Teen dating violence is a concern that may stem from childhood abuse or other experiences with violence. Battering in teen relationships is very different from intimate partner violence that occurs between adults. The issue of teen dating violence requires national attention and prevention efforts that need to continue focusing on adolescent violence within the larger context of family violence.

The nature of intimate partner violence and sexual violence makes such problems difficult to study. Consequently, much remains unknown about the factors that increase or decrease the likelihood that males will behave violently toward females, the factors that endanger or protect females from violence, and the physical and emotional consequences of such violence for females and their children.

15-37. Reduce physical assaults.

Target: 25.5 physical assaults per 1,000 persons aged 12 years older.

Baseline: 31.1 physical assaults per 1,000 persons aged 12 years and older in 1998.

Target setting method: Better than the best.

Data source: National Crime Victimization Survey (NCVS), U.S. Department of Justice, Bureau of Justice Statistics (rates per 1,000).

Persons Aged 12 Years and Older, 1998	Physical Assaults Rate per 1,000
TOTAL	31.1
Race and ethnicity	
American Indian or Alaska Native	DSU
Asian or Pacific Islander	DSU
Asian	DNC
Native Hawaiian and other Pacific Islander	DNC
Black or African American	33.7
White	31.1
Hispanic or Latino	25.6

Persons Aged 12 Years and Older, 1998	Physical Assaults Rate per 1,000
Not Hispanic or Latino	31.5
Black or African American	DNA
White	DNA
Gender	
Female	24.3
Male	38.3
Select populations	
Adolescents aged 12 to 15 years	71.2
Adolescents aged 16 to 19 years	74.7
Young adults aged 20 to 24 years	54.8

DNA = Data have not been analyzed. DNC = Data are not collected. DSU = Data are statistically unreliable.

15-38. Reduce physical fighting among adolescents.

Target: 33.3 percent.

Baseline: 36.6 percent of adolescents in grades 9 through 12 engaged in physical fighting in the previous 12 months in 1997.

Target setting method: Better than the best.

Data source: Youth Risk Behavior Survey (YRBS), CDC, NCCDPHP.

Adolescents in Grades 9 Through 12, 1997	Fighting in Past 12 Months Percent
TOTAL	36.6
Race and ethnicity	
American Indian or Alaska Native	DNC
Asian or Pacific Islander	DNC
Asian	DNC
Native Hawaiian and other Pacific Islander	DNC
Black or African American	DNC
White	DNC
Hispanic or Latino	40.7
Not Hispanic or Latino	DNC
Black or African American	43.0
White	33.7

Adolescents in Grades 9 Through 12, 1997	Fighting in Past 12 Months Percent
Gender	
Female	26.0
Male	45.5
Select populations	
9th grade	44.8
10th grade	40.2
11th grade	34.2
12th grade	28.8

DNA = Data have not been analyzed. DNC = Data are not collected. DSU = Data are statistically unreliable.

15-39. Reduce weapon carrying by adolescents on school property.

Target: 6 percent.

Baseline: 8.5 percent of students in grades 9 through 12 carried weapons on school property during the past 30 days in 1997.

Target setting method: Better than the best.

Data source: Youth Risk Behavior Survey (YRBS), CDC, NCCDPHP.

Students in Grades 9 Through 12, 1997	Weapon Carrying on School Property in Past 30 Days Percent
TOTAL	8.5
Race and ethnicity	
American Indian or Alaska Native	DNC
Asian or Pacific Islander	DNC
Asian	DNC
Native Hawaiian and other Pacific Islander	DNC
Black or African American	DNC
White	DNC
Hispanic or Latino	10.4
Not Hispanic or Latino	DNC
Black or African American	9.2
White	7.8

Students in Grades 9 Through 12, 1997	Weapon Carrying on School Property in Past 30 Days Percent
Gender	
Female	3.7
Male	12.5
Family income level	
Poor	DNC
Near poor	DNC
Middle/high	DNC
Select populations	
9th grade	10.2
10th grade	7.7
11th grade	9.4
12th grade	7.0

DNA = Data have not been analyzed. DNC = Data are not collected. DSU = Data are statistically unreliable.

In 1998, physical assault victimization among adolescents took place twice as often as in the general population of persons age 12 years or older. Assaults were significantly higher among males. While the total assaults for blacks and whites and Hispanics and non-Hispanics were similar, aggravated assault was higher for blacks than whites (11.9 versus 7.0 per 1,000), and simple assault was higher for non-Hispanics than Hispanics (23.9 versus 19.5 per 1,000). Assaults were higher for those with lower household incomes; rates of assault victimization decreased from 54.2 per 1,000 persons in households with annual incomes of less than $7,500 to less than 30 per 1,000 persons in households with annual incomes greater than $35,000.[72a]

In 1997, 36.6 percent of students in grades 9 through 12 had been in a physical fight one or more times during the 12 months preceding the survey.[73] Overall, male students were significantly more likely than female students to have been in a physical fight. This difference was identified for all racial and ethnic and grade subgroups. Overall, African American and Hispanic students were more likely than white students to have been in a physical fight. Male and female students in grade 9 were more likely than male students in grades 11 and 12 and female students in grade 12 to have been in a physical fight. Male and female students in grade 10 were more likely than male and female students in grade 12 to report this behavior.

Weapon carrying on school property during the 30 days before the survey was 8.5 percent nationwide. Overall, male students were more likely than female students to have carried a weapon on school property. This difference was identified for white and Hispanic students and all grade subgroups. African American female students were more likely than Hispanic and white female students to have carried a weapon on school property.[74]

Violence prevention programs for youth need to focus on strategies that reduce involvement in physical fighting and discourage weapon carrying on school property. Strategies to reduce weapon carrying on school property, physical fighting, and resulting injuries among youth should begin early in life and must be tailored to youth of widely varying social, economic, cultural, and ethnic backgrounds.[75] As with other areas of violence and abuse, carefully controlled studies to evaluate the effectiveness of various strategies and interventions are needed. Physicians and other health professionals are in a position to provide effective primary prevention messages to youth and their families. Also, ED workers treating adolescents with fight-related injuries can practice secondary interventions, as they do with victims of child abuse, sexual assault, or attempted suicide.

Related Objectives From Other Focus Areas

1. Access to Quality Health Services

1-3.   Counseling about health behaviors

1-11.   Rapid prehospital emergency care

1-12.   Single toll-free number for poison control centers

7. Educationai and Community-Based Programs

7-3.   Health-risk behavior information for college and university students

8. Environmental Health

8-13.   Pesticide exposures

8-24.   Exposure to pesticides

8-25.   Exposure to heavy metals and other toxic chemicals

18. Mental Health and Mental Disorders

18-1.   Suicide

18-2.   Adolescent suicide attempts

20. Occupational Safety and Health

20-1.   Work-related injury deaths

20-2.   Work-related injuries

20-5.   Work-related homicides

20-6.   Work-related assaults

26. Subtance Abuse

26-1.   Motor vehicle crash deaths and injuries

26-5.   Alcohol-related emergency department visits

26-6.   Youth riding with a driver who has been drinking

26-7.   Alcohol- and drug-related violence

Terminology

(A listing of all abbreviations and acronyms used in this publication appears in Appendix K .)

Age-adjusted injury rate: An injury rate calculated to reflect a standard age distribution.

Attempted rape: Includes males and females, heterosexual and homosexual rape, and verbal threats of rape.

Graduated licensing laws: Require young drivers to progress through phases of restricted driving before they are allowed to get their unrestricted licenses. Such restrictions include a mandatory supervised driving period, night driving curfews, limits on teen passengers riding with a beginning driver, and a lower blood alcohol concentration (BAC) level for teens than for adults.

Homicide: Fatal injury intentionally caused to one human being by another.

Impaired driving: Driving while under the influence of alcohol or drugs.

Injury: Unintentional or intentional damage to the body resulting from acute exposure to thermal, mechanical, electrical, or chemical energy or from the absence of such essentials as heat or oxygen.

Intimate partner(s): Refers to spouses, ex-spouses, boyfriends, girlfriends, and former boyfriends and girlfriends (includes same-sex partners). Intimate partners may or may not be cohabitating and need not be engaging in sexual activities.

Intimate partner violence: Actual or threatened physical or sexual violence or psychological and emotional abuse by an intimate partner.

Motorcyclist: Includes both operator and rider (passenger).

NCUTLO: National Committee on Uniform Traffic Laws and Ordinances.

Pedalcyclists: Riders of bicycles and tricycles.

Premature death: Dying before life expectancy is reached.

Primary enforcement: A stipulation of a safety belt use law that allows law enforcement officials to stop a driver solely on the basis of a safety belt law violation.

Rape: Forced sexual intercourse, including both psychological coercion and physical force. Forced sexual intercourse means vaginal, anal, or oral penetration by the offender(s) and includes incidents of penetration by a foreign object.

Risk factor: A characteristic that has been demonstrated statistically to be associated with a particular injury.

Secondary enforcement: A stipulation of a safety belt use law that allows law enforcement officials to address a safety belt use law violation only after a driver has been stopped for some other purpose.

Sexual assault: A wide range of victimizations separate from rape and attempted rape. Included are attacks or attempted attacks of unwanted sexual contact between the victim and the

offender that may or may not involve force; includes grabbing or fondling. Verbal threats also are included.

Suffocation: Includes inhalation and ingestion of food or other objects; accidental mechanical suffocation; suicide and self-inflicted injury by hanging, strangulation, and suffocation; assault by hanging and strangulation; and hanging, strangulation, or suffocation undetermined whether accidental or purposely inflicted.

Target population: The group of persons (usually those at high risk) whom program interventions are designed to reach.

Trauma registry: A collection of data on patients who receive hospital care for certain types of injuries, such as blunt or penetrating trauma or burns. Such collections are designed primarily to ensure quality care in individual institutions and trauma systems but also provide useful data for the surveillance of injury and death.

Unintentional injury: A type of injury that occurs without purposeful intent.

Vehicle miles traveled (VMT): The miles of travel by all types of motor vehicles as determined by the States on the basis of actual traffic counts and established estimating procedures.

Violence: An act carried out with the intention or perceived intention of causing physical pain or injury to another person.

Vulnerable populations: Refers to children, elderly

persons, and persons with disabilities.

Years of potential life lost (YPLL): A statistical measure used to determine premature death. YPLL is calculated by subtracting an individual's age at death from a predetermined life expectancy. The Centers for Disease Control and Prevention generally uses 75 years of age for this purpose (for example, a person who died at aged 35 years would have a YPLL of 40).

References

1. Centers for Disease Control and Prevention (CDC), National Center for Health Statistics (NCHS). Deaths: Final Data for 1997. *National Vital Statistics Reports* 47(19), June 1999.

2. Houk, V.; and Brown; S.T.; and Rosenberg, M.; One fine solution to the injury problem. *Public Health Reports* 102:5, 1987

3. Baker, S.P.; O'Neill, B.; Ginsburg, M.J.; and Li, G. *The Injury Fact Book*, 2nd ed. New York: Oxford University Press, 1992.

4. CDC. *Health United States, 1999*. Hyattsville, MD: U.S. Department of Health and Human Services, 1999.

5. U.S. Department of Health and Human Services (HHS), National Institutes of Health, National Institute on Alcohol and Alcoholism. *Ninth Special Report to the U.S. Congress on Alcohol and Health from the Secretary of Health and Human Services*. NIH Pub. No. 97-4017. Washington, DC: the Department, 1997.

6. HHS, CDC, National Center for Injury Prevention and Control. Ten Leading Causes of Injury Deaths.

7. Schappert, S.M. Ambulatory care visits to physician offices, hospital outpatient departments and emergency departments: U.S., 1995. NCHS. *Vital and Health Statistics* 13(29):1-38, 1997.

8. National Safety Council. *Accident Facts*. 1995.

9. National Safe Kids Campaign. *Childhood Injury Factsheet*. Itasca, NY: the Council, 1997.

10. Moscicki, E.K.; O'Carroll, P.W.; Rae, D.S.; Roy, A.E.; Locke, B.Z.; and Regier, D.A. Suicideal Ideation and Attempts: The Epidemiologic Catchement Area Study. *Report of the Secretary's Task Force in Youth Suicide*, Volume 4. Washington, DC: U.S. Department of Health and Human Services, January 1989.

11. Indian Health Service (HIS). Injury Prevention Program. *Injuries Among Native Americans and Alaska Natives*. Rockville, MD: IHS, 1997.

12. United States Fire Administration. *Curious Kids Set Fires*. Washington, DC: Federal Emergency Management Agency, 1990.

13. CDC, NCHS. Deaths: Final Data for 1997. *National Vital Statistics Report* 47(10):1-104, 1999.

13. National Safety Council. *Accident Facts*. Itasca, IL: the Council, 1993.

14. Livingson, I.L., ed. *Handbook of Black American Health: The Mosaic of Conditions, Issues, Policies, and Prospects*. Westport, CT: Greenwood Press, 1994.

15. Anderson, R.N.; Kockanck, K.D.; Murphey, S.L. Report of final mortality statistics, 1995. *Monthly Vital Statistics Report* 45(suppl. 2):11, 1997.

16. CDC. *Morbidity and Mortality Monthly Report* 47(10):193, 1998.

17. HHS, CDC. Ten Leading causes of death, 1995. Atlanta, GA: the Department, 1997.

18. McLoughlin, E.; Annest, J.L.; Fingerhut, L.A.; et al. Recommended framework for presenting injury mortality data. *Morbidity and Mortality Weekly Report* 46(RR-14), 1997.

19. Cummings, P.; Grossman, D.C.; Rivara, F.P.; and Koepsell, T.D. State gun safe storage laws and child mortality due to firearms. *Journal of the American Medical Association* 278(13), 1997.

20. Chaloupka, F.J.; Saffer, H.; and Grossman, M. Alcohol control policies and motor-vehicle fatalities. *Journal of Legal Studies* 22:161-186, 1993.

21 Cook, P.J., and Moore, M.J. Economic perspectives on reducing alcohol-related violence. In: Martin, S.E. *Alcohol and Interpersonal Violence: Fostering Multidisplinary Perspectives*. Based on a workshop on alcohol-related violence sponsored by the National Institute on Alcohol Abuse and Alcoholism, May 14-15, 1992. NIH Pub. No. 93-3496, Rockville, MD: National Institutes of Health, 1993.

22. National Center for Injury Prevention and Control. *Best Practices for Preventing Violence by Children and Adolescents: A source book*. Atlanta, GA: Centers for

Data as of November 30, 1999

Disease Control and revention, 1999 (in press).

23. Rice, D.P.; Mackenzie, E.J.; and Associates. *Cost of Injury in the United States: A Report to Congress*. San Francisco, CA: Institute of Health and Aging, University of California and Injury Prevention Center, The Johns Hopkins University, 1989, p. 143, 163.

24. NCHS. National Vital Statistics System, unpublished data, 1999.

25. Kraus, K.F.; Black, M.A.; Hessol, N.; et al. The incidence of acute brain injury and serious impairment in a defined population. *American Journal of Epidemiology* 119:186-201, 1984.

26. Annest, J.L.; Mercy, J.A.; Gibson, D.R.; and Ryan, G.W. National estimates of nonfatal firearm-related injuries. *Journal of the American Medical Association* 273(22):1749-1754, 1995.

27. CDC. Rates of Homicide, Suicide, and Firearm-related Death Among Children - 26 Industrialized countries, 1950-1993. *Morbidity and Mortality Weekly Report* 46(5):101, 1995.

28. Fingerhut, L.A.; Ingram, D.D; and Feldman, J.J. firearm and nonfirearm homicide among persons 15 to 19 years of age: differences by level of urbanization. United States 1979-89. *Journal of the American Medical Association* 267(22):3048-53, 1992.

29. Max, W., and Rice, D.P. Shooting in the dark: Estimating the cost of firearm injuries. *Health Affairs* 12(4):171-185, 1993.

30. NCHS. *Vital statistics mortality data, underlying cause of death, 1962-97.* [Machine-readable public-use tapes.] Hyattsville, MD: U.S. Department of Health and Human Services; 1999.

31. Litovitz, T.L.; Smilkstein, M.S.; Felberg, L.; et al. 1996 annual report of the American Association of Poison Control Centers Toxic Exposure Surveillance System. *American Journal of Emergency Medicine* 15(5):447-500, 1997.

32. National Safe Kids Campaign. *Poisoning Fact Sheet*. September 1997.

33. HHS, NCHS, National Vital Statistics System, 1997, Washington, DC.

34. National Safe Kids Campaign, December 1998.

35. National Highway Traffic Safety Administration (NHTSA), Fatality Analysis Reporting System (FARS), 1998. HHS, NCHS, National Vital Statistics Systems, 1998: Washington, DC.

36. NHTSA. *Traffic Safety Facts 1998: Pedestrians*. Washington, DC: the Administration, 1998.

37. NHTSA. *Traffic Safety Facts 1998*. Washington, DC; the Administration, 1998.

37. NHTSA. *Traffic Safety Facts 1998: Older Population*. Washington, DC: the Administration, 1998.

38. Advocates for Highway and Auto Safety. *Safety Belt Fact Sheet*. 1998.

39. NHTSA. *Traffic Safety Facts 1997: Children*. Washington, DC, the Administration, 1997.

40. NHTSA. *Traffic Safety Facts 1998: Motorcycles*. Washington, DC; the Administration, 1998.

41. NHTSA. *Traffic Safety Facts 1998: Young Drivers*. Washington, DC; the Administration, 1998.

42. NHTSA. *Traffic Safety Facts 1998: Pedalcyclists*. Washington, DC; the Administration, 1998.

43. Insurance Institute for Highway Safety. *Facts 1996 Fatalities: Bicycles*. Arlington, VA: the Institute, 1997.

44. CDC. Injury-Control Recommendations: Bicycle Helmets *Morbidity and Mortality Weekly Report* 44(RR-1), 1995

45. National Safe Kids Campaign. *State Bike Helmet Legislation*. Winter 1998.

46. Karter, M.J. *Fire Loss in the United States, 1998*. Quincy, MA: National Fire Protection Association, 1999.

47. Hall, J.R. *The U.S. Fire Problem and Overview Report. Leading causes and other patterns and trends*. Quincy, MA: NFPA.

48. CDC, NCHS. *Mortality Data Tapes*. Hyattsville, MD: the Center, 1998.

48a. Hingson, R., and Howland, J. Alcohol and Non-Traffic Unintentional Injuries. *Addiction* 88(7):877-883, 1993.

49. Cummings, S.R.; Rubin, S.M.; and Black, D. The future of hip fractures in the United States. Numbers, costs, and potential effects of postmenopausal estrogen. *Clinical Orthopedics* 252:163:166, 1990.

50. Englander, F.; Hodson, T.J.; and Teregrossa, R.A. Economic dimensions of slip and fall injuries. *Journal of Forensic Science* 41(5):746-773, 1996.

51. Tinetti, M.E., and Speechley, M. Prevention of Falls Among the Elderly. *New England Journal of Medicine* 320(16)1055-1059, 1989.

52. NCHS. *National Mortality Data*. Hyattsville, MD: the Center, 1997.

53. U.S. Department of Transportation. *Boating Statistics 1992*. Pub. No. COMDTPUB P16754.8.

Washington, DC: the Department, 1993.

54. NCHS, *Mortality Data Tapes.* Hyattsville, MD: the Center, 1996.

55. American Academy of Pediatrics. *Injury Prevention and Control for Children and Youth,* 3rd ed., 1997.

*\56. Sacks, J.J.; Lockwood, R.; Hornreich, J.; and Sattin, R.W. Fatal Dog Attacks, 1989-94. *Pediatrics* 97:891-895, 1996.

57. Not in text.

58. NCHS. Mortality data tapes for number of deaths. U.S. Bureau of Census population estimates: Intercensal data are used for 1984-89. Decennial census data are used for 1990. Demo-Detail postcensal population estimates are used for 1991-93.

59. Singh, G.K.; Kochanek, K.D.; and MacDorman, M.F. Advance report of final mortality statistics, 1994. *Monthly Vital Statistics Report* 45(3S). Hyattsville, MD: National Center for Health Statistics, 1996.

60. NCHS. *Mortality Data Tapes.* Hyattsville, MD: the Center, 1994.

61. CDC. *National Summary of Injury Mortality Data, 1987-1994.* Atlanta, GA: National Center for Injury Prevention and Control, 1996.

62. World Health Organization. *World Health Statistics Annual, 1994.* Geneva, Switzerland: WHO, 1995.

63. HHS, Administration on Children, Youth, and Families. *Child Maltreatment 1997: Reports from the States to the National Child Abuse and Neglect Data System.* Washington, DC: U.S. Government Printing Office, 1999.

64. Federal Bureau of Investigation. *Crime in the United States: 1996.* Washington, DC: U.S. Government Printing Office, 1997.

65. Bureau of Justice Statistics. *Violence-Related Injuries Treated in Hospital Emergency Departments.* Washington, DC: U.S. Department of Justice, August 1997.

66. Straus, M.A., and Smith, C. Family patterns and primary prevention of family violence. *Trends in Health Care, Law & Ethics* 8(2):1-25, 1993.

67. How violent are American families? Estimates from the National Family Violence Survey and other studies. In: Straus, M.A., and Gelles, R.J. (eds.). *Physical Violence in American Families: Risk Factors and Adaptations to Violence in 8,145 Families.* New Brunswick, NJ: Transaction Publishers, 1990, 95-112.

68. Gazmararian, J.A.; Lazorick, S.; Spitz, A.M.; Ballard, T.J.; Saltzman, L.E.; and Marks, J.S. Prevalence of violence against pregnant women. *Journal of the American Medical Association* 275:1915-1920, 1996.

69. Hotaling, G.T., and Sugarman, D.B. An analysis of risk markers in husband to wife violence: The current state of knowledge. *Violence and Victims* 1:101-124, 1986.

70. U.S. Department of Justice, Bureau of Justice Statistics. *Crime Victimization in the United States, 1994.* Washington, DC: the Bureau, 1997.

71. Bachman, R., and Taylor, B. The measurement of family violence and rape by the redesigned national crime victimization survey. *Justice Quarterly* 11:701-714, 1994.

72. Kilpatrick, D.G.; Edmunds, C.N.; and Seymour, A.K. *Rape in America: A Report to the Nation, 1992*: pg 2.

72a. DOJ. *Statistics. Criminal Victimization 1998: Changes 1997-98 With Trends, 1993-98.* Pub. No. NCJ-176353. Washington, DC: the Department, July 1999.

73. CDC. Youth Risk Behavior Surveillance - United States. *Morbidity and Mortality Weekly Report* 1(SS03):1, August 14, 1998.

74. CDC. CDC Surveillance Summaries, August 14, 1998. *Morbidity and Mortality Weekly Report* 47(No. SS-3):7-8, 44, 1998.

75. National Center for Injury Prevention and Control. *Best practices for preventing violence by children and adolescents: a source book.* Atlanta, GA: the Center, November 1999 (in press).